AMERICAN
HUMOR MAGAZINES
AND
COMIC PERIODICALS

AMERICAN HUMOR MAGAZINES AND COMIC PERIODICALS

Edited by
David E. E. Sloane

Advisory Editor, Stanley Trachtenberg

Historical Guides to the World's Periodicals and Newspapers

Greenwood Press

New York • Westport, Connecticut • London

Library of Congress Cataloging-in-Publication Data

American humor magazines and comic periodicals.

(Historical guides to the world's periodicals and
newspapers, ISSN 0742-5538)
  Bibliography: p.
  Includes index.
  1. American wit and humor—Periodicals—History.
2. American wit and humor—Periodicals—Bibliography.
3. American periodicals—History. 4. American
periodicals—Bibliography.   I. Sloane, David E. E.,
1943–   . II. Series.
PN4880.A46   1987   051   86–27155
ISBN 0–313–23956–8 (lib. bdg. : alk. paper)

Library of Congress Catalog Card Number: 86–27155
ISBN: 0–313–23956–8
ISSN: 0742-5538

First published in 1987

Greenwood Press, Inc.
88 Post Road West, Westport, Connecticut 06881

Printed in the United States of America

∞™

The paper used in this book complies with the
Permanent Paper Standard issued by the National
Information Standards Organization (Z39.48–1984).

10 9 8 7 6 5 4 3 2 1

Copyright Acknowledgments

The editor gratefully acknowledges permission to use portions of the following copyrighted
material:

Philip Hichborn, " 'Tis a Lovely Lady," *Harvard Lampoon*, 19 April 1928. Reprinted with
permission.

John Updike, "Lines in Favor of Deposed Kings," *Harvard Lampoon*, September 1952, and
"Lampy's Doggerel Guide to English Literature," *Harvard Lampoon*, September 1953.
Reprinted with permission.

Michael O'Donoghue, "The Vietnamese Baby Book," *National Lampoon*, January 1972.
Reprinted with permission.

Contents

For Bonnie and Rachel

Foreword

American Humor Magazines and Comic Periodicals is a unique chronicle of one of the liveliest subgenres in American literature. Since Frank Luther Mott's definitive *History of American Magazines* began to appear in 1938, periodicals have become an increasingly inviting area of scholarly investigation. The material has reflected all aspects of our regional culture, but the consequent amount and necessarily broad geographic distribution have made it difficult to assemble and organize in one readily accessible source. Greenwood Press's series of extended bibliographies on localized fields within the broad category of periodicals is intended to fully realize the potential of Mott's work by providing a factual framework and supporting documentation for subsequent studies of individual periodicals, editors, and authors. *American Humor Magazines* is an exciting contribution to this project because it adds so much information that is genuinely fresh and new to the study of American life and humor while taking account of much that went to make up its history.

Humor magazines have provided an extraordinary breadth in reflecting American modes of thought, political interests, and social concerns, serving at once as both a critical and cohesive agent. Here they are traced to 1765, thirty years before the first periodical Mott identified in this genre. From that point on, a chronological review of the magazines in this volume, supplemented by the chronological listing supplied following the genre essays, reveals the gradual changes in social emphasis from political to domestic to sexual concerns. What was to become a characteristic American skepticism may be seen developing in the acerbic political rhetoric, which in the first two decades of the nineteenth century often looked ultimately to the courts rather than the press for a remedy. Comic magazines and periodicals were also an outlet for the first stirrings of sexual liberation which were frequently met by local anti-vice boycotts and, particularly during the first quarter of the twentieth century, by attempts at suppression by postal authorities. David E. E. Sloane's introduction does much to focus these issues and to provide a theoretical framework for the individual essays that follow.

The subjects treated in these journals provide a running commentary on our nation's history. The politics and social life of the Federal era are mirrored in Washington Irving's *Salmagundi* and in the Washington *Champagne Club* and similar periodicals; the Civil War intruded into the pages even of *Vanity Fair*; *The Knickerbocker* magazine and the *Spirit of the Times* dominated the comic assessment of our growth in the years between 1830 and 1860. The colorful New York *Bee* reflected the feeling about the Spanish-American War, while Thomas Nast and Joel Chandler Harris along with *Life*, *Puck*, and *Judge* brought an often satiric irreverence to current events and the corruption they concealed. From the 1930s to the 1960s and beyond, from *Ballyhoo* to *The Realist*, and, more recently, *Mad* magazine and the *National Lampoon*, comic magazines served as gadflies of our national institutions. From racial concerns to sexual fantasies, a full range of these magazines is identified and documented.

American Humor Magazines and Comic Periodicals also provides in-depth studies of individual magazines that expand our awareness of important comic representations of American life. B. P. Shillaber's *The Carpet-Bag*, Lewis Gaylord Clark's *Knickerbocker*, and Norman Anthony's *Ballyhoo* emerge as significant centers of social influence. Other seemingly ephemeral journals from *Abracadabra* to *Moonshine* and from *Jubilee Days* to *Ziffs* take on definition they have never previously been accorded. Added to these essays is a rich source of information in the brief listings of post–1900 magazines, virtually unobtainable in local libraries. This wealth of information along with the concluding articles on related forms of periodical literature noted for humor and with copyright entries compiled by Bonnie Fausz Sloane round out the picture of humorous periodical publication in America in a way that will not only afford pleasure in its own right but will also serve as a necessary starting point for any further investigations in the field.

This depth of information is in all cases presented in an accessible, eminently readable style that makes the history of American humor magazines an exciting story itself as well as part of a broader survey documented in the Greenwood series on American magazines. Taken singly or in concert, they afford a unique conception of our nation as reflected in its periodical literature.

Stanley Trachtenberg

Preface

American Humor Magazines and Comic Periodicals seeks to provide a comprehensive survey of its field, assessing over two hundred years of publication in this genre through examination of the individual magazines. An introductory essay discusses the development of humor magazines in historical and cultural context. Individual magazines are presented in four sections. Part I contains over one hundred substantial articles on representative important magazines, many of which are mentioned in the Introduction. These entries end with "Information Sources," comprising bibliography, index sources, reprint editions, and location sources, and "Publication History," comprising title changes, volume and issue data, publisher and place of publication, editor(s), and circulation. Forty-eight scholars have helped prepare and present this information.

Part II consists of about four hundred briefer entries, many on important minor journals (some of which are also noted in the Introduction), which round out the picture and more fully define the universe of humor magazines and comic papers. Their briefer treatment does not reflect an editorial judgment of their value; rather, it results from the paucity of reliable information available. Entries in Part II do not have appended compilations of data, but similar information is interpolated into the texts wherever possible. Many of these journals deserve fuller treatment, and it is hoped that their inclusion here will stimulate further study. (Note: those entries in Part II that do not list the name of a contributor were provided by the editor.)

Part III provides two listings of additional titles. The first presents titles that have been identified from copyright lists but have not been analyzed; this compilation should help students of comic periodicals trace additional sources, though it is possible that two or three of the inclusions will not prove humorous upon further study. The second listing comprises titles of magazines compiled from popular or informal sources but not fully verified. Available information is given, but this list may have ghosts and a variety of inaccuracies. Nevertheless, as the information is available, it seems reasonable to offer it—*caveat emptor*.

Excluded from all the above categories are magazines that fall under the rubrics of college humor magazines (with the exception of the *Harvard Lampoon*, which is included in Part I): comic books, counter-culture comix, almanacs, and scholarly magazines. These groups of periodicals belong to separate fields and are worthy of study and compilation on their own. The present volume includes as Part IV three comprehensive essays: on college humor magazines, scholarly humor magazines, and humor in American almanacs.

A chronological list of magazines by initial publication date is designed to aid readers who wish to survey the field in historical perspective. Included are magazines noted in Parts I, II, and III, but not IV. A selected bibliography provides important reference sources on American humor, American periodicals, and American humor periodicals supplementing the more specialized sources appearing with entries on individual magazines. These reference sources are cited frequently throughout the text; please refer to the Selected Bibliography for full citations.

The apparatus of this volume is designed to be as simple as possible. Asterisks appear beside the first citations of magazine titles described more fully elsewhere in the text (magazines marked with one asterisk are described in Part I, and those marked with two asterisks are described in Part II). Alternate titles of journals are noted in the text or appended data of the entries; access to alternate titles is possible through the subject index, which also indexes various names, terms, and topics. Designation of library locations by alphabet letters—as in DLC for District of Columbia, Library of Congress—follows the *Union List of Serials*; a key to library location codes commonly used in this volume precedes Part I. In using the information on reprint editions noted in the appended Information Sources, it is noteworthy that, although Readex Microprint has reprinted items in Brigham's list of periodicals through 1820 (see Selected Bibliography) and University Microfilms has reprinted a comprehensive group up to 1850 and certain major journals thereafter, some libraries, such as the New York Public Library, routinely microfilm their own holdings and other libraries will frequently do so on request (although the cost may be high). Their resources are discoverable only through individual correspondence, and sometimes multiple requests are needed before a response is gained.

This editor hopes that he and his contributors have developed a unique reference tool for the study of American humor magazines. Nevertheless, yet other humorous magazines remain even to be located, and new magazines continue to appear. Continued research in this field is to be encouraged.

Acknowledgments

Many librarians, booksellers, antique and comic-book dealers, and scholars contributed to the making of *American Humor Magazines and Comic Periodicals*. The University of New Haven aided this work directly with a summer research fellowship and several supporting grants. It helped directly in a second way through its fine library staff at the Marvin K. Peterson library, including Eric Johnson, now of the University of Bridgeport Library, Jean Rainwater, and present reference librarian Suzanna Gonzalez. I am also grateful to Dean Joseph Chepaitis, Dr. Paul Marx, and Dr. Phillip Kaplan, President of the University of New Haven, for their continuing support. I am indebted to Dr. Jean Henry and Dr. Benjamin Fisher for reading and commenting thoughtfully on drafts of my own introduction. Editor Marilyn Brownstein of Greenwood Press and Dr. Stanley Trachtenberg of Winthrop College, advisory editor for this volume, also gave generously of their ideas and experience. Bonnie Fausz Sloane worked extensively on the frustrating job of collecting and verifying references and proofreading texts and deserves special recognition for this labor, as well as for her compilation of the Copyright List.

A large number of libraries responded generously to pleas for help. Johanna Goldschmid of the San Francisco Public Library was especially helpful, as were librarians at the John Hay Library at Brown University and Harvard's Houghton Library. David Fraser of the Historical Society of Pennsylvania, JoAnn Sardo of Charlton Press, and librarians at the Library of Congress, the New York Public Library, the American Antiquarian Society, the Meine Collection at the University of Illinois, Yale University's Sterling Library, the University of Mississippi Library, the Boston Public Library, the Boston Athenaeum, and others aided with use of their staff and resources.

Because there is no single primary collection of American periodical humor, and much of the material after the 1920s (and in many cases before then) is unavailable through the conventional research tools and processes, I am indebted to several private sources, among them Leopold Fechtner of Queens, New York; Ed Ricciuti of Long Island, New York; Herb Galewitz of Orange, Connecticut; Betty Messenger of Backdate Magazines in Granby, Connecticut; and Leonard Thompson of the Antiquarian Old Book Store of Portsmouth, New Hampshire. They were particularly helpful and kind, among many other collectibles dealers providing source materials.

The late Frank Luther Mott deserves special recognition for his five-volume *History of American Magazines*; this work requires no superlatives here to attest to its many values. However, thanks are due to Mildred Wedel and the Joint Collection University of Missouri Western Historical Manuscript Collection-Columbia and State Historical Society of Missouri Manuscripts and its director, Cindy Stewart, and her fine staff. Their permission and aid in using Professor Mott's notes added even more information to this study. Needless to say, Mott's papers contain further contributions by Walter Blair and Franklin Meine, and acknowledgment of their work is also due. The scholars who have written entries for this volume are named with each entry, and I am grateful to them for their extreme grace under editorial pressure. Dr. George Test, Dr. Michael Butler, and Richard West, editor of *Target* Magazine, have been especially generous with their unconditional support and unseen work. I am also grateful to the many kind people who supported this work while it was being completed during a visiting professorship at the University of Mississippi, in Oxford, Mississippi, during the spring of 1986.

At Duke University, during my graduate student years in 1964–1966, Professor Clarence Gohdes, long-time editor of *American Literature*, strongly encouraged his graduate students to study American literary history through its less obvious byways, particularly including the periodicals of the late nineteenth century. A special word of thanks from this author is offered here for Dr. Gohdes's long-lasting and much-appreciated influence.

Introduction

Ellis Parker Butler, in "Pigs Is Pigs" in the otherwise unfunny *American Magazine* of 1905, showed the self-defeating stupidity of a railroad company which refused to allow guinea pigs to travel as pets at the lower rate; "pigs is pigs," they reasoned, and must travel at "live stock" rates. A comic riot of fast-breeding "live stock" guinea pigs overwhelmed their stationmaster. The concept delighted its age and was Butler's chief claim to fame in a long career as a humorous magazine writer. "Pigs Is Pigs" is particularly American in its skepticism toward rules and management decision-making processes; complementary pieces are easy to find in the *Yankee Notions** of the 1850s and the *Farmer's Weekly Museum** of the 1790s, among hundreds of others. American humor—the American comic vision—is a special blend of ethical and political impulses unique to the democracy for which it stands. For a hundred years before national politicians screamed like liberty's eagle, crowing the special virtues of God's footstool, American comedians responded to the overblown pretensions of self-interested manipulators with vulgar pragmatism and deadpan ironic common sense. For each attack on Hitler in Norman Anthony's *Der Gag Bag* and *Ballyhoo** in the 1930s, and before Anthony in *Americana** early in the decade, a corresponding cartoon attack on "Buck" Buchanan—the doughface president who weakened the North through inaction on the eve of Lincoln's inauguration—can be found in *Vanity Fair,** otherwise painfully neutral, in 1859. Americans held their social and political values strongly and found humor a means to state their values both directly and indirectly through burlesque and ironic understatement. First, Federal politics, then American social life, next international politics, and finally sex and physical sexual and personal mores have provided American humor with its driving vigor. A persistent willingness to put democratic values ahead of personal well-being gives Americans both deadpan humor and an ability at satire and burlesque which is dramatized in the two-hundred years of American comic periodicals studied here. If Freud is correct that humor is a means of assimilating the unpalatable, new, and frightening, Americans in their humor magazines have shown a remarkable persistence in providing their own gadflies in a still ongoing tradition.

American comic periodicals represent a melange of disparate elements as vigorous, as vital, and as irrepressible as the American democratic spirit. Humorous journals occur among the earliest American periodicals, even before the Revolution. They present national mythic tall tales, dialect and local figures, and jaundiced portraits of political and economic corruption for the amusement and correction of their targets as well as their reading public. Their history of libel and legal obscenity battles convincingly demonstrates their social force. To the present day, thousands of wits have been involved in the creation of such magazines, including the most thoughtful and critical of major authors in American cultural history. Millions of copies of humor magazines have been sold, and even more distributed. They have appeared in all sizes, in every combination of papers and formats, and in newspaper, tabloid, magazine, and book forms. They have created, borrowed, burlesqued, or stolen their materials from domestic politics, social and ethnic classes, international interaction, and European and American models; frontier and city, and every other corner of their milieu, have been tapped. Unlike some other literary forms, they have been aimed not at the literati or at a coterie, but at the general public, and they broadly reflect American values in various political, economic, social, and sexual transitions as few other media in our history. Perhaps the greatest testimony to their importance as an irritant at the limit of social acceptability is their exclusion from libraries, making them one of our most ephemeral, though most persistent, literary products.

The styles of humor magazines follow the general development of American history: first, they were Federalist in orientation, and later, international and political following the Civil War. Reflecting the changing social life of the 1890s, they show high life appearing side by side with local color elements at the turn of the century. Later, the Jazz Age and the Modern Age magazines offer their mix of city life, war humor, and sex gags.

From 1765 through 1820, comic periodicals showed a distinct tendency toward the satiric in social and political content. Even in this early period, sarcastic Goeffrey Juvenal in the Philadelphia *Critic*** could slander J. K. Paulding as "The Cabbage Bard," and Robert Rose in *The Port Folio** in 1810 could parody "Ode to the Raritan" in a more localized Philadelphia piece, "To a Market Street Gutter." Numerous magazines were overtly allied with political viewpoints, most notably *The Wasp** of 1802 and William Cobbett's antidemocratic papers, although there were plenty like *Moonshine** in 1807 to fill the need for clever foolery. Washington, D.C.'s *Champagne Club*** of 1834 is typical of the transition to a lighter social-political humor as the Federalist period ended. By the 1830s and 1840s, an increasing amount of humor was directed at cultural events and theatrical personages, most notably P. T. Barnum, the New York stage, and English romances. "Seeing the Elephant" became a stock phrase for initiation into the big city, and there was an *Elephant** comic magazine, and a

Humbug's American Museum,** applying the skeptical concepts of the showman to American society. The Civil War, of course, absorbed attention in the years between 1859 and 1865, and provides a watershed from serious and elevated foolery to popular joke magazines including *Yankee Notions** and *Frank Leslie's Budget of Fun.** Following the Civil War, the humor of the literary comedians was increasingly based on clever language and literary and social burlesque. But it was not without heart, as in the *Yankee Notions* anecdote of 1866 in which a Negro porter describes the difference between "Yankee and Southerner." He notes that the aristocratic Southerner tips him when he does a service, but the democratic Yankee asks him about his grandmother and grandfather. The tight Yankee anecdotes would blend into the crackerbarrel humor tradition at the end of the century.

With the advent of *Life,** *Puck,** and *Judge** in the 1870s and 1880s, humor magazines at last tapped the greatly expanded middle-class readership of America, portraying upper and lower class foibles and follies for the amusement of the middle class—and, perhaps surprisingly, upper and some lower class readers as well. Politics, both national and international, became major themes in the boldly colorful, heavily cartoon-laden comic magazines of the 1890s. An even more significant change was coming. With the advent of the Gibson girl in *Life* in the 1880s, sexual comedy focusing on the female form began to expand its role in humor magazines, and grew in influence and obviousness through the teens and Roaring Twenties. When local yokel humor in journals like W. J. Arkell's *Sis Hopkin's Own Book*** came up to date in the teens, the synthesis was accomplished by uniting *Sis Hopkin's* readership with the audiences of *Judge's Library** and *The Magazine of Fun*** to create *Film Fun,** flourishing from 1916 to 1942—a montage of movie out-takes of pretty starlets in skimpy clothing accompanied by gag lines. Yet, even then, regional humor publications like *Sagebrush Philosophy** (1904–1910), *Hot Dog*** in the 1910s and 1920s, and the *Arkansaw Thomas Cat*** (1890–1948)—itself a local booster—carried a viewpoint as opposed to complacent boosterism and narrow small-town Babbittry as H. L. Mencken's in *The American Mercury** beginning in 1924. Alternatively, *Captain Billy's Whiz Bang** in sexy humor, *The New Yorker** in uncompromising wit and urban sophistication, and *Ballyhoo* in burlesques of advertising culture set new styles for the twentieth century, followed after World War II by *Mad*—"What, me worry?"—and *National Lampoon*—"Buy this magazine or we'll shoot this dog"—the two current reigning monarchs of the humor magazine realm—purposely offensive in content, but accepted by a mass readership, and as characteristic of the modern era as their predecessors were of earlier times.

The history of American humor periodicals begins with the publication of three weekly issues of the Philadelphia *Bee** by William Honeycomb in 1765, correcting in acid satire the foibles of the governors of Quillsylvania but maintaining loyalty to the King. The *Bee* establishes humor magazines as among the earliest American periodical publications. Unlisted by Frank Luther Mott, the dean of scholars on American magazines, it is older than all but twelve titles in his authoritative *History of American Magazines*, but its existence establishes humor as a primary mode of expression in American periodical history. The short-lived Philadelphia *Bee* can also be used to define the type in America. It states its volume and issue number and periodicity. Its interests, appropriate to the eighteenth and nineteenth centuries, are predominantly political. The editor also commented at the end of Number 3 that his friend "Isaac Bickerstaff" worried that he had not stayed windward enough of the libel laws. The magazine's method is consistently comic or satiric; burlesque is used, and fanciful scenes, exaggeration, and humorous literary allusion figure regularly in the language, even though the full run is only three numbers amounting to twenty-four pages. Beyond this technical definition, it also appeared to be generated primarily by a single wit and showed the characteristically short life of pre-Civil War American humor magazines, only a handful of which survived beyond a year.

The second candidate for inclusion in this study is the *Omnium Gatherum** of Boston in 1795, which lasted for ten numbers but which managed to include at least one of the greatest New England tall tales in its brief life—the story of the hunter who reaps all the game of a fecund wilderness by the chance rebound of one stray shot. *Omnium Gatherum* also experimented with local types and edged toward backwoods dialect, foreshadowing the strengths of American humorous joking and tale-telling in the nineteenth century. By this time, however, the Federal period and the expansion of urban political interests and a cultured class allowed for the development of a more sophisticated political and social satire.

Joseph Dennie is probably the first important humorous magazine editor. His career began in the 1790s as a humorous writer of satiric essays by "Captain Farrago." His talent brought him the editorship of *The Farmer's Weekly Museum*, beginning in 1796. Published in Walpole, New Hampshire, from 1793, the *Farmer's Weekly Museum and Lay Preacher's Gazette* provided Dennie and his friend Royall Tyler with a forum to attack "Great cheats" while only "little rogues" must stand in the pillory, among other social abuses. Dennie had originally published his "Farrago" and "Lay Preacher" essays with the *Farmer's Museum*, but based on their success he attempted his own magazine, *The Tablet*,* in Boston in 1795. Dennie and Tyler, his co-contributor, both moved to the Philadelphia *Port Folio*, which Dennie endowed with its characteristically acrid and conservative flavor from 1802 through 1808. After Dennie was suppressed, and ultimately removed by death, it continued only in muted form. Few other writers had Dennie's brilliance, although William Cobbett was another writer-editor of such vindictive power as to require notice. Cobbett's *Peter Porcupine's Gazette*, beginning in 1797, and *Rush-Light*,* started just after the turn of the century, were politically motivated and driven by the force of exaggerated invective which ultimately brought Cobbett's destruction through libel suits.

True to the best tradition of controversial satire, both Dennie and Cobbett attracted legal attention. Dennie was under indictment in 1804 for sedition, based on his sarcastic treatment of democracy; Cobbett was forced to flee the country to escape the consequences of his legal battles, particularly his loss of a libel suit against Dr. Benjamin Rush, whom he had virulently attacked for using the ancient method of bleeding as a medical practice. In 1765, even Honeycomb's *Bee* registered its sensitivity to legal pressure in Bickerstaff's fear that the printer would be persecuted until he exposed the anonymous editor. In fact, John Peter Zenger's *Weekly Journal* in the 1730s used a significant amount of satire, and this irritant as much as any other may have invoked the animosity of the British justices who, in attempting to suppress it, contributed to the first great American defense of freedom of the press: Andrew Hamilton's summation at Zenger's trial for sedition in 1735. Such persecution underscores the controversial social and political nature of humor and humorous periodicals in America. Mott's account of Zenger's case in *American Journalism* makes clear how close satire was to sedition throughout the early period. Following these precedents, humor magazines have persistently operated at political, social, and sexual frontiers, and their persistence attests to the doggedness of dissenting opinion within American society.

The beginning of the nineteenth century saw a profusion of comic forms, including the comic paper, the magazine, the songster, and the comic almanac. Almanac humor, like college humor and academic humor, represents a subset unique unto itself. In the mainstream, comic periodicals were largely directed at social or political targets, taking an educated tone. *Salmagundi*,* created in 1807–1808 by Washington Irving and James Kirke Paulding, stands as the leading proponent of Addisonian irony in the Federalist period, although oriented more toward social manners than political morals. Nemo Nobody's *Something** in Boston in 1808 may have been the first humor magazine to set up burlesque columns of "Letters to the Editor" showing completely opposite demands from various readers, and it too lamented "The moth is the female that's dazzled by glare, / And fashion the blaze that consumes." Earlier in the decade other politically oriented satirists had already appeared, including *The Wasp* in 1802 and *The Corrector** in 1804; *The Barber Shop*,* kept by Sir David Razor, slashed British and American social idiosyncracies in 1807–1808. A number of similar titles came forth to illustrate the critical intention of comic journalism in the Federal era.

Of greatest significance in this period is the Philadelphia *Tickler*,* produced as a comic newspaper by George Helmbold under the pseudonym Toby Scratch'em, from 1807 until his departure to fight in the War of 1812, and resumed as the *Independent Balance* in 1817 and conducted by Helmbold until his death. Helmbold's *Tickler*, though unstudied by scholars, is one of a handful of important comic periodicals that tapped all the potential subjects and modes of its era. Not only did *The Tickler* provide elevated satire and humor derived from European sources and the classics, but Helmbold also printed doggerel verse and ironic dialect from popular sources. In one example, Skip the Magpie, in a bird apologia, blamed his thieving ways on bad parental education—a social issue that is still moot. Dastardly Duane of the *Aurora Borealis** was lashed along with the "embargaroons" and the list of "prizes drawn in the state office lottery" by lawyers of infinite silliness. Helmbold burlesqued and openly attacked political corruption in Philadelphia municipal contracts. In his paper he established and sustained the comic components of later American humorists of significance, including the literary comedians and Mark Twain. When Joseph C. Neal, the "charcoal sketcher," pioneered the portrayal of vulgar urban types in the Philadelphia papers of the 1830s, he may well have been joining the influences of Helmbold and Irving in a new American fusion—a fusion that brought him the title "The American Dickens." Neal's political failures, like the magpie, blamed their parents.

Toward the end of the Federalist period of magazine humor, the Boston *City Firefly** for 23 November 1822, offers evidence of the potency of American comic magazines in two items on attempts to repress them. It notes that Mr. Hall, the publisher of the *Castigator*, was in jail for three months for libel. It added that Buckingham of *The Galaxy*** had also been arraigned for libel, and it went on to libel Buckingham in turn as a defaulter and private imposter. Similar papers are prominent. Baltimore and Boston each offered a *Scourge*,* in 1810 and 1811, respectively, and Merrill Butler of the Boston *Scourge* was imprisoned for libel. New York's Federalist leader Alexander Hamilton defended *The Wasp*'s editor Harry Croswell from libel in a case that dragged on from 1802 to 1804, but with less success than Andrew Hamilton in the Zenger case; Croswell was convicted. Helmbold was forced to make at least one retraction in *The Tickler*, and perhaps more, to escape libel suits. The editor of the Philadelphia *Luncheon* was forced to retract a libelous article and cease publication after six months of life ending in January 1816. Tim Touchstone of the 1811 *Scourge*—Merrill Butler, just mentioned—reported a physical attack on his person by one of his satiric targets. Strongly phrased invective was often the currency of debate in the age before burlesque, and comic periodicals were obvious targets for legal retribution. The Tweed Ring, as is widely known, attempted to suppress Thomas Nast and Frank Leslie after the Civil War. Another period of intense suppression occurred when the postal authorities and city mayors and vice leagues tried to stem the flow of sexuality in the 1910–1930 period. Humor magazines throughout the history of the genre have experienced attacks from their angry butts.

The 1820s and 1830s were decades of transition in the history of American comic periodicals. Humor broadened, and the growth of American cities offered both a wider audience and more subjects. Washington's political life led to the birth of the *Champagne Club* (1834–1835) to attack the capitol's newly polished society. Boston had its *Club-Room*** from February to July 1820 as a lightly humorous outlet for local literati. Philadelphia's *The Ariel** (1827–1832) and Baltimore's *Baltimore Monument** (1836–1838) included humorous material but also pioneered the fictional and humorous in combined format typical of the twentieth century's *Saturday Evening Post*.** Cincinnati had its *Mirror** from 1831 to 1836, and New Orleans boasted George W. Kendall's *Picayune** from

1837 on. By the 1840s, comic papers treated theatrical events, burlesqued political and social topics, and offered a wide range of fictional and general news; among the most acerbic were journals such as *The Elephant, Humbug's American Museum,*** *The Bubble*** on the ephemeral side, and *Judy,** *The John-Donkey,** and *Yankee Doodle.** As far west as Oregon, Charles Pickett in Oregon City, population 400, laughed at the territorial legislature in Indian dialogue in his handwritten *Flumgudgeon Gazette*** in 1845.

The most significant of the comic papers before the Civil War is B. P. Shillaber's *The Carpet-Bag** (1851–1853), standing comfortably between such representative examples as Irving's *Salmagundi* in the Federal period and Louis H. Stephens's *Vanity Fair*, during the Civil War era. Shillaber was the father of Mrs. Partington and her plaguey boy Ike, those bellwethers of the confusing growth from country village to suburb and city which overtook the Northeast in the pre-Civil War years. Hoping for a national readership, Shillaber placed mistress Partington on the masthead of *The Carpet-Bag* as first among equals, for he published many authors from the regions, including John Phoenix, Samuel L. Clemens in his first appearance in a national magazine ("The Dandy Frightening the Squatter"), Charles F. Browne and "Ethan Spike"—Matthew Whittier, the poet's brother, along with the acerbic reviews of Assistant Editor Charles G. Halpine. Unfortunately, *The Carpet-Bag* gathered no substantial paying audience either locally or from the railroad travelers which it hoped to amuse. Other papers of note in this period included Wardle Corbyn's *Figaro!** in New York in 1850–1851, William Mathews's *Yankee Blade** (1842–1856), and T. W. Strong's *Yankee Notions** (1852–1875), a useful compendium and long-lasting reprinter of humor material. Although *Young Sam*** sneered that "Strong's Weakly" (*Yankee Notions*) had a "PUNCH-y appearance," in crude graphics and reportorial anecdotes it caught both the impact of the age of Barnum and the irony of secession. The *Yankee Blade*, a treasure trove of Yankee humor, provided the story of the greenhorn who sees his first cotton mill and is told about a youth who was snatched into the machines and woven into No. 16, super extra, cotton warp yarn—subsequently bought in bunches by the departed's mother and fellow students as remembrances. Richard Dorson in *Jonathan Draws the Longbow* rightly identifies this tale as a source for Mark Twain's similar story in *Roughing It*.

Two magazines in the 1800–1860 period require special attention for the position they hold in the history of American humor: New York's *Spirit of the Times** and *The Knickerbocker** magazine, both of which ran from the 1830s into the 1860s. Enthusiastic recipients of regional pieces, both magazines significantly advanced American humor by giving a wide range of comic authors access to their pages. William Trotter Porter's *Spirit of the Times* (1831–1861) was oriented toward horsemen and sportsmen, particularly the Southern planter population. It thus gathered into its columns the comedy best represented by Thomas Bangs Thorpe's "The Big Bear of Arkansas," the quintessential Southwestern humor story. Among other Southwestern humorists, it offered Thorpe,

C.F.M. Nolan, Johnson Jones Hooper, and George Washington Harris, not to mention sketches by such Northeastern writers as Philadelphian Joseph C. Neal, which often went West as exchange clips and came back East as anonymous Western sketches.

Lewis Gaylord Clark's New York *Knickerbocker* magazine (1833–1865) was more closely aligned with Washington Irving and the genteel humor of the urban literati, although it too featured regional comedy of note and also boasted the best of the literary comedians, John Phoenix, Doesticks, Charles G. Leland, and Frederick S. Cozzens, both in direct publication and in snips in its editorial columns. Clark's selected *Knick-Knacks from an Editor's Table* (1853) is characterized by the picture of old Knick falling off a pitifully undersized donkey on the ride to Dobbs Ferry, overlooking the Tappan Zee, laughed at by his son, young Knick—evidence of the domestic comedy to come in the ensuing decades. Leland became editor at the outset of the Civil War but left *The Knickerbocker*, as he had just left *Vanity Fair*, because he could not push it into a more radical political alignment; Leland's harshest satire was only to find a home briefly in Boston's *The Continental Monthly*,** where some of his comedy looks forward to the twentieth-century cynicism of American black writers. Neither *Spirit of the Times* nor *Knickerbocker* could withstand the economic and philosophical pressures of the Civil War; perhaps these two journals lasted so long because they captured the general material and audience that Shillaber's *Carpet-Bag* had failed to obtain. They are not solely humorous, but the significance of the humorous material they printed establishes them as landmarks in the field.

Vanity Fair (1859–1863), Louis H. Stephens's humor magazine, has perhaps enjoyed the highest standing among Civil War era publications. Stephens's cartoon attacks on President James Buchanan and King Cotton showed a brilliantly innovative imagination. Departing from a fixed cover, *Vanity* caricatured different literary and political personages each week, and its prose content was always consistently high. Artemus Ward's (Charles Farrar Browne) vulgar Old Showman letters were the best the age had to offer, and Charles Arnold as McArone and E. C. Stedman were almost equal to him in talent. Others had dealt with urban themes in burlesque vulgar language, notably *The New York Picayune** (1847–1859) under C. H. Levison and Doesticks, and its counterparts. Others told jokes and offered comic cartoons, for example, *Frank Leslie's Budget of Fun* (1859–1878) and *The Phunny Phellow** (1859–1876). But few seem to have attempted so consistently a high quality of literary humor and graphic excellence based solely on new and original material. Ward's letters and literary burlesques and McArone's travesty of war treatises were deftly comic prose. Rapidly escalating paper costs and the split in *Vanity*'s readership, due to the war, doomed it.

Both South and North had their humorous representations during this period, although the South could hardly offer a Bill Arp for every Artemus Ward. Thomas Nast's depictions of Confederate atrocities in *Harper's Weekly* were noted by Lincoln as his best recruiting tool. Frank Leslie's papers were uncompromisingly pro-Union. *The Plantation*** (1860) of Eatonton, Georgia, was a well-edited, although brief, representation of the Southern humorous sensibility toward literary culture in the face of Yankee vulgarity. Few papers could afford not to take positions, and *Vanity Fair*, followed by *Mrs. Grundy*,* with some of the same main contributors, was undoubtedly weakened by its attempted moderation. *Bugle-Horn of Liberty** in 1863 was intended as a Southern answer to *Vanity Fair* nonetheless. *Southern Punch*,* founded in Richmond, Virginia, in 1863, predictably folded in 1865.

By the 1870s, American critics were beginning to ask why the country could not sustain a comic magazine. The question was a nebulous one because of the exuberance of the genre, but it took on point when individual examples were contrasted with London's *Punch*, which had lasted for over thirty years. After weak beginnings in 1841, barely saved by George Cruikshank's "Comic Almanac," *Punch* by the 1860s was a boisterous and lusty provider of British satire, both a manifestation of English superiority and a gadfly to the social conscience of John Bull. Almost since its founding, it had influenced the format of American humorous publications, although in the matter of cover material, for example, *Vanity Fair* proved itself far more flexible than the unchanging puppet show which provided *Punch* covers into the 1950s. Commentator William Raynor seems to have raised the question of survivability in 1872 with a list of 84 comic periodicals in *Notes and Queries*: only three, *Frank Leslie's Budget of Fun, Nick Nax*,* and *Phunny Phellow* were identified as American (New York, specifically). Frederic Hudson, in "The Comic Paper Question," an earlier *Scribner's* article reprinted in his *Journalism in the United States from 1690 to 1872* (1873), claimed that American humor was so generally distributed among various quarters that no one magazine could contain it as a commercial venture. *Vanity Fair* and *Mrs. Grundy* (1865) provided his chief examples, along with *The Jolly Joker*,* *Momus*,** *The John-Donkey*,* the St. Louis *Puck** and the Mobile *Punster*, and, finally, *Punchinello*** (1870), which he considered heavily backed with $50,000, but which still became a case of infant mortality with but a single volume in print, a sad showing compared to *Punch*, which was then in its twenty-ninth year.

Brander Matthews responded to Raynor's list in the August 1875 issue of the *American Bibliopolist*, citing with varying degrees of accuracy forty-six American comic journals, excluding a dozen or so annuals. He drew directly on Orpheus C. Kerr's "The Mystery of Mr. E. Drood," a Dickens rewrite from *Punchinello* in 1870, for the undertaker's lament. Touring the gravesites, the undertaker intones the names on the headstones: "Next, Original Projector of an American *Punch*; next, Projector of Rural Newspaper; next, another Projector of American *Punch*—indeed, all the rest of that row is American *Punches*." Matthews wrote, "And Mr. Newell is right; the history of comic journalism in America is merely a list of tombstones." Catchy as this line is, it hardly takes into account the history of American periodicals generally and the consequences of collecting subscription fees after, rather than before, delivery, as had been the early custom. Advances in printing technology, decreases in paper prices, and the postal act of 1879 creating second-class mailing for periodicals all contributed to increased viability for magazines, along with changes in American subscription habits. The expansion of great Northern cities with their mass transit systems also allowed for newsstand sales, which brought about a revolution in advertising, merchandising, cover decoration, cover posters (which themselves became the object of a collecting fad around 1895)—and in content suited to mass readership as well. Later, non-bookstore/print-shop sales, as in drugstores, also contributed to broadening the content and ever increasing flamboyance in cover styles of American humor magazines in the great age of illustrated weeklies and monthlies at the turn of the century. The St. Louis *Puck*, mentioned in passing by Hudson, would usher in the New York *Puck* of Joseph Keppler and A. Schwarzmann and the great trio of American humor magazines to dominate the era from 1880 through the First World War.

The 1870s mark a second major transition in American humor and American periodical publishing. Just as the 1830s had seen the end of the Federalist era, so the 1870s marked the change from the older concerns with social identity and national politics—the pre-Civil War and Civil War matter—to the newer subjects of social and sexual morality and, later in the century, international politics. *Punchinello* (1870), with the best staff of *Vanity Fair* transferred to its ranks, is a throwback to the viewpoint of the Civil War, emphasizing national social and political events and prose. Politically, *Thistleton's Illustrated Jolly Giant*** in San Francisco in the early 1870s is transitional; rabidly anti-Irish and anti-papist, it is harbinger to the international political themes prominent later in the century. But *Champagne*** (1871) and *The New Varieties*** (1871–1875) give clear evidence of the coming age of the Gibson Girl, dominanted by cartoons of sloe-eyed busty women in underdresses whenever the opportunity—and there were many—arose. *Champagne* focused on the racy life of the upper classes, whereas *The New Varieties* battened on the sensational crimes and melodramatic theatricals that appealed to the lower social orders. *The New Varieties*, like the *Police Gazette*, showed vice in such lurid detail that the prospective sinner, titillated by the full and comprehensive knowledge of the degradation he was escaping, could shun it the more successfully. *Chic** in 1880–1881 was a slightly more sophisticated follower of the same line.

Also during the post-Civil War era, along with the opening of a wider social subject matter than that approached in the 1850s of the idealistic "Young America" movement, there was a tremendous explosion in the popular offerings of reportorial wits. No longer coffee house correspondents in the style of Joseph Addison and Richard Steele, the newspaper reporter/humorist of the post-Civil War era dwelt on the mundane problems of the enlarging class of wage-earning homeowners. From 1820 through the 1860s, a significant focal point of humorous periodicals was the political-social experience reflected in American mores. Before becoming books of humor, Jack Downing's letters from Portland, Maine, were originally newspaper productions; Artemus Ward's letters went to the

Cleveland *Plain Dealer*. *Graham's*, *Harper's*, and other general magazines of the 1850s maintained brief humor columns. In the 1860s, Henry Clapp's *Saturday Press* (where Mark Twain's "The Notorious Jumping Frog of Calaveras County" first appeared), the New York Sunday *Mercury*, and a host of other papers offered pages devoted largely to humor items. Humor columns appeared everywhere. Needless to say, whole books have been devoted to Mark Twain's writings for various western papers in the 1860s; Bill Nye, Robert J. Burdette, and others like them attained national identity through newspaper humor. By the middle 1870s, Street and Smith's *New York Weekly* offered a humor page, with Doesticks and Josh Billings as regulars.

In the 1870s there was a tremendous expansion in newspaper humor writing across the entire range of newspaper and magazine publishing. More of these later columns were comic moralisms and the comedy of middle-class life. "Brick" Pomeroy claimed national attention from the pages of the La Crosse, Wisconsin, *Democrat* beginning in 1860, the same town that spawned *Peck's Sun* (1874–1894), later of Milwaukee. Bill Nye emerged with the Laramie, Wyoming, *Boomerang** in 1881, the same year that Alexander Sweet and John Armoy Knox began their humorous newspaper *Texas Siftings*,* a year before Opie Read's *Arkansaw Traveler** and two years before William Marshall's *California Maverick*.** Mott lists a number of other regional publications; many more lie in state historical archives for the 1880–1930 period awaiting discovery by dedicated regional scholars. Walter Blair, in "The Popularity of Nineteenth-century American Humorists" (1931), extends the list of papers with significant humor columns and columnists even further, adding the Burlington, Iowa, *Hawk-Eye* man, Robert J. Burdette, and the *"Danbury* (Connecticut) *News* Man" among others. Many of these humorists are less likely than Burdette and Danbury's James M. Bailey to be found in even comprehensive humor anthologies of the period including *Mark Twain's Library of Humor* and A. R. Spofford's *Library of Wit and Humor*, although some will be found there. *Thistleton's Illustrated Jolly Giant* wanted to be considered a part of this melange, stoutly insisting that it was a newspaper and not a magazine. Such a profusion of talent spawned reprinters who were magazines: *Tid-Bits*,* for a time in the middle 1880s, and *Wit and Wisdom*** (1881), a useful and intelligent selector that dedicated itself to scissoring the newspaper exchanges and providing brief feature articles on prominent local comic reporters.

Commercial humor publications had existed, and continue to exist, supporting various advertisers. Almanacs shared common commercial applications throughout our literary history. *The Curiosity Shop*** in 1856 seems to be the first of a group of humor publications intended solely to boost a business—the Boston Museum, similar to Barnum's museum in New York. *Old Abe*,** subtitled the "War Eagle," was a joke paper boosting George Kelly's dry-goods store in Philadelphia around 1879. Chicago's *Hot Soldier*** at the turn of the century also belongs in this category, along with *Duke's Mixture Magazine*,** bringing humor to the tobacco-lover. *World's Fair Puck*,* *The Carnival of Authors***

(centennial in Philadelphia), and *Jubilee Days*,* all fit in the special events category. Even Thomas Edison got into the business with *Grid*, copyrighted Volume 1:1 (October 1919) quarterly through July 1920, to "disseminate some sense and a little nonsense among users of storage batteries." The *Bughouse Bugle* was issued by the Columbia Nut and Bolt Company, Bridgeport, Connecticut, copyrighting Volume 3:3 for July 1922. *Cackles* in 1908, however, appealing though the title is as a humor publication, was only the "illustrated magazine of poultry," without humor as far as copyright information supplies. Lavoris, International Fruit World, and several contemporary companies have all indulged in this subgenre.

The triad of great American magazines of the later nineteenth century, *Puck* (1877–1918), *Judge* (1881–1937), and *Life* (1883–1936), emerged from the seeming chaos of humorous voices with personalities that marked comic publishing in America for the following fifty years. *Puck*, *Life*, and *Judge* portrayed an upper-middle-class experience organized by social expectations of economic well-being. Born on the eve of the great age of color lithography and American illustration, they brought the issues of national political morality to the nation in bold and colorful caricatures in an extraordinary range of colored comic editorial cartoons. None of the three was particularly promising at the outset. *Puck* had lasted only briefly as the German-language St. Louis *Puck* in 1871. Only when Joseph Keppler seasoned it in New York and involved editors Sydney Rosenfeld and Henry Cuyler Bunner did it become a major success, backing Democratic politics. *Judge*, financially unsuccessful at first, was formed by a dissident group of *Puck* artists led by J. A. Worth and including E. W. Kemble, Frank Beard, and later Grant Hamilton. Under W. J. Arkell, it received the patronage of the Republican party to counter *Puck* and also acquired its motif of humor at the expense of tramps and "darkies," later expanded into a country humor mode with authors like E. P. Butler. *Life*, a product of three Harvard men, chose its targets wherever it found a social cause. Charles Dana Gibson's cartoons were first bought not because they were publishable but to encourage the young cartoonist to do better; it was only later that his drawings took on the epoch-defining archness that made them unique. Nevertheless, in the mix of upper crust, localist, and political humor, bolstered by their colorful, strongly opinionated cartoons, the three magazines found mass audiences and developed a set of graphic interests that recognized the new social, economic, and political forces of the era in which America became a major international power.

The tradition of cartoon editorializing for social causes began in the 1850s with Frank Leslie's attacks on swill-milk in New York City—milk licensed by the corrupt city government but taken from cows fed on diseased refuse. Thomas Nast's cartoons for the Union, and later against Tammany Hall, established the importance of American comic art as a political tool, despite the relative lack of success later of Nast's own magazine. With *Puck*, Keppler's strength as a cartoonist was mated with the wit of H. C. Bunner. Although all critics agree that Keppler's cartoons represented a genuine break with the traditional comic magazine format of London's *Punch*, which had dominated American comic magazines for the past thirty years, not all agree that Bunner, who generated significant amounts of comic prose, was equally important. John A. Mitchell's ideas of graphic art and John Kendrick Bangs's editorial abilities gave an equally marked character to *Life*, although Charles Dana Gibson, first appearing in *Life* in 1887, is its most important graphic contributor. Gibson's high-eyebrowed young ladies and Richard "the Lion-Harding" Davis model-men permanently pickled the complacent social superiority of the American newly rich. Evocative in themselves, they adapted well to humorous headings that sometimes expanded into dramatic vignettes burlesquing the spoiled well-to-do, and they blended satisfactorily with a wide variety of other socially critical material. *Judge*'s battery of cartoonists is a register of important American graphic artists in the later nineteenth century. The long lives of the three periodicals were well earned by their conceptualization of an age—an age that died, however, in the hub-bub of the Roaring Twenties. Only a reminiscence of *Puck* survives—the New York *Puck* building—but a healthy advertising corporation carries on the name, standing behind the Sunday "funnies" as "Puck, the Comic Weekly."

While *Life*, *Puck*, and *Judge* captured the age and chronicled its transformation into the twentieth century, a variety of forces stimulated brief-lived competitors. Closer to *Life* was the Chicago *Rambler*** from 1884 to 1887, claiming to be the only Western paper sold on the Manhattan Elevated. An actual *American Punch** was attempted in Boston from 1879 to 1881, but, true to Orpheus C. Kerr's portrayal in "The Mystery of E. Drood," it became extinct in two years. In Texas, *Texas Siftings* was followed in the 1890s by *The Rolling Stone*,* where O. Henry first sought recognition. The most garish colors of the era were the bright yellows in the New York *Bee* of 1898–1899, with its bold cartoons on American imperialism—graphics that out-pucked *Puck*.

In addition to the journals cited above, other regional magazines have added local spice to American comic periodical history. The *California Maverick* is an obvious example in 1883–1886. San Francisco and Chicago have been particularly prolific in comic literature, some of it with ethnic or anti-ethnic flavor. San Francisco's *Wasp*,** Chicago's *Carl Pretzel's Pook*,** and the *San Francisco Puck* are notable examples of later nineteenth-century comedy with a basis in regional or local events and personalities, and Chicago's *Rambler*, already cited, was an outstanding production. The most bizarre offspring of the major national magazines—in this case a foreign occurrence—is the *Tokyo Puck*,** which appeared around 1908–1909 in Japanese and English. It attacked American racism as manifested in naval and armaments policy, and it responded with harsh antagonism to physical attacks on Japanese and Chinese immigrants on the West Coast. It was directly motivated in format, artwork, and subject matter by *Puck*, a curious sidelight on continental publishing history.

Also of significant interest are the regional little magazines for their iconoclastic skepticism toward moral and literary censorship. The original *Calgary Eye Opener** from Canada was cast in this mold, as was Wyoming's *Sagebrush*

*Philosophy** (1904–1910), and the *Kansas Knocker** (1900–1901). Cleveland's *Hot Dog*** combined racy humor with a few girlie photos to get itself in trouble with the censors, as did the Midwest's *Jim Jam Jems.** The *Arkansaw Thomas Cat* from 1890 to 1948 was another of the sharp-tongued, iconoclastic, and crusty vernacular voices that upheld values at once more liberal and more conservative than the self-serving babbittry surrounding it. Without slighting Mencken and George Jean Nathan's contribution to American periodical humor in modernizing traditional skepticism to fit twentieth-century life, other sources may be said to have preceded them. *Sagebrush Philosophy*, among several of the others, foreshadows both the philosophy and style of *The American Mercury*. It warned its readers on the cover of each issue to consider the mummy, he ain't had no fun for five thousand years, a suitably slangy 1904 updating of the *Philadelphia Repository*'s wry comment in 1800 that marriage has many pains, but celibacy has no pleasures.

Resistance to the comic viewpoint of the twentieth century also began to appear, and with good reason. Present in a number of humor magazines, particularly the publications by Arkell such as *Judge's Library*,** are a number of racial and social stereotypes that seem grating to the modern eye. Jews have big noses, Negroes have liver lips. At a higher social level, the languid laxity of some of the marriage-oriented cartoons in the Gibson style suggested a widening skepticism toward conventional morality. In the same period, the first concerns were expressed about the violence and disrespect toward elders prominent in many comics. One such article, by Professor A. O. Leutheusser, appearing in *The Illustrated Home Journal* for 1907, noted skepticism toward city government as dominated by pug-nosed Irish immigrants, violence against fathers and elders, and disrespect for ministers, citing Yens Yensen, The Newlyweds, and Happy Hooligan comic strips. The vice league attacks on Mencken, post office attacks on several humor magazines, and the local and federal government investigations into comic books of the 1930s and 1950s came out of this continuing concern with the "influence" of comic magazines—the presumption being that visual humor formed rather than reflected contemporary social ideas and that suppressing the expression would suppress the reality.

The period following World War I—the Jazz Era—produced several magazines that are significant in themselves, although they never developed into major commercial successes. The *Art Young Quarterly* (1919–1922), beginning as *Good Morning*,* with its "Poor Fish" representing the common man/taxpayer/ sucker was a socialist publication—a sure circulation-killer for political reasons— but with impressively rough charcoal drawings expressing bold political skepticism. *Americana* (1932–1933) took a political/existential slant under editor Alexander King; ominously insightful, its graphics and captioned photos brought European sophistication to bear on American common life, as well as identifying European events that presaged World War II. Each of these journals reflects a vital part of its era, providing the modern reader with an unparalleled view of this later transitional age. *Hello, Buddy*** was a tiny, cheap magazine printed and distributed by disabled vets, and carried the pessimistic humor of war's victims late in the twenties. *Ziffs** (1924–1926) was typical of the breezier twenties magazines but with a higher level of content than any of its contemporaries.

Collegiate humor marked the Roaring Twenties with its peculiar cachet as well, taking up in sexual iconoclasm where *The American Mercury* left off. The field of collegiate humor can be traced well back into the nineteenth century with *Acta Columbiana* and the *Harvard Lampoon* and before, but it was in the 1920s that the co-ed was melded with the Ziegfield girl, and Gibson's Richard Harding Davis male degenerated into John Held, Jr.'s jellybean-headed undergraduate. From the 1920s through the early 1950s, several hundred college humor magazines offered a jazzy mix of the puerile and the sophisticated. The humor of dating and seduction was more pronounced in the 1920s and 1930s than later, but staples included the D+ English mark on a Washington or Lincoln speech, the he/she kissing or sex-banter joke, and the story of a crazy fraternity bash on a Saturday night. Outside the colleges, however, *Cartoons and Collegian Fun*,** *College Humor*,** *College Humor and Sense*,** *College Life*,** *College Comics*,** and *Campus Comics Quarterly** brought this humor to the general public in the 1930s; they were superseded in a brief renaissance in the 1950s and 1960s by a trickle of similar material in *College Laughs** and *Campus Jokes and Cartoons*.** Collegiate humor represents a field unto itself and displays a far greater uniformity of style and theme than is common in other subcategories, but most of the significant writers and cartoonists of the twentieth century appeared first in a college humor magazine.

Life, *Puck*, and *Judge* lived well into the twentieth century, although modern readers only recognize the later pictorial *Life* of Henry Luce as inheritor of the old comic magazine name. Norman Anthony, himself central in an understanding of the new comic tradition cropping out in the 1930s, has commented that *Esquire** and *The New Yorker** took away their remaining readership as well as drawing off readers of his new-styled *Ballyhoo* in the middle 1930s. *Ballyhoo* itself, however, deserves most attention for reformulating humor magazines into the mode dominant throughout the remainder of this century. It, and numerous followers with names like *Bunk*,** *Aw, Nerts!*,** and *Hooey** abandoned typographical formality and squared layouts, scattering gags and cartoons across pages in unexpected slants and overlaps. Anthony's content in *Ballyhoo* matched his layouts in outrageous burlesques of conventional advertising and commercial slogans, freeing the comic periodical medium in ways that he had been prevented from attempting in *Life*. Anthony was not able to repeat his success in *Hellzapoppin'*, *Der Gag Bag*, or *Funnybone Quarterly*,** but *Ballyhoo* alone establishes his importance as a twentieth-century innovator in comic magazine format and ideology. *Ballyhoo*'s innovations made possible the later, bolder, and broader changes in *National Lampoon* and *Mad* in inventing their own formats and employing crudely vulgar and unpleasant material as a counter-irritant to the prevailing cultural blandness they saw around them.

Sophisticated comic magazines proliferated in the twentieth century along with their vulgar counterparts. *Vanity Fair* and *The Smart Set** suggest the upper crust orientation by title alone. *The New Yorker* is particularly notable for lengthy pieces of urban whimsy and comic fiction, and its success spawned similar publications like Philadelphia's *Town Crier.*** Although at first its primary claim seemed to be merely to that sophisticated wit pioneered by such publications as San Francisco's *The Lark** and *Epi-Lark* and some of the Greenwich Village "Little Magazines," *The New Yorker*'s E. B. White, James Thurber, and Peter Arno defined an evanescent milieu of civilized self-assertion—a world equally accepting of White's sense of mortality and emotional vulnerability and of Arno's walrus-mustachioed, top-hatted rake in full rut after the genus Chorus Girlus Americanus—everything a matter of amusement once its premises are accepted. At a more popular level, George Horace Lorimer's *Saturday Evening Post,** Reader's Digest,*** and *Collier's* used humor to express the popular American middle-class sense of social and patriotic values. Various hard-bound anthologies of their cartoons offer continuing evidence of their success with suburban, army/ service, and domestic themes. None of these three qualifies as a humor magazine as such, but each employed humor as an important component of the package offered to readers.

Appealing to yet another audience, the crackerbarrel influence also strengthened noticeably in comic magazines at the turn of the century. Local savants with names like Uncle Josh and Uncle Ben, offering countrified epigrams flowing from the inspiration of Josh Billings and Sam Slick before them, were extraordinarily prominent in the later 1890s. *Sis Hopkin's Own Book, The Magazine of Fun*, and several similar titles under the Arkell firm now separated from *Judge*—Arkell having been bumped out of his *Judge*ship in 1898—succeeded such jocular, locally flavored magazines as *Uncle Remus' Magazine** (1907– 1909) and *Colonel Rollingpin's Annual*. When *Judge's Serials*** merged with the first two named in July 1915 to create *Film Fun*, it would be fair to say that the Jazz Age was initiated in American humor magazines. *Film Fun* lasted to 1942 with its splashy and often flashy array of starlet photos and funny captions, always featuring to greater or lesser degree the humor of dating, mating, or sex, but really depending on cheesecake throughout its run. The lineage is as stated, even if the derivation of cheesecake from crackerbarrel seems odd enough.

The American cartoon also came of age around 1900. Cartoons had occupied their own annual publications as early as David C. Johnston's *Scraps*** from 1828 to 1848, and dominated most of the content of *Humbug's American Museum*. Following the Civil War, breakthroughs in modern printing techniques enabled *Life, Puck, Judge*, and numerous others to offer cartoons of a variety and colorfulness previously unknown. So important did the cartoon become as a form of comic art that museums in both Port Chester, New York, and San Francisco, California, are now dedicated to it. A brief glance at the cartoon face on the February 1932 *Life* will reveal the lasting influence of even a transient visual experience—the face is clearly the ancestor of *Mad*'s Alfred E. Newman.

H. H. Windsor's *Cartoons Magazine** (1912–1922), a sister publication of *Mechanics Illustrated*, was one of the finest and most thoughtful reprinters of cartoons in this age. *Cartoons*, including a special *War in Cartoons* in 1914, often listed as a separate publication, was especially sensitive to politics and social experience. From the 1950s on, cartoon magazines have been prevalent in cheaper formats featuring gals and gags. They are often without other comic prose text or social interest beyond their orientation toward the girlie themes of interest to their readership. Although Crestwood, Minoan Publications, Humorama, and similar publishers offered multiple titles along these lines in the 1960s and 1970s, they have largely disappeared in the 1980s.

Captain Billy's Whiz Bang and a handful of other publications in an easily concealed digest size, including *The Flapper,** Jim Jam Jems*, and later *Smokehouse Monthly,** Calgary Eye Opener*, and *Red Pepper,*** carried the banner of sexy humor into the 1920s, not without significant attacks by the U.S. Post Office. *Jim Jam Jems* was under indictment for four years in the teens before being vindicated of charges of obscenity, and censors frequently cited it along with *Hot Dog* and *Captain Billy's Whiz Bang* among publications they would like to suppress. *Flapper's Experience* in 1925 was declared unmailable by the Post Office on the grounds of obscenity, as was *Film Fun*, although both were found to be mild by judges and juries, and *Ballyhoo* fared similarly at the hands of federal prosecutors in the 1930s. In fact, other publications, especially along the "arts beautiful" and physical culture lines, were far more sexual in content. A wide range of spicy story, pulp magazines also became prominent in the later teens and twenties, some of which are comic, others of which are simply sexsational. "Breezy," "Paris," or "Broadway" were often the title indicators of such content, including *Brevities,*** a tabloid also known as *Broadway Brevities*, *Broadway Nights,** Broadway Nightlife,** Broadway Breeze,** Paris Follies,** Paris Thrills,*** and *Paris Nights.*** The forties expanded the "Girls and Gags" format, with *Grin,* Gayety,** and similar tabloids being tyical.

The 1930s publications were followed in the 1950s with the second wave of *Breezy,** Paris Life***—claiming to be the American edition of *La Vie Parisian*—and similar cheesecake and cartoon magazines. *TV Girls and Gags*** and *Cartoon Cuties* belong to the 1950s; and *Gals and Gags*** and *Comic Cuties*, with racier photos among the cartoons, to the late 1960s. The so-called art photo and titillating story magazine of the earlier part of the century crossed into the humor field on various occasions. Otherwise, the emphasis on nudie photos and sexual acts in cartoons emerged in the late 1950s and 1960s with such titles as *Comedy Riot,** Zowie,** Gaze,** Romp,** Zip,*** and *Stare,*** and others from Humorama, Health Knowledge, and similar purveyors of bimonthly digests of adult sexual cartoons and gags.

The 1970s and 1980s saw the fullest physicalization of sexual humor, with jokes about the sex act, bodily parts, and related details. With the advent of *Screw,** Hustler Humor,*** and *Sex to Sexty,*** and the transformation of *Cartoon Carnival* and *Good Humor*** into adult humor magazines, the breaching of this last social taboo—physical sexuality—through humor was accomplished, although humor magazines can hardly be considered pioneers, and their overall readership may be in significant decline.

The Second World War had its own sort of influence on humor magazines. The war trimmed the number of the 1930s Jazz Era pulps, finishing the winnowing process begun in the Depression. Large folios with names like *War Laffs*** and *TNT*** emerged, combining cartoons and pin-ups in thirty- or thirty-six-page, cheap-paper tabloids. Service cartoons touched on the GI and the Gob on leave, army and civilian jokes, and officer/soldier jokes. Another group of magazines like *Army and Navy Grins*,*** in digest-sized one-hundred-page pocket magazines, offered all cartoons, one to a page with scattered, poorly printed color cartoons, and wartime themes as the usual subject matter. Wacs and fat generals and soldiers and training camps predominated in these cheap-paper magazines with bright covers and crude printing. Among the oddest are publications like *BlackOut*,*** which carried civil defense instructions among the air-raid jokes. The best is the 1941 *Hooey*** Annual with a cutout cover allowing the reader to lift a flap and see goose-stepping Hitler being goosed by an angry goose. As one one-time magazine-format publication was titled, *Humor Is Our Ally*.

As Bill Mauldin brought his GI Joe dogface from "Up Front" to "Back Home," American humor periodicals also attempted to return to domestic materialism, although several service-oriented cartoon digests lasted into the 1950s. Dell attempted to resurrect *Ballyhoo* under the uninspired editorship of cartoonist Bill Yates, and its mildly inoffensive satire corresponds to humor popularized in the great mass fiction magazines including the *Saturday Evening Post* and *Collier's* which dominated American magazine publishing with light fiction endorsing traditional values and viewpoints.

The dominant style in humor magazines after 1950 is as unpromising as the style of comic papers must have seemed two hundred years ago. At one end of the spectrum lies blatantly sexual *Screw* with its focus on physical sexuality but its consistently sarcastic tone; at the other end, *Laugh Factory*** magazine, a bimonthly satire magazine covering multiple targets, but with no bite or real intelligence, seemingly directed at a teenage population. In between lie such offerings as *CARtoons*** and *Cartoon Cavalcade*, specializing in cars and sexy humor, *Sex to Sexty*,*** and *National Lampoon* and *Mad*, still healthy as satiric commentators on the American scene. The success of *Mad* and *National Lampoon* is at least partly based on the high level of content; more than one *Mad* grotesque comic strip was merely a reprinting with comic images of such classics as Longfellow's "The Wreck of the Hesperus." They updated the burlesques practiced by William Makepeace Thackeray in the 1840s and Bret Harte in the 1860s to the American literary environment of the 1950s and 1960s. In the 1960–1980 period, a large handful of scholarly and professional humor magazines existed; the college humor magazine of the 1930s has never reappeared with its earlier strength except in various April Fools' Day issues. The counter-culture comix maintain a following both as new issues and as reprints and collectibles—the X at the end of "comix" designed to indicate their antisocial dissenting position even while they ape the comic book format which strenuously endorses American values through stylized melodrama. They are probably the strongest subgenre at the present time, and like college humor and comic books, they offer enough material for a separate study.

National Lampoon and *Mad* Magazine continue in the middle 1980s as the dominant public humor magazines on American magazine display racks. *National Lampoon* retains its long-standing format of burlesquing serious social ills. "Bum U." is advertised for training street people in a 1986 issue; Superman is changed into Goldman, a Jew who buys off criminals; "Misfortune" burlesques *Fortune*'s applause of capitalists in a lengthy magazine burlesque section. *Mad* maintains a similar format, with "Zonk Me Out to the Ballgame" converting an old popular classic to a drug motif, burlesques of TV ads and series, and Don Martin cartoons. Most of its imitators in the 1960s and 1970s are merely memories, although *Cracked*** lives on. The more intellectual humor magazines which lived briefly during the period have expired, with the exception of a few scholarly and trade-oriented humorous periodicals. *The New Yorker* in 1985 initiated its return to humorous commentary after years as an increasingly serious opponent of American international political policies.

American humor magazines and comic periodicals thus contain much of the American spirit of independence from restraint in personal and political life. Their record of legal troubles in itself provides a study of our changing cultural expectations. The continuity of humor as a periodical medium provides a valuable focus for the history of dissent and commentary in the democracy. Their intrinsic interest, as well as the intrinsic interest of the biographies of the people who made them, is no less impressive. George Helmbold's *Tickler* and *Independent Balance* deserve a major study, as does Lewis Gaylord Clark's *Knickerbocker* and Norman Anthony's *Ballyhoo*. Helmbold, Clark, and Anthony might each be assigned a place in comic periodical publishing equal to William Trotter Porter's and his *Spirit of the Times*, without diminishing in any way Porter's special importance in opening the frontier humor of the Southwest. The regional little magazines like *Sagebrush Philosophy* and the *Arkansaw Thomas Cat* should be more highly prized and more carefully studied than they have been up to the present. A number of characteristic and charismatic regional humor magazines await identification. The recent era of sexual comedy over the past sixty years has yet to be defined in historical terms. In fact, brief studies of many aspects of twentieth-century humor magazines are notable for their lack of rigor and intelligence in assessing the uses of comic periodicals for a variety of purposes. The counter-culture comix movement needs a suitable chronicler, as does the college humor movement before it, although some anthologies at least help to define them. More important, the complete cataloguing and evaluating of humor magazines is far from complete, and the vast profusion of comic magazines in the twentieth century appear even less likely to be collected than their counterparts in previous eras.

Library Location Codes

Union List of Serials codes are used when convenient to identify library locations. The following codes are used in entries in this book; please refer to the *Union List* for any codes not found here; libraries named infrequently are cited by name.

CL	Los Angeles Public Library
CSmH	Huntington Library, California
CSt	Stanford University
CtHW	Trinity College, Hartford
CtY	Yale University
CU	University of Connecticut
CU-BANC	University of California-Berkeley
CU-S	University of California-San Diego
DCU	Catholic University, Washington, D.C.
DeWI	Wilmington Institute Free Library, Delaware
DLC	Library of Congress
GA	Atlanta Public Library, Georgia
IAU	University of Iowa
IC	Chicago Public Library
ICN	Newberry Library, Chicago
ICU	University of Chicago
IEN	Northwestern University, Evanston, Illinois
INE	Evansville Public Library, Evansville, Indiana
IU	University of Illinois
KMK	Kansas State University

KPT	Pittsburg State University, Kansas
MB	Boston Public Library
MBat	Boston Athenaeum
MBU	Boston University
MdBE	Enoch Pratt Free Library, Baltimore
MH	Harvard University
MiD	Detroit Public Library
MiU	University of Michigan
MnU	University of Minnesota
MoK	Kansas City Public Library
MWA	American Antiquarian Society
N	New York State Library, Albany
NB	Brooklyn Public Library
NbU	University of Nebraska
NcD	Duke University
NcU	University of North Carolina, Chapel Hill
NHi	New York Historical Society, New York, N.Y.
NIC	Cornell University
NjP	Princeton University
NjR	Rutgers University
NN	New York Public Library
NNC	Columbia University, New York, N.Y.
NOneoU	State University of New York-Oneonta
OC	Cincinnati Public Library
OCl	Cleveland Public Library
OCLW	Case Western Reserve University
OClWHi	Western Reserve Historical Society, Cleveland
OO	Oberlin College
OrU	University of Oregon
OU	Ohio State University
PHi	Pennsylvania Historical Society
PP	Philadelphia Free Library
PPi	Carnegie Library, Pittsburgh
PPL	Library Company of Philadelphia
PPuLC	Union Library Catalog of Philadelphia
PSC	Swarthmore College
PU	University of Pennsylvania
RP	Providence Public Library, Rhode Island

RPB	Brown University
ScU	University of South Carolina
TxU	University of Texas
UI	University of Illinois
ViU	University of Virginia
WaU	University of Washington
WHi	State Historical Society of Wisconsin, Madison

Part I
MAGAZINE PROFILES

A

ABRACADABRA

Abracadabra was a short-lived compendium of political satire, wit, and pure nonsense published in Portland, Maine, during the summer of 1808. Appearing at the height of President Jefferson's embargo, *Abracadabra* featured short essays on social and political issues with a strong Federalist bias. With much of its political satire masked by metaphor, *Abracadabra* is an interesting example of the use of humor to soften opposition polemics in an era when the legitimacy of political opposition was not yet firmly established. Only two issues were published; the first appeared on 16 June 1808, and the last on 21 July 1808.

The background of *Abracadabra* is obscure. The publisher was William Weeks, who probably also took a hand in the writing. The authors are unknown. In the pages of *Abracadabra* they are identified only as "Messieurs A, B, and C." "We shall keep ourselves shrouded in a mantle of mystery," they proclaimed, "in the manner of congress in the year 1808." The name *Abracadabra* was adopted to add to the air of mystery. In the first number the authors promised to write on any topic that interested them, and they instructed readers not to "attempt to fathom our intentions . . . we are not to be *guess'd at*." *Abracadabra* can hardly be described as a periodical. "Though we have called this a periodical publication," the authors declared in the first issue, "yet we must here unsay it, as we shall not appear at any stated periods—perhaps once in a month—perhaps twice—or in fact, whenever we feel ourselves sufficiently ripe for an essay." Only one more issue appeared, and that some five weeks later. The reasons for the early demise of *Abracadabra* are as obscure as its origins.

Each issue of *Abracadabra* was made up of sixteen pages measuring 4½" × 7", bound in pamphlet form. Individual copies were sold at the Haymarket Street printing shop of J. McKown for nine pence. Both numbers of *Abracadabra* contained four essays of about four pages each. Most are nonsensical, but a few include references to social and political issues of the day. Two essays in the second issue, "A Sentimental Journey to the Hog Islands" and "Patty Clover, A North-Easter Tale," are satires on the idea of rural virtue. Among the veiled political comments in *Abracadabra* is an essay linking Jefferson with Napoleon, and another describing a fanciful stage version of Jack and the Beanstalk as a satire on Jefferson's foreign policy.

Information Sources

INDEX SOURCES: None.
REPRINT EDITIONS: Readex Microprint.
LOCATION SOURCES: MB,NN.

Publication History

MAGAZINE TITLE AND TITLE CHANGES: *Abracadabra*, 16 June–21 July 1808.
VOLUME AND ISSUE DATA: Irregular; Volume 1, 16 June–21 July 1808.
PUBLISHER AND PLACE OF PUBLICATION: William Weeks, Portland, Maine.
EDITOR: Unknown.
CIRCULATION: Unknown.

Jack D. Warren, Jr.

THE AERONAUT

The Aeronaut was a manuscript periodical written and circulated in New York City from 1816 to 1822 by a group that called itself "an Association of Gentlemen," "a Literary Association," and finally "the Literary Club." That the last name may have been derived from the London social group founded by Samuel Johnson is suggested by the Augustan tone of much of the periodical's contents. Johnson, Joseph Addison, and Richard Steele are specifically mentioned in the first issue (18 May 1816) as "illustrious models" for what the association was attempting; the association's members hoped "to catch a spark of that etherial flame which plays around the departed glories" of their great predecessors. They would do this by writing about the world from the point of view of the aeronaut, who "may soar on high, emulating the bird of Jove, or keep along the ground, fearful to rise to too great a height. He has an opportunity of beholding nations & countries & seas spread as in a map before him; of inspecting the manners of mankind, and making observations on their employments & their pursuits."

The first volume of *The Aeronaut*, consisting of eighteen issues, was produced by three writers, each signing with a different initial. A fourth writer was added during the compiling of the second volume, and new writers appeared at irregular intervals thereafter, but there seems never to have been more than a handful of participants in the project. Most issues were individual efforts, though occasional collaborations did occur. The contents included essays on manners and morality, discussions of literature, travel narratives, short stories, translations (especially from Greek and Latin literature), original poetry, parodies, and burlesques. Much of the comic material, concentrated especially in Volume 4, consisted of contrived letters to the editor bearing such signatures as "Thunderlug Agonistes," "Harry Smockface," "Timothy Dullard," and "Bridget Simple." These letters were used to create amusing character sketches and to comment on contemporary life in New York. There were also scattered examples of satire in the styles of John Dryden, Alexander Pope, and Henry Fielding and of unflattering imitations of the first generation Romantics.

The handwritten issues of *The Aeronaut* appeared at intervals varying from one day to several weeks, with later issues occurring less and less regularly. The final issues, in fact, bear no dates at all, but it seems probable that no new numbers were written after 1822. The last reliably numbered issue, Number 195, was dated 30 September 1822. Issues were apparently circulated by hand, and several bear the notation that they were to be returned to 52 Wall Street, though the significance of that address is uncertain. Except for rare pen sketches and the Literary Club logo, which appeared only in later volumes, *The Aeronaut* was not illustrated.

Information Sources

BIBLIOGRAPHY:
Edgar, Neal L. "Aeronaut." *A History and Bibliography of American Magazines 1810–1820.* Metuchen, N.J.: Scarecrow Press, 1975, pp. 90–91.
Gregory, Winifred, ed. "*Aeronaut*, A Periodical Paper, by an Association of Gentlemen." *Union List of Serials in Libraries of the United States and Canada.* New York: H. W. Wilson Co., 1927, p. 23.
Kribbs, Jayne K. Entry No. 5. *An Annotated Bibliography of American Literary Periodicals, 1741–1850.* Boston: G. K. Hall, 1977, p. 1.
INDEX SOURCES: Table of Contents at the end of each volume (1–7) or the beginning of each volume (8–12), except none available for Volume 13; General Index for Volumes 1–6 at the end of Volume 6.
REPRINT EDITIONS: University Microfilms.
LOCATION SOURCES: Columbia University.

Publication History

MAGAZINE TITLE AND TITLE CHANGES: *The Aeronaut: A Periodical Paper, By an Association of Gentlemen,* Volume 1; *The Aeronaut: A Periodical Paper, By a Literary Association,* Volumes 2–5; *The Aeronaut. By a Literary Association,* Volume 6; *The Aeronaut,* Volumes 7–12; *Aeronaut,* Volume 13.
VOLUME AND ISSUE DATA: Irregular, eighteen issues per volume, for Volumes 1–3 (18 May 1816–28 June 1817); irregular, twenty-two issues per volume, for Volumes 4–6 (1 July 1817–4 October 1817); irregular, thirty issues per volume, for Volumes 7–8 (No. 121, 6 October 1817–No. 178, 11 August 1818, complete, except No. 162, 3 July 1818, which is blank; No. 179, 15 August 1818, is also blank; No. 180, undated, is missing entirely); irregular, fifteen issues, for Volume 9 (c. September 1818–30 September 1822); irregular, issue numbers omitted and

number of issues uncertain, for Volumes 10–13 (most dates omitted; nearly all
those included conflict with dates of earlier volumes).
PUBLISHER AND PLACE OF PUBLICATION: The Literary Club, New York.
EDITOR: Unknown.
CIRCULATION: Unknown.

Robert H. O'Connor

THE AMERICAN MERCURY

H. L. Mencken's *The American Mercury* was a journalistic phenomenon during
the 1920s. Highly popular with a youthful, metropolitan, upper-middle-class
readership, it embodied a spirit of opinionated iconoclasm that made it an
essential force in shaping the tastes and moral attitudes of an entire generation.

The inception of the *Mercury* was Alfred Knopf's desire to have a prestige
periodical associated with his family's publishing company. At that time, Henry
Louis Mencken, whose books Knopf had been publishing for some years, and
George Jean Nathan were editing *The Smart Set*.* Knopf first attempted to
purchase and upgrade that magazine. When his purchase offer was rejected,
Mencken, who wished to free himself from *The Smart Set*'s pulp associations,
convinced Knopf that a new venture was preferable. Knopf agreed and formed
an equal-thirds partnership with Mencken and Nathan; their collaboration resulted
in a polished monthly modeled in broad outline on the *London Mercury* and the
Mercure de France.

From its first issue of January 1924, the *Mercury* exhibited a lively eclecticism
that placed it between established organs of commentary and opinion—*Nation*
and *New Republic*—and such high-quality literary journals as *Harper's* and
Atlantic. Knopf, in a prepublication press release, described the *Mercury*'s aim
as being "to offer a comprehensive picture, critically presented, of the entire
American scene." Coverage, he promised, would range over science, the fine
arts, literature, politics, and industrial and social relations. The point of view
would, in Knopf's words, be that of "the civilized minority." Within this
overview there was plenty of room for disagreement. Nathan, equating
"civilized" with "cultivated," pressed Knopf for an emphasis on the fine arts,
with only modest journalistic overtones. Mencken, however, envisioned a more
robust editorial focus, what he called in a first issue editorial "a realistic
presentation of the whole gaudy, gorgeous American scene." For Mencken,
Knopf's civilized minority meant what Charles Graham Sumner had once called
"the forgotten man," or, in Mencken's terms, "the normal, educated, well-
disposed, unfrenzied, enlightened citizen of the middle minority," whom
Mencken believed could be found among scientists, artists, and businessmen
with imagination, the kind of independently minded skeptic who was annoyed
by Prohibition on the one hand and the threat of Comstockery on the other. In
short, Mencken's ideal reader was, if not Mencken himself, then someone very
much like him.

The differing editorial philosophies proved irreconcilable. Following a year of increasing strain, Mencken convinced Knopf that a choice had to be made. In February of 1925, Nathan agreed to vacate his co-editorship and continued as a contributing editor only. Charles Angoff, a recent Harvard graduate, was hired as an editorial assistant with responsibility for office management in New York, thus freeing Mencken to continue residence in Baltimore with only occasional trips north to oversee the composition of each issue. With the reorganization, the *Mercury* was fully transformed into a clear expression of one man's interests, attitudes, and personal style.

Knopf's printing standards, always high, were brought fully to bear on the *Mercury*. For as long as he had an interest in the publication, it displayed exemplary execution. The format, designed by Elmer Adler, was a stunning $10^3/_{16}'' \times 7''$ Garamond-set, double-column issue, featuring fully sewn construction, fine Scotch featherweight paper, and a scrolled Paris green cover that became an emblem of intellectual coming-of-age on American college campuses. The overall effect of the magazine's appearance was one of quiet refinement and substantial conservatism. Yet the book belied its cover. Inside was a consistent 128 pages of commentary as fresh and as controversial as anything on the American scene.

Mencken's close control over the editorial focus was both the great strength and great weakness of the *Mercury*. He wrote virtually all the copy for two of the regular departments: a monthly editorial in which he used current events as a springboard for preaching his personal philosophy of materialism and Social Darwinism, and "The Library," a column of book reviews that were often patronizing lectures aimed at spreading the gospel of literary naturalism. He also selected all copy for a third department, called "The Arts and Sciences," which featured a collection of brief essays on varied subjects whose more common categories over the years revealed the unique mix of Mencken's personality traits and intellectual interests. Medicine was a frequent topic, a probable result of his somewhat morbid hypochondria. The history of journalism and printing technology were addressed with some frequency; so, too, were the American language and Black history and culture. The "Arts and Sciences" essays were written by authorities in their fields, often drawn from the academic community.

The literary focus in the *Mercury* also mirrored Mencken's thinking. He was notoriously contemptuous of poets and never gave more than a page or two in any one issue to their work. Fiction tended toward second-rate social realism or narrations of personal experience by amateurs trying to break into the business. There were occasional publishing coups; Eugene O'Neill's *All God's Chillun Got Wings* first appeared in the *Mercury*, a result primarily of Nathan's influence. Theodore Dreiser made infrequent appearances, as did Sherwood Anderson, F. Scott Fitzgerald, Vachel Lindsay, Langston Hughes, Countee Cullen, and Dorothy Parker. Nonliterary subjects were occasionally covered by the likes of Clarence Darrow, W.E.B. Du Bois, Max Eastman, Joseph Wood Krutch, Edward Sapir, Ernest Boyd, and James M. Cain. But in spite of such an impressive contributors list, the vast majority of items were written by relative unknowns, including some associates from the *Smart Set* days and newspaper writers from Mencken's Baltimore circle. For as long as Mencken controlled the *Mercury*, content reflected his point of view and embodied his vivid writing style. The contributors who were regularly published were those who could imitate Mencken or who were hungry enough not to care how heavily their work was revised. For the most part, the elite writers of the period, literary and nonliterary alike, steered clear of Mencken's draconian editorial control.

Perhaps the only contributor to make an impact on the magazine's style was Nathan. As a contributing editor, he had control of two of the magazine's departments: "Clinical Notes" and "The Theatre." "Notes" was a carryover of the "Répétition Genérale" from *The Smart Set* and consisted of satirical observations and opinions of a tersely cynical sort. The format was better suited to Nathan's wit than to Mencken's heavy-handed sarcasm, and so Nathan was given control of the department until his eventual departure in 1930. "To speak of morals in art is to speak of a clergyman in a bawdyhouse," he could write with a characteristically acid tongue. "This is perhaps why argument for morals in art is considered by its numerous sponsors to be so credible." And again, "Criticism is the art wherewith a critic tries to guess himself into a share of an artist's fame." Nathan's theatrical reviews were perhaps his most entertaining contributions to the *Mercury*. Limited to reviewing the Broadway stage, he nevertheless had a national readership whose attention he held by playing up the art of cutting down. His reviews were regularly more entertaining than informative and relied heavily on insult humor for their effect. Virtually anything was fair game. Of James Joyce's *Exiles* he wrote, "Joyce has removed the drama from the blend and left only the words, chiefly inactive verbs." Nathan particularly delighted in skewering mediocre performances. Of Bertha Kalich's starring role in Jacob Gordin's *The Kreutzer Sonata* he observed, "she moans, shrieks, groans, puffs, heaves and ululates like a calliope with a painful stomach ache. Called upon to express heart-rending woe, she lets loose a series of noises indistinguishable from a prepschool college yell." Though Nathan regularly fell short of brilliant, cutting wit, the lightness of his phrasing balanced Mencken's verbal broadaxe, making his departments some of the most popular portions of the magazine.

Yet in the end, the *Mercury* took its character from Mencken. He had a love/hate relationship with American culture. Politically, he abhorred the egalitarianism of democracy while defending (and exercising) its promised liberty of thought and action. Such fierce individualism found expression in a persistent iconoclasm that informed the spirit of the magazine. Acerbic political profiles were regularly featured. Essay topics were wide-ranging. Herbert Little took on the Supreme Court in "The Omnipotent Nine." Margaret Cobb cast a chilling eye on the Daughters of the American Revolution in "The Soviet of Lady Patriots." Arthur Cramp analyzed "Food Fads and Nutrition Nonsense," while Vilhjalmur Stefansson asked, "Are Explorers to Join the Dodo?" What united all such efforts was Mencken's rigid imposition of a highly entertaining spirit of sarcasm. During his reign as editor, the *Mercury* devoted thirty to forty percent of each issue to debunking and satire, all in the service of an editorial philosophy, articulated by Mencken in the first issue, to the effect that "the world ... is down with at least a score of painful diseases, all of them chronic and incurable; nevertheless, [the editors] cling to the notion that human existence is predominantly charming."

Such cynicism, wedded to a flamboyant journalistic style and a gift for phrase making, made Mencken a huge success with the apostate younger generation of the twenties, who copied his use of the horse-laugh as a rhetorical weapon, and who delighted in his lively yokel-baiting.

Mencken's targets were any and all examples of the follies of "the booboisie," by which term he meant a rising tide of group-think Americans comprising, in his view, the Ku Klux Klan, Methodists, Midwestern cowherds, prohibitionists, Coolidge Republicans, back-slapping lodge-joiners, and small-town Chamber of Commerce "wowsers," indeed, any group whose reputed babbittry, jingoism, fundamentalist piety, prejudice, or provincialism could be vividly stereotyped.

Although Mencken solicited satires to fill the *Mercury*'s roster of stereotypes, including a series of seven "American Portraits" (The Labor Leader, The Washington Job Holder, The Editorial Writer, Medicinae Doctor, Babbitt Emeritus, The Advertising Agent, The Country Banker—all published in 1924), his most effective weapon in his crusade against "Homo Boobiens" was the "Americana" department, which he and Nathan had begun while with *Smart Set*. "Americana" consisted simply of clippings, as many as half sent in by readers, which the editors arranged alphabetically by state of origin and published with brief, frequently ironic prefaces. For example:

TEXAS

From an harangue to the Kiwanis Club of San Antonio by Major William G. Morgan, U.S.A.

"The ignorance of the American people as regards their own ignorance is a remarkable thing."

The point of "Americana" was to expose stupidity and narrow-mindedness, and it succeeded admirably. No feature of the *Mercury* was more influential in the magazine field, if imitation is any measure.

One of the most celebrated episodes in the history of American journalism involved the *Mercury*. In September 1925 Mencken published an essay by A.L.S. Wood called "Keeping the Puritans Pure," which included a scathing word portrait of the Reverend J. Franklin Chase, secretary of the Boston-based New England Watch and Ward Society. Chase, who had placed Mencken on a target list for his published views on the Scopes trial in Dayton, Tennessee, saw an opportunity to act when he received word that the April 1926 issue of the *Mercury* would print a slightly fictionalized essay by Herbert Asbury called "Hatrack," about a small-town prostitute who serviced her clients in the town cemeteries. Chase gave public notice that Watch and Ward would bring legal action against any newsdealer in Boston who sold a copy of the issue, thus effectively banning the *Mercury* in Boston.

Mencken, advised by Knopf and attorney Arthur Garfield Hays (who had sat as defense counsel with Clarence Darrow at the Scopes trial), arranged to travel to Boston and personally sell to Chase a copy of the offending issue, thus creating a test case that might help stem a rising tide of censorship inspired by social reform movements of the period. The sale occurred on Boston Common with all due publicity, following which Mencken was summarily marched off to jail by the vice squad. The case wound up on the docket of Judge James Parmenter, who, after reading "Hatrack," dropped all charges against Mencken, saying of the *Mercury*, "there is nothing in its appearance or make-up which would suggest that it is anything but a serious magazine."

Chase renewed the attack by rushing to New York to persuade the postmaster to bar the April issue from the mails, thus laying the groundwork for revocation of the *Mercury*'s second-class mailing privilege. Mencken again went to court and won an injunction against Chase and the Watch and Ward, enjoining them from further interference with the magazine. To soften their embarrassment before the eyes of the nation, Watch and Ward turned on Chase as a scapegoat, effectively ending his influence and, some historians have argued, contributing to his death later that year.

Mencken was motivated in this period by a sincere desire to defend freedom of the press. It took courage to engage in battle with the powerful Chase. Mencken was at risk in going to Boston and probably avoided imprisonment only because of the interference of a sympathetic court officer who is said to have shifted the Hatrack case, as it came to be called, onto the docket of the liberal Judge Parmenter. Nevertheless, the national publicity was less than sympathetic. Many newspapers, from whose editors Mencken expected support, openly suggested that he had orchestrated the entire affair as a publicity stunt to increase circulation. Mencken was deeply disappointed by what he considered a professional betrayal and had to take what comfort he could from the fact that, without his intending it, sales of the *Mercury* soared, eventually reaching a peak circulation of 84,000 in early 1928.

The period surrounding the Hatrack case marked the pinnacle of the *Mercury*'s popularity and prestige. Even Mencken's harshest critics—and there were many—had to acknowledge the magazine's influence. College humor magazines copied the *Mercury* with tedious regularity. Publications as diverse as *Life*,* *The New Yorker*,* *Bookman*, *North American Review*, *New Masses*, and *McNaught's Monthly* openly imitated (sometimes for the purposes of parody) elements of the *Mercury*'s format and editorial stance. The *Saturday Evening Post*** went so far as to institute an "Americana" department of its own designed to shore up the very sacred cows Mencken took most delight in knocking down. Mencken responded by engaging the *Post*'s ultraconservative editor, George Horace Lorimer, in a journalistic war that lasted through most of 1927. For months Mencken and Lorimer fired editorial cannonades at each other to the delight of the American reading public.

Success was short-lived, however. Circulation began to decline almost as soon as it peaked and continued to decline unchecked for the remainder of the life of the magazine. The aging Victorianism that had so irritated Mencken in the teens and early twenties was, by the end of the decade, too dated to serve as a believable target for the *Mercury*'s sarcasm. Mencken's reputation was also undergoing a change. The man whom Walter Lippmann had referred to in 1926 as "the most powerful influence on this whole generation of educated people" was by the early thirties something of a public goat, primarily because of his glaring failure to acknowlege the reality of the Great Depression. Moreover, Mencken's attentions were divided at the time. The increasing intimacy of his relationship with Sara Haardt, leading to their marriage in 1930, and several subsequent trips abroad provided pleasant distractions for Mencken. In his absence, editorial policy that had once been brilliantly suited for the spirit of an age all too quickly ossified and found history passing it by. Nathan's complete dissociation from the *Mercury* in 1930 brought about an end to "Clinical Notes." Angoff, now in charge, disliked the cut and paste work of "Americana," and allowed that department to shrink. Fiction, never the *Mercury*'s strong suit, was used with increasing frequency to fill out issues. The conservative half of the American public continued to see Mencken as a Godless Darwinist, while the liberal half interpreted his failure to address the problems of the Depression as tacit approval of the policies of big business. Under such circumstances and facing the serious illness of his wife, Mencken lost heart, finally announcing his retirement from the *Mercury* on 6 October 1933.

Knopf continued publication with Henry Hazlitt as editor, replaced after four months by Angoff. Angoff responded by giving the magazine a clearly leftist slant, which so alarmed Knopf that he sold out in 1936 to Paul Palmer of the *Baltimore Sun* papers. Palmer reduced the *Mercury* to digest size and lowered the newsstand price from fifty cents to a quarter. No publishing maneuvers, however, could recover the *Mercury*'s glory days, and Palmer eventually sold it to Lawrence Spivak in 1939. In the next two decades the *Mercury* changed hands numerous times, slowly acquiring an unsavory reputation as an ultraconservative propagandistic journal and addressing itself to the most extreme of those elements in American society that Mencken had so forcefully opposed. Eventually, it passed into the hands of an organization known as the Legion for the Survival of Freedom, in Torrance, California.

Information Sources

BIBLIOGRAPHY:
Angoff, Charles. "From Mencken . . . to Maguire: The Tragedy of the *American Mercury*." *ADL Bulletin* 14 (May 1957): 4–6.

———. *H. L. Mencken: A Portrait from Memory*. New York: Thomas Yoseloff, 1956.

Bode, Carl. *Mencken*. Carbondale, Ill.: Southern Illinois University Press, 1969.

Douglas, George H. *H. L. Mencken: Critic of American Life*. Hamden, Conn.: Archon Books, 1978.

Fecher, Charles A. *Mencken: A Study of His Thought*. New York: Alfred A. Knopf, 1978.

Hobson, Fred C., Jr. *Serpent in Eden: H. L. Mencken and the South*. Chapel Hill: University of North Carolina Press, 1974.

Manchester, William. *Disturber of the Peace*. New York: Harper Brothers, 1950.

———. *The Sage of Baltimore*. London, New York: Andrew Melrose, 1952.

Mott, Frank L. "The American Mercury." In *A History of American Magazines, 1905–1930*. Cambridge, Mass.: Harvard University Press, 1968, 5:3–26.

Peterson, Theodore. *Magazines in the Twentieth Century*. Urbana: University of Illinois Press, 1964.

Singleton, Marvin K. *H. L. Mencken and the American Mercury Adventure*. Durham, N.C.: Duke University Press, 1962.

Stenerson, Douglas C. *H. L. Mencken: Iconoclast from Baltimore*. Chicago: University of Chicago Press, 1971.

INDEX SOURCES: *Readers' Guide* to 1961; also indexed by volume.

REPRINT EDITIONS: University Microfilms.

LOCATION SOURCES: CL, DLC, GA, ICU, MBU, NN, OCl, TxU, WaU, and over three hundred others.

Publication History

MAGAZINE TITLE AND TITLE CHANGES: *The American Mercury*; *The New American Mercury*, December 1950-February 1951 only.

VOLUME AND ISSUE DATA: Monthly, 1924–1962. Three volumes annually, 1924–1940; two volumes annually, 1941–1961; annual volumes 1962–current. Quarterly, 1963–current. Publication irregular 1962–current.

PUBLISHER AND PLACE OF PUBLICATION: 1924–1935: Alfred A. Knopf, New York. 1935–1936: L. E. Spivak, New York. 1936–1939: Paul Palmer, New York. 1939–1950: L. E. Spivak, New York. 1950–1951: Clendin J. Ryan, New York. 1952–1960: J. Russell Maguire, New York. 1960–1962: Defenders of the Christian Faith, Oklahoma City. 1963–current: Legion for the Suvival of Freedom, McAllen, Tex.; Houston; Torrance, Calif.

EDITORS: Henry Louis Mencken and George Jean Nathan, 1924–1925; H. L. Mencken, 1925–1933; Henry Hazlitt, 1934; Charles Angoff, 1934–1935; Paul Palmer, 1935–1939; Eugene Lyons, 1939–1944; L. E. Spivak, 1944–1950; William Bradford Huie, 1950–1953; John A. Clements, 1953–1955; J. R. Maguire, 1955–1957; William La Varre, 1957–1958; Maurine Halliburton, 1958–1960; Gerald S. Pope, 1960–1962; Marcia C. Matthews, 1963; Jason Matthews, 1963–1964; Edwin A. Walker, 1964–1965; La Vonne Doden Furr, 1967–current.

CIRCULATION: 15,000 in January 1924; 42,000 in December 1924; 84,000 in 1928; 42,000 in 1932. The price was fifty cents an issue, five dollars a year.

Gary Engle

THE AMERICAN PUNCH

An unabashed imitation of Britain's most popular comic periodical, *The American Punch* was issued as an advertising vehicle by the Photo-Electrotype Company, a Boston engraving firm, beginning in January 1879. With graphics produced by the company's patented Mumler process, *The American Punch* featured illustrations copied from European periodicals as well as original drawings and full-page political cartoons addressing a wide range of political and social issues, but it was often criticized for "pirating" illustrations and text. Prose and comic verse, mostly puns, comic vernacular letters, and columns featuring social satire and sociopolitical commentary rounded out each issue. Publication was taken over by the J. A. Cummings Engraving Company in January 1881. Despite a drastic cut in the format to make the magazine pay for itself, *The American Punch* failed to attract a sufficient audience; publication ceased in March 1881.

The leading figure in the establishment of *The American Punch* was Boston inventor-entrepreneur William H. Mumler, founder of the Photo-Electrotype Company. Capitalizing on the popularity of Britain's *Punch*, the magazine served as a promotional forum for engravings produced by the Mumler process under the editorial guidance of William Henry Allen, with illustrations, prose, and comic verse copied from American and European sources, particularly *Punch*. Allen became advertising manager in March 1879, and Mumler himself edited the monthly until Earl Marble, art and drama critic of *The Boston Budget* and a widely published comic poet, assumed that post beginning with the May 1879 number. Attacks from the press forced the editors to publish more original material beginning with the September 1879 issue, but the focus of *The American Punch* remained advertisement for the Photo-Electrotype Company and the Mumler engraving process. Copy was produced as inexpensively as possible. *The American Punch* was never a profitable enterprise.

Published monthly, *The American Punch* was initially made up of sixteen quarto pages measuring 11″ × 18″, costing fifty cents a year. The cost of producing more original material was given as the reason for raising the price to one dollar a year in September 1879. Individual copies were sold for five, and, subsequently, ten cents. In January 1881, the format was cut to eight pages and the cost was reduced to five cents an issue in an effort to make the magazine profitable.

Although the scope of *The American Punch* was purportedly national, much of the material reflected the Boston social and political scene, and circulation was largely limited to the Boston area. The combination of text and illustrations was a conscious imitation of its British model. For the first year, the front cover featured a grinning Punch jester presiding over a mischievous band of imps.

Inside, a full-page advertisement for the Photo-Electrotype Company was followed by several pages of short comic pieces in prose and verse, including such regular items as "Lectures by Mrs. Thrashum," a burlesque on high society Boston, and "Marbles," a collection of puns drawn from American newspapers and magazines. Comic correspondence such as "The Grievances of a Billiard Ball" and letters from "The Liar's Club" were frequent, and satiric pieces on the Boston literati and leading journalists of the day were offered occasionally. The political alignment of *The American Punch* was nominally Republican; the magazine generally expressed hard money, high tariff views, although attacks on Republican presidential candidate James G. Blaine, administration Indian policy, liberal pension legislation, and restrictive Chinese immigration laws were common. References to state and local politics were frequent; scathing attacks on Massachusetts politician General Ben Butler appeared regularly. Commentary on political issues appeared in short pieces of comic verse, cartoon captions, or prose items of two to five paragraphs occupying a column or so. Generally, only the verses were credited to authors. Space fillers were provided by bits of comic verse and short puns.

The American Punch was profusely illustrated, in keeping with its status as an advertising forum for the Photo-Electrotype Company, which produced the engraving plates and "upon whose resources *The American Punch*depend[ed] entirely for its outfit." Most of the small illustrations accompanying the shorter items were borrowed, as were some of the cartoons, a number of which were taken from *Punch* itself. *The American Punch* regularly included two and sometimes three full-page political cartoons in each issue, mostly the work of Carl Claus. These cartoons focused on a variety of social and political issues, including the plight of the working man, Chinese immigration policy, and federal pension legislation. General Ben Butler appeared in one cartoon as a merchant captain bringing in a cargo of "rag-babyisms, Commune Kearneyisms, Disgruntled Republicanisms, and Democratic Rowdeyisms." A number of cartoons attacking Federal Indian policy included a poignant full-page drawing of the arrest of Chief Standing Bear for attempting to plow land on his reservation. The editors offered "duplicate electrotypes of the cuts in *American Punch*" for sale to the press, another evidence of the underlying concerns of the magazine.

Information Sources

INDEX SOURCES: None.
REPRINT EDITIONS: None.
LOCATION SOURCES: DLC Volumes 1–2 (partial), Volume 3; MBat Volumes 1–3; MH Volume 1.

Publication History

MAGAZINE TITLE AND TITLE CHANGES: *The American Punch*, January 1879-March 1881.
VOLUME AND ISSUE DATA: Monthly, January 1879-March 1881.

PUBLISHER AND PLACE OF PUBLICATION: January 1879-December 1880: The
  American Punch Publishing Company, Boston. January-March 1881: J. A. Cum-
  mings Engraving Company, Boston.
EDITORS: William M. Mumler, January-April 1879; Earl Marble, May 1879-March
  1881.
CIRCULATION: Unknown; advertising rates suggest printings of several thousand copies.

Jack D. Warren, Jr.

AMERICANA

In the early 1930s, *Americana*, subtitled "satire and humor," offered a grim
view of the world, limned out in boldly dark-crayoned cartoons and acerbic
prose. Editor Alexander King, later a television gag writer and author of *May
This House Be Safe from Tigers*, announced, "We are Americans who believe
that our civilization exudes a miasmic stench and that we had better prepare to
give it a decent but rapid burial." He was joined at the funeral by "laughing
morticians" including George Grosz, European refugee, illustrator, and Jungian
author of *The Book of the Id*, and Gilbert Seldes, author of editorials indicting
the political-economic system inside the monthly's front covers. The monthly
itself was thirty-six pages in a two-column, 9″ × 12″ format, at fifteen cents an
issue; James J. Borup was the publisher from its beginning in November 1932.

Grotesquely distorted caricatures, full-page in stark black and white, heavily
flavored *Americana*. Nordley's cartoons are most dramatic, with a harshness of
line that matched the harshness of the sociopolitical prose, although early covers
by W. Steig followed *The New Yorker.** King claimed to have developed the
comic mode uniting a photograph with an unrelated comic caption, claiming it
as a "legitimate" art form, and the only way for his magazine to survive as a
primarily pictorial commentator. Some photographs carried their own pessimism;
crowded Coney Island beaches juxtaposed against crowded New York cemetaries
conveyed an obvious message, as did a double-page spread showing an old man
in a graveyard hunched over a copy of *Life.**

George Grosz, James Thurber, e. e. cummings, Gilbert Seldes, and Nathanael
West, along with King and others, provided the prose. One of the standing jokes
revolved around the ASPCI, the association for the prevention of cruelty to
intellectuals. Grosz, in a major statement, denied a belief in progress but pleaded
for even a tiny place for survival in the great scheme of things. Franklin D.
Roosevelt was linked to Stalin, Hitler to Mussolini, and Al Capone was drawn
in, all connected to the wealthy and the powerful. Under the title "Pigs is risen,"
"Boosevelt," Norman Thomas asleep, and boodling politicians were jeered.
Theodore Dreiser was derided as an unspeakably bad writer for the "junk he
drools outs," but comparison with Sinclair Lewis could make even him look
like an artist. The Fascists were seen as the worst: "Peacock Hitler, charl'tan,
scoundrel clown / the ass of envy." Even an October 1933 "Hollywood" number
showed the movie moguls being led spiritually by Mickey Mouse.

The Hollywood number proudly announced that *Americana* was changing
from a monthly to a weekly format, but the November 1933 issue seems to have
been the last published, giving it a run of thirteen issues from November to
November, 1932–1933.

Information Sources

INDEX SOURCES: None.
REPRINT EDITIONS: None.
LOCATION SOURCES: RPB, NN, ViU.

Publication History

MAGAZINE TITLE AND TITLE CHANGES: *Americana*, November 1932 to November
    1933.
VOLUME AND ISSUE DATA: Monthly, Volume 1:1, November 1932–Volume 2:1,
    November 1933.
PUBLISHER AND PLACE OF PUBLICATION: Americana Group, New York.
EDITOR: Alexander King.
CIRCULATION: Unknown.

David E. E. Sloane

THE ARIEL

The Ariel, which appeared, with very few exceptions, on alternating Saturdays
from 14 April 1827 through 24 November 1832, was a miscellany of literature
and news that included both original and reprinted material. It was published in
Philadelphia "at the office of the *Saturday Bulletin*" and contained "Selected
Tales, Essays, Biographies of Distinguished Females and of Eminent Individuals,
Reviews of New Books, Literary Notices, Poetry, Original and Selected,
Anecdotes, and a Choice Selection of Miscellaneous Reading, Calculated to
Raise the Genius and Mend the Heart." These heterogeneous items, varying in
length from a few lines to several pages, were notably lacking in controversial
content and appear originally to have been intended as light reading for a female
audience. The preliminary issue of 14 August 1827, in fact, actively sought
submissions from women and promised "to be more than commonly attentive
to the effusions of their muse, 'with pencil dipt in light.' " When the first regular
issue appeared on 5 May 1827, however, this explicit appeal to women had been
dropped, and what had at first been a "Ladies' Literary Gazette" became, more
simply, a "Literary Gazette."

   Although comic material might appear anywhere in the magazine, it was most
often included, especially during the magazine's early run, in a "Humorous"
column on or near the final page. The column bore the inscription, "Prithee,
Poins, lend me thy hand / To laugh a little," and contained well-traveled
anecdotes of famous men, hoary jokes, and such light verse as the following
(entitled "An Equal Couple"):

> 'Tis odd this pair can ne'er agree,
>   Although so equal in their lives:
> The very worst of husbands he,
>   And she the very worst of wives.

The jokes often turned on puns, like the tale of a merchant who attacked the notion that birds are carefree by pointing out that "they have their Bills to provide for as well as we." The anecdotes frequently concerned English men of letters, though the 24 January 1829 and 7 February 1829 issues included Davy Crockett stories. The 7 February issue contained the famous boast that Davy "could wade the Mississippi with a steamboat on his back, whip his weight in wildcats, and 'ride a streak of lightning barebacked.' "

Published by Elwood Walter and later by Edmund Morris, its only editor-in-chief, *The Ariel* altered formats several times during its five-and-a-half-year existence. It appeared in two-column, three-column, and four-column versions, and each issue contained either eight or sixteen pages. Issues varied in size from a minimum of 5″ × 8″ to a maximum of 8″ × 10″. Excellent copperplate engravings were included in approximately every third issue, and many of the other issues were also illustrated. A column of responses to readers indicates that the magazine was distributed nationally, the annual subscription rate being one dollar during the first year of publication and $1.50 thereafter. Difficulties with the collection of overdue subscription money led to the magazine's termination on 24 November 1832.

Information Sources

BIBLIOGRAPHY:
Kribbs, Jayne K. Entry No. 88. *An Annotated Bibliography of American Literary Periodicals, 1741–1850*. Boston: G. K. Hall, 1977, pp. 16–17.
Titus, Edna B., ed. "Ariel." *Union List of Serials in Libraries in the United States and Canada*. New York: H. W. Wilson Co., 1965, p. 475.
INDEX SOURCES: None.
REPRINT EDITIONS: University Microfilms.
LOCATION SOURCES: CtY, DLC; scattered volumes elsewhere.

Publication History

MAGAZINE TITLE AND TITLE CHANGES: *The Ariel. And Ladies' Literary Gazette*, Preliminary Issue; *The Ariel. A Literary Gazette*, Volume 1; *The Ariel. A Literary and Critical Gazette*, Volume 2; *The Ariel. A Semimonthly Literary and Miscellaneous Gazette*, Volumes 3–5; *The Ariel. A Semi-Monthly Literary and Miscellaneous Gazette*, Volume 6.
VOLUME AND ISSUE DATA: Preliminary Issue (14 April 1827); semi-monthly, twenty-six issues per volume, for Volumes 1–5 (5 May 1827–14 April 1832); semi-monthly (except that Issue 12 appeared one week after Issue 11 and three weeks before Issue 13), sixteen issues per volume, for Volume 6 (28 April 1832–24 November 1832).
PUBLISHER AND PLACE OF PUBLICATION: 14 April 1827–22 September 1827:

Elwood Walter, Philadelphia. 6 October 1827–24 November 1832: Edmund Morris, Philadelphia.
EDITOR: Edmund Morris.
CIRCULATION: Unknown.

Robert H. O'Connor

THE ARKANSAW TRAVELER

The Arkansaw Traveler was typical of the regional humorous newspapers of the late 1800s, usually one- or two-man operations of eight folio size pages, six columns to a page, with little in the way of illustration. *The Traveler* was imitative of *Texas Siftings,** the *Detroit Free Press*, the *Burlington Hawkeye*, and others, and gained national prominence for its editor, Opie Read. The periodical declined when Read left it to write novels and become a Chautauqua lecturer.

Opie Read had been raised on hardscrabble Tennessee and Kentucky farms, and his rangy build and honest face gave him a rural appearance. His education came from a typesetter's case, and during the 1870s he worked as a tramp printer in the South. Eventually, he became a reporter and editor in cities such as Cleveland and Little Rock. His brother-in-law, P. D. Benham, a Little Rock businessman, suggested that they pool their talents and bring out a "humorous and literary journal," and *The Arkansaw Traveler* was born on 4 June 1882.

The Traveler was issued every Saturday and cost five cents a copy, two dollars a year. Read and Benham were listed as the publishers, and Little Rock remained the place of publication until replaced by Chicago in 1887. The blurb for *The Traveler* advertised that it was "Full of Original Humor, Literature, and General Information. And Replete with clippings from the best publications of the world. A paper for the Households. A paper for the People! Non-Political, Non-Sectarian, but with decided and well expressed views on every subject of national importance." Its advertising rates were $1.50 an inch for the first insertion and one dollar an inch for each subsequent insertion. Within two years ads occupied about one-fifth of the paper. These were mainly for patent medicines, sewing machines, and watches, with a few local ads.

The Traveler soon became well known throughout the country. The New York humor magazines, such as *Puck** and *Life,** clipped from it, and in San Francisco Ambrose Bierce relied on it to swell out *The Wasp.** It was also successful in Arkansas and within six months claimed a circulation larger than that of any paper in the state. Read was later to claim that circulation grew to 85,000 within three years, but this is doubtful. That figure would equal the circulation of *Puck*, the most successful humor periodical of the time. George P. Rowell's *American Newspaper Directory* for the year 1885 credits *The Traveler* with only 25,000.

Read's contribution was considerable; he wrote about ten full-length columns (one-third of the paper) every week. The most distinctive feature was the traditional traveler sketch done in the Southwest humor tradition—a dialogue between a cultivated traveler and a backwoods squatter. This dialogue was to set the pattern for the skits that were to make *The Traveler* famous. At the top of page one of every issue, *The Traveler* printed a musical stave with the notes of the first several bars of the tune against a background picture of the traveler, the squatter, his cabin and family. The squatter invariably lived in a leaky shack, had several hounds and more children, a still that he wished to keep hidden, and a wife as hospitable as himself. The traveler made no headway at all against this bluff of taciturnity until he either produced some whisky or else exhibited some talent that won the squatter's admiration.

Most of Read's writing appeared on the first page. Besides the traveler sketches, there were anecdotes and short stories in Negro dialect, a column called "Plantation Proverbs," also in Negro dialect, and a column of paragraphs called "Limnings." Page three usually carried an original poem and a short story, which were seldom humorous but usually sentimental and melancholy. On page four Read had a column or two of editorials. Two-thirds of the paper was made up of clippings from other newspapers and magazines that were on *The Traveler*'s exchange list.

The Traveler was not universally popular. In its early years the clergy frequently attacked it for its "coarseness," but others complained that the paper was too refined. One wrote: "I like *The Traveler* very well but I find one fault with it. You clip above the majority of your readers. I like to see clean articles but I don't want them to be so refined and high toned that I can't understand them. Give us something of the rip-roaring order and I can get you fifty subscribers in my neighborhood."[1]

As the issues and volumes multiplied and Read's sketches of the backwoods squatter achieved a national reputation, another type of criticism began to develop. Up-creek politicans, skilled at demagoguery, claimed that Read's purpose was to ridicule the farmers. It was said that one fellow was elected to the legislature on his promise that he would tie a rope around Read's neck and lead a mule out from under him.[2]

Frank Luther Mott attributes the move of the *The Traveler* to Chicago to Read's fear of reprisals such as the above. This might have been a factor, but there were certainly other reasons. Read himself mentions that the magazine's patronage was scattered throughout the country and owed no specific allegiance to Arkansas. Moreover, *The Traveler* had outgrown the facilities of the local post office. Read and Benham were encouraged by the example of *Texas Siftings*, which had left its home in Austin, moved to New York, changed its format to that of an illustrated humor magazine, and had quickly become a circulation leader. Finally, Read was ambitious and was looking for opportunities to expand his talent. He had begun to write novels and had the feeling, common enough at the time, that Chicago would become an important literary center.

When Read and Benham set up headquarters on the seventh floor of the Calumet Building, their dateline of 14 May 1887 carried Chicago as well as Little Rock. It later became Chicago alone. The newspaper soon began to reflect the move. Many of the anecdotes and sketches were set in Chicago restaurants and hotels and cable cars. There was also occasional comment on Chicago politics, especially the boodling aldermen, sometimes accompanied by crude black and white cartoons, the first illustrations *The Traveler* had ever carried. But the newspaper stayed fundamentally the same. Read still continued his backwoods sketches and Negro dialect stories. He also kept one eye on Arkansas. Perhaps he felt guilty about the move because he began to make more and more laudatory comments about the state and ran frequent blurbs about its great potential.

The people of Arkansas also kept one eye, jaundiced, on *The Traveler*. If they were angry with Read before, they were incensed now, and for all his praises of their state, they were not pacified. The attack was led by the clergy, the politicans, and the country editors, whom Read had ridiculed. One politician wrote *The Traveler*: "Cowards, afraid longer to remain in the state, you have taken refuge among the Yankees to make fun of us."[3]

In the fall of 1888 the paper absorbed *The Illustrated Graphic News* and changed the format considerably. There were now illustrations of Chicago monuments and other local phenomena. There were copies of old masters and sentimental pictures of sad young ladies, little children, kittens, and sheep. Read had advertised that the new magazine would contain sixteen pages, but the size was not increased because the page was cut in half from folio to quarto. *The Traveler* had moved into the class of the illustrated humor magazines. It added a "Drummer Department," edited by E. R. Pritchard.

Read left *The Traveler* in 1893 to devote his time to fiction and lecturing. With his departure the paper became less literary and more a comic journal. More cartoons and more jokes were used, and the sketches shrank in length. The magazine was becoming an urban joke book, useful for salesmen and speakers, but without a regional character. The circulation shrank too, to only 12,000 by 1900. By 1906 *The Traveler* had become a monthly, and in 1916 it ceased publication altogether.

As recently as 1945 the Stein Publishing House of Chicago issued a reprint of "Jokes, monologues, funny anecdotes, flashes of wit, original cartoons selected from the *Arkansaw Traveler*. Introducing the quaint wisdom of Opie Read."

Notes

1. *The Arkansaw Traveler* 7 (24 October 1885): 1.
2. Opie Read, *I Remember* (New York: R. R. Smith, 1930), p. 186.
3. Ibid., p. 194.

Information Sources

BIBLIOGRAPHY:
Allsopp, Frederick. *History of the Arkansas Press*. Little Rock, Ark.: Parke-Harper Publishing Co., 1922, p. 375.

Baird, Reed M. "Opie Read: An American Traveler." *Tennessee Historical Quarterly*
    33 (Winter 1974): 410–28.
Linneman, William R. "Opie Read and *The Arkansaw Traveler*." *Midwest Folklore* 10
    (Spring 1960): 5–10.
Read, Opie. *I Remember*. New York: R. R. Smith, 1930, pp. 179–99.
INDEX SOURCES: None.
REPRINT EDITIONS: First six numbers reprinted for the Arkansas State Capitol gift
    shop.
LOCATION SOURCES: IU: Volumes 1–19 (1882–1891); Volumes 33–37 (1906–1910).
    DLC: Volumes 12–20 (1888–1892).

Publication History

MAGAZINE TITLE AND TITLE CHANGES: *The Arkansaw Traveler*, 4 June 1882–
    1916.
VOLUME AND ISSUE DATA: Weekly, semi-annual volumes. Volume 1:1, 4 June
    1882–Volume 20:520, 30 May 1892. Monthly with annual volume. Volumes 33–
    37, July 1906-July 1910.
PUBLISHER AND PLACE OF PUBLICATION: June 1882–7 May 1887: Opie Read
    and P. D. Benham, Little Rock. 14 May 1887–1916: Chicago.
EDITORS: Opie Read, 1882–1893; unknown, 1893–1916.
CIRCULATION: 25,000 in 1885; 12,000 in 1900.

William R. Linneman

AURORA BOREALIS

In January 1849, the *Aurora Borealis* joined over fifty weekly papers then being
published in Boston. Founding editor and publisher Jonathan Kelly admitted in
the 2 June issue, "It is hardly conceivable that Boston can keep up the large
raft of papers now published in the city," but he felt confident that his would
be one of the new papers that would crowd out the "inferior" ones. It was to
be conducted, Kelly had announced, in the manner of the highly successful New
York *Spirit of the Times*,* an honor the *Spirit* returned by reprinting a piece or
two from early issues. Looking over the flattering things that other papers had
to say about the *Aurora Borealis*, many of which he reprinted, Kelly asked
rhetorically in the 24 February issue, "How *can* I fail to make a good paper?"
Just how he failed is not clear, but in any case the *Aurora Borealis* did not last
the year.

Like so many of the magazinists in general and of humor magazines in
particular, Jonathan Kelly had a checkered career. Among other things, he had
been an itinerant actor, a perfumer, and a shopkeeper, and he had held a variety
of positions on a variety of publications, none of them for long. The *Aurora
Borealis* was his most ambitious undertaking and came at a time when Kelly
must have felt particularly prosperous with the popularity of his humorous
sketches in the *Spirit*, *The Yankee Blade*,* and other publications, under such

pseudonyms as "O.K.," "Carro Gordo," "Jack Humphries," "J.F.K.," and "Falconbridge."

The *Aurora Borealis* consisted of eight, four-column quarto pages that measured 14″ × 19″, and it sold for five cents a weekly copy, two dollars for a year's subscription. In a preface to *The Humors of Falconbridge* (1856), a collection of Kelly's writings published a year after his death, his anonymous biographer allowed that the *Aurora* "really was one of the most handsome humorous journals ever commenced in the United States, but it was very expensive" and thus had to be abandoned.

Very few copies are extant, but they suggest that another reason for its demise is that Kelly tried to make his weekly be too many things to too many of the Bostonians who made up his primary audience. According to its subtitle, it was a weekly magazine not only of "Humorous and Entertaining Sketches" but also of "Travels, Narratives, etc." It usually carried a serialized adventure or romantic story, such as "Adventures in Texas," by "Stampede," and "Fatal Evils," by Benjamin King Brown. Other stories were clearly educational: "The Oldest American Actor," for example, and "Burial Ground of the Natchez," which included illustrations, rare for the *Aurora Borealis*. Editorial opinion was not featured, but Kelly did not hesitate to express his ideas when he felt an issue such as a controversial boxing match between Yankee Sullivan and Tom Hyer required it.

As for humor in the *Aurora*, Kelly tried to keep it original and at a high level, with only occasional borrowings from *The Knickerbocker** and *Punch*. Correspondents from New York, Philadelphia, and Washington, D.C., contributed original and amusing reports of events in those cities, but only "Glances of the Empire City" by "A. Gothamite" endured. Kelly regularly provided a long story printed under his favorite pseudonym, "Falconbridge," the kind of story that would be collected in *The Humors of Falconbridge*. "A Leg of Mutton," for example, appeared in both. Other writers included "Ollapod," "Spasm," and "Captain Cotton."

Although successful as a humorist and a writer of popular literature of many types, Kelly had little luck with sustaining more ambitious ventures such as the *Aurora Borealis*. Always "ready to enlist in any new enterprise," says his biographer, "he was led to abandon those occupations, which, if persevered in, would probably have been triumphant."

Information Sources

BIBLIOGRAPHY:
"A Biographical Sketch of the Late Jonathan Kelly." In *The Humors of Falconbridge*. Philadelphia: T. B. Peterson, 1856, pp. 21–28.
INDEX SOURCES: None.
REPRINT EDITIONS: None.
LOCATION SOURCES: The American Antiquarian Society has three issues.

Publication History

MAGAZINE TITLE AND TITLE CHANGES: *Aurora Borealis*, a Weekly Magazine of
   Humorous and Entertaining Sketches, Travels, Narratives, etc., 27 January 1849–
   after 2 June 1849.
VOLUME AND ISSUE DATA: Weekly.
PUBLISHER AND PLACE OF PUBLICATION: Jonathan Kelly, Boston.
EDITOR: Jonathan Kelly.
CIRCULATION: Unknown.

Cameron C. Nickels

B

BALLYHOO

Ballyhoo revolutionized the humor of *Judge** and *Life** into a sexier, livelier format that set a paradoxically bright tone for the Depression era which enveloped its founding. "Ballyhoo," with the publication of a book by that name attacking advertising in 1927, succeeded "humbug" as a standard American term for puffery, but carried a festival air of brightness as well. When Norman Anthony brought forth *Ballyhoo* the magazine in August 1931, the title was natural for its mix of sophisticated burlesque humor and roundhouse satire on conventional advertising.

Ballyhoo's multi-colored cover boasted that it was a new humorous magazine edited by Anthony, who had been involved with humor magazines since Wall Street's *The Lamb*** in 1916, *Film Fun** in the twenties, and *Wit o' the World***; he was most known as a fugitive former editor of *Life* and *Judge*, where he wrestled with other editors to develop fresh humor to replace the stuffiness of the older humor magazines. *Ballyhoo* added on the back, "Kept fresh by cellophane," and Anthony even contrived to get some of the initial sellout run of 150,000 copies cellophane wrapped for distribution. The bright patchwork cover was an unmistakable and outstanding feature, copied by the gamut of *Ballyhoo*'s numerous followers, framing a poster-style cover, 8½″ × 11½″. Inside, *Ballyhoo* was dominated by cartoons by Russell Patterson, Jack Markow, Ralph Fuller, and C. W. Anderson, among others listed under the heading of "gag men" in the December 1932 number, and by its burlesques of trendy advertisements of the day.

Although Mott considered *Ballyhoo* a proponent of outhouse humor, there was only a moderate number of nudie and sex cartoons, barring the "Nudist" number, and the range of comedy was fairly wide across a spectrum of upper and middle crust America, with a decided emphasis on urban and literate experience as opposed to the down-hominess of the crackerbarrel tradition. *Ballyhoo* was a breezy Broadway exposer of babbittry, the Booboisie, politicians, and the advertising con men of its generation, but it used a parody touch significantly lighter than H. L. Mencken's in *The American Mercury,** Art Young's, or Alexander King's in *Americana.** Jazz Era cartoons and slapstick anti-Prohibition sentiment predominated. Burlesque promotions offered advertisers a five billion circulation by 1939 and blamed a sudden downcurve in *Ballyhoo*'s fake growth chart on imitation of *The New Yorker,** with which it had very slight visual affinities in its choice of graphic artists. A cigarette ad for "Old Colds" boasted "not a cough in a coffin''; a Simon and Schuster book of *Ballyhoo* ads rushed into print in 1931 featured its shot of a baby from the rear, under the legend "Keep Kissable.'' Cartoons dominated, irregularly splashed across pages, in full page, and in various sizes throughout the magazine. Copy was limited to the brief and the sharp, and Anthony's awareness of cultural position is outlined by the four magazines he nominated for oblivion in issue one: *Vanity Fair** for pseudo-gentility, *Life* for losing John Ames Mitchell's spirit and Charles Dana Gibson's illustrations, *Arts Beautiful* for its hypocritical prostitution of naked bodies, and the *Congressional Record* for recording trivia. "For your inconvenience,'' *Ballyhoo* grudgingly offered subscriptions at $1.50 a year, but suggested buying it on the newsstands, at fifteens cents a copy.

   Anthony's briskly irreverent formula worked astoundingly well for George Delacorte and Dell Publishing Company. Delacorte liked the rowdy and bawdy tone as a reflection of the college humor he knew in the twenties at Harvard and Columbia, and Anthony's predisposition favored and expanded that orientation. Success was already certain when the sixth number went to press at two million copies, and the magazine plunged along through the Depression, upping its subscription price to $1.80 in 1934, but keeping its boisterous anti-advertising burlesques and its varied cartooning in format. A Broadway show backed by Anthony—and introducing a young comic named Bob Hope—carried the same name, and Delacorte brought forth *Hullabaloo*** as his own competition to get the jump on numerous followers. The imitators of *Ballyhoo*, according to Anthony, were smutty where *Ballyhoo* was risque, and analysis bears him out, but it was *Ballyhoo* that had to defend itself against obscenity charges in a Washington court and was acquitted. Although Anthony was worried about a "Lady Pipperal'' ad punning on being a "sheet house,'' the government attorneys ruined their own case by attempting to give a noncomic analysis of a cartoon showing the National Bolt and Nut Company president holding up a small object and saying, "Gentlemen, prepare for a laugh, this is one of our competitor's nuts.'' The jury laughed the case out of court. In fact, as Mott suggests, and Anthony himself regretted, the bathroom stigma remained permanently locked with the magazine's image, however incomplete as an assessment of its real power. *Ballyhoo* actually threw a wide net across American society, with its own version of Mr. Zero, the Poor Fish, and other representations of the faceless common man. *Ballyhoo*'s Elmer Zilch was perpetuated as the stock comic figure—partly boss, partly uncle, partly middle-class man; he became a figurehead of the new generation. A mix of cartoon humor covered husbands and wives, dating and promiscuity, and the urban and suburban scene; girlie cartoons continued as a leitmotif.

During 1935, *Esquire*,** combining features of *Vanity Fair* and *Ballyhoo*, posed a challenge to Anthony which he recognized but failed to meet, except with a digest-sized *Mr.*** which Delacorte allowed only a year's run. *Ballyhoo* went into digest size and format in February 1937. In his autobiography Anthony admits that his attention wandered from the magazine and it was allowed to become stale. With prose articles and cartoons set up as full-page items, the smaller *Ballyhoo* seemed less zippy than its predecessor, although it labored after a breezily irreverent tone. The May 1938 number was the most potent, featuring a variety of jokes, burlesque ads, and articles on the theme "When Japan Conquers America." Miss Universe, inside the front cover, was a deathshead with a rose clenched between its teeth. By 1938 circulation was dipping, after hovering around 100,000 for most of *Ballyhoo*'s run, and Delacorte let Anthony go at the end of the year. A burlesque *Reader's Digest*** failed to save it, and the last issue, in February 1939, was a mock issue of Henry Luce's *Life*.

In the winter of 1953, Delacorte brought *Ballyhoo* back as a quarterly under the editorship of Bill Yates. Michael Berry, Reamer Keller, VIP, and a row of cartoonists and writers listed on the title page, carried the tenor of the magazine up to the 1950s visually. Prose increased with comic interviews and takeoffs on general magazine literature of the *Saturday Evening Post*,** *Ladies Home Journal* variety—"We Saved Our Marriage, Darn It!," "Hitler Ain't Dead" as told to Jesse James, and issues devoted to topics like "Space" taking off on the science fiction and futurist boom of the early fifties. In addition to the burlesque advertisements, real advertisements took over dominant cover positions and sobered the magazine, now a child of the fifties, squarer in shape at 8½" × 11"and less adventurous in cover design than its parti-colored progenitor and more juvenile in its orientation; gone were the risque cartoons of the thirties to competitors in the style of *TV Girls and Gags*.** Gone, too, was the vitality of Anthony's conception, transformed into a watery blend of *Saturday Evening Post* and *Mad* Magazine.*

Information Sources

BIBLIOGRAPHY:
Anthony, Norman. *How to Grow Old Disgracefully*. New York: Duell, Sloan & Pearce, 1946.
Pringle, Henry. "The Anatomy of Ballyhoo: A New Type of Magazine—Smutty or Smart?" *Outlook* 160 (6 January 1932): 13–14.
INDEX SOURCES: None.
REPRINT EDITIONS: None.
LOCATION SOURCES: DLC, MnU 1–2, NN 1–15, ViU 1–2, 4.

Publication History

MAGAZINE TITLE AND TITLE CHANGES: *Ballyhoo*.
VOLUME AND ISSUE DATA: Monthly, Volume 1:1, August 1931–Volume 16:1, February 1939; quarterly, Volume 1:1, Winter 1953–Volume 1:5, Winter 1954.
PUBLISHER AND PLACE OF PUBLICATION: Dell Publishing Co., New York.
EDITORS: Norman Anthony, 1931–1938; Albert Rosa?, 1938–1939; Bill Yates, 1953–1954.
CIRCULATION: 100,000 average, 1931–1939, with high around 2 million in 1932–1934; later, unknown.

David E. E. Sloane

BALTIMORE MONUMENT

An editorial in the inaugural issue of the *Baltimore Monument* explicitly conveys the magazine's aim to "erect a fabric of Literature that shall not deteriorate from the high honors of the 'Monumental City.' " Its founder T. S. Arthur and its editors hoped to uncover Baltimore's hidden talent; thereby they would enhance their city's reputation for "Virtue, Patriotism, (and) Learning." The magazine carried informal essays, literary reviews, recipes, and anecdotes; humor emerged as a natural byproduct. Appearing in the first issue, "Mourning the Dead" by Benjamin Brief ridicules the wearing of mourning attire. In the grand style of Jonathan Swift, the essayist shows the inconveniences of the practice. Another early issue contains a whimsical treatise on time by James Kirke Paulding, who was the most notable contributor from a list including T. S. Arthur, William H. Carpenter, Park Benjamin, Anna H. Dorsey, and Lydia Jane Pierson. Other essays testifying to the humorous vein of the *Monument* are such pieces as "The Chess Game," which depicts gaming as "a fascinating sin," and "Managing a Husband," which in addition to offering advice on dealing with spouses mentions the *Southern Literary Messenger* and *Godey's Ladies' Book*. Despite the merits of these entries, most of the *Monument*'s comic material is contained in anecdotes and fillers, literary ancestors of the witticisms in the *Reader's Digest*.** The anecdotes feature such famous persons as painter Gilbert Stuart, George IV, and Frederick III of Prussia.

The editors strove to combine "the light and the beautiful" in the *Baltimore Monument* and presented their material in a newspaper format. For the three dollar subscription, readers could enjoy not only sundry pieces of literature, but also steel and wood engravings and pieces of music. Although the magazine was short-lived, Mott views it as Baltimore's best literary periodical, rivalled only by the *Emerald*.

Information Sources

BIBLIOGRAPHY:
Mott, Frank Luther, "Baltimore Monument." In *A History of American Magazines, 1741–1840*. Cambridge, Mass.: Harvard University Press, 1957, 1:381.

INDEX SOURCES: Title index with each volume.
REPRINT EDITIONS: University Microfilms.
LOCATION SOURCES: DLC, MdBE, Peabody Institute, NcD, NjR, Omaha Public
    Library, WHi.

Publication History

MAGAZINE TITLE AND TITLE CHANGES: *Baltimore Monument: A Weekly Journal,
    Devoted to Polite Literature, Science, and the Arts*, October 1836–September
    1838; *Baltimore Literary Monument*, October 1838–October 1839.
VOLUME AND ISSUE DATA: Weekly (October 1836–September 1838); monthly (Oc-
    tober 1838–October 1839); Volumes 1–4, October 1836–October 1839.
PUBLISHER AND PLACE OF PUBLICATION: 1836–1838: David Creamer, Baltimore.
    1838–1839: T. S. Arthur, Baltimore.
EDITORS: J. N. McJilton and David Creamer, 1836–1838; John N. McJilton and T. S.
    Arthur, 1838–1839.
CIRCULATION: Unknown; according to the editors, "respectable."

E. Kate Stewart

THE BARBER'S SHOP

The Barber's Shop was a theme periodical designed to trim its subjects down
to size with satire. Armed with "edge tools" that included puns, poetry, and
pot-shotting correspondence, proprietor "Sir David Razor" crusaded against the
British, rival editors, and other proclaimed evils, while riding proudly on the
coattails of *Salmagundi.**

The *Shop* appeared at Salem, Massachusetts, in four undated issues during
1807–1808. Each number contained sixteen pages of single-column typography,
with puns and fractured bits of Latin inevitably italicized for emphasis. Artwork
appeared rarely, limited to a few engravings of ships, birds, and musical notes
meant for decoration. Sir David cited the price of different issues as "twelve
and a half cents" and "ninepence."

The overall makeup of his publication was as inconsistent as the price. The
first number, capitalizing on the "barber" pun and its double-edged trade
vocabulary, promised an establishment endowed with regular characteristics.
There was an ornate mirror to attract the attention of customers who normally
could not tolerate "plain reflections." The editor described an adjoining
"Library" and a window from which patrons could "behold the passing crowd,
and speculate on their follies and fashions." But the narrow theme proved too
confining. Two numbers marked the duration of standard initial features such
as "Chit Chat," a series of anecdotes laced with comic vernacular, and
"Lathering the British," a column of inflammatory comment reflecting tensions
that preceded the War of 1812. Sir David devoted much of his third issue to an
uneven collection of letters. And he filled the fourth with a long, parenthetical
essay introducing a dueling, but unrevealed, correspondence between himself
and "Thomas Brainless, Esq.," editor of a Salem publication entitled *The Fool.**

Razor considered his *Shop* a cut above *The Fool* and on a par with other comic periodicals of the time. He specifically mentioned *Thunderclap* ("which left a nauseous stench"), *My Pocket Book* ("exhibited in Philadelphia for the entertainment of the multitude"), and Boston's *Thistle* ("none but a Jack-ass can relish it").[1] His attitude toward *Salmagundi* was admiring to the point of blatant imitation. To match Launcelot Langstaff's popular stable of contributors, Razor devised the likes of "David Razor, Junior" ("a young shaver, of promising talents"), "Humphrey Dasher" ("one of my journeymen who is quite a blade"), and correspondents "Dick Cowlick" and "Will Waxend." The young Razor's contribution, "The Stranger Under Water," was a mockery of John Carr's *The Stranger in Ireland*, which had also been parodied in *Salmagundi*.

The flavor of Sir David's satire was often diluted by attempts to belittle large, general groups. In between his frequent attacks on the British, he derided women and foreigners of several nationalities. He used verse to skewer lawyers, turncoats, sluggards, and henpecked husbands. His final issue contained a sharp rebuttal directed toward the "Boston reviewers," a stroke betraying a poor reception for the *Shop* in literary circles and a reason for its abrupt disappearance.

Note

1. A 146-page volume entitled *My Pocket Book* was written by Edward Dubois under the pseudonym "A Knight Errant" and published in New York in 1807. Composed in the form of short memoranda for a planned "Quarto Volume," the book was one of several parodies of John Carr's *The Stranger in Ireland* to appear at the time.

Information Sources

INDEX SOURCES: None.
REPRINT EDITIONS: University Microfilms.
LOCATION SOURCES: DLC (No. 1 only), NN.

Publication History

MAGAZINE TITLE AND TITLE CHANGES: *The Barber's Shop*, 1807–1808.
VOLUME AND ISSUE DATA: Four issues. Exact publication dates unknown.
PUBLISHER AND PLACE OF PUBLICATION: Unknown; Salem, Mass.
EDITOR: "Sir David Razor."
CIRCULATION: Unknown. Price is cited as twelve and a half cents and "ninepence."

Stuart A. Kollar

THE BEE (New York)

The Bee "Illustrated Comic Weekly" of 1898 was one of the largest and brightest of American comic weeklies during its eleven-week flight from 16 May to 2 August 1898. At five cents, its three-column, $10'' \times 15''$ format was boldly marked by dramatic and colorful front and back cover cartoon caricatures oriented toward the politics of the day and heavily influenced by the Spanish-American

War. It claimed to be an illustrated weekly of no party, although its stands tended to be anti-workingman and pro-American, even if a naive editorial in the second number wondered whether we couldn't fight Spain without hating Americans who happened to be Spanish.

From the first, *The Bee* was conscious of circulation and promised not to actively solicit advertising until it had reached 100,000. Color cartoons like one of a sleazy Uncle Sam eyeing a Feejee maid labeled "colonial expansion" were the main circulation booster. The first ads appeared on 29 June with Teddy Roosevelt in a full-page heroic cartoon on the cover with the admonition that America needed men of his stamp, even if he did lack a sense of the ridiculous. On 16 July *The Bee* noted that some persons still didn't see its purpose and reaffirmed that it represented no cause but sought only to tell the truth and be cheerful—always an unfortunate position for American comic periodicals.

Among the authors and departments, four stand out. James L. Ford is most notable. Charles Battell Loomis offered a number of pieces, including a dialect poem "When North and South Unite": "We teach the world a heap er things when North an' Saouth unite." "Lonergan's Letter" covering graft and corruption at New York City Hall became a regular feature, along with "Dialogues on Draughtsmen," covering illustrators' life. W. C. Munkittrick and W. C. Gibson also appear to have been among the writers. One cartoon of a sidewalk sandwich board offered "When you remember the Maine don't forget that Snooks' hats are only a dollar." In August, *The Bee* boasted the largest circulation ever for a weekly paper of its age, with no moldy jokes, a major innovation in the rapid processing of color cartoons for timely news, and lively satire on living personalities. Nevertheless, it ended with the 9 August number. The dash of its color cartoons alone, however, establishes its importance. An unpublished note in Mott's papers at the University of Missouri indicates that "Cory," formerly an illustrator with the New York *Journal*, was editor, owner, and publisher; this would be J. C. Cory.

Information Sources

INDEX SOURCES: None.
REPRINT EDITIONS: None.
LOCATION SOURCES: DLC, NN, CtY (Nos. 1–6), ICN (Nos. 1–4).

Publication History

MAGAZINE TITLE AND TITLE CHANGES: *The Bee*.
VOLUME AND ISSUE DATA: Weekly, Volume 1: 1–11, 16 May–2 August 1898.
PUBLISHER AND PLACE OF PUBLICATION: The Bee Publishing Co., New York.
EDITOR: J. C. Cory.
CIRCULATION: Unknown.

David E. E. Sloane

THE BEE (Philadelphia)

The Bee, printed in Philadelphia by Anthony Armbruster in 1765, stands as the first American humor magazine, only the thirteenth magazine attempted on the continent. Its run extended through three Tuesday issues, 12 February 1765 (Vol. 1:1), 19 February (Vol. 1:2), and 7 March (Vol. 1:3). Each issue was eight pages in octavo, 6¼" × 3¾". In its scant twenty-two pages, *The Bee* made for lively stinging of the colonial governors and Quaker parsons and all "great Folks who stick themselves up for Quality, and turn up their Noses at honest Mechanics," according to the pseudonymous editor, William Honeycomb.

The editor, even in describing himself, managed to be both elusive and allusive in the first number. In the second, he printed a burlesque letter defending the governor of Quillsylvania province which listed a variety of crimes, all under the banner of Pope and Hudibras—"Yes, while we live no rich or noble Knave; / Shall walk the World in Credit to his Grave." In the third number, he describes a tavern scene which he notes "Isaac Bickerstaff" was fearful had not kept enough windward of the law:

> The Provincial Praetor . . . shortly after his arrival in Quillsylvania invited all the Drunkards, Whoremasters, profane swearers, Rakes, Bucks, Bloods, fops, Jemmies, Fidlers, Topers, Whores and profligates of all sorts and sizes to meet with him once a week at the sign of the Bagpipe and Hitchman in Harris-Street.

For the next issue, which is not bound in the volume and may never have appeared, Honeycomb advertised "The Giant's Eulogy; or, the Scunk's Lamentation over his deceased friend," refuting the pamphlet "A Humble attempt at Scurrility" printed for J. B. in Coffee-house street, Printer and Publisher to the three dirty Parsons in Quillsylvania.

The Bee took the part of the common mechanic against government and religion at a time when periodicals were considered de facto enemies of the state. Lyon Richardson notes a likeness in its style to pamphlets by Isaac Hunt, but Hunt, John Dickenson, and others all used a similarly satiric style. Armbruster the printer is known to have done other job printing work for Joseph Shippen, Jr., although it is not clear that this allies him to a political party or its authors. *The Bee*'s tone is sharply satiric with wittily exaggerated rhetoric, and its viewpoint makes it an appropriate forerunner of other important Philadelphia humorous papers, William Helmbold's *The Tickler** and *Independent Balance** and Joseph Dennie's *The Port Folio** in the 1800–1825 period. Copies are housed at the Pennsylvania Historical Society and the Rare Book Room of the New York Public Library.

Information Sources

BIBLIOGRAPHY:
Richardson, Lyon. *A History of Early American Magazines, 1741–1789.* New York: Thomas Nelson and Sons, 1931, pp. 140n.–41n.
INDEX SOURCES: None.
REPRINT EDITIONS: None.
LOCATION SOURCES: NN-Rare Book Rm., DLC, PP, PHi, PPuLC.

Publication History

MAGAZINE TITLE AND TITLE CHANGES: *The Bee.*
VOLUME AND ISSUE DATA: Weekly, Volume 1:1–3, 12, 19 February, 7 March 1765.
PUBLISHER AND PLACE OF PUBLICATION: Anthony Armbruster, Philadelphia.
EDITOR: William Honeycomb, pseud.
CIRCULATION: Unknown.

David E. E. Sloane

LARAMIE BOOMERANG

The Laramie (Wyoming) *Boomerang* was founded in early 1881 by Albany County Republicans as an answer to the locally prominent daily *Times*, a Democratic newspaper. Laramie's other Republican paper, the once competitive *Sentinel*, had dropped its daily edition in 1879, and thus there was no longer a daily Republican counterpart of the *Times*. The first editor of the *Boomerang* was the famous American humorist Edgar Wilson (Bill) Nye.

Born in Maine in 1850 and raised in Wisconsin, Bill Nye had come West to Laramie in the Spring of 1876 to find work. Soon he was associate editor of the *Sentinel*, where he worked for three years before resigning to run for the legislature (unsuccessfully) and serve as lawyer, justice of the peace, U.S. land commissioner, and popular correspondent for other newspapers throughout the country. He was thus experienced and available when the *Boomerang*'s founders were looking for an editor. The *Boomerang* began publication on 11 March 1881, as both a daily and weekly, with Nye earning a salary of $150 a month. With characteristic wit, Nye announced the following prospectus in the first issue:

> We will spare our readers the usual programme of what we intend to do hereafter as a moulder of public opinion. We do this partly because we haven't clearly outlined our course yet in our own mind, and partly because some one might keep a file of the paper and annoy us with it in the years to come.
>
> In all political questions which may arise the Boomerang will be Republican. We also intend to give due credit for what we copy from exchanges.
>
> We shall, in addition to the above, perform several startling tricks of square-toed integrity which will arouse the wonder and surprise of those who have known us in the past.
>
> With many thanks to the host of patrons and friends who have contributed to

the very pronounced succcess of this enterprise, and with the earnest hope that they will not be disappointed, we advance to the foot-lights and hesitate a moment until the thunders of applause have died away in the distance.[1]

Nye took great personal interest in the operation of the paper. He named it himself (after his pet mule Boomerang), went to Chicago to select the presses and other equipment, and was even largely responsible for selecting the quarters for the editorial offices. One site was the upper floor of a livery stable, a location that caused the good-humored Nye to erect a sign outside instructing *Boomerang* customers either to take the stairs at the back of the stable or "twist the tail of the iron-gray mule and take the elevator." Apparently, his humorous outlook often helped offset the sometimes overpowering scent emanating from below.

The popularity of the *Boomerang* rested solely on Nye's humorous columns. Otherwise, as Wyoming historian T. A. Larson has pointed out, it was "a pretty ordinary western small-town paper."[2] Those columns consisted largely of clever prose sketches, essays, burlesques, and other satires written in relaxed style, informal structure, and humorous tone (yet with art and design). These pieces were published daily and then collected for a whole page of humor in the weekly edition. They covered a variety of topics, from politics to the travails of a frontier editor, but focused mainly on what was germane to the West: mines and mining, Indians, outlaws, the Mormons and Chinese, women of the West, local customs and special events, the fickle weather, and the rugged land itself. No matter what the subject, however, Nye's emphasis is almost always on people. As he once wrote, "During my short but eventful life I have given a large portion of my time to studying human nature. Studying human nature and rustling for grub, as the Psalmist has it, have occupied my time ever since I arrived at man's estate."[3]

By Nye's second year as editor, the *Boomerang* had become nationally famous and even enjoyed some foreign subscriptions. Major dailies throughout the country arranged exchanges. Its popularity notwithstanding, financial difficulties with the operation of the paper and Nye's own severe illness in 1882 with cerebrospinal meningitis spelled an end to the paper's brief period under his tutelage. Nye was forced to be inactive throughout the Winter and Spring of 1882–1883 and then got into a financial squabble with the ownership of the paper over back funds allegedly owed him. Forced because of his illness to move to lower altitudes, Nye closed out his business with the paper in the Summer and Fall of 1883 and left Laramie for his home in Hudson, Wisconsin, and then went on to the New York *World* as Sunday columnist.

The Laramie *Boomerang* still publishes, carrying on its banner head the words "Founded by American Humorist Bill Nye in 1881."

Notes

1. Quoted from Cheyenne *Daily Sun*, 16 March 1881 (Hebard file, University of Wyoming Library, p. 14). *Boomerang* files from Nye's time are not extant.

2. T. A. Larson, "Laramie's Bill Nye," *The Denver West—1952 Brand Book* (Denver: The Westerners, 1953), p. 44.

3. Bill Nye, "Some Overland Tourists," *Bill Nye and Boomerang* (Chicago: Belford, Clarke, 1881), p. 229.

Information Sources

BIBLIOGRAPHY:

Chaplin, W. E. "Bill Nye in Laramie." *Second Biennial Report, State Historian of Wyoming.* Sheridan, Wy.: Mills, 1921–1923, pp. 142–58.

———. "Some of the Early Newspapers of Wyoming." *Wyoming Historical Society Miscellanies.* Laramie: Laramie Republican, 1919, pp. 7–24.

———. "Some Wyoming Editors I Have Known." *Annals of Wyoming* 18 (January 1946): 79–87.

Kesterson, David B. *Bill Nye.* Boston: Twayne Publishers, 1981.

———. *Bill Nye: The Western Writings.* Boise, Idaho: Boise State University, 1976.

Larson, T. A. "Laramie's Bill Nye." *The Denver West—1952 Brand Book.* Denver: The Westerners, 1953, pp. 34–56.

INDEX SOURCES: None.

REPRINT EDITIONS: None.

LOCATION SOURCES: There is no extant file of the issues of the *Boomerang* edited by Bill Nye in 1881–1882. However, the University of Wyoming library holds the account books of the *Boomerang* during its early years and also has an excellent collection of Nye materials, including letters, documents, and works both on and by Nye.

Publication History

MAGAZINE TITLE AND TITLE CHANGES: Laramie *Boomerang*, 11 March 1881–   .

VOLUME AND ISSUE DATA: Volume 1, 11 March 1881 to present.

PUBLISHER AND PLACE OF PUBLICATION: Albany County Republicans of Laramie, Wyoming. Incorporators: M. C. Jahren, Robert Marsh, Henry Wagner, A. S. Peabody, J. J. Strode.

EDITORS: Bill Nye, editor and manager; Robert G. Head, City Editor.

CIRCULATION: Locally about 150 to 200 ("counting dead-heads," wrote Nye). National and international circulation unknown, though apparently fairly extensive.

David B. Kesterson

THE BUGLE-HORN OF LIBERTY

The Bugle-Horn of Liberty: A Humorous Paper, Devoted to Fun, Fact, and Fancy, along with Richmond's *Southern Punch,* was the Confederacy's answer to *Vanity Fair** and the plethora of other comic periodicals that opened in the North just before and during the Civil War. Humorous commentary on the social

and political scene, comic vernacular letters from imaginary Southern in-
fantrymen, mock epic, heroic, and amatory verse, and Johnsonian witticisms
dominated its attempts to shore up a Southern morale that was beginning to sag
under the reversals of the war. Within three issues of its first publication,
however, the rapidly inflating cost of paper and the general economic chaos in
the South abruptly halted publication.

Published in Griffin, Georgia, by Hill and Swayze, *Bugle-Horn* appeared in
August 1863, with the expressed purpose of challenging Southern writers to
create a purely Southern literature. The submerged pun in its title proposed to
bring the "horn" of schoolday writing purpose to use in the militant call of
Southern liberty:

> We are establishing an extensive publishing house, and of such a character as to
> make use of almost any kind of productions, thus affording an opportunity to all
> to promote the literary taste of the country. Writers, come forward and take a place
> in our ranks.

Not surprisingly, then, the cover of the first two issues was blazoned with a cut
of a semi-naked turbaned figure variously labeled Abraham Lincoln and Horace
Greeley. As self-chosen champion of Southern literature, *Bugle-Horn*'s humor
focused on Confederate social concerns:

> "Father, are there any niggers in our Congress?"
> "No my son—why do you ask . . . "
> "Because the papers said the other day that the members of the Federal Congress
> *kicked* Mr. Brown's *Bill* out of the house."

Interspersed with graveyard humor invoking the hardships of military service
and with satiric jabs at war profiteers and draft evaders are salutes to the *elan*
of the Southern forces:

> One day . . . General Lee's hat having fallen off, a young Lieutenant stepped
> forward, picked it up, and presented it to him.
> "Thank you, *Captain*," said the General inadvertently.
> "In what regiment sir?" inquired the Lieutenant, quick as lightning. The General
> smiled and forthwith promoted the witty youth.

And pervading each issue are broad jabs at genteel society in general. When a
lady resident of Griffin asks why the Army needs female nurses, the surgeon in
charge quietly mocks the distance between the soldier and the civilian: "It is
sufficient for you to know, madam, that *we* desire them."

Concluding the third issue are an announcement of the purchase of a thousand
dollars of printing equipment, an advertisement for the first of a series of original
regional publications, and a solicitation for further manuscripts. Paper costs,
however, rose fourfold in September 1863. Between August and September the

doubling of subscription costs from twenty-five cents to fifty cents (from two to five dollars a year) signaled severe problems for publishing in the South, and the lack of original material and the decrease in the number of sketches in the October issue were ominous. The November issue apparently never appeared.

In format, the paper consisted of sixteen quarto pages, three columns to a page, a style that imitated Joseph Addison Turner's *Countryman*. Bound volumes were not available. In addition to the recurring Lincoln-Greeley caricature, unsigned original pen sketches were common in each number. Standard printer's engravings also appeared as filler, so much so that the last issue included a parody of Confederate cavalry officers by interspersing such familiarly conventional sketches in a text describing the various personal accoutrements that a well-known Southern major needed to win his battle for a lady's eye.

The *Bugle-Horn*'s most distinguished contributor was Bill Arp (Charles Henry Smith), who promised to appear in each number. Along with his tales of "Konskripshun" and the exploits of the "Konfederate Hos Kavalry," the paper printed satirical letters from the Kilroyish Elihu Squiggs, who, living on "half a dozen bread pills" a day, exposes camp life and tells of beating back the "Cholera epidemic" of invading Yankees with the "iron pills" provided in every infantryman's cartridge box. Whimsical verse such as "Outside of a Horse: An Equinine Reminiscence" and "Paddy O'Connor, or Love and Bad Luck" round out the literary offerings by the likes of "Nix Simpkins" and "John Happy." The review of drama in each issue oddly provides billings in the North as well as in the Confederacy.

The most impressive and effective feature article, however, was the monthly expropriation of Artemus Ward's Boston *Post* column. Scathing looks at Union draft laws that allowed exemptions for men who held stock in the Vermont Railroad and that excluded the mentally deficient and those "who deliberately voted for John Tyler" must have had an effect on Southerners which was hardly a part of Ward's original intentions. The Confederacy, of course, was also facing harsh conscription laws by 1863. This fact, the paper's first editorial explains tongue in cheek, accounts for its apparent lack of an editor: "We have made up our mind, owing to the tightness of the times, and the scarcity of the article in question (all in the army) to dispense with that seeming inseparable appendage." The fundamental seriousness built into the joke is underlined by the October editorial's explanation for the issue's tardiness. The *Bugle-Horn*'s offices were impressed, at least temporarily, for use as part of the much-needed hospital moved into Griffin in the Summer and Fall of 1863. The November number apparently became another victim of the military and economic disasters that would soon lead to the Confederacy's collapse.

Information Sources

BIBLIOGRAPHY:
Blair, Walter, "The Popularity of Nineteenth-Century Humor." *American Literature* 3 (1931): 175–94.

Flanders, Bertram Holland. "*Bugle Horn of Liberty*: A Confederate Humorous Magazine." *Emory University Quarterly* 9 (1953): 79–85.

Mott, Frank L. *A History of American Magazines, 1850–1865*. Cambridge, Mass.: Harvard University Press, 1957, 2:185.

INDEX SOURCES: None.
REPRINT EDITIONS: None.
LOCATION SOURCES: DLC, NB, GA, NcD.

Publication History

MAGAZINE TITLE AND TITLE CHANGES: *The Bugle-Horn of Liberty: A Humorous Paper, Devoted to Fun, Fact, and Fancy.* August 1863-October 1863.

VOLUME AND ISSUE DATA: Monthly, Volume 1:1, August 1863–Volume 1:3, October 1863.

PUBLISHER AND PLACE OF PUBLICATION: Hill and Swayze, Publishers, Griffin, Georgia.

EDITOR: Unknown.
CIRCULATION: Unknown.

David W. Hiscoe

C

CALGARY EYE OPENER

The *Calgary Eye Opener* existed in two forms. The original was Canadian around the turn of the century, typical of the regional iconoclasts in the States, but especially Canadian and less usual in the more conservative Canadian environment. The later *Eye Opener* was a product of Captain Billy Fawcett's wife, competition to his *Whiz Bang** in the 1920s and 1930s.

Bob Edwards, founder, publisher, editor, and staff of the *Calgary Eye Opener* from 1902 to 1922, was an Alberta native (1864–1922). A heavy drinker who wrote in favor of temperance, Edwards was a sarcastic satirist who drew the praise of the New York *Bookman* and made his newsless newspaper the most widely read Canadian newspaper west of Winnipeg with a circulation of 7,000 in 1907. Impatient for a better deal for the poor, Edwards contended that wealth carried responsibility, not license: on Fords he chanted, "The Ford is my jitney, I shall not want . . . Yea, though I walk through the valleys, I am towed up the hills." He counseled solemnly, "Never trust a man whose dog has gone back on him." More significant was his general viewpoint: "A little learning is a dangerous thing but a lot of ignorance is just as bad." The last issue appeared on 29 July 1922, twenty years after its beginnings, when Edwards, just elected to provincial government, died of drinking-related illness. Grant MacEwan's *Eye Opener Bob; The Story of Bob Edwards* (Edmonton: Institute of Applied Art, 1957), the source of this information, covers the history fully.

The second *Calgary Eye Opener*, published by the Bob Edwards Publishing Company, of Minneapolis, Minnesota, descended directly from the first. The Canadian edition claimed Harvey Fawcett and Mrs. Kate Edwards as editors in the July 1929 number (Vol. 26:41), twenty-five cents, 6" × 7", filled with sexy gags and single-entendre jokes and gag cartoons along the theme of sex play. The "American" edition was edited by Annett[e] Fawcett, the wife of Wilford

H. (Harvey) (*Captain Billy's Whiz Bang**) Fawcett; she soon divorced the veteran and published it on her own as the Henna-haired Hurricane of Laughter and Joy. The first numbers actually seen are Volume 29:83 (December 1932) and Volume 32:8 (October 1933), twenty-five cents, monthly, 5½″ × 8¼″. "A good resolution is like a chorus girl—easier to make than to keep," is typical of the casual sex jokes of the magazine. It was still going strong in April 1939 (Vol. 38:2), in the same format, at the same price. *Eye Opener's Red Pepper Annual* at thirty-five cents, one hundred pages, in the same size but with more cartoon gags, was another byproduct of this magazine. It lasted several years, but only the 1933 edition has been seen.

Information Sources

BIBLIOGRAPHY:
MacEwen, Grant. *Eye Opener Bob; The Story of Bob Edwards*. Edmonton: Institute of
      Applied Art, 1957.
INDEX SOURCES: None.
REPRINT EDITIONS: None.
LOCATION SOURCES: None.

Publication Data

MAGAZINE TITLE AND TITLE CHANGES: *Calgary Eye Opener*, c.1902-c. April
      1939).
VOLUME AND ISSUE DATA: Weekly, c. 1902–29 July 1922; monthly, July 1929
      (Vol. 26:41)-April 1939 (Vol. 38:2).
PUBLISHER AND PLACE OF PUBLICATION: 1902–1922: Bob Edwards, Calgary,
      Alberta, Canada; Bob Edwards Publishing Co., Minneapolis, thereafter.
EDITORS: Bob Edwards, 1902–1922; Harvey Fawcett and Kate Edwards, 1922–1929;
      Annette Fawcett, c.1930–1939.
CIRCULATION: 7,000 in 1907, significantly higher in 1920s and 1930s.

David E. E. Sloane

CAPTAIN BILLY'S WHIZ BANG

Few periodicals reflect the post-World War I cultural change in American life as well as *Captain Billy's Whiz Bang*. To some people *Captain Billy's* represented the decline of morality and the flaunting of sexual immodesty; to others it signified an increase in openness. For much of the early 1920s, *Captain Billy's* was the most prominent comic magazine in America with its mix of racy poetry and naughty jokes and puns, aimed at a small-town audience with pretensions of "sophistication." *Captain Billy's*, founded and edited by Wilford H. Fawcett, also served as the first, and flagship, magazine of Fawcett Publications, which later included magazines such as *True Confessions* and *Mechanix Illustrated*. The magazine has earned a permanent niche in America's cultural history in *The Music Man* (supposedly set in 1912, seven years too early); in the recitation attached to the song "Trouble," Professor Harold Hill warns the unsuspecting mothers of River City: "Heed the warning before it's too late! Watch for the tell-tale signs of corruption! . . . Is he memorizing jokes out of Capt. Billy's Whiz Bang?"

Captain Billy's Whiz Bang began modestly. Returning home to Minneapolis after World War I, Captain Wilford Hamilton Fawcett, a former police reporter for the *Minneapolis Journal*, found himself out of work. He opened a tavern for soldiers, but this venture was closed by Prohibition. After that venture failed, Fawcett was left without work and with few funds. In 1919 to amuse himself and his hospitalized ex-servicemen friends, he began mimeographing and distributing sheets of off-color jokes and verses that he had learned in the service from his fellow doughboys. From these meager beginnings in 1919, the magazine, named for a World War I artillery shell (which, as it passed went Whiz, then Bang!), was started with an initial press run of 5,000 copies at a price of twenty-five cents. At first largely sold in Midwestern hotel lobbies, the magazine proved popular and the readership began to climb, as a result of which Fawcett was forced to hire other jokesmiths. In 1923, the readership of *Captain Billy's Whiz Bang* had climbed to 425,000, but by the middle of the Roaring Twenties the humor was beginning to lose some of its novelty and shock value, and by 1930 circulation slumped to only 150,000. By the early 1930s, the magazine had numerous competitors, including the successful *Ballyhoo** and the *Calgary Eye Opener*,* operated by Fawcett's ex-wife Annette Fisher Fawcett, whom Captain Billy had fondly referred to in the pages of his magazine as "the henna-haired heckler." Despite published reports that the magazine died in 1932, an issue from August 1936 has been seen. Brothers Roscoe and Harvey joined Captain Billy, and his four sons also joined and eventually ran the firm. Roscoe Fawcett, W. F. Fawcett's son and circulation manager for Fawcett Publications, recalls that it was published until the early 1940s—although by then it was a shell of its former self.

From the beginning the magazine seemed primarily targeted at a rural audience and prided itself on its "farmyard fun and filosophy." Fawcett correctly recognized the void in the published American humor of the period and set about to fill it. The humor, mild by contemporary standards, was saucy for the early part of the decade. *Captain Billy* was very careful to avoid offensive language and, unlike some competitors, never ran afoul of postal regulations for mailing obscene material, although some issues were held up until they were corrected. The early years with their doggerel poetry and rather naive sexuality (by contemporary standards, at least) are rather charming. By the middle of the decade Fawcett added erotic pictures of the movie starlets of the period (for example, Louise Brooks and Dorothy Dix), some even with bare breasts, and the humor became increasingly coarse. By the thirties the magazine became dominated by rather explicit cartoons, and the humor also became increasingly explicit, losing its subtlety. For a reader who wishes to understand the aesthetic contribution of *Captain Billy's* to American culture, one must begin with the opening volumes.

Much of the material was set at the "Whiz Bang Farm," supposedly in Robbinsdale (now a Minneapolis suburb), and involved Gus and Olaf, the hired men, Deacon Callahan, his daughter Lizzie (on whom men constantly had designs), and Pedro, the Whiz Bang Bull. (It was reported that rejection slips explained to authors that "Pedro, the Whiz Bang bull, didn't like this one.") Much of the humor depended on knowing the obscene joke that *Billy's* milder version referred to. In the words of *Captain Billy's* subtitle, the magazine was "an explosion of pedigreed bull" (or "bunk") as in this representative joke from January 1921:

The other day Adam approached Peter at the pearly gates and said: "I should very much like, Peter, to get a pass the first of the year to revisit my old haunts on earth."

"Nothing doing, Adam. You started too much trouble down there when you were a young man."

"Aw, Pete, be a good sport and let me go."

"What do you want to go down there for anyhow?"

"I want to turn over a new leaf."

From June 1923, we find this rather blue witticism:

"Why, hello," said the first poor working girl; "you must have struck it rich since I saw you last! Them jools, them furs, them everything!"

"Oh, haven't you heard?" said the second poor working girl. "I've got a new position!"

From the poetry corner in January 1921:

I had a flower garden,
But my love for it is dead,
'Cause I found a bachelor's button
In my black-eyed susan's bed.

No one will ever accuse *Captain Billy's* of excess creativity, yet the jokes—and the fact that they were printed—made a considerable impression on many a teenage boy. The magazine may be likened to *Playboy* in its role in male adolescent culture—just as the loosened sexual mores of the 1920s might be compared to those of the 1960s.

In addition to those jokes that, by later standards, would surely be considered sexist, the magazine also included jokes that ridiculed Blacks, Jews, and, not surprisingly considering its Minnesota locale, Scandinavian immigrants. Such jokes were common in jokebooks of the 1920s and, at the time, were far less controversial than the lewd material.

While *Captain Billy's Whiz Bang* was not overtly political, Fawcett had a strong patriotic streak. On the inside cover he described his magazine as "edited by a Spanish and World War Veteran, and dedicated to the fighting forces of the United States.'' He quotes former President Theodore Roosevelt: "We Have Room for but One Soul Loyalty and That is Loyalty to the American People.'' In addition, W. H. Fawcett was vigorously "wet" or anti-Prohibition, and devoted several of his editorial columns, "Drippings From the Fawcett," to that cause. For example, in 1928 when the State of North Dakota almost repealed Prohibition, Fawcett wrote:

> North Dakota! I am prouder of you than my red-headed wife is of her new pair of Montgomery Ward corsets with straps and surcingle attached. I am glad to know that the light of intelligence is slowly entering your dumb old skull. . . . What I am trying to get at is that the smellers and the sniffers have filled the Great American saps with baloney that rural America is unanimously for prohibition.

Fawcett also wished to represent rural Americans in his attacks on urban financiers.

Despite the tame content of the magazine by later standards (even those of a decade later), the early issues were roundly condemned by those who were attempting to rid American newsstands of smut. According to Frank R. Kent, writing in the *Baltimore Sun*:

> [There] are a whole flock—fifteen or twenty—monthlies of the "Hot Dog," "Red Pepper," "Whiz Bang" type, which add to the suggestiveness of the French a coarseness and vulgarity that are entirely American. All of these periodicals are openly and frankly pornographic. . . . They are of the type that have to be read by stealth and hidden in the desk. . . . It is an unenviable distinction, but we do seem to have taken the lead in lewdness away from the French. It is not a pleasant thing upon which to reflect (*Literary Digest*, 19 September 1925, p. 33).

In the mid–1920s authorities in Hudson, New Jersey, indicted and convicted three newsdealers for distributing and selling *Captain Billy's Whiz Bang* (among other magazines). However, it is not clear whether some other magazines on the list, such as *Artists and Models*, were not more to blame for the conviction. Still, the consensus in some quarters was that *Captain Billy's* was smut and should be prohibited.

Captain Billy's Whiz Bang is notable in American magazine publishing not only for its content, but also for being the cornerstone on which the Fawcett publishing empire was built. Nearly half a million copies at twenty-five cents each provided a sound base for W. H. Fawcett to expand his publishing business. In retrospect, the Fawcett magazine in this early period that has had the greatest impact on American publishing was *True Confessions*. Like most popular cultural phenomena, *Captain Billy's Whiz Bang* had a short period of impact. Although it continued publishing for over two decades, throughout much of the period it was just another low-brow humor magazine. Yet in its early years, it reflected and possibly helped to foster a loosening of American mores and a slight lifting of our Victorian sensibilities.

Information Sources

BIBLIOGRAPHY:

"America First—in Lewd Literature." *Literary Digest* 86 (19 September 1925): 33.

"Animated Annette." *Time* 20 (4 July 1932): 21.

"Captain Billy Goes West." *Time* 35 (19 February 1940): 61.

"The Fawcett Formula." *Time* 45 (19 March 1945): 63, 64, 66.

"Fawcett Publications." *Tide* 19 (1 March 1945): 56, 58, 60.

"Hooey." *Time* 18 (14 December 1931): 41–42.

Peterson, Theodore. *Magazines in the Twentieth Century*, 2d ed. Urbana: University of Illinois Press, 1962, pp. 284–87.

"The Story of Fawcett World Library." *Book Production Magazine* (August 1964): 42–45.

"Up From Whiz Bang." *Newsweek* 27 (25 March 1946): 64.

Villard, Oswald Garrison. "Sex, Art, Truth, and Magazines," *Atlantic* 137 (March 1926): 388–98.

"Whiz-Banger." *Time* 16 (29 December 1930): 19–20.

INDEX SOURCES: None.

REPRINT EDITIONS: None.

LOCATION SOURCES: A nearly complete edition of *Captain Billy's Whiz Bang* is available at the Minnesota Historical Society Library, St. Paul, Minnesota.

Publication History

MAGAZINE TITLE AND TITLE CHANGES: *Captain Billy's Whiz Bang*.

VOLUME AND ISSUE DATA: Monthly, some confusion in the volume numbering. Volumes 1–15 (1919–1932); Volumes 7–11 (1932–1936) (c. September 1919-c. August 1936). According to Roscoe Fawcett, W. H. Fawcett's son and Fawcett circulation manager, the magazine began in May 1919 and ended in 1942 or 1943. The tenth Anniversary issue was published in October 1928, even though there is no indication that the publication began before late 1919.

PUBLISHER AND PLACE OF PUBLICATION: Wilford H. Fawcett, Robbinsdale, later Minneapolis; Greenwich, Connecticut.

EDITOR: Wilford H. Fawcett (aided from 1920 to 1935 by brother, Roscoe Fawcett).

CIRCULATION: Varies; apparently 425,000 in 1923; 150,000 in 1930.

Gary Alan Fine

THE CARPET-BAG

Although an attempt to establish a comic journal in Boston failed in 1845, the founders of *The Carpet-Bag* were confident of success in 1851. The earlier journal, the *Jester*,** had sought to be an American *Punch*, whereas in its prospectus *The Carpet-Bag* promised grave as well as humorous matter, instruction as well as amusement, and, withal, a literary journal of quality and variety that would be "an agreeable fireside and wayside companion" to the reader. The name was adopted to indicate "the miscellaneous character of a good paper into which are crowded a variety of things necessary for comfort and happiness while on the highway of life" (Vol. 1:1, p. 5). *The Carpet-Bag* soon proved to be a much more humorous than grave journal: "our correspondents—jolly fellows—have had it their own way," the editor wrote in graceful capitulation as the paper entered its second year of publication, "and we have become almost unwittingly, but agreeably, the dispensers of their heartiness" (Vol. 2:1, p. 4). That heartiness brought widespread recognition and appreciation but few paying subscribers. A dealer in Columbus, Ohio, reported sales of fifty copies per week at probably five cents each; yet the paper never had more than four hundred subscribers at two dollars per year, and so it died. The editor, Benjamin Penhallow Shillaber, attributed its demise partly to the increased humorous content, partly to an extended political satire of the Scott-Pierce presidential campaign that offended both Whigs and Democrats in 1851–1852, and partly to severe editorial conduct by the junior editor, Charles G. Halpine, who bought a quarter interest in the publication on 19 June 1852.

The philosophy of *The Carpet-Bag* derived from its unflagging determination to win enough paying subscribers to finance a publication of quality. Public approval was frankly courted in the editor's columns where many declarations are made of "humble efforts to please" and of striving "hard to win public approval" (23 March 1851). In the "Close of Volume One" the editors look back to note that "the effort to please has been incessant" (27 March 1852). The first issue of Volume 2 renews the commitment: "With the breath of popular favor we shall live" (31 April 1852). Though two of the original founders had departed, the "Close of Volume Two" a year later confirms the paper's singular goal: "One thing is very certain," the editors note, "we have tried to please . . . to cater to your good-natured taste."

An article reprinted in the first issue from the *Glasgow Citizen* entitled "The Philosophy of a Little Carpet-Bag" reveals how *The Carpet-Bag* sought to win readers: "A little carpet-bag is almost always indicative of a short and pleasant excursion. No painful ideas of stormy seas or dreadful accidents on far-off railway lines are suggested by it . . . a gentleman with a little carpet-bag may be said to contemplate about a couple of shirts' absence from home" (Vol. 1:1, p. 4). A solicitous companion devoted to pleasing, then, *The Carpet-Bag* avoided "painful ideas" and followed a safe course. To its readers it continually pledged "harmless witticisms," "good jokes," "pleasant satire"—anything "cheerful" that appealed to "good-natured taste."

The ideal reader is described in the thirty-first issue. Above a caption "Portrait of the Man Who Can See Fun in the Carpet-Bag" is the smiling image of a jovial man at rest in a comfortable chair, *The Carpet-Bag* in his hand. "To be happy is his governing principle," the article proclaims. "Moroseness and ill-nature he holds in abhorence as hostile to the good of man." Attention is called to his face. "He loves to laugh, but not boisterously. You can read his mirth in his eyes and upon his lips before you hear him laugh." He is, in brief, the amiable humorist as the eighteenth and nineteenth centuries idealized him. The editors of *The Carpet-Bag* catered to that amiability. In the fifty-second issue Shillaber declared that nothing would be published to "wound the sensibilities of individuals" (Vol. 1:52, p. 4). Satire thus attacked broad rather than particular subjects; cartoons jibed mildly at the harmless fashions and foibles of the general public. The journal also promoted morality by amiable example. "Vice," Shillaber announced, "has no palliator in our humble sheet." Fourteen weeks later Shillaber ostentatiously welcomed the genteel daughter test: "We mean," he wrote, "to produce a paper for you, reader, that you can carry into your family and place before your wife and daughter, with the knowledge that it contains no poisons for their minds or morals . . . that its fun will be genial and wholesome" (Vol. 2:14, p. 4). Happily, for all its probity and inoffensive amiability, *The Carpet-Bag* was a surprisingly vigorous, genuinely comic paper. "Ben Barleycorn" praised it justly in these comic lines: "The man of sense, the wit, the wag, / All love to read the Carpet Bag" (Vol. 1:10, p. 8).

The achievement of a national reputation was a historically important development. It came about partly because *The Carpet-Bag* sought the largest possible audience. Two of the original founders, George K. Snow and Silas W. Wilder, had secured widespread circulation with their Boston *Pathfinder* and the *Pathfinder Railway Guide*. The *Guide* made a profit from advertising and was distributed without cost to travelers; wherever the rails went, the *Guide* went. The specific hope was that *The Carpet-Bag* could win a good portion of the *Guide*'s audience as paying subscribers. The general hope was that those rails would lead to a large national audience ready to support a lively, quality publication. From the outset Shillaber, as editor, had his eye on the nation at large. He welcomed exchanges with other publications because they helped to make *The Carpet-Bag* known far beyond the reaches of Boston. The Clemens brothers, for example, reprinted items from it in the Hannibal *Journal*. Shillaber also encouraged writers from every region and published them. *The Carpet-Bag* soon boasted some one hundred contributors, many of whom were writers of talent and reputation. Probably no other publication of the time provided an outlet for so much talent. Indeed, a most important historical contribution of the paper was its publishing young writers who were to achieve fame in subsequent decades: Charles G. Halpine (Private Miles O'Reilly), Charles F. Brown (Artemus Ward), and "S. L. C." (Mark Twain).

For all its national interests, *The Carpet-Bag* was founded in Boston with Yankee owners, editors, and a host of eager Down East contributors who immediately capitalized on a rich regional content. Among them were Matthew F. Whittier (Ethan Spike) and "Betsy Sprigg" who captured Yankee talk in print. "A Letter from Ethan Spike" is a fresh, funny use of the well-established rustic epistle (Vol. 1:33, p. 7). Sprigg's "Widow Waddle's Sentiments on Wearing the Breeches" simultaneously illustrates the comic possibilities of homespun talk and a subject matter that amused the age (Vol. 1:13, p. 3). A spoof on shipbuilding, "The Yellow-Squall-Hound" by Benjamin Drew (Trismegistus), epitomizes the humor of New England fishing ports. The *Hound* is a remarkable mackerel boat with "a keelson, two sister keelsons, and one brother and nephew keelson" (Vol. 1:13, p. 5). Most famous of all was Mrs. Partington (Shillaber) who, moving from a Down East village to Boston, responded to experiences of town and country with hilariously malapropish yet authentic Yankee speech.

Rivalling, as an embodiment of Yankee humor, such established male characters as Jack Downing and Sam Slick, Mrs. Partington first appeared in the Boston *Post* in 1847 and achieved national fame before the advent of *The Carpet-Bag*. It is clear that the new publication counted on her to enhance its chances of success. The prospectus announces exclusive rights to humorous pieces featuring her. The first issue also celebrates her new role in a long poem: "Mrs. Partington's Dream: or the Opening of the Carpet-Bag" (Vol. 1:1, p. 2). More striking, the picture of her with nephew Ike is prominently displayed in the paper's handsome masthead where it visually confirms a permanent association between Mrs. Partington and *The Carpet-Bag*. The picture of the kindly old lady and the mischievous boy is richly suggestive today because it recalls Shillaber's influence on Mark Twain's creation of Aunt Polly and Tom Sawyer. One of the most interesting sketches about Mrs. Partington that Shillaber wrote for the paper is "Mrs. Partington's Phrenology"; it accounts for her comic eccentricities by making droll references to her "very eneven head" (Vol. 1:51, p. 5).

Emphasis on humor helped to assure that *The Carpet-Bag* would be a national as well as regional journal because laughable local-color pieces contributed to the larger perspective. "How to Load a Gun" by "Carlos" displays the Irishman as comic bumbler (Vol. 1:29, p. 8); humorists of the Old Southwest were yarning off similar tales featuring the type. While maintaining its regional flavor, the whimsical depiction by "Chub" (Charles Farrar Brown, who later added the *e* to Brown) entitled "An Old Fashioned Husking" typifies rural life in midcentury America. George Horatio Derby's burlesque "A New Military Uniform" transcends regionalism. "The Botherum Pootrum" by "Peter Snooks, Esquire" (John C. Moore)—"a chapter in chickencraft"—is characteristic of the ubiquitous tall tale. A vivid picture of a male fighting cock stands atop the article, readily supporting Snooks's contention of sizes ranging from 16 inches to 25 feet and weights ranging from 6 to 100 pounds. The mighty Botherum eats corn, old hats, shoes, and stray socks; its voice when it crows surpasses the sound of any steam locomotive (Vol. 1:52, p. 8).[1] Sketches such as these, other anecdotes, jests, and tales of fishing, hunting, and courting express national as well as regional tendencies in the emerging humor of America.

Writers from outside New England broadened and enriched *The Carpet-Bag*. Southern writers sent in pieces; and M. Quad of the Detroit *Free Press* always found Shillaber eagerly awaiting his "Travels in the West." Typical of the Quad pieces is a sketch dated 16 October 1851 from Leavenworth, Indiana (Vol. 1:32, p. 7). More copiously indicative of the paper's national perspective are the many references to other sections and rising cities—New York, Washington, D.C.,

Baltimore, Richmond, Virginia, Detroit, St. Louis, and other cities in the Midwest and California. The mock political campaign of Ensign Jehiel Stebbings lightheartedly parodied the contest between Generals Winfield Scott and Franklin Pierce but damaged the paper. The response shows the national impact of *The Carpet-Bag*, as citizens everywhere protested or approved. (See, for example, "Our Candidate," Vol. 1:31, p. 4; 1 November 1851.)

The format of *The Carpet-Bag* was especially attractive. J. Wolcott designed a striking masthead that depicted the uppermost part of a carpet bag with hand grasping the leather handles. Two scenes are depicted in oval "frames" on either side of the inch-high letters of the title. On the left, Mrs. Partington and Ike are seated at a parlor or kitchen table. On the right, two signs stand above a doorway to the street, one advertising the *Pathfinder* office, and the other, *The Carpet-Bag*. The paper itself consisted of eight small folio pages of about 12″ × 16″, divided into four columns. The printing was excellently done on white paper of good quality. Illustrations took up no more than ten percent of the total space, but they were well executed by some of the best graphic artists of the day. *The Carpet-Bag* sold for two dollars per year per copy, five copies to one order for eight dollars and ten copies to one order for fifteen dollars. Two annual volumes at two dollars each were issued, one at the end of each completed year of the paper's existence.

The Carpet-Bag placed notable emphasis on poetry, devoting perhaps a third of the total space to verse. Some of it was melodramatic, sentimental, elegiac, and occasionally solemn. Even such wits as Shillaber and Benjamin Drew occasionally wrote sentimental verse about youth and old home town. Drew's recollection of his boyhood days on Cape Cod is about as good as *Carpet-Bag* writers could be in this mode (Vol. 1:34, p. 6). However, the greater amount of verse was light, in keeping with the paper's expressed desire to cultivate cheerfulness. Thus, in many humorous poems sentiment is more often made fun of than indulged in, as these titles indicate: "Love vs. Roast Onions," "Lament of the Disconsolate Loafer," and "My Heart's Delight," a lyric celebrating a young girl's greatest charm—her money. In the second issue the paper met one of the age's expectations of humorous verse, a parody of "The Raven." The importance of verse to *The Carpet-Bag* is underscored by the Great Union Poem, a collaborative effort of 53 stanzas entitled "Jethro Hornbeam," by various pseudonymous poets (28 February 1852). Artemus Ward (Chub) contributed a nine-line stanza beginning "When through the cow-path street called Washington / He walked one afternoon with loitering gait" (XIV); other regular contributors to the journal wrote verses (Vol. 1:48, p. 5). Shillaber, who acknowledges two stanzas "By the Editor," later confessed to writing twenty-nine under many aliases. The editor's great labor on the poem suggests the importance of humorous verse to *The Carpet-Bag*.

Among other notable features of the journal were excellent book reviews, a variety of material about Mrs. Partington, humorous accounts of contacts with the spiritual world, and a series, with illustrations, of *The Carpet-Bag* "family."

The "family" sketches played mildly amusing games with the pseudonymous identities of the paper's chief contributors while introducing them to the readers.

Most important, however, was the wealth of material exploiting vernacular speech in apparently realistic events and settings. Twain's one contribution and the ten pieces contributed by Artemus Ward between 27 December 1851 and 25 December 1852 reflect aspects of that trend. Half of Ward's sketches humorously satirize drinking and drunkards. "Oil vs. Vinegar; or the Rantankerous Lecturer" (19 June 1852) presents a lively interchange between a temperance lecturer who speaks for proper establishment folk and "Uncle Thad," a village native whose vernacular speech frustrates, if it does not subvert completely, the moral position of the temperance lecturer (Vol. 2:12, p. 2). As the younger writers perfected their skills, some of them, like Ward, exploited the latent energies of American vernacular speech that are revealed in hundreds of tales and sketches like "Oil and Vinegar."

In addition to apprentice writers like Halpine and Browne, *The Carpet-Bag* benefitted from the contributions of better known writers. These included J. T. Trowbridge, "Paul Creyton," author of juvenile stories, poems, and novels; women poets such as Mrs. Louise Chandler Moulton, "Ellen Louise," who became a household name in America; and Elizabeth Akers Allen who, as "Florence Percy," achieved an international reputation. Other writers whom Shillaber singled out in his autobiographical "Experiences During Many Years" include Tobias H. Miller, "Uncle Toby," Charles G. Eastman, "Guess Who," J. Q. A. Griffith, whose "Bumpus Reports, Hilary Term" find humor while exploring legal minds, and Fred T. Somerby, "Cymon," who originated some of the most imaginative hoaxes or "sells" of the midcentury. Like Somerby, Benjamin Drew knew Shillaber from earlier days on the Boston *Post*; and it was he, rather than Somerby, who originated the campaign hoax of Jehiel Stebbings, fictitious hero of a bogus "Aroostook War." Little did these witty, humor-loving old friends realize that a lighthearted spoof of a presidential campaign would anger contending parties and hurt *The Carpet-Bag*.

Although the first issue of *The Carpet-Bag* lists S. W. Wilder and Shillaber as editors, and although Halpine became associate editor and took on the responsibilities of editor for a brief time while Shillaber was away, Shillaber was almost always completely in charge. Content, format, and style reflect his influence. That both Artemus Ward and Mark Twain found him receptive probably derives as much from their brevity and short, clear sentences as from the content of their work. The illustrations also reflect Shillaber's editorial taste. On occasion he singled out for praise such well-known illustrators as Hammat Billings, D. C. Johnston, G. H. Rouse, J. Wolcott, and Frank Bellew. Although these artists possessed distinctive styles and in other journals depicted individuals admirably, their work for Shillaber reflects his governing philosophy of humor. Background details or animal figures are depicted in abundant detail, but people are presented as types. When sport is made in *The Carpet-Bag*, it is of general rather than particular targets.

For all his commitment to *The Carpet-Bag*, Shillaber, whose "Experiences" were published in the *New England Magazine* in the 1890s, gave a judicious rather than an inflated assessment of it. He believed that it brought together the largest number of professional and amateur writers ever to contribute to one publication and that it advanced the careers of deserving young writers, while helping to prepare for a readier acceptance of native humor. Before the advent of *The Carpet-Bag*, he further observed, the place of humor in American news-papers and journals had not been established; nor had the humorous column become a prominent feature. *The Carpet-Bag* also awakened creators of humor, encouraging them to write better and to attempt new things. If the experiment of publishing "an exclusively humorous paper" had failed, it was because public sentiment was not ready for it in the 1850s: "There was a lurking feeling of suspicion and doubt about it, it being a new departure in Boston, and a fear lest levity should usurp the place of more staid customs that had crystallized with the years."[2]

In a sense public fears were accurate, if not fully justified. For all of Shillaber's devotion to the values of the genteel establishment, a subversive irreverence was working in the humor of *The Carpet-Bag*, undermining those "staid customs" of many years. The promise of that irreverence is notable in the vernacular humor. The mildest and least irreverent of that vernacular humor, the Ruth Partington sketches, were collected by Shillaber into an often-reprinted book, the *Life and Sayings of Mrs. Partington*, in 1854; hence, *The Carpet-Bag* pro-vided much of the material that constituted the first book-length work in American literature to contain a fully developed humorous woman character. But the per-vasive influence of *The Carpet-Bag* on the American public and the press best testifies to the paper's historical influence. Few publications existing for so brief a time have exercised so lasting an influence.

Notes

1. This piece had a further life, being partly reprinted, with full reference to *The Carpet-Bag*, in Geo. P. Burnham's *The History of the Hen Fever* (Boston: James French and Co., 1855), pp. 92–97.

2. Benjamin Penhallow Shillaber, "Experiences During Many Years," *New England Magazine* 9 (October 1893): 157.

Information Sources

BIBLIOGRAPHY:

Austin, James C. *Artemus Ward*. New York: Twayne Publishers, 1964, pp. 22–29.

Blair, Walter. *Native American Humor*. New York: American Book Co., 1937, pp. 43, 113–16, 23, 49–51, and passim.

Blair, Walter, and Hamlin Hill. *America's Humor: From Poor Richard to Doonesbury*. New York: Oxford University Press, 1978, passim.

DeVoto, Bernard. *Mark Twain's America*. Boston: Little, Brown, and Co., 1932, 88–90.

Hamilton, Sinclair. *Early American Book Illustrators and Wood Engravers 1670–1870*.

Princeton, N.J.: Princeton University Press, 1958, pp. xliii, 71–72; xxxix, 48, 74–77; xxxvi, 137, 140, 162–63 and passim.

Meine, Franklin J. "American Comic Periodicals; No. 1—The Carpet-Bag." *Collector's Journal* 4, No. 3 (October-November-December 1933): 411–13.

Mott, Frank L. "The Carpet Bag." In *A History of American Magazines, 1850–1865.* Cambridge, Mass.: Harvard University Press, 1957, 2:180–81.

Murrell, William. *A History of American Graphic Humor.* New York: Whitney Museum, 1933, pp. 181–82, and passim.

Reed, John Q. *Benjamin Penhallow Shillaber.* New York: Twayne Publishers, 1972, pp. 22–27, and passim.

Shillaber, Benjamin Penhallow. "Experiences During Many Years." *New England Magazine* (June 1893-May 1894), 8 (1893): 511–25, 618–27, 719–24; 9 (1893): 88–95, 153–60, 529–33, 625–31; 10 (1894): 29–36, 247–56, 286–94.

Stewart, George R. *John Phoenix, Esq. The Veritable Squibob: A Life of Captain George H. Derby, U.S.A.* New York: Da Capo Press, 1969; repr. Henry Holt and Co., 1937, pp. 80–81, 212, 225, and passim.

INDEX SOURCES: None.

REPRINT EDITIONS: Readex Microprint.

LOCATION SOURCES: DLC, ICU, MB, MWA, NN, IU, and seventeen other libraries list holdings.

Publication History

MAGAZINE TITLE AND TITLE CHANGES: *The Carpet-Bag*, 29 March 1851–26 March 1853.

VOLUME AND ISSUE DATA: Weekly, annual volumes, Volume 1: 1, 29 March 1851–Volume 2:52, 26 March 1853.

PUBLISHER AND PLACE OF PUBLICATION: Snow and Wilder; Wilder and Pickard, Boston.

EDITORS: Silas W. Wilder and Benjamin Penhallow Shillaber, 1851–1853; Charles G. Halpine, Associate Editor, 19 June 1852.

CIRCULATION: 400 known subscribers; advertising rates unknown; railroad distribution; extensive "Exchanges" with other publications.

Clyde G. Wade

CARTOON CARNIVAL

Caravan Books first copyrighted a humor magazine under this title in October 1955 in a 7¾" × 10¾" format. But Charlton Publications in Derby, Connecticut, took over the title and ran it together with *Good Humor*** beginning in the Spring of 1962 and continuing through the present. The story of *Cartoon Carnival* and *Good Humor* as tandem bimonthly publications demonstrates the cost factors that figured in the survival of magazines oriented toward adult sexual humor in the 1960–1985 period. Its humor at first tended toward light sexual comedy including the proposition at a party, honeymoon expectations at the threshold doorway, and light social and dating situations. Over the years, the beauties and cuties became lusher, following the style of Bill Wenzel and others, and the honeymoon performance jokes moved inside the bedroom and finally into the nuptial bed itself, where they remain at present. Other areas of sexual and dating activity underwent a similar maturation and physicalization.

Cartoon Carnival as developed by Charlton appeared once in combination with *Good Humor* in the Winter of 1960, but was published as number 1 by Charlton, quarterly, Winter 1962. The print run was 86,000 and sales amounted to 27,500; later print runs increased to 100,000 with sales following up to 40,000; by the late 1960s, print runs were closer to 125,000 with sales around 50,000 to 55,000 bimonthly. Both *Cartoon Carnival* and *Good Humor* converted to alternate bimonthly publications in June 1967, becoming siamese twins in the later 1970s after *Good Humor* had a brief fling as a men's magazine. The later 1970s, however, showed sales in the 20,000 to 30,000 range and the 1980s have shown occasional dips into the teens. Since 1979 the two magazines have used the same editor and the same material, and have been, in fact, a single publication under two titles with only the slightest differences in format. The present price is $1.75 per issue. Ten to thirty gags and cartoons with sexual orientation are pasted up per page and come from various sources; it has only front and back cover advertisements and an unlisted editorial staff. Editor JoAnn Sardo is responsible for these and two other publications, edited by selecting cartoons submitted through the mail. *Cartoon Carnival* continued in January 1986 under a new name, *Comedy Capers*, with the same inside material, and was suspended with Volume 25:125 for March 1987.

Information Sources

INDEX SOURCES: None.
REPRINT EDITIONS: None.
LOCATION SOURCES: Charlton Press.

Publication History

MAGAZINE TITLE AND TITLE CHANGES: *Cartoon Carnival* to November 1985; *Comedy Capers* thereafter.
VOLUME AND ISSUE DATA: Quarterly, Volume 1, Winter 1962; bimonthly, Numbers 17, August 1967,–118, November 1985; *Comedy Capers* suspended with Volume 25:125 (March 1987).
PUBLISHER AND PLACE OF PUBLICATION: Charlton Press, Derby, Connecticut.
EDITORS: "Wild Bill" Anderson, 1970s; JoAnn Sardo, 1983–1987.
CIRCULATION: 50,000–60,000, 1960s; 40,000, early 1970s; 20,000, late 1970s; 15,000–20,000, 1980s.

David E. E. Sloane

CARTOONS (CARTOONS MAGAZINE/WAYSIDE TALES AND CARTOONS)

Although *Life*,* *Puck*,* and *Judge*,* among others, were dominated by their special brands of cartoons and cartoonists—particularly Charles Dana Gibson and Zim (Eugene Zimmerman), from 1912 through 1922 *Cartoons Magazine* must be identified as the leading serious publisher of cartoon humor and commentary, with accompanying periodical coverage of leading world and national social and political events. H. H. Windsor was the editor and publisher of the Chicago monthly, priced first at fifteen cents and later at twenty-five cents, and frequently numbering 150 pages of densely packed cartoons and news features in its 7" × 9¾" format. In the later teens, T. C. O'Donnell became Windsor's managing editor. The Roaring Twenties may have proved hard on the serious side of the magazine, however. Windsor died in 1924, and the format may have shifted into *Cartoons and Collegian Fun* (c. 1926) and *Cartoons and Movies Magazine* (c. 1925) published by Hubbard Publications in New York City.

Windsor was committed to the cartoon as a journalistic form, subtitling his magazine, "A magazine of cartoons from periodicals and newspapers," priced at $1.50 per year. From the first 8½" × 11", 66-page issue in January 1912, it took three years for the *Cartoons* format to emerge. At first, national and international cartoons were reprinted on heavy but cheap paper, but a slick-paper center section was added featuring the best of the national editorial cartoons. Gradually, background articles and items on individual cartoonists became more noticeable. Volume 4 brought a size change to 7" × 9½" and an improvement in paper quality. More important, interpretive articles and cartoons were now grouped around a theme such as "The Railroads' Toll of Death," or "The New Styles." Discussion and interpretation of major world events and social issues through the cartoon medium were fully established as the magazine's special focus.

Most notable was the November 1914 issue titled *"The War in Cartoons Magazine"* on the cover. Illustrated articles dealt with the Napoleonic Wars in caricature, *Punch*'s "New Rakes Progress," and a wide coverage of war issues on the newly opened European front. Although *Cartoons* included display advertisements and classifieds, as with other numbers, this number proclaimed no "clubbing" or premiums to increase subscriptions. William T. Jefferson's "The New Religion" from the Davenport Democrat, "meaning the worship of the gun," was the first page of text, boxed, and had the force of a *Cartoons* editorial. In December, "The War in Cartoons" was the heading of another editorial from the *Lutheran Observer*, commenting that the cartoon has become "an established feature of modern journalism": "They have humor in them, of course, but it is a grim, sardonic, bitter humor . . . the bewildered surprise of those who are looking on the unbelievable." Other features dealt with Daumier and the Franco-Prussian War, America's unreadiness for war, the national elections, and a further array of war-related topics. In the years before Mickey Mouse, *Cartoons* noted Wallace Carlson's coup in animating cartoons of the 1914 World Series within hours of the four-game series.

Cartoons, unlike later magazines bearing the name, was a philosophic examiner and employer of news cartoons. It was neither a trade journal nor a light, society-oriented laugh book. After T. C. O'Donnell became Windsor's managing editor in the late teens, added to the masthead were the side comments "The

Passing Show in Cartoons'' and ''Telling it with a Chuckle.'' The focus remained on serious newspaper editorial cartoons, however, each group of cartoons carrying by-lined text. The heavy lines of the charcoal graphics in editorial cartoons, accompanying the discussions of topics, maintained the serious tone of the magazine in topics from the Irish Sinn Fein movement through isolationism, early air transportation, naming the baby, and the daylight savings repeal movement. A few cartoons drawn for *Cartoons* were by various hands, but the mass were taken from national and English and European newspaper sources. O'Donnell edited an informal column toward the back of the magazine, but he did not set as serious a tone as Windsor had at the outbreak of the war.

Cartoons was united with *Wayside Tales* in 1921 and ended in December of that year. *Wayside Tales and Cartoons* offered unimpressive adventure stories and local humor, with a few jokes and cartoons divorced from political and social issues. Another Windsor publication in a similar format but with a different topic—*Popular Mechanics Magazine*—continued in print long after this period.

Information Sources

INDEX SOURCES: Table of Contents at front of each issue.
REPRINT EDITIONS: University Microfilms.
LOCATION SOURCES: IC, IAU, MH, MBat, NjP list the longest runs among about
    thirty libraries with holdings under *Wayside Tales*.

Publication History

MAGAZINE TITLE AND TITLE CHANGES: *Cartoons*, Volumes 1–3:5, January 1912-
    May 1913; *Cartoons Magazine*, Volume 3:6-Volume 19:12, June 1913-June 1921;
    Cartoons Magazine and Wayside Tales, Volume 20:1, July 1921; *Wayside Tales
    and Cartoons Magazine*, Volume 20:2-Volume 20:6, August 1921-December
    1921.
VOLUME AND ISSUE DATA: Monthly, Volume 1:1, January 1912–Volume 20:6,
    December 1921.
PUBLISHER AND PLACE OF PUBLICATION: H. H. Windsor, Chicago.
EDITOR: H. H. Windsor.
CIRCULATION: Unknown.

David E. E. Sloane

CHIC

Chic was the first imitator, in a long line of imitators, of *Puck** of New York. It copied *Puck*'s size (11″ × 15″), *Puck*'s format (lithographed front and back cover and centerspread cartoons, all in color, plus woodcuts within) and *Puck*'s editorial content (humorous short prose and poetry).

Chic made its debut on 15 September 1880, in the midst of the presidential campaign. Politics provided *Chic* with much of its cannon fodder. The weekly appears to have preferred General Winfield S. Hancock, the Democrat, to his Republican opponent, Congressman James A. Garfield. But *Chic* was not too enamored with either side and was, in a general view, nonpartisan. The rest of *Chic*'s editorial matter was given over to social humor and the discussion of such matters of the day as the trend of rich Englishmen marrying American women, the photography craze, and interest in Sarah Bernhardt. Charles Kendrick, a good caricaturist who had previously done freelance work for Harper's and Leslie's publications, was *Chic*'s chief cartoonist. He was assisted by C. W. Weldon, Livingston Hopkins, and an artist who signed himself J. B.

Lasting only a year, *Chic*, Volume 1:1 (15 September 1880) through Volume 2:38 (1 June 1881) sold at ten cents per copy and was published by the Chic Publishing Company, of New York. Intending to compete with the three major cartoon magazines of its era, it presented itself in their format with sixteen pages—the middle two being given to a large cartoon, and the last page and front page also featuring boldly colored, politically oriented cartoons; three pages of ads filled up the back of the magazine.

Kendrick's cartoons were most notable, and it affected a breezy style in jokes aimed at Garfield, Roscoe Conkling, and Jay Gould. In April 1881, *Chic* complained that the Manhattan Elevated Railroad was making rapacious demands in return for displaying the magazine on their newsstands—demands it could not meet. By 3 May, *Chic* expanded to eighteen pages, claiming a growth in advertisers and patronage. It furnished such comic bits as the Great American Novel, published in "spasms" rather than chapters, along with major social-economic cartoons such as Gould and Vanderbilt as spiders in telegraph webs in the 12 January issue. Democrats and Wall Street cheats came in for much of its humor, some of it in doggerel verse. Lack of circulation on the railroad newsstands, however, probably killed it.

Information Sources

INDEX SOURCES: None.
REPRINT EDITIONS: None.
LOCATION SOURCES: DLC.

Publication History

MAGAZINE TITLE AND TITLE CHANGES: *Chic*.
VOLUME AND ISSUE DATA: Weekly, 15 September 1880–1 June 1881. Volumes are
     numbered 1 and 2, and issues 1 through 38.
PUBLISHER AND PLACE OF PUBLICATION: Chic Publishing Co., New York.
EDITOR: Unknown.
CIRCULATION: Unknown.

Richard Samuel West

CINCINNATI MIRROR

Editor William D. Gallagher proclaimed the *Cincinnati Mirror* a "voice in the wilderness," when he patterned his magazine after the Eastern literary periodicals in October 1831 for his Western, largely female audience. For $1.25 annually, the quarto *Mirror* became the first magazine of note in the Cincinnati literary renaissance of the 1830s and 1840s which launched Harriet Beecher, Caroline Lee Hentz, and other notables. On the way, Gallagher absorbed the *Ladies' Parterre* and the *Ladies' Museum* and added Thomas Hopkins Shreve as editor in 1833. Although front-page matter was dominated by writers of the East, including Edgar Allan Poe and James Kirke Paulding, original materials from James Hall, Timothy Flint, and Gallagher also appeared, and the journal reached a circulation of 2,000 early in its career. In the Spring of 1836, a feud between editors and publishers caused Gallagher's resignation in April and Shreve's in May, leading to the end of the magazine on 17 September 1836. An attempted change to newspaper format under new editor James Reese Fry in June brought on its demise.

Although the *Mirror*'s jocular cup did not overflow, many of the essays—reminiscent of Charles Lamb—and some of the poetry were humorous. The first volume contained a comical account of bachelor life and a satirical piece, "A Quaker Jumping a Ditch." "Coquetry," "Female Swindlers," and "The Salted Pudding" offered a variety of humor; the last poem, possessing shades of Joel Barlow's *The Hasty-Pudding*, relates misadventures with breakfast cereal. Samuel Warren's *Diary of a Physician* from *Blackwood's* probably inspired "Diary of a Pedestrian" and "Diary of a Lawyer."

Indicative of the *Mirror*'s character was the restrained spirit of satiric irreverence detectable in each issue's back matter, comprising reviews, columns, sketches, and miscellany: "sensible communications, even when coarsely written, will always be preferred to the namby-pamby ravings of moon-sick rhymsters and romancing idiots." The resultant potpourri of literary humor included parodies of sentimental verse, domestic and rural sketches featuring Dutch and Yankee stereotypes, sporting stories, steamboat adventures, and local-color sketches in the manner of Joseph G. Baldwin and Augustus Baldwin Longstreet. Gallagher and Shreve actually wrote much of this material under the pseudonyms of Hazlewood Buckeye, Esq., John Greenleaf Buckeye, and Dr. Greasequack.

Information Sources

BIBLIOGRAPHY:
Coyle, William, ed. *Ohio Authors and Their Books, 1796–1950*. Cleveland: World Publishing Co., 1962.
Mott, Frank L. *A History of American Magazines, 1741–1850*. Cambridge, Mass.: Harvard University Press, 1938, 1:389, 801.
Rusk, Ralph L. *The Literature of the Middle Western Frontier*. New York: Columbia University Press, 1925, 1:163, 188.
INDEX SOURCES: Title index with each volume.
REPRINT EDITIONS: University Microfilms.
LOCATION SOURCES: OClWHi has the only complete run; also CtY, DLC, MWA, NN, and roughly ten other libraries.

Publication History

MAGAZINE TITLE AND TITLE CHANGES: *Cincinnati Mirror and Ladies' Parterre*,
   October 1831-November 1832; *Cincinnati Mirror and Ladies' Parterre and Museum*, November 1832-September 1833; *Cincinnati Mirror & Western Gazette of
   Literature, Science, and the Arts*, September 1833-September 1835; *Buckeye and
   Cincinnati Mirror*, October 1835-January 1836.
VOLUME AND ISSUE DATA: Semi-monthly and weekly, annual volumes. Semi-
   monthly, Volume 1:1 (1 October 1831)–Volume 3:26 (27 September 1834);
   weekly, Volume 3:1 (5 October 1833)–Volume 5:17 (23 January 1836); weekly
   except for a six-week hiatus, Volume 5:1 (30 January 1836)–Volume 5:34 (17
   September 1836).
PUBLISHER AND PLACE OF PUBLICATION: Wood and Stratton, Cincinnati, Ohio.
EDITORS: William Davis Gallagher, 1831-April 1836; Thomas Hopkins Shreve, 1833–
   May 1836; Joseph Reese Fry, 23 May 1836–17 September 1836.
CIRCULATION: Approximately 2,000.

E. Kate Stewart and Gary Engle

CITY FIRE-FLY

In a brief prospectus, the pseudonymous editor of Boston's *City Fire-Fly*,
Philemon Flash, acknowledged more competing publications than the public had
a "disposition to support." Its standard fare, in a quarto-sized, six-cent issue,
was gossip about young ladies in compromising positions, brief riddles, satires
on droning clergymen, and phony medical advertisements, and it displayed
affinities with its rival publications. Comic tag names recalled similar techniques
in the Boston *Castigator*, edited by Lorenzo Hall, a prime target of the *Fire-
Fly*'s abuse. Parodies of "Ship News" imitated such sober information in Nathan
Hale's Boston *Daily Advertiser*, and mock literary notices aped the format of
columns in Joseph Tinker Buckingham's *New-England Galaxy*. Emphasizing
satire and gossip over political squabbles, the editor announced his desire to
reform rather than to defame, to "apply the knife and the caustic" if the case
demanded.

Two controversies occupied the *Fire-Fly* over several issues, each involving
rival editors in libel suits. A Methodist minister, the Reverend John Maffitt, had
sued Buckingham, who had accused the divine of fraud, lechery, and hypocrisy.
Hall had been sued by Colonel Amos Binney after a charge of conflict of interest
over dealings with the state bank. As the *Galaxy* and other Boston papers
stockpiled evidence against both men, the *Fire-Fly* ran an advertisement claiming
that the hypocrisy of seeking asylum in libel prosecution had run its course. A
New Year's 1823 address to patrons suggested that three months' performance
promised even greater comic delights, but the pungent, fast-paced *Fire-Fly*
ceased publication the following month.

Information Sources

INDEX SOURCES: None.
REPRINT EDITIONS: None.
LOCATION SOURCES: MB; Numbers 1–9, Massachusetts State Library; Number 6, DLC.

Publication History

MAGAZINE TITLE AND TITLE CHANGES: *City Fire-Fly, and Humorous Repository* (19 October 1822–15 February 1823).
VOLUME AND ISSUE DATA: Weekly, 19 October 1822–15 February 1823.
PUBLISHER AND PLACE OF PUBLICATION: Publisher unknown, but availability of subscriptions was advertised at Book Stall near Mr. Kidder's office, Old Market St., Boston.
EDITOR: "Philemon Flash" (identity unknown).
CIRCULATION: Unknown.

Kent P. Ljungquist

COMIC MONTHLY

One of the longest-lived of the Civil War era publications, *Comic Monthly* lasted from March 1859 (Vol. 1:1) through 1881 (Vol. 23), although the last seen is Volume 21:5 for November 1880. It had an 11½" by 15¾" format and later made variations to 11" × 15". *Comic Monthly* was produced by a prominent humor publisher in New York, J. C. Haney, at 75 cents a year, then one dollar and $1.25 by 1866; later it cost five cents a number. It was in newspaper style, with sixteen pages and three columns, and was printed on newsprint, though in stiffer paper in the 1880s. Claiming at first to be apolitical, when it finally became political in 1861 it supported the hanging of rebels and freeing the contraband, a viewpoint less boldly stated, however, than *Vanity Fair*'s* War Democrat position and undoubtedly less damaging to its circulation.

Some of the best illustrators of the era graced the *Comic Monthly*'s pages. Thomas Nast did covers in 1859, and Frank Bellew followed in 1860, although theatrical rather than political figures dominated. A cartoon sequence of six boxes often showed up on the last page. By the mid–1870s, political targets like Boss Tweed drew more attention from Frank Beard, including a Tweed Extra for April 1872. Frederick Opper caricatured Roscoe Conkling in an 1876 cover. Double-page center cartoons were a regular feature.

The humor was also aligned with the literary comedians; Artemus Ward, Petroleum V. Nasby, Orpheus C. Kerr, and Doesticks were frequently reprinted; Mark Twain pieces were borrowed; and short novels were burlesqued. Old Abe jokes and Yankee dialect speech were prominent in the earlier period. In the later period, middle-class social life got attention. Other subjects included back-country courting, target excursions, lawyers, hoop skirts, and Boston life. One philanthropic farmer was cited for mesmerizing his pigs before killing them.

Reprinting remained a feature of its humor, including tall tales from Dan Marble a generation earlier, Frank Forester, Josh Billings, and Spoopendyke. In "Muscular Christianity" a conductor beats up a tough in church and says, "Never mind, parson . . . I've punched him and he's got to show coin" to ride the holy through-line. Frank Beard's chalk-talk lecture on Tammany was puffed as well.

Information Sources

INDEX SOURCES: None.
REPRINT EDITIONS: None.
LOCATION SOURCES: DLC, NN, and MWA have brief broken runs; scattered copies
    at two or three other locations.

Publication History

MAGAZINE TITLE AND TITLE CHANGES: *Comic Monthly.*
VOLUME AND ISSUE DATA: Volume 1:1, March 1859–Volume 21:5, November 1880,
    continuing to Volume 23 (1881).
PUBLISHER AND PLACE OF PUBLICATION: J. C. Haney, New York.
EDITOR: J. C. Haney?
CIRCULATION: Unknown.

David E. E. Sloane

THE CORRECTOR

The Corrector was established in 1804 by the pseudonymous Toby Tickler primarily to foster the political efforts of Aaron Burr. Like other publications that appeared on the New York political scene in the early 1880s, its vicious and scurrilous satire was far from subtle. The newspaper expired, along with Burr's political aspirations, when Burr lost the election of 1804.

The Corrector was born out of factional strife. The first few years of the nineteenth century found New York politics dominated by the aristocratic Clinton and Livingston families. The Republican party was comprised of several factions engaged in bitter rivalry. George Clinton, seven-term governor, and his nephew DeWitt Clinton, Mayor of New York City, put forth the easy-going Morgan Lewis as the nominee of the Clinton-Livingston faction. Aaron Burr, former Vice-President of the United States, and also a Republican, sought the governorship of New York as a means of regaining his failing political stature. Arrayed against Burr were many enemies, including the Clintons and their allies and Alexander Hamilton, who had much influence over the Federalist vote. Burr, running as an independent, and Lewis, the Republican candidate, were soon engaged in what was to be one of the bitterest political campaigns in American history. The Clinton-Livingston machine, working through James Cheetham, editor of the *American-Citizen*, hurled outrageous charges against Burr in editorials, broadsides, and pamphlets. The Burrites responded in kind with *The Corrector*.

Toby Tickler, Esq., whose identity has never been ascertained, elucidated the philosophy of his semi-weekly newspaper in the first issue. Although claiming to be "under the influence of no party or sect," Tickler threatened to expose the political wrongdoings of the Livingstons and Clintons, as well as every other "less hardened offender." In the ensuing weeks Tickler and a host of other pseudonymous writers were true to the stated editorial policy, hurling a barrage of inflammatory, insulting, and offensive accusations against the Clintons, Morgan Lewis, James Cheetham, and their crowd.

The newspaper was issued in four three-column quarto pages, continuously paged through the run of ten numbers. No price was listed, although the tabloid was sold at the bookstore of Stephen Gould and Company, the printer. A note in the first issue promised that its size would increase "as soon as the expense is authorised by public patronage," but it remained four pages per issue until its demise.

During its run *The Corrector* singlemindedly reported on the vicissitudes of the anti-Burrites, not hesitating to print the names of supposed political wrongdoers. Original articles, almost always signed by a one-word pseudonym such as Mentor, Maxim, or Cujus, and reprints of articles favorable to Burr or critical of Clinton and Cheetham appeared in each issue. The last page usually printed the various Independent Republican nominations of Burr for governor.

As the election neared, the articles grew hotter and more libelous. Direct threats were made to Clinton's partisans, and Morgan Lewis was warned against defaming Burr and consorting with Cheetham unless he wanted to see nine personal anecdotes in print. A series of reprinted articles by "Brutus," dating from 1802, and letters from "Coelius" added fuel to the already raging political fires, and the fifth issue, dated 11 April 1804, introduced Touchstone Tickler, Toby's supposed cousin, who supplied lists of new books, plays, and artworks, all highly derogatory of Burr's opponents. A later issue featured a letter from Bickerstaffe Tickler, Toby's uncle.

Since illustrations did not yet appear in journal publications, Tickler's foes were spared visual attack. But articles that referred to the Clinton faction members as "Monkey Dick," "Ourang Outang," "Col. Blubber," "Yahoo," and "Greasy Porpoise" were offensive enough. At least one libel suit was brought against the printer; the issue of 18 April stated that Isaac Clason had "commenced an action" for being identified earlier as a "late German convict." A note in issue Number 5 (11 April) informed readers that this would probably be the last number published by S. Gould and Company, although Gould was still listed as publisher in the final issue.

There was no warning given that issue Number 10 dated 26 April would be the final one. The polls for the New York gubernatorial election closed on that day, and within five days the results showed Burr losing the election to Lewis by almost 9,000 votes. Its *raison d'etre* thus removed, *The Corrector* ceased as suddenly as it had begun, taking with it the identity of Toby Tickler, Esq. Its limited focus and scurrilous humor precluded its continuation, since the loss of the election also meant the end of Burr's political career. *The Corrector* remains today as a curiosity from the most defamatory and journalistically violent political decades in the history of our country.

Information Sources

BIBLIOGRAPHY:

Brigham, Clarence S. *History and Bibliography of American Newspapers, 1690–1820*. Hamden, Conn.: Archon Books, 1962, 1:619.

Fox, Dixon Ryan. *The Decline of Aristocracy in the Politics of New York*. New York (Columbia University): Longman, Green and Co., 1919, p. 66.

Mott, Frank L. "Comic Periodicals." In *A History of American Magazines, 1741–1850*. Cambridge, Mass.: Harvard University Press, 1938, 1:170, 792.

Parmet, Herbert S., and Marie B. Hecht. *Aaron Burr; Portrait of an Ambitious Man*. New York: Macmillan, 1967, p. 198. (Mistitled "The Collector," but the correct title is given in a footnote.)

INDEX SOURCES: None.

REPRINT EDITIONS: University Microfilms.

LOCATION SOURCES: Complete runs can be found at the MWA, NHi, DLC, East Hampton Free Library, CtY, and MBat.

Publication History

MAGAZINE TITLE AND TITLE CHANGES: *The Corrector*, 28 March–26 April 1804.

VOLUME AND ISSUE DATA: Semi-weekly, Wednesday and Saturday, Number 1, 28 March–Number 8, 21 April 1804. Tuesday and Thursday, Number 9, 24 April–Number 10, 26 April 1804.

PUBLISHER AND PLACE OF PUBLICATION: "Printed and published by S(tephen) Gould & Co.," New York.

EDITOR: "Toby Tickler, Esq." (pseudonym).

CIRCULATION: Unknown. No advertising.

Eric W. Johnson

COZZENS WINE PRESS

Cozzens Wine Press was a loosely defined serial whose publication spanned the 1854 to 1861 period. Published monthly by wine merchant Frederick Swartwout Cozzens at 73 Warren Street in New York, the *Wine Press* consistently featured articles about grapes, wine, liquors, and other alcohol-related topics. It furnished discussions of wines from America, foreign countries, and antiquity, and it included serious poems praising grapes, editorials on wine tariffs, hints for making punch, and essays on such unrelated topics as bullfighting and coffee-houses. In addition, it featured homilies, humorous anecdotes and stories, essays, biographical sketches of famous Americans, conundrums, words of advice, and anything else Cozzens cared to include. Satire, however, is largely absent; in a public lecture given in 1857, Cozzens asserted his belief that satire is only "a rogue in armor, while a buffoon not seldom proves a philosopher in disguise."

The publication consisted of eight octavo pages, devoted mostly to advertisements for wines, liquors, and "segars." Humorous drinking songs sometimes dominated the pages, and there were selections from such figures as Swift, Thackeray, and Longfellow. Also included were submissions by readers and by less well-known writers. In general, the content does not appear to have been restricted by preconceived editorial policies.

The humor in the *Wine Press* frequently centers around drunkenness and/or sex. In a typical conundrum, for instance, Old Hurricane asks when a ship may be said to be in love. After rejecting such answers as, "When she wants to be manned"; "When she's tender to a man of war"; and "When she makes much of a fast sailor," Old Hurricane proclaims that a ship is in love when "she's attached to a buoy."

Cozzens, an original member of New York's Century Club, began his literary career with a comic imitation of Edmund Spenser in *Yankee Doodle** (1847) and contributed both anonymously and under a pseudonym to *The Knickerbocker* Magazine.* He achieved a national reputation as a humorist with *The Sparrowgrass Papers; or Living in the Country* (1856). Cozzens's New York wine cellar was a frequent meeting place for various literary figures, including Washington Irving and T. B. Thorpe. Thorpe reminisced in 1874 that "there were rare gatherings in his [Cozzens's] celler, where wit was expended that was as rich and mellow as his own 'best brands.' "

Information Sources

BIBLIOGRAPHY:

Johnson, Allen, and Dumas Malone, eds. *Dictionary of American Biography.* New York: Charles Scribner's Sons, 1929, 2:490–91.

Mott, Frank L. *A History of American Magazines, 1850–1865.* Cambridge, Mass.: Harvard University Press, 1938, 2:183, 211.

"Mr. Fred S. Cozzens' Lecture on Wit and Humor." *New York Daily Times*, 28 January 1857.

Wilson, James G., and John Fiske, eds. *Appleton's Cyclopedia of American Biography.* New York: D. Appleton and Co., 1888.

INDEX SOURCES: None.

REPRINT EDITIONS: None.

LOCATION SOURCES: CU-BANC, NN, N, CSmH, NNC, and Buffalo and Erie County Public Library.

Publication History

MAGAZINE TITLE AND TITLE CHANGES: *Cozzens Wine Press*, 20 June 1854–20 May 1861.

VOLUME AND ISSUE DATA: Monthly, Volume 1:1, 20 June 1854–Volume 7:12, 20 May 1861.

PUBLISHER AND PLACE OF PUBLICATION: Frederick Swartwout Cozzens, New York.

EDITOR: Frederick Swartwout Cozzens.

CIRCULATION: Unknown.

Richard Alan Schwartz

————— **E** —————

THE ELEPHANT

The Elephant is a footnote to the career of Cornelius Mathews, early champion of literary Americanism, and represents his last attempt to stay in the magazine business after the failure of *Yankee Doodle*.*

Although *The Elephant* has the characteristic Mathews social and political concerns, it is more generally humorous. Its objectives were to illustrate the "follies of public men, public institutions, and [are] intended as a *hit* at the times." Furthermore, *The Elephant* is to provide "miscellaneous news, wit, jokes, satire, and the general humorous characteristics of the country" as well as "The Promotion of Happiness, The Cure of Cross Husbands, and Scolding Wives, and Practical Patriotism." In one of its many altercations with the rival magazine, *The John-Donkey*,* the general characteristics of its humor are also maintained: "*The Elephant* is the only entirely comic paper in the country whose humor is broad and comprehensive, like the eternal ocean itself; and when *The Donkey* concludes to stand up to the rack of real wit, instead of dealing in pointless scraps of personality and caricature, there may be a small chance for him, and then *but* a small one!"

The Elephant describes itself as consisting of "eight large and handsomely printed pages; and each number will contain numerous comic designs, drawn and engraved by the first artists in America." The front page features a laureled, scribbling, genial-looking elephant with figures proceeding around the margins and across the top—jesters, musicians, masquers, magicians, and sylphs (some suggesting the style of Clarence Day) engraved by J. A. and D. E. Read. Cartoons are mainly political "hits of the times." One featured Horace Greeley as a bear in a cave with Clay standing outside, captioned "Fetching Him Out." Another showed a court martial featuring General Stephen W. Kearny and Senator Thomas Hart Benton. Included are poems, sketches, tall tales, dialect stories, a regular feature "Our Column of Fun," with tired anecdotes, the best of which are those of Mrs. Partington. There are theater reviews praising the Christy Minstrels over the Astor Palace Opera, articles on burning issues of the day such as chloroform, the amalgamationists, and Dr. Collyer and the "Model Artists" who shocked the city with their deshabille. An obligatory "olla podrida" section appears; a characteristic Mathews feature, "Our Walk About Town," includes effective descriptions, one of a poor Irish immigrant woman and a handless and legless Mexican War veteran reminiscent of Birdofredum Sawin. Aside from Mathews's one poem attributed to Thomas Dunn English of *The John-Donkey*, and the pieces from other works and magazines in "Our Column of Fun," contributors have not been identified.

The Elephant was published by Wm. H. Graham at the Tribune building in New York and claimed agents in a dozen major cities as far west as St. Louis and as far south as New Orleans "and by booksellers throughout the U.S." One possible sign of the range of its distribution is perhaps its only claim to a bit of fame: the last number contains a sketch entitled "Scene on the Ohio," which was picked up by the Bloomington, Iowa *Herald* (13 February 1849) and in turn was a source, according to Fred W. Lorch, for one of Mark Twain's first published pieces, "The Dandy Frightening the Squatter." Whatever its scope, however, it was clearly New York-based, judging by its special features.

The Elephant is never attributed to Mathews in correspondence, whereas all of Mathews's other work of that time is mentioned somewhere as Donald Yanella points out. Moreover, the internal evidence of Mathews' editorship is not compelling. Some of this evidence consists in continuities between *The Elephant* and *Yankee Doodle*, which Mathews is known to have edited. *The Elephant* was issued (first number, 22 January 1848) close upon the failure of *Yankee Doodle* (last issue 2 October 1847). Another continuity is in the title and the purpose of "seeing the elephant" that the title suggests: a series of *Yankee Doodle* articles had been entitled "Various Attempts 'To see the Elephant,' made in the city of New York. In the Spring and Summer of 1847, by Joshua Greening of Esopus." Although the meaning of the phrase is not exact, it seems to have suggested a more worldly attitude than the social and political satire of *Yankee Doodle*, a broadened appeal that Mathews might have thought would boost circulation. Internal evidence rests mainly in the typical Mathews's style and targets. The internal evidence is complicated by the following squib, which seems to be a mock denial of Mathews's editorship:

Now we—the *Elephant*, unhesitatingly assert that Mr. Mathews, with all his fun, and the John Donkey admits that he *is* funny—a quality no one pretends to award to the "long eared gentlemen"—*does not* edit the "Elephant" but is the *bona-fide* editor of the John Donkey. We are much afraid however that Mr. English will have serious cause to regret the peddling hand he has taken in managing the outdoor business of The Donkey—and that, instead of his notorious patronymic of *Dun English*, we shall be necessitated to write him—Dun Brown!

It was this sort of humor that probably killed *The Elephant*. *The Elephant* seems to have been in financial trouble very quickly, if one can judge by measures such as a ten dollar prize for a piece of humor and, beginning with the third number, a supplement entitled *The City Advertiser*.

Information Sources

BIBLIOGRAPHY:

Lorch, Fred W. "A Source for Mark Twain's 'The Dandy Frightening the Squatter.' " *American Literature* 3 (November 1931): 300–13.

Mott, Frank L. *A History of American Magazines, 1741–1850*. New York: D. Appleton and Co., 1938, 1:780, 809.

Stein, Allen F. *Cornelius Mathews*. New York: Twayne Publishers, 1974, pp. 22, 164n.

Yanella, Donald. "Cornelius Mathews: Knickerbocker Satirist." Ph.D. diss., Fordham University, 1971, pp. 202–205, 233–39.

INDEX SOURCES: None.

REPRINT EDITIONS: University Microfilms.

LOCATION SOURCES: Beinecke Library, Yale University.

Publication History

MAGAZINE TITLE AND TITLE CHANGES: *The Elephant*, 22 January 1848–19 February 1848.

VOLUME AND ISSUE DATA: Weekly for five numbers.

PUBLISHER AND PLACE OF PUBLICATION: William H. Graham, New York.

EDITOR: (Probably) Cornelius Mathews.

CIRCULATION: The editor claims a circulation of 5,000 with expectations of 10,000, but the expectations were unfulfilled.

James Lester Busskohl

EVERY BODY'S ALBUM

The twelve issues of *Every Body's Album* in 1836 and 1837 represent the "reputable" strain of American humor. The magazine, billed as "a humorous collection of tales, quips, quirks, anecdotes, and facetiae," relied heavily on foreign sources and showed little or no vulgarizing folk or frontier influence. Although most of the content was in the form of prose sketches and stories, it also published poetry, music, and a generous number of cartoons and illustrations.

Despite strong ties to Philadelphia, the magazine had a distinctly international flavor. Published by Charles Alexander, who was involved in a number of publishing ventures in the 1830s, the magazine made extensive use of the sketches of Joseph C. Neal, many of which were later reprinted in *Neal's Saturday Gazette*. Alexander was editor of the *Gentleman's Vade Mecum* and its successor *Philadelphia Saturday News* for which Neal served as assistant editor. Also involved with Neal and Alexander was Morton McMichael, former editor of the *Saturday Evening Post*,** and editor with Neal of the *Saturday News* after

Alexander withdrew, and still later associated with Neal in publishing *Neal's Saturday Gazette*. Neal contributed seventeen sketches to *Every Body's Album*, and McMichael contributed one. Neal's pieces dealt with marginal Philadelphia types, later dubbed ironically "City Worthies," and the sketches represent the magazine's most important contribution to American humor. Occasional articles on aspects of life and culture in Philadelphia (for example, the history of firefighting in the city) also tie the magazine to the City of Brotherly Love. Of Thomas S. Davis, who is listed on the title page as the collector of the contents of the magazine, nothing is known.

Other American writers published in *Every Body's Album* included Silas Pinckney Holbrook, William E. Burton, comic actor and author, and Robert Walsh, praised by Edgar Allan Poe as "one of the finest writers, one of the most accomplished scholars . . . in the country" (quoted in *National Cyclopedia of American Biography* 5:357). The magazine also relied on cartoons, illustrations, jokes, fillers, and other miscellaneous items that were common in newspaper and magazine exchange.

The European flavor of the magazine came from reprints of Boccaccio, a Tom Brown translation of a tale by Paul Scarron, woodcuts from the London *Satirist*, a ballad by Thomas Hood, and a translation from *La Garde National* with woodcuts of an article on an "automated" chess player, a famous hoax of the day. Also notable were selections by Charles Dickens, Douglas Jerrold, Charles Whitehead, and various other English writers of the time. In the twelve months the journal existed, only one selection by each was published, but Dickens's piece is the "Misplaced Attachment of John Dounce," included in *Sketches by Boz*, and Jerrold's contribution is "The Wine Cellar," which anticipates Poe's "The Cask of Amontillado," but with a mock-moral ending. Charles Whitehead, author of a popular burlesque biography of hangman Jack Ketch, was a friend of Dickens and Jerrold, and all were publishing in popular new London magazines such as *Bentley's Miscellany* and the *New Monthly Magazine*. In addition to these writers, *Every Body's Album* also published a piece by John Poole, identified as the "author of Paul Pry," a popular play of the previous decade. Other British writers include William Howitt, Ann Marie Hall, whose husband edited the *New Monthly Magazine*, William Lennox, Frederick Marryat, and Alfred Tennyson.

In its first issue *Every Body's Album* stated that it "intended to gratify all tastes, and please all readers. . . . We challenge the age to produce a greater variety of all that can amuse and gratify." And variety it certainly produced. A typical seventy-odd page issue contained a dozen or more prose pieces with several pages of verse interspersed, a popular song—including words and music, one or more cartoon series, caricatures, and other woodcuts illustrating the prose selections, and numerous squibs as page fillers. All of this was rounded off with a full page of jokes on the last page. Humorous stories and sketches appeared cheek by jowl with short biographies of Oscoela, Hannah Dunston, Tom Thumb, Simon Bolivar, Napoleon and his family, and Benjamin Franklin. Cartoon sequences included "Six Stages of Drunkenness," ten cartoons picturing "The Adventures of a Day," all humorous, and "Diversions of Old Nick," on the temptations and disruptions of the devil. The songs were sometimes familiar, including "Old King Cole" and "John Gilpin," sometimes romantic, as "Lovely Jean" and "Had I a Heart," and sometimes cruel as "The Extravagance of Jim Crow" and "Three Jewesses. A Comic Song." If the claim to variety was met in the kinds of material published, the claim was not fulfilled in the kinds of humor published. *Every Body's Album* contained no cartoons of political figures, local or national, and no jokes aimed at parties, factions, or causes. Instead, there were Irish dialect jokes, jokes at the expense of Blacks and foreigners, and accounts of violent outlandish happenings in such strange places as Maine, Kentucky, and Tennessee. The butts of the humor were unsurprising: drunkards, doctors, women, married life, and foreigners.

Of the native comic types that appeared in the nineteenth century—violent frontiersmen, garrulous widows, Yankee sharpsters, and so on—*Every Body's Album* produced nothing. Single pieces by new and popular English comic writers could not rescue the magazine from its traditional and conventional material. Neal's pieces, available at the same time in the *Daily Pennsylvanian* and across the country through exchange reprints, were very popular. But his sketches of an opportunistic politician—"Adventures of Peter Brush"—, a bully—"Orson Dabbs, the Hittite"—, his braggart but cowardly admirer—"Rocky Smalt; or, the Dangers of Immitation"—, an ineffectual aesthete—"Olympus Pump; or, the Poetic Temperament"—, among others, present neither indigenous American types nor sufficiently vital characters. *Every Body's Album* attempted to achieve variety so as to please everybody, but the attempt resulted in blandness and lack of focus. Clearly not for everybody, it died unannounced with the twelfth issue.

Information Sources

BIBLIOGRAPHY:

Mott, Frank L. *A History of American Magazines, 1741–1850*. Cambridge, Mass.: Harvard University Press, 1938, 1:425.

Murrell, William. *A History of American Graphic Art*. New York: Whitney Museum, 1933, 1:157.

Oberholtzer, Ellis P. *The Literary History of Philadelphia*. Philadelphia: Jacobs, 1906.

Sloane, David E. E. "Joseph C. Neal." *Dictionary of Literary Biography: American Humorists 1800–1950*. Ed. Stanley Trachtenberg. Detroit: Gale, 1982, 2:344–49.

INDEX SOURCES: None.

REPRINT EDITIONS: University Microfilms.

LOCATION SOURCES: CtHW, MH, DLC, MnU–1.

Publication History

MAGAZINE TITLE AND TITLE CHANGES: *Every Body's Album*, July 1836-June 1837.

VOLUME AND ISSUE DATA: Monthly, Volume 1:1, July 1836–Volume 2:6, June 1837.

PUBLISHER AND PLACE OF PUBLICATION: Charles Alexander, Philadelphia.

EDITOR: Thomas S. Davis (?). Davis is not anywhere listed as editor, but his name appears four times on the cover of Volume 1 and three times on the cover of Volume 2.

CIRCULATION: Unknown.

George A. Test

F

THE FARMER'S WEEKLY MUSEUM

The Farmer's Weekly Museum, a newspaper with modest literary pretensions, was published in Walpole, New Hampshire, from 1793 to 1810. In its early years it had only local interest with no remarkable aspects other than its association with its founder, Isaiah Thomas, the noted patriot, printer, editor, publisher, and historian who eventually founded the American Antiquarian Society. The *Museum*'s final decade was also undistinguished, but for a brief period from 1797 to 1799, under the editorship of Joseph Dennie, it achieved a national readership and became one of the more critically respected journals of the period.

Dennie moved to Walpole in the Autumn of 1795 following an abortive editorship of Boston's *The Tablet*.* His intention was to practice law, but he found a literary career more compatible with his taste for tavern life. In October of 1795 he submitted a piece to the *Museum* which became the first in his series of familiar essays, *The Lay Preacher*. This series continued with great frequency until mid–1797, by which time Dennie had assumed the editorship and appeared less regularly thereafter.

From its inception, the *Museum* tried to embody Thomas's founding philosophy that journalism must be as entertaining as it was informative. Toward that end its first editor, David Carlisle, filled each four-column folio issue with news scissored from a wide range of publications and chinked the gaps with original essays, ads, and humor. Regular captioned features included Miscellanies, Poetical Repository, European Intelligence, and Entertaining Scraps.

Dennie's contribution as editor was to extend the commercial basis of the publication and play up its entertainment function. In a front-page editorial of his first issue he announced that "Politiks, Biography, Economicks, Morals, and Daily Details will be restrained to the first pages" where these seriously treated topics fought for space with notices of stray livestock and ads for Doctor Lee's True Billious Pills. Dennie's other innovation was to gather all literary matter onto the back page, which he headed with an elaborate illustration of a fruit basket and wine goblets backed by a floral festoon. The Dessert, as the page was titled, contained reviews, verse parodies, pseudonymous essays (The Meddler, The Hermit, Americus, Solomon Fodder, Charles Chatterbox, Peter Quince, Peter Pencil, "From the Desk of Beri Hesdin," and others), and a joke column captioned "Nuts." Consistent quality on the page could be found in the frequent "From the Shop of Messrs. Colon and Spondee," Dennie's and Royall Tyler's collaborative pastiche that ranged with urbanely satiric wit over the fashions, manners, and literary tastes of the day.

The *Museum*'s greatest contribution, however, was *The Lay Preacher*. Of the 117 pieces Dennie eventually wrote in the series, 90 were published in the *Museum*. Inspired by Laurence Sterne's *The Sermons of Mr. Yorick*, building on his own experiments with characterization in his earlier *Farrago* series, and drawing on his personal experience as a lay preacher in Claremont, New Hampshire, Dennie developed the essays as an extended character study of a type common in eighteenth-century literature: the aging bachelor and reformed misogynist who, in the afternoon of life, grows fondly indulgent in the company of women. Each essay was headed by scriptural text and had a clear moral intent involving the pleasures of rural life and the virtues of industry, modesty, and sobriety. But the source of charm in the pieces largely responsible for their wide popularity was their florid, even overwrought, style and their tendency to digress into comic irrelevancies. Occasionally, Dennie used *The Lay Preacher* as a pulpit from which to vent his considerable anti-Jacobinism, but these instances were the exceptions that underscored by contrast the abiding whimsicality of the series. *The Lay Preacher* is now regarded as the most significant belletristic achievement in America before the efforts of the *Salmagundi** writers and Washington Irving, who openly acknowledged Dennie's influence.

Information Sources

BIBLIOGRAPHY:

Buckingham, Joseph Tinker. *Specimens of Newspaper Literature: With Personal Memoires, Anecdotes, and Reminiscences.* Boston: C. C. Little and J. Brown, 1850, 2:174–220.

Ellis, Harold Milton. *Joseph Dennie and His Circle: A Study in American Literature from 1792 to 1812.* Austin, 1915; rpt. New York: Johnson Reprint Corp., 1972.
———. "Introduction." *The Lay Preacher by Joseph Dennie.* New York: Scholars' Facsimiles and Reprints, 1943.

Granger, Bruce. *American Essay Serials from Franklin to Irving.* Knoxville: University of Tennessee Press, 1978.

Mott, Frank L. *A History of American Magazines, 1741–1850.* New York: D. Appleton and Co., 1938, 1:223–46, and passim.

INDEX SOURCES: None.
REPRINT EDITIONS: Readex Microprint.
LOCATION SOURCES: DLC, MWA, OClWHi, and fifteen others.

Publication History

MAGAZINE TITLE AND TITLE CHANGES: *New Hampshire Journal; or, the Farmer's Weekly Museum*, 11 April 1793–4 April 1794; *New Hampshire and Vermont Journal; or, the Farmer's Weekly Museum*, 11 April 1794–28 March 1797; *Farmer's Weekly Museum: New Hampshire and Vermont Journal*, 4 April 1797–25 March 1799; *Farmer's Museum; or Lay Preacher's Gazette*, 1 April 1799–8 September 1804. Other slight changes.

VOLUME AND ISSUE DATA: Weekly, Volume 1:1, 11 April 1793–Volume 16:52, 15 October 1810. Suspended 3 April 1807–17 October 1808.

PUBLISHER AND PLACE OF PUBLICATION: Isaiah Thomas and David Carlisle, Walpole, New Hampshire.

EDITORS: David Carlisle, 1793–28 March 1797; Joseph Dennie, 4 April 1797–25 March 1799; Carlisle thereafter.

CIRCULATION: Unknown. By 1800 the paper was soliciting advertisers with the claim of "an extensive circulation throughout the United States." The annual subscription rate was $1.50.

Gary Engle

FILM FUN

Film Fun may be the oldest, longest lived, and best of all the film-oriented humor magazines, lasting from 1915 through September 1942, the last issue being Volume 72, Number 641, and still selling for ten cents an issue. *Film Fun* was genuinely film-oriented, rather than being solely a cheap excuse for cheese or sleazecake photography. Its comic photocaptions on film out-takes often show clever puns and imagination, although relatedness of caption to photo varied greatly depending on the editor at the time. Its garish girlie covers maintained the tone of the twenties long before and after that era, and its flapper/courtship/general interests belied serious criticism. Scholars and critics have ignored it.

The origins of *Film Fun* lie with *Judge's Serials*** and *Judge's Library: A Monthly Magazine of Fun*,** an 1887–1912 spinoff of *Judge** which became *The Magazine of Fun*** from August 1912 (No. 281) through June 1915 and became *Film Fun* thereafter. The first ten numbers of *Judge's Serials* were quarterly from November 1887 through January 1890, at which time it became a monthly as *Judge's Library* (Nos. 11–280). *Sis Hopkin's Own Book*** was also combined with the others at a later time, leading to a heavy input of crackers among the movie stars and *Film Fun*'s emphasis on "the happy side of the movies." Monthly numbering is consecutive, making the earliest issue of *Film Fun* seen April 1916 (No. 325), although it presumably began with the July 1915 issue (No. 316).

The 1916 *Film Fun*, with cover by Flohri, who had done the Sis Hopkin's illustrations, sold at ten cents in standard size, 8″ × 11½″. Elizabeth Sears was editor, and Grant Hamilton was art director, with Leslie-Judge as publishers. Articles were light photojournalism on movie stars. Some cartoon sequences and general family humor jokes filled up the magazine, together with stills from current films. By the mid-twenties, Kendall Banning was editorial director and Norman Anthony was secretary for Leslie-Judge; George Mitchell was editing *Film Fun* in a racier manner, with sensuous flapper covers and full-page photo-notes on individual films. Jokes were of the sort like "she has a nice leg—you don't know the calf of it" variety. The tone was kept light, and "fillums" were subjected to reader reviews as well as photo coverage. Orientation was toward the movies, and relatively little humor, as such, appeared. The price was twenty cents throughout this period. It took a brief fling at semi-monthly publication in 1928 under editor Curtis Mitchell and pushed its appeal to collegiate readers with racy captions on its film cuts and more prose columns. Its cutie covers regularly appeared on dormitory walls during this period, but it relapsed to monthly status by 1929.

By the early 1930s, the Dell Publishing Company under George Delacorte had taken over *Film Fun* from "Film Humor, Inc." and Lester Grady was editor. Covers featured models like Alice Anthon under bathing suit titles like "Knotty but Nice!" for a typical nautical theme. By this time *Film Fun* had become a romping Gold Digger humor magazine, far from the original Sis Hopkin's connection. Starlets and Chorines in silk teddies and in provocative stills from movies were splashed across its pages with tongue-in-cheek captions and gags. One photo of W. C. Fields spanking Gracie Allen with a cane, from Paramount's release *International House*, has Gracie asking if the doctor was disappointed when he examined Fields's wife; Fields responds, "Yes, he found me at home!" The caption and photo have no particular connection. Other gags are similar; one notes that desirable producers have good reputations—and will therefore pay a starlet more hush money to keep them intact. By 1939, *Film Fun* was being published by Film Fun Publishing Company, and the price had returned to the original ten cents. Victor Bloom was the editor and cheesecake was blending with sleazecake, although the photo/comic caption format remained much the same. A few cartoons appeared, and one girlie caption commented that when a girl wants a man she can live up to, she better marry an aviator. In 1940, *Film Fun* experimented with a photo pin-up cover but returned to the more luscious illustrations. Under Bloom's editorship, sequences of photos, still with gag captions, replaced the random scattering layout of earlier issues, but the girlie emphasis was constant. By 1942, Charles Saxon had become editor, and the 1930s girlie-gags format was modernized with cartoon pieces, humorous articles, and gag bits; it continued to present essentially the same sense of humor as in the past two decades, but was racier and jokier. The last issue seen is September 1942.

The Library of Congress has a partial set of *Film Fun*; the New York Public Library at Lincoln Center could locate only one volume of its listed holdings; the Union List also cites NNC.

Information Sources

INDEX SOURCES: None.
REPRINT EDITIONS: None.
LOCATION SOURCES: DLC, partial; NN, one volume only found, NNC.

Publication History

MAGAZINE TITLE AND TITLE CHANGES: *Film Fun*, July 1915-September 1942.
VOLUME AND ISSUE DATA: July 1915 (No. 316?)-September 1942 (Vol. 72:641).
PUBLISHER AND PLACE OF PUBLICATION: 1915-1925?: Leslie-Judge Co., New
    York; 1926?-1938: George Delacorte as Film Humor, Inc. and later Dell Pub-
    lishing Co., New York; 1939-1942: Film Fun Publishing Co., Dunellen, N.J.;
    1942: Charles Saxon.
EDITORS (Dates in several cases are approximate): Elizabeth Sears, 1916-?, George
    Mitchell, 1924-1928, Curtis Mitchell, 1928-c.1930, Ernest V. Heyn, 1930, Lester
    Grady, 1931-1938, Victor Bloom, 1939-1941, George Saxon, 1942.
CIRCULATION: Unknown.

David E. E. Sloane

THE FOOL

The Fool, a little-known periodical, was published in Salem, Massachusetts, in 1807. It was published only from February to April, and only three numbers of the magazine were ever published. These numbers appeared monthly, the first in February and the last, appropriately, on April Fool's Day.

The names adopted for the editor and the title of the paper indicate the publication's lack of seriousness. *The Fool*'s editor, the pseudonymous Thomas Brainless, Esq., Lld., Jester to His Majesty the Public, includes in the first issue of the paper a prospectus dated 1 January 1807 for the "new and useless paper" (No. 1, p. 1). In this sketch, the editor outlines the objective of the publication: to devote itself to "everything but matter of fact, expression of decided opinion, and serious discussion" (No. 1, p. 1).

True to its promise, *The Fool*'s twelve pages contain humorous entries relating to weather and fashion as well as ridiculous advertisements for products, contests, and presentations. One advertisement offers a ten dollar bottle of medicine guaranteed to do everything from curing gunshot wounds to clearing the brain. The ad further promises that the inexpensive potion will be wrapped in a twenty dollar bill to "prevent counterfeits" (No. 2, p. 6). Also included are bits of short fiction and poetry, comic literary and wedding notices, and letters. *The Fool*'s treatment of these topics suggests that the paper satirized the miscellaneous magazines of the day dealing seriously with such subject matter (See Hoornstra, p. 86).

The Fool followed no definite format in organizing its humorous content. In fact, in the January 1 prospectus Brainless states that the paper is to be "of no particular form or size, issued at irregular intervals; and the price to be left to the generosity of its patrons" (No. 1, p. 1). Despite the editor's statement *The Fool* did maintain some degree of regularity. The first pages of the three numbers are similar in that each bears the title of the magazine, the date of issue, and the name of the editor.

The Fool's editor claims to have included material from a variety of contributors who used pseudonyms such as Thomas Thumb, Solomon Strait-Jacket, and Simon Simple. All of the material in *The Fool*, however, probably came from a single source. The material has a distinctive flavor, partly created by the repetition of certain words such as *enigmatic* and *conundrum*. Moreover, Bonaparte provides a recurring theme throughout the paper.

The editor of *The Fool* cautions against speculation as to either his identity or that of his contributors. In the second number of the paper, Brainless chastises those who seem unable to "repress an idle curiosity" and calls them fools (No. 2, p. 5). Perhaps the warning did indeed discourage further conjecture, or perhaps whatever interest might have existed merely died after *The Fool*'s publication ceased. Whatever the reason, sources to date seem to offer no clue as to the identity of *The Fool*'s creator.

Information Sources

BIBLIOGRAPHY:

Hoornstra, Jean, and Trudy Heath, eds. *American Periodicals, 1741–1900: An Index to the Microfilm Collections*. Ann Arbor, Mich.: University Microfilms International, 1979.

Kribbs, Jayne K., ed. *An Annotated Bibliography of American Periodicals, 1741–1850*. Boston: G. K. Hall and Co., 1977.

INDEX SOURCES: None.

REPRINT EDITIONS: University Microfilms.

LOCATION SOURCES: Libraries listing holdings include MH, MWA, DLC, NN, ViU, Massachusetts Historical Society, Kent State University, University of North Carolina, and University of Oregon.

Publication History

MAGAZINE TITLE AND TITLE CHANGES: *The Fool*.

VOLUME AND ISSUE DATA: Monthly; No. 1, February 1807; No. 2, 23 March 1807; No. 3, 1 April 1807.

PUBLISHER AND PLACE OF PUBLICATION: Unknown; Salem, Massachusetts.

EDITOR: Thomas Brainless (pseud.), Esq., Lld., Jester to His Majesty the Public.

CIRCULATION: Unknown.

Debra Brown

FRANK LESLIE'S BUDGET OF FUN

Although copies are extremely scarce now, *Frank Leslie's Budget of Fun* seems to have enjoyed a long run from January 1859 through June 1878 (Nos. 1–243) as a monthly humor paper. Issues were sixteen pages in newspaper format well suited to its political burlesques, 11½" × 16½", in three columns with copious comic illustrations of various sizes. In 1859 it sold for six cents a copy—which in 1861 it boasted was a miracle of cheapness considering how many points of Western civilization were shown up in its slashing, dashing, flashing, crashing, lashing, gashing humor. In 1871, an annual subscription cost $1.50, and 1875 saw it at fifteen cents a copy. Its focus was on the social, literary, and locally interesting, although during the Civil War period it was strongly pro-Union. Burlesque novels carried titles like ''The Bandit Barber of Weehawken.'' Frank Leslie's Copperhead flag combined the snake and the dollar sign, and one cartoon suggested Northern antislavery impatience by the image of Lincoln in a life-bouy letting Sambo drown at sea.

Frank Leslie, born Henry Carter of Ipswich, England, on 29 March 1821, was an English engraver who abandoned the family name to avoid embarrassing the family by his trade. After emigrating to America in 1848, he gained experience with P. T. Barnum's *Illustrated News* in New York, where Charles G. Leland was editor, and with Frederick Gleason in Boston before starting his own paper in 1854, *Frank Leslie's Ladies' Gazette of Fashion*. In December 1855, *Frank Leslie's Illustrated Newspaper* appeared as a sensational weekly featuring engravings of popular and notorious events weeks before competitors. Popular appeal, lively graphic interest, and simple themes raised circulation to well over 100,000, a large number before the Civil War, and provided Leslie with the money to finance other ventures, including *Frank Leslie's Budget of Fun* (1859–1878) and *Jolly Joker** (1862–1878). Leslie himself died on 10 January 1880, but the firm was carried on by his second wife. Bankruptcy in 1877 probably accounted for the death of *Jolly Joker* the following year; in 1878 as well, *Frank Leslie's Budget of Fun* became *Frank Leslie's Budget*, yet later renamed *Frank Leslie's Budget of Wit*. The Judge Company under W. J. Arkell bought several periodicals from the Leslie Company in 1889, but Frederic L. Colver took over the remainder in 1895 and seems responsible for the demise of the paper.

The humorous formula of *Frank Leslie's Budget of Fun* was always flexible enough to attract a Northern general audience of moderate education. As ''The Comic History of the Month,'' *Budget* spent time on the Civil War and later offered front-page cartoons by Joseph Keppler treating Grant's politics with a heavy hand. But the focus remained general more than political, with ''Flashes of Wit'' columns offering dialect jokes, a mix of puzzles, and stories about city and regional characters, often featuring dialect language or amusing actions. *Budget* advertised itself as having the wit of the Paris *Charivari* and the artistic power of England's *Punch*, although it does not seem to have followed particularly closely the Paris and London counterparts. Exalted burlesque style and comic dialect poetry consistently made a muting offset to cartoons like the cover of the March 1871 number showing Grant wooing a caricature Negro maid labeled Santo Domingo. ''Jehial Slab's Remarks'' on ''The Santo Domingo

Muddle'' began, ''Men very often go into business as though they had the most implicit faith that God in some way would prosper laziness.'' The comment is representative of the saltiness which makes Leslie's humor appealing.

Frank Luther Mott has described *Budget* as subliterary and inartistic. Careful study of the magazine by later critics, however, may reveal a significant world view with a strong sense of social and political accountability. *Leslie's Weekly*— *''Frank Leslie's Illustrated Newspaper''*—treated fully by Mott—can be credited with active social concerns; Thomas Nast and Frank Leslie, in attacking the selling of diseased milk in the late 1850s, brought about a significant improvement in health standards in the face of an antagonistic city government. Leslie's sense of the interests of his popular audience by no means panders to its worst elements. Further study may not be easy, however, as only broken runs exist. The title was changed to *Frank Leslie's Budget* in 1878 and later to *Frank Leslie's Budget of Wit*, which ceased in April, 1896.

Information Sources

BIBLIOGRAPHY:
Mott, Frank L. ''Leslie's Weekly.'' In *A History of American Magazines, 1850–1865*. Cambridge, Mass.: Harvard University Press, 1938, 2:452–65; *Budget of Fun*, passim, as indexed.
Stern, Madeleine B. *Purple Passage: The Life of Mrs. Frank Leslie*. Norman: University of Oklahoma Press, 1953.
INDEX SOURCES: None.
REPRINT EDITIONS: None.
LOCATION SOURCES: DLC, ICU, INE, NB, MWA, and one or two issues at a few other locations.

Publication History

MAGAZINE TITLE AND TITLE CHANGES: *Frank Leslie's Budget of Fun*; continues after June 1878 under other names.
VOLUME AND ISSUE DATA: Monthly, Numbers 1–243, January 1859-June 1878.
PUBLISHER AND PLACE OF PUBLICATION: Frank Leslie, New York.
EDITORS: Unknown. (Thomas Powell shortly after the Civil War, according to Mott.)
CIRCULATION: Unknown.

David E. E. Sloane

G

YE GIGLAMPZ

During the Summer of 1874 a reporter for the daily and Sunday Cincinnati *Enquirer* and a local commercial artist invested their meager savings and enormous energy into the short-lived, illustrated comic weekly *Ye Giglampz*. The young co-editors, Lafcadio Hearn and Henry Farny, who would gain international reputations, respectively, as a minor man of letters and a painter of the American West, sought to provide a local audience with art, literature, and satire. Hearn and Farny, the principal editorial staff in this venture, were attracted by a mutual interest in the human condition, the arts, and a desire for independence from the commercial restrictions of established Cincinnati publishing. The publication lasted only nine weeks but afforded both men the opportunity to experiment. While Hearn wrote sensuous and provocative stories, Farny contributed cartoons on subjects ranging from the Society for the Prevention of Cruelty to Animals (SPCA) to the Reverend Henry Ward Beecher. Although the publication suffered terminal financial ills, it was not money but an editorial diversion that proved fatal.

Lacking the necessary funds for the venture, Farny approached E. H. Austerlitz, manager of the Western German Advertising Agency, and C. A. Honthum, foreign and amusement editor of the Cincinnati *Courier* who, according to Hearn, agreed to found an illustrated journal, hire an editor, and "remunerate the Bohemian artist (Farny) for his labor—not as a recompense for his philanthropy, for philanthropy scorns pecuniary compensation, but merely 'for lost time' in the education of the human race." E. H. Austerlitz and Company initiated the periodical *Kladderadatsch* in German. *Ye Giglampz* succeeded it, the title referring to spectacles of huge and owlish description. Lafcadio Hearn, later known for his Japanese collections of descriptive sketches, essays, folk tales, and ghost stories, accepted Farny's offer to become co-editor of the weekly for an unspecified amount of money to be paid from the pocket of E. H. Austerlitz. Because Hearn was not ready to resign his job and paycheck at the *Enquirer*, however, he agreed to furnish the journal with "fun during the day and hunt up horrors for the *Enquirer* during the night." Hearn was concerned, and justifiably so, about the circumstances of his part-time employment and the future of the weekly: "The Giglampz," he noted, "had no sinking fund, no subscription list, no subscribers, no advertisers, no exchanges, no canvassing agents, no business management."

Few conclusions about policy and tone were decided upon prior to publication except that it was "to be devoted to art, literature and satire, and to be excruciatingly funny without descending to coarseness or salacity," according to Hearn. Farny chose *Punch* as his model over Hearn's preference for the *Paris Charivari*.

Volume 1, Number 1 of *Ye Giglampz*, dated 21 June 1874, indeed proclaimed on the cover page that it was "A weekly illustrated journal devoted to art, literature and satire." The issue, 14⅝" × 10¾", was smaller than the remaining eight issues. In addition, it was the only number to use a three-column format. Hearn contributed most of the editorial copy, fourteen of the nineteen articles, and notes ranging in length from one-sixth column to two and two-thirds columns. Farny did all of the art, although he only signed the two-page centerfold cartoon, a standing feature of the eight-page illustrated comic weekly. All of the articles were satirical, if not humorous. There were two articles on Great Britain (including commentary on a *Punch* cartoon), a piece on spiritualism, and a short two-paragraph note on Colonel George Ward Nichols (referred to as "Nickels"), a local patron of the arts, written by Farny.

Hearn's first editorial, "Salutary. By a celebrated French Author. A friend of Giglampz," exemplifies his flowery writing style in combination with fantasy, gruesome narrative, and the absurd, later seen in such stories as "The Tale a Picture Tells" and "Fantasy of a Fan," originally entitled "The Smell of a Woman."

Number 2 of *Ye Giglampz*, dated 28 June, had some minor physical changes. The size of the paper was increased to 15¾" × 11⅛", with four instead of three columns per editorial page.

Farny's cover art consisted of four sketches under the major cutline "Leaves from a Builder's Portfolio and Beauties of American Architecture." The controversial sketches showed a bridge collapsing and people tumbling into a canal, people falling through a collapsed church floor, water rushing through a break in a dam, and people fleeing from a collapsing house. The centerfold cartoon depicted a member of the SPCA, another favorite target of *Ye Giglampz* editors, whipping his horse while in chase of a mule-drawn street wagon driven hard by a smiling driver. The cartoon on the back cover was classic Farny. "The Scarlet Letter" had the Reverend Henry Ward Beecher on a platform (stockade behind him) with hands held in front and an "A" on his chest. Mr. Giglampz

(Hearn) was in the lower left of the cartoon. Hearn asked Farny to make him one of the spectators, and the bespectacled face was easily recognizable.

Hearn's "Fantasies for Summer Seasons" was published as "Fantasies for Sultry Seasons" in *Ye Giglampz*, Number 4, dated 12 July. They were very bold, if not pornographic, for the puritanical Cincinnati of the 1870s. Hearn's elaborate description of the tropical environment must have truly been a fantasy for Cincinnati readers. The main character lay naked on a "soft bed of fresh palm-leaves." Hearn was only setting up the reader for commentary on missionaries: "Nasty, horrid people, who won't let anybody dance the hula-hula or enjoy lomi-lomi, and who want everybody to wear clothes and be slaves and look miserable." The tropics were attractive to Hearn. His fantasies took him away from the grime and soot and trying weather of Cincinnati from which his frail body shrank.

At a time when the editorial copy was improving and the few advertisers continued to support the weekly, there was still concern about the publication's health. The staff was optimistic about the attention its editorial copy received. The *New York Herald* had for some time been exchanging its *Weekly* with *Ye Giglampz* and was using some of the articles. The staff considered this to be a great step at last toward education of the human race. At the moment when financial stability seemed to be the only thing holding the bold weekly from success, an editorial decision was made that would bring it to eternal sleep.

On the day before the deadline for the eighth issue, the steamer *Pat Rogers* caught fire and burned out of control on the Ohio River. Farny dispatched an artist who returned with a series of sketches. The coup beat the local dailies with a breaking news story: the two-page centerfold displayed the sketches of the "Burning of the Steamer Pat Rogers." Unfortunately, for eight weeks the editors of *Ye Giglampz* had been trying to convince the public that their publication was a sophisticated vehicle for art, literature, and satire. Shifting to hard-breaking news confused and appalled the readers. Hearn explained the public's reaction: "The mourning American public failed to see the high artistic merits of these cartoons. It felt its holiest feelings had been horribly outraged." There was no effort in the editorial columns of issue eight to explain the intention of the sketches. Only a short note on page two mentioned the centerfold: "Subscribers and purchasers of the *Giglampz* should be careful to see that they get the 'Pat Rogers' cartoon with this week's issue. We mean it to go with the paper."

The other contents of Number 8, dated 9 August, were virtually overlooked. Hearn's weird story of Loki's evil children, from a Scandinavian folk tale, entitled "Eddaic Fragments," and a reprint of one of his *Enquirer* articles, "Eyes. Their Meaning, Power, and Beauty," were overshadowed by the Pat Rogers cartoon. Hearn claimed that that week *Ye Giglampz* lost five hundred subscribers in addition to the already deserting anti-temperance patronage.

At a point when the weekly could have become a viable publication, an editorial misjudgment proved fatal. Thus ended Hearn's first public experiment with the style and theme found in his later more literary work and an historical collaboration between two men who later gained individual international recognition for their talent.

Information Sources

BIBLIOGRAPHY:

Hughes, Jon Christopher. *Ye Giglampz*. Cincinnati: Crossroads Books with the Public Library of Cincinnati and Hamilton County, 1983.

INDEX SOURCES: None.

REPRINT EDITIONS: A facsimile of the nine numbers is included in *Ye Giglampz* by Jon Christopher Hughes (Cincinnati: Crossroads Books with the Public Library of Cincinnati and Hamilton County, 1983).

LOCATION SOURCES: The Public Library of Cincinnati and Hamilton County has the only complete set of the originals. Numbers 1–8 belonged to Lafcadio Hearn and carry his margin notations. Both the library and the Cincinnati Historical Society have photostats.

Publication History

MAGAZINE TITLE AND TITLE CHANGES: *Ye Giglampz*, 5 July 1874–16 August 1874.

VOLUME AND ISSUE DATA: Weekly, Volume 1:1, 5 July 1874,–Volume 1:9, 16 August 1874.

PUBLISHER AND PLACE OF PUBLICATION: E. H. Austerlitz and Co. (Volume 1:1–6); H. F. Farny and Co. (Volume 1:7–9); Cincinnati, Ohio.

EDITORS: Henry Farny and Lafcadio Hearn.

CIRCULATION: Unknown.

Jon Christopher Hughes

GOOD MORNING and ART YOUNG QUARTERLY (THE SOLDIER)

Art Young, Midwestern socialist farmboy and progressive cartoonist, founded *Good Morning* in New York in 1919. It was titled after the Pear's Soap commercial, and *Art Young Quarterly* was its successor in 1922. The inability of *The Liberator*, a socialist periodical, to pay its contributors was a major stimulus to the founding of the periodical, along with Young's desire to be more free-wheeling and less serious in his treatment of capitalist excesses. Young's intention was "to satirize the whole capitalistic works," including armaments, unemployment, plutocrats and bureaucrats, war and war profiteering, and religious hypocrisy. The Harding inaugural number for 15 February 1921 showed nine pages of parading figures, including starving schoolchildren worshipping a garlanded hog labeled "the packing trust." A "God" number for 1 July 1920 covered the news story of Jesus Christ and praised Pilate for keeping law and order. Carl Van Doren, among others, recognized the originality of Young's "Poor Fish," a common man-fish cartoon figure keeping his money tight and his mouth shut in the face of overwhelming plutocratic power.

Good Morning, Volume 1:1, issued 8 May 1919, was a sellout issue with a printing of 10,000. It achieved 4,000 subscriptions, along with newsstand sales, in its first year, but money problems dogged it as they did all such socialist-leaning publications and humor publications. Young did the editing and cartoons, with Harry Engels as publisher, weekly through October 1919 and then irregularly; it became semi-monthly in May 1920, monthly for August, September, and October, and then died. The Good Morning Publishing Company attempted the *Art Young Quarterly* as a revival at twenty-five cents a copy, 7½″ × 11″, thirty-six pages, with Volume 1:1 (First Quarter 1922) being a review issue of the last six years of Young's military-oriented work under the title "The Soldier." The next quarter promised "The Poor Fish," but it never appeared. Greenwood Press reprinted the run as part of a series of socialist periodicals, with an introduction by Daniel Aaron, in 1968; see also John N. Beffel, *Art Young: His Life and Times* (New York: Sheridan House, 1939), Young's autobiography as edited by John N. Beffel.

Information Sources

BIBLIOGRAPHY:
Aaron, Daniel. "Introduction," in *Good Morning* (Reprint edition). Westport, Conn.: Greenwood Press, 1968.
Beffel, John N., ed. *Art Young: His Life and Times*. New York: Sheridan House, 1939.
INDEX SOURCES: None.
REPRINT EDITIONS: Greenwood Press, 1968.
LOCATION SOURCES: CSmH, DLC, NN, PU.

Publication History

MAGAZINE TITLE AND TITLE CHANGES: *Good Morning*, 1919–1921; *Art Young Quarterly*, 1922.
VOLUME AND ISSUE DATA: Weekly, Volume 1:1, 8 May 1919-October 1919; irregularly through October 1920; *Art Young Quarterly*, First Quarter, 1922.
PUBLISHER AND PLACE OF PUBLICATION: 1919–1920: Harry Engels, New York. 1922: Good Morning Publishing Co.
EDITOR: Art Young.
CIRCULATION: 10,000.

David E. E. Sloane

GRUMP

With the comprehensive motto "For people who are against all the DUMB THINGS that are going on," *Grump* took on what it saw as the inordinacies of advertising, politics, education, feminism, and various trends and fads of the mid–1960s. In an era sometimes characterized by violent political activity and changing sexual mores, *Grump* professed to represent the "moral middle." It objected to the "proliferation of venality" and "excesses of . . . consumer culture." But "Good Grumpers," editor Roger Price noted in the first issue, "are not cynics or misanthropes. They grump because they truly love the world and hate to see it exploited by Loonies, Louts and Crap Artists."

Early issues carried grumps solicited from humorists Al Capp, Steve Allen, Shelley Berman, and Henry Morgan, and writers Isaac Asimov and Jacques Barzun. Mini-grumps contributed by readers ran as a regular feature. A variation on the grumps was the Nagonna's collection, readers' negative reaction to the imperatives of the time: "I'm NAGONNA ask Westinghouse what I can be sure of"; "I'm NAGONNA burn my draft card, my public library card, my social security card, my credit card, my student activity card, my alien registration card, my YMCA card or my French Post Card." Continuing the tradition of Jonathan Swift and H. L. Mencken with their Yahoos and Boobs, Price created the Roobs, the lowest common denominator of mass consumer culture whose favorite topic of conversation is "teevee" and whose cuisine consists of "French-fried Anything with catsup, Barbecued Anything, Instant Anything, Hamburgers, Canned Spaghetti and Pizza."

Contributors included Allan Sherman, Jean Shepherd, Don Adams, Robert Osborn, and Henry Miller, none of whom appeared more than once. Regular contributors were Judith Rascoe, later a short story and screen writer, Bill Majeski, later a television comic writer, and cartoonists and illustrators Jack Nelson, Donald Silverstein, and Stan Mack. *Grump* was profusely illustrated, containing at various times cartoon strips, single panel cartoons, comic photos ("The Care and Feeding of Pet Clams"), and, occasionally, "Droodles," described by Price as a "sub-art form owned and operated" (that is, invented) by him. "Droodles" also appeared as a syndicated newspaper feature for five years. *Grump* came in two sizes, the standard 8½" × 11" magazine or the double standard that opened up to tabloid size. The magazine format normally yielded thirty-two pages, and the tabloid format sixteen. The first anniversary issue (No. 7) contained 64 pages. *Grump* carried no advertising.

Information Sources

BIBLIOGRAPHY:
"Humor in the Moral Middle." *Time* (15 April 1960): 48, 51.
Morton, Charles W. "The Case for *Grump*." *Atlantic* 218 (September 1966): 115–16.
INDEX SOURCES: None.
REPRINT EDITIONS: None.
LOCATION SOURCES: CU-S, KMK, MH, OrU (all partial series).

Publication History

MAGAZINE TITLE AND TITLE CHANGES: *Grump*, May 1965-May 1966(?).
VOLUME AND ISSUE DATA: Bimonthly from May 1965, first issue unnumbered but consecutively thereafter to Number 11 (?).
PUBLISHER AND PLACE OF PUBLICATION: Roger Price, New York.
EDITOR: Roger Price.
CIRCULATION: 46,000 (April 1966).

George A. Test

H

HARVARD LAMPOON

"Professor Norton was lecturing upon the Fine Arts in Holden Chapel, one day in January, 1876," recalled John Tyler Wheelwright, Harvard class of 1876. "[when] Ralph Curtis snapped at me a little three-cornered note—come to Sherwood's room after lecture—we are to start a College *Punch*." That day was born a new humor magazine, the *Harvard Lampoon*, which first reached Harvard undergraduates as a twelve-page, double-column magazine on 10 February 1876. It sold for twenty-five cents a copy; 1,200 copies were printed, and all were sold in Harvard Yard by the next day. In addition to Curtis '76, Wheelwright and Samuel Sherwood '76, the first "editors" included Edward Sanford Martin '77, Edmund Marsh Wheelwright '77, Arthur Murray Sherwood '78, and, as "Business Editor," William Sigourney Otis '78. In the inaugural issue, the editors, anonymously, stated their mission:

> It is not our purpose to vie with the pessimistic and Nestorlike tone of the *Nation* nor the twaddle of the *Saturday Evening Gazette*, and we cannot hope to attain the poet-laureatism of the *Advocate* nor the high moral and aesthetic tone of the *Crimson*, but we shall try, with trenchant pencil and sarcastic pen, to hit off the foibles of our "little world," and to open a field where the last jest at the club-table and the latest undergraduate freak may find a fitting place.

They hoped not only to print their jests but also to expose folly:

> We propose to have a cut at everything about us that needs correction. All the affectation, all the snobbishness, all the censoriousness, which hovers about the College and occasionally crops out in her journals—everything of this order we propose to set up as a mark for our darts of withering sarcasm and remorseless irony.

Yet their cuts were not meant to draw blood, nor even to bruise the skin. "The very lightness of our material," the editors assured readers, "will make any injury a slight one."

For well over a hundred years, the *Harvard Lampoon* has remained faithful to its original mission. Many of its staffers became famous writers, such as George Santayana '86, John Reed '10, John P. Marquand '15, Robert Sherwood '17, David McCord '21, and Michael Arlen '52. Contributors have relished their role as brash, irreverent mockers of the Harvard establishment, while at the same time, of course, enjoying all the privileges bestowed on those attending America's premier university. Although editors have periodically renewed the pledge to "correct" abuse, the promises are issued only to assert the conventional pose of the satirist as a fearless and feared critic. In practice, the *Harvard Lampoon* is not a satirical magazine since it has no official point of view. Its point of view is solely to be funny, but also to appear as wicked as possible in being so—and to have great fun producing the whole zany enterprise. Befitting such aims, since the beginning the magazine's masthead mascot has been a grinning devil dressed in Elizabethan-era motley—"Lampy," who is shown guiding a ship of fools above the logo "Vanitas" and the motto: "Youth at the Prow and Pleasure at the Helm." By 1890, the Yard's new jester acquired a suitable companion and foil—the equivalent to *Punch*'s Toby: a bespeckled ibis, an extinct bird which, it should be emphasized, was timid and fed in shallow waters.

During the *Harvard Lampoon*'s first quarter century, the main targets were freshmen, "grinds," "sports," anyone foolish enough to attend any other Ivy League institution, and "certain Harvard professors." Themes followed the seasonal rhythms of campus life, beginning with "welcoming" freshmen in early fall, deflating football rivals in late fall, exposing lapsed New Year's resolutions at midyear, and finally decrying the injustices of section exams in the spring. It was published biweekly until recently, and in format it imitated, and even parodied, the standard features of established weeklies and monthlies, such as *Harper's Weekly*. "Correspondence" featured "Dear Lampy" letters (fictitious) from imaginary alumni. "Odds and Ends" included mock gossip overheard in dormitory alcoves. Under "Morceaux," the editors printed "in"-yard jokes, while in "Exchanges," they compiled compliments, again fictitious, collected from envious editors of rival Ivy League publications. By the end of the nineteenth century, "special numbers" were common, and five became regular seasonal productions: "Freshmen," "Football," "Christmas," "Class Day," and "Graduation."

Befitting a fledgling youth-oriented magazine, many early issues had to be padded with doggerel, mock schoolboy songs, short jokes and parodies of stand-ard authors from the curriculum such as Wordsworth and Tennyson, as well as popular favorites such as Poe and Longfellow. Occasionally, a particularly clever student would venture into extended literary parody, a mode that over the many decades would become one of the magazine's best features. "Busted; or, the Dean's Revenge" (18 May 1877), a melodrama in blank verse, made light of a familiar campus complaint. "The Death of Sir Cuttenthroat, A Legend of the Third Crusade" (21 December 1899), a mock epic in fourteener couplets, trampled both archaic literary conventions and contemporary administrative "cutthroats." A rather witty and ambitious series began in the 20 October 1895 issue called "A History of Harvard College from Prehistoric Times to the Present," by Alfred Kean Moe '97, who also drew the illustrations. It begins with early Cambridge:

> It was a golden age, thickly studded with mosquitoes and malaria, but happy because of the unknown horrors of hour exams,—an age which was snugly wedged in between the glorious periods of the Hundred Years' War and the founding of the "old Harvard."

Such mock histories, loaded with "in" jokes, look ahead to *The New Yorker**-style parodies, such as Donald Ogden Stewart's mock-Wellsian history *Parody Outline of History* (1921).

Contributors strained to affect the self-conscious pose of the blasé, world-weary clubman. It appeared first in "On the Pleasures of Suspension" (20 April 1876), which began: "I have passed a charming month. . . . No vender of useless articles invades my sanctum. No Jew, reeking with cheap cigar smoke, steals in my absence my pipes and coats." The haughty, arrogantly WASP attitude bespoke membership in an elite society in which contributors and readers alike belonged. To the University at large, outside their own ivied precincts, contributors wanted the magazine to be regarded as a kind of wicked, wayward stepchild who delighted in upsetting a rigidly parental faculty and better behaved progeny— namely, the *Harvard Crimson* and the *Harvard Advocate*, or "Mother *Advocate*." Both of these older and more dignified magazines were regularly attacked, usually portrayed, especially in cartoons, as dowdy New England grannies. The pariah's fate was always a self-serving fiction, however, since *Crimson* and *Advocate* editors usually championed the *Lampoon*'s cause and many of their staffers also contributed to the humor magazine.

By the turn of the century, the *Harvard Lampoon* was well established and even prosperous. Advertising pages were expanded from two to three or four pages, front and back, and included an increasing number of ads for the fancier goods and services, including ads promising vacations at the classier hotels in New York City. In 1909, the magazine moved from makeshift digs in Harvard Yard to new headquarters a block away, at 44 Bow Street and into a Flemish styled neo-Gothic and turreted fortress, itself a parody of a medieval manor. "The Castle," still *Lampoon* headquarters, was financed by William Randolph Hearst '86 and built by Edmund Marsh Wheelwright, Architect, one of the magazine's founders.

Although the magazine became successful as a diverting campus bulletin, it lacked any sustained literary distinction during its first quarter century. It was rescued from terminal blandness almost singlehandedly by the president (that is,

editor) from the class of 1912, Robert C. Benchley. Benchley pledged the
Harvard Lampoon to satirical "correction," but in practice he indulged his
special gifts for inspired whimsy. First of all, he set a new standard for arresting
comic imagery. He began his first editorial:

> The freshman class is upon us. The 1915 movement surges through the sacred
> precincts of the yard, under the effete elms and the optimistically umbrageous
> oaks, crashes noisily against faculty. . . . Poor, greenish protoplasmic beings afloat
> in an unfamiliar and tremendously magnified rain drop! (18 September 1911, p. 15).

Instead of perpetuating the pose of the haughty Harvard clubman, Benchley
exposed the bewildered late-adolescent quivering underneath. He became himself
the model of the campus bumbler, in his own cartoons and in "Benchley"
caricatures perfected by Gluyas Williams '11, who would later become Benchley's illustrator. Benchley introduced "Moments at the Courses," in which
the bewildered clubman is shown floundering in Economics 18 or English A.
He perfected the "How to" parody that would graduate with him into the pages
of *The New Yorker*. "How to Become a Graduate Student" (21 October 1911),
for example, bears the Benchley mark: "On a little card, you write your name,
address, home address, business address, mail, summer, female, winter addresses, your father's name, his address, and the length of his belt, your mother's
name at frequent intervals through her life" (p. 52). Out of these burlesques
would emerge Benchley's bumbling "little man" casuals, popular later in *The
New Yorker*. Benchley also initiated the now-famous magazine parodies with a
meticulous and witty send-up of *Life** (3 March 1911), the established national
humor magazine, once edited by *Lampoon* co-founder, Edward Sanford Martin.
Beginning in 1920, the *Lampoon* ran a magazine parody every year, and over
the years, the more influential magazines such as *Time* and *Newsweek* would be
parodied several times.

Prior to the 1920s, lampooners cast a disdainful eye toward the world beyond
the Yard—when they bothered to look at all. But the dramatic rise of a new
consumer culture after World War I teased them out of their edenic innocence.
Writers and cartoonists seemed happily seduced since every new craze or controversy obliged all would-be wits with rich new sources of comic material.

Contributors doted particularly on the new "motion pictures." The literary
classics that used to be broadly burlesqued were now scrambled into celluloid
hash, beginning with *Hamlet* "retold" as a movie thriller (9 March 1917). The
old Bret Harte vehicle, the "condensed novel," was updated and turned into
mock movie scripts (22 May 1921). The trite, sentimental plots of silent film,
the gushy heroines, the male heart-throbs, the hysterical fans—anything "Hollywood" proved to be inspired stuff, even though nothing much memorable
came of it. Perhaps the magazine's most brilliant artistic performance was its
learned parody of *Photoplay* complete with full-color illustrations (31 March
1926). The *Harvard Lampoon* has been going to the movies regularly ever since;

since 1940 it has run a special "number" honoring the more egregious follies of Hollywood-produced pop culture and solemnly touting "the worst movies of the year."

Until the mid–1920s, the *Harvard Lampoon* imitated styles of humor and illustration in the better established magazines. Contributors followed *Punch* and its American imitators, *Puck** and *Life*, mixing jest, verse, and cartoon; but they ignored *Punch*'s avowed liberalism and the pointed criticism of the American humor magazines. The illustrations, particularly in the earliest years, were dominated by full-page block-printed portraits that were stiltedly realistic and all too static, in the style of *Harper's Weekly*, with the joke a two-line snippet of dialogue printed below. The artwork, however old-fashioned and derivative, was usually more accomplished than the jokes they illustrated, which often turned on some egregious pun. In time, the illustrations shrank in size and became less realistic, more animated, more self-consciously stylized or surreal, as master caricaturists like Gluyas Williams arrived to make the pictures themselves witty or zany, thus achieving some balance between visual and verbal humor in the magazine. During the 1920s alcove-bred doggerel also gave way largely to *vers de société* and romantic lyrics in a campus cavalier vein. Some of the hitherto established features disappeared and new ones appeared, part of a conscious effort to break free of campus provincialism and to appear more cosmopolitan. "In"-Yard tales made way for lengthier narratives about Harvard men bustling about in the world of commerce in which contributors would soon become powerful members. Advertising pages were greatly expanded, so that in size the *Harvard Lampoon* rivalled New York-based national glossies like *Vanity Fair*.* In short, the magazine, while remaining a campus-based collector of jests, was also striving to seem more urbane. Its new model was clearly *The New Yorker*, founded in 1925, several of whose first contributors were former "poonies," most notably Benchley and Sherwood. The first of the *Lampoon*'s many send-ups of *The New Yorker* was "The *New Yorker* of Boston" (19 April 1928), in which contributors faithfully reproduced the literary and cartoon styles, the format, and even the typescript. One of the wittier entries was Philip Hichborn's parody of Dorothy Parker's "'Tis a Lovely Lady":

> Lady, once I held you so—
> I could never let you go,
> And the charms were never broken
> Once the magic words were spoken.
> Take a wreath and lay it here,
> Touch the laurel, shed a tear,
> For since I never could forget you,
> I'm goddam glad I never met you.

To many such aspiring wits, then and since, *The New Yorker* was the company they wanted to work for after graduation.

During the social and political upheavals of the 1930s, while the ship of state appeared to flounder, the Bow Street ship of fools kept a steady course, with Pleasure ever at the helm. Contributors had always relished attacking politicians and exposing political corruption, and they had found ready-made targets in the Boston Statehouse, Tammany Hall, and the administration of U. S. Grant. True to the principle of impartiality, they avoided taking sides, choosing instead to lampoon all prominent personalities with evenhanded derision. Hence, they spared neither Harding, Coolidge, nor "Herby Hoover," although they were unusually aggressive in ridiculing presidential candidate Franklin D. Roosevelt, portraying him in cartoons as a hypocritical populist too cozy with the lower classes (28 September 1932). A "Politics Number" (11 October 1928) was an occasion to plague both political houses; an "Election Issue" (2 November 1932) was an occasion to launch rival "parties," such as the Unemployed Socialite Party or Do Nothings and the Scholastic Labor or No-deb Party. An "Obscene Number" (16 February 1933) was an occasion to promote the book-burning of the Peek and Carp Sodality. While Jews and blacks figured prominently in crude caricature in earlier times, the 1930s offered up "Japs" and Germans, who became stock characters in mock radio dramas and sportscasts. They, like other non-Harvard groups, were put through their farcical paces, made to serve the ends of easy laughter. Not even Hitler's cataclysmic transgressions seemed to faze lampooners, who found him merely clownish—another fool good for a laugh or two. The haughty clubman's stance, insisted on since the magazine's inception, required unswerving devotion to *indifference*. Indeed, at the height of the Depression, when taking sides seemed in order, "Indifference" was celebrated as the Harvard's man's highest virtue: "Harvard indifference is not only an attitude. It is a complete Philosophy of Life; it is your Ontology and Cosmology. It is your very Life Blood" (19 September 1934).

After World War II, the *Harvard Lampoon* shed much of its clubman snobbishness, perhaps because many contributors were veterans and hence older and less inclined to strike undergraduate elitist poses. "In" jokes, light verse, and cartoons continued to abound, but the stories became more complicated and more heavily plotted, with better rounded characters given to subtler emotions. Many were comedies of situation that turned on climactic ironies visited on Harvard look-alikes grappling with success or failure. The increasing dominance of comedy of manners again showed the influence of *The New Yorker* and of literary-minded presidents of the *Lampoon* of prewar days, such as Nathanael Benchley '38, whose own stories often fit *New Yorker* formulas. The magazine's self-consciously cosmopolitan tone was sustained after the war under the presidency of George Plimpton '48, whose stories, like "Evangeline and the Boa" (22 September 1949), dealt with chance encounters among sophisticates and leaned heavily on surprising turns of plot.

But the *Harvard Lampoon* reached a second peak of remarkable literary sophistication, thanks to the prolific output of its most accomplished contributor, the president from the class of 1954, John H. Updike. "The reason he took a scholarship to Harvard (instead of one to Cornell)," reported interviewer Jane

Howard, "was that he wanted to do cartoons for the famous *Lampoon*, which had nurtured Robert Benchley and other of his idols." He was elected to the Literary Board as a freshman, rose to the position of Narthex (the officer in charge of club functions)—and a new position inaugurated in January 1934— as a sophomore, then became Ibis (by his time, the officer in charge of *Lampoon* management), and finally president (editor) in December of his junior year. During his four years, Updike contributed over one hundred cartoons and occasional drawings, sixty poems, twenty-five articles and short stories, and also furnished seven color illustrations for the magazine's cover.

Like the Benchleys, Plimpton, and other literary-minded and talented *Lampoon* leaders, like Clement Wood '47, Updike avoided the stance of the wicked, world-weary clubman. The droll, understated wit of his cartoons showed the influence of *New Yorker* minimalists like Whitney Darrow, Jr., and William Steig. His poems were in the tradition of *Lampoon* verse: brief, clever, topical, and self-consciously "literary." He was certainly precocious, even ostentatiously so. "Lines in Favor of Deposed Kings" (September 1952) displayed Updike's soon to be celebrated gift for word play:

> Farouk, a cabbage sort of king
>   Rotund and slightly green,
> When Egypt nestled neath his wing
>   Was flagrant and obscene.
> Now would I hail him as a pal
>   Long lost and seldom seen;
> So would I greet ex-king Talal,
>   The Jordan Schizophrene.

Even his doggerels sound more polished, and many still give pleasure, such as "Lampy's Doggerel Guide to English Literature" (September 1953), which bows to Benchley and to that other zany wit (and Harvard alum), Ogden Nash:

> "This Century"
> Everything began
> When Whitman wouldn't scan
>
> Dickinson and Crane
> Had inner pain.
> Williams and Frost
> Just plain felt lost.
>
> A jaded zealot
> Is T. S. Ealot
> These days Pound
> Just sits around.

Updike also perfected "At the Pleasures" series and launched an editor's column, "Vanitas," which ran in the magazine for years. His articles under "Coming Distractions," which touted imaginary film versions of the classics, carried on an old *Lampoon* tradition and anticipated the prose parodies he contributed to the "Talk of the Town" in *The New Yorker* during his early staff years. Many of his stories are too topical to be of much interest today, but several are as subtle in development of theme and character as his later professional stories. In "The Peruvian in the Heart of Lake Winnapasaukee" (September 1953), Updike skillfully counterpoints a strange foreign camper, a foreigner, in search of himself and the narrator, an obtuse camp registrar unable to recognize the discovery when it comes. In "The Sunshine Poet" (December 1952), he uses fast-paced repartee to unmask the latest college circuit-rider, the pretentiousness of much modern poetry, and its easily charmed devotees. In "Little Schism" (April 1953), an unprecedented 6,000 words long, he uncovers the petty animosities that result when a congregation divides over whether an ancient weathervane on their church steeple should be replaced with a cross of gold (copper) or of silver (stainless steel). The emotional "schisms" of failing Christians that Updike examined here look ahead to more complicated explorations in his suburb-situated novels, such as *Rabbit, Run* and *Couples*.

Updike's accomplished parables about upwardly mobile neurotics spoke prophetically to the 1950s, a period of schisms between public duties and private aspirations that burdened individuals and produced both "the organization man" and the "lonely crowd." The consequent rise and influence of ambitious sociological studies and pop psychology, prompted by the publication of the Kinsey Report, opened up a rich new vein for social satire and parody. In an "Erotica" issue (December 1958), lampooners exploited the breaking down of sexual taboos by joking about them in cartoon and verse. Writers parodied the sex reports, having fun with the public's newfound fascination with the forbidden. The issue was loaded with parlor games, one including playing cards in four suits: Extroverts, Diverts, Inverts, and Converts. The immense popularity of *Games People Play* by psychologist Eric Berne inspired a whole series of mock games which, like the magazine parodies, carried the *Lampoon* well into the 1960s. By 30 March 1967, "Games" received an issue of its own, one of the *Lampoon*'s most wicked productions. A few of these like "Black Death" showed uncommon cleverness in the writing:

> "Burghers" and "Rats" slug it out in a faithful vinyl replica of a medieval town.
> Adapted from the French game, *La Peste*, Black Death affords many hours of
> historically accurate enjoyment as the burghers try to slough off the Rats on each
> other and the Rat hordes struggle to occupy the entire town. Sets include a dozen
> life-sized Burgher dolls and 100,000 corduroy rats.

Others depended on striking the right conceit, such as "The Great Game of Absolution and Redemption," based on Monopoly. The draw cards were "Sin" and "Miracle" and at the end: "When all the players have died or completed the proper number of circuits, the pieces shall be put away, and the Predestination cards shall be turned over. If the cards read 'damned,' and most do, the player loses.'' A few game parodies in the issue brazenly assaulted yet-unspoken taboos, such as ''Unwed Mother,'' featuring ''Bickering, Contraception and Libido Cards,'' along with these directions:

> The artificial insemination card is played in the same manner as the hysterical pregnancy card. It can be countered *only* by one of the two abortion cards. Again if a challenged player lacks an abortion card, she may bicker for it; if she fails to obtain it, she is considered impregnated and is stoned (p. 21).

The *Harvard Lampoon* always strained to be cheerfully abusive toward everyone but never with such abrasiveness as in the mid–1960s. A new, more open society created a climate of ''anything goes,'' which prompted lampooners to push against the boundaries of good taste—and, as in ''Unwed Mother,'' to step blithely over them. Deepening American military involvement in Vietnam produced coarse whimsy and mock-Kafka farce, evidence that writers were provoked by worsening crises, not really shaken by them. Illustrators played up the horrid human consequences of American foreign policy, sometimes with ghoulish glee, as in ''Red Guerilla Number'' (25 February 1965). Yet contributors again followed *Lampoon* tradition and refrained from taking any political position editorially—except to do so in a mocking parodistic vein. For example, the magazine requested that the Geneva Convention on Indo-China adopt the Shirley Temple Plan: ''Mao and LBJ should each leave an old sweater in the jungle, 100 miles apart. Con Edison will build a huge trench halfway between them, filled with muddy, guppy-infested water. . . . Shooting will be done with the right index finger.'' As the war escalated, so too did interest in mocking the combatants, culminating in ''The Overkill Number'' (January 1968) in which writers ridiculed nearly every facet of the American effort—yet remained scrupulously ''indifferent.'' By the middle 1960s, the *Lampoon* became more avowedly hostile, more eager to offend, perhaps goaded by the perception that political events in Southeast Asia were spinning out of control. The new aggressiveness seems to have been organized under the tenure of President Jonathan Cerf '68 and included the exceptionally talented wits, Henry Beard and Douglas Kenney. They were the contributors mainly responsible for the misogynist bawdry and anti-Catholic satire as well as for the *Lampoon*'s most successful magazine parody, the 1968 send-up of *Time*, which became a huge best-seller. After graduation, they would become the nucleus of the spinoff humor magazine, the *National Lampoon*,* where ''bad taste'' humor would reach new heights, as well as garner considerable profits.

As the nation settled back into a complacent, rather self-indulgent mood after the civil rights struggle and the resolution of the Vietnam War, so too did the *Harvard Lampoon*, retreating to more campus-oriented topics. Lampooners feasted on the new fads and fashions, bad movies (and by now television), parodied new literary favorites, groused about Yard types—in effect, returned to playing the court jester in the magazine's original plan. Perhaps when *Lampoon* management sold its name to the *National Lampoon* corporation, keeping rights to its magazine parodies, it bequeathed to its new child its subversive, anarchic personality. Succeeding classes of talented undergraduates worked hard thereafter to be scandalous, even giving an issue over to it ("Sacrilege," December 1976). But such features as "Excommunication, and How You Can Avoid It" lack the slashing anti-Catholic bite of Kenney's pieces from the 1960s. "The Adventures of Christian Scientist," a mock Superman comic, is visually accomplished but verbally bland, letting fundamentalists off easily. The "Downtrodden Number" (May 1980) is only predictably scandalizing. As in the past, the writing is overshadowed by the artwork, which has benefitted from ever more refined methods of color reproduction.

While the magazine maintains its century-old pose of the indifferent clubman, the WASP bigotry of former times has gone. The groups that the Harvard man used to disdain haughtily—Jews, blacks, and women—now take leading roles on the magazine. In 1981, the *Harvard Lampoon* elected its first woman president, Lisa Henson '82. The prominence of Blacks and women shows in the heavier doses of topical jokes and cartoons that turn on racial or feminist attitudes and issues. Jewish humor also abounds, as in the "People Are Funny" issue (April 1980), which echoes nightclub comedy patter and TV sitcom put-downs. At present, the *Lampoon* is published bimonthly, it is thinner than at any time since the 1890s, and thin also in wit; it is, however, thick with spectacular graphic work that fits well with the slick ads, stunning testament to the dominance in America of a technologically advanced *visual* culture. Despite its present lack of literary distinction, the *Harvard Lampoon* strives to be decently irreverent, holding up an extraordinarily long tradition. A huge endowment permits the magazine to adhere to high production standards; meanwhile, the "Castle" awaits the arrival of the next Benchley or Updike.

Information Sources

BIBLIOGRAPHY:

Andersen, Kurt B., et al., eds. *The Harvard Lampoon Hundredth Anniversary Issue*, Cambridge, Mass.: Harvard Lampoon, 1976.

Bunce, Douglas, et al., eds. *The Harvard Lampoon Seventy-Fifth Anniversary Issue*. Cambridge, Mass.: Harvard Lampoon, 1952.

English, R. McC., et al., eds. *The Harvard Lampoon Fiftieth Anniversary Issue*. Cambridge, Mass.: Harvard Lampoon, 1926.

Lampy's Early Days. Cambridge, Mass.: Harvard Lampoon Society, 1909.

McCoy, Robert. "John Updike's Literary Apprenticeship in the *Harvard Lampoon*." *Modern Fiction Studies* 20, No. 1 (Spring 1974): 3–12.

Santayana, George. "The Lampoon from 1883 to 1886." In *Reminiscences and a List of Editors of the Harvard Lampoon, 1876–1901*. Cambridge, Mass.: Privately Printed, 1901.

INDEX SOURCES: None.
REPRINT EDITIONS: See anniversary editions above.
LOCATION SOURCES: Pusey Archives Library-Harvard, partial CtY.

Publication History

MAGAZINE TITLE AND TITLE CHANGES: The *Harvard Lampoon*, February 1876
    to present.
VOLUME AND ISSUE DATA: Volumes 1–9 (1876–1880, ten issues per year), First
    Series; Volumes 1–   (1881–   ), Second Series, published bimonthly or monthly
    irregularly between 1951 and 1966; now published five times per year.
PUBLISHER AND PLACE OF PUBLICATION: The *Harvard Lampoon*, Cambridge,
    Massachusetts.
CIRCULATION: Not available.

Thomas Grant

HUMBUG MAGAZINE

Humbug Magazine, which ran for eleven numbers in 1957–1958, was the creation
of the artists who had originated and made a success of *Mad*.* Although similar
to its predecessor in look and choice of material, *Humbug* appears to have been
aimed at a slightly more adult audience. It printed the parodies of films, television
programs, comic strips, and advertisements which characterized the older
magazine; in other features it also revealed an awareness of political, social, and
economic conditions of its times. *Humbug* was unusual in that it was owned by
its artists—a fact attributable to the disastrous history of *Trump*, another short-
lived humor magazine of the fifties with which they all had been associated.

In 1956, Hugh Hefner, publisher of the very successful *Playboy*, essentially
bought the staff of *Mad* to produce his own humor magazine. Harvey Kurtzman,
a founder of *Mad* who had resigned over a policy dispute, was the editor of the
new publication originally to be called *X* but finally released as the well-produced,
expensive-looking *Trump*. The first issue appeared in January 1957.
Unfortunately, the distributor of the magazine, the American News Company,
went into bankruptcy shortly after, and the second issue of *Trump* did not reach
newsstands until March. By that time, the magazine was about $95,000 in debt
and Hefner ceased publication. In September of 1957, Kurtzman, Harry Chester,
and artist Will Elder, who had known each other since they were students at
New York High School of Music and Art, together with artists Arnold Roth and
Jack Davis, two more castaways from the *Trump* sinking, formed the company
which published *Humbug*. Kurtzman was editor-in-chief; Chester, manager;
Davis and Elder, staff artists; and Roth and Al Jaffee, another alumnus of *Mad*
and the High School of Music and Art, editors. This was essentially the staff
of the magazine throughout its history. In later issues, Davis, Elder, Jaffee, and
Roth were all designated assistant editors, and L. Auerbach was hired as art
director.

The first nine issues of *Humbug* were printed on comic book stock at comic book size and measured approximately 6½″ × 9½″. The format was changed with Number 10 when, in order to escape the comic book section of the newsstand and find its proper readership among those looking through "larger, more sophisticated publications," *Humbug* increased in size to approximately 8⅜″ × 10¾″ and was printed on better quality paper. Numbers 1 through 10 were thirty-two pages long. *Humbug* Number 11, which included fifteen pages of material from *Trump*, contained forty-eight pages. The price of the small *Humbug* was fifteen cents per issue; the subscription rate was two dollars for fourteen issues. The larger magazine cost twenty-five cents; a subscription was three dollars for fourteen issues. *Humbug* carried almost no advertising—none unrelated to the magazine or associated enterprises like a *Humbug* anthology, *Humbug* jewelry, or *Humbug* Christmas wrapping paper designed by Jaffee. Ballantine Books published a paperback reader of material drawn from early issues. The last issue of the magazine advertised the first nine numbers bound into a hardcover book selling for $2.50. That the circulation figures of the magazine were disappointing is suggested by its short run and by Kurtzman's editorial comment that of his three magazines, *Humbug* printed "the very best satire of all, which of course now sells the very worst of all."

In addition to Kurtzman, Elder, Davis, Jaffee, and Roth, regular contributors to the magazine were R. Blechman, one of whose singular cartoons was printed practically every month, and Lawrence Siegel, an alumnus of the University of Illinois' humor magazine *Shaft*, who did most of *Humbug*'s print parodies and who ranged through targets like the best-selling novel *Marjorie Morningstar*, O. Henry's "Gift of the Magi," army field manuals, television network censors, Jim Bishop's *The Day Lincoln Was Shot*, and—in a Dick and Jane version of the play—*Hamlet*. Harry Purvis was a less regular contributor with a series entitled "Favorite Formulas for Finishing Films." As with *Mad* and *Trump*, parody was the dominant type of humor in *Humbug*. Jack Davis and Bill Elder's treatments of movies, television programs, commercials, and comics were frequent features. Davis also authored a running spoof of movie clichés entitled "You Know Who Gets Killed." Each issue of the magazine contained at least one advertisement parody and a magazine parody, the targets of which ranged from *Consumer Reports* through cheap song lyric magazines, car magazines, and muscle magazines to the *New York Daily News'* "Year in Review." *Humbug*'s satire was socially aware but fairly mild. The magazine gibed at *Confidential*-type exposé magazines, lodges and fraternal organizations, turkey carving, Miami, and doctors' fees. Roth did cartoons on American holidays and history. Perhaps the sharpest comment in the magazine came in "The *Humbug* of the Month Awards." Some of these went to fake Santa Clauses; Leona Gage, the Miss USA who turned out to be a Mrs.; and television interviewer Mike Wallace. Others went to Orval Faubus, who was declared Humbug of the year; to "panicky patriots . . . who give to our missile program so generously of their emotions and without whose contributions we could do"; and to the "Economy Optimists . . . who say everything is going to be ALL right."

Readers' reactions to *Humbug* reveal the nature of the times in which it tried to exist and suggest the reasons for its short life. One reader wrote: "Between *Humbug* and *The New Yorker*, life can go on." Another: "You have placed your explosive satire beneath our most sacred cows, and have blasted those idols with the mercilessness they deserve." "We did that? ! ! ! " the editors replied. Jabs at Orval Faubus drew a large and nasty reaction, however. Including the name of Pope Pius XII in a parody of Leonard Lyon's gossip column drew threat of cancellation from a reader, as did a cover showing Sputnik peeking at the bathing girl in "September Morn." A mother in Chicago promised to report the magazine to a morals committee which would in future "watch" the store where it was sold. A reader who objected to a comic alphabet drawn by Roth which included "C—Holy See" and "O" as in Oly Man" wrote to communicate the collective wrath of "approximately 150 members of the AVMC, in Baltimore."

The existence of such attitudes toward *Humbug*'s style of humor no doubt helped prevent the magazine from catching on as it deserved. The recession of 1957, however, seems to have been primarily responsible for its demise. Recession jokes increase in later issues of *Humbug*. The cover of the last issue shows the head above the nose of a man drowning in red ink. Kurtzman's farewell entitled "We're Beat" reads: "As we stated to our readers in *Humbug* #1, page 1, quote: 'We won't write for morons. We won't do anything just to get laughs. We won't be dirty. We won't be grotesque. We won't be in bad taste. We won't sell magazines.' *Humbug has not let its readers down!*"

Information Sources

INDEX SOURCES: None.
REPRINT EDITIONS: None.
LOCATION SOURCES: Spencer Research Library at the University of Kansas; none listed in *Union List of Serials*.

Publication History

MAGAZINE TITLE AND TITLE CHANGES: *Humbug Magazine*, August 1957-August 1958.
VOLUME AND ISSUE DATA: Monthly, eleven issues, March and July 1958 skipped; August 1958 cover dated October.
PUBLISHER AND PLACE OF PUBLICATION: Humbug Publishing Co., New York, and Derby, Connecticut.
EDITORS: Harvey Kurtzman. Assistant Editors: Jack Davis, Will Elder, Al Jaffee, and Arnold Roth.
CIRCULATION: Unknown.

Michael D. Butler

I

THE IDIOT

Samuel Simpleton offered the 52 issues of his weekly *The Idiot*, subtitled "The Invisible Rambler," to his Boston audience from 10 January 1818 through 2 January 1819. At $1.50 a year, six cents an issue, in three-column, 10″ × 12″ format, *The Idiot* was an early proponent of the position that most news is boring and useless, particularly including ship arrivals, foreign wars, and the like. During the summer, the cheeky editor mused that "For the past six weeks not a single death has occurred in New London," and the great sea serpent scare of Boston Harbor was the subject of ironic comment running through several months. Communications not immoral, slanderous, or invective were welcomed with the 16 May number. Subscribers as of the Fourth of July were listed at 1,400. With the final announcement of discontinuance in Number 52, the editor commented that he had to generate too much of the copy himself without contributions and was transferring the establishment to the *Kaleidoscope.*** Thus ended one of New England's better comic offerings of the early period.

The Idiot's masthead showed a simpleton at his writing desk but rejected college students and literary men in favor of plain style and simple readers. A family of Simpletons was conjured into being who would report doings from various areas: a traveler to Ohio, a New England preacher to the Indians, a collegian, and similar New England stock figures of the early nineteenth century. A number of dialect pieces showed Negroes, sailors, and common folk in short pieces like one where two Blacks duel over a woman by shooting at coconuts, but she goes off with a third man by the time they return, refusing to endorse a "white sabage cus'um." Filler news stories caricatured contemporary papers with unbelievable items on turkeys with three necks and four gizzards. A good Vermont story from Graham's told of a farmer who avoided being excommunicated for a Sunday bear shoot by standing in the back of the church during the sermon and drawing a bead on the preacher with his rifle.

By the late Spring, regular departments had emerged on "Theatrical Remarks," "Humour," and "Uncle Sam's Weekly Summary," covering international politics. Uncle Sam amended Alexander Pope democratically to "Whatever is *POPULAR*, is right!" concerning the witchcraft persecutions and Sabbath laws of a hundred years before. But *The Idiot* followed Joseph Dennie's lead in the *Farmer's Weekly Museum*;* he attacked the practice of letting "Great men" fail for $50,000 or $100,000 and depriving widows and orphans of their hard-earned pittance while the rich man retains his carriage and silk stockings. Slavery received antagonistic comment. Shakers, the Boston sea serpent, Western immigration, and comic-moral reflections on seduction were notable subjects, and the sudden honoring of Christmas as a feast-day was noted with bemusement. A suffering pastor responded to his choir with a misread litany, "Lord, have mercy on these poor, miserable singers." The Chillecothe *Supporter* was quoted in September for a tall tale from the West in which the death of Daniel Boone took place so naturally that his friends found him the next day stiff and cold but still positioned in the act of aiming his rifle. Clips from other papers appeared, but the author also offered items from *Joe Miller* and *Colman's Broad Grins* among other English sources. Uncle Jerry Simpleton's *Tour to the Ohio* was promised as a book available at N. Coverly's bookstore in Milk Street the week after the paper's final issue, and Coverly may have been connected with the paper.

Information Sources

INDEX SOURCES: None.
REPRINT EDITIONS: Readex Microprint, under Boston *Mirror*.
LOCATION SOURCES: Long runs at MB, MH, MiD, DCU, and one or two copies at
     DLC, MWA.

Publication Data

MAGAZINE TITLE AND TITLE CHANGES: *The Idiot; or Invisible Rambler*.
VOLUME AND ISSUE DATA: Volume 1:1–52, 10 January 1818–2 January 1819.
PUBLISHER AND PLACE OF PUBLICATION: Unknown, Boston.
EDITOR: Samuel Simpleton, pseud.
CIRCULATION: 1,400.

David E. E. Sloane

INDEPENDENT BALANCE

George Helmbold's *Independent Balance* of Philadelphia stands with Helmbold's Philadelphia *Tickler** as one of the most mature of the earlier American comic papers treating American social and civil life through humor. Helmbold established the *Independent Balance* on 20 March 1817 under the editorship of "Democritus the Younger—a lineal descendent of the laughing philosopher."

Helmbold died early in the Fall of 1821, leaving the paper in the hands of S. Helmbold, his brother, who ran it from 17 October through 5 December to aid George's widow and orphan, and probably thereafter. On 19 February 1823, the subscription price was lowered to four dollars a year, and on 28 May, L. P. Franks became publisher, moving the publication date to Saturday, and for a period mastheading Dietrich Knickerbocker the Younger as editor. The paper survived through 4 December 1830, whole Number 607, with Franks, former owner of the Philadelphia *Luncheon*, editing as "Simon Spunkey, Esq." after 29 October 1824. In its later years, however, the *Balance* was more political and less humorous than it had been under the hands of the Helmbolds.

Helmbold returned from the War of 1812 with consciousness intact but with his Philadelphia *Tickler* long since lapsed. On his return from the war, he opened a tavern, the Minerva, in October 1815, hoping to serve his fellows from the war and to pay off his *Tickler* debts. The poor pay of the newspaper business was always a problem for him; nonetheless, he brought out the *Independent Balance* in a format that was similar to his previous paper, four 11" × 19" pages in four colums, published every Wednesday at 32 Cherry Street, next to his residence, at five dollars a year. The first volume concluded on 8 April 1818 with 1:52.

The paper covered much the same content as the *Tickler*, with the masthead showing a hunter shooting folly on the wing. The 20 December 1820 number showed a "Southron's" coat of arms with a slaver beating a Negro and shooting and caning opponents under a wreath of slave chains—early hostility to slavery for a Northern paper. By 1821, he was complaining about subscribers not paying. He continued to reprint humor items from other papers. The 17 October 1821 issue offered a verse drama in which a Yankee thinks of immigrating to Illinois or Alabama to escape the poor land. Throughout, American subject matter, civil events, and social attitudes provided the chief focus of the paper, and this focus continued when George's brother took over in December, reassuring correspondents of anonymity. True to George's conduct of the *Balance*, the new editor wrote that the manner or style of his composition may not suit courtly ears, but that in matter he stood on high ground and served the public good— only the fool, hypocrite, or rogue would be made uncomfortable. An awareness of American "types" also continued, with Yankees, Dutch, and other American characters and subjects making up many of the paragraphs and clips from a wide variety of writers and newspaper sources. One heading was "Steamboats, Alligators, Buffaloes, & c." Some limits were maintained; on 19 December 1821, an article by "Timothy Tickle" was noted as being turned down because it was too abrasive for publication.

After L. P. Franks took over the paper, it became significantly less lively. There was less variety of matter and somewhat more of a political direction. On 22 November 1823, Franks was forced to retract a personal attack—a pun on a Mr. Bomeisler as a bamboozler—typical of the kind of problems Franks had run into on the *Luncheon*. Physically, the paper retained its format, and aside from the lessening of the humor and the turn toward the political, it remained relatively the same through its remaining run. However, Franks' course may have been the better one economically, considering that the paper lasted until 4 December 1830.

Information Sources

BIBLIOGRAPHY:

Becker, Gloria. University of Pennsylvania Dissertation in Progress on Pennsylvania commerce and milling.

Scharf, J. Thomas, and Thompson Westcott. *History of Philadelphia*. Philadelphia: L. H. Everts and Co., 1884, 1:989.

Smyth, Albert H. *The History of Philadelphia Magazines*. Philadelphia: Robert M. Lindsay, 1892, pp. 184–85.

Publication History

MAGAZINE TITLE AND TITLE CHANGES: *Independent Balance*, Volume 1:1, 20 March 1817 to New Series 27—whole Number 607—4 December 1830, with some minor irregularities in publication dates.

VOLUME AND ISSUE DATA: Volume 1:1, 20 March 1817 to Number 607 4 December 1830.

PUBLISHER AND PLACE OF PUBLICATION: G. Helmbold to Volume 5:236, 17 October 1821, when S. Helmbold becomes publisher; L. P. Franks from Volume 7:5(Number 315) on 28 May 1823–4 December 1830, whole Number 607; Philadelphia.

EDITORS: G. Helmbold to Number 236; S. Helmbold to Number 315; L. P. Franks under various pseudonyms.

CIRCULATION: Unknown.

David E. E. Sloane

J

JIM JAM JEMS

Jim Jam Jems was a pocket-size, unpretentious Midwestern journal of opinion, founded and exclusively written by Sam H. Clark (alias Jim Jam Junior) in 1912. Clark's short essays condemned all deviations from virtue—political corruption, corporate greed, consumer scams, cruelty to the downtrodden, obscenity in print and on stage—and celebrated the much rarer examples of human kindness and heroism.

Clark was a seasoned newspaperman who felt his opinions unduly constrained by editorial policy in his regular line of work. *Jim Jam Jems* was to be an outlet where he could "write just whatever we damn please and say as much." The magazine was subtitled "A Volley of Truth" and later, "Sam Clark's Volley of Truth." *Jim Jam Jems* was not intended to make money beyond the costs of publication, and it contained no advertising. It was sold only on newsstands and direct from the publisher until 1922 when Clark finally agreed to offer subscriptions. The source for the meaningless title was an earlier unpublished book in support of Prohibition by Clark's father—hence Clark's alias, Jim Jam Junior.

Jim Jam Jems was published monthly with occasional special issues, such as one for Mothers' Day. From 1925 to 1927 publication was irregular, in part because Clark had founded another magazine, *Follyology*, which was intended, in contrast to the heavy irony and sarcasm of *Jim Jam Jems*, to be Clark's "playground" for "humor, sentiment and pointed comment." Clark published *Follyology* for ten months (May 1924 to February 1925) and then sold it to Myron Zobel of Associated Distributing Corporation. According to a dismayed and disgusted Clark, *Follyology*'s purchasers turned it from a "clean, wholesome publication" to a rag along the lines of *Hollywood Confessions*.

Jim Jam Jems was often confused with the suggestive and barnyard humor magazines which proliferated on newsstands in the early 1920s and which it resembled in size and general format. It was often included on police lists of banned magazines in cities all over the country. These episodes always ended with the removal of the ban after Clark's vigorous protests to the authorities.

A more serious attempt at the suppression of *Jim Jam Jems* occurred late in 1922 when John S. Sumner of the New York Society for the Suppression of Vice succeeded in having *Jim Jam Jems* labeled obscene and dealers who refused to discontinue sales arrested. Clark traveled from South Dakota to New York to post bail for his dealers, "went into court and came out with a clean bill of health and certificate of good character." In the July 1925 issue Clark differentiated his magazine from its lewd imitators: "*Jim Jam Jems* stands alone in its field. We have kept it clean. The double meaning story, the sex-fiction obscenity, the nude pictures, the suggestive charicature [*sic*] . . . have been excluded from our magazine. Truth and Sentiment and Sunshine—that is all."

In the October 1928 issue Clark apologized to readers for the delay that his illness had caused in the issue's appearance. As it turned out, this was to be the last issue. At the end of the year Wilford H. Fawcett, publisher and editor of *Captain Billy's Whiz Bang*,* the type of magazine Clark had scorned, purchased *Jim Jam Jems*, and it ceased to exist.

Information Sources

BIBLIOGRAPHY:
Peterson, Theodore. *Magazines in the Twentieth Century*. Urbana: University of Illinois Press, 1956, p. 266.
INDEX SOURCES: None.
REPRINT EDITIONS: University Microfilms.
LOCATION SOURCES: DLC.

Publication History

MAGAZINE TITLE AND TITLE CHANGES: *Jim Jam Jems*, January 1912-October 1928.
VOLUME AND ISSUE DATA: Monthly, Volumes 1–17; Library of Congress/ University Microfilms set lacks January 1923, February, May, August, November, December 1925, March-June 1926; publication suspended July 1926-December 1927.
PUBLISHER AND PLACE OF PUBLICATION: Sam H. Clark and C. H. Crockard, Bismarck, North Dakota.
EDITOR: Sam H. Clark.
CIRCULATION: Unknown.

Jean Rainwater

JINGO

Jingo was a magazine with a mission: to flail the skins off of the Democrats and Mug-Wumps in general and their candidate for President, Grover Cleveland, in particular. Owned and edited by Bostonian G. Walter Turner, *Jingo* was first issued on 10 September 1884, in response to the Mug-Wump bolt from the

Republican party ranks and to Cleveland's nomination by the Democrats. *Jingo*'s three-color cartoons and nearly all of its editorial matter were unrelentingly political. The magazine did not so much support Republican candidate Blaine as it attacked Cleveland and his liberal Republican supporters. In the cartoons, *Jingo*'s artists (most notably James A. Wales, late of *Judge*,* made the most of Cleveland's virtual admission to having fathered an illegitimate child. In the text, Turner hammered away at the immorality of those who opposed Blaine in long political essays, some with satirical overtones, some simply political assaults. The last issue, Number 11, appeared right after the election. Because the magazine had made Blaine's victory its sole purpose, Blaine's defeat meant *Jingo*'s end.

   Jingo, "a journal of politics and humor," was published by the Art Newspaper Company of Boston from Volume 1:1 (10 September 1884) weekly through at least Number 11 (18 November 1884), the whole run existing at DLC. In folio at 10½″ × 14″ at ten cents, shortly lowered to six cents, *Jingo* offered garishly colored covers and political cartoons boosting Blaine, the tariff, manufactures, and the American home against Cleveland, whisky, John Bull, and poverty for American workingmen. Obviously oriented toward the election of 1884, one cartoon showed Columbia as a pretty girl pursued over a precipice by Cleveland and another thug on horseback. Some longer burlesque fiction appeared in addition to prosaic "Whittlings," but the colored double-page center cartoon and the cover cartoons, all on political themes, dominated the journal. It claimed a circulation of 30,000 and a readership of 100,000, but the promised change of format following the election of the Democratic pirates was a change to no format, and it disappeared.

Information Sources

INDEX SOURCES: None.
REPRINT EDITIONS: None.
LOCATION SOURCES: DLC.

Publication History

MAGAZINE TITLE AND TITLE CHANGES: *Jingo*.
VOLUME AND ISSUE DATA: Weekly, 10 September 1884–18 November 1884. Volume 1 as issued includes eleven numbers.
PUBLISHER AND PLACE OF PUBLICATION: Art Newspaper Co., Boston.
EDITOR: G. Walter Turner.
CIRCULATION: 30,000.

Richard Samuel West

THE JOHN-DONKEY

The John-Donkey brayed for the understanding of its fellow jackasses with mock irony for less than a year, in 1848, but in that short period it established itself as the outstanding comic paper up to that time in America. The cover of each issue featured the musing donkey, Dr. John-Donkey, portrayed full length,

surrounded by silhouettes of himself in varied activities reflecting the life of his
fellow editors and politicians whom he loved to mock. His motto, "Stand up
to the rack, fodder or no fodder," was a challenge for plain dealing and integrity
rather than self-serving hypocrisy of the kind he saw motivating the likes of
Rufus Wilmot Griswold and the New York Historical Society, on the local level,
and a host of political posturers nationally and internationally. Dr. John-Donkey
offered his universal vegetable pill, in his advertisements, as the universal remedy
of the time. The pill offered was one which noted that the British for all their
pompous claims that they did not tolerate slavery imprisoned their children in
mines below ground. The attack was backed with doggerel verse and caricatures,
"Cartoons for the English House of Commons," which established the ass as
a thoughtful humanitarian.

In specific gibes, the *Donkey* could be sharply pointed, particularly toward
other members of the press, which he contended were eager to join in any
asininity. After noting that Edgar Allan Poe had been seen going up Broadway
making a study of guardrails, *The John-Donkey* returned some weeks later to
comment that Poe had been defended against *John-Donkey*'s implication of
drunkenness by a country paper—a worse humiliation than the original attack.
The Webster-Calhoun debates were burlesqued, and one of *John-Donkey*'s full-
page cartoons showed James K. Polk sucking eggs labeled Texas, Mexico, and
Cuba. Classing P. T. Barnum and R. W. Griswold together in their pursuit of
"Washington's Leather Breeches," *John-Donkey* brayed that both would fail in
their quest—"We have the breeches!" Griswold seemed to be singled out for
special abuse for his pompous posing. It considered Greeley a poor imitation of
Don Quixote and offered a serial burlesque of him in that role. The journal
thought William Lloyd Garrison a madman, but when a Boston paper sneered
at fallen soldiers in the Mexican War, *John-Donkey* defended them as committed
to their country, regardless of the cause.

National politics increasingly became *John-Donkey*'s focus. It showed
particular awareness of the issues surrounding American expansionism and trade
and money policies, although it generally burlesqued the proponents rather than
the issues. Thomas Hart Benton, Lewis Cass, James Buchanan, and James K.
Polk received special opprobrium in cartoons and texts. Boston as a cultural
center was equally obnoxious, and in its dying bray, *John-Donkey* promised that
if he rose from the flames, like a "funny-ass" he would return to his scorn of
Boston ladies like Eppie Sargeant (Mr. Epes Sargent of the Boston *Transcript*)
and others of type, male and female. If Boston was scorned, however, self-
serving hypocrisy was a target anywhere. A purposefully crude cartoon of
William Penn winking to his brother Quakers as he cheats the Indians, "Penn's
Treaty with the Indians," deserves special recognition for its use of inartistic
art to enhance its sarcasm. (One of the stick figure Indians thumbs his nose in
the near background as the treaty is handed over.) *John-Donkey* attacked the
Boston papers for attacking New York and treating the rest of the United States
as an appendage of eastern Massachusetts; their provincialism, he claimed,

described the Puritans' cant, hypocrisy, and thievery as if it was pure religion, manly action, and justice. In "Dialogues of the Dead—No. 1" he has Charon musing that the "D——dYankees" were negotiating with him to trade his ferry for a steamboat after selling a load of high-grade coal to Pluto for hell-fires and renaming Proserpina's villa "The American Hotel." The Yankees threatened if he didn't negotiate that they would "annex these regions to the United States" in the manner of jingoistic warriors eyeing Mexico and the Caribbean.

An impressive humanist perspective runs throughout the comedy of *John-Donkey*. The paper opposed hanging and satirized the barbaric act. It hated the exploitation of child labor, or of any laborer, but was willing to see laborers and immigrants as boors also. With regard to British critiques of American kindness in warfare with the Mexicans, it commented that such so-called American stupidity was more humane than the savagery practiced by the British and French in killing off the women and children of surrendering opponents. Its bold sarcasm was oriented toward bettering the human condition in the best and most visionary sense, and few other humor magazines so consistently presented their viewpoint in comic and burlesque commentary on contemporary events.

Although *The John-Donkey* was brilliant, its life was short. The first issue, edited by Thomas Dunn English and George G. Foster, both talented comic editors, came out on 1 January 1848; it brayed its last on 21 October with Volume 2:17. G. B. Zieber in Philadelphia and George Dexter in New York were the publishers, and the orientation of *John-Donkey* seemed almost as much toward New York as to Philadelphia and Pennsylvania, its apparent primary home. In its 7½" × 11" format, it sold for six cents, three dollars per year in advance. Each issue offered a page of advertisements, four or five pages of comic text, and a cartoon printed on a full page with a blank page backing it, followed by one or two more pages of advertisements. C. A. Hinckley and F.O.C. Darley provided the engravings. In May, *John-Donkey* reported that seven libel suits had been filed against it, and it seems likely that intense legal pressure forced it out of existence. Special issues appeared for 1 April and 4 July.

Information Sources

BIBLIOGRAPHY:

Mott, Frank L. *A History of American Magazines 1741–1850*. Cambridge, Mass.: Harvard University Press, 1938, 1:780–83, and passim.

Smyth, A. H. *Philadelphia Magazines and Their Contributors*. Philadelphia: Robert M. Lindsay, 1892.

INDEX SOURCES: None.

REPRINT EDITIONS: University Microfilms.

LOCATION SOURCES: CtY, MH, MB, PP, and ten other libraries list holdings.

Publication History

MAGAZINE TITLE AND TITLE CHANGES: *The John-Donkey*.

VOLUME AND ISSUE DATA: Volume 1:1, 1 January 1848–Volume 2:17, 21 October 1848.

PUBLISHER AND PLACE OF PUBLICATION: G. B. Zieber, Philadelphia; George
     Dexter, New York.
EDITORS: Thomas Dunn English and George G. Foster.
CIRCULATION: 12,000.

David E. E. Sloane

THE JOLLY JOKER

In 1899, celebrating the three-month anniversary of the New Orleans *Jolly Joker*,
the editor Edwin D. Elliott pledged to "make it worthy the patronage of every
Southern person who believes in home enterprise." At that time he seemed to
have launched a successful venture. He claimed to be making a profit already
and boasted of gaining 367 subscribers—many from Alexandria and Shreveport,
Louisiana, which his agent had visited—since the previous semi-monthly issue.
Before the end of the year *The Jolly Joker* became a weekly.

Apparently, the public agreed with Elliott that a magazine double the size but
half the price of *Puck** or *Judge** was worth purchasing, but their decision may
well have been based more on its regional sympathies than on the quality of the
humorous material. In the editorial columns, Elliott called for the development
of Southern business and industry and supported New Orleans civic
improvements. Despite the claim that the weekly was nonpolitical, Elliott
encouraged Southerners to remain with the regular Democratic party rather than
form self-defeating factions, and he objected to William McKinley's policies,
which offended Southern sensibilities. When he briefly adopted Sidney Storey
as co-editor in January 1900, the regional focus widened. A one-page "Land
Department" carried advertisements for real estate in Louisiana and Mississippi
but offered to list "properties for sale throughout our Southern States." The
editors asked correspondents to send them news "from every town in the South."

Hoping to boost circulation to 10,000, Elliott and Storey announced a
subscription contest. They also began to include opera and theater notices, news
about New Orleans civic clubs, household hints, and moral instruction for
employees, husbands, wives, and children—all to make theirs "an interesting,
clean family paper which will be acceptable in every respectable home." The
new life lasted only a few weeks. Extant issues following Storey's departure
show that Elliott greatly increased the number of reprinted humorous items.
Either he had to rely on these as filler since he was without Storey's assistance,
or he hoped this change would gain subscribers to offset the magazine's unsound
financial condition. Although *The Jolly Joker* was published for at least fourteen
months, Elliott ultimately found the New South insufficiently interested in
supporting its own regional humorous magazine.

Relatively little of the humorous material reflects the regional editorial policy,
and little is original. In addition to frequent anecdotes about life in New Orleans,
there are occasional jokes about Confederate soldiers or about Blacks. Only
rarely is one of the many reprinted humorous items attributed to a Southern

newspaper. An original cartoon—almost always political—fills the front page of each issue, some commenting on New Orleans civic problems, as do smaller cartoons on inside pages. Just as many poke fun at the English in the Boer War; other original cartoons condemn McKinley's policy in the Philippines. Henry G. Grelle, an artist for the *New Orleans Item*, is the most frequent contributor of such drawings. Only one of the photographs which appeared from time to time is humorous, and that is an example of racist humor. Despite requests for original contributions, only one signed article in the available issues was written for the magazine. Entitled "A Woman Hater" by Vic. J. S., it recounts a situation reminiscent of William Tappan Thompson's well-known "Major Jones Pops the Question."

Reprinted cartoons and jokes provide most of the humor in *The Jolly Joker*. Each extant issue in the first volume contains thirty to fifty small cartoons about general, nonpolitical subjects. In contrast, the first issue which Storey co-edited has only one. The number quickly rises to between ten and twenty in the following issues. *Ally Sloper*, *Judy*, the *New York Journal*, and the *New York World* are frequently cited sources. Most issues also carry cartoons with English captions that are credited to such German-language periodicals as *Fliegende Blätter*, *Heitere Welt*, and *Humoristische Blätter*. One political cartoon shows "the French view of the Boer War," but no other material is identified as French, despite the influence of French culture in New Orleans.

The Jolly Joker's reprinted short jokes, riddles, and puns are all nonpolitical. These pieces from acknowledged and unacknowledged newspapers and humorous magazines appear on almost every page of the first volume. Beginning with the second volume, most are placed together as "Humorous Squibs." An "Irish Wit" column—the only attempt to classify material by subject—appears infrequently. Through Volume 2:6, the total of these miscellaneous items per issue varies between thirty-five and forty-five. In the two latest available issues—those after Storey's departure as co-editor—the totals increase sharply to sixty and then to over one hundred.

Although *The Jolly Joker* always sold for five cents per copy, the annual subscription price rose from $1.50 to two dollars when Storey became co-editor. No change had occurred several months earlier when the magazine's frequency increased from semi-monthly to weekly. After Storey left, Elliott returned the magazine to its original price to attract needed subscribers. The pages measure 25 cm × 34½ cm and vary in number from twelve to twenty per issue.

Information Sources

INDEX SOURCES: None.
REPRINT EDITIONS: None.
LOCATION SOURCES: Howard-Tilton Memorial Library, Tulane University: Only scattered issues; Volume 1:2 (15 January 1899), 6 (1 April), 16 (1 September), 22
  (6 November); Volume 2:3 (13 January 1900), 5 (27 January), 6 (3 February), 8
  (17 February), 9 (24 February).

Publication History

MAGAZINE TITLE AND TITLE CHANGES: *The Jolly Joker, an Independent, Up-to-Date Humorous Journal.*

VOLUME AND ISSUE DATA: Annual volumes; semi-monthly from January 1899 through at least Volume 1:16; weekly by Volume 1:22; life span is unknown because the first and last issues are not extant; 24 February 1900 (Vol. 2:9) last issue seen.

PUBLISHER AND PLACE OF PUBLICATION: Edwin D. Elliott, New Orleans.

EDITOR: Edwin D. Elliott; briefly joined by Sidney Storey as co-editor (beginning with Volume 2:3, and ending by Volume 2:8).

CIRCULATION: Unknown; the editors requested "correspondents to send us items of news from every town in the South."

David C. Estes

JUBILEE DAYS

Edited by William Dean Howells and Thomas Bailey Aldrich, with illustrations by Augustus Hoppin, *Jubilee Days* was a collection of short essays, comic gossip, jokes, bright remarks, humorous poems, and cartoons which provided daily comment on the "World's Peace Jubilee and International Music Festival," held in Boston from 17 June to 4 July 1872. At the time of its publication, the *Boston Globe* declared *Jubilee Days*, "bright and readable," its "whole tone . . . light airy, pointed and graceful." Just as pertinent is the report of a New York paper that copies of the comic paper made a significant contribution to the litter swept up at the end of each festival day. Despite the talents and accomplishments of its contributors, the favorable reactions of contemporary readers, and the real virtues of the paper, it was only moderately successful at realizing the comic potential of the truly fantastic event of which it was a part.

The Peace Jubilee was the creation of Patrick Sarsfield Gilmore, an Irish immigrant who became one of the nation's leading bandmasters during the 1850s and first established the military band as a legitimate indoor concert entity. In 1869, Gilmore staged a musical jubilee in Boston to celebrate the dawning of national peace, gathering a 1,000-piece orchestra for the event. In 1871, when the United States and Great Britain signed the Treaty of Washington, Gilmore undertook the production of an even greater event. For the World's Peace Jubilee and International Music Festival, a colosseum seating 100,000 people was built and an orchestra of 2,000 players and a chorus of 20,000 singers were gathered.

The Jubilee was an event of national interest. New York papers published daily accounts of both musical events and the doings outside the colosseum where crowds were entertained by religious services, minstrel shows, "relicts of the Chicago fire," shooting galleries, a whirligig, a hot air balloon ride, and "hundreds of lager beer stands." New York coverage was generally rude; the *Herald* referred to the festival as a "huge Celtic joke" unequaled since the South Sea Bubble, "the Great Musical Panjandrum," "Boston Buncome," "Gilmore's

Babel.'' Sarcastic reporting increased as the festival failed to fulfill its backers' hopes.

Jubilee Days, the creation of James R. Osgood, a leading Boston publisher and proprietor of the *Atlantic Monthly*, appeared every day except Sunday between 17 June and 4 July 1872 for a total of sixteen issues. According to Thomas Bailey Alrich, the paper was a "moderate" financial success and was reprinted in a bound volume after the Jubilee ended. The price was ten cents a copy; the first number announced the availability of subscriptions. In format, *Jubilee Days* consisted of four pages measuring 7¾" × 11⅛" printed on a single folded sheet. The first and third pages were taken up by full-page Augustus Hoppin cartoons. The second and fourth pages were three columns each. The second page carried two to two and one-half columns of editorial matter; the remainder of the third column consisted of small advertisements. The fourth page of each issue contained a small Hoppin cartoon with two columns of text below it. The third column on the page was advertisements. The tenth number contained an inserted two-page illustration of the Jubilee Ball; the third page substituted text for its usual cartoon.

The writing of *Jubilee Days* was required to fit into a similarly rigid pattern. Each issue began with one to two columns of genial and relatively polite informal essays. Topics included the concerts or related Jubilee matters like items swept up by the "broomists," beer selling, press coverage—particularly in the New York papers, the American Marine Band's inferiority to European military bands, or the balloon ride. Some essays wandered off into considerations of American tourists in Europe, New York reviews of Charles Dudley Warner's books, and Horace Greeley. The essays were usually followed by an "Etc." column of short quips and bright remarks. "Etc." went beyond festival matters and, in addition to remarks on the "Anvil Chorus" and absentee critics who wrote reviews of concerts they did not attend, also commented on who was or was not attending the Jubilee, negativism in the New York papers, international events, and information found in European magazines. Scattered among its columns were brief observations on the Pope, the Paris Commune, Clarence King's *Mountaineering in the Sierras*, Dr. Mary Walker—America's first woman doctor—and Horace Greeley. A few comic poems appeared between "Etc." and the regular "Personals" feature. Both a social column and a parody, "Personals" commented on who would and ought to attend the Jubilee, and on New York critics, Greeley again, and a Black woman lawyer who had begun practicing in Washington, D.C.

The editors of *Jubilee Days*, Howells and Aldrich, were regular employees of Osgood. Howells was in his first year as editor of the *Atlantic*, and Aldrich, who had published several volumes of verse and *The Story of a Bad Boy*, was editor of Osgood's *Every Saturday*. One item suggests that friends and colleagues like Mark Twain, Bret Harte, and Charles Dudley Warner contributed, but Howells and Aldrich probably wrote most of the paper themselves. Aldrich said that his contributions measured seventeen and a half feet when measured with a piece of string. The opening essays were probably by Howells, with Aldrich handling "Etc.," "Personals," and the humorous poems.

Augustus Hoppin's drawings were the most notable feature of the paper. Hoppin had worked for *Young America*, said to be the first American rival to *Punch*, and for its successor *Yankee Notions*.* He was a regular illustrator for *Putnam's* and *Harper's Weekly* and books including Benjamin Shillaber's Partington works, from which he borrowed "Ike" for a *Jubilee Days* drawing. A publisher's note at the front of the bound edition calls Hoppin's contributions a pioneering step in illustrated daily journalism. His three daily pictures were engraved in three hours by the Chemical Engraving Company. Of varying quality in inspiration and execution, they touch on the great drum and pipe organ, the massed "Anvil Chorus," Professor Allen's balloon ride, late arrivals to the festival, the scarcity of lodging in Boston, and the amount of beer drunk at the Jubilee. Patrick Gilmore is celebrated in one of several cartoons treating him as Hercules completing his labors. Scoffers of the "outland" press are also attacked. The dominant motif of the drawings during the last week is fatigue, with the last showing the artist sprawled at his desk.

Jubilee Days was an amusing but restrained comic paper. Because of its authors' taste and the defensive posture they were forced into by outside criticism of the extravaganza, they did not do comic justice to the World's Peace Jubilee and International Music Festival. The final word is Mark Twain's, who said of the National Peace Jubilee that it was "an unintentional but complete, symmetrical and enormous burlesque which shamed the poor inventions of the sketchers and scribblers who tried to be funny over it in magazines and newspapers," words equally true of its international follower.

Information Sources

BIBLIOGRAPHY:
"Augustus Hoppin." *National Cyclopedia of American Biography.* New York: James T. White, 1907, 9:483.
Greenslet, Ferris. *The Life of Thomas Bailey Aldrich.* Boston: Houghton Mifflin, 1908, pp. 191–92.
Mott, Frank L. *A History of American Magazines, 1865–1885.* Cambridge, Mass.: Harvard University Press, 1938, 3:266.
New York Herald. 18 June–5 July 1872.
New York Tribune. 18 June–5 July 1872.
"Patrick Sarsfield Gilmore." *National Cyclopedia of American Biography.* New York: James T. White, 1907, 3:292–293.
Twain, Mark. "Memoranda." *The Galaxy*, 10 (July 1870): 137.
INDEX SOURCES: None.
REPRINT EDITIONS: None.
LOCATION SOURCES: DLC, ICN, MWA, RPB, and roughly twenty other locations.

Publication History

MAGAZINE TITLE AND TITLE CHANGES: *Jubilee Days*.
VOLUME AND ISSUE DATA: Daily, Volume 1:1 to Volume 1:16, 17 June to 4 July 1872.
PUBLISHER AND PLACE OF PUBLICATION: James R. Osgood, Boston.
EDITORS: Thomas Bailey Aldrich and William Dean Howells.
CIRCULATION: Unknown.

Michael D. Butler

JUDGE

Judge began in 1881 when a group of cartoonists led by James Albert Wales at *Puck**, the successful humor magazine launched in 1877, seceded to found what they hoped to be an even greater success. Several contributors were already well-established cartoonists, including Thomas Worth, who had done the "Darktown" Negro travesties for Currier and Ives, and Livingston Hopkins and Frank Beard, both seasoned writers and artists.[1] The magazine mixed harsh editorial diatribes, satirical cartoons, ethnic and politically topical jokes, and assorted doggerel in order both to enlighten and to entertain its readers. The new venture seldom matched its longer established rival in verbal wit and imaginative satire, but it often outshown *Puck* in cartoon art. At first the magazine flourished; later, its fortunes fluctuated in the highly competitive humor magazine market. However, it outdistanced *Life** before the century was out and by 1912 sprinted ahead of *Puck*. *Judge* hit its stride during the 1920s and early 1930s but faded in the late 1930s, lingering on obscurely until 1949.

On 29 October 1881, *Judge* first appeared as *The Judge*, a sixteen-page quarto with full-page chromolithograph front and back covers and center spread; it sold for ten cents. It featured tri-columns tightly packed with short paragraphs of "judgments" attacking New York politicians, followed by Aesop-like "Fables," which were really only more political comment thinly disguised with a concluding "moral," "Conundrums," which were only loaded questions designed to tease gossip-searching readers, and mock "Proverbs" loosely in the style of Poor Richard. Filler was supplied by "Our Popular Farces," "Our Cards Received," and "Whiffs and Correspondents." These features were interspersed with assorted doggerel and cartoons, most of them keyed to a two-character dialogue with punch line—the "Pat and Mike" format that the magazine did much to popularize. The last two pages were reserved for ads; later, ads would fill up the first two pages as well.

The magazine, like *Puck*, followed the example of *Punch* by adopting a resident comic overseer—"The Judge," a smirking Falstaffian figure in black robe and specs who, on the inside cover, peered down on the world from a lofty court bench. "I have started this paper for fun," announced "The Judge" in the first issue; "money is no object" (p. 2). The 7 April 1883 issue added that he would dedicate the magazine to the best quality and to good taste: "It is the Judge's ambition to live abreast of the present age, or ahead of it, . . . to be independent in thought and action, to employ the very best American literature and artistic talent, and to make a comic periodical which no gentleman will be ashamed to read in the family circle" (p. 2). While the many short features supplied the fun, "The Judge" himself supplied the stern disapproval, with harsh, sometimes cantankerous opinions on the corruptions and follies of the day. Despite his puckish grin, he wielded a heavy gavel and was often given to sweeping denunciations sent down from on high. On 14 April 1881, "The Judge" demanded that President Chester Alan Arthur fire his entire cabinet (p. 2). In the occasional feature "Judge at the Play," he aggressively assumed the role of cultural arbiter and delivered rather severe indictments (and occasional praise) of current New York productions. He was more severe on the "foreign element" then crowding into New York, and he enjoyed posing as a patriotic Irish-American playing to Anglo xenophobia among his readers. In "Jews in Congress" (20 January 1883), he was openly anti-Semitic. Mixed in with such harangues were celebrations, such as one about the completion of the Brooklyn Bridge (26 May 1883) in which "The Judge" recounted walking across the new span and savoring the commuter's independence from ferry boats (p. 2). He could also temper acerbity with engagingly irascible wit, as when he savaged the American tourist abroad:

[He] goes about Europe with a drawn revolver, making hotel clerks and others get down on their knees and beg his pardon. He is a bully and . . . smells of whisky and is voluble with a course and forbidding mouth: It is the scream of the eagle with a new and a more objectionable loudness than the original one (11 October 1890, p. 2).

While the writers strove for wit, and often succeeded, the cartoonists carried the magazine's political points most memorably, with brightly colored full-page chromos that quickly became *Judge*'s most accomplished feature. *Judge* cartoons centered on vivid caricatures of well-known local, state, or national politicians. Stilted in pose, they were surrounded by elaborately filled-in backgrounds, with their crime or folly allegorically marked. The satirical point was seldom subtle, but the artwork was always ambitious and often visually stunning. The cover of the first issue by J. A. Wales showed "Two Political Dominos," the Democratic and Republican parties, leaning against their party headquarters, each posted with a notice: "No Bosses." Early cartoon targets were President Ulysses S. Grant, Samuel Tilden, Charles Dana, Robert G. Ingersoll, and Grover Cleveland, with frequent assaults on bossism, especially at Tammany Hall. The great Blaine-Cleveland contest of 1884 gave sharp focus to inspired caricature. The Republican party found humor magazines useful to its own political fortunes. The party managed to force a reorganization of the Judge Company under a new editor, Isaac M. Gregory, who had been editor of the Republican-oriented *Elmira Ga-*

zette and Free Press. He hired away from *Puck* three more of its chief cartoonists: Bernard Gillam, Eugene Zimmerman, and Grant Hamilton, the last of whom stayed with *Judge* for over twenty-five years, serving for many years as its art editor.[2]

The Republican party had made a shrewd investment; *Judge* therefore abandoned its vaunted "independence" and instead stood staunchly for "the party of 1860," frequently reiterating its support for Republican party principles and especially championing "protection" and "prosperity." Decisive in the election of William McKinley in 1896 was Grant Hamilton's "full dinner pail" series, which became a Republican campaign logo and later a theme and even a campaign symbol touting both magazine and the Republican party well into the Roosevelt and Taft administrations. The Free Silver position of McKinley's opponent, William Jennings Bryan, was the target of much editorial ridicule; caricaturists frequently clowned with his giant head and grimly pious demeanor. In return for its support of the winning party, *Judge* enjoyed a boom in advertising and circulation, which rose to 50,000 and then to 85,000 after the McKinley campaign of 1896.[3] By 1900, "The Judge" had acquired a jester's mace and a companion (an owl), as well as regal fur-lined robes that made him look like one of the "bosses" the cartoonists enjoyed caricaturing.

In the new century, chromolithograph political cartoons continued to be the magazine's best feature. New artists included E. Flohri, Art Young, "Gus" Dirks, and James Montgomery Flagg. Black and white cartoons abounded, with "Pat and Mike" dialogue underneath, usually aimed at women, Blacks, and immigrants. Ethnic humor, since it depended mostly on malapropisms, was designed to be both entertaining and satirical. A recurring joke featured lower class Irish workers at a construction site:

> *Sucey*—"Th' men shtruck fer an increase at twinty cints a day."
>
> *Callahan*—"An' did yez git it?"
>
> *Ducey*—"We did. Th' boss put in twinty dagoes wid scints that wud knock ye down" (15 December 1900, unpaged).

In addition to such jokes, the cartoonists in black and white and the versifiers followed the middle class to the suburbs, recording their mishaps and foibles with gently mocking jibes.

In 1909 the publishing company of the magazine was reorganized as the Leslie-Judge Company, and its Republican party partnership was dissolved.[4] Editorially, the magazine remained staunchly middle-of-the-road Republican, standing for "adequate protection to home industry, for money based on the gold standard, and for fair, honest treatment for labor and capital alike" (29 October 1910, unpaged). But the sometimes strident partisanship became less pronounced as the magazine, under a new editor, James M. Lee, strove to return to its earlier independent position. Lee wished to serve the cultural tastes of a wider readership as well as the artistic needs of his contributors. He introduced many nonpolitical features such as "Judge's Women's Department," a parody of the *Perfect Ladies' Companion*; "Not According to Webster's," a new feature devoted to puns and word play; and "Cap and Gown Similes," featuring parodies of popular poets such as Edwin Markham. While the color cartoonists continued to attack corrupt public officials, other contributors concentrated on mocking social strivers and pretenders to cultural eminence. In "Poets," for example, W. B. Kerr defined the "near-poets,"—a species to be found weekly in *Judge*'s own pages—with memorable wit:

> The near poet is born with the inclination of a poet and the disposition of a parrot, and writes poetry by the simplified method. He hasn't any license to be a poet, but he takes more poetic licenses than any other kind. A real poet can write poetry that others cannot understand, but the near-poet perpetuates rhymes he himself doesn't understand (9 October 1909, unpaged).

Other signs that the magazine was turning away from Republican partisanship were its theme issues—not politically topical but socially seasonal ones: "Midsummer," "Christmas," and "Cracker" (i.e., Independence Day) as well as special "Numbers" like "Summer Girl." Such general humor appealed to popular taste and to advertisers. Lee also inaugurated the "Prize Picture Puzzle Contest," which was calculated to boost circulation, and "The Caricature Series," which sought to attract new talent among art students throughout the country. Among new contributors was versifier Carolyn Wells; Albert Bigelow Paine, Twain's biographer, contributed quatrains. Homer Croy wrote a feature, "Watching Our Funny World Go By," and John Kendrick Bangs, well-known humorist who had helped to found *Life*,* the rival humor magazine, also made frequent appearances. Henry James made a few contributions, one of which was prose doggerel, "Clearing Up the Mystery" (30 October 1909), examining whether Cook or Peary discovered the North Pole:

> Each explorer got some sledges, skimmed the edges, as he followed out his quest. But who got there and who faltered, who was ernest and who altered . . . who by frozen chains was haltered, is the theme discussed with zest. Some try for prizes polar get it in the plexus (solar) or surprise the willing molar with a chunk that can't be chewed. We don't know who's had this sorrow; maybe we shall know to-morrow, and of trouble we won't borrow, by assertions bald and rude (unpaged).

Around 1910 *Judge* changed its format from aggressive political satire and "funny" ethnic jokes to learned parody, urbane wit, and slicker advertising that would appeal to an increasingly urban and suburban readership. The stark, simplistic allegorical cartoons of Hamilton and Gillam seemed old-fashioned in the new century and gave way to the more romantic, often erotic, illustrations drawn by Flagg and his imitators, Albert Hencke and Edna Crompton. Flagg's covers featured voluptuous beauties bathed in soft pastels; they represented a new sophistication in magazine art that would later become a distinguishing mark of *Vanity Fair** and *The New Yorker.** Inside, the short jabbing paragraphs of political comment were replaced by romantic vignettes and short stories which dealt primarily with the perils of courtship suffered by urbanites with whom the readership could identify. J. A. Waldron contributed many pieces such as "Idle Conversation" (11 April 1914) about two college girls who seek adventures denied to the preceding generation, insisting that "we women are going to be real people before we become grandmothers" (unpaged). In "Her Love Cure," by Jane Vivian (17 January 1914), a matchable man learns to love high-brow culture when a beautiful millionaire girlfriend of his sister's takes an interest in him. These stories doted on current social fashions as well as reflecting changing moral attitudes; they often catered to the desires and fantasies of the magazine's acquisitive, upward-bound middle-class readers. New features included "The Modern Woman" by Ida Husted Harper and "The Speed Fiend" by Walt Mason; Mason paid weekly homage to that perilous new invention, the automobile.

Editorially, "The Judge" continued to strike with a heavy gavel, widening his authority to include a "judging" section on the "motion picture" by 1914. Generally, however, the magazine was moving closer to adopting the values of the upper and middle-class readers which its contributors hoped to reach. While it had once vigilantly defended the eternal verities of family life and railed against divorce, "The Divorcee's Dictionary" (2 July 1910) advocated free choice, with the writer mildly disdainful of both marriage and divorce. On the brink of World War I, the reformer's zeal so assiduously nurtured during the magazine's first quarter century largely evaporated. In 1914, even "The Judge" himself inexplicably vanished, and the magazine's surrender to fashionable wit and humor was complete.

The war years offered obliging satirical topics for editorialists, such as Kaiser Wilhelm but the prevailing comic tone was announced in the magazine's new subtitle: "The Nation's Perpetual Smileage Book." Circulation continued to soar, rising to 250,000 by 1923, when the price was increased to fifteen cents. In 1922, *Judge* merged with *Leslie's Weekly* under a new publisher, Douglas H. Cooke, and a new editor, Norman Anthony, then a freelance artist.[5] Anthony compartmentalized the magazine, adding many new short features, such as Dogs, Yanks, Wheezes, Lawyers, Food, On the Farm, and Matrimony, among others. Editorially, Anthony supported mainline Republicanism, backing Coolidge, attacking "bossism," and urging repeal of Prohibition. He added more "smileage" with humor gleaned from campus humor magazines, crossword puzzles, more contests, and increased space for black and white cartoons, many featuring "Mabel and Madge," a pair of dim-witted urban single girls, who, like "Pat and Mike," fell comically into malapropisms. Typical is one frame showing the two long-legged beauties commenting on an eligible young man who has just passed by:

Mabel—"Is he on the football team?"

Madge—"Oh, yes! He's some kind of a drawback."

(23 August 1923, p. 24)

Anthony also introduced "High Hat" by "Judge, Jr.," a rakish man-about-town who commented impudently about current New York shows and nightclubs; illustrations were by Jefferson Machamer. The feature anticipated the more refined, more restrained "Talk of the Town" feature of the rival *New Yorker* (founded in 1925). Indeed, Anthony completed the magazine's metamorphosis into a polished, high-toned magazine of fashionable and topical wit and fashion ads. "The World's Wittiest Weekly," beamed the cover of 29 March 1924—pitched to an urbane city-bred audience. *Judge* contributors enjoyed parodying *New Yorker* writers, such as "Porothy Darker," and in the 23 October 1926 issue, contributors parodied *Vanity Fair* with "In Anity Fair." The most polished piece was "Cloudburst," a poem by Edna St. Vincent Oleolay:

> Skies darken,
> Thunder
> Peals in the distance,
> Streaks of lightning
> Rip the heaven,
> A drop of water
> Splashes
> Against my cheek
> It looks like—
> Rain. (p. 7)

During the twenties, *Judge* hit its stride with accomplished, well-balanced features written by a wide variety of stylists. Feature writers included Stephen Leacock, Walter Trumbull, Kenneth Roberts, and Stephen Vincent Benet. New artists included the veteran Gellett Burgess of *Lark** fame, Oliver Herford, Gardiner Rea, John Held, Jr., Harry Grant Dart, Theodore Geisel (Dr. Seuss), and Ralph Barton. Heywood Broun edited a sports column; Walter Prichard Eaton wrote capsule book reviews; radio and the automobile were covered in a chatty manner by various hands. George Mitchell surveyed Hollywood regularly, but with little "judgment" of current movies, doting instead on gossip about current movie personalities. "The Judge's" gavel was passed to George Jean Nathan who contributed an acerbic "Judgment of the Shows" column from 1922 to 1935. William Norris Houghton, and then Pare Lorentz, wrote "Judging the Movies" during the same period, with Lorentz rivalling Nathan as an incisive critic of popular entertainment. "The Judge" himself reappeared in 1923 behind his high bench and resumed his editorial duties.

During this fertile period, one of *Judge*'s zaniest writers was S. J. Perelman, a recent Brown graduate whom Norman Anthony had hired in 1925 to contribute cartoons. The cartoons were unmemorable, but Perelman's knack for funny names was already well practiced—"Pierre de la Matzos," a wife named "Dementia"—as were his puns, which seemed to overshadow the usually thin story lines. In "Are You a Good Skate?" (28 July 1928), Perelman spun a mock history of "the finny sport" (p. 18), while in "Perelman's Children's Weekend

Guide,'' a mock outdoorsman recommended swordfishing, of which there are two kinds: ''(a) sabres and (b) rapiers, and it is certainly a glorious feeling to sail in from the sword grounds in your creel stuffed with good fat swords and the knowledge that 'to the victor belong the foils' '' (p. 31). Many of these sketches were collected in Perelman's first book, *Dawn Ginsbergh's Revenge* (1929). Perelman left *Judge* in 1929 to go to Hollywood and returned a celebrity when, in 1935, he appeared, perhaps as a jest, in a Dole Pineapple Juice ad in the magazine, touted as the ''famous humorist and Paramount Studios writer.''

The Great Depression devastated the humor market. *Judge* had to lower its price to a dime to increase circulation; but the remedy failed. The magazine became a monthly in July 1932 at fifteen cents.[6] Established features survived, notably, ''Judge at the Bench,'' ''High Hat,'' and the ''Judging'' sections. They were now handled by new writers—Ted Shane on books, Rex Deane on sports, and later Dana Gale replacing Nathan on drama. Pare Lorentz continued to judge Hollywood fashions uncompromisingly and crusaded for sober realism in the movies which would be more reflective of the hard realities of the time. He also campaigned against censorship, taking on Will Hays and the producers in their efforts to stiffen the audience viewing code. Dr. Seuss drew cartoons and an occasional cover. Other cartoonists included Colin Allen and Rodlow Willard, as well as *New Yorker* staffers William Steig and Whitney Darrow, Jr. Baird Leonard created ''Mistress Pepys' Journal,'' a masterful Pepys parody that mocked social-climbing gossips while serving their cause. Parke Cummings contributed ''Let's Put It This Way,'' a humor column about the current state of English. The genial banter of these features was offset by sober pages devoted to ''How Good Is Your Bridge Game?'' by Sidney Lenz. The popularity of this feature prompted the inclusion of an ambitious series beginning in January 1933 called *Dial, a Monthly Magazine of Contract Bridge*, edited by Philip Hal Sims, a thick insert supplanting Lenz's column. Percy Crosby began ''Knuckles and Feathers'' in 1932, a combative, Mencken-like column in which he fought for liberal and pro-Roosevelt causes. Later, Crosby's ''Skippy Dialogues'' featured a smart-alecky, streetwise fifth grader who, like an urban Huck Finn, provided an innocent, unvarnished view of adult foibles and hypocrisies. In ''Radio— and What to Do About It,'' Don Herald took on Father Joseph Coughlin and often delivered sharp remarks about politics and the media:

No longer will cigar-chewing small-time, behind-the-scenes, machine politicians meet in hotel rooms and burn holes in the rug and leave bottle rings on the dresser top and choose pasty-faced nincompoops for high public office. From now on, we're going to do our own judging, and the judging is going to be done largely on the basis of radio showmanship (January 1937, p. 21).

As the thirties waned, several of these contributors were *Life* staffers who came over to *Judge* after that humor magazine ceased publication in 1936 and *Judge* bought the subscription lists and features. ''*Judge* has only one serious mission in life,'' insisted the editors in the November 1936 issue, ''that of converting folks to fun'' (p. 28). The merger ought to have doubled the fun; instead, it shrank, reduced to old formula cartoons, much bland chatter, and fewer judgments. ''The Judge'' himself disappeared once again, perhaps a casualty of the renewed policy stressing humor to lighten spirits during increasingly grim times. A few new features strained to be provocatively denunciatory, only to sound merely abusive. In a monthly feature, ''God Forgive Me. . . . '' A. D. Rothman, under the guise of candor implied by his title, vented his prejudices, singling out women who presumed to seek careers outside their proper sphere. His misogynist wit prompted many replies by women who sometimes wittily unmasked male hypocrisies without really disturbing prevailing social views. As the Depression worsened, *Judge* cloaked its cynicism and maintained a smiling face.

That elusive comic overseer, ''The Judge'' himself, reappeared in 1937 along with a new publisher and editor, Harry Newman, former publisher of the journalists' trade paper, the *Fourth Estate*. He added the subtitle, ''The National Magazine of Humor, Politics and Satire,'' raised the price to twenty-five cents, and, in December 1938, switched to a larger format. He brought back ''name'' humorists such as former contributors Stephen Leacock and Carolyn Wells as well as F. P. Adams, Milt Gross, and even Fred Allen occasionally. Possibly Newman sought to move the magazine, which had once prided itself on being a critical outsider, closer to its hoped-for, yet diminishing, audience—older readers, more conservative, and certainly more politically influential. In his publisher's forum, ''The Senator at Large,'' Newman advocated centrist Republican positions on the rejuvenation of capitalism, but he also lectured, often pompously, the powerbrokers he purported to know intimately. The column assumed a large importance in the magazine but quickly degenerated into musings and oracular predictions. Newman apparently thought so well of his influence that he introduced the ''High Hat'' award, a kind of *Time* Man-of-the-Year imitation, given to distinguished Americans, from Howard Hughes to Norman Rockwell. ''The Judge'' himself found his smile again as the Depression lifted; he turned his attention more to crises abroad, with regular harangues against Hitler, particularly his anti-Semitic policies. The Falstaffian wit, who in the last century used to play up his Irish roots and rail against overly ambitious Jews, came in the late 1930s to the impassioned defense of another persecuted ''race.''

Newman's attempts to add patrician eminence to the magazine and to curry favor with the great could not, however, forestall *Judge*'s decline. It wasted away in 1939. In May 1941 *Judge* went back to the short format and became thinner on a bland diet of campus humor, cartoons, and anonymous contributions. Its collapse was perhaps best typified by the ''Judging the Movies'' feature, which degenerated into studio-produced quotations from the stars on the set. *Judge*'s glory years had passed, and so had its twilight. Another world war hastened its death, and afterwards distinguished cartoon and verbal wit and humor would survive and flourish mainly in higher toned, studiously higher brow magazines such as *Esquire** and *The New Yorker*.

Notes

1. Frank L. Mott, *A History of American Magazines*. Cambridge, Mass.: Harvard University Press, 1957, 3:552.

2. Ibid., p. 553.

3. In 1887, the Judge Company began *Judge's Library: A Monthly Magazine of Fun*,** which reached a circulation of 100,000 in 1898. It was retitled *The Magazine of Fun*** in 1913 and ended publication in June 1915. In 1893, the Judge Company began *Judge's Quarterly*, which reached a circulation of 60,000 in 1899 and continued publication until 1917 (Mott, *A History of American Magazines*, p. 554).

4. Mott, *A History of American Magazines*, p. 555.

5. Ibid.

6. Ibid., p. 556.

Information Sources

BIBLIOGRAPHY:

Anthony, Norman. *How to Grow Old Disgracefully*. New York: Duell, Sloan and Pearce, 1946.

Crosby, Percy L. *Dear Sooky*. New York: G. P. Putnam's Sons, 1929.

———. *Skippy: The Complete Compilation, 1925–1926*. Westport, Conn.: Hyperion Press [no date].

Flagg, James Montgomery. *Yours Truly, and One Hundred Other Original Drawings by Celebrated American Artists*. New York: Judge Co., 1908.

Meyer, Susan E. *James Montgomery Flagg*. New York: Watson Guptill, 1974.

Mott, Frank L. *A History of American Magazines*. 5 vols. Cambridge, Mass.: Harvard University Press, 1957.

Perelman, S. J. *The Last Laugh*. New York: Simon and Schuster, 1978.

Robinson, Jerry. *Skippy and Percy Crosby*. New York: Holt, Rinehart and Winston, 1978.

INDEX SOURCES: None.

REPRINT EDITIONS: University Microfilms.

LOCATION SOURCES: Approximately one hundred libraries list holdings.

Publication History

MAGAZINE TITLE AND TITLE CHANGES: *The Judge*, 1881–1885, 1938–1949; *Judge*, 1886–1937. Subtitles vary.

VOLUME AND ISSUE DATA: Volumes 1–177 (1881–1941); weekly, 1881–1931; monthly, 1932–1949. Volume 76 incorrectly published as Volume 75. October and November 1938 issues never published.

PUBLISHER AND PLACE OF PUBLICATION: 1881–1909: Judge Co. 1910–1917: Leslie-Judge Co.: 1927–1931: Judge Publishing Co. 1932–1949: Judge Magazine, Inc., New York.

EDITORS: J. A. Wales, 1881–1885; I. M. Gregory, 1886–1901; Henry Tyrrell, 1901–

1907; Burges Johnson, 1908; James Melvin Lee, 1909–1912; Carleton G. Garretson, 1912–1917; Douglas H. Cooke, 1922–1927; Norman Anthony, 1927–1928; Jack Shuttleworth, 1929–1936, 1937–1938; Monte Bourjaoly, 1936–1937; Robert T. Gebler, 1938–1939; and Harry Newman, 1937–1949.
CIRCULATION: 85,000, 1896; 250,000, 1923.

Thomas Grant

JUDY

On 28 November 1846, scarcely seven weeks after *Yankee Doodle** announced itself to New York readers in response to the need for a distinctively American satiric journal, Henry Grattan Plunkett brought out the first issue of *Judy*, with an identical format and an identical program. Although Judy, pictured on the cover as a dowdy and domesticated old maid, promised to eschew the "extravagances" and wild ways of her "husband," Punch, she and her journal clearly hoped to prosper in an imitation of the London *Punch*. The Irish-born Plunkett, who would earn a slender reputation as a poet and dramatist under the pseudonym H. P. Grattan, had himself been an early contributor to *Punch* before he immigrated to America. But the prospective imitators of *Punch* were legion in the United States throughout the nineteenth century. After eleven issues, *Judy*'s ownership changed hands; after thirteen weekly issues, *Judy* perished, a victim of unfortunate timing, fierce competition, and the inability to move beyond the style of her English model.

In many ways, *Judy* deserved a better fate. Although she adopted the same format as *Yankee Doodle*, with twelve double-columned pages measuring 9″ × 11¾″, throughout her run, she was more attractive, more professionally illustrated, and more confident of her editorial purpose. Early on, Plunkett announced *Judy*'s lofty goals: "Her intention is not the publication of a mere comic-almanac—a hash of broad humorous jests for the unthinking crowd. She has a much higher and worthier aim. . . . pointed wit, good-humored satire and well-directed ridicule." A later statement focuses on the satiric purpose which Plunkett had in mind: "It is Judy's province, good-naturedly, to correct all sorts of public abuses—to expose impudent assumption. . . . to tear the lion's skin from the carcass of the ass—to oppose oppression in every shape—defend the weak—sustain the poor—expose vice and promote the cause of virtue and morality."

With such an extravagant sense of her mission, *Judy* scarcely knew where to turn her corrective gaze first. Although her primary target, particularly in the full-page political cartoons, was the Mexican War, a single issue finds broadsides directed at President James K. Polk, General Zachary Taylor, Henry Clay, Daniel Webster, W. B. Astor, Horace Greeley, P. T. Barnum, the performance of Charles Kean as King John on the New York stage, a purported sequel to *The Leatherstocking Tales* by James Fenimore Cooper entitled "Worsted Garter," the "science" of phrenology, and assorted Whigs, Abolitionists, Nativists, Loco

Focos, and Shaking Quakers. *Judy*'s tone could occasionally be innocuous, as when she asserted that "a Kean desire to make money" would be the death of Shakespeare's fame. More often, she was acerbic in her attacks on offensive behavior. Of the Shakers, she insisted that "Nothing can be more positively outrageous to every feeling of decency and sense of propriety than the disgusting exhibition of those fanatical mountebanks." *Judy* poses, then, as the defender of a standard of taste, decency, and propriety, but so determined did she seem to be to castigate everyone, that she ultimately exerted her cankered muse effectively on no one.

Judy's weekly format remained remarkably consistent, considering that early on Plunkett must have begun to worry about circulation and the journal's inability to fill more than two pages of inexpensive advertising, while competitor *Yankee Doodle*'s more expensive advertisements always filled three or more pages. Readers were offered weekly "lectures" on Nature, Conscience, Prudence, or Happiness, which mocked the abstruse metaphysics of the Lyceum movement. Each week found "Chapters on Natural History," a continuation of the work of "Monsieur de Buffoon" on the American character. *Judy* mocked the aristocratic pretensions of her readers in "Advice to Young Men of Fashionable Habits: Showing the Proper Method of Using Walking Canes, Umbrellas and Half-Lighted Cigars." Each issue concluded with the "Medical Dictionary," a hodge-podge of terrible puns, mangled etymology, and dubious medical information: "OSSIFICATION (from *os*, a bone and *facio*, to make) The French Revolution was a grand Ossification, as it made BONY-PART." The pages of the journal were liberally sprinkled with unsigned sketches, brief songs, riddles, and puns.

But *Judy* offered her most vigorous satire each week when she turned her sights, as a struggling outsider, on the New York journalistic establishment. Her particular targets were Horace Greeley and his *Tribune*, and *Judy*'s primary competitor, *Yankee Doodle*, also published in the Tribune Building. The first issue offered "Intercepted Correspondence" in which "Doodle Doo" begs around town for "a joke or two" for his next number. Issue 3 informed her readers "that in order to moderate the pungency of soda water, the custom of labeling the bottles with an epigram or 'witty' paragraph from *Yankee Doodle* has been adopted." *Judy* expressed utter disbelief when *Yankee Doodle*'s mediocrity was expanded to a sixteen-page format, and she later published weekly epitaphs for it only days before her own extinction.

Never once did *Yankee Doodle* respond in print to any of the jibes of its less successful rival, and *Judy* could not long survive by printing satiric barbs which missed their mark. Ultimately, *Judy* was unable to secure her proposed stature as an American *Punch* because she was unable to generate any original or distinctively American humor. In the first issue, editor Plunkett asserted that "Judy, although of foreign birth, resolves to patronize native talent." But none of the thirteen issues contains signed material or any hint of the particular native talent who contributed to the journal. Moreover, the editor, in each of his columns, clings to the Latinate and highly artificial diction which he felt appropriate to a near relation of *Punch*. Although one feature, entitled "Negro Advice," feebly attempted a Black dialect, *Judy* was much too busy parodying Horace and Shakespeare to seek out American characters.

Judy's failure is instructive of the intensely competitive conditions of New York journalism in the mid-nineteenth century. The journal was unable to reach beyond the confines of New York culture to the various regions of the United States for her incidents and characters, and her version of New York cosmopolitanism was inadequate to attract the national circulation necessary for survival.

Information Sources

BIBLIOGRAPHY:
Mott, Frank L. *A History of American Magazines, 1741–1850*. New York: D. Appleton and Co. 1938, 1:425–26.
INDEX SOURCES: None.
REPRINT EDITIONS: University Microfilms.
LOCATION SOURCES: Complete holdings of *Judy* are available at CtY, NN, and IU.

Publication History

MAGAZINE TITLE AND TITLE CHANGES: *Judy*, 28 November 1846–20 February 1847.
VOLUME AND ISSUE DATA: Weekly, Volume 1:1–13.
PUBLISHER AND PLACE OF PUBLICATION: Burgess and Stringer, New York.
EDITOR: Henry Grattan Plunkett.
CIRCULATION: Unknown.

Lorne Fienberg

K

THE KANSAS KNOCKER: A JOURNAL FOR CRANKS

Short-lived but lively, *The Kansas Knocker* provided a forum for current and future Kansas politicians as well as a vehicle for the average citizen who wished to "knock" in 1900. A knock was usually a humorous criticism of some problem ranging from the sociopolitical to everyday domestic situations. The journal's motto, "Knock and things will come your way," was dramatized by Myron A. Waterman, the magazine's illustrator, who depicted a man knocking on a door labeled "Success." For fifteen cents per 3½" × 8¼" copy or half a dollar for the entire and only year of its existence, the reader of the *Knocker* might enjoy prominent writers in, and occasionally outside, the state giving vent to their pet peeves on national and regional issues. Turn-of-the-century Kansas, still a hotbed of Populist politics, provided a fertile setting for wide-ranging opinions both political and domestic.

Kansas Supreme Court Chief Frank Doster, a career Populist, set the tone for the magazine's contributors in its second issue when he pointedly stated: "I am a knocker by instinct and professionally. I am not satisfied with things. I don't like the existing order. Give me the raw material to work with and I can make a great deal better world than this." Among the targets for Doster's humorous complaint were the college student who "takes up too much room and make [*sic*] too much noise, and costs too much money" and the old men who plagued the efforts of recuiters for the Spanish-American War: "Old bald-headed relics of the Mexican and Civil War, . . . sans teeth, sans eyesight, sans sense, sans everything necessary for the arduous duties of a soldier." Doster singled out Confederate General Joseph Wheeler as particularly representative for his "pertinacious insistance on considering himself still alive and on earth instead of dead to all intents and purposes." Indeed, Doster, who frequently stated that "the rights of the user are paramount to the rights of the owner," was constantly defending himself, in the *Knocker* and elsewhere, against charges that he was a "radical socialist."

The *Knocker* invited writers to "choose their own subjects and knock as they see fit." Such notables as John J. Ingalls, William Allen White, Elbert Hubbard, Jerry Simpson, E. W. Howe, and Annie L. Diggs rapped back on a variety of topics, as befitted their political or personal perceptions at the time. Ingalls, from Atchison, served eighteen years as Republican state senator until his defeat in 1891 by Populist William A. Peffer of Topeka. When reporter J. F. Jarrell and state bank commissioner Myron Waterman planned a small quarterly magazine, they wrote to Ingalls, who was in the West, for a contribution. His classic "The Jesus Business" criticized self-righteous politicians in Topeka who were then praising the efforts of Dr. Charles Sheldon (author of the famous *In His Steps*), who edited the Topeka *Capital* paper for one week, in his judgment, "as Jesus would have run it." This initial contribution encouraged the editors' efforts, and Ingalls's use of the word "knock" in the first sentence of his article provided them with the name for their publication.

William Allen White, Emporia *Gazette* editor who wrote "What's the Matter with Kansas?" (a powerful attack against Populists whom he instructed to "raise more corn and less hell"), wrote "The Gentle Art of Knocking," which encouraged positive thinking in the state. White proposed a ten dollar fine to be levied on all "non-gentle" knockers. Jerry Simpson of Medicine Lodge, nicknamed "Sockless Jerry" during his victorious 1890 congressional campaign against a wealthy Republican foe, redefined his role as critic of the status quo in government in his "The Knocker Who Knocks on the Knocker." E. W. Howe, Atchison *Daily Globe* editor and author of *The Story of a Country Town* (1883), provided distinctive regional criticism befitting his nickname "The Squire of Potato Hill." Eugene Fitch Ware, known as "Ironquill" and author of the popular lines "And Dewey feel discouraged? I Dew not think we Dew!" from his poem "Dewey was the Morning" (1898), contributed a "Knock on Stepping Stones" to the July 1900 issue of the magazine. Elbert Hubbard, perhaps best known for his "A Message to Garcia" (1899) and editor of the *Philistine*,* contributed a typically esoteric piece titled "On Profane Swearing" to the October 1900 issue. Personal hygiene, education, and other mundane topics of the day were "knocked about" by a variety of other local writers.

Editors Jarrell, who also edited *The Red Ball* for the Santa Fe Railway Company, and Waterman, who earlier illustrated White's and Albert Bigelow Paine's *Rhymes by Two Friends* (1893), willingly experimented with the format of their magazine in an attempt to establish its readership. A twenty-five dollar prize was offered for the best knock, which would be published in the October 1900 issue. Contestants had to limit their knocks to less than 1,000 words. In keeping with the spirit of the event, the editors did not anticipate an entry from rival Colonel Marsh Murdock, editor of the Wichita *Eagle*, who "could not keep sentences within 100 words to save his life." Contest judges included Henry J. Allen, then secretary to Republican Governor Eugene Stanley and later governor himself from 1919 to 1923; Arthur Capper, editor of the Topeka *Mail & Breeze*, who would later serve as Republican governor from 1915 to 1919 and state senator for thirty years until 1949; and Charles Session, Kansas City *Journal* editor. John P. Fritts of Topeka won with his classic knock "A Week with the Woman 'Jiner,' " a diatribe in rural Kansas dialect against the activist women who joined many clubs and other causes. As a result, her family crumbled within seven days. Over four hundred entries came from across the state and as far as Guthrie, Oklahoma. They knocked the *Knocker* itself, campaign liars, bums, and women who complain endlessly about their "ailments and miseries."

The special experimental January 1901 issue, the final *Knocker*, featured a dozen knocks, all invited from female authors. Included were both editor Jarrell's wife and Governor Eugene Stanley's wife who wrote "Trials of a Housekeeper." The most distinguished female knocker was Annie L. Diggs of Topeka, the state librarian. Nicknamed "Little Annie," the five-foot, ninety-three-pound biographer of "sockless Jerry" Simpson spoke along with Mary Elizabeth Lease, who opposed White's pacifism and encouraged farmers to "raise less corn and more hell," on behalf of Populism, earlier in the decade. Mrs. Diggs composed a knock entitled "New Words and Books." The female knockers complained not about men, but about women who used their mothers as scapegoats, held afternoon tea receptions, nagged their husbands, and complained about their housework. Despite such spirited contributions, Volume 2 of the *Knocker* never appeared, the victim of limited readership and the editors' passing fancy. As a financial venture, *The Kansas Knocker* was a dismal failure with only a few hundred subscriptions and little advertising. However, as a Kansas literary venture the publication greatly increased the state's reputation. Nearly every daily newspaper in the United States printed Ingall's article, and several others were widely reprinted. One other article nearly led to a shooting.

Occasionally more vindictive than humorous, but always controversial, and attracting some of the area's sharpest wits, *The Kansas Knocker* provided a far less bloody forum for Republican and Populist antagonists than did the House of Representatives in 1893 when the parties clashed with fully armed sergeants-at-arms in addition to the governor's militia. Far from the conservative or tornado-plagued image frequently perpetuated about Kansas, the *Knocker* was generated by a colorful and tumultuous heritage.

Information Sources

BIBLIOGRAPHY:
Broadhead, Michael J. *Persevering Populist: The Life of Frank Doster*. Reno: University of Nevada Press, 1969, pp. 127–29.
Clanton, O. Gene. *Kansas Populism: Ideas and Men*. Lawrence: University Press of Kansas, 1969.
" 'Kansas Knocker' Lived Only One Year But 'Twas Potent While It Lasted." Topeka *Journal*, 14 April 1928.
Richmond, Robert W. *Kansas: Land of Contrasts*. Saint Charles, Mo.: Forum Press, 1974.

Williams, Burton J. *Senator John James Ingalls: Kansas' Iridescent Republican*. Law-
    rence: University Press of Kansas, 1972.
INDEX SOURCES: None.
REPRINT EDITIONS: None.
LOCATION SOURCES: Kansas State Historical Society, KMK, NN, ICN, New York
    State University at Albany Library, and San Francisco Public Library.

Publication History

MAGAZINE TITLE AND TITLE CHANGES: *The Kansas Knocker: A Journal for
    Cranks*, April 1900-January 1901.
VOLUME AND ISSUE DATA: Quarterly, Volume 1:1, April 1900; Number 2, July
    1900; Number 3, October 1900; Number 4, January 1901.
PUBLISHER AND PLACE OF PUBLICATION: J. F. Jarrell and Myron A. Waterman,
    Topeka, Kansas.
EDITORS: J. F. Jarrell and Myron A. Waterman, 1900–1901.
CIRCULATION: 3,000.

Gregory S. Sojka

THE KEEPAPITCHININ

During its short existence *The Keepapitchinin* provided the early Utah settlers
with a humorous commentary on both Mormonism and Utah society in general.
Subtitled "A semi-occasional paper, devoted to cents, scents, sense and
nonsense," it served as a voice of orthodox Mormonism and addressed serious
subjects in a far from serious tone.

The Keepapitchinin first appeared in 1867 as a crudely produced four-page
broadside, half of which was devoted to advertisements. Its chief editor was
"Uno Hoo," in actuality George J. Taylor, eldest son of John Taylor, apostle
and eventual president of the Latter-day Saints. Other pseudonymous contributors
included Charles Savage, George M. Ottinger, Joseph C. Rich, Heber J.
Richards, and Orson Pratt, all talented and influential Saints. The first issues
were indeed semi-occasional, and their humor ranged from the topical (hog-
weighing in Kansas) to the racist (an exaggerated Black dialect speech by one
M. Lillywhite). In 1870, however, with the first issue of Volume 2, *The
Keepapitchinin* improved its type and expanded its comical coverage.

The paper thereafter appeared on the first and fifteenth of each month. Each
issue was comprised of four three-column pages, measuring 41 cm, and was
illustrated with woodcut cartoons. Individual issues cost ten cents; a year's
subscription was $1.50. Advertisements were restricted to five lines at fifty cents
per line.

With the advent of the Godbeite New Movement, an organized reaction by
William Godbe and others against the restrictions imposed by Mormon leaders
on the life and thought of their followers, the paper received further impetus for
survival. Since its editors embraced orthodox Mormonism, they continually
lampooned the pretentious intellectualism and spiritualistic leanings of the "New

Move'' (as they called it) with outrageous articles and cartoons. Items of local satire included a purported monster in Bear Lake and the perils of sleigh riding in Rush Valley. At the same time the paper widened its range of fire and burlesqued such celebrities as Henry Ward Beecher and one J. P. Newman, a minister who came to Salt Lake City to debate Brigham Young on polygamy; satirized the writings of Anthony Trollope and Frederick Marryat (as Another Trollop and Captain Marrowfat); and featured humorous up-to-date bulletins on the Franco-Prussian War. It also reprinted essays and poems by Mark Twain, Josh Billings, Artemus Ward, and Bret Harte.

The Keepapitchinin did not survive long after the collapse of the Godbeite New Movement; its last regular issue appeared on 15 February 1871, although a special edition was published on 4 July of that same year. Taylor intended to revive it at a later date but never did so.

Although its humor was uneven and at times crude, and its illustrations primitive, *The Keepapitchinin* was one of the first humor magazines to appear from the West. It served as a humorous escape for the Utah settlers, if only for a short time, from the rigors of pioneer life.

Information Sources

BIBLIOGRAPHY:

Alter, J. Cecil. *Early Utah Journalism: A Half-Century of Forensic Warfare, Waged by the West's Most Militant Press.* Salt Lake City: Utah State Historical Society, 1935, pp. 317–18.

Matthews, J. Brander. "The Comic Periodical Literature of the United States." *American Bibliopolist* 7 (August 1875): 200.

Mott, Frank L. "The Comics." In *A History of American Magazines, 1865–1885.* Cambridge, Mass.: Harvard University Press, 1938, 3:266.

Walker, Ronald W. "The Keep-A-Pitchinin or the Mormon Pioneer Was Human." *Brigham Young University Studies* 14 (Spring 1974): 331–44. (Reprints issue of 4 July 1871.)

INDEX SOURCES: None.

REPRINT EDITIONS: None.

LOCATION SOURCES: Partial runs can be found at the University of Utah and CtY.

Publication History

MAGAZINE TITLE AND TITLE CHANGES: *The Keepapitchinin; a Semi-Occasional Paper, Devoted to Cents, Scents, Sense and Nonsense,* 1867?–4 July 1871.

VOLUME AND ISSUE DATA: Irregular for Volume 1, 1867?–1868?. Semi-monthly, Volume 2: 1, 1 March 1870–Volume 2:24, 15 February 1871. Volume 3:1, 4 July 1871.

PUBLISHER AND PLACE OF PUBLICATION: George J. Taylor, the Great Western Emporium, South Temple Street, Salt Lake City, Utah.

EDITOR: "Uno Hoo" (George J. Taylor).

CIRCULATION: Unknown.

Eric W. Johnson

THE KNICKERBOCKER

From 1833 to 1865 *The Knickerbocker* offered staple reading for American and British audiences. Deriving its name from Diedrich Knickerbocker, Washington Irving's genial historian-folklorist, the magazine came naturally to be associated with humor and with attitudes of the "Knickerbocker" writers, who were chiefly from New York City and State. These figures carried along the traditions of Dutch geniality, slow-paced but industrious living, and a strain of waggish humor underlying seeming slow-witted personalities. To suppose that humor and artistic substance are synonymous in *The Knickerbocker*, however, is erroneous, as the quality of comic productions diminished during the career of the periodical. Such bawdy, coarse, irreligious tall tales as appeared, for example, in another New York journal, William T. Porter's *Spirit of the Times*,* adumbrating the art of Mark Twain, are not evident in *The Knickerbocker*. Significantly, the magazine's demise coincides with the advent of rowdy literary comedy during the 1860s.

The Knickerbocker nonetheless carries a threefold significance for American literary humor for the three decades before the Civil War. First, although contributions from well-known American comic writers were generally not of their authors' finest quality, they were part of the periodical's attempts to promote a genuinely American literature. Second, Lewis Gaylord Clark, the most famous editor of *The Knickerbocker*, attracted attention to the journal by means of his "Editor's Table" columns. There, satire, parody, and wry gossip furnished typical comedy. Third, reviews of humorous works, essays treating the comic, and occasional pertinent remarks offer barometers to a powerful segment of literary taste in mid-nineteenth-century America.

The founders of *The Knickerbocker*, Peabody and Company of New York City, and early editors like Charles Fenno Hoffman and Lewis Gaylord Clark wanted to foster a solid national American literature in their journal. Imitations of European models, especially in the 1830s, the extravagances of "German" or Gothic productions, and the puerilities of "Fashionable Novels" were deplored. Although Irving had refused the editorship of the magazine, his spirit hovered over its general ethos. The models touted by *The Knickerbocker* often exemplified a genuine comic sense—Irving himself, the English Oliver Goldsmith and Charles Lamb, and the Americans Fitz-Greene Halleck, James Kirke Paulding, and Robert C. Sands—but sustained vicissitudes in reputation before the magazine ceased publication. By the 1860s, an aura of fading and staling had set in for the venture. Another weak cause that *The Knickerbocker* doggedly supported was the literary reputation of the editor's twin, Willis Gaylord Clark, who had brought out a series titled "Ollapodiana" in early numbers, before his early death, in 1841, from tuberculosis. Those pallid imitations of Lamb's "Elia" essays soon fell from fashion, although the surviving Clark brother never ceased to champion them and their author in lachrymose terms. A survey of numerous changes in ownership and many financial problems connected with *The Knickerbocker* reveals that policies were often undercut by exigencies that were not altogether under editorial control.

The history and development of humorous elements in *The Knickerbocker* demonstrates that, if the magazine did not succeed in publishing great comic items per se, it did touch on pulses of such materials in the Anglo-American literary scene. The early years of "Old Knick," as the magazine was dubbed by affectionate admirers, were prosperous insofar as reputation was concerned, and many then-famous names appeared: William Cullen Bryant, James Fenimore Cooper, Washington Irving, William Leete Stone, James Kirke Paulding, William Gilmore Simms, Henry W. Longfellow, John Greenleaf Whittier, plus well-known British authors, like William Wordsworth, Robert Southey, and Edward Bulwer-Lytton. In the 1830s and 1840s, humor was much discussed and brought to the fore. Paulding's first contribution, "A Ramble in the Woods on Sunday, and What the Writer Saw and Heard There" (January 1833), mingles realism and fantasy as animals assume human dimensions. Whimsy of this variety recurs throughout the history of the magazine. Geniality characterizes most of the comic writing in these years of *The Knickerbocker*, devolving from the strong influence of Irving. His own contributions, later published in volume form as *Wolfert's Roost* (1855), deal with varied legends, as well as with New York in the time of Governor Peter Stuyvesant, the crabbed, lame, old Dutchman ultimately defeated by the English. Stuyvesant's spectre had been invoked in the "Introduction" to Volume 1 of *The Knickerbocker* (January 1833), wherein he confronted the editor with questions about the need for yet another American literary journal. He vanished when the editor mentioned Irving's name, and perhaps Irving later remembered this gambit.

A hallmark of *The Knickerbocker* is a familiarity with American literary culture. Often in later issues some earlier circumstance or article is recalled. Contributors also seemed to know much about the careers and publications of their contemporaries, and these topics often furnished materials for mirth. Parody is frequently the form for such attention. Longfellow's "Hiawatha" and "The Skeleton in Armor" were lampooned thus, and Poe's verse, notably "The Raven," several times elicited parodies. Walt Whitman's "Song of Myself" was used up in July 1860. An unlikely target for humor, Hawthorne's *The Marble Faun*, was furnished an amusing conclusion in that same issue. Elsewhere, however, Hawthorne was perceived as a comic author, one who manifested "quiet humor." Clark also serially burlesqued country newspapers in "The Bunkumville Chronicle" (1849), which mocked standard editorials, news features, advertisements, reviewing practices, and hackneyed style and format generally in the journalist's trade.

Less pleasant humor in *The Knickerbocker* includes Clark's recurrent thrusts at William Gilmore Simms and Edgar Allan Poe, who ran afoul of his anger when they wrote unfavorably about the New York literati. Simms had been well received by Clark until 1842, when he wrote negatively about the Northern literary establishment. Thereafter, Clark missed no chance to make Simms look foolish. His vitriol culminated in the observation, "But whoever looks for humor in Mr. Simms might as well look for a smile in the jaws of an alligator," in April 1846. Poe's treatment in *The Knickerbocker*, as an interloper on the American literary scene, whose drunkenness and other undesirable traits, principally an inability to distinguish verse from true poetry, were ridiculous, is not unique. Other periodicals took up cudgels against this often savage critic, whose own imaginative work made easy prey for parody and satire. The attacks by Thomas Dunn English and others on the staff of *The John-Donkey** (1848– 1849) make what appears against Poe in *The Knickerbocker* seem mild. Poe's unflattering comments on Willis Gaylord Clark's work and his general antipathies toward literary circles revolving around Lewis Gaylord Clark and contributors to "Old Knick" combined to create a hostile return of his notoriously acid literary criticism.

In addition to parodic verse, epigrammatic wit in rhyme frequently appeared in *The Knickerbocker*, a carryover from the days of Alexander Pope and his American disciples, Fitz-Greene Halleck, and less well-known versifiers. Comic dialect poetry and prose also grew popular, and "John Phoenix" (G. H. Derby), "K. N. Pepper" (James Morris), John G. Saxe, and Charles Godfrey Leland contributed their wares. Oliver Wendell Holmes also published light verse here, but, again, these pieces are not among his best writing. Leland took over editing the magazine when Clark retired, and his own humorous propensities were among the strengths of the declining years of the enterprise.

Leland's comic serials, *The Mace Sloper Papers* and *Meister Karl's Sketch Book*, contain miscellaneous prose pieces loosely unified by a central character. *Meister Karl* (1855) is styled after Bulwer-Lytton's sketches of a "metaphysical," or not strictly realistic, nature. A travel book of sorts, this work also includes tales of the frontier-humor stamp, with rural sports and hunting as prominent elements. Leland calls on the Irving who had created Diedrich Knickerbocker and *Tales of a Traveller* as an inspiration. Like Irving, he blends foreign adventure with "Yankee Stories," and sometimes theorizes about humor. Leland's fame may be greater because of *Hans Breitman's Ballads*, but his *Knickerbocker* work offers important insights concerning the concept of mirth demonstrated in his verse.

"The Editor's Table," Lewis Gaylord Clark's signal contribution, became for many the highlight of *The Knickerbocker*. Clark's own predilections for Lamb, Dickens, Irving, and other watered-down heirs of neo-classic humor mingled there with his interests in the increasingly popular American varieties of colloquial humor, often involving idiosyncratic spelling, dialect, and a larger share of horseplay than he generally printed. His parody of newspapers led in the early 1850s to a like project, "The Bunkum Flag-staff and Independent Echo," slyly burlesquing such cherished ideas as American patriotism, currency reform, and the Constitution. The dialect humor and phonetic spelling, however, seem feeble imitations of stronger works like James Russell Lowell's *The Biglow Papers*. Clark's greater success with "The Editor's Table" doubtless stemmed from the mix of humor with more sober fare. The attention accorded current literary personages and events, repeated notice and clips of comic publications, and reminiscences (particularly about previous work and writers in *The Knickerbocker*), make these columns central for any current study of nineteenth-century American humor and humorists. "The Editor's Table" was modeled on the popular "Noctes Ambrosianae," from the Scottish *Blackwood's Edinburgh Magazine*. Although Clark did not present as many characters as were featured in the "Noctes," his subjects resembled those found there, as does his use of the editor's persona. Clark also initiated a serial "Editorial Narrative of the *Knickerbocker Magazine*," which ran from 1859 to 1861, thereby outlining much of the history and identifying many of the unsigned pieces that had appeared over the years. This work also sheds light on humor of the period.

If general literary criticism in *The Knickerbocker* is unimpressive, the number of book reviews treating the comic and the number of other observations on humor are impressive. They give the magazine status as a measurer of cultural taste. Vernacular yarns, like those George Washington Harris elsewhere spun through the medium of Sut Lovingood, or those by Johnson Jones Hooper, Thomas Bangs Thorpe, and Mark Twain, constituted no great bulk in "Old Knick," but they were recognized as signal texts in American writing. Side by side with reprints of Charles Lamb, Oliver Goldsmith, and other more refined purveyors of humor, works by "John Phoenix" (George Horatio Derby), Thomas Bangs Thorpe, "K. N. Pepper" (James W. Morris), C. G. Leland—these two did produce dialect mirth—William Gilmore Simms, and Herman Melville were reviewed in terms that highlighted their comic elements. Hawthorne's tales, moreover, were designated humorous in reiterated commentary in *Knickerbocker* columns. The notices of Melville and the attention to Hawthorne's humor are noteworthy.

Additional value in *The Knickerbocker* is discernible in essays centering on or in interspersed remarks concerning humor. For example, Claude Halcro's "Laughter" in August 1854 attempts to categorize types of laughter and those who laugh. Laughter originates in wit. Responding in December, Charles A. Munger, in "A Second Chapter on Laughter," deems laughter a socially unifying force. He also notes that some restraint in comic presentation is necessary. Equally worthwhile, Richard Haywarde's "On Wit and Humor," in December 1850, distinguishes the immediacy of humor from the delayed reaction (and doubtless more unconscious attempt after comedy) within wit. Humor relates to pathos, and wit to causticity. Among less extensive treatments of humor, *The Knickerbocker* demonstrates recurring fascination with the grotesque, the parodic, and the bizarre. An excellent exemplification of such inclination appears in the review of W. M. Thackeray's *Vanity Fair* in September 1848. Satire and political humor by Robert C. Sands elicits repeated commendation, as do the contents of the *Spirit of the Times*. Objections to coarse mirth may be illustrated by the strictures leveled against Simms's tale, "Calayo," in March 1846. Conversely, Thomas Bangs Thorpe's "dry humor" in *The Hive of the Bee-Hunter* and the "Rabelaisian" characteristics of C. G. Leland are praised—respectively, in April 1854 and February 1856.

Several general conclusions concerning the role of *The Knickerbocker* among nineteenth-century American periodicals may be drawn. The spirit of New York Knickerbocker writers pervaded the career of the publication. Clark never altogether shook off his early predilections for the type of comic art manifested by Goldsmith, Lamb, Irving, and their heirs. At least he departed little from that variety of humor in terms of what he published in "Old Knick." He might have more actively fostered the growing popularity of "Big Bar," or rougher, more coarse writing, but Clark failed to capitalize on what he himself often admired in his "Editor's Table" and in the literary notices he brought out. By keeping a distance from such literary fare, he doubtless brought about the eventual downfall of *The Knickerbocker*. Nonetheless, the magazine stands out among many others in its day in furnishing a register of opinion about humor, just as in its comic publications it reflects a type of literary taste current over several decades. Most of the foremost names among humorists of the mid-nineteenth century—Lamb, Irving, Dickens, Thackeray—as well as others of lesser magnitude were in some way connected to the journal. The failure to go along with the times, however, combined with financial disasters, brought its demise in 1865.

Information Sources

BIBLIOGRAPHY:

Anonymous. "Filching From Old Knick." *The Boston Aurora Borealis*, Number 5 (24 February 1849): 38.

Anonymous. "Knickerbocker Literature." *Nation* (5 December 1867): 459–61.

Dunlap, Leslie W., ed. *The Letters of Willis Gaylord Clark and Lewis Gaylord Clark*. New York: New York Public Library, 1940.

Francis, John W., George P. Morris, Rufus W. Griswold, Richard B. Kimball, and Frederick W. Shelton, eds. *The Knickerbocker Gallery: A Testimonial to the Editor of The Knickerbocker Magazine from Its Contributors*. New York: Samuel Hueston, 1855.

Leland, Charles G. *Memoirs*. London: Heinemann, 1893.

McHaney, Thomas L. "An Early 19th Century Literary Agent: James Lawson of New York." *Papers of the Bibliographical Society of America* 64 (2nd quarter 1970): 177–92.

Miller, Perry. *The Raven and the Whale: The War of Words and Wits in the Era of Poe and Melville*. New York: Harcourt, Brace, and World, 1956.

Moss, Sidney P. *Poe's Literary Battles: The Critic in the Context of His Literary Milieu*. Durham, N.C.: Duke University Press, 1963; rptd. Carbondale and Edwardsville: Southern Illinois University Press, 1969; London and Amsterdam: Feffer and Simons, 1969.

———. *Poe's Major Crisis: His Libel Suit and New York's Literary World*. Durham, N.C.: Duke University Press, 1970.

Mott, Frank L. "The Knickerbocker Magazine." In *A History of American Magazines, 1741–1850*. New York and London: D. Appleton and Co., 1930, 1:606–13.

Nethery, Wallace. *Charles Lamb in America to 1848*. Worcester, Mass.: Achilles J. St. Onge, 1963.

Pritchard, John Paul. *Literary Wise Men of Gotham: Criticism in New York, 1815–1860*. Baton Rouge: Louisiana State University Press, 1963.

Roche, Arthur John III. "A Literary Gentleman in New York: Evert A. Duychinck's Relationship with Nathaniel Hawthorne, Herman Melville, Edgar Allan Poe, and William Gilmore Simms." Ph.D. diss., Duke University, 1973.

Sloane, David E. E., ed. *The Literary Humor of the Urban Northeast, 1830–1890*. Baton Rouge: Louisiana State University Press, 1983, pp. 313–319.

Spivey, Herman Everette. "The Knickerbocker Magazine, 1833–1865: A Study of Its History, Contents, and Significance." Ph.D. diss., University of North Carolina, 1938.

Tebbel, John. *The American Magazine: A Compact History*. New York: Hawthorn Books, 1969, pp. 49, 61–62, 70–80, 82, 87, 96.

Thorpe, Thomas Bangs. "Lewis Gaylord Clark." *Harper's New Monthly Magazine* 48 (March 1874): 587–92.

INDEX SOURCES: Title index bound at the beginning of each volume.

REPRINT EDITIONS: University Microfilms.

LOCATION SOURCES: MH, MWA, NN, NHi, PU, PP, NjP, NcD, NcU, TxU, ViU, and approximately forty other libraries.

Publication History

MAGAZINE TITLE AND TITLE CHANGES: *The Knickerbocker; or, New-York Monthly Magazine*, January 1833-September 1862 ["*Knickerbacker*" in Volume 1]; *The Knickerbocker Monthly; a National Magazine of Literature, Art, Politics, and Society*, October 1863-February 1864; *The American Monthly Knickerbocker. Devoted to Literature, Art, Society, and Politics*, March 1864-June 1865; *Federal American Monthly*, July-October 1865.

VOLUME AND ISSUE DATA: Monthly, Volume 1:1, January 1833–Volume 66:9, October 1865.

PUBLISHER AND PLACE OF PUBLICATION: 1833–1834: Peabody and Co. 1834–1839: L. G. Clark and Clement M. Edson. 1840–1841: L. G. Clark. 1841–1842: John Bisco. 1842–1849: John Allen. 1849–1857: Samuel Hueston. 1858–1860: John A. Gray. 1861: J. R. Gilmore. 1862: Morris Phillips. 1862–1863: J. H. Elliot. 1864–1865: John Holmes Agnew. New York.

EDITORS: Charles Fenno Hoffman, January-March 1833; Samuel Daly Langtree, April-September 1833; Timothy Flint, October 1833; Samuel Daly Langtree, November 1833-April 1834; Lewis Gaylord Clark, May 1834-December 1860; Willis Gaylord Clark, Associate Editor, 1834–1841; James D. Noyes, Associate Editor, 1858–1859; Kinahan Cornwallis, January 1861-September 1863; Kinahan Cornwallis and Lewis Gaylord Clark [Charles Godfrey Leland assisted during part of 1861-September 1862], October-December 1863; J. Holmes Agnew, January 1864-October 1865.

CIRCULATION: Unknown. Advertising rates suggest printings of several thousand.

Benjamin Franklin Fisher IV

L

THE LARK

" 'Who'll be the Clerk?' 'I' said *The Lark*." So reads the title page of the first issue of Gelett Burgess's and Bruce Porter's nonsense magazine, *The Lark*, which was published in San Francisco by printer and bookseller William Doxey and enjoyed a successful run of monthly publications between May 1895 and April 1897 before its editors tired of their play and clipped its wings. They issued a sequel in May 1897, a single issue of *The Epilark*, which also bore Doxey's imprimatur. And in 1898 Burgess, Carolyn Wells, a regular contributor to *The Lark*, and Oliver Herford published a single, April Fools' issue entitled *Enfant Terrible!*

A playful absurdity underlies all of these efforts. As Bruce Porter commented in the prologue to the first issue of *The Lark*, the magazine had "no more serious intention than to be gay—to sing a song, to tell a story;—and when this is no longer to our liking—then this little house of pleasure will close its doors." In a later interview Burgess added, "*The Lark* lived because of its beautiful optimism, being at the same time a sort of joke in earnest and a protest against journalism that is merely commercial." The absurd spirit applied even to the magazine's cost: in its first year single issues sold for a nickel, but an annual subscription for the monthly cost a dollar. Not until the second year, when the price of a single issue doubled to ten cents, did subscribers come out ahead. Much to the editors' surprise, the magazine proved popular enough that in the first year a number of people were willing to accept a forty-cent loss in order to subscribe. The cover of *The Epilark* advertises a yearly subscription rate of one dollar, even though only one issue was ever printed, or even planned.

The pages of *The Lark*, sixteen square, unnumbered, unjustified, unevenly cut, book-sized, duodecimo sheaves, with printing on only one side, were made from bamboo paper that Burgess and Porter had purchased in quantity in

Chinatown. The bamboo caused problems by shattering the type face, until the printers changed to a different printing method. According to Wells, the pages would crumble if someone simply looked at them. Banished from these pages were any submissions with political content or anything possessing an identifiable theme. Instead, readers found Burgess's illustrated Goop poems, such as "I'd never dare to walk across / A Bridge I could not see, / For much afraid of falling off, / I fear that I should be." We also find nonsense stories; relatively long narrative poems, like "The Ambitious Shepherd," a parody of a fairy tale; spurious ballads like "Tyrante," sung to the tune of "Lord Randal"; and impure maxims, like those in "Inexpensive Cynicisms": "A Lark in the Hand gathers no Moss," "Profit is not without Honour save in Boston," and "Of two Devils choose the Prettier." *Epilark* and *Enfant Terrible!* generally provide more of the same. The six-page, illustrated *Enfant Terrible!* plays on the idea of the precocious child gone amuck and uses a ship's setting.

Gelett Burgess was the driving and sustaining force behind *The Lark*. He assumed responsibility not only for writing many or most of the pieces (sometimes under assumed names), but also for doing illustrations and sometimes designing the covers. Burgess, a native Bostonian, was twenty-nine years old when he began *The Lark*. Like his wild predecessor in California humor, George Horatio Derby, Burgess was a civil engineer, having graduated from the Massachusetts Institute of Technology in 1877. After graduation he worked for the Southern Pacific Railway Company for three years and then, for the next three years, taught civil engineering at the University of California at Berkeley. During the period that he was editing *The Lark* he also designed furniture and "other articles of use and beauty." In the year of *The Lark*'s demise, 1897, Burgess wrote for *Criterion*, becoming a favorite of the young H. L. Mencken, and for *The News-Letter* and the *Woman's Home Companion*. At the time of his death in 1951, he had published over thirty-five books, many of them featuring the Goop characters he introduced in *The Lark*.

A particularly good example of *The Lark*'s humor is the *Petit Journal des Refusees*, an apparently nonexistent magazine Burgess advertised in *The Lark*'s sixth issue. It was to be published by one James Marrion II of San Francisco and to be comprised solely of articles rejected by other journals. Burgess tantalizes his readers with two sample offerings: "The Naughty Archer," which had been refused by *The Congregationalist* and *The War Cry*, and "Our Clubbing List," which had been refused by *The Complete Alphabet of Freaks*. The first verse of the former poem reads, "I'd love to hunt for angels, / And shoot them on the wing; / I'd love to see them hop around / And yell like anything." The second poem anticipates the alphabet humor of Edward Gorey with such rhymes as "*B* is for *Beardsley*, the idol supreme, / Whose drawings are not half so bad as they seem"; *S* is for *Stevie Crane*, infant precocious, / Who has written some lines that are simply ferocious"; and "*L* is for *Lark*, and the fellows who planned it. / Say even they cannot but half understand it."

In the pages of *The Lark* proper, and *The Epilark*, Burgess and his cronies fly highest. Although Burgess's own personal favorites were "A Boy's Will Is the Wind's Will" and the "Song for the New Year," he is best remembered for "The Purple Cow," which ultimately gave the name to a genre of nonsense rhymes. Appearing in the first issue, and accompanied by Burgess's illustration, the poem reads, "I never Saw a Purple Cow; / I never Hope to See One; / But I can Tell you, Anyhow, / I'd rather See Than Be One." Carolyn Wells answered with her own version, "The Purpil Cowe" in the eighteenth issue, and Burgess himself revealed in *The Epilark* what may have been a genuine frustration at being continuously identified with the poem. His sequel shows a peevish sketch of himself and goes, "Ah, yes I wrote the 'Purple Cow' / I'm Sorry, now, I wrote it; / But I can tell you Anyhow / I'll Kill you if you Quote it!"

Contributor Carolyn Wells was also among the initial subscribers. Bowled over by the zany humor in the first offering, she volunteered her own talents for subsequent issues. Burgess replied with a list of things *The Lark* would not accept, including submissions from women writers. But Wells persevered and broke into *The Lark* in the fourteenth issue. She was singled out for special honorary mention in the nineteenth issue, in the form of Burgess's piece, "H.R.H., The Princess Perilla." Wells also wrote several books of nonsense, parodies for *Bookman* magazine, and contributions to the *Philistine*,* *Uncle Remus Magazine*,* and the *Saturday Evening Post*,** as well as being assistant editor for *The Browning Magazine*. Her 1908 parody for *The Post*, "The Rubaiyat of Wall Street," was perhaps inspired by earlier parodies by her fellow governors of the *Enfant Terrible!*; Herford had written "The Rubaiyat of a Persian Kitten" in 1904 for *Collier's*; in the same year Burgess published *The Rubaiyat of Omar Cayenne*.

The Lark was surprisingly successful and had a nationwide circulation of about 5,000. Part of its success may have been due to the entrepreneurial instincts of its publisher, William Doxey. Doxey described his role to the *San Francisco Call*: "I found these young men with matter of merit . . . but they did not seem to know just how to handle it, so I took it up and published *The Lark* first jointly with them and then myself." For the initial issues Burgess and Porter had to guarantee the first hundred dollars of expenses.

But *The Lark* was profitable, if unlikely to make its founders' fortunes. Moreover, it was admired by other comic magazines of the period that shared its spirit. *The Chap-Book* in Chicago commented that "Its friends will be appreciative" before adding "but there will not be many of them." *The Lark* was also reviewed in such diverse newspapers as the *Richmond Times*, the *San Francisco Examiner*, the *Boston Budget*, the *Washington Capital* and the *Chicago Journal*. The *San Francisco Call* ran a lengthy article eulogizing *The Lark* upon the cessation of the magazine's publication. Of course, *The Lark*'s appeal was largely limited to a fairly elite, erudite readership. To appreciate parody, after all, one must be familiar with the original on which the spoof is based, and nonsense often appeals most to those who have surfeited on serious literature and ideas. Burgess himself acknowledged that the magazine was part of a "revolt against the commonplace.'' *The Lark* is provoking in that it and other nonsensical publications of the time satisfied some antirational need of the intellectual elite in the mid–1890s. Though neither profound nor enduring in their own right, the nonsense pieces in *The Lark, The Chap-Book*, and the *Philistine*, and other magazines of their ilk, because of their popularity among the intellectual elite, prompt us to reexamine the *fin-de-siecle* period of American history and to ask why some segments of the intelligentsia, well before Dada and existentialism, would reject reason and all vestiges of seriousness in favor of pure fantasy and nonsense. In that respect, *The Lark* and its cohorts acquire a relevance which their founders would have found alarming.

Information Sources

BIBLIOGRAPHY:

Bachus, Joseph M. "Gelett Burgess: A Biography of the Man Who Wrote 'The Purple Cow.' '' Ph.D. diss., University of California at Berkeley, 1961.

Blair, Walter, and Hamlin Hill. *America's Humor: From Poor Richard to Doonesbury.* New York: Oxford University Press, 1978, pp. 375–80.

Bragdon, Claude. "The Purple Cow Period." *Bookman* 49 (1929): 475–78.

Burgess, Gelett. " 'The Lark,' an Amateur Journal." *Academy* 57 (1898): 212.

Dresner, Zita Zatkin. "Carolyn Wells." In *Dictionary of Literary Biography*, Volume 21: *American Humorists, 1800–1950*. Detroit: Gale Research Co., 1982, pp. 556–60.

"Editor Burgess Kills 'The Lark.' '' *San Francisco Call*, 31 March 1897.

Linneman, William R. "Satires of American Realism, 1880–1900." *American Literature* 34 (March 1962): 80–93.

Mott, Frank L. *A History of American Magazines, 1885–1905*. Cambridge, Mass.: Harvard University Press, 1957, 4:386–88 and passim.

Wells, Carolyn. "What a Lark!" *Colophon*, Part 8, 1931.

Wenke, John. "Gelett Burgess." *American Humorists, 1800–1950*, Stanley Trachtenberg, ed. (Detroit: Gale Research, 1982), 1:68–76.

INDEX SOURCES: None.

REPRINT EDITIONS: *The Lark* and *Epilark*, Kraus Microforms. *Enfant Terrible!*, none.

LOCATION SOURCES: *Lark* and *Epilark* at Arizona State University, Pasadena Public Library, San Francisco State University, University of California-Berkeley and Irvine, ICN, MBU, University of Houston, Michigan State University, University of Wisconsin-Milwaukee, N, University of Rochester, and approximately thirty-six other libraries list holdings. *Enfant Terrible!* at NjP, NN, N, NcD, ViU, CU-BANC.

Publication History

MAGAZINE TITLE AND TITLE CHANGES: *The Lark*, May 1895-April 1897; *The Epilark*, May 1897; *Enfant Terrible!*, 1 April 1898.

VOLUME AND ISSUE DATA: *The Lark*, monthly, annual volumes Volume 1:1, May 1895–Volume 2:24. *The Epilark* is collected as Number 25 in Volume 2. *Enfant Terrible!*, single issue, labeled Volume 1:1, on cover.

PUBLISHER AND PLACE OF PUBLICATION: *The Lark* and *Epilark*, William Doxey, San Francisco. *Enfant Terrible!*, R. H. Russell, New York.

EDITORS: *The Lark* and *Epilark*, Gelett Burgess and Bruce Porter. *Enfant Terrible!*,
    Gelett Burgess, Carolyn Wells, Oliver Herford.
CIRCULATION: Approximately 5,000.

Richard Alan Schwartz

LAUGH BOOK MAGAZINE

Dedicated to providing "something for everyone," *Laugh Book Magazine* began in Wichita, Kansas, in 1933 as a local gossip sheet, evolved into a collection of jokes for servicemen, and finally matured into a popular low-brow magazine with an international circulation. Also known as *Charley Jones' Laugh Book Magazine, Laugh Book* was a 5" × 6¾" digest published by Charley Jones and edited by Ken Berglund, originally the Jayhawk Press, of Wichita, Kansas. In its heyday, *Laugh Book* was 3¼" × 6¼", one hundred pages, at thirty-five cents a copy, quarterly. It featured sex and bathroom humor: "I bet you marines kissed girls all over the map, and other places too," or, Anthony to Cleo on the absence of bathrooms in her palace, "This place is uncanny." The later squared-off monthly magazine added pages of mail-ins and humorous clips from the newspapers; humor was consequently more general.

In July 1933, with only six cents in his pocket, an out-of-work printer named Charley Jones took the suggestion of a friend in the theatre business to create a "throw-away" magazine for theatrical advertisements. Named *Downtown Wichita*, this modest publication was enlarged when Jones added a "tattle-tale column" exposing local political corruption and other shenanigans. From $32.50 for the initial issue, costs grew to exceed $40,000, and so did revenue. Jones developed a large printing business, which in turn gave birth to *The Latrine Gazette* in World War II. First sold exclusively to Army PXs, the *Gazette* moved to the Navy as *Head Liners*, and *Head Liners* became *Laugh Book Magazine*, with public newsstand sales in January 1944.

At first a dollar-a-year quarterly, *Laugh Book* soon became a monthly publication with a $3.60 annual subscription. Its circulation grew so rapidly that Jones incorporated a printing plant named the Jayhawk Press with fifty employees in order to meet the needs of his growing readership. When his readership declined, the plant failed in 1950. Mounting financial problems, changing morality and tastes, and failing health forced Jones to conclude publication with the April 1964 issue, printed in his basement. Jones's low-brow policy may have ultimately contributed to *Laugh Book*'s demise. His restrictions on quality were minimal. "If a joke was dirtier than it was funny," Jones said, "then it wasn't for us."

For a quarter, during the war, lonely servicemen obtained over one hundred pages of jokes liberally spiced with moderate sexual humor guaranteed to make a soldier forget the girlfriend who married the civilian at home. Dedicated to the Latrine Orderly, the "Army's greatest strategist," the *Gazette* enabled servicemen to laugh both at the bureaucracies of military life and at themselves.

The first two volumes of the *Laugh Book* in 1944 and 1945 promised to continue the traditions of *Downtown Wichita* and the *Gazette*. Over two thousand readers sent one dollar for a subscription to what would become a quarterly in 1946. Another half-million, claimed the ever-optimistic Jones, could have been sold except for paper shortages.

Jones solicited material from his readers, and in exchange for a published joke, gag, verse, short limerick, or cartoon returned a small sum of cash. Thus, *Laugh Book* reflected the humor of "Main Street America": "the guy or the gal who keeps a smile eternally upon the map of America." This format provided abundant humor at a moderate price. Other special features included games or puzzles (prizes for their solutions were free subscriptions to *Laugh Book*); Earl Wilson's "Requoted Quotes," beginning in 1951, selected from his column "It Happened Last Night"; a section devoted to the old *Gazette* through the 1950s; "The Reader's Page" (a forum for subscribers); a "Pinup of the Month" snapshot which was later replaced with racier photos of Hollywood starlets; and the omnipresent "Letter From Charley," where the publisher would chat about current events, offer publishing news, and even relate humorous anecdotes of his own. Reflecting the wide circulation, later *Laugh Books* included advertisements for published collections of party humor, speakers' jokes, and the increasingly popular pin-ups of young actresses such as Sophia Loren, Marilyn Monroe, and Diana Dors.

Despite its national popularity, *Laugh Book* showed a particular middle-of-the-country, Kansas humor frequently playing on the naiveté and country-bumpkin image of the Great Plains farmer. But the humor was often a sly turnabout on snobbish, metropolitan elitism. For example, a girl from the East arrives in Kansas and falls victim to her ignorance while working in a feed store. When a farmer asks for some "shorts" (ground corn) for his pigs, the girl replies, "I'm sorry, but we are out of pig shorts. How about some nice brassiers for your cows?" The humor also revealed a native, horse-sense intelligence. One story claims that Kansans know the difference between a politician and a lady. If a politician says "yes," he means "maybe." If he says "maybe," he means "no." If he says "no," he's no politician. If a lady says "no," she means "maybe." If she says "maybe," she means "yes." And if she says "yes," she's no lady.

Kansas humor frequently joked about the weather and landscape and other hardships experienced during pioneer days. A traveler once asked a Kansas farmer why he had a hole in the roof of his sod home. "It's a crowbar hole," he answered. "What's it for?" asked the visitor. "Every morning I stick a crowbar through it, and if it doesn't bend, then it's not too windy to go out." Kansans recognized their divergence from the Northeast: "I grant that you will seldom see / A poem lovely as a tree; / But Kansas plains being as I know'em, / You'd better settle for a poem." Southeastern Kansas, long noted for its coal production, originated a story about two coal-mining partners who were attending a revival service. One partner joined the church and urged his companion to follow his good example. "I can't do it, John," replied the partner. "Who'll do the weighin' if I join?" When a deceased Kansan approached the gates of eternity, he remarked, "Ah! I never thought heaven could be so much like Kansas." "Son," replied the gatekeeper, "this isn't heaven."

Laugh Book's humor also reflected prevalent, mid-American prejudices. "Rastus" and other Black characters became the targets of humor directed toward their stupidity, poor speech, and greed. Midwestern attitudes toward Washington, D.C., mirrored contemporary conservative attitudes: A reporter tells Vance Packard, author of *The Status Seekers*, how to identify Capital politicians: "When a Republican serves a drink, he measures with a jigger; a Democrat just pours." Marilyn Monroe's divorces, Bridget Bardot's seductive towels, and John F. Kennedy's speeches became the magazine's jokes. Readers of the March 1961 issue had "nothing to worry about," according to one story; "President-elect Kennedy has promised to look after us from the cradle to the grave, and Khrushchev has promised he will bury us."

Throughout its twenty years, the *Laugh Book* served as a measuring stick and reflector of America's popular culture. Charley Jones provided a "rags-to-riches" story of one man's persistence, and his *Laugh Book* represented a period when people could chuckle about sex and society without being lewd and offensive.

Information Sources

INDEX SOURCES: None.
REPRINT EDITIONS: None.
LOCATION SOURCES: Kansas State Historical Society.

Publication History

MAGAZINE TITLE AND TITLE CHANGES: *Laugh Book*, 1944–1951; *Laugh Book Magazine*, 1952–1964.
VOLUME AND ISSUE DATA: Quarterly, unnumbered January 1944–Volume 7: 5, 1952. Monthly, Volume 7: 6, 1952–Volume 19: 1964.
PUBLISHER AND PLACE OF PUBLICATION: Charles "Charley" E. Jones, Joste Publishing and Jayhawk Press, Wichita, Kansas.
EDITORS: Charles E. Jones, 1944–1952; Ken Berglund, 1953; Ted O. "Junior" Thackrey, 1953; Ceora R. Raymond, 1964.
CIRCULATION: Approximately 100,000 during the 1950s, according to paper sales records.

Gregory S. Sojka

LIFE

Life Magazine was designed as an American *Punch*; more properly, it was an outgrowth of the *Harvard Lampoon*,* which itself was a copy of *Punch*. *Life* stood as a challenge to the recently successful *Puck** and *Judge**, both of which were full of color, 9″ × 12″, and full of raucous humor. *Life*, on the other hand, was smaller (8½" × 11"), black and white, and self-consciously genteel. It ultimately succeeded so well that it became the most influential cartoon and literary humor magazine of its time, and—a fact forgotten today—itself served as the model for another humor magazine, *The New Yorker*.*

The obvious favorable climate for cartoon-publishing ventures, and especially the success of *Puck*, *Judge*, and the *Harvard Lampoon*, bore greatly on the mind of John Ames Mitchell, an architect and book illustrator, in the early months of 1882. While preparing a book on society cartoons, he reflected on the new advances in means of reproduction work—the process of zinc-etched engraving— and he decided to start a magazine. It was, he later remembered, "one of those ideas that once in possession lays hold for victory." He envisioned it as an American version of *Punch*, the London humor magazine.

Growing more and more enthusiastic about the idea, but without any knowledge of printing, editing, publishing, or managing a magazine, he sought his friend, publisher Henry Holt, for advice. Holt had himself entertained a similar idea—that of publishing a journal of humor, satire, and reviews. Too prudent a businessman to invest in such chancy areas, he instead tried to convince Brander Matthews, later a respected essayist and critic, to start such a venture. Mitchell and Matthews had very different ideas, however, and the three parted company on the subject.

Besides Mitchell's lack of expertise in the area, there were other negative factors, chief among them being the very high mortality rate among humorous papers in America. *Puck*, however, had managed to survive, its display of sheer talent fostering a healthy circulation and political influence. As Mitchell's dream included bypassing color (*Puck*'s selling point) and concentrating on the new photo-engraving process of reproducing black and white cartoons (woodcutting had been the chief method until this time), his friends predicted another early gravestone in the journalistic graveyard.

But Mitchell had a firm ambition and a $10,000 inheritance with which to further it. He convinced Edward S. Martin, a friend of Harvard days who had helped to found and publish the *Lampoon*, to cast his lot with the venture, and Martin enthusiastically began a search for contributors. The first steps were being taken, but a publisher was still needed. This was no easy task; much later, in one of his editorials, Mitchell described the arguments which a professional in the field had given him:

"As I understand, you mean to give the public a periodical about half the size of *Harper's Weekly*, *Puck*, or *Judge*, and yet you ask the same price for it. Now, to get that price, your smaller publication must be unquestionably better in quality, both artistic and literary. Have you secured the men whose work and reputation will assure you that position?"

"No. The artists are not to be had."

"And the literary men?"

"The same with them."

"That's bad enough. Is your own experience in journalism such as to warrant you in going ahead under such . . . peculiar circumstances?"

"I have no experience in journalism."

"None whatever?"

"None whatever."

The man of experience indulged in a smile, but a smile of sadness and pity.

"Would you mind telling me," he asked, "just to gratify my curiosity—on what are you building your hope of success?"

"On the fact that there being an unoccupied field for it. If such papers can thrive in Europe, there must be a place for one in America."

"Previous efforts have demonstrated the reverse, and they have done it pretty clearly."

"But this paper will be a very different thing from any of its predecessors—of a higher grade and far more artistic."

"How can that be when the best men hold aloof?"

"That will occur only at the beginning. I think it will prove an opportunity for talent now unrecognized to come to the front."

Again the business manager smiled the sorrowing smile.

"All that you have said is pure theory, without a single fact on which it would be safe to risk a dollar. Take my advice and drop the whole business while you can. A year from now you will be amazed that you ever seriously thought of it."

When I stepped out upon the sidewalk after this interview, I said to myself:

"Probably the advice is good, but if I listen to reason I shall weaken."

After several attempts and similar conversations, the press of Gillis Brothers agreed to publish a magazine—providing payment was made in advance. While hundreds of smaller problems remained, two larger ones loomed immediately: finding a man for the business department and finding a title for the magazine. Martin somehow secured one of his Harvard friends, Andrew S. Miller, who had worked for the New York Daily *Graphic* and a large advertising company. "Not handicapped by any experience in the business," he was in perfect harmony with his partners. Naming the paper was also important, and Mitchell and Miller decided, from many possible choices, on *Life*—"a comprehensive title that left nothing out." It was also properly philosophical.

Mitchell, as managing editor, was ready as ever to roll, so with Martin searching frantically for copy which seemed not to exist, and Miller for advertisements which must have had equally effective hiding-places, and himself in similar straits in the Art Department, he somehow produced the first issue on 4 January 1883. To quote Mitchell's account:

The first number bore the date of January 4, 1883. The others followed with confusing rapidity. Friday, the day we went to press, seemed to come around three times a week. The first number probably from its novelty, sold reasonably well. The second issue showed a falling off. When the returned copies come back they showed that not a quarter of the edition had been sold. Of the third issue, nearly all returned upon our hands. And when the returns of the fourth and fifth came in, the three anxious men who counted them made the blood-curdling discovery that the unsold copies outnumbered the editions printed! Six thousand had been issued, and there were six thousand two hundred returns. It seemed for a moment that miracles were being resorted to that *Life*'s defeat might be quicker. A more careful examination, however, showed the extra copies were from previous editions.

For six months sales were almost literally nil. Nonetheless, the trio managed to turn out the issues week after week. Editor Mitchell attributes it to Miller's miraculous talent for convincing advertisers to buy space. In this way they kept revenues coming in and kept alive a magazine that wasn't selling. The situation was very depressing for quite a while. Mitchell later recalled: "It was alarming to reflect upon the number of intelligent Americans who got along comfortably without purchasing our paper."

Mitchell and Martin themselves were not beyond performing miracles. Rather amateurish artists were recruited from the ranks of the *Harvard Lampoon*, including Henry McVickar and F. G. Attwood—but there were some excellent cartoonists, some established, some with very promising futures. Among them were E. W. Kemble, destined to become one of the all-time great cartoonists and illustrator of Mark Twain stories; Palmer Cox, who would become famous with his "Brownies"; and Charles Green Bush, later an outstanding editorial cartoonist with the *New York Herald* and *World*. Other early artists included W. H. Hyde; Charles Kendrick; W. A. Rogers, soon to succeed Thomas Nast at *Harper's Weekly*; and Gray Parker. Mitchell himself drew many of the early cartoons.

Martin was having similar luck in the literary department. Besides his own essays and poems, which brought considerable attention, he secured work from Brander Matthews; John Kendrick Bangs; James Whitcomb Riley; Tom L. Masson; and Robert Bridges, later editor of *Scribner's Magazine*. Predictably, there was also a heavy assortment of Harvard talent.

It wasn't until June that an increase in sales was noticed. It was really about time, considering the crude but obvious talent and many favorable reviews from such sources as *The Critic*,* the *New York Sun*, and even its rival, *Puck*. By August, there were still no profits, but no more losses, and early in its second year, *Life* passed the quite respectable 20,000 mark in circulation.

Mitchell had divided the concern into three parts: he held half-interest, while Martin and Miller had a quarter apiece. *Life*'s little mascot, a cupid, was flying unassisted.

In its infancy, *Life* pledged to be independent in political matters and was held to its promise by the practical necessity of not offending potential readers. The irrepressible Mitchell and Martin attacked both Democrats and Republicans. By mid–1884, the magazine was solvent enough—and outraged enough—to join the fight against the corrupt Republican presidential candidate James G. Blaine. Many Republican and Independent journals revolted against the scandal-ridden candidate, and *Life* audaciously drew a double-page cartoon of a parade of independent and "mugwump" papers—including *Harper's Weekly*, The *New York Times*, and *Puck*—all being led by *Life*'s little cupid!

Perhaps Mitchell and Martin had Democratic tendencies from the start, but their support for Cleveland in 1884 marked the start of a definite Democratic bias that lasted until the New Deal, with the allowances of "vacations" during the Populist Bryan's campaigns.

Life was being noticed and was gaining influence. By 1885 its appearance was slick and no longer amateurish. In 1886, Henry Holt started publishing the first of a dozen or so annual collections of drawings titled *Good Things from Life*. A measure of its growth is indicated by *Puck*'s attitude toward it. In *Life*'s struggling days, the senior cartoon paper had kind words for the journal, but now that *Life* was a strong competitor, *Puck* ran cartoons with stiff figures cut out of mail-order catalogues as parodies of *Life*'s art and called the magazine "our esteemed black and white contemporary." (*Life* replied, addressing its elder as "our colored contemporary.") In 1887 a battle arose between the two magazines over a *Life* cartoon which *Puck* charged was in bad taste. The cartoon showed the *Puck* mascot in a gutter and Robert Louis Stevenson (representing the *Century* magazine) as a homosexual (6 January 1887). *Life* denied that the drawing was meant to represent those situations, with *Puck* answering that "our younger brother" had, therefore, hired cartoonists who didn't know what they were drawing.

Ironically, at this same time, *Puck* was negotiating (unsuccessfully) to contract this very cartoonist. He preferred to stay with *Life*, a decision that turned out to be very lucky for *Life*.

About one year earlier, in 1886, this frustrated and disappointed cartoonist had climbed the stairway to Mitchell's office at 1155 Broadway to leave drawings for inspection—drawings that had been rejected by a dozen other magazines. A few days later the depressed artist climbed the stairs to methodically pick up his portfolio, expecting it to be accompanied by the inevitable rejection slip. He had finally decided to go home to Flushing, throw his art away, and follow his father's advice by getting into some "decent" business. He was led into Mitchell's office and waited in silence—a seeming eternity—while the editor examined the drawings slowly. Through his beard and with a twinkle in his eyes, Mitchell announced: "We're taking this one, Mr. Gibson." Charles Dana Gibson had sold his first drawing to *Life* for four dollars.

The next week Gibson returned with a portfolio of many drawings, dashed off on the basis of confidence in sales; not one was acceptable. Mitchell, sensitive to the eighteen-year-old Gibson's disappointment, took him to lunch. Thus started a warm relationship, a touching devotion (that, among other things, prevented Gibson from going to high-paying *Puck*), and a career that saw Gibson become America's most popular cartoonist, fashion dictator for a generation of men and women, and eventually take control of *Life* itself after Mitchell's passing.

Before long, Gibson's cartoons were a weekly feature; their subject matter was high society, and by the 1890s the "Gibson Girl" had become a national institution. And so had *Life*. With its success came cocksureness, and commentary filled its pages as much as humor. It attacked corruption, tariffs, monopolies, laborers, immigrants, Bostonites, the English, Jews, the *New York Sun*, and the *New York World*. Other objects of its attack were society's "400," Christian Scientists, Museum proprietors, the censor Anthony Comstock, and the art arbiter di Cesnola.

In 1887, Mitchell initiated the "Fresh Air Fund" for the "Life's Farm" program, by which hundreds of tenement children would go to New York or Connecticut farms for two-week periods. This program continues today, always receiving generous help from public subscriptions.

By the mid–1890s, *Life* was a major voice in the magazine world. In large part this was due to the Gibson Girl cartoons. Songs were written about her, her pictures were framed all over the land, thousands of girls dressed and carried themselves like the Gibson Girl, and thousands of men shaved their moustaches, beards, and sideburns and squared their shoulders, just like Gibson's cartoon heroes. In this period of economic depression, Mitchell decided to splurge and employed the half-tone heliograph method of engraving to accommodate wash drawings, so that watercolors could be reproduced in grays in addition to the black and white pen-and-ink work. This type of work was given almost wholly to the "society artists" who preferred paint over pen and ink. These artists who spoofed the "400," the *nouveaux riches*, and the fortune-hunters included Van Schaik and Albert Wenzel; holdovers from early days who still dealt with these themes were W. H. Hyde and Francis Gilbert Attwood.

The art staff and contributors list expanded in the mid–1890s to include Oliver Herford, who often wrote essays or verse to accompany his wispy pictures; Albert S. Sterner, a painter and illustrator for the *Century* and *Harper's*; Frederick T. Richards, a comic artist who was to succeed Attwood in the monthly commentary page after Attwood's death in 1900; Charles Howard Johnson, an unpolished but prolific artist, whose frequent appearances in *Life* are probably attributable to a friendly prejudice on Mitchell's part; Michael Angelo Woolf, who drew pathetic slum kids—early social commentary in cartoons; Hy Mayer, whose unorthodox style bespoke European training; F. P. W. ("Chip") Bellew, whose father was a pioneer American cartoonist and who died prematurely in 1894; and T. S. Sullivant, appreciated for his wild exaggerations and outlandish animals, obviously from his beginnings a genius. Sullivant drew for *Life* well into the 1920s.

Other cartoonists were A. D. Blashfield, who by this time had developed his delicate shading technique and was turning out dozens upon dozens of the cupids that became *Life*'s mascot; C. J. Budd, who was fond of superimposing photographs over his wash drawings; O. Toaspern, who employed a pebbleboard-and-crayon technique—a masterful caricaturist; and the young James Montgomery Flagg, at this time given mostly to illustrated puns.

On the literary side, "Droch" (Robert Bridges) was a widely respected book reviewer who was succeeded late in the 1880s by J. B. Kerfoot after Bridges's engagement as editor of *Scribner's* magazine. James Metcalfe's theater reviews were becoming more and more outspoken; Williston Fish and James L. Ford were two bright additions.

The magazine was so successful that in 1893 a new home was sought for its offices. Land was purchased at 19 West 31st Street in New York City, but in the midst of planning a headquarters, the Depression struck. Finally, in May 1894, the staff moved into the Life Building, complete with a statue of Cupid over the portals.

As *Life* did not rely on the novelty of color, it was not badly hurt by the advent of colored comic strips. Indeed, newspaper cartoonists such as Rudolph Dirks, Carl Schulze ("Bunny"), and C. W. Kahles freelanced for *Life*.

Editorially, *Life* stood by President Cleveland during his second term, depression and all, and abhorred the Populist movement and William Jennings Bryan. Having no love for William McKinley and his high-tariff policies, *Life* nevertheless fought Bryan as savagely as any Republican journal. Cartoons of him generally included stormy skies and a few anarchists in the background. The Spanish-American War provided another reason, however, to turn the criticism toward McKinley. *Life* was violently anti-imperialist, antiwar (this war, at any rate), and anti-jingo. No Johnny-come-lately as "Colonel" Bryan himself was, *Life* took a firm stand and remained consistent before, during, and after the "splendid little war's" duration. It parted company with *Puck* and *Judge* on this issue but agreed with many of the Eastern liberal journals, notably the *Nation*. The ensuing struggles in the Philippines caused *Life* to link the United States with the British, with their Boer War (another atrocity in its eyes), and publish cartoons of Uncle Sam as a bloody-handed murderer—the modern Hun.

The Roosevelt years (1901–1909) brought more new cartoonists to the magazine as well as a new editorial flavor. It was the era of the Muckrakers, and reform was in the air. *Life* had always supported reform, whether civil service, tariff, or monetary. Now attention was focused on trusts and social problems. The Fresh Air Fund was a recognition of urban problems, but now *Life*, like millions of its countrymen, saw in the government a potential instrument for reform of social ills. New cartoonists included C. Allan Gilbert, who is famous for "All Is Vanity," the still-popular picture of a woman sitting at a table mirror, forming the image of a skull; Rudolph Dirks, creator of the *Katzenjammer Kids*; his brother Gus, delineator of comic bugs; William H. Walker, an artist who produced very unattractive work but was a standby for years; his brother A. B. Walker; Will Crawford, who produced marvelously cross-hatched historical cartoons; Art Young, whose cartoons in this decade reflect his drift toward socialism; Orson Lowell, one of the better imitators of Gibson; an improved James Montgomery Flagg; and Walt Kuhn, later a painter, now a cartoonist of birds and bugs.

Of course, Gibson was still there, and the period from 1900 to 1905 was his most successful. He had produced a wildly popular series entitled "Mr. Pipp" in 1899 and was elected to the American Institute of Arts and Letters in the same year, and the Society of Illustrators in 1902. In 1904, the blossoming *Collier's* magazine tried to sign Gibson to an exclusive contract, but once again he would not leave the General, as Mitchell was called. Finally, he signed an agreement to draw exclusively for *Life* and *Collier's*, the latter magazine paying $100,000 for one hundred drawings over the space of several years. In a few years Gibson grew tired of the pen-and-ink work which had served him—and his magazine—so well, forsook an income of approximately $75,000 per year, and went to Europe to learn to paint. *Life* missed him but by no means collapsed. Its page count increased with each issue.

The biggest increase in the advertising columns came from cameras, liquors, and especially automobiles. By 1908 each issue had dozens of car ads, many in color, and issues frequently focused on the new phenomenon. Advertising was so heavy that in 1912 *Life* ran a "great auto race"—to see which manufacturer bought the most space in its columns. *Life* had quality ads, and an upper-middle-class audience. These expansions, coupled with the addition of even more popular features (such as Wallace Irwin's "Letters of a Japanese Schoolboy"), led George Harvey, editor of *Harper's Weekly*, to declare in 1913: "The most successful 10¢ weekly is *Life* . . . "

Life's social consciousness grew notably in the early 1900s. Around 1907 cartoons that were not meant to be funny began to appear. These were cartoons of gloom and pessimism, such as Art Young's "This World of Creepers—Afraid of the Almighty, the Unknown, and Themselves." Or Balfour-Ker's "From the Depths" showing a fist of one of many enslaved workers emerging through the floor they are supporting, on which dances a party of society people. Tom L. Masson, the brilliant managing editor, took on Ellis O. Jones, a socialist, as contributing editor, and it was in these years that *Life* began its policy of publishing points of view different from its editorial stance—especially when the editors leaned in a certain direction but dared not make it formal editorial policy.

The height of *Life*'s success came during the years immediately preceding America's entry into the Great War. In 1916, circulation reached 150,000, and issues ranged from fifty to more than one hundred pages. (Although advertising was a boon, the magazine's strength lay in circulation. *Printer's Ink* magazine estimated that in 1893, *Life* made a profit of $100,000, one-third of which was from circulation. Until the early teens, *Life*'s circulation rested at 60–70,000 over a decade.) All in all, the magazine was very comfortable, mature, and accepted as an institution by the public.

The most published *Life* artists in the teens were Fred G. Cooper (who designed the logo and drew hundreds of spot cartoons); Edwin Blashfield; Angus Mc-Donnall; Victor Anderson; Paul Goold; Donald McKee; Paul Reilly; Anton Otto Fischer; Paul Stahr; Walter Tittle; Orson Lowell; R. M. Crosby; Art Young; Otho Cushing (whose figures always resembled Greek statuary); the Walker Brothers; Harrison Cady (strangely mixing cute bug cartoons with strong anti-Semitic perorations); Frederick T. Richards; Ellison Hoover; R. B. Fuller; Percy

Crosby; Carl Anderson; Walt Kahn; T. S. Sullivant; and Charles Dana Gibson, who returned to the pen and to *Life* around 1910.

It was about this time that the war broke out in Europe, and for John Ames Mitchell, the cause of "humanity versus Germany" became the greatest of his life, superseding *Life*'s Farm, anti-vivisection ("if good for a horse, why not for a man?"), opposition to serums and inoculation, and other crusades. *Life* had always been Germanophobic and Francophilic; Mitchell's position was probably influenced very little by the fact that *Life* had large sales in England. Some contributors took anti-interventionist stands (but not for long, Ellis O. Jones being fired in 1916 for pacifist views), but through *Life*, Mitchell and Miller, together with Theodore Roosevelt and Elihu Root, were the earliest voices in favor of preparedness and, later, of intervention. Some savage cartoons appeared against its hero, Woodrow Wilson, for his weak and contradictory stands (largely forgotten today) before 1917.

Mitchell threw his magazine's full effort into the fight for preparedness against the amazing incompetency of the administration. His heart went out to the land where he had studied art for two long periods in his halcyon student days, and he established the French Orphan's Fund through *Life*. Immediately $200,000 was collected, and in 1918, *Life* supported 2,800 French children.

Mitchell died on 29 June 1918, not living long enough to see the Germans defeated, but long enough to see his cherished publishing dream become not only a reality, but also a respected institution. Success had not come single-handedly, but he had been the captain of the ship, involving himself with every page and every drawing, and leaving his mark on everything. And that was the problem that confronted *Life* after his death: he left too great a void. Charles Dana Gibson—once again drawing exclusively for *Life*—assumed the art editorship which Mitchell had never left, regardless of his other duties. Its flavor therefore remained somewhat intact, and it was in good hands. The company was reorganized with Miller as President (having served previously as Secretary and Treasurer), James S. Metcalfe as Secretary, and Masson as Managing Editor.

But Miller survived Mitchell by only a year and a half, and the staff—that family-like group of workers—was hit with the news that the Miller estate had put the magazine on the auction block. After many conferences and much planning, the staff combined behind Charles Dana Gibson; the syndicate went to the auction in 1920 to bid against agents for Doubleday, Page and Company. Gibson outbid Doubleday, Page, finally paying one million dollars.

In another reshuffling at the top, Gibson was made President of the company. Le Roy Miller became Secretary/Treasurer; Frank de Sales Casey became Art Editor, and Martin remained as Editor until 1922.

Through all this confusion, *Life* was still being put out weekly, now selling for fifteen cents. Just as Warren Harding's "Return to Normalcy" really wasn't a return to anything, so was it hard for *Life* to remain constant. In one sense, this shift was good, for many of the changes were due to the infusion of new talent miraculously appearing after the war. New signatures on cartoons included

Rollin Kirby, the brilliant *New York World* editorial cartoonist; Gluyas Williams, whose economy of line was to gain him fame in illustrating Robert Benchley's work; John Held, Jr., to be famous for flapper cartoons; Percy Crosby and his *Skippy*; H. T. Webster, creator of "The Timid Soul"; Norman Rockwell, painting his earliest covers; and more of T. S. Sullivant's genius. Of course, Gibson was active again.

The literary staff made more impressive gains, however, their new luminaries including Franklin P. Adams, Corey Ford, Montague Glass, Will Rogers, Dorothy Parker, Robert Benchley, Robert E. Sherwood, Ring Lardner, Marc Connelly, and George S. Kaufman.

The twenties began poorly for *Life*. From a circulation of nearly one-half million in 1920, sales dropped to 227,000 in 1922. In 1925 Andrew Miller's widow asked the courts to appoint a receiver for the company and set a "reasonable" salary for Gibson who was said to be getting $30,000 a year for contributions and $20,000 as President. The suit was withdrawn immediately, but it had the intended effect of shaking things up. Editors were Louis Evan Shipman and Robert E. Sherwood between 1922 and 1929; Oliver Herford and Lucinda Flynn were managing editors.

Its troubles are literally unexplainable; it was at the time a very smart and slick magazine. Its rival, *Judge*, was crude and cheaper-looking, but surged past it in sales. *Life* may simply have been too genteel for the speakeasy generation; apparently, *Life* wasn't changing—life was changing. A new format was tried in 1928 and flopped; *Life*'s "Will Rogers for President" campaign attracted some attention, but all to no avail. By 1929, sales had slipped to 113,000. At this point Charles Dana Gibson turned over the presidency to Claire Maxwell.

It was Maxwell who lured Norman Anthony away from *Judge* where he had been editor for five years and had changed it into a zany success-sheet for the college crowd. Maxwell observed his rival's success and the large part Anthony played in it. Gibson assured the new editor that he was set for a long time and would have a free hand in revamping the magazine to make it turn the corner. Anthony accepted the editorship. Aside from putting Gibson to work again and retaining E. S. Martin's editorials, he threw tradition out the window. The accent was more on youth and drinking and New York's recommended night spots. The cartoons were wilder and more risqué. His staff was interchangeable with *Judge*'s: R. B. Fuller; G. B. Inwood; Frank Hanley; Dr. Seuss; Donald McKee; Paul Reilly; and Gardner Rea. In addition, the whole format was changed, and text took a back seat to cartoons.

According to Anthony, sales during his first six months rose from 40,000 to 100,000. Advertisers, however, resented the dominance of the racier new material and, as Anthony reported, "their howls of anguish could be heard way up in Maine where Charles Dana spent his summers." Finally, Anthony got the word that he was out; he immediately sued, claiming a verbal contract for $35,000 per year plus ten percent of the profits, which was what Gibson had offered. *Life* put up a fight but then asked Anthony to drop his suit, which he did.

This episode probably hastened *Life*'s inevitable demise. Bolton Mallory became editor for two years, and the cartoonist George T. Eggleston succeeded him and returned the conservative appearance until 1936 when it was gaining in circulation as a monthly. Eggleston went on to a brilliant career as editor, writer, and Revisionist historian. Gibson retired, but Edwina was drawing her delightful dog cartoons; Marge spoofed society before going to the *Post* and *Little Lulu*. Percy Crosby kept *Skippy* going; and Milt Gross, Dr. Seuss, and Don Herold continued each in his own zany way. S. J. Perelman, Frank Sullivan, George Jean Nathan, Robert Benchley, and Dorothy Parker, along with the inevitable E. S. Martin, provided the literary humor and commentary.

Life was now a quiet, amusing, conservative (it was anti-FDR) magazine starting on the upswing when, in 1936, its owners gave in to offers from Time, Inc., to buy the title. It seemed that the old cupid was simply too weary from the turmoil of the last dozen years. Its subscriptions and features went to the ailing *Judge*, and its name to a proposed picture magazine. Henry Luce of Time, Inc., paid $92,000 for *Life*. Ironically, Clare Booth, whom he married in 1935, told her husband after the purchase of *Life* that in 1933, while she was Managing Editor of *Vanity Fair*,* she wrote a memo to her chief, Condé Nast, urging him to buy *Life* (available then for $20,000) and turn it into a picture-news magazine.

What killed *Life*? Initially, it relied too much on John Ames Mitchell. Then it vacillated between retaining its traditions and catering to a new audience. E. S. Martin felt that the chief reason was the passing of the old staff (he was the sole survivor and wrote a eulogy in the last issue, November 1936), as well as the changing world: "a distracted world that does not know which way to turn or what will happen to it next." Or perhaps after having lived a long, busy, rich, rewarding, and happy life, it simply died a natural and honest death.

Information Sources

BIBLIOGRAPHY:

Anthony, Norman. *How to Grow Old Disgracefully*. New York: Eagle Books, 1946.

Downey, Fairfax. *Portrait of an Era as Drawn by C. D. Gibson*. New York: Scribner's, 1936.

Ford, James L. *Forty-Odd Years in the Literary Shop*. New York: E. P. Dutton, 1921.

Marschall, Richard E. "Selected Humor Magazines, 1802–1950." In *Dictionary of Literary Biography*, Vol. 2, *American Humorists 1800–1950*. Detroit: Gale Research Co., 1982.

Martin, Edward Sanford. Editorial in *Life*. January 1923.

———. "*Life Reincarnate*." *Life*, November 1936 (Special Supplement).

Mitchell, John Ames. "As *Life* Runs On." *Life*, 26 December 1901.

———. "The History of *Life*." *Life*, 10 January 1908.

———. "How *Life* Began." *Life*, 12 January 1893.

———. "Thirty Years." *Life*, 10 January 1908.

Mott, Frank L. *A History of American Magazines, 1865–1885*. Cambridge, Mass.: Harvard University Press, 1957; 4:556–568, and passim.

Peterson, Theodore. *Magazines in the 20th Century*. Urbana: University of Illinois Press, 1956.
Rogers, W. A. *A World Worth While*. New York: Harper's, 1922.
Wood, James Playstead. *Magazines in the United States*. New York: Eagle Books, 1946.
Young, Art. *On My Way*. New York: Horace Liveright, 1928.
INDEX SOURCES: None.
REPRINT EDITIONS: University Microfilms.
LOCATION SOURCES: Approximately one hundred libraries list holdings.

Publication History

MAGAZINE TITLE AND TITLE CHANGES: *Life* (4 December 1883-November 1936).
VOLUME AND ISSUE DATA: Weekly, semi-annual volumes. Volume 1:1, 4 January 1883–Volume 98:2560, 27 November 1931. Monthly, annual volumes, Volume 98:2561, December 1931–Volume 103:2620, November 1936.
PUBLISHER AND PLACE OF PUBLICATION: 1883–1932: Life Publishing Co., New York. 1932–1936: Life Magazine Co., New York.
EDITORS: E. S. Martin, 1883; Henry Guy Carleton, 1883–ca. 1888; Frank White, ca. 1888–ca. 1890; John Kendrick Bangs, ca. 1890–ca. 1896; E. S. Martin, 1896–1922; Louis Evan Shipman, 1923–1925; Robert E. Sherwood, 1925–1929; Norman Anthony, 1929–1930; Bolton Mallory, 1930–1932; George T. Eggleston, 1932–1936.
CIRCULATION: 50,000, 1890; 150,000, 1916.

Richard E. Marschall

LIFE'S COMEDY

One of the many spinoffs from *Life*,* *Life's Comedy* of 1897 through 1899 was a twenty-five cent quarterly featuring reprinted cartoons from its parent magazine. Charles Dana Gibson—clearly taking the lion's share—O. Toaspern, A. B. Wenzell, and H. B. Wechsler were most prominent in comic drawings categorized under headings like "The American Girl," "Belles and Beaux," and "Our Bachelors," all reflecting the artistic and social conventions of the Gibson girl era. Bicycle and courting jokes abound, among other topics; an aquatint of a woman in a bathtub is captioned "Summer Resort"; a dowager in torn clothes announces it was not a cable car accident but rather a bargain basement sale which tore her clothes. Although the first page was decorated with an escutcheon showing a pig and beer steins opposite another showing a railroad and dice, harsher social critiques are supplanted by upper-middle-class topics related to recreation, courtship, and allied social and family situations.

Information Sources

BIBLIOGRAPHY:
Mott, Frank L. "Life." In *A History of American Magazines, 1885–1905*. Cambridge, Mass.: Harvard University Press, 1957; 4:556–68, and passim.
INDEX SOURCES: Artists listed at front of each volume.

REPRINT EDITIONS: None; the Scribner edition is supposed to be a reissue of a Life
    Publishing Company edition.
LOCATION SOURCES: DLC lists only complete run; also CtY, MB, OCLW, OrU,
    PPi, MnU.

Publication History

MAGAZINE TITLE AND TITLE CHANGES: *Life's Comedy*.
VOLUME AND ISSUE DATA: Volumes 1–3 (February, May, August, November),
    1897–1899.
PUBLISHER AND PLACE OF PUBLICATION: Life Publishing Co.; Charles Scribner's
    Sons, New York.
EDITORS: J. A. Mitchell and Andrew Miller.
CIRCULATION: Unknown.

David E. E. Sloane

M

MAD

First a comic book and later an 8″ × 10½″ magazine, Harvey Kurtzman's *Mad* burst upon the American scene in the early 1950s, aimed primarily at readers ranging in age from ten to twenty. Its "What, me worry?" attitude soon disturbed adults already concerned about the impact of comic books on America's youth. In addition to making fun of American popular culture, *Mad*—unlike the Hardy Boys or Horatio Alger books—seemed to be attacking capitalism, consumerism and advertising, government, education, the family, and authority in general. Concerned parents and watchdogs of public morality argued that *Mad* inculcated destructive habits, that it taught teenagers cynicism and, ultimately, disengagement. Over thirty years later, it is still difficult to assess *Mad*'s cultural impact. By itself, it did not shape a generation. Nevertheless, its consciousness of itself as trash, as comic book (later as magazine), as enemy of parents and teachers, and even as money-making enterprise thrilled young people across America.

Mad proved to be one of the two new smash-hit phenomena in the post-World War II magazine business, the other being Hugh Hefner's *Playboy*. Over the years, its scattershot targets included Lyndon Johnson, Barry Goldwater, Fidel Castro, Lassie, railroad timetables, and *Look* Magazine, as well as the classics and a wide variety of other forms of literature. For many, word inventions such as "veeblefetzer," "furshlugginer," "ecch," and "potrzebie" (which could be applied to anything) became part of the language. *Mad*'s frenzy always ran the risk of less than universal appeal, but its secret, saving ingredient was its artwork. In addition to attracting first-rate caricaturists, *Mad* influenced a generation of artists, writers, and media people who grew up with it. *Mad* remains alive and well. Al Feldstein is only its second editor, and William Gaines remains *Mad*'s publisher, although E. C. Publications is now part of Warner Communications,

Inc. Some thirty years after its founding, *Mad*'s spirited burlesques still provide telling commentary on American mores and manners.

Mad's preeminence in its field derives from its pioneering of the sophisticated comic book. Newspaper comic strips have usually had a sizable adult readership, whereas comic books have been aimed primarily at a juvenile and adolescent audience. With its combination of visual media and narrative, the comic-book format proved effective in an age which, under the influence of television and the movies, was becoming increasingly visually oriented. Many of the more sophisticated and intelligent high school and college students found the satirical pieces in commercial magazines like the *Saturday Evening Post*** and *The New Yorker** too tame for their tastes. Humor magazines had two serious limitations: visual humor was limited largely to one-frame caricatures and cartoons; narrative humor was largely verbal. *Mad* synthesized the satirical and humorous approach of the humor and general magazines with the narrative-visual continuity of comic books, thus creating a new medium that made possible a more extended form of verbal and visual humor. To effect this combination, *Mad*'s creators had to develop new comic structures exploiting the joint possibilities of verbal and visual humor. The most important of these was *Mad*'s version of the burlesque, a mainstay of the magazine since its beginning.

The first issue of *Mad* was dated October-November 1952 but appeared in August, postdated as comic books always are. It cost a dime, and its format was that of a regular comic book—thirty-two pages, newsprint, four colors. By its sixth anniversary issue in 1958, *Mad* printed 1.3 million copies, a one hundred percent increase over the comparable issue for 1957. In 1960, *Mad* had a circulation of over 1.4 million. By 1968, each of its eight issues a year sold for "30 cents cheap." Its circulation was 1.7 million, with only three to four percent of this figure through subscriptions. *Mad*'s staff estimated its hand-to-hand readership to be six million plus. In 1971, the magazine reached 2.15 million sold issues. By the late 1970s, *Mad*, according to its staff, sold as many as two million copies a month in the Summer and at Christmastime and 1,650,000 copies during the slower school months. As always, it still contained no advertising.

From the beginning, *Mad*'s days as a comic book were numbered. During the early 1950s, critics of comic books began attacking the sex, violence, and sensationalism that were often essential ingredients of many of the comic books that flooded the market. Ironically, the theme of *Mad* Number 5 happened to be a satire on the sex and violence themes objected to by the guardians of public morality. Critics screamed not only at its contents, but also at the cover which depicted a corpse with an ax and arrows embedded in its skull, something in a perambulator drinking blood from a plasma bottle, and a man in the background hanging a small girl by the neck.

The Comics Code Authority, a censorship body, had been formed in October of 1954, and the public outcry against comic books eventually drove E. C. Publications' best sellers—crime and horror comics—from the newsstands.

Publisher Gaines discontinued all his comic books except *Mad* in 1955. With Issue 24 (July 1955), *Mad* was converted to a twenty-five cent, large format, black and white magazine with "name" humor talent (like Ernie Kovacs and Bob & Ray) on the cover to give it adult drawing power and a certain hint of respectability.

Over the years, *Mad* was called many negative things by its critics. Yet, ironically, it was publicly described in 1967 as a purveyor of old-time religion. In an "exposé" in *The Christian Century*, Vernard Eller maintained: "The moral code reflected in the pages of *Mad* is strait-laced enough to put to shame any Sunday school paper in the land. *Mad* takes out after alcohol, tobacco, drugs, licentiousness, deceit, hypocrisy. . . . Nor does it overlook the issues of social morality. . . . *Mad* represents as old-fashioned a morality as is currently in circulation."[1] "Beneath the pile of garbage that is *Mad*," concluded Eller, employing one of *Mad*'s own favorite descriptions of its contents, "there beats, I suspect, the heart of a rabbi."[2]

As a comic book, *Mad* had focused its satire on other comics. As a magazine, it continued its satires in comics style, but quickly broadened its range to take on television shows, the movies, products, advertisements, politicians, celebrities, and fads, all of which remain its staple diet today. Just after *Mad* became a magazine, editor Harvey Kurtzman, who had been instrumental in shaping the new format, argued with publisher Gaines over control of the magazine. Leaving *Mad*, Kurtzman edited several new satire magazines which failed to catch on; he also created the "Little Annie Fanny" stories in *Playboy*. He was replaced by Al Feldstein, still *Mad*'s editor in the 1980s.

Mad was Kurtzman's brainchild. During the early 1950s, he was editing two war comic books, *Two-Fisted Tales* and *Frontline Combat*, for the E. C. comic book company. At first, the initials "E. C." on comic book covers stood for "Educational Comics." When M. C. Gaines began E. C. in the mid–1940s, the company was indeed educational, publishing comic-book versions of the Bible and American history. After Gaines's death in 1947, his son William shifted the firm's emphasis toward commercial romance comics, westerns, and crime titles, and "E. C." came to stand for "Entertaining Comics." In 1949, horror stories edged into E. C.'s crime comics, and in 1950, E. C. began publishing three unabashed horror titles and science fiction comics.

Kurtzman, an E. C. editor, worked on the science fiction comics before taking over the company's war comic books. He emphasized realism in his work about men at war, an approach requiring much research. In 1952, he decided to create a comic book that he could write without leaving his room, drawing on "All the junk I'd been accumulating from childhood."[3] As a result, Kurtzman and a small staff of E. C.'s top-rated comic-book artists—Bill Elder, Wallace Wood, and Jack Davis—decided to experiment with a different kind of comic book. William Gaines gave them their freedom, and, without doubt, much of *Mad*'s later success came from E. C.'s initial willingness to let four young men try a format that was not guaranteed to make money.

If the most obvious meaning of *Mad* was "crazy" (i.e., confused by the absurdities of modern existence), the connotation of anger was never entirely absent. Its full title—*Tales calculated to drive you mad. Humor in a jugular vein*—warned the reader about the kind of humor it cultivated. Although it took a few issues for the format to become established, *Mad* would achieve its greatest fame as a purveyor of parody and satire. The original concept, revealed on the editor's page of the first issue, was: "A comic book! Not a serious comic . . . but a Comic book . . . a comic mag based on the short story type of wild adventure that you seem to like so well." In essence, the early *Mad* based its material on a style that had already been established by the war and science fiction comics previously edited by Kurtzman. "Blobs," a science fiction takeoff (drawn by Wallace Wood) in the first issue, was only a little weirder than the stories in E. C.'s *Weird*. Humorous details in the drawing and script created a comic effect and set the tone for the early issues, which existed in a limbo halfway between previous E. C. titles and the *Mad* that was to come.

Beginning with the first issue, Kurtzman introduced a mysterious and zany character named Melvin, who became an identifying character-logo for *Mad*. A full face shot of Melvin did not appear until the twenty-third issue of *Mad*. Although later issues always carried Melvin's picture, they never referred to his name, only to his famous motto: "What, me worry?" During the 1960s, Melvin became Alfred E. Newman, a grinning, gap-toothed teenager who usually appeared on *Mad*'s covers in one fantastic role or another.

The first parody in the definitive *Mad* style was "Superduperman," delineated by Wallace Wood for the fourth issue. Although it was Bill Elder who finally gained the greatest reputation for his ability to burlesque other comics in *Mad*, Wood established the trend in issues 4 through 11. Elder began his attacks on other comics with "Woman Wonder" in the tenth issue and fully matured with "Starchie" (No. 12), which gave the impression that it had been drawn in a moment of madness by an "Archie" staff artist. Elder imitated the style of the artist he was mocking, while Wood drew the characters in his own style, supplying enough original detail to make apparent the source: both forms of caricature were devastating. Although parodies were outnumbered by other humorous approaches, they set *Mad*'s tone. The characters became self-conscious commentators on their own formats. "Mickey Rodent" hatched a plot to regain the popularity he had lost to "Darnold Duck," while "Superduperman" was aware of the Superman lawsuit against Captain Marvel.

The high point of the *Mad* comic book was reached with the seventeenth issue. Elder's "Bringing Back Father" has Jiggs reacting to his wife with real resentment and real injuries, finally hiring a group of thugs to reestablish himself as the head of the family. Kurtzman and Wood's "Julius Caesar" uses the then-current film version of Shakespeare's play as a springboard for a treatment with *Mad*'s techniques. Jack Davis's "What's My Shine" courageously depicted the Army-McCarthy hearings as a television panel show. *Mad* thus established another comic-book landmark by taking on a real and powerful politician.

From the very first as a magazine, *Mad* was arranged in "departments." A typical *Mad* magazine of any vintage might contain ten to twenty departments, from a "Terror Dept." to a "Scenes We'd Like to See Dept." to a "Davy Crockett Dept." to a "Don Martin Dept.," reserved for an artist who proved to be a great favorite of *Mad* readers. The "department" format and the wide range of subject matter covered have remained typical over the years.

Mad has long attacked the irrelevant gimmicks and deceptive practices of American advertising. Its burlesques of advertisements combine verbal and visual satire. The magazine's back cover has frequently been devoted to a full-color burlesque of a current advertising campaign. Another type of *Mad* advertisement takes the form of a direct satire on advertising's deceptive practices; a more or less straight version of an ad is presented, followed by a series of pictures which illuminate the true character of whatever is being advertised.

Also used to good advantage (especially during the seventies) were what might be called *Mad* newsreels. A sequence of photographs is accompanied by captions that bring out the satirical point. The words of some traditional song or speech would be juxtaposed against contemporary photographs to reveal how traditional feelings or beliefs are being violated in today's world. *Mad* delighted in setting the words of the Ten Commandments over current news photographs.

Some of *Mad*'s features edged away from burlesque and parody toward direct satire of particular American institutions. A connected series of short one- to four-picture gags frequently illustrated in mosaic style different aspects of a particular institution. David Berg, a major *Mad* contributor, made great use of this kind of direct satire. His portrayal of American life was central to the general mood or unity of *Mad*'s satirical attitudes.

In its sixth anniversary issue in 1958, *Mad* conjured up such magazines as *Caveman's Weekly* (sample article: "Is the Stone-Ax the Ultimate Weapon?") and the *Pilgrim's Home Journal* (featuring "I Should Have Kept My Mouth Shut," by John Alden); gave advice on how to play golf ("The grip should be about the same as one would use clutching a dead trout"); and quoted some woman-meets-native dialogue from *National Osographic*, which captured the inarticulateness of its era: "Evelyn stepped forward and asked in Swahili, 'What I want to know, and I want you to give me a straight answer, is—I mean—I want to know if you really got cannibals up this way. I mean I heard the rumble. I know the story.' "

During the 1960s, burlesques continued to be *Mad*'s principal stock in trade. The drawings were imitations of the rotogravure sections in Sunday newspapers. The style of *Mad* in the sixties was heavily marked by the film and television satires by caricaturist Mort Drucker; the way-out humor of Don Martin, whose work is one of the best examples of sick humor in comics style; and "The Lighter Side of . . . " feature by David Berg, which directed its barbs at the life-styles found in suburban America.

As its circulation and notoriety grew, *Mad* continued to parody anything and everything. But when *Mad* needled Madison Avenue, doctors, and other well-worn targets to the tune of Irving Berlin's "There's No Business Like Show Business" and other popular songs, Berlin and twelve music publishers (representing Richard Rodgers and Cole Porter among others) filed suit, charging infringement of copyright. In 1964, the U.S. Court of Appeals in New York found in favor of *Mad* in the case of *Berlin et al. v. E. C. Publications*. Upholding a lower court decision, Judge Irving R. Kaufman wrote: "Parody and satire are deserving of substantial freedom both as entertainment and as a form of social and literary criticism."

Mad burlesques during the 1960s—such as Mort Drucker and Arnie Kogen's burlesque of *Butch Cassidy and the Sundance Kid*—illustrate how much more sophisticated the magazine had become since the early fifties. Drucker's style of visual parody is richer and more subtle in its range of expression than the grotesque caricatures of the earlier *Mad*. The main object of satire in "Botch Cassidy and the Someduncе Kid" (No. 136, July 1970) is the film's attempt to make a humorous and lyrical statement out of materials of the traditional Western. At one point, Botch's gang is fleeing a posse. As Botch and Someduncе exchange one-line gags, one of the outlaws says: "It's times like these that I miss the biting, satirical humor of Roy Rogers and Dale Evans!" When Botch and Someduncе are trapped on a high cliff by the posse, Botch absolutely refuses to jump until Someduncе says:

Hey did you hear the one about these two traveling salesmen—?
I'LL JUMP!! I'LL JUMP!!

"Botch Casually" represents a main type of *Mad* burlesque. The object of satire is more the formal characteristics of the parodied work than the values they represent. These are, on the whole, friendly satires instead of attacks.

Yet many of *Mad*'s television and movie burlesque of the seventies are far more biting attacks on the fake values and hypocrisy that the satirized works present. Angelo Torres and Stan Hart's "Room 22222zzzz" (No. 136, July 1970), a takeoff on a television series about an integrated high school, is a representative *Mad* attack on the mass media's fashionable, escapist version of contemporary themes and social relevance during the seventies. For example, a Black student and Mr. Dixie, the Black teacher, have the following conversation:

Hey, Mr. Dixie! How come when the program opens each week, we show White couples and Black couples, but no Mixed couples—like maybe a White girl and a Black boy.

Because this is TV—not movies! and TV still isn't ready to show what Democracy is really all about! In fact, it's amazing that we can even show that this school is totally integrated!

Yeah, especially when it's actually located in an all-White suburban area, and no Blacks live anywhere near it!

Today, *Mad* demonstrates less interest in the more extravagant and grotesque forms of humor which it utilized during the 1950s to lampoon American culture. More revolutionary forms of comedy have emerged in the underground press to compete with the milder mockery of *Mad*. Nevertheless, *Mad*'s running critical commentary on the American scene continues to delight millions of readers.

Notes

1. Vernard Eller, "The '*Mad*' Morality: An Exposé," *The Christian Century* 84 (27 December 1967): 1647.

2. Ibid., p. 1649.

3. Quoted in Tony Hiss and Jeff Lewis, "The '*Mad*' Generation," *New York Times Magazine* (31 July 1977): 16.

Information Sources

BIBLIOGRAPHY:
Barrier, Michael, and Martin Williams. *A Smithsonian Book of Comic-Book Comics*. New York: Smithsonian Press, 1981, pp. 295–98.
Cawelti, John G. "The Sanity of *Mad*." In *American Humor: Essays Presented to John C. Gerber*, ed. O. M. Brack, Jr. N. p.: n. p. 1977, 171–88.
Crawford, Hubert H. *Crawford's Encyclopedia of Comic Books*. Middle Village, N.Y.: Jonathan David Publishers, 1978, pp. 294–95, 300–301, 306.
Daniels, Les. *A History of Comic Books in America*. New York: Outerbridge and Dienstfrey, 1971, pp. 66–70.
Eller, Vernard. "The '*Mad*' Morality: An Exposé." *The Christian Century* 84 (27 December 1967): 1647–49.
Flagler, J. M. "The *Mad* Miracle." *Look* 32 (19 March 1968): 46, 48, 50.
Hiss, Tony, and Jeff Lewis. "The '*Mad*' Generation." *New York Times Magazine* (31 July 1977): 14, 16, 18–20.
Morton, Charles W. "The Case for *Mad*." *Atlantic* 212 (19 March 1963): 100.
Pilpel, Harriet. "When Is a Parody a Plagiarism?" *Publishers' Weekly* 184 (30 December 1963): 31.
Reitberger, Reinhold, and Wolfgang Fuchs. *Comics: Anatomy of a Mass Medium*. Boston: Little, Brown and Co., 1971, pp. 62–65.
Skow, Jack. "*Mad*: Wild Oracle of the Teenage Underground." *Saturday Evening Post* 236 (21–28 December 1963): 62–65.
Thompson, Don, and Dick Lupoff, eds. *The Comic-Book Book*. New Rochelle, N.Y.: Arlington House, 1973, pp. 301–304.
INDEX SOURCES: None.
REPRINT SOURCES: None.
LOCATION SOURCES: Eight libraries list holdings: CL, DLC, University of Iowa, University of Kansas Libraries Lawrence, NN, OU, Pennsylvania State University, and ViU.

Publication History

MAGAZINE TITLE AND TITLE CHANGES: *Mad* (comic book), Numbers 1–23, October-November 1952–May 1955; *Mad* (magazine), Numbers 24– , July 1955- .

VOLUME AND ISSUE DATA: Bimonthly, October-November 1952–September-Oc-
    tober 1958; eight times a year, November 1958–   .
PUBLISHER AND PLACE OF PUBLICATION: William Gaines, New York.
EDITORS: Harvey Kurtzman (1952–1956); Al Feldstein (1956–   ).
CIRCULATION: 1.4 million in 1960; 1.7 million in 1968; 2 million in 1977; 2 million
    in 1982. *Mad* has never accepted advertising. Most of its sales are newsstand
    sales.

L. Moody Simms, Jr.

MOONSHINE

Moonshine, an 1807 periodical of only five issues, took its title from the
superstition that a person exposed to the rays of the moon became insane. The
journal of the "Lunarian Society," *Moonshine* burlesqued the numerous
scientific organizations of the early nineteenth century and treated literature, the
sciences, the law, and social customs with sophisticated irreverence. Contributors
attempted to "manufacture a few easy jokes," so that people might forget the
great calamities of life—spoiled clothing, failure in love, or financial reverses.
Critical of European affectation and open displays of wealth or learning,
Moonshine noted that membership in the Lunarian Society came automatically
to the person who traveled to London and Paris and repeatedly told anecdotes
of his tour.

The Lunarians claimed as their vice-president Copernicus Ptolemy, who held
membership in 16 royal societies, 43 academies, and 121 "anacreonic societies,"
and who was a fellow of the Society of Noah's Ark (FSNA). Other than Noah
and the Man in the Moon, only Vincent Lunardi, the secretary of the Society,
and Henry Henpeck, a troubled husband bound by the "Gordian tye" of
marriage, appeared by name as contributors to *Moonshine*. The opening essay
exploited contemporary enthusiasm for Egyptology aroused by the discovery of
the Rosetta Stone in 1799. After a report of a fragment of supposed Pharaonic
lore, the piece compared wit to a bridle that could be used for leading a foolish,
goose-like population. Puns, allusions to the classics, adaptations of literary
masterworks, and exaggerations of professional cant appeared in all issues. The
influence of the law straddled "across Calvert Street like a modern Colossus";
another essay depicted a lawyer "praying for a continuance" in the case of his
death.

In format, *Moonshine* appeared in one-column pages. Individual copies sold
for twelve and one-half cents. Each of the first two issues contained sixteen
pages, but the remaining three had eight each. As *Moonshine* had announced,
the third number, for 9 July 1807, sold with the first issue of the *Baltimore
Magazine*. Samuel Jefferies of Baltimore, Maryland, was noted as the publisher;
Jefferies and his partner printed the magazine. According to the publisher, readers
demanded more than the offerings possible in a purely humorous magazine; the

opportunities for a catholicity of literary themes and subject matter lay beyond the scope of *Moonshine*.

The phrase in Greek on the cover of the first issue—"five dark-blue beans in a dark-blue pouch"—suggests that, despite the initial advertisement promising as many as ten issues, *Moonshine* was intended to have a five-issue run. Whether such a conclusion is warranted, the high-comedy aspect of the periodical contributed to its demise; the nature of its satire commanded a limited audience, and the smallness of the area of distribution doomed *Moonshine* from its beginning.

Information Sources

INDEX SOURCES: None.
REPRINT EDITIONS: University Microfilms.
LOCATION SOURCES: DLC, MB, Boston Public, MBat, and New York State Institute of Psychiatry; first issue at MWA.

Publication History

MAGAZINE TITLE AND TITLE CHANGES: *Moonshine*, 20 June 1807 to 23 July 1807.
VOLUME AND ISSUE DATA: Volume 1:1, 20 June 1807–Volume 1:5, 23 July 1807.
PUBLISHER AND PLACE OF PUBLICATION: Samuel Jefferies, Baltimore, Maryland.
EDITOR: Unknown.
CIRCULATION: Unknown.

Thomas Hunter Stewart

MRS. GRUNDY

Mrs. Grundy, which had a short but happy life during the Summer of 1865, was an extension of *Vanity Fair*.* Artists Henry L. Stephens and Edward F. Mullen, and editor C. D. Shanley were all alumni of *Vanity Fair*. Other artists were A. L. Carroll, Augustus Hoppin, Edwin Forbes, and Thomas Nast. The magazine advertised the "highest order of talent" in both pen and pencil, and in a few weeks was claiming to be "equal to *Punch*." Nast drew the initial cover which was used for each of the twelve issues. It shows the character of Mrs. Grundy, on stage, facing an audience of many famous contemporary men and women.

Mrs. Grundy's format was similar to that of other imitations of *Punch*. It was a twelve-page quarto with a middle unbacked cartoon. The magazine sold a three-month subscription for two dollars, although it did not live that long. In its first issue (8 July 1865), the magazine set out its aims in heroic couplets: "Step forward, Politicians, great and small; / Dame Grundy has a paragraph for all." In addition to politicians, it promised to keep an eye on clergymen, professors, editors, and almost every other occupation. "We have for every class our special critics, / Whose keen eyes scan, unwarped by specious glamour, / All themes, from Ethics down to English Grammar." Its aims were to dispel illusions and to reform abuses, but with good nature. It borrowed its motto from a then-current speech: "Malice toward none, but charity for all" (p. 3).

So overwhelming was the response that *Mrs. Grundy* had to print a cautioning poem the next week. The editors reasoned that many of the contributions had been inspired by "naught but Cupidity," for what was sent was a "mass of Stupidity." Contributors were to avoid the sentimental, keep vapidity out of jokes, and acidity out of satires (p. 16).

Light verse was probably the best feature of the magazine, and there were several occasional poems in each issue. Sometimes these were translations or mock-translations of German or Latin poems, complete with the original language version. Some of the poems were dialect monologues: Yankee, Negro, Irish, German. There was a poem about the Atlantic Cable, written from the point of view of a fish, who wonders what that thing is that looks like a snake. There was a mock epic about a fight between two New York fire companies, and poems about the smells and sounds of the city.

> How sweet to my Nose are the Smells of the City,
> From the scarce perceived Flavor of mouldering Kitty
> To the full-bodied Stench of the Horse that lies dead. (p. 44)

Reconstruction politics was a big topic. The personalities most frequently mentioned were President Andrew Johnson, Secretary of War Edwin Stanton, Secretary of State William Seward, and Generals William T. Sherman and U. S. Grant. Editor Horace Greeley, financier Jay Cooke, and poet Walt Whitman also came in for notice. The editorial for the first issue was a nonhumorous poem, "A Reunion Carol for July 4, 1865." The cartoon showed the personification of Peace reuniting the country.

Much of the subject matter in *Mrs. Grundy* involved New York City. There were jokes and sketches about the garbage, police, councilmen, and the newspapers. There were cartoons and editorials about the hazards of railroad travel, and the dishonesty of Wall Street bankers. There was also material about high society, summer resorts, and fashions. "Some strong-minded women with short hair, and weak-minded men with long hair, have been holding a 'Convention' again on the subject of Short Petticoats and 'women's right' to wear them" (p. 4).

The editorials were usually done in a light style, sometimes set in verse. Two editorials were done in the form of letters to the dowager, Mrs. Grundy. One from a Miss "Flora Parvenue," was about the burning of the United States Hotel in Saratoga. It told about her plight, relegated as she was to a second-rate hotel where there was nobody worth talking to or dancing with, after she had bought eleven trunks of dresses from Paris. The other letter was from a bachelor about the most sensational event of the Summer of 1865: the trial of Mary Harris in Washington D.C., for the murder of her ex-suitor.

Both of these letters were illustrated by Thomas Nast. In addition to the frontispiece, Nast contributed twelve sketches and drawings, four of them middle cartoons, to *Mrs. Grundy*. The literary contributions to the magazine were unsigned, and many of the drawings were not initialed. However, each of Nast's contributions was signed "Th. Nast" or initialed "TN."

Nast drew middle cartoons about railroad disasters and Wall Street bankers. He also contributed sketches about fashions, resorts, and tourists. There is an amusing illustration of a poem about "The Saengerfest" (p. 43), a week-long celebration of German singing—and drinking—societies in New York.

Nast's work for *Mrs. Grundy* is very different from the type of drawing he was doing at the same time for *Harper's Weekly*. It is more humorous and lighthearted, and shows no awareness of the war and Reconstruction. The smaller page of *Mrs. Grundy* forced Nast to concentrate his message; he did not have the luxury of the two folio pages of *Harper's Weekly* to expand his theme. Nast's association with *Mrs. Grundy* probably accelerated his development from an illustrator to a cartoonist.

Mrs. Grundy expired after twelve weeks, its income from circulation barely able to meet the expenses. The magazine appealed to a limited audience—the literati and cognoscenti—and the average reader probably had difficulty appreciating its humor.

A week after *Mrs. Grundy*'s demise, *Harper's Weekly* (30 September 1865) printed a cartoon showing a policeman talking to Mrs. Grundy.

"Well, Old Woman, What's the matter with you?" Mrs. Grundy. "Oh, Sir! I've been dreadfully deceived. My name is Mrs. Grundy. Those young fellows running down the street there decoyed me from my home to 132 Nassau Street. They said they wanted to know what I had to say; so I told them all I knew—which was precious little—and—and—now that I can say no more, they say it don't pay, and they put me out of doors." N.B.—The poor old lady is since dead of a new disease called "undeveloped humor."(p. 624)

Information Sources

BIBLIOGRAPHY:

Carroll, A. L. "Can a Humorous Periodical Succeed in America?" *Round Table* 2 (21 October 1865): 97–98.

Mott, Frank L. *A History of American Magazines, 1865–1885*. Cambridge, Mass.: Harvard University Press, 1957, 3:265.

Paine, Albert Bigelow. *Th. Nast: His Period and His Pictures*. Gloucester, Mass.: Peter Smith, 1965, p. 100.

INDEX SOURCES: None.

REPRINT EDITIONS: None.

LOCATION SOURCES: ICN, MH, MWA, NN, NIC, RPB, UI.

Publication History

MAGAZINE TITLE AND TITLE CHANGES: *Mrs. Grundy*, 8 July 1865–23 September 1865.

VOLUME AND ISSUE DATA: Weekly, Number 1, 8 July 1865–Number 12, 23 September 1865. Bound in one volume.

PUBLISHER AND PLACE OF PUBLICATION: Mrs. Grundy Publishing Co., 132
    Nassau Street, New York.
EDITORS: Dr. Alfred L. Carroll, Charles Dawson Shanley. Assistants: Howard Irving,
    Ashley W. Cole, George Phoebus.
CIRCULATION: 6,000(?).

William R. Linneman

___ N ___

NAST'S WEEKLY

The accidental fulfillment of a life-long ambition, Thomas Nast's *Nast's Weekly* began publication during the election campaign of 1892 and ran for six months, appearing every Saturday from 1 September 1892 until 4 March 1893. Supported almost entirely by Republican presidential hopes, the paper could not survive the Democratic electoral victory on 8 November and the final edition was issued on Inauguration Day, 1893 as, for the second time, Grover Cleveland took the oath of office.

Nast had long dreamed of a paper of his own, free of editorial or public pressure, that would place principles before personalities. A standard-bearer of Radical Republicanism for twenty-six years with *Harper's Weekly*, Nast embodied a passionate, often myopic, black and white political morality. He had fewer and fewer sympathizers as the intense and clearly defined divisions of the Civil War and Reconstruction blurred and the "bloody shirt" was buried. Even during his greatest years with *Harper's*, Nast had frequently been at odds with the more temperate editorial policies of long-time *Harper's* editor George William Curtis. Curtis always felt, and repeatedly tried to convince the Harper brothers, that Nast's savage satire should be restrained by political caution, and it was only through the mediation of Fletcher Harper that Nast and Curtis were able to remain on the same paper.

As early as 1884, while still drawing for *Harper's*, Nast, hoping to raise the capital to finance a journal of his own, had rashly invested in the firm of Grant and Ward, losing almost everything when Ward proved to be a scoundrel. The election of that year in which both Nast and *Harper's*, unable to stand the Republican "Plumed Knight," James C. Blaine, joined the Mug-Wumps in support of Cleveland, commercially damaged *Harper's* and increased Nast's political isolation. Nast again came out for Cleveland in 1888, and the Republican liberals were for a time dubbed the "Nast-T" party, but, for the first time, Nast found himself on the losing side in an election. Resented by the Republican faithful—*Judge** in particular took Nast to task—and unable to reconcile himself to Democratic and Tammany administrations, Nast found himself without an audience. Without Fletcher Harper, and facing popular professional competition from the Democratic *Puck** and the Republican *Judge*, which had begun featuring colored lithographs, Nast in his later years experienced increasing personal disappointment and professional obscurity. Moving from journal to journal, often hired by editors of failing papers who hoped that his name would revive moribund circulation, Nast seldom lasted in a job more than a few weeks before bankruptcy or an editorial crisis, often brought on by his own inflexible convictions, forced him once again to move on.

Thus in March 1892, Nast received a letter from the editors of the *New York Gazette*, a four-page daily begun in 1889, promising Nast a "free rein." Hired as an illustrator, Nast was soon the *Gazette*'s chief creditor and by the end of April was in possession of the paper itself. Having at last the chance that in better years had escaped him, Nast put a second mortgage on his house, set up his son, Thomas Nast, Jr., as publisher and hired Morrison Renshaw as editor. Unfortunately, as Albert Paine notes in his biography of Nast, "There have been a great many bad combinations in publishing enterprises, but probably never a worse one than that which took over the remnants and fortunes of the *Gazette*" (p. 538). None of the principals had any practical knowledge of publishing. In addition, Nast, always the impolitic crusader for municipal reform, returned to a theme that had provided some of his first successful material with *Harper's* and *Leslie's Illustrated Weekly* and began printing pages of "police scandal" which caused the paper to be "discontinued" by the distributors. Although the paper stumbled through the Summer of 1892 on vague hopes of assistance from Charles Henry Parkhurst and other prominent leaders of New York reform, little help actually materialized. The *Gazette* would have died of its own accord by August had it not been an election year; Nast's attacks on current Tammany "Boss" Richard Croker, and his return to the Republican fold in support of President Benjamin Harrison persuaded the Republican party to "guarantee" a circulation of 100,000 for the paper through the election. Now to be called *Nast's Weekly*, the paper's prospectus in the first issue under the new masthead announced: "The aim of the paper will be to promote and defend the cause of good government, National, State and Municipal. . . . The features of the paper will be of a political, social, literary, domestic and humorous character, and special articles from time to time, on chosen subjects, by prominent writers will appear." A later editorial goes on to say: "We propose to steer a course between conservatism and aggressiveness. The channel between them is broad enough, but here and there are reefs we fain would avoid."

The election and national political issues dominated *Nast's Weekly*. The McKinley Tariff, the healthy condition of business under the Harrison administration, and "His Dignity," Grover Cleveland, were the common editorial topics. The lead editorial in the first issue, "Has Cleveland's Head Been Turned?" (by a third nomination), sets a motif that reappears through the entire run up to Inauguration Day. It is probable that Nast, remembering the outcry of "Caesarism" when his idol Ulysses Grant sought a third term, added a healthy vigor to this charge.

Nast's Weekly's attention to municipal affairs consisted mainly of attempts to stir up a reform fervor over local gambling dens, police brutality, and pool halls. But even such "social" comment was usually tailored to make political points. Nast was a Republican by persuasion as well as party. Democracy in general and Tammany in particular were, he felt, at the heart of public vice, municipal malfeasance, and national disunion. To Nast, Tammany and Democratic corruption went hand in hand with Southern secessionist treachery—never far from his mind or pen. Drawing a parallel between Republican protective legislation and the Summer's quarantine against a worldwide cholera epidemic, the *Weekly* editorialized, "Quarantine against Democracy is as necessary to the future prosperity of the country as quarantine against cholera—and more so."

Philosophically centered on Nast's independent, often ferociously aggressive, conservatism, *Nast's Weekly* was editorially formatted around his illustrations. Each issue contains up to a dozen drawings, from small pieces accompanying a particular column, to large double-page center spreads and supplements. A front-page drawing, usually a half-page portrait under a Nast-like owl in a jester's cap, set the editorial theme each week, and the point was driven home by the centerpiece. The large drawings very closely resemble Nast's usual format with *Harper's*—oversize single pages here measuring 10" × 13". Moreover, in a manner surely calculated to call up unpleasant associations in the minds of his readers, Nast's drawings hearken back twenty years to the battle with Bill Tweed and the Tammany Ring. Not only do the usual Nast images and style appear— the Tammany Tiger, Uncle Sam, the Republican elephant, and the Democratic donkey—but the pictures of Cleveland with his "head turned," all the way around, are very like the earlier drawings of Tweed with a money bag where his head should be.

In other ways the drawings compare less favorably to the best of Nast's *Harper's* work. Nast had never gotten used to the techniques of photochemical reproduction which required drawing in pen and ink on paper for transference to copper plates for printing. Until *Harper's* took up the photoengraving process in 1880, Nast had most often drawn in soft pencil directly on the boxwood blocks that would then be cut down and locked in the printing frame. His hand was stiff with the steel pens of the new technique, and the contrast is clearly seen when an old drawing from *Harper's* is reproduced in *Nast's Weekly*.

Physically, the paper started out at sixteen pages counting front and back covers, folded in octavo and printed in two columns for editorials and three for back pages. After the election issue of 12 November, as economies had to be practiced, the paper came out in only eight pages with no supplements. Paine suggests that the letterpress was donated by Charles Fairbanks and Leon Mead, and the printers are identified in an advertisement as the Stuyvesant Press, incorporated 1891, of New York City. The first few issues are plain newsprint but most of the run is on paper with a slightly glossy finish, similar to paper used on the *Gazette*. The price remained five cents a copy, $1.50 for six months and $2.50 for a year. No colors were used, the only unusual feature being a photograph of the Manola-Mason Company Performers in the theater section of issue 21.

Apart from politics, the paper also featured pages of "General Comment," paragraphs on timely topics, and witty, one-line remarks prone to political allegory. The Lizzie Borden murder trial, the Corbett-Sullivan prizefight, the Homestead Strike, the DeLesseps Canal Scandal, and John Bull baiting over the annexation of Hawaii (the paper looked favorably on proposals for a similar arrangement with Canada)—all came in for consideration. Column fillers consisted of coy doggerel or slightly naughty jokes. A "Players" section was devoted to short theater notes and a page of theater ads. The pieces of a literary character were, in the early issues, one-page stories said to be translated from "French Novels," but this section disappeared after 12 November. Thereafter, the literary pieces are for the most part sentimental or humorous verses signed frequently by Leon Mead. Two eulogies by James Whitcomb Riley appear, "Tennyson" in Number 6 for 22 October, and "Caroline Scott Harrison" (the First Lady), in Number 9 for 3 December.

Advertisements and frequent self-promotional pieces provide a clear gauge of the *Weekly*'s financial precariousness. Although many of the commercial advertisers remained to the end, a full page of railroad ads and schedules disappeared immediately after the election. As the situation grew worse, quasi-editorials on the virtues of newspaper advertising began offering inducements to would-be advertisers—free illustrations, contests, and a suggestion that the paper would be expanded and brought out in color. But even before the election the "guarantee" to advertisers had slipped to 50,000 copies, and afterwards, without even this largely fictitious circulation, the paper could not continue very long. Paine notes that no creditors went unpaid when the paper finally went under, but the paper's failure left Nast in a position from which he never completely recovered.

The political issues of the early 1890s, the protective tariff, business, and the National Bank, hotly debated as they were in Congress and the press, were not as dramatic and not as easily caricatured as secession, slavery, and ostentatiously corrupt municipal managers. The heroes and villains of post-Civil War and Reconstruction politics, who through Nast's pen had peopled the pages of *Harper's Weekly*, were gone by the time he got the chance to start his own paper. Gone too were the great editors, Bryant and Bennett, Curtis, and Greeley (killed it had been said by disappointment and Nast's pencil) were all dead, and journalism was becoming more a profit-minded incorporation than a platform for editorial opinion and politically partisan polemic. Especially in the popular imagination Nast's reputation already belonged to another era; the Democrat Cleveland's second inauguration spelled the end of Nast's once formidable influence on national politics.

Information Sources

BIBLIOGRAPHY:

American Newspaper Annual. Philadelphia: N. W. Ayer & Son, 1890.

Christmas Drawings for the Human Race. With introduction and epilogue by Thomas Nast St. Hill. New York: Harper and Row, 1971. Reprint of 1890 edition with new introduction and foreword.

Harper, Joseph Henry. *The House of Harper*. New York: Harper and Bros., 1912.

Keller, Morton. *The Art and Politics of Thomas Nast*. New York: Oxford University Press, 1968.

Mott, Frank Luther. *American Journalism*. 3d ed. New York: Macmillan Co., 1962.

Paine, Albert Bigelow. *Th. Nast, His Period and His Pictures*. Gloucester, Mass.: Peter Smith, 1967. Reprint of 1904 edition.

Vinson, J. C. *Thomas Nast, Political Cartoonist*. Athens, Ga.: University of Georgia Press, 1967.

INDEX SOURCES: None.

REPRINT EDITIONS: None.

LOCATION SOURCES: The University of Minnesota Special Collections, Wilson Library, in Minneapolis holds the only bound run of *Nast's Weekly*. Their holdings include two extra copies of issue number 3 for 1 October 1892. Nast used these copies in planning the 12 November election issue, pasting up drawings from other issues and other papers, as well as pencilling in margin notes and directions to the printers.

The University of Iowa Main Library in Iowa City holds a microfilm copy of Minnesota's holdings. DLC and NN hold partial runs of the *Gazette*.

Publication History

MAGAZINE TITLE AND TITLE CHANGES: *Nast's Weekly*, 1 September 1892–4 March 1893.

VOLUME AND ISSUE DATA: Twenty-five numbers of one volume, issued every Saturday for twenty-five weeks.

PUBLISHER AND PLACE OF PUBLICATION: Thomas Nast, Jr., New York.

EDITOR: Morrison Renshaw, 1 September–10 December 1892. No editor appears on the masthead after 10 December, but there are indications that Leon Mead took over at least some of the editorial duties.

CIRCULATION: The first three numbers advertise a "guaranteed" circulation of 100,000 which slipped to 50,000 by October 1892. It is unlikely that actual readership ever approached either of these figures.

Eric Austin

NATIONAL LAMPOON

The *National Lampoon* began in 1970 as a spinoff of Harvard's campus humor magazine. In its first year, it attracted a huge national audience by attacking everything and offending everybody. Its primary targets have remained adolescence, pop culture fads and fashions, best-sellers, celebrities in politics, and the media—virtually anything tainted by commercialization. It is not a satire magazine since it has no official point of view, and its editors and writers have pointed out that *National Lampoon* plays no favorites, assaulting everyone with perverse evenhandedness in a tone of cheerful nihilism. It revels in *lampooning* in its original seventeenth-century sense of attack that is personal and even scurrilous—the pleasure derived from the French, *lampons*, "let us drink." Indeed, contributors like to appear to be inebriates of scorn, too drunk on heaping abuse to worry at all about correcting it.

The magazine was founded by three Harvard graduates—Henry Beard, Doug Kenney, and Rob Hoffman—who worked on the *Harvard Lampoon** as undergraduates in the late 1960s. They had produced several successful full-scale magazine parodies and believed a national humor magazine could achieve commercial success. They approached Matty Simmons and Leonard Mogul, owners of Twenty-First Century Communications, publishers of *Weight Watchers* and *Ingenue*—the company that printed and distributed the *Harvard Lampoon* parodies. Later, Simmons and Mogul would produce *National Lampoon* anthologies and popular movies written by *Lampoon* staffers. Simmons and Mogul agreed to provide Beard, Kenney, and Hoffman with capital and publishing expertise. The five men worked together for almost a year, creating a format; the first issue of *National Lampoon*, "A Humor Magazine for Adults," appeared on the stands in April 1970.

In format, the monthly borrowed liberally from its parent, the campus-based weekly, opening with a mock "editorial," followed by fictitious letters, monthly columns by regular contributors, and feature-length topical satires interspersed with cartoons, jokes, and quotes. Just as the *Harvard Lampoon* published "theme" issues keyed to the academic calendar, such as fall "Football" and spring "Graduation" as well as special "Numbers" like "Elections," so too did its national spinoff, with "theme" issues keyed to national trends, such as "Paranoia," "Nostalgia," and even "Bad Taste." *National Lampoon* also maintained the campus tradition of highly literate magazine parody, initiated by Robert Benchley with his parody of *Life** in 1912, with send-ups of established monthlies such as *The New Yorker*,* *Esquire*,** *American Bride, Cosmopolitan* and, more recently, the *L. L. Bean Catalog*. In all of these, even the art designs and the typography were meticulously parodied.

The magazine was originally co-edited by Beard and Kenney. Hoffman, the first managing editor, left in 1971. Kenney left a year later, but occasionally contributed, and Beard remained as editor-in-chief from 1972 until 1975. During these first years, the magazine tried to maintain its Cambridge pedigree, despite the move to Madison Avenue. As if bowing to high-brow Harvard tradition, Richard Armour, Harvard alumnus turned academic dean and humorist, inaugurated the magazine with "Sex Through the Ages," a mock-anthropological survey of mores in the style of Benchley. Other traces of self-conscious Harvard Yard cleverness included "Whitehouse Heartbreak," a "true romance" starring Julie Nixon and David Eisenhower, and the "discovery" of "Kuka Sutra, Dirty

Book of the Gods.'' The wittiest of these early efforts was Doug Kenney's monthly column, ''Mrs. Agnew's Diary,'' an American version of ''Mrs. Wilson's Diary'' from the British satire magazine, *Private Eye*. In it, the wife of the former Vice-President is portrayed as a self-consumed dim-witted gossip who burbles about squint-eyed ''Spiggy'' and about her own misalliance with the Famous Writers School.

Other Harvard alumni soon joined the staff, most notably Christopher Cerf and George Trow, and helped to keep the Harvard high-brow wit polished. The absence of a talented art director showed, however, in inferior layouts, which resembled those in underground, fugitive magazines. In 1971, Michael Gross became art director and transformed *National Lampoon* into a visually sophisticated magazine rivalling the high-brow magazines it parodied. Among the more artistically stunning was Bruce McCall's art deco ''Bulgemobile'' series, in which he assaulted 1940s and 1950s megalomania for chrome behemoths by parodying auto advertising hype of the day. In the May 1974 issue, he featured the Mogul V–24 Sedanola, the Nabob V–16 Sleekster, and others—new cars that say, ''Get out of my way.'' Other connoisseurs of *schlock* soon followed, most notably Wayne McLoughlin in his mock art deco renditions of American icons. As if redesigned by a commercial developer gone berserk, ''Architectural Freaks'' shows the St. Louis arch, for example, with one leg bent up, topped by a revolving diner crowned by a neon sign, ''Eat.'' Such accomplished graphic art showed the influence of *Esquire* and *New York* magazine art departments and won *National Lampoon* eighteen awards for magazine design.[1]

Despite the imaginative writing and the impressive artwork, wit and cleverness alone were not spicy enough to keep a national humor magazine alive. The necessary sauce was sexual humor, meant to appeal to the less elitist tastes of a wider audience. According to market research, the average *National Lampoon* reader was, and remains, white, male, and twenty-two.[2] Matty Simmons laid down only one ground rule: the humor ''can be sick, but it must also be funny,'' adding that ''tits and ass are what sells.''[3] The first issues provided plenty of both while striving to be both funny and ''sick''; but the magazine languished. Tits and Ass were featured in the September 1970 issue with ''Racquel Welch Laid Bare'' and a ''sick'' emphasis supplied by a ''Screen Slime'' section, ''MGM Scandal Auction: Morbid Memories from Hollywood's 10-Carat Golden Age''—highlighting the ''Fatty Arbuckle Coke Bottle.'' The cover proclaimed boardroom devotion to sexual humor with Minnie Mouse touting ''Mouse Knockers'' in tassles and G-string. The result was a $10 million lawsuit, record sales, and an unforgettable marketing lesson.

Thereafter, *National Lampoon* became more self-consciously ''sick'' as well as unabashedly sexist, seeking to grab readers' attention without losing advertisers. New features appearing in the mid–1970s featured ''macho'' humor in the illustrated color cartoon format, ''Foto Funnies,'' that stressed male embarassment before a female bare-breasted, and topical jokes that relied on newswire photos incongruously juxtaposed with balloon captions. *Playboy* cartoonist Gahan Wilson joined the first year, contributing many of his distinctively ghoulish, vomit-green jokes, and, in 1977, minimalist Sam Gross began a "sick" series in which he enjoyed mocking the conventional pieties Americans hold toward the aged, the handicapped, and the defenseless. One of these, about a legless frog confined to a wheelchair and forced to bus trays in a restaurant specializing in frog legs, elevated the amputee into a *Lampoon* mascot that has since adorned a line of fashion apparel advertised in the magazine—also lampooning the lucrative Izod alligator. Other regular cartoonists included Rick Meyerowitz; Charles Rodriguez, whose "Dirty Duck" series about a leering Disney webfoot who looks like Groucho Marx showed the influence of George Herriman and Don Marquis; and Bobby London, whose "Cheek Vizard" featured a streetwise Pogo in Black dialect. Even the ads, many of which were for high-class goods such as stereos and scotch, included girlie magazine ads promoting condoms, "cremes," and "specialty cards." The magazine that began as part *Harvard Lampoon* and *Esquire* became more like *Playboy*—a slick "entertainment" magazine for males who had outgrown *Mad** but who were still in the market for visual chuckles and broad farce.

Inevitably, the market demand to appear shocking forced contributors to push against the boundaries of reader tolerance—and then step boldly across them. One of several instances occurred in the January 1972 issue which featured Michael O'Donoghue's "The Vietnamese Baby Book," a mock scrapbook of a war casualty whose mother had been raped by a G.I. Its handprint is missing a finger, its first word is "medic" and its favorite nursery rhyme is:

> Willy Calley, pudding and pie,
> Shot the boys and made them die.
> When the girls came to surrender,
> Willy just ignored their gender.

The magazine had snapped at American foreign policy, but with no special relish, feeding on any dish available. While the O'Donoghue piece was interpreted as heralding a commitment to Swiftean satire, it may have merely licensed assaults on the defenseless and vulnerable. In "Famine Circle" (July 1974), a starving African woman tells how "she feeds a family of 17 by talking about food" and "The Joys of Wife Tasting" (June 1974) cunnilingus is graphically shown as a connoisseur's method of discriminating among "vintage" mates. O'Donoghue spoke for fellow practitioners when he said: "What I do is baby seal humor. I try to leave blood on the floor."[4]

In 1975, Twenty-First Century Communications (now *National Lampoon*, Inc.) bought Beard, Kenney, and Hoffman's interest in the publication. Beard resigned as Editor-in-Chief and from 1975 to 1978, *National Lampoon* was run by an editorial committee, the most prominent members of which were Tony Hendra, Sean Kelly, and Brian McConnachie. Circulation peaked in 1974 at about a million and began to decline rapidly during this period, when the magazine seemed to suffer from a lack of leadership. In 1978, Managing Editor P. J. O'Rourke was appointed Editor-in-Chief and remained in this post until 1981. He created new features and rearranged the contents, setting the format that generally holds at present: News on the March, Straight Talk, Canadian Corner, True Facts, Editorials, Letters, Features, Foto Funnies, and Funny Pages. Circulation stabilized, leveling off at its present half million. The Harvard tradition of learned parody was upheld by Ellis Weiner, a frequent contributor to *The New Yorker*. Wilson and Gross carried on with their ''sick'' humor. Feminist cartoonists became regular contributors, most notably Clair Bretécher and Shary Flennikin, both of whom dwelt on comic mishaps and hang-ups suffered by young women, drawn in the style of Jules Feiffer.

During this period, the sexual humor that had made *National Lampoon* a publishing sensation began to dominate the magazine. Many of the contributors were Irish upper class ex-Catholics who doted on male phobias about ambitious, and potentially threatening, outsiders, namely, homosexuals and women— ''homos'' and ''porkers,'' to use the parlance of the magazine. The ''Gay Issue'' (May 1977) featured ''Queen Kong'' and ''Better Homes and Closets, the Idea Magazine for Women of All Sexes.'' The September 1978 issue highlighted ''Homo Fashions for Fags and Queens'' while in the May 1980 issue, ''On the Most Liberated Gay Street in New York,'' one can find the latest gay status symbol, ''a perfectly scaled model ship custom built for your anus.'' Women were always fair game, but more recently they have become regular objects of misogynist bawdry, as in O'Rourke's ''Planet of the Naked Women'' and John Hughes's ''My Vagina'' (April 1979). The latter attacks males who yearn for a sex change, but in terms that are frankly scurrilous: ''I was a guy and who the fuck but a girl would ever want to be a girl except a homo, and I am *not* a homo.'' Even the ads, or mock ads, took an aggressively misogynist line, typified by one in the September 1975 issue that showed a stranded woman motorist about to be gang-raped. The caption read, echoing publisher Simmons's call for humor that sells: ''When you've got Pack CB radio, you've got the world by the tits.''

Arthur Lubow called *National Lampoon* humor ''screw you humor'' because ''it victimizes society's victims.''[5] It is also preoccupied with creature functions and body orifices and thus seems to appeal to younger males. As ''baby seal hunter's humor,'' it represents a backlash at 1960s-era seriousness. Its most studious and prolific practitioner, O'Rourke, favors bawdy tales of female conquest which feed middle-class male nostalgia for simpler times, before women's lib and Vietnam. In his ''King of Sandusky, Ohio'' series and in such prolix ''memoirs'' as ''How to Drive Fast on Drugs While Getting Your Wing-Wang Squeezed and Not Spill Your Drink'' (March 1979), O'Rourke sounds like a more sexually oriented Jean Shepherd, another early *Lampoon* contributor, and writes in the hyped-up paranoid style of the so-called new journalists such as Tom Wolfe and Hunter Thompson. Yet such macho tales about taboo-breaking in the suburbs and backwaters of middle America reveal, after all, the magazine's *raison d'etre* since its inception: to be outrageous and shocking, but appear wickedly clever and insouciant in the process. "This may sound square," O'Rourke confessed, "but if the magazine has a real target, it symbolically is our parents."[6]

The *National Lampoon* continues to be eclectic and, to some extent, unpredictable. It depends on heavy doses of adult comics and broad sexual farce; yet it remains devoted to sharply focused parody and high-brow wit that occasionally pays homage to its Harvard roots.

Notes

1. Mopsy Strange Kennedy, "Juvenile, Puerile, Sophomoric, Jejune, Nutty—and Funny," *New York Times Magazine* (10 December 1972): 106.

2. Ibid.

3. P. J. O'Rourke, ed., *National Lampoon, Tenth Anniversary Year* (February 1980): 10.

4. Arthur Lubow, "Screw You Humor," *New Republic* (21 October 1978): 19. Baby seals are clubbed to death for their pelts, a practice that has drawn the anger and protest of animal-loving and social liberal groups.

5. Ibid.

6. Franz Lidz, "Winning Through Denigration," *Johns Hopkins Magazine* (June 1980): 20.

Information Sources

BIBLIOGRAPHY:
Anson, Robert Sam. "The Life and Death of a Comic Genius." *Esquire* (October 1981): 37–46.
Kennedy, Mopsy Strange. "Juvenile, Puerile, Sophomoric, Jejune, Nutty—and Funny," *New York Times Magazine* (10 December 1972): 34–35, 102–109.
Lidz, Franz. "Winning Through Denigration." *Johns Hopkins Magazine* (June 1980): 14–20.
Lubow, Arthur. "Screw You Humor." *New Republic* (21 October 1978): 18–22.
O'Rourke, P. J. "Introduction." *National Lampoon Tenth Anniversary Anthology, 1970–1980*. New York: Simon and Schuster, 1979.
Rovit, Earl. "College Humor and the Modern Audience." In *Comic Relief: Humor in Contemporary American Literature*, ed. Sarah Blecher Cohen. Urbana: University of Illinois Press, 1978.
Schwartz, Tony. "College Humor Comes Back." *Newsweek* (23 October 1978): 88–97.
INDEX SOURCES: None.
REPRINT EDITIONS: None.
LOCATION SOURCES: University of Connecticut, 1970–1971, 1974–1979; University of Hartford, 1980–1982.

Publication History

MAGAZINE TITLE AND TITLE CHANGES: *National Lampoon*, April 1970 to the present.

VOLUME AND ISSUE DATA: Monthly, Volume 1:1, April 1970–Volume 1:99, July 1978; Volume 2:1, August 1978–   .

PUBLISHER AND PLACE OF PUBLICATION: NL Communications, New York.
EDITORS: Henry Beard and Douglas Kenney, 1970–1972; Henry Beard, 1972–1975; Editorial Committee, 1975–1978; P. J. O'Rourke, 1978–1981; Gerald Sussman, 1981–1983; L. Dennis Plunkett, 1984– .
CIRCULATION: 500,000 (estimated).

Thomas Grant

THE NEW HAVEN GAZETTE AND THE CONNECTICUT MAGAZINE

The New Haven Gazette and The Connecticut Magazine was one of several periodicals to flourish briefly in New England after the Revolutionary War. Like its Hartford counterparts, the *Connecticut Courant* and *The American Mercury*,* it provided an obliging vehicle for satire produced by a group of Yale College alumni known as the "Connecticut Wits." The Wits were not full-time writers; they included a doctor, a lawyer, and other professional men who characterized their occasional literary efforts as "hotchpot." This word adequately describes the style and makeup of the *Gazette* itself. Edited by Yale tutor Josiah Meigs, it offered humor stirred into an eclectic recipe of news, philosophy, correspondence, and verse meant to satisfy Federalist tastes in a time of perilous political instability.

During its initial two years of publication (1784–1786), the *Gazette* contained almost nothing but news. But the 15 February 1786 issue added "The Connecticut Magazine" to the masthead, introducing an expanded format and promising "amusing and instructive articles" without the distracting presence of advertising. Meigs and co-publisher Eleutheros Dana banished ads to a supplement, hoping their format would attract contributors "of genius and ability."

The remodeled *Gazette* appeared weekly, with an annual subscription rate of nine shillings. It contained eight three-column quarto pages, with typography uninterrupted by supplementary art. The editorial slant was moralizing and provincial, directing regular attention to deteriorating economic conditions in neighboring states. Meigs often filled the gray front page with installments of long essays such as his own "Observations on the Present Situation and Future Prospects of This and the United States," which he published over the signature "Lycurgus."

Short comic items including reprints from British and American periodicals appeared as filler inside, scattered between reports of legislative proceedings, shipping news, obituaries, and other features. Anecdotes using puns and comic vernacular struggled for attention, sometimes plainly labeled ("Humorous Story"), but often separated from serious material by only a pair of rules or a little extra lead.

Meigs reserved more prominent editorial play for political satire meant to shape public opinion. This humor was frequently packaged as literary burlesque, using florid verse and prose to condemn wrong-thinking individuals,

Massachusetts mobs, Rhode Island paper money, or federal impotence. Attribution was usually fictitious. But the actual authors included Joel Barlow, Timothy Dwight, Dr. Lemuel Hopkins, David Humphreys, and John Trumbull— the self-styled Connecticut Wits.

Dwight's mildly satirical series, "The Friend," dominated the front page beginning on 23 March 1786 under the by-lines, "James Littlejohn, Esq." and "John Homely." Later during the year, excerpts from Trumbull's Revolutionary War poem, *M'Fingal*, were reprinted with admiring editorial comment. The Yale men contributed correspondence and poetry lampooning local figures such as Judge William Williams, who on 23 November was consoled in an ironic letter from "Benevolence, Junior" professing to defend him against the attacks of "the wicked wits."

The group's most influential effort was a parody of Alexander Pope's *The Dunciad* entitled *The Anarchiad: A Poem on the Restoration of Chaos and Substantial Night* co-authored by Barlow, Hopkins, Humphreys, and Trumbull. Anonymously presented as an ancient manuscript recovered from ruins in "the western country," the mock epic ran in twelve installments between 26 October 1786 and 13 September 1787. With episodes containing visions of chaos in Massachusetts and Rhode Island, the poem assigned thin aliases to victims of its ridicule. The harassed Judge Williams appeared as "William Wimble," and General James Wadsworth, an opponent of strong central government, was dubbed "Wronghead." Although precise attribution for most numbers has never been established, the Wits' biographers agree that the poem was widely reprinted and received with interest by readers weary of economic depression. Still feigning innocence in 1820, Trumbull himself wrote, "The publications of these gentlemen were supposed, at the time, to have had considerable influence on the public taste and opinions." (*Poetical Works*, I). The series appeared before and during the Constitutional Convention of 1787. William K. Bottorff, in his introduction to the Scholars Facsimile edition of *The Anarchiad*, suggests that it may have had a unifying influence on the Connecticut delegation, whose "Connecticut Compromise" helped save the convention from failure.

In the *Gazette*'s second year, the publishers lowered its price to seven shillings and admitted advertising to the back pages. Meigs's increasing preoccupation with politics took a toll on the anecdotes; the index for Volume 1 lists twenty-two, while Volume 2 contained only ten. In Volume 3 he eliminated the ads again, returning the price to nine shillings. The final issue appeared on 18 June 1789.

Information Sources

BIBLIOGRAPHY:

Cowie, Alexander. *John Trumbull: Connecticut Wit*. Westport, Conn.: Greenwood Press, 1972. Reprinted from University of North Carolina Press, 1936.

Ford, Arthur C. *Joel Barlow*. New York: Twayne Publishers, 1971.

Holliday, Carl. *The With and Humor of Colonial Days*. New York: Frederick Ungar Publishing Co., 1912.

Howard, Leon. *The Connecticut Wits*. Chicago: University of Chicago Press, 1943.

Mott, Frank L. *A History of American Magazines, 1741–1850*. New York: D. Appleton and Co., 1938, 1:31n, 788.

Osterweis, Rollin G. *Three Centuries of New Haven, 1638–1938*. New Haven, Conn.: Yale University Press, 1953.

Riggs, Walter G., ed. *The Anarchiad: A New England Poem (1786–1787)*. Gainesville, Fla.: Scholars Facsimiles and Reprints, 1967.

INDEX SOURCES: Annual index included in Volume 1:52, 15 February 1787, and Volume 2:45, 27 December 1787.

REPRINT EDITIONS: University Microfilms.

LOCATION SOURCES: Sixteen libraries list partial holdings. The most complete can be found at CtY, MB, WHi, and OU. MWA is the only source for any portion of Volume 4.

Publication History

MAGAZINE TITLE AND TITLE CHANGES: *The New Haven Gazette*, 1784–1786; *The New Haven Gazette and The Connecticut Magazine*, 15 February 1786–18 June 1789.

VOLUME AND ISSUE DATA: Weekly, annual volumes, with an index for Volumes 1 and 2.

PUBLISHER AND PLACE OF PUBLICATION: Meigs and Dana (Josiah Meigs, Eleutheros Dana, Daniel Bowen), New Haven, Connecticut.

EDITOR: Josiah Meigs.

CIRCULATION: Unknown.

Stuart A. Kollar

THE NEW YORKER

Not to be confused with the short-lived *The New-Yorker* (with a hyphenated title), *The New Yorker* is one of America's longest running and most successful comic journals.[1] For many readers the most distinctive feature of the magazine is its cartoons. However, *The New Yorker*'s success is based on a foundation much more solid than just providing a weekly collection of good cartoons; it is directly attributable to the dream and hard work of Harold Wallace Ross, an improbable candidate to be the founding editor of what would come to be one of America's wittiest and most sophisticated magazines. Opinionated, exasperating, distrustful, and cantankerous, only someone like Ross, who was fond of claiming "I'll hire *anybody*," and who in the early years of the magazine seemed intent on proving that statement, would have hired Ross.

Ross's connection with the celebrated Thanatopsis Literary and Inside Straight Club, a group of literati, including Alexander Woollcott, Franklin P. Adams, George S. Kaufman, Robert Benchley, and Dorothy Parker, who met at the Hotel Algonquin in New York City, led to his founding of *The New Yorker* in 1925. Through this group Ross became acquainted with Raoul Fleischmann, a millionaire baker, who agreed to provide $150,000 backing for Ross's proposed journal. Ross had carried around the dummy of his magazine for two years before he finally found his backer.

The early months of *The New Yorker* were almost fatal. Issue Number 1 carried the cover date of 21 February 1925, and 15,000 copies were sold.[2] The magazine's title had been suggested by John Peter Tuohey, a Broadway press agent and *Saturday Evening Post*** writer, and the first cover featured a drawing by Rea Irvin of a supercilious nineteenth-century dandy observing a butterfly through a monocle. Eustace Tilley, as the fop on the cover was christened by Corey Ford, appears at the top of the "Talk of the Town" page each week, and the anniversary issue each year repeats the original cover.[3] By the third issue sales had dropped to 12,000, and only 10,500 copies were sold the following week. In late April the magazine had only 8,000 readers and was losing $8,000 a week. In August, circulation was down to 2,700. Ross and Fleischmann declared the magazine defunct, but then changed their minds. The budget was cut to $5,000 a week, Fleischmann was persuaded to contribute more money (ultimately $560,000), and $60,000 was allocated for full-page newspaper advertisements.

The publication of Ellin MacKay's "Why We Go to Cabarets, A Post-Débutante Explains," in the first year's Thanksgiving issue is credited with being the event that saved *The New Yorker*. MacKay, a former debutante who would become Mrs. Irving Berlin in 1926, stirred up a Park Avenue audience with her essay about why young women from New York's high society would rather go to a night club than contend with the stag lines at private parties.

With minor variations *The New Yorker*'s format has remained essentially the same from the beginning. The inaugural issue contained thirty-two three-column pages measuring $8\frac{1}{4}'' \times 11''$. The first textual material was titled "Of All Things" and contained the magazine's prospectus. This was followed by the "Talk of the Town" section, which was signed "The New Yorkers." Other regular departments in the early years were "Profile," "The Story of ManhattanKind," and "Behind the News." Lois Long, who married co-staffer cartoonist Peter Arno, created the "Tables for Two" and "On and Off the Avenue" columns. The night club gossip of the former department and the good taste exhibited in the latter, a buying guide, attracted readers and provided the journal with stability. *The New Yorker* remained thirty-two pages long until 6 June 1925 when it was cut to twenty-four pages. On 10 September 1925 the length was increased to forty pages, and it has varied since. Until the 11 May 1925 issue, newsstand copies were available on the Tuesday following the cover date. Subsequent issues have been available on the Friday before.

After the first issue, "The Talk of the Town" was the first editorial content until the "Goings on About Town" department was moved to the front on 12 December 1925. This order became permanent with the 30

January 1926 issue. Beginning with this issue through the 7 January 1926 number, the names of "Advisory Editors" were printed above the "Talk of the Town" title. Those listed were Ralph Barton, Marc Connelly, Irving Kaufman, Alice Duer Miller, Parker, and Woollcott. (Woollcott was replaced by Hugh Wiley in August 1925.)

Recent issues of *The New Yorker* (1983–1984) have consisted of 74 to 220 pages (though the number has approached 250 in the past). The cover prices for individual copies have ranged from fifteen cents for the first issue to the current $1.50, a one thousand percent increase over 59 years. The subscription rate for the first year was five dollars; that rate now runs as high as thirty-two dollars a year.

Until March 1969 no masthead or table of contents was included in the magazine. Ross once toyed with the idea of using symbols next to the titles to indicate whether a piece was humorous, or whatever, but the idea was never implemented. There is still no identification of the editor-in-chief or fiction, nonfiction, or art editors printed anywhere in the journal. Even after a table of contents was added, contributors' names were not listed for years. In fact, one of the attractions of *The New Yorker* that has been mentioned by S. J. Perelman and others was the intellectual guessing game prompted by the periodical's practice of printing authors' names only at the ends of their contributions. Readers either had to turn to the end of a piece to see who wrote it, or they could try to determine authorship from the topic and style. The printing of the writer's name at the end is still in force, even though the information is now also available in the table of contents.

Items listed in the table of contents fall into three categories: regular departments and various kinds of reporting (on politics, or full-length theater, dance, film, music, art, and book reviews, for instance), indicated by plain titles; personal experiences and reflections and works of fiction and poetry, enclosed within quotation marks; and poems further differentiated by the denotation poem within parentheses following the title. Credit is given to the cover artist, as well as to the artists responsible for the drawings and cartoons that appear in the issue (No distinction is made between the creators of the drawings and the cartoonists).

Other than advertising, the first actual content in today's *The New Yorker* is always the "Goings on about Town" department, which consists of an alphabetically arranged listing of events currently running in New York City. The arrangement is by the categories of "Theatre," "Dance," "Night Life," "Art" (with the subcategories "Galleries"—by location, such as uptown and so forth—"Museums," "Libraries"), "Music," "Sports," "Et Alia" (prose readings, lectures, walking tours, auctions, and similar activities), and "The Movie Houses," all of which give the title, date, time, address, telephone number, a synopsis of the event and participants, and other pertinent information but no prices. The "Night Life" section notes that it is comprised of a "highly arbitrary listing" and warns in a wonderfully understated way that the information contained in the column should be approached cautiously: "Musicians and night-club proprietors live complicated lives that are subject to last-minute change; it is therefore always advisable to call ahead." "Goings on about Town," sandwiched between myriads of advertisements, is followed by the review sections, other departments on an irregular basis, poetry, and "casuals," as Ross called the journal's prose pieces.

Even today, when the journal's humorous prose has diminished in both amount and quality, the cartoons set *The New Yorker* apart from its few competitors. Ross was not, as is sometimes claimed, the inventor of the one-line cartoon. This was an important part of the format of humor magazines before *The New Yorker* came into being, including two of the publications for which he had previously served as an editor, *Stars and Stripes* and *Judge*,* but the form certainly flourished under his guidance at *The New Yorker*.

The New Yorker's format reflects its editorial content. No blurbs appear on the front cover intended to grab a reader's attention. Similarly, other than the front cover and a portion of the advertisements, the magazine does not use color. The black and white pages are clean and quiet, as is the prose, and there are no subheads shouting at the reader. Makeup editor Carmine Peppe helped devise this approach.

Born in Aspen, Colorado, in 1892, the son of a militant anti-Mormon, Ross worked on the Salt Lake City *Tribune*, the San Francisco *Call*, and other newspapers. During World War I, he edited the United States Army's *Stars and Stripes*. After the war Ross married newspaperwoman Jane Grant, who insisted that they live in New York. He tried to establish a civilian version of *Stars and Stripes*, called *Home Sector*, in 1919, but the magazine folded. He then worked for the *American Legion Weekly*, which he left when he perceived that the journal was turning political.[4] In 1924 he accepted the editorship of *Judge*, one of the nation's foremost humor magazines at the time, where he bought his first piece from Perelman.

Ross never tried to cater to an audience. Contending that he would not edit his journal "for the old lady in Dubuque," Ross, contrary to many of his contemporaries, claimed that "An editor prints only what pleases him—if enough people like what he likes, he is a success." In *The New Yorker*'s prospectus he said that the magazine "will be a reflection in word and picture of metropolitan life. It will be human. Its general tenor will be one of gaiety, wit, and satire, but it will be more than a jester. It will not be what is commonly called radical or high-brow. It will be what is commonly called sophisticated. . . . It will hate bunk. . . . Its integrity will be above suspicion." In the editorial statement published in the premiere issue of the magazine, Ross said that *The New Yorker* would have "a serious purpose but . . . will not be too serious in executing it. It hopes . . . to keep up with events of the day." At the same time, the staff refused to deal with sensationalism purely for the sake of sensationalism. The journal, Ross claimed, would "publish facts that it will have to go behind the scenes to get, but it will not deal in scandal for the sake of scandal. . . . It is not engaged in tapping the Great Buying Power of the North American steppe region by trading mirrors and colored beads in the form of our best brands of hokum."

The chief element in *The New Yorker*'s phenomenal success was Ross's approach to editing; "Use the rapier, not the bludgeon," he advised his writers. To help them hone their prose, he edited it meticulously. Manuscripts were returned to their authors with lists of numbered comments that sometimes were as long as the manuscripts. Ross also established a special department, modeled after a similar department at the *Saturday Evening Post*, to check every fact. Four-letter obscenities and material with any sexual connotation were barred.

Ross had some misgivings about his ability to manage a journal. To overcome his apprehensions he was willing to hire almost anybody who showed up at his office. Many employees were brought into the organization high on the editorial ladder, regardless of their journalistic experience.[5] Sooner or later most either worked themselves down to a more suitable level or left the magazine, but it is clear that Ross both attracted and fostered the most important American humorists for over thirty years, and that they either knew or found out what they had to do to make the magazine a success. Ross not only allowed his talented staff to perform but he also forced them to meet their potential.

William Shawn served as Editor-in-Chief of *The New Yorker* for over thirty years (Ross served in that capacity for twenty-six years), having accepted the position on 21 January 1952. A "Talk of the Town" reporter in 1933, his association with the magazine extended over more than half a century. A whole generation of *The New Yorker*'s readers grew up reading the journal published under Shawn's editorship, and probably without ever having seen an issue edited by Ross (Robert Gottlieb is Shawn's successor).

Besides editor Gottlieb, the magazine's managers today include Peter F. Fleischmann (Raoul Fleischmann's only son), chairman; George J. Green, president; and Robert F. Young, advertising director. The journal's editorial "rabbit-warren" offices have been located at 25 West 43rd Street in New York City almost from the first (For a very short time they were housed in a building just a couple of blocks away, on West 45th Street).

Not much is known about Shawn, a very private man. Born in Chicago in 1907 as William Chon (he changed the spelling of his name so that his readers would not think he was Chinese), Shawn had minimal journalistic experience when he joined the magazine after moving to New York to compose music. Ross's hand-picked successor, he continued many of the magazine's characteristics that were established under Ross. Both men had developed writers under their tutelage, though in different ways. Shawn was more intellectually inquisitive than his predecessor. Whereas Ross was a stickler for details ("Was Moby Dick the whale or the man?"), Shawn was more concerned with whether an author said what he intended to say. He was also more politically oriented than Ross —it was Shawn who convinced Ross to devote an entire issue to John Hersey's 30,000-word "Hiroshima" in August 1946, and during both the Vietnam era and the Watergate affair *The New Yorker*, particularly in the "Notes and Comments" department, spoke out against the immorality of these events.

The overuse of commas in *The New Yorker*, a source of many jokes and parodies throughout Ross's editorship, diminished under Shawn. So, too, many readers believe, did the amount of humor. However, Shawn may not be at fault. As early as the mid–1940s, Ross recognized and bemoaned the dwindling of humorous pieces and the increasing amount of "grim stuff." Times, taste, and authors change, and the more serious world of World War II and after may not lend itself to the happy-go-lucky, juvenile humor that appeared in *The New Yorker*'s early pages. There are still spots of humor in the magazine, though entire humorous essays are infrequent now.

Many of America's most important prose writers have worked for or contributed to *The New Yorker*. As suggested above, the list is a who's who of American humorists in the middle of the twentieth century: Benchley, S. N. Behrman, Sally Benson, Connelly, Clarence Day, Ralph Ingersoll, Nunnally Johnson, Kaufman, Ring Lardner, Lois Long, H. L. Mencken, Parker, Perelman, Leonard Q. Ross (the pen name of Leo C. Rosten), Thorne Smith, Jean Stafford, Frank Sullivan, Thurber, E. B. White, Woollcott. Some of the more famous pieces that have appeared on the magazine's pages include "Pal Joey," "My Sister Eileen," and Day's "Life with Father."

In addition, many other distinguished authors' works have appeared in *The New Yorker*. Among these have been Sherwood Anderson, James Baldwin, Rachel Carson (*The Silent Spring*), John Cheever, Robert M. Coates, Clifton Fadiman, F. Scott Fitzgerald, Ernest Hemingway, Hersey, Shirley Jackson (her "The Lottery" caused a major brouhaha), A. J. Liebling, Mary McCarthy, John McNulty, Lewis Mumford, Irwin Shaw, Rebecca West, and Edmund Wilson. Samuel Beckett's playlet *Catastrophe* was published in *The New Yorker*, as have been over one hundred pieces each by Truman Capote, John O'Hara, and J. D. Salinger. The high quality of contributions has continued. Recently, there has been a short story by Wright Morris, a fine piece by Alice Adams, and a long article on Kansas City by Calvin Trillin. Regular contributors include Brendan Gill (since 1936), Penelope Gilliatt, Pauline Kael, Molly Panter-Downes (her "Letter from London" began in 1939), Edith Oliver, and George Steiner. The magazine also invites freelance submissions of both serious and light fiction (1,000 to 6,000 words in length) and factual pieces (3,000 to 10,000 words). Longer pieces and "Talk of the Town" are written by the staff, though ideas for the "Talk of the Town" department and most of the journal's fillers are purchased.

Typical *New Yorker* casuals are characterized by human, cultivated, sensitive qualities. The style maintained is one of lyrical softness. The authors assume an unhurried, gentle, relaxed, urbane prose. Occasionally, of course, a manic humor breaks through the superficial "pretense of controlled humor." If the writers sometimes appear a bit dilettantish, they are seldom foppish, silly, or stupid; quiet as opposed to ranting, they are amused, yet wistful; they are romantic; they are wise but at times innocently foolish. If their personae are pretentious at the beginning of a story, they are not pretentious at the end. And all of the action commonly occurs in a New York City setting. Although the perspective is bohemian New York (whether the tale takes place in New York or London or Paris or Columbus, Ohio), a world of books and films, the theater, and Greenwich village, it is not seedy—ritzy shops, hotels, and restaurants are mentioned frequently.

As is the case with the magazine's contributors of humorous prose, the list of cartoonists whose work has appeared in *The New Yorker* reads like a who's who. In the early years this included Peter Arno (Curtis Arnoux Peters) who coined the phrase "Well, back to the old drawing board" as the caption for his 1941 drawing of a relatively unconcerned man in a suit and hat carrying a roll of blueprints under his arm and walking away from the scene of the crash of a fighter plane while military men and an ambulance rush toward the crushed aircraft and the pilot is seen descending by parachute in the background. According to legend, Arno labored over one of his captions for three years. Other noteworthy cartoonists were Charles Addams, Whitney Darrow, Jr., Chon Day, Robert Day, John Held, Jr., Syd Hoff, Helen Hokinson (who specialized in society matrons and flappers), Arnie Levin, George Price, Gardner Rea, Ronald Searle, William Steig, Saul Steinberg, Richard Taylor, and Thurber. Some, like Addams, are still contributing, along with current artists George Booth, Dana Fradan, William Hamilton, Edward Koren (whose fuzzy characters are an unmistakable trademark), Charles Saxon, and Robert Webber. Over the years Eldon Dedini, Anatol Kovarsky, Robert Kraus, Frank Modell, and James Mulligan have also produced a number of memorable cartoons. In 1981 the magazine had forty cartoonists under contract, meaning, essentially, that *The New Yorker* has first-refusal rights to all of their cartoons. The journal only accepts a small number (perhaps three) of freelance cartoons a year, preferring to rely on artists who can produce superior material over an extended period rather than on one-shot submissions.

Between 1925 and 1975 *The New Yorker* published approximately 40,000 cartoons, most of them under the supervision of James M. Geraghty, the journal's art editor from 1939 through 1972. In Geraghty's opinion, *The New Yorker* cartoons are zanier and less topical today than in the past. He prefers cartoons "connected with reality" and drawing "a little moral lesson." Among the most enthralling cartoons are Addams's dark picture of two unicorns standing on a rock gazing at the ark as it sails away and the water rises about them; Joseph Mirachi's drawing of two scowling men on ladders at opposite ends of a large animal's skeleton, each about to affix a skull to his end, with the caption reading "Yeah? Well, I've forgotten more about paleontology then you'll ever know"; Robert S. Grossman's alien crawling away from a wrecked flying saucer in the middle of a desert and calling "Ammonia! Ammonia!"; and Robert Day's representation of a huge suburban area with rows of look-alike houses and a woman saying to a postman, "I'm Mrs. Edward M. Barnes. Where do I live?" The essence of the magazine's cartoon humor is whimsical and witty, and includes artistic and literary allusions; it looks at everyday events of the upper middle class to mock pretentiousness, foolishness, business, suburbia, the sexes, politics, and modern society. These are the same topics that provide the humor for the journal's prose pieces.

Of all of the prose writers who have contributed to *The New Yorker*, three men stand out as having made the largest imprint and as being most representative of the journal's tone: White, Thurber, and Perelman.

Elwyn Brooks White joined *The New Yorker* staff in 1926. Ironically, while of all of the journal's contributors he may have had the greatest influence on the magazine, his contribution may also be the most difficult to verify. Hired at thirty dollars a week, White was responsible for much of the magazine's editing, and he helped Ross establish the approach that still characterizes *The New Yorker*'s prose. Justly famed for his own essays and for his children's novels *Stuart Little* and *Charlotte's Web*, he is known for his textbooks on the writing process as well. White's sense of humor can be seen in his tag line comment appended to a "newsbreak" ("unintentionally humorous items from various newspapers and magazines" used by *The New Yorker* as fillers) describing the coats of two lost foxhounds in very colorful terms. "Those aren't dogs, those are nasturtiums," White commented. Possibly more important than White's editorial skills were his contributions to the "Talk of the Town" department, particularly the "Notes and Comments" section that appears on the magazine's first page of actual text, for it was this that set the tone for *The New Yorker*'s content and approach. As Thurber says in *The Years With Ross*, "through the years [White's "Notes and Comments"] has left its firm and graceful imprint on American letters and every now and then has exerted its influence upon local, or even wider, affairs." The format and the success of the "Talk of the Town" constitute an example of how well Ross chose men who shared his vision of *The New Yorker* and were equipped to execute that vision. In the 1924 prospectus it is stated that "There will be a personal mention column—a jotting down in the small-town newspaper style of the comings, goings and doings in the village of New York. This will contain some josh and some news value." During the eleven years that White ran the department, he provided what Ross wanted, and the tradition that he established continues. Russell Maloney took over the "Talk of the Town" editorship in 1935. Yet even today the department retains much of the flavor introduced by White, that of a small-town newspaper reporting on current events in a folksy way that implies that the writer and reader know each other, share the same beliefs, and are on familiar terms. The "editorial we" is used throughout. Parenthetically, Katharine Angell, a talented literary editor on the journal for years, married White (she and Alva Johnston set the pattern for the "Profile" entries); her son, Roger Angell, is a *New Yorker* contributor.

James Thurber's impact on *The New Yorker* was immeasurable. Like White, he joined the staff in the magazine's formative period, in 1927, and as an active and long-time member of the editorial staff, he was a primary factor in determining the journal's "style"—even serving as managing editor for a while. Most important, however, were his 364 signed and unsigned casuals and 307 drawings. "The Secret Life of Walter Mitty," a classic fantasy, became the most famous piece of fiction ever published in *The New Yorker*. Thurber's drawings reflected the view of life, and in particular the battle of the sexes, that occupied his attention in his prose. One of the most famous is a rendering, published in January 1932, of a man and a woman in bed, with a seal looking over the headboard behind them. The woman grumbles: "All Right, Have It Your Way— You Heard a Seal Bark!"

Sidney Joseph Perelman's relationship with *The New Yorker* was different from that of White and Thurber, and consequently his contribution was of a different nature. Since Perelman was not a member of the editorial staff, he did not exert the kind of influence in this area that White and Thurber did. Instead, his contribution came in the form of his casuals that were published in the journal. Between 13 December 1930, when his first piece appeared in *The New Yorker*, and 10 September 1979, forty-nine years later, when his last piece appeared—barely over a month before his death—Perelman contributed 278 casuals to the magazine. In many ways the pieces that were printed with his signature at the end have come to be regarded as representative of *The New Yorker* humor. "The Idol's Eye" is the finest example of the "manic humor" that sometimes burst forth from the magazine: Snubbers relates an improbable tale of how his grandfather managed to steal the huge, flawless ruby that served as the eye of a temple idol. It is a plot straight out of the B-movies and serials of the 1930s and 1940s, even to the particular of a mysterious face appearing in the dark outside the window.

When *The New Yorker* was established, the editorial and advertising departments were assigned offices on different stories to insure that they would be separated. Ross did not want to provide the advertising department with any opportunity to exert an influence over the editorial department. Amusingly, this separation extended to the point that the two staffs seldom even met. Once, when an advertising man ventured upstairs, Ross chased him away, and A. J. Russell, former president of *The New Yorker*, has been quoted as saying that the only time he and Ross ever spoke was when they said hello at the magazine's annual birthday party.

Ross was particular about what products could be advertised in his journal too. James Playsted Wood has noted, in *Magazines in the United States*, that *The New Yorker* places restrictions on advertising: "It will allow no exaggeration, superlatives, or innuendoes. It eschews feminine hygiene, bad breath, body odors, and patent medicines. It will picture nothing which is worn beneath a woman's slip. . . . it has rejected all cigarette advertising [since the publication of the Surgeon General's report] . . . [and] Liquor advertising is strictly limited to 16 percent of the advertising pages" (p. 272). While these strictures are still generally in effect, a color photograph of a female model wearing Maidenform panties and bra appeared in 1983.

Although the magazine regularly turns down advertising, since the mid–1940s the percentage of nonadvertising pages has ranged from forty-two to forty-five, while the percentage of advertising pages has run between fifty-five and fifty-eight. Of the 150 pages in a September 1983 number, 47⅓ are devoted to color advertising and 41⅓ to black and white advertisements. There are eleven pages of art, one short poem, and twenty-one pages of prose text.

The New Yorker's advertising rates have climbed steadily. In 1929 advertisers were charged $598 a page (gross advertising earnings were $1,929,964), and the circulation hit 80,000. Newsstand and subscription revenues were $197,149 and $139,985, respectively. With circulation at 125,000 in 1934, advertising rates stood at $550 to $880 per page, depending on whether the ad was in the in-town edition or in the national edition (Vogue was then charging $1,500 and the New York Times received $2,131). On a "per thousand readers" scale, The New Yorker was paid $8.85 as opposed to the New York Time's $5.45.

By 1947, based on a circulation increase from 260,000 to 315,000 (seventy percent of whom lived outside Manhattan), its rates were raised from $1,800 to $1,975. Although the "per thousand" figure had dropped to about $7.05 a page, it was still expensive. (Other mass magazines averaged $2.67.) The advertising income had increased fivefold since 1927, from $900,000 to $4 million. However, the number of pages of advertising carried had expanded only from 1,175 to 2,500. In 1966 The New Yorker earned $23,390,000 from 6,114 pages of advertising. The following year marked the tenth consecutive year that the magazine was the nation's leader in the amount of advertising carried. It is estimated that the magazine's 1983 revenue included 53.6 million advertising dollars. In 1984 The New Yorker charged $10,200 for a full-page black and white advertisement, and $16,200 for a four-color advertisement. (Compare this to the magazine's entire budget in 1925, which started at $8,000 a week but was cut to $5,000 a week that summer.) The number of advertising pages carried in The New Yorker is among the highest in the publishing industry.

If the evidence represented by its longevity, circulation, and advertising revenue was not sufficient to demonstrate the success, and importance, of The New Yorker, the journal has received serious attention from Advertising Age, The American Mercury,* Cosmopolitan, Fortune, Harper's Magazine, Herald-Tribune Books, Horizon, The New York Times Book Review, Newsweek, The Saturday Review, Wall Street Journal, and Women's Wear Daily. Two staff members, Thurber and Gill, have written books about the magazine, a dissertation has been completed, and chapters in several books have been devoted to it. The Bombay Times calls the magazine part of American social history, and the Spectator in London labels the journal "an important part not only of American culture but of Western culture generally."

The Saturday Review attributes The New Yorker's success to three factors: Ross's sense of perfection; the "number and variety of items in each issue";

and the increasing "complexity of action" that lies behind the magazine's weekly publication. This third item is possibly an outgrowth of several of Ross's traits combined with a wide audience and broadening of subject matter. Ross loved accuracy, and he loved his magazine and staff. The pride in accuracy has produced a careful attention to detail that is not always found elsewhere.[6] This instills a feeling of good workmanship that is complemented and emphasized by the editorial care given to the writing style. *New Yorker* staffers are loyal to their magazine, and Ross's, and after him Shawn's, attitude toward contributors and staff alike has been instrumental in reinforcing this feeling for the journal. Ross once refused to accept White's resignation because, he asserted, "This isn't a magazine—it's a Movement!"

On the wall of his office Ross displayed a framed sentence from an editorial about *The New Yorker* that had been published in the Lynchburg, Virginia, *Advance*: "It is a supposedly 'funny' magazine doing one of the most intelligent, honest, public-spirited jobs, a service to civilization, that has ever been rendered by any one publication." Ross must have felt that this was, indeed, what he was doing, and he must have been pleased to know that others recognized his work; he would surely be pleased to know that the traditions are continuing intact.

Notes

1. *The New-Yorker* was a five-cent weekly newspaper specializing in a "bright, spicy, and interesting" as well as a "varied budget of gossip." Publication under the editorship of Harry Wilson Walker began on 6 March 1901. Horace Greeley was the publisher. In 1904 R. W. Criswell became editor and publisher. The periodical, which never exceeded a circulation of 20,000 according to Frank Luther Mott, "perished" two years later.

2. The account of the number of copies printed ranges from 12,000 to 18,000, and the date that the magazine was actually available at newsstands is uncertain, since it has been described as occurring on both 12 February and 19 February.

3. Actually, Cory wrote a series of advertisements for *The New Yorker* burlesquing the "Pulp-to-a-Great-Institution" concept through a dilettantish character named Eustace Tilley. The name was mistakenly applied to Irvin's cartoon character.

4. Ironically, during the McCarthy era it was claimed that *The New Yorker* was Communist-inspired.

5. The role of Ross's managing editor was filled by many men labeled "Jesuses" and "Geniuses." Along the way the musical chairs approach engulfed Joseph M. March, M. B. Levick, Arthur Samuels, Bernard A. Bergman, Stanley Walker, Ik Shuman, Philip D. Hoyt, and St. Clair McKelway. There is no official record of other names or exact dates.

6. Past experience has shown that most journals keep poor or no records. This is not true at *The New Yorker*. I am grateful to Elizabeth Hughes and her staff for willingly providing valuable information for this entry.

Information Sources

BIBLIOGRAPHY:

Bernstein, Burton. *Thurber: A Biography*. New York: Dodd, Mead, 1975.

Blair, Walter, and Hamlin Hill. *America's Humor: From Poor Richard to Doonesbury*. New York: Oxford University Press, 1978.

Churchill, Allen. "Ross of the *New Yorker*." *The American Mercury* 67 (August 1948): 147–55.

Fainberg, Andrew. "Still at the Old Drawing Board." *Horizon* (January 1981): 54–61.

Gill, Brendan. *Here at the New Yorker*. London: Michael Joseph, 1975; New York: Random House, 1975.

Hughes, Lawrence M. "North American Steppes Yield Gold to Mr. Tilley." *Advertising Age* (1 December 1947): 1, 50–52.

Kramer, Dale. *Ross and the New Yorker*. Garden City, N.Y.: Doubleday, 1951.

———, and George R. Clark. "Harold Ross and *The New Yorker*." *Harper's Magazine* 186 (1 April 1943): 510–21.

Maloney, Russell. "Tilley the Toiler." *The Saturday Review* (30 August 1947): 7–10, 29–32.

Nerney, Brian James. "Katharine S. White, *New Yorker* Editor: Her Influences on the *New Yorker* and on American Literature." Ph.D. diss., University of Minnesota, 1982.

"The New Yorker." *Fortune* 10 (August 1934): 73–80, 82, 85–86, 88, 90, 92, 97.

The New Yorker Album of Art and Artists. Greenwich, Conn.: New York Graphic Society, 1970.

The New Yorker Album of Drawings, 1925–1975. New York: Viking Press, 1975.

Rutledge, Howard, and Peter Bart. "Urbanity, Inc." *Wall Street Journal* (30 June 1958): 1, 6.

Spiller, Robert E. et al. *Literary History of the United States*. New York: Macmillan Co., 1974; 4th ed., rev., pp. 164–66, 210, 751, 752, 755, 757, 1378.

Thurber, James. *Credos and Curios*. New York: Harper and Row, 1962.

———. *The Years with Ross*. Boston: Little, Brown, 1959.

White, E. B. *Letters of E. B. White*. Ed. Dorothy Lobrano Guth. New York: Harper and Row, 1976.

Wood, James Playsted. *Magazines in the United States*. New York: Ronald Press, 1971. 3d ed., pp. 256–76, 327, 434, 438.

Yates, Norris. *The American Humorist: Conscience of the Twentieth Century*. Ames: Iowa State University Press, 1964.

INDEX SOURCES: Robert O. Johnson, *An Index To Literature In The New Yorker*. Metuchen, N.J.: Scarecrow Press, 1969–1976. Volumes 1–15 include 1925–1944 (published 1969); Volumes 16–30 include 1944–1955 (1970); Volumes 31–45 include 1955–1970 (1971); Volumes 41–50 include 1970–1975 (1976); Robert O. Johnson, *An Index to Profiles in the New Yorker*. Metuchen, N.J.: Scarecrow Press, 1972; *Reader's Guide to Periodical Literature*.

REPRINT EDITIONS: University Microfilms.

LOCATION SOURCES: Available at most libraries; see *Union List of Serials*. (There are over 2,000 public, academic—not including professional schools such as medicine and law—and armed services libraries in the United States; it is estimated that ninety percent of these carry *The New Yorker*.)

Publication History

MAGAZINE TITLE AND TITLE CHANGES: *The New Yorker*, 21 February 1925 to
    present.
VOLUME AND ISSUE DATA: Weekly.
PUBLISHER AND PLACE OF PUBLICATION: The New Yorker Magazine, New York.
EDITORS: Harold W. Ross, 1925–1951; William Shawn, 1952–1987; Robert Gottlieb,
    1987 to present.
CIRCULATION: 506,038.

Steven H. Gale

THE NEW YORK PICAYUNE

One of the longest running, least available to scholars, and most important of
the comic papers in showing the shift in Northeastern literary humor toward
literary comedy is *The New York Picayune*, edited and published by J. C. Levison
in New York City throughout the 1850s, subtitled "The American Pick." In its
last phase, it was 11½" × 16¾", four columns in format, selling at three cents,
often publishing a second edition and adding a "Pictorial Picayune" for the
holidays—the one seen selling for six and one-fourth cents. Levison's illustrated
papers offered critical and sarcastic commentary on city and state corruption,
burlesques of sappy literature, and major social and economic phenomena, such
as one cartoon showing unsafe railroad cars as death vehicles. In the middle
1850s, the "Pick" claimed a circulation of 40,000, establishing it as a relatively
widely read humorous paper, and its longevity suggests that it was profitable.
Mortimer C. Thomson—"Doesticks"—became one of its important writers, and
eventually joined Levison in a partnership arrangement.

The "Pick" regularly reviewed New York theater events, including the moral
dramas at P. T. Barnum's Museum, and otherwise fitted itself to contemporary
public events. *Punch* was roundly attacked for its politics on Cuba, and local
types like the shyster lawyers hanging around the Tombs, New York's local
prison, were satirized in poetry and illustrations. As early as 1855, it was
concerned about the drift toward conflict over the slavery issue. "Chips from
other Blockheads" borrowed longer comic paragraphs from other sources even
as its title burlesqued *Yankee Notions'* * "Chip Basket." Levison himself was a
talented burlesquer in Negro dialect and produced his "Julius Ceasar Hannibal"
sketches in rich abundance. These sketches were reprinted in book form as *Black
Diamonds*, credited as one of the earliest sources of Black minstrel material and
comic dialect. In 1856, Doesticks was a regular contributor—one of the first of
the racy, colloquial literary comedians to achieve a major reputation. John
Brougham and J. C. Haney were also regular contributors, along with the
illustrators Frank Bellew and T. B. Gunn. A "Pictorial Picayune" was also
offered for the holidays. Mott (2:181–83) reviews further components of this
journal.

The New York Picayune, is one of the more important comic journals of the pre-Civil War period, even though it is now almost unobtainable, except for a large unsorted batch of issues from 1851 through 1859 at the American Antiquarian Society. At one time or another it appears in three different sizes and at various prices. Its importance lies in its shift from political to social issues, featuring the comic cartoons of Frank Bellew and the columns of Doesticks and Julius Ceasar Hannibal—Mortimer Thomson and W. H. Levison, the leaders of the movement toward urban literary comedy in New York in the 1850s.

The paper began in January 1847 (according to Mott, in order to advertise a patent medicine) and was edited for a time by Joseph Scoville until Levison took over in 1852. The first issue seen is Volume 2:16 (19 April 1851) in six-column newspaper format, four pages measuring 15¾" × 22". It sold at two cents a copy or one dollar a year. Woodward and Company, the original publishers, boasted a circulation of 30,000 weekly. Sketches of city figures were mixed with digests of foreign and domestic news. Typical items were the "Dashes about Town" series by "The Doctor," literary humor about New York middle-class life. Julius Ceasar Hannibal also offered his series of burlesque scientific discourses in comic Black dialect. The last seen in this size is Volume 4:33 (13 August 1853), priced at three cents an issue. *The Pictorial Picayune* was a semi-annual version designed to provide a giant tabloid holiday issue for the Fourth of July and New Year's. Number 7 was for 4 July 1854 and Number 11 was issued 1 January 1857, both priced at six cents and 23" × 16¾", with an emphasis on graphic comedy and text; another Number 7, presumably of a later series, was issued for the Christmas and New Year's week of 1859–1860.

The later *Picayune* is of most interest to historians, for in 1857 it was edited by Doesticks, then the leading American literary comedian, and "Triangle," the symbol used by the illustrator Bellew. By then it was in Volume 8, with Number 31 dated 25 July 1857. It was of a smaller size at 10½" × 7½", but expanded to sixteen pages, the last two of which were advertisements. Humor in 1857 focused on the Mormons and the current commercial panic. In addition, Krautsalaat wrote on the problems of city deliveries, John G. Saxe offered poems, and the editors claimed an "apolitical" orientation. The new series of the acclaimed Doesticks letters began appearing on 5 December 1857, and Doesticks and Triangle continued as editors into 1858. The *Picayune* jumped in size to 16¾" × 11½" with the 17 April 1858 issue, but only eight pages. Soon after on 15 May 1858, it began its most significant social foray with a front-page cartoon by Triangle attacking the sale of swill-milk (milk from cows fed on swill and other refuse and a major menace to the health of the poor in New York City), thereby inaugurating a major social campaign that was hotly contested over a sustained period. The last issue seen is Volume 11, Number 13, for 26 March 1859, and it ended with the 18 February 1860 number.

Information Sources

BIBLIOGRAPHY:
Mott, Frank L. *A History of American Magazines, 1850–1865*. Cambridge, Mass.: Harvard University Press, 1938, 2:177–84.
INDEX SOURCES: None.
REPRINT EDITIONS: The New York Public Library has microfilmed its holdings; *Chips from Uncle Sam's Jack-Knife; or Slices from the N. Y. Picayune* (New York: Dick and Fitzgerald, n.d.) was a 94-page paperback book selling for twenty-five cents in garish yellow, blue, and red covers featuring excerpts from the paper—RPB holds a copy.
LOCATION SOURCES: MWA, DLC, MH, and NN have varied runs; three other libraries have one or two issues.

Publication History

MAGAZINE TITLE AND TITLE CHANGES: *The New York Picayune*.
VOLUME AND ISSUE DATA: Volume 1:1, January 1847–Volume 12:17, 18 February 1860.
PUBLISHER AND PLACE OF PUBLICATION: 1847–1853: Woodward and Hutchings. 1853–1857: Woodward, Levison, and Robert Gun. 1857–1860: Levison and Thomson, New York.
EDITORS: Joseph A. Scoville, ?–1852; William H. Levison, 1852–1857; J. C. Haney, c.1857; F. Bellew and M. Thomson, 1857–1860 (Dates require confirmation).
CIRCULATION: 40,000.

David E. E. Sloane

THE NEW YORK PICK

The New York Pick was a weekly illustrated newspaper published from 1852 to 1854. It provided Joseph A. Scoville (1811–1864) a comic organ to advance "purely American" themes after his flight from *The New York Picayune.**
Scoville, *Pick*'s editor and publisher, had been secretary to John C. Calhoun and was frequently embroiled in controversy, both personal and political, although he claimed not to fuss with politicians, whom he called "crawling, winding men." For Clay and the great national spokesmen of the pre-doughface era he had great admiration, and he wrote of Clay's death that presidents might die and be replaced, but there was only one Clay. The liveliness of *Pick* and its general intelligence make this a worthwhile compliment.

The *Pick* saw first light on Saturday, 21 February 1852, as a four-page newspaper of six columns measuring roughly 19″ × 20″, selling for two cents a copy or a dollar per year. As Scoville noted, the paper was sold at a loss, but the advertisers and shilling-a-line notices carried it. His last two pages in each issue offered two or three columns of advertisements in addition to the popular puzzles and rebuses which amused readers in the middle of the nineteenth century. The editor's concerns were featured prominently in the editorial column, "Mr. Pick in his Sanctum," in commanding position at the top left of page one. Other columns answered correspondence from readers and carried a variety of comic fictions, jokes, theatrical notices, and sophisticated local matter. The illustrations maintained the appearance of uncommonly crude woodcuts, and although Scoville claimed that he would upgrade them, their roughness remained constant. Nevertheless, distribution in nine cities on the Atlantic seaboard carried *Pick* fairly far for a paper with a decidedly New York orientation. Scoville advertised that his first issue sold 24,000 copies and the second 30,000, a hefty figure for the early 1850s.

"Mr. Pick" was a cultivated commentator on both the national scene and New York City life visible on Broadway and the Bowery. The "Five Points" of New York—a geographic locale—was described as a man with a thumb on his nose and fingers outstretched in the classic skeptic manner. Double-column cartoons on the front page addressed national themes and suggested the intent of *Pick* to take its place as the American comic illustrated newspaper, a claim reserved for *Puck** two decades later. Both visual jokes and comic copy boosted Americans over foreigners with a robust nationalism that bordered on the xenophobic. Among others, *Pick* attacked mustachioed Italians who had nothing better to do than walk around New York seducing foolish women. *Pick*'s comic serial "The Romance of the Mustache" meandered through various issues burlesquing city social life; proceeding at the rate of only a lengthy paragraph or two per week, it was less urgent on the issues of foreigners and New York socialites. A poem datelined Williamsburg—another New York district—chanted "A Yankee girl is the girl for me, / Away with your foreign flirts."

The editor also claimed to care little for politics. Noting the obvious, however, he wrote, "Mr. Pick advises the Whig leaders to take warning in time, or prepare to vacate their fodder at the public crib." Scoville's political experience might have suggested to his peers that his concern about party unity was pertinent. On a grimmer local note, a cartoon showed the milkmaid of the poor as a death skeleton, drawn by Read, striking the theme which *Frank Leslie's Weekly* made a major social campaign later in the decade—the "swill-milk" abuse that poisoned New York's residents. *Pick* was ahead of its time as a social reformer.

Information Sources

BIBLIOGRAPHY:
Mott, Frank L. *A History of American Magazines, 1850–1865*. Cambridge, Mass.: Harvard University Press, 1938; 2:179–183.
INDEX SOURCES: None.
REPRINT EDITIONS: University Microfilms.
LOCATION SOURCES: NN.

Publication History

MAGAZINE TITLE AND TITLE CHANGES: *The New York Pick*.
VOLUME AND ISSUE DATA: Volume 1:1, 21 February 1852–Volume 1:43, 11 December 1852 last seen; the common ending date is given as 1854.

PUBLISHER AND PLACE OF PUBLICATION: Joseph A. Scoville, New York.
EDITOR: Joseph A. Scoville.
CIRCULATION: 24,000–30,000.

David E. E. Sloane

NICK NAX (FOR ALL CREATION)

William Levison and J. C. Haney combined to edit *Nick Nax* or *Nick Nax for All Creation* monthly from Volume 1:1, May 1856; a Volume 18:1 for May 1872 is cited in a list of American comic periodicals in *Notes and Queries* (15 June 1872) compiled by William Raynor; it merged into *Comic World* after the December 1875 issue (Vol. 20).

Nick Nax featured the general humor of the cities and the regions, with jokes reflecting local life more than political affairs. Doesticks, Artemus Ward, Oliver Wendell Holmes, and other anecdotalists and literary comedians were frequently reprinted. Jokes and characters actually seemed fresh. One story described a rich man complaining to friends that he couldn't marry off his three daughters with $10,000 each; an Irishman stepped up to him and made a respectful bow, saying ''I'll take two of them.'' Longer stories and poems of country folk humor were also frequent in the randomly organized double-column mix of stories, pictures, and illustrated cartoons. The cost was ten cents for the 7¼" × 10¾", thirty-page issues, one dollar per year.

Yankee sharper stories were well represented in *Nick Nax*, including one in which a "Landlord Gratified" is conned by a Yankee he was chaffing for a trick. The Yankee says he will get gin out of one end of a wine barrel and brandy out of the other; drilling one hole, he asks the landlord to hold it to save his liquor; drilling another hole, he leaves the landlord holding both holes while he goes—permanently away—to get bowls; the landlord has to treat all around to be released from the trap (Vol. 2:2, p. 54). Ross and Tousey, publishers of other humorous works, were the agents.

Information Sources

INDEX SOURCES: None.
REPRINT EDITIONS: None.
LOCATION SOURCES: MWA, Volumes 1:2; DLC, IAU, NN, OClWHi have partial
    listings.

Publication History

MAGAZINE TITLE AND TITLE CHANGES: *Nick Nax* or *Nick Nax for All Creation*.
VOLUME AND ISSUE DATA: Volume 1:1, May 1856–Volume 20:8, December 1875.
PUBLISHER AND PLACE OF PUBLICATION: Levison and Haney, New York.
EDITORS: William Levison and J. C. Haney.
CIRCULATION: Unknown.

David E. E. Sloane

THE ———

Washington, D.C., in the 1820s was an isolated rural community peopled by transient politicians riven by sectional factionalism. John Quincy Adams became President in 1824 with the backing of Henry Clay, who some thought had been promised the position of Secretary of State by Adams for his support. This coalition momentarily slowed the growing Jacksonian movement but insured that Adams's hopes for the government were not to be realized. A national university, national scientific explorations, a Department of Interior, and government-backed improvements of transportation, all advanced in Adams's first Annual Message, were doomed by a Congress packed with the opposition party, the first time in the history of the country that the President's party did not dominate Congress.

Into conditions rife for satire came The ———, edited by "Nonius Nondescript" and published by Pishey Thompson, an Englishman in his early forties who ran a bookstore on Pennsylvania Avenue. Thompson had come to the United States in 1819 and during his twenty-seven years of residence was an acquaintance of Daniel Webster, Henry Clay, Edward Everett, and other leading politicians. Thompson was apparently a bookish person having occupied his time in England before coming to the United States by collecting material for a history of the area of Lincolnshire where he was born. The ——— is sprinkled with epigraphs drawn from works by George Crabbe, Oliver Goldsmith, Sir Walter Scott, William Shakespeare, Thomas Sheridan, Thomson, Virgil, and William Wordsworth. Latin and French tags stud the prose and poetry. The lack of title for the eight issues is explained by an epigraph that appeared on each cover: "What's a name? 'A word, and a word can be abused.' " This effacement extends to the name of the ostensible editor, Nonius Nondescript, the faceless persona to whom most of the selections in the magazine are addressed.

In order to comment on life in the inchoate capital, Thompson created several outsider personae. At a time when the Yankee commentator was widely used, The ——— presented John Ouisconsin, the "Backwoodsman in Washington," his brother Job, Clara from Illinois, and several other pseudonymous correspondents. John Ouisconsin writes flawless prose but is socially inept, retailing his problems learning how to dress correctly, how to behave at dinner, and how to make his way in the Washington social whirl. Job, his brother, writes in dialect, posing innocent questions about reports on the rowdiness and factionalism of congressional proceedings. Much of the humor is broadly directed at a parvenu society. (Ouisconsin falls down the stairs the first time he wears new boots with military heels, drinks the water in the finger bowl, etc.) The satire of politics tends to be muted, although a sketch in the 18 February issue (p. 1) mocks the prevailing attitude that exploiting Indians was widely acceptable behavior. The issue was then much in the public view as the result of Georgia's usurpation of land belonging to the Creek Indians. The ongoing dispute about whether the United States should send a "mission" to a meeting of Latin American nations in Panama was referred to as "*Panammunition . . . priming* to *keep up* congressional *gunning.*" Sketches of congressional figures attacked, without naming, a "Gratiano" described as a "libertine in language," a "practiced prodigal" (p. 68), and a Congressional Bore, a master of timely tags and cliches (p. 79). But *The* —— also contained occasional encomiums as well as a meditation on Mount Vernon honoring the first President.

Each issue of *The* —— was twelve pages long inside a cover that contained the title, the name of Nonius Nondescript, the epigraph, and publisher's information. The selections were usually signed with pseudonyms and presented as epistles to Mr. Nondescript. Most of the material was in prose, although each issue contained at least one poem. There were no illustrations.

The eighth and last issue closed with an eighty-four line poem, "Valedictory," a good-humored catalogue that captures the varied and contradictory life of Washington in the 1820s:

> Farewell to long speeches! Farewell
> to strange faces! Oratorical tropes,
> and rhetorical graces! Farewell to
> the statesmen, so various in powers!
> Farewell to the tongue that would wag
> on for hours!

Information Sources

INDEX SOURCES: None.
REPRINT EDITIONS: University Microfilms.
LOCATION SOURCES: KMK, NN, NOneoU, and eight other libraries.

Publication History

MAGAZINE TITLE AND TITLE CHANGES: *The* —— (18 February 1826–18 May 1926).
VOLUME AND ISSUE DATA: Bi-weekly, Volume 1:1, 18 February 1826–Volume 1:8, 18 May 1926.
PUBLISHER AND PLACE OF PUBLICATION: Pishey Thompson, Washington, D.C.
EDITOR: "Nonius Nondescript."
CIRCULATION: Unknown.

George A. Test

O

OASIS

The plan for the *Oasis: A Monthly Magazine Devoted to Literature, Science, and the Arts* (first published 12 August 1837) called for a publication containing mostly original pieces that avoided sectarian and political issues. An editorial in the second issue stressed that the *Oasis* had begun with the editors' desiring to delight and instruct, not to provide information only. Among its essays on a variety of subjects and its poetry, musical selections, biographical sketches, literary criticism, and news, the *Oasis* offered solemnity as well as amusement.

As the number of its issues increased, the *Oasis* turned frequently to other publications, principally the *Knickerbocker* magazine. Contributors included Ellery Channing, Robert Southey, and Dorothea Hemens, and credits frequently appeared for the *Edinburgh Review* and the *Yale Literary Magazine*. Perhaps sixty percent of its material was humor, largely reprinted from other publications.

The second issue of the *Oasis* included an essay on spiders, characterizing them from behavioral traits. Although many persons detest the arachnids, the writer says, spiders exemplify industriousness and perseverance. Because they work in wine cellars they are convivial; because they may be found in ruins they love nature; and because they spin webs behind old paintings they love art. In November 1837 the *Oasis* printed some "extracts from the Posthumous works of a fellow still living." The seventh issue contained an essay that proved to be a joke on the reader. Credited to the *Gentlemen's Magazine*, "The Alligator" narrated in conspicuous malapropisms how a maid was eaten by a crocodile with "as much ease as you would eat a buttered muffin." In the end the reader learns that the maid had not been carried away by a crocodile, but had eloped through an alley fence with a man who had courted her there. He was the "alley-gate-r."

The twelve issues of the *Oasis* appeared in three-column pages, sixteen per issue. In order to accommodate the musical scores that appeared regularly, pages were printed in imperial octavo. The advance subscription cost was $1.50, but the price rose to two dollars when the magazine had run three issues. The final number of the *Oasis* appeared on 28 July 1838, the magazine's demise resulting from an apparent lack of finances. Having received "little assistance from patrons," the editors noted their inability to continue their enterprise.

Information Sources

INDEX SOURCES: Title index with Volume 1.
REPRINT EDITIONS: University Microfilms.
LOCATION SOURCES: MWA, NN, and WHi.

Publication History

MAGAZINE TITLE AND TITLE CHANGES: The *Oasis: A Monthly Magazine Devoted to Literature, Science, and the Arts*, 12 August 1837–28 July 1838.
VOLUME AND ISSUE DATA: Volume 1:1, 12 August 1837–Volume 1:12, 28 July 1838.
PUBLISHER AND PLACE OF PUBLICATION: George Henry, Oswego, New York.
EDITORS: Joseph Nelson and John S. Randall.
CIRCULATION: Unknown.

Thomas Hunter Stewart

OMNIUM GATHERUM

Omnium Gatherum gathered a variety of humorous materials into its one volume from November 1809 to October 1810. Published in Boston by T. Kennard, it filled 4″ × 7″ pages with wit from England and America, including local items, as well as more serious material. Its tenth number reprinted George H–ll's (cited as the Vermont Nimrod) original Vermont tall tale from the *Farmer's Almanac*:

> I was once passing down the banks of the Hudson in search of game, and suddenly heard a crackling on the opposite bank. Looking across the river, I saw a stately buck, and instantly drew up, and let fly at him. That very moment a huge sturgeon leaped from the river in the direction of my piece. The ball went through him, and passed on. I flung down my gun; threw off my coat and hat, and swam for the floating fish, which, mounting, I towed to the bank, and went to see what more my shot had done for me. I found the ball had passed through the heart of the deer, and struck into the hollow tree beyond, where the honey was running out like a river! I sprung round to find something to stop the hole with, and caught hold of a white rabbit—It squeaked just like a stuck pig; so I thrash'd it away from me in a passion at the disappointment, and it went with such force that it killed three cock partridges and a woodcock (Vol. 1:10, p. 455).

Other items offer social and political content, as when a spinster refuses to sit beside a judge on the bench because "There are old women there enough already"; another "Affecting Anecdote" (Vol. 1:5, pp. 255–56) describes a poor Englishwoman's hanging after she steals to support his babies following her husband's impressment—typical of Mark Twain's later indictments of early British law. Undistinguished serials by "Merry Andrew" beginning in the fifth number and "A Juvenile Traveler" in the seventh attempted to offer original material mediating between a large number of serious items on commerce, law, criminal justice, and biographical items, including a reprinting of Gilman's biographical sketch of Timothy Dexter (Vol. 1:8, pp. 337–45).

Information Sources

INDEX SOURCES: None.
REPRINT EDITIONS: University Microfilms.
LOCATION SOURCES: MWA, CtY, MH, and NN.

Publication History

MAGAZINE TITLE AND TITLE CHANGES: *Omnium Gatherum*.
VOLUME AND ISSUE DATE: Volume 1:1–12, November 1809-October 1810.
PUBLISHER AND PLACE OF PUBLICATION: T. Kennard, Boston.
EDITOR: T. Kendall(?).
CIRCULATION: Unknown.

David E. E. Sloane

THE OUTSIDER'S NEWSLETTER

The Outsider's Newsletter (*ON*), founded in 1962, was a weekly version of *Monocle*.** Under the motto, "All we know is what we don't read in the papers," *ON* professed to supply news and comment not available in the "inside" stories contained in "such sheets as *Time*, and *I. F. Stone's Weekly*." *ON* was also dedicated to combatting what it called the "information surplus," a condition that had produced an "over-informed" citizenry and groups such as "the Rand Corporation and the C.I.A." The targets of its satire and humor were political figures around the world, government and business organizations, the media, and social problems such as automation, integration, and women's rights. Its contents consisted of an ironic and comic running commentary on the news of the world between early 1962 and mid-June 1964.

Charles DeGaulle, Harold MacMillan, Fidel Castro, Mme. Nhu, sister-in-law of South Vietnam's President Diem, and other world figures were regularly mocked on the pages of the *Outsider's Newsletter*. President John F. Kennedy and members of his family, President Lyndon Johnson, members of Congress, and Cabinet members all found themselves targets of *ON*. When the Wheeling Steel Company raised the price of steel against the agreement made by the large corporations, Marvin Kitman, *ON* staff member, lauded Wheeling for its spirit of free enterprise and placed an order for a ton of steel to be shipped to his home in Leonia, New Jersey. *ON* opposed the piecemeal method of cutting the federal budget and recommended that the State of California be cut from the

Union since it received more federal money than any other state. *ON* made fun of the entire presidential nomination process when Kitman entered the primary in New Hampshire in December 1963. For months thereafter, *ON* carried the correspondence with the Republican party, copies of news clippings generated by Kitman's action, and news of actions and reactions to the jape. During the New York City newspaper strike in 1962 *ON* published parody issues of several New York papers.

The size of *The Outsider's Newsletter*, 4¼" × 9½", merely added to the humor of a newspaper parody. *ON* began with eight pages but Volume 1:29, went to sixteen pages. Page one always contained a cartoon or other illustration relating to the lead item. In addition to such graphic satire, *ON* ran cartoons ("Superkahn" by Ed Koren) and untitled cartoon series by Lou Myers. "Superkahn" purported to be the adventures of Herman Kahn, futurist founder of the Hudson Institute, a "think tank." *ON* rarely published photographs, but it reproduced news clippings and correspondence for comic purposes and used a variety of techniques to achieve its satire. Kitman wrote a column, "By Jingo," as did David Cort, "A Simpleton's Newbook," and Jerry Doolittle, "The Mess in Washington." "A Letter from Kyuichi" purported to be from a minor Japanese politician whose problems and actions often paralleled those in the American scene. Among other things, C.D.B. Bryan wrote the continuing adventure of James Bland, Agent 008, and sometimes Trixie Malloy, "Girl Free-Lance Undercover Agent and Inventor," a parody of spy-adventure fantasy and a device for commenting on British and international politics. Imaginary dialogues between famous persons took place in "Outsiders Newsreal," and short verse appeared under "Poems of Protest." At least sixty percent of the content was unsigned.

Information Sources

INDEX SOURCES: None.
REPRINT EDITIONS: None.
LOCATION SOURCES: IEN, IU, KPT, MH, PSC, CU.

Publication History

MAGAZINE TITLE AND TITLE CHANGES: *The Outsider's Newsletter* (no week or
    month listed for 1962–19 June 1964).
VOLUME AND ISSUE DATA: Weekly, annual volumes, Volume 1:1, 1962–Volume
    2:31, 19 June 1964.
PUBLISHER AND PLACE OF PUBLICATION: Monocle Periodicals, New York.
EDITOR: None listed. Staff: Victor S. Navasky, Richard Lingeman, C.D.B. Bryan,
    Marvin Kitman, Eleanor Dienstag, and Phil Gips, and Lou Klein (art).
CIRCULATION: 2,000.

George A. Test

P

PHILISTINE

In many ways, the success of the *Philistine*, according to Frank Luther Mott, was a catalyst causing an explosion of other little literary magazines around the turn of the century. Founded by three western New Yorkers, the magazine soon became a soap box for Elbert Hubbard, whose Roycroft commune in East Aurora was a focus for much of culture-hungry middle America during the early twentieth century. For most of its life, Hubbard wrote each issue himself. Leslie Stephens had defined "philistine" as a term of contempt applied by prigs to the rest of their species, and Hubbard was content to be whatever the prigs were not and proudly proclaimed his "philistinism" while encouraging others to join. He didn't always take himself or his cause too seriously, but the *Philistine* became the foundation of his Roycroft enterprise. Through it he attacked pretense and mediocrity in American life and letters while advertising the products and philosophies designed to correct it.

Elbert Green Hubbard was born in Bloomington, Illinois, on 19 June 1856, and sold soap door to door as a youth. Later, his advertising genius helped enrich J. D. Larkin and Company, a maker of office furniture. In 1884, Hubbard, while still married to Bertha Crawford, met a young high school teacher named Alice Moore, who would bear him a daughter. In 1904, after a scandalous lawsuit and divorce, they would marry; Alice, a writer and reformer herself, was to have a significant and as-yet unexplored impact on Hubbard's intellectual growth.

Near the end of 1892, having published his first novel the year before, Elbert Hubbard sold his interest in the Larkin Company to embark on a literary career. His attempt to enroll at Harvard failed when the university refused to accept him as a regular student. He attended some classes while continuing his novel writing, but he soon became frustrated with academic life. Although failing to find a publisher for a series of impressionistic journeys to the homes of the great, his

Little Journeys to the Homes of Good Men and Great, in 1894 he left for England and Ireland to gather material. In England he met William Morris and visited his Kelmscott commune at Hammersmith. This experience influenced the founding of his Roycroft commune, named after two seventeenth-century English bookbinders.

Upon his return, the idea for the *Philistine* was implemented. Three men were involved in its founding; besides Hubbard, there was William McIntosh, managing editor of the *Buffalo Evening News*, and Harry P. Taber, a poet-printer-journalist from East Aurora. Hubbard's story is that the *Philistine* was initially intended as a one-issue venture, sent in magazine form to 2,500 carefully selected patrons only to gain second-class mailing privileges. Not only could he advertise for his upcoming *Little Journeys* series soon to be published by G. P. Putnam's Sons, but he could also take some pot shots at the literary establishment. Taber later claimed that the idea for the *Philistine* was his, and he was listed as editor in early issues. Until March 1896, the magazine was copyrighted in his name. The early venture was probably not singlehanded, but Hubbard soon gained control of the publication. In 1896, he proposed to his Boston friend Walter Blackburn Harte that they merge the *Philistine* with Harte's *Fly Leaf*, started in December 1895, and work as partners. Harte moved to East Aurora, but Hubbard changed his mind about the partnership and offered him a salaried position instead. They quarreled, and the joint venture was abandoned.

In format, the *Philistine* was pocket-sized, 4¾" × 6¼", with a sand or cream-colored cover. After the first three issues, its size was slightly reduced, and beginning in September 1895, the magazine was printed on Dickinson's handmade paper and bound in a coarse brown butcher-type wrapping. In the August number, Hubbard announced that its successful reception warranted this improvement, and he boasted that "the proofs submitted to the publishers promise a periodical unequalled among all the rough paper magazines in America for typographical beauty." The squarish black text type resembled a Jenson typeface, and large ornamental factorums served as initials.

The title blazed in red on the covers of the first three issues with the subtitle "A Periodical of Protest," and its claim was to be "Printed Every Little While for The Society of The Philistines and Published by Them Monthly." After the third issue, the title was printed in black with a red ornamental "P." The first and second issue covers quoted John Calvin: "Those Philistines who engender animosity, stir up trouble and then smile." Hubbard later wrote:"We called it the *Philistine* because we were going after the Chosen People in literature. . . . The Smug and Snugly Ensconced denizens of Union Square called me a Philistine, and I said, 'Yes, I am one if a Philistine is something different from you!' "

Cover quotations for the first two years came mostly from Shakespeare and the Bible, with a bit of William Thackeray, Omar Khayyam, and Charles Lamb for variety. As Hubbard's voice began to dominate, some covers showcased the type of epigram which would later make him famous and would become prominent in his writings, especially in the *Philistine*. The cover of the February 1898 issue warns; "Those who really do not know how to take this magazine, had better not."

McIntosh led the first number with his essay "Philistines Ancient and Modern." To Hubbard, Taber, and McIntosh, Philistines were cultural outsiders, heroes battling hypocrisy, false values, and pretense. Hubbard's first essay blasted the English notion of erecting monuments. The thirty-two page initial effort contained poetry by McIntosh, Joy Cartman, Joy Trolleyman, Francis W. Bourdillon, and Rowland B. Mahoney, and advertising for Hubbard's *Little Journeys* and Thomas B. Mosher's *Bibelot*.** Stephen Crane would shortly be added to the list of contributors. The issue ended with Hubbard's first "Side Talks . . . " column, consisting of brief and biting attacks on Hamlin Garland, William Dean Howells, Mark Twain, and, in later issues, Harry Thurston Peck of the *Bookman*, Edward Bok of *Ladies' Home Journal*, and Richard Watson Gilder of the *Century*, *S.S. McClure's*, *Scribner's*, *Godey's*, and *Peterson's*. Other contributors during the *Philistine*'s first five years included Walter Blackburn Harte, Joaquin Miller, Eugene Field, Carolyn Wells, William Marion Reedy, Ouida, Frank Putnam, Bliss Carman, Walter Storrs Bigelow, Emma Eggleston, Michael Monahan, William A. Payton, George Turner Phelps, W. F. Wheatley, Jr., and Irving Bacheller. After 1901, Hubbard wrote most of each issue himself, but those contributing most frequently after that year included Hugh O. Pentecost, Benjamin De Casseres, Marilla Ricker, and Richard Le Gallienne.

The first three back covers advertised Hubbard's *Little Journeys*, and continued to feature ads, poetry, and satirical cartoons. Later poets included Eleanor B. Caldwell, Grace Hibbard, John Mack, Jr., Sarah Norcliffe Cleghorn, Harold MacGrath, John Oakman, Lavinia S. Goodwin, Myrtle Reed, C. P. Nettleton, and Stephen Crane. Throughout 1898–1899, W. W. Denslow's color and black and white satiric cartoons became more prominent, on back covers and within the magazine itself. Some of his sketches accompanied Crane's poetry. By 1899, the back covers also offered boldly printed quotations by notables such as John Ruskin and William Morris in addition to anonymous epigrams by Hubbard himself.

In the *Philistine*'s early days, Hubbard had sold all advertising space for five hundred dollars to Fred Gardner of Chicago, who then resold it at his own rates. As the *Philistine*'s circulation grew, Hubbard refused to abide by the contract, and, after losing three expensive lawsuits, bought out Gardner for a huge amount. The *Philistine*'s advertising initially aimed at a small bookish audience, but as circulation grew, it focused more on the middle and upper middle classes. By May 1897, three bicycle ads listed prices ranging from sixty to one hundred and fifty dollars. In the same issue, two New York health sanitariums advertised. Hubbard was able to attract such clients as Tiffany's, Gorham Silver, Baldwin Pianos, American Telegraph and Telephone Company, the Chalmers Car Company of Detroit, and other top businesses. In 1910 he advertised an eighty-six foot cruiser built by the Racine Boat Company of Muskegon, Michigan, sleeping eight and selling for over $2,000.

Subscription rates were one dollar yearly and soon included "Health, Success, and Love vibrations that are sent daily to all subscribers at 4:00 P.M., Eastern Time. (If shy on vibrations, please advise.)" Single copies sold for ten cents. Within the first year, Hubbard announced the formation of the Society of Philistines (International), later dubbed the American Academy of Immortals, "An association of Book Lovers and Folks who Write, Paint and Dream . . . Organized to further Good-Fellowship among men and women who believe in allowing the widest liberty to Individuality in Thought and Expression." Life memberships cost ten dollars and included all available back issues and all future issues for one hundred years (soon changed to "ninety-nine years—but no longer"). Membership in the American Academy of Immortals was easy to maintain. After paying his subscription fee, each member's duty consisted in "living up to his highest Ideal (as nearly as possible) and attending the Annual Dinner (if convenient)."

The *Philistine*'s scope, although initially limited to those rejected writers, artists, and intellectuals disenchanted with the current cultural scene, soon reached out to encompass much of middle America. Hubbard had probably seen the *Yellow Book* while in England, and the American *Chap-book* also influenced the *Philistine*. Like those, and Thomas B. Mosher's *Bibelot*, the early *Philistine* had a narrow audience. However, the success of Hubbard's publication was to encourage numerous imitators. While the *Chap-book*'s circulation, for example, never seemed to top 16,500, the *Philistine*, by 1905, counted itself among some twenty magazines whose yearly sales exceeded 100,000.

The most lively and wittiest feature from the beginning was Hubbard's own "Side Talks With The Philistines." Often the column would have a subtitle such as "Being Sundry Bits of Wisdom Which Have Been Heretofore Secreted, And Are Now Set Forth In Print"; or later, "Being Soul Easement . . . And Wisdom Incidentally." Titles evolved and disappeared until it finally settled down as "Heart to Heart Talks with Philistines by the Pastor of His Flock." By about 1900, it was not only the main feature of the magazine, but often the only one.

These witty, brilliant, sometimes banal columns would typically contain one or two short philosophical essays on current news, on the death of prominent persons, or on observations Hubbard made during business or lecture trips. He commonly chastised doctors, lawyers, and ministers, while commenting on imperialism, child labor, evolutionary theory, feminism, marriage and divorce, education, crime and criminals, conspicuous consumption, religion, and life in general. Some shorter essays were preachments or parables, true parodies of a pastor talking to his flock. Hubbard responded to letters of criticism and praise, commented on the literary scene, and wrote witty epigrams. These sayings were later bound into *The Roycroft Dictionary*, similar to, yet not as biting as Ambrose Bierce's *The Devil's Dictionary*. He wrote brief biographies of people he met in his travels, especially businessmen, and some of these later became *Little*

Journeys or were printed as promotional pamphlets. He reported on visitors to his growing Roycroft Campus and talked about other happenings in and around the shops. The news was chatty, and regular readers felt as if they were insiders and belonged, as Hubbard intended.

Hubbard's most famous essay, "A Message to Garcia," was originally simple preachment in the March 1899 *Philistine* which consisted entirely of a "Heart to Heart Talk . . . " column. Even Hubbard was surprised at the success of this essay, focusing on an heroic event in the Spanish-American War and glamorizing individual responsibility and success. It transformed his current image as an eccentric American imitator of William Morris to that of "Fra Elbertus, the Sage of East Aurora." With his new nationwide reputation came the backing of business and industry and the rapid growth of his Roycroft enterprises. Even by the end of its first year, the *Philistine* was less a pamphlet of protesting voices than it was a vehicle for Elbert Hubbard. However, by 1902, most of the crude yet witty barbs were gone, and Hubbard was writing: "Beware of the paper or person that mud-balls people. The epithet a man applies to another usually fits himself best. We describe that which we see." Now that he was a part of the establishment, it was difficult to attack it.

In the Spring of 1915, Elbert and Alice Hubbard sailed on the *Lusitania* for Europe to gather information about the war, which Hubbard opposed. Hubbard hoped for an interview with the Kaiser, the object of much recent criticism in his *Philistine*. When on 15 May, the *Lusitania* was sunk by a German U-boat and the Hubbards were not among the survivors, the Roycrofters knew that the man and the magazine had been one, and any attempt to continue its wit and humor without "Fra Elbertus" would be futile. The last *Philistine*, a July memorial issue, told readers: "The *Philistine* had been Hubbard's armor, his shield, and his sword for long years. He has left us for a Little Journey, we know not where. He may need his *Philistine*, and so with tears on it we give it to him." The *Fra* was carried on as a nonhumorous successor by Edward (Felix) Shay for two years after Hubbard's death.

Information Sources

BIBLIOGRAPHY

Allen, Frederick Lewis. "Elbert Hubbard." *Scribner's* 104 (September 1938): 12–14, 49–51.

Balch, David Arnold. *Elbert Hubbard: Genius of Roycroft.* New York: Stokes, 1940.

Champney, Freeman. *Art and Glory: The Story of Elbert Hubbard.* New York: Crown Publishers, 1968.

Crumrine, Janice G. "Personality Development and Social Change: A Study of the Intersection of History and Biography." Ph.D. diss., State University of New York at Buffalo, 1975.

Hamilton, Charles F. *As Bees in Honey Drown: Elbert Hubbard and the Roycrofters.* Cranbury, N.J.: A. S. Barnes and Co., 1973.

————. *Roycroft Collectibles.* New York: A. S. Barnes and Co., 1980.

Heath, Mary Hubbard. *The Elbert Hubbard I Knew*. East Aurora, N.Y.: Roycroft Press, 1981[1929].

Hopkins, John Stephen. "Elbert Hubbard and the American Business Creed." Master's Thesis, Brown University, Providence, R.I., 1970.

Hubbard, Elbert. *The Roycroft Shop: A History*. East Aurora, N.Y., Roycroft Press, 1909.

Jackson, Holbrook. *The Eighteen Nineties: A Review of Art and Ideas at the Close of the Nineteenth Century*. New York: Alfred A. Knopf, 1972.

Mott, Frank L. "The Philistine." In *A History of American Magazines*, 1885–1905. Cambridge, Mass.: Harvard University Press, 1957, 4: 639–48.

Shay, Felix (Edward J.). *Elbert Hubbard of East Aurora*. New York: William H. Wise and Co., 1926.

Stott, Mary Roelofs. *Rebel with Reverence: Elbert Hubbard, a Granddaughter's Tribute* Watkins Glenn, N.Y.: Century House Americana Publishers, 1975.

INDEX SOURCES: Julia Ditto Young, *Philistine Index and Concordance*. East Aurora, N.Y.: Roycroft Press, 1905.

LOCATION SOURCES: 123 libraries list holdings. The most complete collections are held by the Art Institute, Ryerson Library, Chicago; IU; ICN; OU; OO; Workingmen's Institute Library, New Harmony, Indiana; Reading Public Library, Pennsylvania; Forbes Public Library, Northampton, Massachusetts; Minneapolis Public Library; and MdBE. The Elbert Hubbard Museum in East Aurora, New York, has the most complete collection of all Roycroft publications.

Publication History

MAGAZINE TITLE AND TITLE CHANGES: *The Philistine: A Periodical of Protest*, June 1895–July 1915. Absorbed the *Fly Leaf* in May 1896.

VOLUME AND ISSUE DATA: Monthly, semi-annual volumes, Volume 1:1, June 1895– Volume 41:2, July 1915.

PUBLISHER AND PLACE OF PUBLICATION: Elbert Hubbard, East Aurora, New York.

EDITORS: Harry Persons Taber, 1895–1896; Elbert Hubbard, 1896–1915.

CIRCULATION: Records were destroyed in a World War II scrap drive; according to its own claims, 1900: 60,000; 1903–1906: 125,000; 1915: 110,000.

Douglas R. Capra

THE PHUNNY PHELLOW

From 1859 through 1876, the Phun of the *Phunny Phellow* was the fun of social and class literary comedy. Relatively racy and fresh, *Phunny Phellow* found New York City urbanized regional subjects: Irish immigrants, pick pockets, green Yankees in the city, street urchins, and allied members of the rogues gallery of the urban Northeast. Literary irony, comic language, and brief comic characterizations typified the paper, and many of its jokes were old standards like the Irishman asking a Negro how long he had been in the country and, getting his answer in a brogue, concluding, "ownly twenty days over, an' tarned like that? I must away back to Ireland again." Comic verse, frequently dealing with the difficult social conditions of the poor, and sentimental romances filled out its pages. "Recipe for a 'Dead Rabbit' " (a poem protesting city street gangs) is the song of a crossing sweeper whose sister has become a whore and whose expectations are a life of thievery, "policy," and "shoulder hitting." Cartoons were in much evidence, including a full-page back cover.

The first issue of Volume 1 has been seen at the New York Public Library, dated October 1859. It is described as a weekly at four cents a copy in an 11″ × 14″, sixteen-page format, varying between two, three, and four columns per page depending on whether or not fiction, jokes, or cartoons were dominant in the layout. Frank L. Mott gives its dates as 1859 through 1876 with Oakie, Dayton and Jones as publishers to 1876 when Street and Smith took it over.

Information Sources

INDEX SOURCES: None.
REPRINT EDITIONS: None.
LOCATION SOURCES: MWA, MnU, OU, RP, and IU list broken holdings.

Publication History

MAGAZINE TITLE AND TITLE CHANGES: *The Phunny Phellow*.
VOLUME AND ISSUE DATA: Volume 1:1, October 1859–? (November 1872 number
    is last noted in several sources—1876?).
PUBLISHER AND PLACE OF PUBLICATION: 1859–1876: Oakie, Dayton and Jones.
    1876: Street and Smith, New York.
EDITORS: Unknown.
CIRCULATION: Unknown.

David E. E. Sloane

PICKINGS FROM PUCK

Begun in 1883, first as an annual but continuing later as a quarterly, *Pickings from Puck*, as its name implies, was a selection of items published by the editors of *Puck** from its weekly—in its own words "a choice collection of preeminently perfect pieces, poems and pictures from *Puck*." In format it looked very much like *Puck*, offering the same large 10″ × 14″ page and often vivid color inside and on its cover. Unlike *Puck*, it did not supply a table of contents or editorial comment, and since it printed previously published material, sometimes materials several years old, it was less likely to treat current affairs with opinion and humor. Nevertheless, it was careful not to use outdated material, and it avoided those political cartoons and jokes that were no longer topical. Nor did it attempt to offer the same regular features as did its weekly parent. However, at sixty-four pages it offered four times as much material as did the weekly. An advertisement for *Pickings* in *Puck* during 1904 claimed that the quarterly "contains more than 200 illustrations by *Puck*'s staff of artists." These artists included the founder of *Puck*, Joseph Keppler, and later his son, Joseph Keppler, Jr., and such luminaries as Frederick Opper, Eugene Zimmerman, Louis

Dalrymple, C. J. Taylor, Frank A. Nankivell, A. B. Shults, Louis M. Glackens, J. S. Pughe, and Hy Mayer. Writers from *Puck* whose work reappeared in *Pickings* included Henry Cuyler Bunner, B. B. Valentine, R. K. Munkittrick, and W. J. Henderson. (For a discussion of the work of these artists and writers, see the entry for *Puck*.) *Pickings from Puck* sold for one dollar per year, or twenty-five cents per copy.

Information Sources

BIBLIOGRAPHY:
For a listing of books treating the whole *Puck* enterprise, see the entry for that magazine.
    However, virtually no mention is made of *Pickings from Puck* itself in these
    sources.
INDEX SOURCES: None.
REPRINT EDITIONS: None.
LOCATION SOURCES: DLC, MiU.

Publication History

MAGAZINE TITLE AND TITLE CHANGES: *Pickings from Puck*, 1883–1914. From
    1883 to 1894 the full title reads: *Pickings from Puck, being a choice collection
    of preeminently perfect pieces, poems, and pictures from Puck.*
VOLUME AND ISSUE DATA: At first, beginning in 1883, *Pickings from Puck* was
    published as an annual. It was published irregularly from 1883 on until it became
    a quarterly in 1891, but Ayers begins to list it in that year as a monthly and
    continues to list it as a monthly until 1905, when he first calls it a quarterly.
    Numbering is irregular, with the issues between the years of 1885 to 1894 called
    2nd, 3rd "crop," and so on. The first issue of 1891 is 6th Crop, Number 1.
PUBLISHER AND PLACE OF PUBLICATION: 1883–1913: Keppler and Schwarzmann,
    New York. 1914: Puck Publishing Company, New York.
EDITORS: Henry Cuyler Bunner, 1883–1896; Harry Leon Wilson, 1896–1902; John
    Kendrick Bangs, 1904–1905; Arthur Hamilton Folwell, 1905–1914; and Hy
    Mayer, 1914.
CIRCULATION: Unknown.

Robert Secor

POLITICAL CENSOR, OR MONTHLY REVIEW

William Cobbett's *Political Censor*, by Peter Porcupine, stands as the first in a series of polemical journals published by the controversial British journalist. In the eight issues between March 1796 and March 1797, Cobbett gave full voice to his hatred of revolutionary France and its sympathizers in the United States. But his controversial and satirical pamphleteering forced him to become his own publisher, so that the *Political Censor* became in effect the apprenticeship for a career of political journalism that ended only with Cobbett's death in 1835. Thus, the contents of the *Censor* combine political news reporting, pamphleteering, and political satire.

Cobbett lived in the United States from 1792 to 1800. Two years after he arrived he began his polemical career. His prickly style of writing soon caused him to be likened to a porcupine. The image of the rough-speaking satirist as a porcupine was traditional since Joseph Hall's *Virgidemiarium* (1597–1598), "The Satyre should be like the Porcupine, / That shoots sharpe quills out in each angry line." Cobbett immediately accepted the description, adopted the nom de plume Peter Porcupine, and advanced it in the last four issues to the title, calling his new magazine, *Porcupine's Political Censor*.

Cobbett originally conceived of his publication as *A Prospect from the Congress-Gallery* and published one issue under that title, but differences with the publisher caused him to abandon that logo. *A Prospect* and most of the first two issues of the *Political Censor* adhered to the original concept, however, being long descriptions of the "Most Interesting Political Occurrences relative to the United States of America," as the subtitle of the magazine stated it. It consisted of seemingly verbatim accounts of debates on the floor of Congress interlarded with critical remarks by Cobbett. Occasionally, Cobbett departed from the minutiae of congressional debate to personify the "suicide" of the *Argus Magazine* of New York, to deliver a mock-speech to Congress, to involve Peter Porcupine in a mock-dialogue with members of Congress, or to publish a vituperative "letter" from a Cousin Hedge-hog.

With Congress no longer in session, in the May 1796 issue Cobbett begins his famous lampoon of Tom Paine. The attack is actually in four parts: "Paine's Age of Reason" and "Epitaph on Tom Paine" (May 1796), the "Life of Thomas Paine Interspersed with Remarks and Reflections" (September 1796), and "Letter to the Infamous Tom Paine in answer to his letter to General Washington" (December 1796). Cobbett calls on all his powers of invective, describing Paine as a "vender of poison," "Mad Tom," "Citizen Common Sense," and a "Frenchified English desperado." Although Paine was still very much alive, Cobbett branded him "politically dead" and therefore rife for an "epitaph," following in the tradition of Jonathan Swift and Benjamin Franklin who "buried" enemies not yet dead. Cobbett's "life" of Paine is a shortened version of a life that had been published by an admirer of Paine but with Cobbett's running commentary as "corrective." Paine was anathema to Cobbett not only for his attack on conventional Christianity in *The Age of Reason* but also for his support of the French Revolution. After attacking all aspects of Paine's life ("See if there be one among the yelping kennel of modern patriots, who is not a bad husband, father, brother or son"), Cobbett concludes that, "Like Judas he will be remembered by posterity; men will learn to express all that is base, malignant, treacherous, unnatural and blasphemous, by the single monosyllable, *Paine*" (September 1797, p. 49).

The remainder of the same issue is taken up with Cobbett's rejoinders to the writers of six pamphlets attacking Peter Porcupine. One of the pamphlets, which Cobbett believed to be by Samuel Bradford, son of the printer from whom Cobbett had earlier parted company, drew some of the epithets that were so characteristic of Cobbett's style: "Sooty Sam, the gosling," and "young Lampblack."

In March 1797 Cobbett discontinued the monthly *Censor* for a daily newspaper that allowed him to comment more immediately on political affairs. In the final issue of the *Censor* Cobbett included a mock-will and testament. Since his inflammatory style usually caused strong reactions, so violent, he claimed, as to threaten his life, it was only fitting that he prepare himself for that eventuality. For all the victims of his satire in the *Censor* he finds appropriately ironic gifts:

> To the editors of the Boston Chronicle, the New York Argus, and the Philadelphia Merchants' Advertiser, I will and bequeath one ounce of modesty and love of truth, to be equally divided between them. I should have been more liberal in this bequest, were I not well assured, that one ounce is more than they will ever make use of . . . "To citizen M[onr]oe, I will and bequeath my chamber looking-glass. It is a plain but exceeding true mirror; in it he will see the exact likeness of a traitor, who has bartered the honour and interest of his country to a perfidious and savage enemy." And so on.

Cobbett's support of all things British, especially of John Jay's treaty with Great Britain in 1796, occasioned a cartoon in which he is pictured in league with the devil causing Liberty to weep over a bust of Benjamin Franklin. Rather, Cobbett responded, "I have endeavored to make America laugh instead of weep" (September 1796, p. 55). Although embedded in detailed political argument, Cobbett displayed a full armory of humorous and satiric techniques. His personae of the forthright, honest, principled ordinary man has more in common with H. L. Mencken than with the satirists of the eighteenth century whom he so admired. Like the "Baltimore Bad Boy," Cobbett has always been overshadowed by reactions to his often outrageous political ideas.

Information Sources

BIBLIOGRAPHY:

Clark, Mary Elizabeth. *Peter Porcupine in America: The Career of William Cobbett, 1792–1800*. Philadelphia: Gettysburg Times and News, 1937; rep. New York: Beekman, 1974.

Cobbett, William. *Life and Adventures of Pete Porcupine*. London: Nonesuch, 1927; rpt. Washington, N.Y.: Kennikat, 1970.

Cole, G. D. H. *The Life of William Cobbett*. London: Collins, 1924; rpt. New York: Russell and Russell, 1947, p. 59.

List, Karen. "The Role of William Cobbett in Philadelphia's Party Press, 1794–1799." *Journalism Monographs* 82 (May 1983).

Mott, Frank Luther. *American Journalism: A History of Newspapers in the United States Through 260 Years: 1690–1950*. New York: Macmillan, 1950, pp. 129–31.

———. *A History of American Magazines, 1790–1850*. Cambridge, Mass.: Harvard University Press, 1957, 1: 157–60.

Reitzel, William. "William Cobbett and Philadelphia Journalism: 1794–1800." *Pennsylvania Magazine of History and Biography* 59 (July 1935): 223–44.

Sambrook, James. *William Cobbett*. London: Routlege and Kegan Paul, 1973, p. 59.

Spater, George. *William Cobbett: The Poor Man's Friend*. London: Cambridge University Press, 1982, 1: 73–75, 80.
INDEX SOURCES: None.
REPRINT EDITIONS: University Microfilms.
LOCATION SOURCES: CtY, MH, MWA, ScU, NN, ICU, NbU, DLC.

Publication History

MAGAZINE TITLE AND TITLE CHANGES: *Political Censor, or Monthly Review*, March, April, May, 1796; *Political Censor or Review*, September 1796 only; *Porcupine's Political Censor*, November, December 1796, January and March 1797.
VOLUME AND ISSUE DATA: Volume 1:1–8, according to December 1796 issue, but issue Number 4 (*The Scare-Crow*) and issue Number 5 (*The Life of Peter Porcupine*) were published as separate works and not as part of the *Political Censor*. Volume 2 included issues Number 1 and 2, January and March 1797. No issues were published in June, July, or August of 1796, although Cobbett apparently conceived of issues 4 and 5 above as part of the series. There was no issue in February 1797.
PUBLISHER AND PLACE OF PUBLICATION: Benjamin Davis, Philadelphia, published the first three issues; William Cobbett, Philadelphia, all others.
EDITOR: William Cobbett.
CIRCULATION: 500 to 2,000, depending on issue.

George A. Test

THE PORT FOLIO

The Port Folio, published in Philadelphia during the first quarter of the nineteenth century, was the first important literary periodical in America. Its founder, Joseph Dennie, chose as his editorial pseudonym Oliver Oldschool, Esq., which served the publication, as Eustace Tilly would serve *The New Yorker** more than a century later, by providing an image of arrogant urbanity and genial good humor from which contributors could take their cue.

Dennie arrived in Philadelphia in 1799 following a successful period in Walpole, New Hampshire, as editor of the highly regarded *Farmer's Weekly Museum*.* He had already earned something of a literary reputation as author of *The Farrago* and *The Lay Preacher*, periodical series of which he would eventually reprint a large portion in *The Port Folio* to widespread popular and critical acclaim. At that time Philadelphia was the recognized literary capital of America, and Dennie found there an atmosphere conducive to his literary pursuits and compatible with his clubman personality. He also found a gap in the literary scene caused by the hasty departure of William Cobbett (Peter Porcupine), the reigning master of satiric invective, who was forced to leave the city following a notorious libel suit brought against him by Benjamin Rush. Ever the opportunist, Dennie wasted no time in putting himself forward as Cobbett's successor.

Dennie was a fine writer, but he was a genius as an editor, with *The Port Folio* being his undisputed masterwork. He had high standards and a gift for imposing a unified editorial vision on diverse voices and subjects without diminishing the variety that kept his journal lively. In a wry and verbose prospectus circulated in 1800 among (as he designated them) "men of affluence, men of liberality, and men of letters," Dennie acknowledged the prevailing dullness and lack of professionalism in American journalism, vowed to deliver a weekly publication that would elude the twin demons of impartiality and controversy, and promised a sincere effort "to relieve the dryness of news, and the severity of political argument, with wholesome morals and gay miscellany— to insert interesting articles of biography, criticism, poetry, and merriment, and 'bind the rod of the moralist with the roses of the muse.' " The prospectus was well enough received that a first issue was published on 3 January 1801. Dennie planned for a first printing of a thousand copies. Co-publisher Asbury Dickins persuaded him to accept a run of 1,500, which proved insufficient to meet demand. A second edition of the first issue was required, and by the Spring of the year the regular edition of each weekly issue consisted of 2,000 copies. This early success attested both to the active nature of the Philadelphia literary scene and to the quality of Dennie's publication.

Early success, however, did not result in financial security. The readership, though international, remained select and never grew much beyond the size established during the first year. The publication was also plagued by the problem of unpaid subscriptions. By 1808 the strains became so severe that Dennie relinquished all financial interest and continued as editor on a salary paid by the then publishers, Bradford and Inskeep. As part of the deal, Dennie allowed *The Port Folio* to become a monthly, beginning in Janury 1809. He remained as editor until his death in 1812, with the last years of his life marked by increasing ill health. Historians now uniformly recognize a gradual decline in quality in *The Port Folio* beginning with the 1809 volume and continuing until its eventual demise in 1827. Dennie was succeeded by Nicholas Biddle, Charles Caldwell, and eventually John Elihu Hall, all respectable literary figures and all lacking Dennie's delight in humor and his gift for imbuing a publication with an irrepressible spiritedness. What began in 1801 as the nation's liveliest general miscellany wound up as a rather tedious literary journal so encrusted with respectability that it could not survive the gradual shift of the American literary scene toward Boston and New York.

The Port Folio began as an eight-page weekly on super royal quarto sheets laid out in a three-column format. Dennie imposed exacting standards on his printers, insisting that the typography be regular, carefully set, and scrupulously proofed, with each column well leaded for clarity of design. In 1806 a New Series was declared, and Dennie shifted to a sixteen-page octavo, two-column format. In 1807 small engravings began appearing on the title pages, but not until 1809 did illustration play a significant role in the publication. By then, each monthly issue, running 80 to 90 pages, featured at least one plate. One of the very few marks of distinction of the post-Dennie *Port Folio* was the quality of illustration, with the best engravers of the day, including David Edwin and James Barton Longacre, well represented. In addition to portraiture, there was a steady selection of landscape plates, with upstate New York, Pennsylvania, and the Western Reserve the most frequent subjects. These landscapes were generally of indifferent quality, but they did prefigure most of the motifs and all of the themes of the Hudson River School.

Although Dennie was editing a self-styled newspaper, it was clear from the beginning that his interests were primarily literary. The first issue, prepared entirely by Dennie and John Quincy Adams, had more than half its eight pages devoted to the first installment of Adams's *Journal of a Tour Through Silesia* and his verse translation of the thirteenth satire of Juvenal subjoined by the Latin text. The remainder of the issue contained an original poem by Dennie, a selection of letters from the estate of Tobias Smollett written by the likes of Samuel Richardson, Thomas Hume, and James Boswell (among others), a department of literary intelligence in which Dennie discussed at length the impending appearance of *The Farrago* and *The Lay Preacher*, and a literary review column titled *An Author's Evenings* in which he exposed his wide-ranging and thoroughly unstructured reading habits. Although a political department was added in the second issue, the periodical never really lost its literary focus. Features that Dennie had developed for *The Farmer's Weekly Museum* were eventually added, including *From the Shop of Messrs. Colon and Spondee* (originally written in collaboration with Royall Tyler but increasingly the product of Dennie's pen), a theatrical department, moral essays, travel, literary and historical biographies, poetry (both original and selected), a wide range of translations, legal intelligence, current events, frequent commentary on fashion, and a wealth of miscellaneous humor ranging from standard Joe Miller jests to excerpts from bizarre wills.

The most frequently published and longest lasting feature, surviving even Dennie's editorship, was *The American Lounger by Samuel Saunter*, an umbrella heading under which Dennie published correspondence and essays of widely varying quality on any subject within the periodical's scope.

Much of the character of the periodical's early years came from Dennie's insistence that *The Port Folio* could at once serve and snub the muse. It was common for academic neo-classical exercises to be printed side by side with risqué doggerel verse. Dennie's early inclusion of selections from the *Lyrical Ballads*, making him one of the first Americans to recognize their worth, did not prevent him from devoting the entire first page of the 18 August 1804 issue to an elaborate and heavily annotated parody titled *A Lyrical Ballad* by one R. Shallow in which the worst of Wordsworth's excesses were spoofed with the relish of a connoisseur. Similarly, the paper's department of literary criticism, which ranged from Thomas Gray and William Godwin to Shakespeare and the classics, was, in moments of whimsy, turned with burlesque effect on such odd texts as a nursery rhyme (14 and 28 July 1804) and an advertisement for a stray horse (28 December 1805 and 11 January 1806). For a brief period in 1804 the humor of *The Port Folio* assumed a decidedly racy tone attributable to a visit to the city by the English poet Thomas Moore, whom Dennie lionized in the pages of the publication. Other literary figures to receive Dennie's nod of approval included Thomas Campbell, Leigh Hunt, and the Salmagundi writers, whom Dennie reprinted, perhaps in flattered response to a visit by Washington Irving who openly modeled his Launcelot Langstaff on Dennie.

One of the more interesting departments developed by Dennie was "To Readers and Correspondents," a personal column of sorts in which Dennie, playing Dear Abby to the Philadelphia literary tyros, dished out encouragement and critiques of submissions. It was an effective method of flattering the contributors for whom he could not find room in the paper and of teasing the imagination of the readership, as he occasionally did by obliquely summarizing submissions too salacious for publication. He also made use of the opportunity to vent a bit of spleen against rival publications, as in the following notice of rejection: "The communication from a writer, who calls himself *Sieyes*, is so putrid with the rottenness of democracy, and has such a horrible stench of the ulcerated lungs of a jacobin bawler, that the *Aurora*, the privy of Pennsylvania, is the only place in which it can be deposited."

Although Dennie was highly opinionated in matters of politics, it could hardly be said that he was a political animal, and his inclusion of a political department was perhaps as much a concession to the journalistic realities of the times as anything else. Still, his editorial integrity saw to it that *The Port Folio* handled politics with the same spirit that governed the literary side. He encouraged political satire from contributors and himself wrote frequent commentary that took particular delight in flogging the spirit of nationalism and liberal republicanism embodied in the Jefferson administration. For Dennie, Thomas Jefferson was a hypocritical slave-owning propagandist, and Monticello was "the favourite haunt of philosophy, liberty, and other French fairies." Dennie was not above printing "Monticellian Sally," a risqué verse satire of Jefferson's widely rumored affair with a household slave, the refrain of which comprised the lines

> Yankee Doodle, who's the noodle?
> What wife were half so handy?
> To breed a flock of slaves for stock;
> A blackamoor's the dandy.

So frequently did Dennie express his basic Anglophilia and his unshakable belief that the American Revolution had been a grave mistake perpetrated by an ungrateful people, that on the carefully chosen day of 4 July 1804, Dennie was indicted for inflammatory and seditious libel. The indictment was in response to a paragraph published in the 23 April 1803 issue in which Dennie stated briefly, and in terms that were for him reasonably restrained, his basic opposition to the concept of democracy. Possibly the outrage caused by the statement was inspired less by what he actually wrote than by the offhand manner of its placement in a column of miscellaneous filler, sandwiched between a theatrical blurb for George Colman's *John Bull; or an Englishman's Fireside* and a capsule review of an unnamed play accused of Catholicism for having left its audience in purgatory. Whatever the motives behind the indictment, Dennie had no trouble earning acquittal when he finally went to trial in 1805. Following the verdict, Dennie leveled a final blast in early 1806 with an announcement that "the editor has been triumphant in his warfare with Democracy, a fiend more terrible than any that the imagination of the classical poets ever conjured up from the 'vasty deep' of their Pagan hell."

The Port Folio was never again to achieve such a level of political intensity. Bradford and Inskeep, as part of their buy-out in 1808, effectively muzzled their editor by insisting on genuine bipartisanship, which accounted for much of the deflation of spirit detectable in the periodical from 1809 on. In fact, there was virtually nothing of controversy, political or otherwise, in Dennie's last years, with the exception of his infrequent renewals of a long-standing feud with Noah Webster, whose efforts to legitimate an American version of the English language deeply offended Dennie's Anglophilia and led to his occasionally publishing sarcastic lists of American verbal atrocities.

A common pattern for journals of the period was to rely on literary clubs for contributions, and *The Port Folio* was no exception. Dennie was the quintessential clubman: a heavy drinker, a fop, a brilliant wit, and a scandalous sophisticate. He drew the livelier sorts in Philadelphia to him like a magnet and formed the Tuesday Club, comprising mostly young lawyers and doctors graduated from the University of Pennsylvania. They met frequently and became the core contributors to *The Port Folio*. A list of the more notable figures who had some association with the club and those who contributed with varying frequency to *The Port Folio* is a "Who's Who" of the legal, medical, and literary communities in Philadelphia during that influential period. Among them were Charles Brockden Brown (an occasional contributor before he began his own *Literary Magazine and American Register* in 1803), Horace Binney, Nathaniel Chapman, Charles Jared Ingersoll, Joseph Hopkinson, Samuel Ewing, John Blair Linn, Sarah Hall, James Abercrombie, Gertrude Gouveneur Meredith, Richard Rush, Thomas Cadwalader, Harriet Fenno, Thomas Isaac Wharton, and Nicholas Biddle. In addition, there was a large and loyal coterie of corresponding contributors stretching from Maine to the Carolinas and as far west as Cincinnati, including John Quincy Adams, Josiah Quincy, John Shaw, Robert H. Rose, and a host of others.

The Port Folio achieved very little of any true distinction following the reorganization of 1809. Dennie's illness, the timidity of the publishers, a growing dependence on the periodical's staid literary reputation, increasing reliance on reprinted selections from conservative European journals, an emphasis on history, science, and the fine arts at the expense of current events and humor, all contributed to the overall lack of distinction. There were, however, a few moments of note. During Charles Caldwell's editorship, there was full and accurate coverage of the War of 1812, and Condy Raguet allowed *The Port Folio* to publish his extensive memoirs of the rebellion in Haiti. In 1820 John Elihu Hall converted *The Port Folio* to a quarterly with no success, resuming the monthly schedule in 1822. The last years saw little of merit save a few pieces on western America provided by Judge James Hall, the editor's brother and founder of the highly regarded *Illinois Gazette*. Publication was sporadic in the final year, with the July 1827 issue being the last.

Information Sources

BIBLIOGRAPHY:

Caldwell, Charles. *Autobiography of Charles Caldwell, M.D.* Philadelphia: Lippincott and Grambo, 1855, pp. 321–48.

Edgar, Neal L. *A History and Bibliography of American Magazines 1810–1820.* Metuchen, N.J.: Scarecrow Press, 1975, pp. 217–20.

Ellis, Harold Milton. *Joseph Dennie and His Circle: A Study in American Literature from 1792 to 1812.* Austin, Tex., 1915; rpt. New York: Johnson Reprint Corp., 1972.

Mott, Frank L. *A History of American Magazines, 1741–1850.* New York: D. Appleton and Co., 1930, 1:223–46 and passim.

Oberholtzer, Ellis Paxton. "The Port Folio." *The Literary History of Philadelphia.* Philadelphia: George W. Jacobs, 1906, pp. 168–88.

Randall, Randolph C. "Authors of the Port Folio Revealed by the Hall Files." *American Literature* 11 (January 1940): 379–416.

Smyth, Albert Henry. "The Nineteenth Century: The Port Folio." *The Philadelphia Magazines and Their Contributors, 1741–1850.* Philadelphia: Robert M. Lindsay, 1892, pp. 86–151.

Wood, James Playsted. "Magazines as National Educators: *The Port Folio* and Its Contemporaries." *Magazines in the United States.* New York: Roland Press Co., 1949, pp. 28–43.

INDEX SOURCES: Poole; also indexed by volume, 1806–1827.

REPRINT EDITIONS: University Microfilms.

LOCATION SOURCES: CU, DLC, IU, MWA, OC, PPL, RPB and approximately 150 others.

Publication History

MAGAZINE TITLE AND TITLE CHANGES: *The Port Folio; The Port Folio and New York Monthly Magazine* (5th Series, Volumes 13–14).

VOLUME AND ISSUE DATA: Weekly, annual volumes. Volume 1–Volume 5, 1801–1806. New (second) Series: Weekly, semi-annual volumes; Volume 1 (6)–Volume 6 (11), 1806–1808. New (third) Series: Weekly, semi-annual volumes; Volume 1 (12)–Volume 8 (19), 1809–1812. Third (fourth) Series: Monthly, semi-annual volumes; Volume 1 (20)–Volume 6 (25), 1813–1815. Fourth (fifth) Series: Monthly, semi-annual volumes; Volume 1 (26)–Volume 20 (45), 1816–1825 (quarterly, 1820–1821). Hall's Second (sixth) Series: Monthly, semi-annual volumes; Volume 1 (46)–Volume 2 (47), 1826–1827. Suspended January-July 1826 and January-July 1827.

PUBLISHER AND PLACE OF PUBLICATION: 1801–1808: Joseph Dennie (with Asbury Dickins, 1801; Elizabeth Dickins, 1802). 1809–1815: Bradford and Inskeep. 1815: Thomas Silver. 1816–1827: Harrison Hall. All in Philadelphia.

EDITORS: Joseph Dennie, 1801–1811; Nicholas Biddle, 1812–1814; Charles Caldwell, 1814–1816; John Elihu Hall, 1816–1827.

CIRCULATION: Two thousand in 1801; 2,500 in 1816. The original price, five dollars per year, increased to six dollars in 1804.

Gary Engle

PUCK

When *Puck* pranced onto the scene in March of 1877, the history of American comic magazines was one of short-lived failures, but Joseph Keppler's offspring would live well into middle age, its last issue appearing in 1918. *Puck* succeeded where others had failed because it was better than its predecessors—with higher standards, better artists, wider interests. The magazine was ready to poke fun at all human folly, as is suggested by its motto from *A Midsummer Night's Dream*: "Oh what fools these mortals be!" Its most distinguishing feature was its magnificently colored lithographs, and with these colored cartoons *Puck* created a genre of vigorous political satire that established an American tradition of comic journalism.

If President Nixon felt himself haunted by Herblock in the daily papers in the 1970s, he could look back almost a century to the candidate James G. Blaine, who was terrorized by *Puck*'s Bernhard Gillam in the 1884 presidential race. *Puck*'s politics shifted from what has been called independent to independent Democratic, thus opposing the political positions of its rival, *Judge*.* As its influence grew, so did its circulation, which was close to 90,000 from the mid–1880s to the mid–1890s. Spinoffs and collections from *Puck* began to multiply, so that at its height the weekly had spawned a monthly (*Puck's Library*,* which reached a circulation of over 60,000 in its own right, before being superseded by *Puck's Monthly Magazine and Almanac*), a couple of quarterlies (*Pickings from Puck** and the later *Puck's Quarterly**), and annuals (*Puck on Wheels*,* *Puck's Annual**). Book collections include Frederick Opper's *This Funny World as Puck Sees It* (1890) and *Puck's Opper Book* (1888), *Mavericks* (1892), short stories by *Puck*'s authors illustrated by *Puck*'s artists, and several short story collections by *Puck* editor H. C. Bunner.

The ingenuity and comic art of its founder, Joseph Keppler, the business acumen of A. Schwarzmann, and the editorial energy and resourcefulness of H. C. Bunner—these were the initial reasons for *Puck*'s success. Keppler, whose first attempts at artistry may have been decorating cakes for his father, a Viennese baker, studied seriously at Vienna's Academy of Fine Arts. He had also done some acting by the time he left Vienna, at twenty-nine, to settle in St. Louis in

1867. After traveling with a touring theatrical company, Keppler began an illustrated lithographic German weekly, *Die Vehme*, in 1869. He felt his two interests were related; he once observed that he developed his taste for color and composition from his experience of group arrangements and scenic design. *Die Vehme*, however, lasted only a year, and so in 1871 he again attempted a comic paper, his first *Puck*; Volume 1 was all in German, and Volume 2 had an English edition as well. This too folded after a year and a half. In 1872, Keppler left for New York, joining the staff of *Leslie's Illustrated*. He still had larger visions for himself, however, and in 1876 he formed a partnership with Schwarzmann, a printer, and resurrected *Puck*.

The first issue, all in German under the editorship of Leopold Schenck, appeared in September 1876. It was well received, so delighting the playwright Sidney Rosenfeld that he pursuaded Keppler to publish an English edition as well, using the same cuts and caricatures. Rosenfeld was signed to edit the first English edition, which appeared in March 1877. Although the German *Puck* continued for about twenty-two years, it was soon eclipsed by its English-speaking younger brother. In 1881, for example, the circulation of the English-language *Puck* was 85,000 while the circulation of the German-language edition held at 19,500.

In format, the new weekly was a sixteen-page quarto, offering a large 11″ × 14″ page, twice the size of the usual magazine, and sold for ten cents. Keppler's cover cartoon—"A Stir in the Roost: What Another Chicken?"—showed an impish Puck hatching out of an egg marked "13 North Williams St.," where the magazine had its first offices. Puck doffs his cap to the roost's other curious chickens, representing such papers as the *Tribune*, *Herald*, *Graphic*, *Leslie's*, and *Harper's Weekly*. Inside the magazine, he announces his appearance:

> I am here. And I don't apologize for being here. I only hope my appearance will be as agreeable to you as it is to me. I have a mission to fulfill. Everybody has; but like almost everybody else I can't exactly tell what that mission is until I have found out definitely myself. . . . I shall have pensive moods—occasionally; no oftener than circumstances compel, but often enough to prove that I have not come merely as a flippant plaything to amuse you in your idle movements, but rather as a pleasant confidential companion, who will be the best natured fellow in the world—if you will only let him ([14] March 1877, p. 2).

Each issue carried a large double-paged political cartoon at its center, as well as a different full-page political cartoon for every cover, and another full cartoon, more likely to be social than political, for the back cover. For the first several years of *Puck*'s existence, all of these large cartoons were drawn by Keppler, who was also responsible for a number of smaller black and white illustrations to accompany text and advertisements. Keppler's cartoons are always skillfully drawn and pointed, but gayer, more graceful, and lighter of touch than those done by Thomas Nast for *Harper's Weekly*. The use of a different cartoon for each cover was a break with the traditional set cover of other magazines, and the color and gaiety of the magazine brought to it a liveliness and appeal that caught the imagination of the American public. Keppler took the political cartoon beyond the French and Italian model of caricature, with its device of exaggeration in heads and legs, and abandoned the overhead loops which the artists of the lithographic sheets had used to encapsulate dialogue, instead creating full backgrounds and detail which made the meaning of his cartoons clear. In 1878, Keppler began to introduce an effective variety of colors by use of two tint blocks, and by 1879 advances in chromolithography allowed him to create the magazine's brilliantly overcolored cartoons.

Second only to Keppler in importance for the artistic success of the infant *Puck* was Henry Cuyler Bunner, who was just twenty-two when he signed on as Rosenfeld's assistant. Shortly thereafter, Rosenfeld left, and Bunner succeeded to the editorship, retaining the post from 1878 until he died in 1896. Well read in Shakespeare and the British poets, as well as in classical literature and the works of contemporary continental authors, Bunner brought a wide frame of reference to his writing. At times his work may have seemed pale besides the pointed satire of Keppler's cartoons—so that Ambrose Bierce fixed him in comic verse as a "Fat-witted fool whose words make weak / The pictures that you [Keppler] make so strong." When Bunner's life was cut short at forty, *The Critic*** (23 May 1896) recognized the unfairness of such comparisons: "To make the fine violinlike tones of his 'comments' heard through all the trumpet-blast of Keppler's cartoons was no easy task, yet Bunner accomplished it." In *Puck*'s first ten years of existence, first as Rosenfeld's assistant and then from 1878 as editor, Bunner was responsible for everything that went into it and was himself chief contributor in prose and verse. Brander Matthews, who contributed to *Puck* and became an intimate of Bunner, was impressed by how much he did for the weekly:

> Whatever might be wanted he stood ready to supply—rhymes of the time, humorous ballads, *vers do société*, verses to go with a cartoon, dialogues to go under a drawing, paragraphs pertinent and impertinent, satiric sketches of character, short stories, little comedies, nondescript comicalities of all kinds. Whatever the demand upon him he was ready and able to meet it; he had irresistible freshness and dauntless fecundity (p. 289).

Matthews concludes by observing that "the average was surprisingly high, and the variety was extraordinary."

With Keppler and Bunner at the helm, *Puck* mixed its drawings and cartoons with small items of comic prose and verse, daffy definitions, puns, satiric comment, light fiction, and theatrical and musical reviews. Each issue had a table of contents and a page of commentary, usually mixing wry observations on topical issues with glosses on the color cartoons of the week. "Puckerings" was a recurring column of comic definitions, observations, and verse. Also as part of a recurring series, the Englishman in America, F. R. Fitznoodle (a creation of B. B. Vallentine) gave in exaggerated accents his thoughts on various aspects of American life. Features like "Answers for the Anxious" offered comic advice to the needy. "Improbabilities," subtitled "Sketches of What We Don't Particularly Expect," presented improbable scenes (not unlike the "Scenes We'd Like to See" in current *Mad** Comics), such as Jay Gould with his hands in his own pockets. *Puck*'s political interests extended to Ireland, whose problems Professor Ephraim Muggins claims to have solved in an issue of 7 April 1880: "We have made a careful diagnosis of the case and have concluded to bring this island over to America." On the national scene, the same issue presented a column of "Presidential Suggestions," in which mock letter-writers, such as D. Tees and Bill Board, make known their presidential preferences. Bill Board seems rather ahead of his time. He suggests that we should look to other than the usual professions for presidential timber, and nominates Edwin Booth and Lawrence Barrett, "the two greatest actors that the world ever saw." Board believes that people would go for such a ticket, since "Deportment and dignity are what is required in the White House, and who, I should like to know, have these qualities more strongly developed than Booth and Barrett?"

Puck's greatest impact, however, was political, particularly during presidential campaigns when it could be devastating in its humor. In the presidential race of 1880, Keppler produced one of his most famous cartoons attacking James Garfield: "Forbidding the Banns." The daring drawing calls attention to the Republican nominee's connection with the Credit Mobilier financial scandal by depicting the candidate in woman's clothes as a blushing bride—and unwed mother. With bridesmaids of Carl Schurz, Secretary of the Interior, and Whitelaw Reid, editor of the *New York Tribune*, and with a clergyman whose head is a ballot box, the bride is about to be wedded to Uncle Sam. But the ceremony is interrupted by the chairman of the Democratic national committee, who rushes in from the rear with hand raised and babe in arms, labeled "$329 Credit Mobilier." In the subtitle for the cartoon, the coy bride protests: "But it was such a little one."

The most effective and memorable of *Puck*'s campaign cartoons, however, appeared in the next election campaign, when on 16 April 1884, Bernhard Gillam represented Blaine as the Tattooed Man, the various charges of corruption, such as "Little Rock Railroad Bonds" and "Mulligan Letters," indelibly etched on his skin. Evoking a painting by Gérôme that had been the sensation of Paris twelve years earlier, in which Hypereides wins a verdict for Phryne by exposing her beauty to the court, Gillam shows Blaine being unveiled by Whitelaw Reid, his face hid in his arm for shame as his tattooed body is exposed before the startled and amused Chicago tribunal. Gillam never let up on the theme, continuing to show Blaine as the Tattooed Man whose supporters cannot rub him clean. They try to do so in one cartoon with *Tribune* Cleaning Fluid, and in another cartoon they look on in horror at the handwriting on the wall depicting his sins, as Blaine tries to cover himself with pages from the *Tribune*. Even after the election, Gillam depicted the Republican candidate by showing only a pair of tattooed legs sticking out of the Salt River. Blaine was furious and had to be restrained by his friends from suing *Puck* for libel, while the grateful Cleveland attributed his winning the presidency to the magazine.

In another effective series of cartoons, Keppler mocked Benjamin Harrison, grandson of "Old Tippecanoe," as Harrison continues to shrink beneath grandpa's oversized hat, until in an 1892 cartoon Uncle Sam peers into the hat, unable to find "Little Ben" at all.

If *Puck* had its favorite targets among political candidates, it also had its favorite issues. It was opposed to free silver, strongly favored reform of the merit system for civil service employees, advocated lower tariffs, and fought to eliminate ballot abuses and to expose political corruption wherever it caught a whiff of it. *Puck* also targeted church abuses (like high pew rents) and camp meetings, and pompous preachers (picturing T. Dewitt Talmadge, for example, as all mouth). More specifically it sometimes attacked the Catholic Church, particularly after the ascent of Leo XIII to the Papacy, and it also had fun at the expense of the Mormons. Among its most serious concerns were the relations between labor, with which it was sympathetic, and the evils of big business, particularly trusts and monopolies. A cartoon of 1 August 1883, "The Tournament of Today—A Set-to Between Labor and Monopoly," shows crowds cheering a joust between the gaunt figure of labor mounted on an emaciated nag, clutching a clearly inadequate mallet labeled "strike," and iron-clad Monopoly. Monopoly brandishes an imposing lance marked "subsidized press," protects himself with a shield marked "Corruption of the Legislature," and rides a towering steed propelled on locomotive wheels. At the same time, *Puck* always cautioned Labor against extremism, suggesting that the boycotter and the anarchist were enemies of the working man. In "It Works Both Ways" (25 November 1885), Eugene Zimmerman depicted a labor union leader wielding a heavy bat labeled "Boycotting," his eyes ablaze, against the sitting figure of puzzled management. In back of the leader are the workingmen themselves cowering behind the swinging bat, while signs on the wall equate "Enforced Idleness for the Manufacturer" with "Enforced Idleness for the Laborer." The danger of the general strike to the public was the subject of "Fearful Consequence of a General Strike" (7 April 1880). The cartoon shows a well-dressed woman and her three prim children shoveling their own coal, robbers mugging their victims before a row of seated policemen, and fashionable ladies parading in their undergarments because tailors are on strike, while directors are hitched to their own railroad cars and a variety of people are forced to struggle with ingenious devices of transportation in the light of the general strike.

In its long run, *Puck* established a stable of writers and artists whose superior work supported the high quality of the magazine. Chief among these was the cartoonist Frederick Burr Opper. Opper joined *Puck* in 1880 and was with the magazine for over eighteen years, leaving to continue his extraordinarily durable career with Hearst before retiring in 1932. In 1943, a poll of active and retired comic artists named Opper the funniest man ever connected with the American daily press. *Puck*'s other leading artists included F. Graetz, who knew no English and had to have ideas for cartoons translated into German for him; J. A. Wales, who joined *Puck* in 1879 but quarreled with Keppler and left in 1881 to found the rival *Judge*; and Bernhard Gillam, who soon after his devastating 1884 caricatures of Blaine defected to *Judge* as chief cartoonist. Wales, in the meantime, made up with Keppler and returned to *Puck*, remaining until he died in 1886. Other luminaries on *Puck*'s art staff included Eugene Zimmerman, Louis Dalrymple, C. J. Taylor, Frank A. Nankivell, A. B. Shults, Louis M. Glackens, J. S. Pughe, Art Young, and Joseph Keppler, Jr., who succeeded his father when the elder Keppler died in 1894. The best known figures on the literary staff were, in addition to Bunner, B. B. Vallentine, R. K. Munkittrick, George Jean Nathan, and Arthur Guiterman. W. J. Henderson was the weekly's leading reviewer of theatrical and musical performances.

By the 1890s, the heyday of the magazine's political influence was over, and it turned increasingly to lighter humor and satire. Among those who made literary contributions was Harry Wilson, who succeeded Bunner as editor in 1896. Eight years later John Kendrick Bangs became editor, and his burlesque view of the London stage (''Alice in Stageland'') became one of the magazine's most popular features. Cartoonists during this period included L. M. Glackens and Grant Hamilton, who made Theodore Roosevelt one of his favorite targets. By the time Arthur Hamilton Folwell became editor in 1905, *Puck* was clearly not the influential magazine it had been in the eighties and nineties. The role it had played so long and so well was taken over in part by the daily papers, which were now publishing their own political cartoons. A weekly with elaborate colored drawings could not remain as fresh and topical as could these papers, and the emphasis which such newspaper entrepreneurs as William Randolph Hearst and Joseph Pulitzer placed on pictorial journalism appealed to the same audience that *Puck* had developed. By 1911, circulation had dipped to 80,000. It did make something of a comeback, however, when the young millionaire Nathan Straus took over as the magazine's publisher, making Hy Mayer its editor for the first issue of April 1914, with Folwell serving as literary editor and Foster Gilroy as general manager. That arrangement stood until Folwell was again appointed editor, beginning with the first issue of 1915. At the end of 1914 *Puck* boasted that in that year of rejuvenation it had quadrupled its circulation and steadily increased its advertising patronage, but that might be largely explained by the fact that the magazine had discontinued its monthly and automatically moved its subscribers over to the lists of the weekly.

Puck now had established regular columns from James Gibbon Huneker, who covered ''The Seven Arts,'' a feature which, in *Puck*'s words ''weighed critically, judged impartially, and labeled plainly, yet entertainingly'' new plays, books, and art exhibits; George Jean Nathan, who had been an editor of *The Smart Set** and contributed to *Puck*'s ''Puppet Shop'' comic paragraphs on new plays and Broadway gossip; and P. A. Vaile, whose regular feature on *"Puck*'s Golf Idiot"* became one of the magazine's most popular humorous columns. *Puck* also signed on Rube Goldberg as a regular at the end of 1914, and he was soon doing double-page color cartoons. Richard Barry contributed social satire; Ralph Barton became Paris correspondent, bringing the war news from Europe, while Dana Burnet translated the news into rhyme. The art department was headed by Mayer, who according to the magazine's advertisements was "America's foremost cartoonist," and included Joseph Keppler, Jr., De Zayas, and Nelson Greene.

The magazine's moment of recovery passed, however, and by 1915 *Puck* was forced to contract its size (to 8" × 12" in 1915 and 7¼" × 10¾" by 1917) and, when the war made paper scarce, to go to a cheaper stock. In 1916, under its last editor, Karl Schmidt, the magazine abandoned color for all but its cover. In 1917, *Puck* was adopted by Hearst, who spruced it up and made it a fortnightly beginning with the 20 June issue, but by the following March it was coming out only once a month. "I have a mission to fulfill," Puck announced in his first English issue, although he did not yet know quite what that mission was to be. We now know that it was to give shape and vitality to comic journalism in America, and when he died after the September 1918 issue, forty-one years later, that mission was fulfilled.

Information Sources

BIBLIOGRAPHY:
Craven, Thomas. *Cartoon Cavalcade*. New York: Simon and Schuster, 1943.
The Critic 2 (25 February 1882): 50.
The Critic 28 (23 May 1896): 362.
Ford, James L. *Forty-Odd Years in the Literary Shop*. New York: E. P. Dutton, 1921.
Hess, Stephen, and Milton Kaplan. *The Ungentlemanly Art: A History of American Political Cartoons*. New York: Macmillan Co., 1968.
Matthews, Brander. "H. C. Bunner." *Scribner's Magazine* 22 (September 1896): 287–95.
Maurice, Arthur Bartlett, and Frederick T. Cooper. *The History of the Nineteenth Century in Caricature*. New York: Dodd, Mead, 1904.
Mott, Frank L. *A History of American Magazines, 1865–1885*. Cambridge, Mass.: Harvard University Press, 1938, 3:520–32.
Nevins, Allan, and Frank Weitenkampf. *A Century of Political Cartoons*. New York: Charles Scribner's Sons, 1944.
Paneth, Donald. *The Encyclopedia of American Journalism*. New York: Facts on File Publications, 1983.
INDEX SOURCES: N. W. Ayers, *American Newspaper Annual*. Philadelphia: N. W. Ayers and Sons, 1880–1918.
REPRINT EDITIONS: University Microfilms.
LOCATION SOURCES: Over 80 libraries list holdings. Most complete are DLC, NN, CL, IC, OC, PPL, OO, and Seattle Public Library.

Publication History

MAGAZINE TITLE AND TITLE CHANGES: *Puck*, [14] March 1877-September 1918.
VOLUME AND ISSUE DATA: The magazine appeared weekly from [14] March 1877
   until 6 June 1917; semi-weekly, 20 June 1917–5 February 1918. From March-
   September 1918 it was a monthly. Volumes are numbered 1–83, Numbers 1–
   2121.
PUBLISHER AND PLACE OF PUBLICATION: 1877–1878: Puck Publishing Co. 1879–
   1913: Keppler and Schwarzmann, New York. 1914–1917: Puck Publishing Co.,
   New York. 1917–1918: International Magazine Co., New York.
EDITORS: Sidney Rosenfeld, 1877–1878; Henry Cuyler Bunner, 1878–1896; Harry Leon
   Wilson, literary editor, 1896–1902; Arthur Hamilton Folwell, literary editor,
   1902–1905, editor, 1905–1914; John Kendrick Bangs, editor-in-chief, 1904–1905;
   Hy Mayer, 1914–1915, with A. H. Folwell as literary editor; Arthur Hamilton
   Folwell, 1915–1916; Foster Gilroy, 1916–1918; Karl Schmidt, 1918.
CIRCULATION: 1881, 85,000; 1886–1907, 89,700; 1911, 80,000 1917, 50,000 (*Puck*
   on 2 February 1915 reported 12,500 as its circulation for 1913).

Robert Secor

PUCK ON WHEELS

Each July from 1880 to 1886 the editors of *Puck** put out a collection of cartoons
and prose designed for summer reading. This summer annual, which was over
a hundred pages in length, unlike its parent organ, had color only on its cover.

Although it took its title (and usually the cover illustration) from the bicycling
craze of the 1880s, the range of *Puck on Wheels* included all summer activity.
In 1882, for example, it treated its readers to "Puck's Summer Resort Guide,"
a "comprehensive summary of the best spots" for vacationing, "calculated to
serve the great summer tourist as a guide, philosopher and friend." The guide
covers several pages, listing spots from A to Z, parodying the usual tourist guide
promises. Washington, D.C., for example, is listed as "a profitable and popular
resort for Congressmen and Senators. . . . Hotels open night and day. Special
rates to lobbyists." Albany, we are told, "is opposite Greenbush, and Greenbush
is opposite Albany most of the time. Forty miles from Saratoga, it would be
better for Saratoga if Albany was further off." The guide recommends Alaska
as a a place with "No mosquitoes—nothing but straight pneumonia." Fall River's
most important products, we learn, "are principally calicoes and factory-girls."

In addition to comic portraits of Puck on wheels, the annual offered humor
and parody concerning all summer sports: baseball, bathing, polo, fishing, tennis,
canoeing, lacrosse, cricket, yachting, and others. The magazine describes cricket,
for example, concluding that it is "not a giddily rapid game. In fact chess is
fast alongside of it" (1884). The editors employed comic dedications for each
issue, so that *Puck* dedicated the 1880 volume to the Metropolitan Baseball Club
"In The Hope that It may Yield him as Many Dollars As the Metropolitan Club
Will the People who Bet Against Them." Inside is a page of cartoons of baseball

players in various predicaments, including "Our abused friend the umpire," who stands helpless while a bat in the hand of an unseen player threatens his head, and fists and fingers are being shaken and pointed in his direction. Opposite is a page of humorous observations relating to baseball.

Not all the humor, fiction, and verse in this annual is related to summer activity, but the editors were careful to make all the humor light summer reading and to direct any satire in the annual at general targets only, unlike the frequently acerbic and pointed political humor of the parent *Puck*. For example, critics are given a comic needle in 1884 with the following rhyme:

> He made a fizzle
> With his chisel
>
> He saw no way on
> With his crayon
>
> Of brush and easel
> No work could he sell
>
> Nor court nor hovel
> Would buy his novel
>
> He failed at teaching
> Likewise at preaching
>
> But now, with genius analytic,
> He's a critic.

Puck on Wheels drew on the stable of artists and writers who worked for *Puck* during the 1880s; readers interested in the summer collection should consult the entry for the parent weekly. Artists whose work can be found in *Puck on Wheels* were F. Opper, J. A. Wales, C. J. Taylor, and F. Graetze. Authors included H. C. Bunner, B. B. Vallentine, B. Zimmerman, and R. K. Munkittrick. John Whitcomb Riley also contributed comic verse.

Information Sources

BIBLIOGRAPHY:
For a listing of books treating the whole *Puck* enterprise, see the entry for that magazine.
However, these sources make virtually no mention of *Puck on Wheels* itself.
INDEX SOURCES: None.
REPRINT EDITIONS: None.
LOCATION SOURCES: Thirteen libraries list holdings. DLC, NN, MB, and NB have complete collections. Incomplete holdings can be found at CU-BANC, CtY, ICU, MiU, NIC, NcU, and St. Louis Public Library.

Publication History

MAGAZINE TITLE AND TITLE CHANGES: *Puck on Wheels*, 1880–1886.
VOLUME AND ISSUE DATA: The volumes are numbered 1–6, with each issue published in July of the year.

PUBLISHER AND PLACE OF PUBLICATION: Keppler and Schwarzmann, New York.
EDITOR: Henry Cuyler Bunner.
CIRCULATION: Unknown.

Robert Secor

PUCK'S ANNUAL

From 1880 until 1887, the editors of *Puck* issued an annual that was in part a parody of the standard almanacs. With a nod to those all-purpose annuals, it announced itself on its first title page as "Being also an Almanac, a City Directory, a Universal Gazateer, a Rhyming Dictionary, a Guide to Draw-Poker and Wall Street, a Table of Logarithms, a Cold Collation, a Jack knife and a Toothpick.'' In its prognostications for the year, it parodied the usual astronomical predictions: "There will be several eclipses during 1880, Miss Jemima Ann of the Avenue will endeavor to eclipse Miss Anna Maria, also of the Avenue, in the elaboration and ornamentation of her fall hat.'' The calendar for the year, presented in two pages, was ornamented with comic verse and remarks.

In the 1882 issue, "Puck's Horoscope'' for the year includes remarks or verses for all the months, as contributed supposedly by famous authors, like Hugo, Tennyson, and Oscar Wilde, who are presented in parody. Each month in the 1883 volume has jokes concerning different countries or nationalities: Poland for January, the French for February, and so on. In the 1885 annual, V. Hugo Dusenbury, P. P. (Professional Poet), offers a full-page poem for each month according to what profession the month belongs to, so that January is described as "The Plumbers Month,'' June as "The Summer Hotel Clerk's Month,'' and November as the "Ward Politician's Month.'' Each of these poems is decorated by an illustration from *Puck*'s artists. Opposite Dusenbury's poem for each month is a full-page parody of a different writer. March is Walt Whitman's month: "O divine woman, to you I sing! / You may not call this singing; but it is the nearest I can come to it.'' June punctures the pretentious obviousness of Martin Farquhar Tupper—for example, 10 June: "The sea is turbulent and strong; but the heart of a man is affected by nicotine in his system.''

Light fiction and comic verse from the writers of *Puck*'s stable, such as Henry Cuyler Bunner, R. K. Munkittrick, W. J. Henderson, and Ford, and comic illustrations from the parent magazine's artists, such as Joseph Keppler, Frederick Opper, Bernhard Gillam, F. Graetz, Eugene Zimmerman, E. S. Bisbee, and L. F. Schliessbach fill the annual. *Puck's Annual* ran about 126 pages, with color used only on its cover.

Information Sources

BIBLIOGRAPHY:
For a listing of works treating the whole *Puck* enterprise, see the entry for *Puck*. These works do not give specific attention to *Puck's Annual* itself, however.

INDEX SOURCES: None.
REPRINT EDITIONS: None.
LOCATION SOURCES: Complete collections are in NN and DLC. Five volumes can be found in CSmH, and single volumes at ICU, MB, MBat, MiU, NIC, and St. Louis Public Library.

Publication History

MAGAZINE TITLE AND TITLE CHANGES: *Puck's Annual*, 1880–1887.
VOLUME AND ISSUE DATA: There are eight volumes, each dated by year from 1880 to 1887.
PUBLISHER AND PLACE OF PUBLICATION: Keppler and Schwarzmann, New York.
EDITOR: Henry Cuyler Bunner.
CIRCULATION: Unknown.

Robert Secor

PUCK'S LIBRARY and PUCK'S MONTHLY MAGAZINE AND ALMANAC

Founded in 1887, *Puck's Library* was the most successful of *Puck*'s offspring, reaching a circulation of over 62,000 by 1890. Smaller in page size than *Puck* at 8″ × 12″, this thirty-six-page monthly sold for ten cents per copy and reprinted items from its parent weekly classified around certain topics. It claimed to present to the reader only those items that were of lasting rather than topical interest, and so it avoided the more immediate concerns and satire, particularly relating to political figures and issues, that *Puck* so frequently treated. "By this arrangement," the editors claimed in their advertisements, "the reader who wishes what *Puck* has to give outside of politics and daily happenings, can have it here in monthly feasts of dainty tidbits."

The monthly was heavily illustrated, with color only on its cover. Each issue was filled with cartoons, jokes, comic sketches, and parodies built around a single theme. Some items were culled from *Puck*'s sport humor, like " 'The National Game.' Being *Puck*'s Best Things About Baseball" (No. 1); and " 'Fun At Zero.' Being *Puck*'s Best Things About Winter Sports" (No. 30). Others were gathered around different ways of American life, like " 'Suburban.' Being *Puck*'s Best Things About the Country of the Commuter" (No. 12); and " 'City Sketches.' Being *Puck*'s Best Things About the Merry Metropolis" (No. 15). Others dealt with stereotypes, like " 'Hayseed Hits.' Being *Puck*'s Best Things About the Merry Rustic and His Ways" (No. 4); and " 'Darktown Doings.' Being *Puck*'s Best Things About Afro (and other) Americans" (No. 36); certain professions, like " 'Show Business.' Being *Puck*'s Best Things About Artists and Fakirs" (No. 22) and " 'Them Lit'ry Fellers.' *Puck*'s Best Things About the World of Pen and Pencil" (No. 60).

Within these and many other categories, the humor ranged freely, so that "Them Lit'ry Fellers" dealt with the newspaper room and the printing office; with how to become a literary fellow and how to identify one; and with editors and humorists as well as poets and novelists, with modern journalism as well as lovers of fiction. Later volumes in the series seemed to be less compulsive about staying with the announced theme, as the editors began to find it difficult to come up with new classifications that allowed enough humorous items to reprint from *Puck* to fill thirty-two pages. By 1904, although the cover was still announcing a particular theme, the monthly itself only had a few items related to it.

As a result, in the January 1905 issue, *Puck's Library* was superseded by *Puck's Monthly Magazine and Almanac*. The issue was double-numbered: Number 211 of *Puck's Library* and Number 1 of *Puck's Magazine*. The page was the same size as it had been for *Puck's Library*, and it remained the same thirty-two pages. In fact, the cover continued to suggest a particular theme—so that the first issue was titled "Jungle Folks" and featured a full-color cartoon of a monkey in a top hat reading an issue of *Puck* to amused jungle folk. What is new in the format, however, is the suggestion of the magazine as an almanac, and like *Puck's Annual** it frequently parodies current almanacs. The first issue presented a full-page calendar for each month, handsomely bordered with illustrations by *Puck*'s artists. The page opposite each calendar was devoted to the month, so that March gives the reader "Ode to March," a series of ten mock predictions under "Weather Forecast" (e.g., "Heavy fogs in London, from *Punch* Editorial Rooms to Foreign Office and back"), and a paragraph of humorous "Fashion Chat for March." January similarly offers an ode and forecast, but instead of fashion chat presents health hints for the month. Each calendar gave "Historical Events and Moral Maxims for Sundays" next to dates—some straight (e.g., Monday, 17 April, "J. Pierpont Morgan born 1837"), others humorous (e.g., Thursday, January 1905, "Henry James splits first infinitive, 1883"). These full-page calendars lasted only seven months, after which they were reduced to half a page on the bottom of the inside cover. *Puck's Monthly* continued for nine years, but by 1913 circulation had dropped to 32,000 and its last issue was published in May 1914. For a discussion of the writers and artists who appeared in *Puck's Library* and *Monthly* from 1887 to 1914, see the entry for *Puck*.

Information Sources

BIBLIOGRAPHY:
For a listing of books treating the whole *Puck* enterprise, see the entry for that magazine.
INDEX SOURCES: Ayers, N. W. *American Newspaper Annual*. Philadelphia: N. W. Ayers and Sons, 1890–1914.
REPRINT EDITIONS: None.
LOCATION SOURCES: Holdings for *Puck's Library* can be found in CtHW, DLC, MiU, MnU, NN, and Hamilton College. Holdings for *Puck's Monthly Magazine and Almanac* can be found in NN and DLC.

Publication History

MAGAZINE TITLE AND TITLE CHANGES: *Puck's Library*, 1887–1904. *Puck's Monthly Magazine and Almanac*, 1905–1914.

VOLUME AND ISSUE DATA: Volumes of *Puck's Library* are numbered consecutively, 1–210. The first twelve volumes of *Puck's Monthly Magazine and Almanac* are double numbered as 1–12 and numbers 211–222.

PUBLISHER AND PLACE OF PUBLICATION: 1887–1913: Keppler and Schwarzmann, New York. 1914: Puck Publishing Co., New York.

EDITORS: Henry Cuyler Bunner, 1887–1896; Harry Leon Wilson, 1896–1903; John Kendrick Bangs, 1904–1905; Arthur Hamilton Folwell, 1905–1914.

CIRCULATION: Unknown. 62,631 as *Puck's Library*. Down to 32,000 by 1913 as *Puck's Monthly Magazine and Almanac*.

Robert Secor

PUCK'S QUARTERLY

Puck's Quarterly coexisted with the weekly *Puck** from April 1896 until its last issue in October 1914. Unlike its parent magazine, *Puck's Quarterly* had no editorial comment or table of contents and, compared to the weekly's frequently stinging satire, consisted mostly of fluff and fillers.

Particularly in its early issues—except for some full-page story comics and cartoons—all sketches, verse, and illustrations were kept very brief. The jokes were often of the "He–She" variety (e.g.: "She. 'I hate that Spoonley girl.' He. 'What for?' She. 'Because she is in love with you.' He. 'But I'm not in love with her.' She. 'If you were, I'd hate you too.' " [April 1896].) Humor and parody were rarely pointed. For example, the January 1908 issue has a page on the "Traits of Well Known Authors," which parodies the gossip and interviews of literary magazines. Thus, we learn that Richard Harding David "dislikes exceedingly to see his books referred to as 'utter rot,' " that Jack London "usually cashes or deposits all checks he receives from his publishers," and it is Mrs. Humphrey Ward's habit when correcting proof from her manuscript "to mark all errors she observes." Similarly, the quarterly pokes harmless fun at its own class of writers when it tells of saying to the College Graduate that what he doesn't know would fill a good many books, only to learn that he intends to fill newspapers with it (October 1908).

Later volumes included some longer light fiction, and H. C. Bunner's popular *Runaway Browns* was serialized through several issues of 1909 and 1910 before being issued in book form. The entry for *Puck* gives a full portrait of the stable of writers and artists who contributed to *Puck's Quarterly*.

Information Sources

BIBLIOGRAPHY:
For a listing of books treating the whole *Puck* enterprise, see the entry for that magazine.
INDEX SOURCES: None.
REPRINT EDITIONS: None.
LOCATION SOURCES: DLC, the only known source, has holdings from 1896 to 1909.

Publication History

MAGAZINE TITLE AND TITLE CHANGES: *Puck's Quarterly*, 1896–1914.
VOLUME AND ISSUE DATA: Volumes 1–75, April 1896-October 1914.
PUBLISHER AND PLACE OF PUBLICATION: 1896–1913: Keppler and Schwarzmann,
    New York. 1914: Puck Publishing Co., New York.
EDITORS: Harry Leon Wilson, 1896–1903; John Kendrick Bangs, 1904–1905; Arthur
    Hamilton Folwell, 1905–1914.
CIRCULATION: Unknown.

Robert Secor

R

THE REALIST

Paul Krassner's *The Realist* began publication in the Summer of 1958 and was issued sporadically throughout the 1960s, finally terminating in 1974. During its early years as a satirical magazine, it featured articles and interviews with Lenny Bruce, Ken Kesey, Terry Southern, Woody Allen, Joseph Heller, Norman Mailer, Dick Gregory, Kurt Vonnegut, Max Shulman, and Jean Shepherd. As a political satire magazine, it goaded America's sacred cows and bulls, including Richard Nixon, J. Edgar Hoover, Joseph McCarthy, Miss Rheingold, telethons, Catholicism and Judaism, Barry Goldwater, Lyndon Johnson, and Walt Disney.

As the Vietnam War became more prominent in the early 1960s, *The Realist* became less satirical and more strident. The editorial bent for black humor became increasingly grim as the war progressed. Its most famous cartoon was one of Uncle Sam lying in a sexual position across a coolie's body labeled Vietnam. The emotional fault lines show clearly in "Confessions of a Guilty Bystander," about the assassination of John F. Kennedy, and by 1967, with "The Parts Left Out of the Kennedy Book," gloomy, biting sarcasm replaces satiric insight. Sex and sexual metaphors were freely used in political commentary.

The Realist was a brilliant political review, akin to England's *Private Eye*. By 1968, it had become so intermittent that the tenth anniversary issue had to be postponed, for two years as it turned out. Krassner's sensitivity to cultural issues is notable even in his discussion of violence in comics, in Number 93 for August 1972. *The Realist* almost always wound together politics, culture, and psychology, as in "Roseamerica's Baby," a burlesque of "Rosemary's Baby" showing the Pope clawing at Miss Liberty's panties and her giving birth to a two-headed monster representing Hubert Humphrey, hung in his own umbilical cord, and Nixon, giving a V-sign and a single-finger sign to a crowd. Such cartooning in a magazine, which Bill Katz in *Magazines for Libraries* recommended as "a first choice for all libraries," suggests the seriousness with which dissenting sexual lampoons could be taken; Katz describes it as second to none as a dissenting magazine from any establishment. Krassner used "Impolite Interviews" to irreverently question figures from Alan Watts to Hugh Hefner; Lyle Stuart republished several of these interviews in 1961 as a book by that name.

The Realist cost fifty cents and was issued in an 8″ × 10″ format, numbered forty-eight pages, and had no glossy covers. Circulation for *The Realist* itself was 100,000. It was published in New York by Realist Association, with Paul Krassner listed as "Editor and Zen Bastard." Publication was suspended in February 1974 with Number 94. It has been reprinted by University Microfilms and selectively in a 1984 collection, *Best of the Realist* (Philadelphia: Running Press).

Information Sources

BIBLIOGRAPHY:
Galligan, Edward L. "*The Realist*, A Journal of Freethought, Criticism and Satire."
    Satire Newsletter 2 (Spring 1965): 82–90.
Katz, Bill. *Magazines for Libraries*. New York: R. R. Bowker, 1969, p. 340.
INDEX SOURCES: None.
REPRINT EDITIONS: University Microfilms.
LOCATION SOURCES: None.

Publication History

MAGAZINE TITLE AND TITLE CHANGES: *The Realist*.
VOLUME AND ISSUE DATA: Summer 1958, irregular, to Number 94, February 1974.
PUBLISHER AND PLACE OF PUBLICATION: The Realist Association, New York.
EDITOR: Paul Krassner.
CIRCULATION: 100,000.

Franz Douskey

THE RED BOOK

The Red Book attempted to bring urbane wit and sophisticated humor to Baltimore, at a time when the city was gaining prominence in the first flowering of literary nationalism. As an emerging metropolitan center with a new self-consciousness of its social classes, Baltimore provided the perfect soil to nurture a periodical aspiring to the stature of Washington Irving's earlier, highly successful *Salmagundi*.* Derivative of English journals like *The Tattler* and *The Spectator*, *The Red Book* found and filled a regional need from 1819 to 1821.

The Red Book contained original poetry, familiar essays, and sketches, and was written and edited by John Pendleton Kennedy—lawyer, politician, and novelist (*Swallow Barn*, 1832; *Horse-Shoe Robinson*, 1835; and *Rob of the Bowl*, 1838)—and by Peter Hoffman Cruse—editor for several years of the *Baltimore*

American and then of the *Patriot*. The editors proclaimed "The World in our opinion needs correction, and we have essayed to use the weapons placed in our hands." Their target, as enunciated in the first issue, was Baltimore society:

Baltimore, it is said abroad, is celebrated for three things—its *music*,—its *churches* and its *military*. In each of these, are strange anomalies. Music is patronized by those who have the least *ear* and the most *money* (which is only another name for discord.) The best *churches* are built by the worst christians; and in the *military* department, it is observed, that all logick is set at defiance in making *majors* of *minors*.

The youthful exuberance of Cruse's poetry proved engaging:

Meanwhile,—that doughty men may know
What doughtier hero is their foe,—
    My height's five feet eleven,
My courage fair, my temper hot,
My hand not bad at pistol shot
    My age scant twenty-seven.

Kennedy's prose took satiric aim at contemporary social, political, and economic mores. In "Market Street Musings," he exposed "the perfect epitome" of Baltimore:

In this motley assemblage, the sourest face I saw, belonged to an old maid who had in her youth been a toast. The most cheerful looking man, was a bankrupt. The busiest matron, a widow who had a young friend about to be married—the wisest looking man was a bank director—the prettiest girl was a young quaker. The most egregious fool—here I am at a loss,—this honor was divided among several candidates.

Other numbers included conventional sketches and essays in the *Salmagundi* and *Spectator* tradition such as "A Full Length Portrait of Mr. Dunder," "Letter to a Young Lady," "From the Observatory," "Lady Fashion and Lady Good Sense," and "The Story of Mr. Bronze" (which owed more than a nod to Sir Roger de Coverly).

Although Kennedy and Cruse had projected twelve numbers of *The Red Book*, only ten were completed. It fell victim to its authors' other interests: Kennedy won election to the Maryland House of Delegates in 1820, whereas Cruse desired to pursue more seriously a career of letters. A pleasant escapade and literary initiation, *The Red Book* was, as Cruse wrote in the last number, "A breath-inflated bubble."

Information Sources

BIBLIOGRAPHY:

Blair, Walter. *Native American Humor*. New York: American Book Co., 1937.

Bohner, C. H. *John Pendleton Kennedy: Gentleman from Baltimore*. Baltimore: Johns Hopkins University Press, 1961.

Kribbs, Jayne K. *An Annotated Bibliography of American Literary Periodicals, 1741–1850*. Boston: G. K. Hall, 1977.

Mott, Frank L. *A History of American Magazines, 1741–1850*. Cambridge, Mass.: Harvard University Press, 1938, 1:172, 706.

INDEX SOURCES: None.

REPRINT EDITIONS: None.

LOCATION SOURCES: Complete Series are at DLC, CtY; incomplete Series are at MdBE, Peabody Institute, Baltimore, and NjP.

Publication History

MAGAZINE TITLE AND TITLE CHANGES: *The Red Book*, 23 October 1819–16 March 1821.

VOLUME AND ISSUE DATA: Irregular. Six numbers published between October 1819 and January 1820 (these were collected and bound by the publisher); three numbers of the second volume at approximately one-month intervals beginning on 3 March 1820; the tenth and last number appeared on 16 March 1821.

PUBLISHER AND PLACE OF PUBLICATION: Joseph Robinson, Baltimore.

EDITORS: John Pendleton Kennedy and Peter Hoffman Cruse.

CIRCULATION: Unknown, though, as C. H. Bohner notes, "it was a popular, and presumably a financial success," the first edition selling out quickly (pp. 39–40). Its distribution seems to have been primarily within a local radius, with copies sent to Boston for review.

William E. Lenz

THE ROLLING STONE

The Rolling Stone was founded, written, illustrated, and in almost every way dominated by a talented young bank clerk named William Sydney Porter. Although the weekly journal lasted only a year and made no great impact on the comic journalism of the day, it holds a significant place in the history of humorous magazines since Porter, who later wrote fiction under the pseudonym O. Henry, served his literary apprenticeship in its pages. While the standard humorous fare of the day—puns, political satire, vernacular and ethnic humor, local color, burlesques on small-town newspapers, and bad verse— predominated, there occasionally appeared sketches that reflect the later style that has come to be associated with the mature O. Henry at his best.

After having worked in the First National Bank of Austin, Texas, for three years, Will Porter took the first major step in his career as a professional writer when, in March 1894, he bought the press of *The Iconoclast*, a radical monthly published by William C. Brann. His friends Will Booth and Herman Pressler signed the note for the $250 purchase price for Porter, and another friend, James P. Crane, joined him as a partner in the new enterprise. Bored and dissatisfied in his job and facing family stresses, Porter embarked on the publishing venture primarily for the pleasure and self-fulfillment it would afford him, though he also seems to have hoped that it would supplement his clerk's salary and perhaps eventually allow him to give up that position altogether. The initial issues of *The Rolling Stone* announce his intention to "fill its pages with matter that will make a heartrending appeal to every lover of good literature," promising that "each number will contain Stories, Humorous Sketches, Poems, Jokes, properly labeled, sidesplitting references to the mother-in-law, the goat, Governor Hogg, and the states of weather and Texas." Although its early numbers contain a substantial amount of humorous news commentary, mostly about state and local politics, from the beginning it was obvious that Porter's penchant was for stories, sketches, and poems, and *The Rolling Stone* became increasingly more belletristic as the year wore one.

Porter published the first two issues under the title *The Iconoclast*, but Brann, who settled in Waco, demanded that Porter relinquish the name. Thus, on 28 April 1894, at Crane's suggestion, Number 3 of the new journal was issued as *The Rolling Stone* with the motto "Out for Moss." It began as an eight-page folio (13" × 20") with five columns per page, but in July Porter changed the format to a twelve-page quarto (10" × 12") with four columns per page; in December he returned to the folio size and eight pages, but in March 1895, changed back to the twelve-page quarto. The prolific illustrations, all drawn by Porter and almost all typical comic magazine fare, were reproduced by inexpensive chalk plates prepared by Dixie Daniels, a printer who became the journal's Business Manager in August after Crane left for Chicago. Although the early illustrations were usually small, most later issues sported front pages devoted entirely to larger Porter drawings.

In addition to preparing the illustrations, Porter, despite retaining his full-time job at the bank, produced all of the journal's copy except for a San Antonio column that ran briefly, occasional bits from such magazines as *Truth* and *Life*,* and the regular use of Bill Nye's syndicated column. His efforts ranged from the curious blend of ethnic humor and literary burlesque in pieces such as "Tictocq, the Great French Detective," and "Hans Von Pretzel, the Great German Detective," to the miscellany column "Vagrant Remarks," to such remarkable early sketches as "Bexar Scrip No. 2692," probably the best of Porter's *Rolling Stone* stories. More typical, however, is the light and imitative "Thomas Toby's Travels," written in the guise of a special correspondent: "William Shakespeare is dead. I have recently visited the house where he used to live. The people there seem to have recovered their wonted cheerfulness after so sad an affair; and indeed were quite lively and chipper" (v. 1:8, p. 3; byline 16 July 1894). Or another regular feature, "The Plunkville Patriot" page that was supposedly reproduced from a small-town newspaper replete with numerous typographical "errors," including mixing the sizes and kinds of type (v. 1:20,

p. 6, for 25 August 1894). He also did a bit of local-color reporting, although "State Saengerfest," the farcical account of an ethnic festival, alienated some German readers. As with most of his writings, this piece grew out of his favorite hobby, "bumming" around town, or, in his own words: "Like the Califf Haroun Al Raschid, but without his power of relieving distress or punishing wickedness, I often stroll about Austin studying human nature and reading many pages in the great book of Man."

In mid-December 1894, during an investigation by a federal bank examiner, Porter resigned his position at the bank, ostensibly to devote more time to the magazine. After Porter was later convicted of embezzlement charges, there was much speculation that he had used bank funds to subsidize the failing magazine. Throughout its short history *The Rolling Stone* had been plagued with financial problems, despite loans from Porter's father-in-law and from a friend, Ed Smith. In January 1895, Porter opened a San Antonio office in the hopes of expanding subscriptions—which never exceeded 1,500—and advertising, and appointed a pretentious Englishman named Henry Ryder-Taylor as co-editor with responsibility for the new San Antonio page. Although the San Antonio office failed to save the faltering journal, Porter's association with that city later bore fruit as the source for several of his short stories. On 30 March, the *Stone* carried an apology for its two-week absence with the explanation that Porter had been ill; also in that number, Ryder-Taylor was demoted to "Manager of the San Antonio Department." Four weeks later, on 27 April 1895, the last issue of *The Rolling Stone* was published.

Dixie Daniels, the former printer and business manager, claimed that the demise of *Rolling Stone* was brought about by a combination of the alienation of the German community in the Austin area and the paper's partisanship in a bitter San Antonio mayoral campaign that was urged on Porter by Ryder-Taylor. Richard O'Connor, one of Porter's biographers, has insisted that its failure was due to Austin's smallness, conservative tastes, and provinciality. While all were probably contributing factors, it seems more likely that poor management, especially in failing to attract more advertisers and subscribers, was the primary culprit. Will Porter was no businessman, but *The Rolling Stone* did provide him with the most valuable literary training he was to receive on the road to becoming O. Henry.

Information Sources

BIBLIOGRAPHY:

Davis, Robert H., and Arthur B. Maurice. *The Caliph of Bagdad*. New York: Appleton, 1931.

Langford, Gerald. *Alias O. Henry*. New York: Macmillan Co., 1957.

Long, E. Hudson. *O. Henry: The Man and His Work*. Philadelphia: University of Pennsylvania Press, 1949.

Mott, Frank L. "*The Rolling Stone*." In *A History of American Magazines, 1885–1905*. Cambridge, Mass.: Harvard University Press, 1957, 4:665–70.

O'Connor, Richard. *O. Henry: The Legendary Life of William S. Porter*. Garden City, N.Y.: Doubleday, 1970.
Ratchford, Fannie E. "*The Rolling Stone*: The Life History of an O. Henry Rarity," *Colophon* 5 (June 1934): Pt. 17 (No. 8).
Tracy, Paul A. "A Closer Look at O. Henry's *Rolling Stone*." Master's thesis, University of Texas at Austin, 1949.
INDEX SOURCES: None.
REPRINT EDITIONS: A number of pieces from the magazine were collected in *Rolling Stones* (New York: Doubleday, Page, and Co., 1912).
LOCATION SOURCES: The University of Texas at Austin holds the only known file of *The Rolling Stone*, and it contains the following: Volume 1:3–9, 11–15, 17–29, 31–32, 34–36; Volume 2:2–4, 6, 9, 12.

Publication History

MAGAZINE TITLE AND TITLE CHANGES: *The Iconoclast*, 14–21 April 1894; *The Rolling Stone*, 28 April 1894–27 April 1895.
VOLUME AND ISSUE DATA: Weekly, annual volumes. Volume 1:1, 14 April 1894–Volume 2:12, 27 April 1895. Volume 2:7–8, 16 and 23 March 1895, were not issued.
PUBLISHER AND PLACE OF PUBLICATION: The Rolling Stone Co. (W. S. Porter, with Hec McEachin, 30 March–27 April 1894); Austin, Texas (Volume 2:1–5, list Austin and San Antonio jointly as places of publication, though actual publication seems to have been only in Austin.)
EDITORS: William Sydney Porter (with Henry Ryder-Taylor as San Antonio Editor, 26 January 1895–30 March 1895).
CIRCULATION: About 1,500.

W. Craig Turner

THE ROVER

A native Yankee humorist, Seba Smith, founder and editor of *The Rover*, gained a nationwide reputation with the "Jack Downing Letters," published in the *Portland Daily Courier* from 1830 to 1833. Smith and his family moved to New York in 1842 with renewed literary ambitions after disastrous financial ventures in South Carolina. *The Rover* was a serious editorial undertaking for Smith, and his connection with the magazine continued from 24 March 1843 until January 1845. A regular contributor to *The Rover*, Smith's wife adopted the pen name of Elizabeth Oakes Smith and soon took her own place among the literati of New York.

The Rover was intended as a choice of tales, sketches, and poems; they did not claim to be original but rather to be for preservation and worthy of being bound into volumes. Besides selected serious works, there were various original comic stories by Seba Smith, John Neal, and Lawrence Labree. They marked a significant transition between rural Down East humor and a new brand of domestic comedy in an urban setting, and Smith seems to have intended to bridge the gap between established literary tastes and popular traditions. Each week, a steel engraving with an accompanying sketch added to the attraction of the magazine, and the first issue of the third volume had Jack Downing's portrait on the cover. Made up of two-column pages, *The Rover* was first twelve and then sixteen pages in length. It sold at six cents an issue in 1843. The subscription price was three dollars a year, a dollar less than the *New York Mirror* and the *Broadway Journal*. By early 1845, the cost was reduced to three cents a copy or one dollar a year in advance.

Among the authors of selected prose and poetry were Charles Hoffman, Washington Irving, William Cullen Bryant, Oliver Wendell Holmes, James Kirke Paulding, and John Greenleaf Whittier. An original whale story by J. N. Reynolds entitled "Mocha Dick of the Pacific" was published on 19 January 1844. It pictured a white whale of prodigious size and strength and was one source for Herman Melville's *Moby Dick*.

Seba Smith's portrayal of New England life combined folk humor with psychological intricacies in numerous, often nostalgic, tales later reprinted in *'Way Down East* (1854): "Aunt Nabby's Stewed Goose," "Polly Gray and the Doctors," "Christopher Crotchet, the Singing Master," "Getting over the Difficulty," or "The Brown Mug." On his part, Lawrence Labree contributed "Zephania Starling," a sketch with Dickensian connotations in which a sly peddler is outwitted by a learned villager, well read in the classics. This and similar stories were directed at a public that welcomed more sophistication in native humor.

The most notable feature of *The Rover* was the resumption of the "Downing Letters" after a gap of eight years. In 1830, Jack had poked fun at Jackson's entourage while upbraiding the new Democrats for their betrayal of Jeffersonian ideals. He reappeared in *The Rover* toward the end of the second volume in a letter dated 1 January 1844. His final contribution was for the last issue of 1844. Beginning with 26 July 1844, the letters were not originally written for *The Rover* but were reprinted from *Bunker Hill*, a weekly magazine published to support James Harper, the Mayor of New York, who came into office as a candidate of the Native American party. Well-known characters such as Joel Downing, Uncle Joshua, Cousin Ephraim, and Aunt Nabby were enlisted to support the nativist cause by opposing immigration and fighting naturalization laws. In a fable about prankish boys who climbed into his apple tree and pelted him with the fruit, Uncle Joshua declared that he would have no foreigners climbing into "the American Tree of Liberty." Propaganda was detrimental to Smith's humor, and he never recaptured the easy-going mood of the earlier series. As a prelude to the letters published in the *National Intelligencer* between 1847 and 1856, *The Rover* already suggested Smith's Whig commitment. Scornful of the divisions among the Democrats before the nomination of James Polk in 1844, Jack made it clear that John C. Calhoun's aim was "to upset the kettle and pour the fat all in the fire." Manifest Destiny thus became Smith's major butt of satire.

Smith's editorship ended on 11 January 1845, with the seventeenth number of the fourth volume. The main reason was his new editorial task for the *New York American Republican*, the organ of the city government. Lawrence Labree, who took over as sole editor, proved less successful. As the last issue appeared in September 1845, it became clear that *The Rover* had lost its satiric appeal after the withdrawal of Seba Smith.

Information Sources

BIBLIOGRAPHY:

Kribbs, Jayne K. *An Annotated Bibliography of American Literary Periodicals, 1741– 1850*. Boston: G. K. Hall, 1977, pp. 147–48.

Rickels, Milton, and Patricia. *Seba Smith*. Boston: G. K. Hall, Twayne Publishers, 1977, pp. 72–80.

Wyman, Mary Alice. *Selections from the Autobiography of Elizabeth Oakes Smith*. Lewiston: Lewiston Journal Co., 1924, pp. 82–95.

———. *Two American Pioneers: Seba Smith and Elizabeth Oakes Smith*. New York: Columbia University Press, 1927, pp. 131–38.

INDEX SOURCES: Title index bound at the end of each volume.

REPRINT EDITIONS: University Microfilms.

LOCATION SOURCES: American Philosophical Society, N.

Publication History

MAGAZINE TITLE AND TITLE CHANGES: *The Rover*, 15 March 1843–13 September 1845.

VOLUME AND ISSUE DATA: Weekly, semi-annual volumes. Volume 1–1, 15 March 1843–Volume 5:26, 13 September 1845.

PUBLISHER AND PLACE OF PUBLICATION: 1843: Labree, Dean and Co. 1844: Dean and Co. 1845: Robinson and Co., New York.

EDITORS: Seba Smith and Lawrence Labree, 1843; Seba Smith, 1844; Lawrence Labree, 1845.

CIRCULATION: Unknown.

Daniel Royot

THE RUSH-LIGHT

This periodical grew out of a lawsuit instituted by Benjamin Rush, the celebrated Philadelphia physician and signer of the Declaration of Independence, against writer/publisher William Cobbett for libel in response to Cobbett's abusive satires of Rush in *Porcupine's Gazette*. Cobbett's outspokenness, combative personality, and reactionary Royalist political views earned him no sympathy in post-Revolutionary Philadelphia, so that when the suit reached court in 1799 the trial proved to be anything but impartial. In order to avoid payment of the settlement against him, Cobbett decamped for New York where he published seven issues of *The Rush-Light* before sailing to England in the Summer of 1800.

Cobbett had several reasons for publishing *The Rush-Light*. The genesis of the project was his desire to have the public hear his side of the story regarding the libel suit. He was also attracted by the opportunity to further vilify Rush as a medical quack and man of questionable ethics, and to harangue a sympathetic New York readership on the virtues of Republicanism. Cobbett peppered all seven issues with his virulent satiric style, sometimes employing his comic persona, Peter Porcupine. The journal's significance today stems from issue Number 3, which Cobbett gave over entirely to an impassioned defense of the publications on which Rush's legal action had been grounded. Through the rhetorical force and eloquence of his argument Cobbett made a powerful statement on the methods and ethics of satire.

Information Sources

BIBLIOGRAPHY:
Butterfield, L. H., ed. "Appendix III: The Cobbett Rush Feud." In *Letters of Benjamin Rush*. Princeton, N.J.: Princeton University Press, 1951, 2: 1213–18.
Mott, Frank L. *A History of American Magazines, 1741–1850*. Cambridge, Mass.: Harvard University Press, 1930, 1:150, 791.
Spater, George. *William Cobbett, The Poor Man's Friend*. Cambridge and New York: Cambridge University Press, 1982, 1:99–109.
INDEX SOURCES: Table of Contents published with each issue.
REPRINT EDITIONS: None.
LOCATION SOURCES: CtY, DLC, MB, MH, NN, PPHi, WHi, and twenty-one others.

Publication History

MAGAZINE TITLE AND TITLE CHANGES: *The Rush-Light/The Republican Rush-Light*, 15 February–30 August 1800.
VOLUME AND ISSUE DATA: Irregular, Volume 1:1–6, Volume 2:1, 15 February–30 August 1800.
PUBLISHER AND PLACE OF PUBLICATION: William Cobbett, New York.
EDITOR: William Cobbett (Peter Porcupine).
CIRCULATION: Unknown.

Gary Engle

——— S ———

SAGEBRUSH PHILOSOPHY

From January 1904 until his death in October 1910, Bill Barlow illuminated Wyoming with fourteen volumes of his uncopyrighted *Sagebrush Philosophy*, claiming that "The Lord never intended that the dissemination of Pure Stuph should be limited by law." M. C. and M. F. Barrow published the little octavo 5″ × 6½″ monthly for ten cents a copy, a dollar a year, "printed on prickly pear papyrus," and intended to have a distinctly wild Western regional flavor. Contemporary idiomatic crackerbox style dominated the journal, composed almost entirely by its editor. He quotes the toast to our wives and sweethearts—may they never meet—and argues against nonsense complaints about husbands acting like bachelors when away from home with the crusty rationale of "what did you expect?" Two- and three-page reflective articles marked the eight pages of each issue, filled out with some one-line jokes and a beer advertisement in later issues.

Sagebrush Philosophy anticipates H. L. Mencken's style in *The American Mercury*,* with the distinct difference that it boosted rather than condemned its region. Political and social nonsense was excoriated pungently, and sarcasm toward the sentimental, the bluestocking, and the hypocritical abounded. The editor described himself as the "apostle of sunshine," and he was an advocate of plain dealing and the enjoyment of the pleasures of life in his broadly sarcastic fulminations. His motto warned his readers to "consider the mummy, he ain't had no fun in 4,000 years." His wife concluded publication with a memorial issue in November 1910 immediately following his death.

Information Sources

INDEX SOURCES: First four years indexed.
REPRINT EDITIONS: None.
LOCATION SOURCES: DLC, NN, ICN, CtY, and RPB hold extensive runs; four other
    libraries list holdings.

Publication History

MAGAZINE TITLE AND TITLE CHANGES: *Sagebrush Philosophy*, January 1904–
    November 1910.
VOLUME AND ISSUE DATA: Monthly, semi-annual volumes. Volume 1:1, January
    1904–Volume 14:11, November 1910, although some numbering irregularity may
    exist.
PUBLISHER AND PLACE OF PUBLICATION: M. C. and M. F. Barrow, Douglas,
    Wyoming.
EDITORS: William Barlow; last issue, Mrs. William Barlow.
CIRCULATION: Unknown. Later issues carried regular advice about obtaining back
    issues. Since it paid its costs after the first few months, regional popularity may
    be assumed.

David E. E. Sloane

ST. LOUIS REVEILLE

The *St. Louis Reveille* was one of the leading regional newspapers publishing
and promoting American humor during the antebellum period. Along with the
New Orleans Picayune,** to which it was often favorably compared, the *Reveille*
is credited with aiding the development of the humorous literature of the Old
Southwest. The more famous nationally circulated sporting paper, the New York
Spirit of the Times,* frequently reprinted humorous stories taken from the
columns of the *Reveille*. With its rich store of humorous and realistic anecdotes
and tales cast for the most part in the vernacular of its region and depicting a
wide range of frontier folk and folkways, the *Reveille*, among a few similar
regional newspapers, offered to the reading public an alternative to the highly
romantic, sentimental literature found in most of the magazines and gift-books
of the day.

Charles Keemle, Matthew C. Field, and Joseph M. Field founded the daily
Reveille in May 1844. Keemle, a native of Philadelphia, came to St. Louis as
early as 1817 and subsequently became a prominent citizen of the city and a
publisher of at least five other newspapers besides the *Reveille* during his career
there.[1] Unlike the Fields, who were free-spirited personalities talented at creative
writing and acting, Keemle was serious minded and less creative. He likely
furnished most of the financial backing for the *Reveille* and dealt with the day-
to-day business details of it, while the Fields, especially Joseph, oversaw most
of the editorial duties of the paper. The three men probably first met in 1835,
when the Field brothers traveled from New Orleans to St. Louis to act in the
theater company of N. M. Ludlow.[2] Joseph and Matthew continued to pursue

their acting careers while working as journalists for the *New Orleans Picayune*, to which they contributed many poems. Only five months after joining the St. Louis enterprise, Matthew Field left the *Reveille* because of poor health, with his brother and Keemle remaining as "proprietors, publishers, and editors" until the paper ceased operation in 1850.

The *Reveille* began as a morning newspaper published every day except Monday. Within two months, the proprietors also began a weekly *Reveille*, published on Mondays, and usually made up of materials that had appeared in that week's daily *Reveille*. By 1847, Keemle and Field added a daily evening edition, a tri-weekly, and even a *Reveille* almanac for Missouri and Illinois. As Frank Luther Mott has noted, the *Reveille* was one of the first daily newspapers in the United States to publish a Sunday issue regularly, an action that proved controversial in the St. Louis religious community and one that Keemle and Field were forced to defend as late as 1849.

In format, the daily *Reveille* consisted of four six-column unnumbered pages. The subscription price was five dollars a year, with single issues for a nickel. Few engravings were included in the paper, but its regular masthead etching showed a young soldier beating a drum, set against a backdrop of cannon, tents, and an American flag—a scene prompting the editors to refer to themselves frequently as "drummers" waking up St. Louis readers early each morning. The weekly *Reveille* consisted of eight five-column quarto pages and sold for three dollars a year. From the outset, the *Reveille* mainly published news and literary selections of regional interest, but with an exchange system involving over one hundred other newspapers by 1847 and with agents in Boston, New York, Philadelphia, Baltimore, New Orleans and Mobile by 1848, the *Reveille* reached a diverse and far-distant readership.

A typical issue of the daily *Reveille* consisted of slightly more than one page of news items and literary selections and nearly three pages of advertisements and announcements. Most news items were taken from exchange papers and appeared as paragraphs in the *Reveille*, although three historic events—the Mormons' movement westward, the Mexican War, and the California Gold Rush—received more space in the form of long news articles and letters from correspondents on the scene. Brief "local" news items (including those concerning crimes and shifty characters in Missouri and the nearby states) and human oddities supposedly observed across the nation (such as a woefully emaciated man who had a 100-foot-long tapeworm removed from his stomach) made reports of sea serpents and the mythical gyascutus altogether plausible to readers and prepared the *Reveille* audience for the comic exaggerations in many of the paper's stories and poems.

From the start, Keemle and Joseph Field had sought "variety" in the newspaper's contents, and the subject matter and techniques of the humor selections varied greatly, but most of the selections were satiric. Many stories satirized fringe religious groups, such as the Millerites, or medical and scientific discoveries. Field's comic story "Establishing the Science," for example, poked fun at the contemporary interest in mesmerism, while an article signed by "O. Hevings" lauded a new telescope that showed moon craters to be huge hog wallows. Despite Keemle and Field's avowed intention to keep the *Reveille* an "Independent" paper politically, they did not try to avoid politics as a subject for humor. "Song of the Runaway" satirized abolitionists, a group that the *Reveille* editors consistently criticized. "Oregon," a "Musical Jeu d'Esprit," with John Bull and Uncle Sam as main characters and the individual states as minor ones, promoted an expansionist role for America in the Oregon Territory. "The Cabinet," a one-column play in miniature, satirized James Polk and his political appointees. The *Reveille* editors especially disliked Polk because of his veto of a "Rivers and Harbors" bill that would have provided funds for the improvement of Missouri waterways. At a time when the public eagerly awaited a "Message" from him Keemle and Field gained revenge on Polk by planting a phony "President's Message" in the *Reveille* in which he reverses his stand on the navigation bill and proposes moving the nation's capital from Washington to St. Louis.

Many of the stories and poems in the *Reveille* offered ethnic and state humor. As in many other humor publications of the time, Irishmen, Frenchmen, and Blacks were frequently targets of humor, and most of the humor of such ethnic pieces was derived more from the peculiar behavior and dialects presented than from well-crafted plots or dramatic situations. Germans were the ethnic group most frequently satirized by *Reveille* writers, probably because of the large German population that had recently settled in St. Louis. A regular "Recorder's Court" column for several years gave the *Reveille* editors a ready forum for having fun at the expense of real-life "foreigners" in their city. Most of the state satire in the paper was directed at illiterate Missourians and Illinois "Suckers," who most often displayed their ignorance and boorish nature when encountering "civilized" society in St. Louis and other cities.

Parodies and burlesques made up another large category of satiric pieces in the *Reveille*. Poems parodied works by Shakespeare, Byron, Wordsworth, Poe, and Longfellow. Shakespeare and Poe were especially popular targets, with three parodies of "The Raven" and two comic *Hamlets*, including "Hamlet's Lunacy For the Consideration of the Commentators," in which the author attributed the Dane's erratic behavior to "dyspepsy." Prose burlesques of popular romantic fiction were also common. Representative is "The Perjured Husband. A Tale in the Magazine Style," which offers eight "chapters" in the space of one newspaper column; and "Strabismus—Or, The Broken Heart. A Tale of Passion," a sensitive account of two lovers, one of whom was cross-eyed. Joseph Holt Ingraham's prolific and poorly written novels of adventure and Ernst T. Hoffmann's German "Fantastic Stories" were likewise burlesqued in the *Reveille*.

Contributors to the *Reveille* included three notable humorists—Solomon Franklin (Sol.) Smith, the editor Joseph M. Field, and John S. Robb. Smith, an actor and theater manager of national reputation, wrote stories mainly describing humorous incidents in his profession. These were later collected and published in his *Theatrical Apprenticeship and Anecdotical Recollections of Sol. Smith* in 1846 and *The Theatrical Journey-Work and Anecdotical Recollections of Sol. Smith* in 1854. Among his *Reveille* contributions, Field ("Everpoint," "Straws") published two famous stories about the legendary riverman Mike Fink—"Death of Mike Fink" and "Mike Fink, 'The Last of the Boatmen.' " "Death of Mike Fink," which he claimed to be a factual account based on details furnished by his partner Charles Keemle, countered an earlier published version of Fink's death by Morgan Neville. Field's stories were collected in *The Drama in Pokerville: The Bench and Bar of Jurytown, and Other Stories* in 1847. Robb ("Solitaire"), a printer and associate editor with the *Reveille* for a number of years, wrote humor stories dealing with rural Missouri life and folkways and adventure stories set in the Western frontier. The best of these tales were published in *Streaks of Squatter Life, and Far-West Scenes* in 1847. Other less renowned humorists who wrote frequently for the *Reveille* included Thompson Westcott ("Joe Miller, Jr.") of Philadelphia and Lieutenant R. S. Elliott ("John Brown"), a member of the Missouri Laclede Rangers during the Mexican War.

Although humor dominated the literary selections in the *Reveille*, the paper offered other types of literature. After satirizing popular romances, the *Reveille* offered serialized romances from 1847 through 1849, and examples of sentimental verse appear throughout its publishing life. Several of the romances of revenge or intrigue were written by the humorists Field and Robb. The *Reveille* encouraged the writing of such tales in 1848 when it sponsored a contest offering a prize of fifty dollars for the "best original story." The prize-winning story and five others of the fifteen submitted were subsequently published.

The *St. Louis Reveille* was a successful venture, competing against twenty-seven other newspapers in the city in 1844, when the paper was founded. Its circulation grew from 1,612 in 1845 to 2,100 in 1847 to a high of perhaps 3,000 by 1848 (when St. Louis had a population of about 50,000 people). The *Reveille*'s business success gained for Keemle and Field an appointment as "City Job Printers" and for the newspaper an awarding of the city post-office printing assignment in both 1847 and 1848 (on the basis of the paper's having the largest daily circulation in St. Louis). The *Reveille* became known across the country for its literary selections. Leading humor publications, including the New York *Spirit of the Times* and the *New Orleans Picayune*, praised it highly and reprinted materials from it frequently. The Boston *Yankee Blade** called the *Reveille* "one of the richest and raciest papers in all Jonathan's dominions, from the Forests of Aroostook to the Halls of Montezuma." No one could have foreseen the tragedy awaiting the flourishing paper. On the night of 17 May 1849, a great fire swept from the riverfront through the city of St. Louis, causing at least $3 million worth of damage according to Field and destroying the *Reveille*'s printing establishment and most of its equipment. Keemle and Field purchased new equipment, moved to a nearby location, and somehow managed to keep the newspaper operating for another seventeen months. The *Reveille* ultimately failed in October 1850, primarily as a result of inadequate insurance that covered only about half of the paper's losses in the St. Louis fire. The *Reveille* was sold to John Frazer, who subsequently merged it with the St. Louis *People's Organ*.

Notes

1. J. Thomas Scharf, *History of Saint Louis City and County* (Philadelphia: Louis H. Everts and Co.), 2: 1596.
2. Ibid., 1: 967–968.

Information Sources

BIBLIOGRAPHY:
Cohen, Hennig, and William B. Dillingham. *Humor of the Old Southwest*. Athens, Ga.: University of Georgia Press, 1975, pp. xv, 96–97.
Mott, Frank Luther. *American Journalism. A History of Newspapers in the United States Through 260 Years: 1690 to 1950*. New York: Macmillan Co., 1950, p. 318.
Spotts, Carle Brooks. "The Development of Fiction on the Missouri Frontier (1830–1860)." *Missouri Historical Review* 29, Pt. 4 (1935): 103.
INDEX SOURCES: None.
REPRINT EDITIONS: None.
LOCATION SOURCES: ICN, MnU, IU, and approximately five other libraries.

Publication History

MAGAZINE TITLE AND TITLE CHANGES: *St. Louis Reveille*, 14 May 1844–6 October 1850.
VOLUME AND ISSUE DATA: Daily, Volume 1:1, 14 May 1844–Volume 7:1976, 6 October 1850.
PUBLISHER AND PLACE OF PUBLICATION: Charles Keemle and Joseph M. Field, St. Louis, Missouri.
EDITORS: Charles Keemle and Joseph M. Field.
CIRCULATION: Approximately 2,100 to 3,000.

Mark A. Keller

SALMAGUNDI

Frank Luther Mott writes that *Salmagundi; Or, the Whimwhams and Opinions of Launcelot Langstaff, Esq., and Others*, written by Washington Irving, his brother William, and his brother-in-law, James Kirke Paulding, and published irregularly in New York from 24 January 1807 through 25 January 1808, was the most famous of all the publications of the satirical kind in the early nineteenth century.[1] Certainly, it was a model for many such publications.

Salmagundi was the heir to and occasionally the competitor of a wide range of fledgling American periodicals. *The Wasp** (edited at Hudson, New York, in 1802 and 1803 by "Robert Rusticoat") and the *Corrector** (edited at New York in 1804 by "Toby Tickler, Esq.") focused primarily on political issues, while Joseph Dennie's *The Port Folio** (Philadelphia, 1807–1811), John Howard

Payne's *Thespian Mirror* (New York, 1805–1806), Charles Brockden Brown's *Literary Magazine and American Register* (Philadelphia, 1803–1807), and the short-lived *The Town* (New York, 1807) emphasized social, literary, and theatrical concerns. Owing a more direct debt to these rather than to the English periodicals of Richard Steele, Joseph Addison, Samuel Johnson, and Oliver Goldsmith (though Laurence Sterne's *Life and Opinions of Tristram Shandy, Gentleman* perhaps towers above all), *Salmagundi* proved an immediate success in New York, a city that briefly outshone Philadelphia as the literary star of the United States during the early 1800s. A measure of its success can be noted in that David Longworth, its publisher (and the owner of the popular New York bookstore The Sentimental Epicure's Ordinary), himself took out a copyright on *Salmagundi* and thereby reaped its financial profits. The authors thus unwittingly gave credence to their glib prefatory contention that they "have nothing to do with the pecuniary concerns of the paper," though they were eventually paid a token one hundred dollars each.[2]

Washington Irving, the chief author of the most memorable *Salmagundi* pieces by Launcelot Langstaff, Esq., and Mustapha Rub-A-Dub Keli Khan, had served his literary apprenticeship by composing the *Letters of Jonathan Oldstyle, Gent.*, for his brother Peter Irving's *New York Morning Chronicle* in 1802 and 1803. These highly conventional satiric pieces, writes Bruce Granger, were "wholly social, three of the essays focusing on manners, the other six on theatrical criticism."[3] James Kirke Paulding, tied to the Irvings by marriage as well as by friendship, felt irresistibly drawn to a life of letters: "Oh—may all the glory and success attend the noble art of scribbling!" he wrote in 1802. "What would become of me without the solace it affords?"[4] William Irving, another of Washington's brothers, not only encouraged Paulding and Washington Irving to write, but also offered to join them by contributing poetry. "The thoughts of the authors were so mingled together in these essays, and they were so literally joint productions," warns Paulding in the 1835 Preface to the New York edition, "that it would be difficult, as well as useless, at this distance of time, to assign to each his exact share."[5] Although the venture in editorship may have appeared truly joint, especially in the early numbers, most of the verse can be attributed to William Irving, the Launcelot Langstaff essays to Washington Irving, and the William Wizard criticism to James Kirke Paulding; the Mustapha letters seem to be the collaborative efforts of Paulding and Washington Irving.

"Our intention," proclaimed the first number,

> is simply to instruct the young, reform the old, correct the town, and castigate the age; this is an arduous task, and therefore we undertake it with confidence. We intend for this purpose to present a striking picture of the town; and as everybody is anxious to see his own phiz on canvas, however stupid or ugly it may be, we have no doubt but the whole town will flock to our exhibition (p. 2).

Conservative in its social satire of "Gotham," Federalist in its political orientation, and good-natured in its literary parodies of competitors like *The Port Folio* and *Town*, *Salmagundi*—literally, slang for a popular hash dish consisting of pickled herring, onions, green peppers, and odds and ends—apparently found a recipe that suited the taste of New Yorkers from its first appearance in 1807. Delighted with the appetite of their audience, the editors quickly served up four numbers composed of a mixture of familiar rather than periodical essays featuring a menu of humorous eccentrics: Launcelot Langstaff, Esq., the central persona who editorialized on a wide range of topics from his "elbow-chair"; Anthony Evergreen, who reported on fashion and style in the town; William Wizard, who furnished theatrical criticism; Pindar Cockloft, whose satiric poems admonished the citizens of a degenerate age; Jeremy Cockloft, whose parodies of travel books began in Number 4; and Mustapha Rub-A-Dub Keli Khan, a Tripolitan prisoner-of-war whose letters home from his cell in New York to his *bashaw*'s slave-driver provided an outsider's view of the "grand scale" of American social, political, and military institutions. These eccentrics, together with other family members and acquaintances of the venerable Cocklofts, made up the primary characters contained in *Salmagundi*.

Cockloft Hall, the hub of literary activity, afforded a sanctuary for the *Salmagundi* personae far enough away from the vagaries of New York to offer the proper perspective. "We beg the respectable old matrons of this city not to be alarmed at the appearance we make; we are none of those outlandish geniuses who swarm in New York, who live by their wits, or rather by the little wit of their neighbors, and who spoil the genuine honest American tastes of their daughters with French slops and fricasseed sentiment" (p. 6). The editors' genuine nationalistic tone struck a responsive chord in harmony with the sentiments of Americans who desired a truly American literature. Yet in case its readers might miss the point of this literary adventure, *Salmagundi* emblazoned its credo just below the mainstaff:

> In hoc est hoax, cum quiz et jokesez,
> Et smokem, toastem, roastem folksez,
>   Fee, faw, fum.

> With baked and boiled, and stewed and toasted,
> And fried and broiled, and smoked and roasted,
>   We treat the town.

Humorous amusement was the goal of *Salmagundi*'s "laughing philosophers," and for quite some time they kept New York society amused by their anonymity; no one outside the immediate circle could with certainty identify the papers' authors. And everyone could with ease identify one or another of the satiric portraits as an acquaintance or enemy. This was all part of the intended stir *Salmagundi* caused, increased by the inclusion not only of exaggerated caricatures but also of real personages. The magazine was a success, as evidenced by the fact that in one day alone eight hundred copies of issue Number 4 were sold. Its 4" × 7" size (with two columns of text) and bright yellow cover attracted attention. In the Spring David Longworth arranged for distribution in Boston, Philadelphia, and other cities where, according to Johanna Johnston, "it was also selling well and stirring speculation."[6]

Salmagundi's fascination with the ladies of New York—who formed a substantial part of its readership—provided a fresh, brash, and decidedly contemporary appeal that accounted in no small measure for its success. The editors recommended *Salmagundi* to all mothers and all daughters; the daughter would be taught "the true line of propriety, and the most advisable method of managing their beaux," while the mothers would be "initiated into the arcana of the bon-ton." In short, "parents shall be taught how to govern their children, girls how to get husbands, and old maids how to do without them" (p. 13). It was not that the girls of Gotham were so terribly delinquent; rather,

> the ladies of New York are the fairest, the finest, the most accomplished, the most bewitching, the most ineffable beings that walk, creep, crawl, swim, fly, float, or vegetate in any or all of the four elements; and that they only want to be cured of certain whims, eccentricities, and unseemly conceits, by our superintending cares, to render them absolutely perfect (pp. 7–8).

To accomplish this, the old bachelor, Pindar Cockloft, urged them to be honestly American:

> Ah, Launce, this poor town has been wofully fash'd;
> Has long been be-Frenchman'd, be-cockney'd, be-trash'd,
> And our ladies bedevil'd, bewilder'd astray,
> From the rules of their grandames have wandered away.
> No longer that modest demeanor we meet,
> Which whilom the eyes of our fathers did greet;
> No longer be-mobbled, be-ruffled, be-quilled,
> Be-powder'd, be-hooded, be-patch'd, and be-frill'd. (p. 39)

Anthony Evergreen commented on the idiosyncrasies of fashionable dress for a morning promenade:

> If the weather be very cold, a thin muslin gown or frock is most advisable, because it agrees with the season, being perfectly cool. The neck, arms, and particularly the elbows bare, in order that they may be agreeably painted and mottled by Mr. John Frost, nose-painter-general, of the color of Castile soap. Shoes of kid, the thinnest that can possibly be procured—as they tend to promote colds, and make a lady look interesting—(*i.e., grizzly*) (p. 57).

Evergreen also reported on the comportment of characters including the fashionable Billy Dimple, Tucky Squash, and Laurella Dashaway at a grand ball he attended with William Wizard, who "thundered down the dance like a coach and six'' (p. 117). The editors were not averse to naming names to pique interest—as in the competition between the rival dressmakers Mrs.Toole and Madame Bouchard—''Mrs. Toole is the tallest, but Madame Bouchard has the longest nose'' (p. 56)—but more frequently they described merely the manners and dress of New York belles and dandies, and thereby furnished fuel for speculation and gossip among cosmopolitan society. But it was under the double disguise of Mustapha Rub-A-Dub Keli Khan that American ladies received the harshest criticism. The letters of this Tripolitan prisoner praised the beauty of feminine New Yorkers but bemoaned the fact that none were fat, that they poisoned themselves with vinegar, pickles, and tobacco to retain their ''skeleton beauty,'' that they painted themselves like Indians on the warpath, and that they considered useful duties thoroughly undignified. Nothing, however, horrified Mustapha more than the assertion that ''at least one-fifth part of them—have souls!'' (p. 50).

Mustapha has no more sympathy for the American system of government. It is, he asserts, a ''*logocracy*, or government of words'' (p. 148). ''This vast empire, therefore, may be compared to nothing more or less than a mighty windmill'' (p. 154). Elections are puppet-shows, economy is the native god worshipped falsely by all, inequality is everywhere evident, and statues are erected and dinners given immodestly to honor the living. President Jefferson is ''a very plain old gentleman'' (p. 52) in red breeches, the voting electorate is a drunken mob, and, as Launcelot Langstaff bitterly notes, in America we all too often see the most immoral man succeed in ''his slimy progress from worm to butterfly'' (p. 358). The conservative, somewhat aristocratic and Federalist bias of *Salmagundi* is clear.

Other essays sought to preserve the customs of the past, to report on the invasion of New York by hordes of Hoppingtots (dancing-masters), to chronicle travels through the countryside (''Princeton—college—professors wear boots!''), to review theater productions (which the reviewer had not seen), or to muse on the foibles of a Cockloft relative who watered and aired his children like vegetables. In all, the papers were a true salmagundi, a highly spiced hash of odds and ends.

At the height of its popularity, and owing in part to the failure of the publisher, David Longworth, to compensate its editors for their work, *Salmagundi* published its last number on 25 January 1808, commending to its readers ''the Bible and almanac, the newspaper and *Salmagundi*; which is all the reading an honest citizen has occasion for'' (p. 473). A second series of *Salmagundi*, written by Paulding alone in 1819–1820 (Philadelphia), met with little success and was quickly discontinued.

Notes

1. Frank Luther Mott, *A History of American Magazines, 1741–1850* (Cambridge, Mass.: Harvard University Press, 1938), 1: 171.

2. William Irving, James Kirke Paulding, and Washington Irving, *Salmagundi; Or, The Whimwhams and Opinions of Launcelot Langstaff, Esq.*, Printed from the Original Edition, with a Preface and Notes by Evert A. Duyckinck (New York: G. P. Putnam's Sons, 1860), p. 2. All references will be to this edition, the page numbers noted parenthetically in the text.

3. Bruce Granger, *American Essay Serials from Franklin to Irving* (Knoxville: University of Tennessee Press, 1978), p. 206.

4. Ibid., p. 203.

5. Quoted by ibid., p. 214.

6. Johanna Johnston, *The Heart That Would Not Hold: A Biography of Washington Irving* (New York: M. Evans and Co., 1971), p. 82.

Information Sources

BIBLIOGRAPHY:

Granger, Bruce. *American Essay Serials from Franklin to Irving.* Knoxville: University of Tennessee Press, 1978.

Irving, William, James Kirke Paulding, and Washington Irving. *Salmagundi; Or, The Whimwhams And Opinions Of Launcelot Langstaff, Esq.* Printed from the Original Edition, with a Preface and Notes by Evert A. Duyckinck. New York: G. P. Putnam's Sons, 1860.

Johnston, Johanna. *The Heart That Would Not Hold: A Biography of Washington Irving.* New York: M. Evans and Co., 1971.

Kribbs, Jayne K. *An Annotated Bibliography of American Literary Periodicals, 1741–1850.* Boston: G. K. Hall, 1977.

Mott, Frank Luther. "Comic Periodicals." In *A History of American Magazines; 1741–1850.* Cambridge, Mass.: Harvard University Press, 1938, 1:170–72.

INDEX SOURCES: Titles listed in Table of Contents in bound volumes: in 1835, "a new edition, corrected by the authors," was published in New York by Harper and Brothers; this was followed by the Duycknick edition in 1860; in 1871 J. B. Lippincott and Company printed a new edition in Philadelphia; and the most recent edition is that by Bruce I. Granger and Martha Hartzog for Twayne in 1977.

REPRINT EDITIONS: The first series is readily available in a modern edition edited by Bruce I. Granger and Martha Hartzog (Boston: Twayne, 1977). University Microfilms offers both series.

LOCATION SOURCES: Nine libraries list holdings for the first series: CtY, DeWI, IU, MBat, MH, NN, OCLW, OClWHi, and PPHi; three list the second series: MH, CtHW, and PPHi.

Publication History

MAGAZINE TITLE AND TITLE CHANGES: *Salmagundi; Or, The Whimwhams And Opinions Of Launcelot Langstaff, Esq., And Others.* First Series: 24 January 1807–24 January 1808; Second Series ("By Launcelot Langstaff"): 30 May 1819–19 August 1820.

VOLUME AND ISSUE DATA: First Series, irregular. Nineteen numbers were published in 1807 as follows: 24 January; 4, 13, 24 February; 7, 20 March; 4, 18, 25 April; 16 May; 2, 27 June; 14 August; 16 September; 1, 15 October; 11, 24 November;

31 December. One number appeared on 25 January 1808. Second Series, semi-
monthly.
PUBLISHER AND PLACE OF PUBLICATION: First Series: David Longworth, New
York. Second Series: Haly and Thomas, New York.
EDITORS: First Series: Washington Irving, William Irving, and James Kirke Paulding.
Second Series: James Kirke Paulding.
CIRCULATION: Unknown, although Johanna Johnston's note that Number 4 sold eight
hundred copies in one day suggests a sizable printing. That David Longworth
arranged for distribution to cities other than New York also indicates a fairly wide
circulation.

William E. Lenz

SATIRE NEWSLETTER

The breakthrough in academic satire criticism in the 1950s and early 1960s with
the publication of studies by Maynard Mack, Ellen Leyburn, Alvin Kernan,
Robert Elliott, Gilbert Highet, and Leonard Feinberg, among others, was
paralleled by an eruption in satire in literature and popular culture (Lenny Bruce,
Catch-22, Robert Crumb, *That Was the Week That Was*, *Dr. Strangelove*, Second
City, *Monocle*,* et alia). Founded in 1963, *Satire Newsletter* became what one
critic called the "official" journal of the art and another called "curious."[1] It
was called curious because it published not only the standard fare of scholarly
journals but also satire itself, thereby becoming an anomaly, a scholarly "little"
magazine. Conceived as a newsletter, the first issue blossomed to thirty-two
pages, and subsequent issues in its ten-year existence went to more than a hundred
pages per issue. Even though it quickly became a full-fledged journal, the original
title was retained, thereby underscoring its atypical nature.

Satire Newsletter served the academic community by publishing articles,
reviews, bibliographies, and several symposia. In addition, it published satiric
sketches, short fiction, and poetry. Loy Otis Banks, Sam Elkin, Charles Clerc,
Charles Genthe, Eleanor Hyde, Alice Wooledge Salmon, and Ken Lawless were
among the short fiction writers published. Poets included David Axelrod, David
Cornel DeJong, Charles Edward Eaton, Norma Farber, Ernest Kroll, Jack
McManis, Robert Mezey, Paul Selver, William Stafford, Lewis Turco, and
David Young. Translations of works by Karl Kraus and Ivan Krylov appeared
for the first time. Articles on satire in Eastern Europe, Chile, *The Realist*,* Black
American literature, American popular culture, and on satirists in Germany,
France, Russia, and classical literature made the contents unusually diverse. The
covers occasionally contained reproductions of graphic satire by George Grosz,
James Gillray, J. J. Grandeville, and Honore Daumier. Illustrations, cartoons
and reproductions of photographs sometimes accompanied articles. The covers
of early issues contained a drawing of an upright human-like figure with a whip
in one hand and a leering mask in the other. The figure had horns, donkey ears,
wings, a fish tail, and dog-like legs that terminated in a hoof on one leg and a

webbed foot on another. The illustration was adapted by George Zimmerman from a medieval drawing and served as the logo for the journal.

Satire Newsletter was discontinued in 1973 as a result of sharp increases in printing costs and losses of subscribers owing to inflation and institutional budget cutbacks.

Note

1. Frederick Kiley and J. M. Shuttleworth, eds., *Satire from Aesop to Buchwald* (New York: Odyssey Press, 1971), p. 484; "Literary Periodicals," *London Times Literary Supplement* (25 March 1965): 239.

Information Sources

INDEX SOURCES: Bibliography, Volumes 1–9, 1963–1973. *Satire Newsletter* 10 Supplement (Spring 1973): 1–33.
REPRINT EDITIONS: Kraus, Volumes 1–5 only (1974).
LOCATION SOURCES: DLC, MnU, NN, CtY, PSC, WaU, and NOneoU are among 103 libraries listing holdings.

Publication History

MAGAZINE TITLE AND TITLE CHANGES: *Satire Newsletter*, Fall 1963-Spring 1973.
VOLUME AND ISSUE DATA: Semi-annual. Volume 1:1 (Fall 1963)–Volume 10:2 (Spring 1973).
PUBLISHER AND PLACE OF PUBLICATION: George Test, Oneonta, New York.
EDITOR: George Test; Poetry Editor: Richard Frost; Assistant Editor: Evelyn Duncan.
CIRCULATION: 280 (December 1964), 523 (January 1971).

George A. Test

THE SATIRIST

The first issue of Albany's *Satirist*, published in 1842, announced its opposition to "the ignorant pretender, the empiric in literature and science." The longest piece in this issue, a tale entitled "My First Party," inaugurated a satirical series to be called "The Sketcher." The tale dealt with a novice in party-going, a young man "not matrimonially inclined," singularly devoting his energies to his "single self." Incorporating swipes at the artificialities of aristocratic entertainments and allusions to the controversy attending the publication of James Fenimore Cooper's *Home as Found*, the sketch contained characteristics of the comic "bachelor tales" that pervaded nineteenth-century periodicals.

Too short-lived to have acquired a distinctive character, *The Satirist*, priced at $2.50 per year, carried topical humor understandable in the local context of rival newspapers. "The Mystic Nook," a satiric miscellany compiled by LeSage, Horace, and Juvenal, aimed to provoke "a hearty laugh at the fallacies of mankind" and "a tear, over their misfortunes." Targets of the column included Thurlow Weed, editor of the competing Whig paper, *The Albany Journal*. Cooper had sued Weed for libel the previous year, his letter of protest appearing in the

4 December 1841, *Albany Argus*, the competing Democratic publication. Apparently in response to this series of suits, *The Satirist* published "Reputation," a solemnly didactic examination of that fragile commodity so recently damaged in the public press. The public appetite for Charles Dickens having been sharpened by installments of *American Notes* and *Barnaby Rudge* in the *Argus*, a poetic "Address to Boz" in *The Satirist* aimed to exploit interest in the British author's upcoming American visit. "The Reform," a comic poem written in response to the *Albany Chronicle*'s apparently incongruous connection between Irish immigrants and the temperance movement, presented a befuddled Devil who could no longer count on the "sons of the Emerald Isle" to join his drinking escapades. The remainder of this quarto-sized satirical miscellany included barbs at the expense of chronic complainers, an exposé of fashionable charity, and a parody of Thomas Campbell's poetry. Diverse in its treatment of literary and political subjects, *The Satirist* apparently did not find a sufficient audience for its forays into high comedy.

Information Sources

INDEX SOURCES: None.
REPRINT EDITIONS: University Microfilms.
LOCATION SOURCES: MB.

Publication History

MAGAZINE TITLE AND TITLE CHANGES: *The Satirist: A Journal of Criticism, Literature and Fine Arts*, 5 February 1842.
VOLUME AND ISSUE DATA: Weekly; Volume 1:1, 5 February 1842.
PUBLISHER AND PLACE OF PUBLICATION: J. Smith and Co., Albany, New York.
EDITORS: "The Mystic Three" (identities unknown).
CIRCULATION: Unknown.

Kent P. Ljungquist

THE SCOURGE (Baltimore)

Published in Baltimore in 1810, *The Scourge* was a journal of social and political commentary that also printed news items and advertisements. Because issues 2 through 20 and issue 26 are the only surviving numbers, the journal's dates of initial and terminal publication are uncertain, but 26 May 1810 is the most likely date of origin, and 24 November 1810 is the last known date of appearance. Edited by the pseudonymous "Titus Tickler," *The Scourge* addressed a broad range of local and national concerns from the pitching of pennies in municipal parks to the sale and ownership of slaves. In articles that varied in length from a few lines to several columns and in tone from the lightly humorous to the righteously indignant, it inveighed against vice and the abuse of human freedom. The journal's "Prospectus" promised that it would never contain any matter that might "cause a blush on the cheek of female innocence and chastity," but it made "no pledge" that the journal would "be free from *all* personalities" since "the *principal* object of the Journal" was "to exhibit the *animal*, Man, in his simple, native attire, divested of the cob-web-covering which pride of office, or the significance of wealth may weave to obscure his deformities." Consistent with this statement of high moral purpose was the journal's motto, "Be just—fear not."

Through various reminders of America's recent revolutionary past, *The Scourge* laid claim to being a patriotic guardian of American principles. Incompatible with those principles and with America's potential greatness were such abominations as the continuation of the slave trade, the interference of France and England with American shipping, and the extortionate abuse of power by certain public officials. *The Scourge* dealt with these matters in articles characterized by an inflexible outrage. Less wrathful and more lightly sardonic were *The Scourge*'s various treatments of such threats to America's moral strength as gambling, drunkenness, and vandalism. In a punning comment on card-playing, for example, one writer speculated that "the inventor of Cards had a moral lesson in view.—Let us suppose he reasoned thus to himself. 'The man who has the HEART, (that is the spirit) to play for DIAMONDS, (that is money) may get into a *quarrel*, which may produce CLUBS, which may occasion the necessity of bringing SPADES, to dig a *grave* for his *carcase*.' "

The Scourge's moralizing does not inspire belly laughs, but shows an ongoing interest in wordplay. Puns were the source of humor, too, in various nonsatiric filler paragraphs scattered among the journal's pages. When one considers its dedication to human dignity, however, *The Scourge*'s most startling attempts at the comic were its occasional inclusions of crude ethnic humor. Parodies of Black and German dialect appeared among the letters-to-the-editor, and a poem entitled "The Jew," printed in the journal's second issue, ended with the title character attempting to turn a profit by buying the clothes of an executed Christian.

Each number of *The Scourge*, presented in a four-column newspaper format, consisted of four pages. Single issues sold for twelve cents, and annual subscriptions were four dollars. The only individual whose association with *The Scourge* has been established with certainty is its publisher, Samuel Magill.

Information Sources

BIBLIOGRAPHY:
Edgar, Neal L. "Scourge." *A History and Bibliography of American Magazines 1810–1820*. Metuchen, N.J.: Scarecrow Press, 1975, pp. 233–34.
Mott, Frank Luther. *A History of American Magazines, 1741–1850*. Cambridge, Mass.: Harvard University Press, 1957.
INDEX SOURCES: None.
REPRINT EDITIONS: Maryland Historical Society Assorted Maryland Newspapers Series, Reel 7.
LOCATION SOURCES: Maryland Historical Society.

Publication History

MAGAZINE TITLE AND TITLE CHANGES: *The Scourge*.
VOLUME AND ISSUE DATA: Weekly (except biweekly between issue 13, 18 August
    1810, and issue 14, 1 September 1810), twenty-six issues per volume?, for Volume
    1 (ca. 26 May 1810–ca. 24 November 1810).
PUBLISHER AND PLACE OF PUBLICATION: Samuel Magill, Baltimore.
EDITOR: "Titus Tickler" (pseudonym).
CIRCULATION: Unknown.

Robert H. O'Connor

THE SCOURGE (Boston)

The Scourge was a satiric political journal published in Boston from 10 August
to 28 December 1811. Its editor, Merrill Butler, who used the pseudonym "Tim
Touchstone," attacked Democratic-Republican policies with such reckless zeal
that he was eventually jailed for libel. The rancorous, self-righteous spirit of the
journal is suggested by its masthead, which showed "Public Justice" whipping
a figure labeled "Vice" and "Scurality," and by its motto, "Weak men demand
our pity—bad men deserve our stripes."

In the journal's first issue, Butler stated that

> The political situation of this countrye and of this commonwealth in particular;—
> the conduct of our national and state rulers; and the lies and intrigues of our leading
> democrats—will form the principal subjects of the Scourge—and, as with energy
> was observed by a celebrated writer, 'What I know to be true, that will I declare';—
> and what I feel to be my duty to represent, that will I have the boldness to publish.

The combative nature of Butler's enterprise is further indicated by his statement,
again in the first issue, that

> Democracy opens a wide field for Satire; yet the Editor of the Scourge feels it will
> be a Herculean task to touch her sensibilities so to the quick, as to make her either
> blush with shame, or retract her errors. The attempt, however, shall be made.—
> The ganntlet [*sic*] of defiance has been thrown at us;—we take it up, and declare,
> that we shall neither ASK, RECEIVE, NOR GIVE QUARTER.

Much of the satire of *The Scourge* was directed against those governmental
policies which the editor saw as pro-French and anti-British. *The Scourge*
abounded in references to the Napoleonic peril and to the viciousness of those
who favored war with England. In the seventh issue, for example, a letter was
printed in which an imaginary "Tom W—," the stereotypic pro-war buffoon,
wrote, "Ef Congris dont ackt like a pac of dam fules, as tha hav dun for fore
or five ears back, thale dicklare wor against Grate Brittun, and then mi frend
we shal hav the plesher I trust of klippin off a fue of the dam tory heds. But
moer of this bime bi." There are promising anticipations of later dialect political
satire in the preceding, but most of the writing in *The Scourge* failed to rise

above the level of personal vituperation. A poem in one issue attacked President James Madison and former Secretary of State Robert Smith as, respectively, a *"Rogue"* and a *"Fool"*; another poem in this issue listed Massachusetts Governor Elbridge Gerry's accomplishments as "Raving, swearing, singing, praying, / Whistling, jumping, sitting, braying, / Laughing, crying, walking, creeping, / Smiling now, and now fast weeping"; a prose passage accused Jefferson of having "paid Callender for defaming Washington" and having "attempted the chastity of his friend's wife." Such items are interesting as radical Federalist political propaganda, but they lack power as satiric literature.

The Scourge was presented in a newspaper format consisting of four pages of three columns each. Individual pages measured 10½" × 18", and each issue concluded with a column or so of advertising. A few issues, sold at ten cents and later at twelve and a half cents a copy, contained primitive political cartoons, but most were not illustrated, except in the masthead. Although references in *The Scourge* itself indicate that Butler was publisher in addition to being editor, Mott (p. 170) calls James L. Edwards publisher, and Jayne K. Kribbs (p. 153) follows his lead. With the jailing of Butler for publishing libelous remarks about Governor Gerry, Aaron Hill, Benjamin Austin, and William P. Whiting, *The Scourge* was able to survive through only two more issues.

Information Sources

BIBLIOGRAPHY:Edgar, Neal L. "Scourge." *A History and Bibliography of American Magazines 1810–1820*. Metuchen, N.J.: Scarecrow Press, 1975, p. 234.

Kribbs, Jayne K. Entry No. 775. *An Annotated Bibliography of American Literary Periodicals, 1741–1850*. Boston: G. K. Hall, 1977, p. 153.

Mott, Frank Luther. *A History of American Magazines, 1741–1850*. Cambridge, Mass.: Harvard University Press, 1957.

INDEX SOURCES: None.

REPRINT EDITIONS: University Microfilms.

LOCATION SOURCES: MWA; scattered issues elsewhere.

Publication History

MAGAZINE TITLE AND TITLE CHANGES: *The Scourge*.

VOLUME AND ISSUE DATA: Irregular (every six to seventeen days), sixteen issues per volume, for Volume 1, 10 August 1811–28 December 1811.

PUBLISHER AND PLACE OF PUBLICATION: Merrill Butler (or James L. Edwards?), Boston.

EDITOR: Merrill Butler (pseudonym, "Tim Touchstone").

CIRCULATION: Unknown.

Robert H. O'Connor

THE SMART SET

The Smart Set first appeared in 1900 as a clever magazine for snobs. It succeeded for a few years as the literary snack of the Knickerbocker leisure class. Then its flavor sharpened, corrupted but never entirely dominated by young editors who believed that the best way to survive fundamentalism, racism, politics,

Prohibition, and other twentieth-century inanities was to laugh at them. The change made for an uneven periodical, with works by H. L. Mencken, George J. Nathan, James Joyce, F. Scott Fitzgerald, Ezra Pound, Theodore Dreiser, and other major figures smothered amid a variety of slight novelettes, short stories featuring surprise endings, and shopping columns seriously describing the novelties "smart" people were buying in New York. Unable to grow and prosper through a quarter-century of publication, the magazine merely mutated, evolving into a self-contradictory product that was eventually abandoned by readers, contributors—and even its own editors.

During its first decade (1900–1911), *The Smart Set* was very much a publisher's magazine. The colorful owner, Colonel William D'Alton Mann, left day-to-day editorial matters largely to his employees. But his narrow conceptual ability and tight budget limited what the staff could do. The architect of a weekly New York gossip sheet called *Tales from Town Topics*,* Mann visualized his new venture as an arty collection of stories, verse, and other light items from wealthy contributors whose high social standing would guarantee readership regardless of their literary abilities. In contrast to the prevailing seriousness of other contemporary periodicals, the entry from the "Ess Ess Publishing Company" was saucy and irreverent, a "Magazine of Cleverness" that offered entertainment without moral baggage. Contributors to early issues included Prince Albert of Monaco, the Infanta Eulalie, and a Mrs. S. Van Rensselaer Cruger.

But editor Arthur Grissom encountered a flaw in the Colonel's founding philosophy: the rich did not write nearly enough to fill a monthly magazine. To answer the demand for manuscripts, he solicited work from professional and unknown writers as well as the blue-bloods, running contests for contributions while the magazine became established. Pseudonyms became a regular feature, masking multiple submissions from authors who successfully mastered the sunny *Smart Set* style. While the high society accent remained, the pages were filled out with work by underpaid beginners who were willing to take a penny a word for fiction and twenty-five cents a line for poetry. According to F. L. Mott, some of the magazine's favorite subjects during this period included social intrigue, love without marriage, and irony at the expense of conventions.

A typical issue sold for twenty-five cents and contained 160 pages of editorial matter, beginning with a novelette and including a play, a dozen short stories (one in French), as many poems, or perhaps an essay, with vignettes, epigrams, and short jokes used to fill the bare spots. The cover featured the oversized "S's" of the title as the habitat of a mischievous Pan, who seemed to have control over the subjects illustrated below—often a fashionably dressed couple. The paper was notoriously bad. But the fiction printed on it included work by O. Henry, Jack London, James Branch Cabell, Ambrose Bierce, and Max Pemberton. The humor of Mann's era showcased R. K. Munkittrick, Sewell Ford, John Kendrick Bangs, Carolyn Wells, Tom P. Morgan, and Alfred Damon Runyon ridiculing the "new woman," lampooning society matters, and grimacing over the crude customs of country bumpkins.

Initially, it all worked. The Colonel celebrated a circulation of 100,000 during his first year and 165,000 by 1905. But his magazine represented a revolving door for editors. When Grissom died in 1901, Marvin Dana took over. In 1904, Dana gave way to Charles Hanson Towne. Towne quit in 1907, to be replaced by young Fred Splint. A year later, Splint was gone, and Norman Boyer stepped aboard. Colonel Mann remained in command while his editorial troops shuttled in and out, keeping a firm hand on the purse strings and generally doing more harm than good. During 1905–1906, he lost a scandalous and well-publicized defamation suit that seriously tarnished his magazine's image. Suddenly, *The Smart Set* was no longer considered "smart." It lost 25,000 readers in 1906, and, as circulation continued to fall, it began to acquire an aroma of thinly veiled pornography. Before resigning in 1907, Towne complained that the magazine had become a "literary Grand Central Station," losing its best writers to *Ainslee's* and other higher paying competitors.

In an effort to imitate a popular feature appearing in *Ainslee's*, the Colonel authorized his current editor to engage a writer capable of contributing a monthly book column. Fred Splint retained someone who, a few years earlier, had unsuccessfully offered poetry to *The Smart Set*, a Baltimore newspaperman named Henry Lewis Mencken. "Write what you damn well please," Splint advised, "as long as it's lively and gets attention." Armed with a high school education, an appetite for books, and a knack for creative phrase-making, Mencken contributed the first of his 182 *Smart Set* book reviews in November 1908. During a visit to New York the following May, he met the magazine's new drama critic, George Jean Nathan. Retiring to a nearby tavern, the columnists quickly agreed that their new employers were fools, but that they could have some fun in spite of the management.

The reviews of Mencken and Nathan failed to reverse the magazine's fortunes. Sales remained sickly, and in 1911 Mann sold out to John Adams Thayer, the gullible co-owner of *Everybody's Magazine*. Thayer took an active interest in *The Smart Set*, devising a new but short-lived credo ("Its Prime Purpose is to Provide Lively Entertainment for Minds That are not Primitive") and chipping in his own monthly column. Advertising surged dramatically, but readership did not. Flaccid editorial leadership inspired Mencken to call the book "a pallid imitation of Smith's *(Ainslee's)* magazine."

Thayer needed a stronger editor; he found one who was titanic. Willard Huntington Wright, an aggressive young Mencken-admirer, accepted the job in 1913 only after his new boss agreed to pay him twice the salary of his predecessor and to stay entirely out of editorial matters. Wright was fired within a year. But during his brief tenure he turned *The Smart Set* into what Burton Rascoe called the "best edited and best remembered of any magazine ever published on this continent" (pp. xxii-xxxiii). Modeling his product after Ford Madox Ford's *English Review*, Wright sought realistic stories from writers who denounced middle-class values and emphasized sexual freedom. He discarded the old penny-a-word policy and soon had Ezra Pound scouring Europe for work by D. H.

Lawrence, Joseph Conrad, Frank Harris, and W. B. Yeats. American contributors included Achmed Abdullah, Floyd Dell, Louis Untermeyer, and Robinson Jeffers. Intent on publishing daring material shunned by other magazines, he even collaborated with Mencken and Nathan on a dummy issue of a satirical weekly to be called *The Blue Review*.

Thayer found all this troubling. The cost alarmed him. When Wright's expensive tastes failed to improve circulation and advertisers began complaining about the magazine's Bohemian flavor, Thayer wasted no time firing the young editor. In his column of March 1914, he apologized for Wright's work, acknowledging that the magazine had become "too serious" about literature. Disturbed by the turn of events, Mencken complained to a friend that *The Smart Set* had become "as righteous as a decrepit and converted madame."

Wright departed, eventually returning to the literary scene as "S. S. Van Dine," author of the Philo Vance detective stories. But his spirit continued to thrive at the magazine, embodied in Mencken and Nathan. They watched with enthusiasm when the stock market slump that accompanied the outbreak of World War I ruined Thayer, forcing him virtually to give *The Smart Set* away to settle a debt with his paper supplier. The new owner, Eugene F. Crowe, engaged Eltinge F. Warner to run the magazine. A businessman with no editorial interests, Warner asked Nathan to edit. Nathan agreed, with the condition that Mencken be appointed co-editor, and the three men settled into a regular, long-distance routine. All Warner did was handle the money. Nathan presided over the New York editorial office, with Mencken, headquartered in Baltimore, acting as first reader and primary rejector of manuscripts. As remuneration, the editors shared one-third of the "profits" plus $100 per month for their columns and a reinstituted cent-a-word for pieces they published under assumed names. These were numerous: M. K. Singleton attributes more than ten items with various by-lines in the November 1914 issue to Mencken alone.

The new editors had little effect on the magazine's basic fare: short stories, a scattering of poems, a few articles, a novelette, a play. The tradition of introducing a few great writers continued, but most of the material came from unknowns and old-line *Smart Set* regulars such as Thyra Samter Winslow.

The most important change from the Mann decade involved a surge in the quality and quantity of *Smart Set* humor. Funny nonfiction appeared more often, fashioned after Wright's satirical "Los Angeles, the Chemically Pure" (March 1913). John Macy described "Blue Boston," and Lewis Sherwin sermonized with tongue in cheek about "The Morals of Mormons." In "Threnody upon a Decadent Art," Joseph Wood Krutch mourned the decline of the once glorious act of suicide. John Macy, in "Rum, Reading, and Rebellion," complained that he found reading impossible under Prohibition and looked forward to the day when he could "go to Paris or Florence or Munich and sit in a cafe next door to a bookstall and read and read and drink and drink and drink."

More of the short stories leaned toward satire. Donald Ogden Stewart, Sinclair Lewis, Ben Hecht, Ruth Suckow, Carl Van Doren, and others ridiculed romantic love, marriage, small-town life, academia, and "success." Fillers used to finish off partial pages offered epigrams, witty definitions, and twisted clichés skewering the same subjects.

Many of these short items were created by the magazine's most prolific humorists, its editors. According to Carl R. Dolmetsch, readers often opened the magazine to the back, "as if it were written in Hebrew or Chinese," to begin "with the cricital essays of Mencken (the last item) or Nathan (next to last)." Dolmetsch aptly describes Nathan's writing as "one long gasp of exasperation at the inadequacies of American drama" (p. 55). A destructive critic, he was especially fond of dismissing a poor production with a single, coined word. "Flapdoodle" or "pish-posh" was sometimes all he needed to say. Mencken, on the other hand, liked to bury pretension and bad writing beneath piles of insulting invective. A slashing writer whose foremost aim was to be amusing, he had great fun at the expense of "The Poets That Bloom in the Spring, Tra-La!" and humbled respected authors simply by subjecting them to a series of horse-laughs.

In addition to their monthly column, Mencken and Nathan wrote many contributions run under the by-line of "Major Owen Hatteras," a sarcastic, collaborated persona who feasted on folly and hypocrisy. "Americana," a series attributed to Hatteras beginning in 1923, consisted entirely of short items, reprinted from newspapers and other sources, illustrating various absurdities of the American scene.

In 1919, the editors inaugurated a regular satirical review entitled "Repetition Generale," in which they tossed "elegant 3½" × 4¾" custard pies at figures guilty of asinine public pronouncements and actions. A 1923 series promoted Mencken and Nathan as candidates for the presidency and vice-presidency of the United States, describing a platform that included changing the face of the Goddess of Liberty as it appeared on coinage to look "less like a senescent school-marm and more like a cutie."

As *Smart Set* humor developed, so did the editors' discontent with the limitations of their magazine. Its two-layered format—stinging satire cushioned within a framework of forgettable short stories—failed to capture many readers (23,000 in 1923) and left the editors looking for a better outlet.

In January 1924, they resigned, using Wright's *Blue Review* as inspiration for *The American Mercury*, a new magazine financed by Alfred Knopf. Knopf had first tried to buy *The Smart Set*, but it was sold instead to William Randolph Hearst. Trumpeting "True Stories from Real Life" without intellectual encumbrances, it enjoyed popular success during the late twenties. In 1929 it combined with *McClure's* in an attempt to invigorate that ailing enterprise. *The New Smart Set* fell, a victim of the Depression, in 1930.

Information Sources

BIBLIOGRAPHY:
Dolmetsch, Carl R. *The Smart Set*. New York: Dial Press, 1966.
Forgue, Guy J., ed. *Letters of H. L. Mencken*. New York: Alfred A. Knopf, 1961.

Logan, Andy. *The Man Who Robbed the Robber Barons*. New York: W. W. Norton, 1965.

Mott, Frank L. *A History of American Magazines*. Cambridge, Mass.: Harvard University Press, 1968, 5:246–272.

Nolte, William H. *H. L. Mencken's Smart Set Criticism*. Ithaca, N.Y.: Cornell University Press, 1968.

Rascoe, Burton. "Smart Set History." In *The Smart Set Anthology*. New York: Reynal and Hitchcock, 1934.

Singleton, M. K. *H. L. Mencken and the American Mercury Adventure*. Durham, N.C.: Duke University Press, 1962.

INDEX SOURCES: None.

REPRINT EDITIONS: University Microfilms.

LOCATION SOURCES: A total of twenty-four libraries list holdings. Complete holdings only at NjP. Other extensive collections are at CU, DLC, IC, MdBE, and MoK.

Publication History

MAGAZINE TITLE AND TITLE CHANGES: *The Smart Set*, March 1900-March 1930; *The New Smart Set*, April-July 1930.

VOLUME AND ISSUE DATA: Monthly. Volume 1, March-June 1900; Volume 2, July-December 1900; Volumes 3–74, January 1901-August 1924, 4 Numbers per volume (56–57 have irregular numbering: September 1918 called Volume 56:1; October-December called Volume 57:2–4); Volumes 75–85, September 1924-February 1930, 6 numbers per volume; Volume 86, March-July 1930.

PUBLISHER AND PLACE OF PUBLICATION: 1900–1911: Ess Ess Publishing Co. (William D'Alton Mann, owner), New York. 1911–1914: John Adams Thayer Corp., New York. 1914–1924: Smart Set Co. (Eugene F. Crowe, Eltinge F. Warner, George Jean Nathan, Henry Louis Mencken, owners), New York. 1924–1930: Magus Magazine Corp. (William Randolph Hearst, owner), New York.

EDITORS: Arthur Grissom, 1900–1901; Marvin Dana, 1902–1904; Charles Hanson Towne, 1904–1907, Fred C. Splint, 1907–1908; Norman Boyer, 1909–1911; Mark Lee Luther, 1911–1912; Willard Huntington Wright, 1913–1914; George Jean Nathan and Henry Louis Mencken, 1914–1923; Morris Gilbert, 1924; F. Orlin Tremaine, 1924–1925; William Charles Lengel, 1925–1928; T. Howard Kelly, 1928–1929; Margaret Elizabeth Sangster, 1929–1930.

CIRCULATION: 165,000 in 1905. Gradually declined to 23,000 in 1923 Grew to 385,000 after sale to Hearst enterprise in 1924.

Stuart A. Kollar

SOUTH CAROLINIAN

Although the Columbia *South Carolinian* ran for two decades beginning in 1838, only the four years 1845–1848 are significant to the history of American comic periodicals. These issues were edited by Adam Geiselhart Summer (1818–1866), who delighted in rough-and-tumble backwoods humor, wrote yarns, and encouraged other writers. The *South Carolinian* contains a large number of original humorous stories and sketches written by Summer and a dozen able friends in upcountry South Carolina, many republished in periodicals across the country, most notably William T. Porter's *Spirit of the Times*.* The *Spirit* reprinted at least two of Summer's own tales, and the *Carolinian* in turn reprinted yarns from the *Spirit*, sometimes "rewritten" by their Carolina authors for the *Carolinian*. The paper had close ties to the *New Orleans Picayune*** and *Delta*, the *Western Continent* (edited by William Tappan Thompson, Summer's friend), and the *St. Louis Reveille*.* In his four-year span as editor, Summer reprinted works by Johnson Jones Hooper, Sol Smith, T. B. Thorpe, John S. Robb, and William Tappan Thompson.

Summer's first issue as editor was 6 February 1845. At this time, the paper was a weekly during all but the state legislative sessions (October-December), at which time it became a semi-weekly. On 25 January 1848 it became a semi-weekly year round. In Summer's first numbers, he was half-owner. For a short period (10 March to 5 May 1847), he sold his half-interest and went home to supervise his farm; but on 12 May 1847 he became the only editor until ending his involvement with the issue of 29 December 1848. Neither the editor who preceded Summer nor the editors who followed him published humor, thus attesting to Summer's key role. The paper's format in 1845 was seven four-column pages measuring 19½" × 24½". The issue of 14 January 1848 changed to six columns measuring 17" × 23", reflecting the new semi-weekly status. The paper cost three dollars—as Summer says, "the cheapest paper in the Southern country." The *Carolinian*'s scope was intended to be sectional and to appeal to planters, but original material was contributed by Northerners and Europeans, including Summer's friends and relatives abroad.

Summer was a successful planter, lawyer, legislator, and avid reader, and the newspaper's objectives reflect its editor's interests, as well as the enthusiasms of the gentleman planter of his day. "Republican and independent," strictly Southern in character, and promoting the "prosperity of the South," the journal was edited according to Summer's "Text Book" of "Free Trade, Low Duties, No Debt, and a Strict Adherence to the Constitution." Summer's aims were to "instruct, amuse, and edify." Agricultural columns accompanied essays on judicial reform. Since it was the official paper of record for the state, it published the proceedings of the Legislature. Literature was not slighted; Summer wrote that he would "give such an amount of Literary matter as will make it an entertaining family visitor," including the comic yarn and genteel fiction, but with a decided predisposition toward the comic.

Through his local literary connections, Summer was able to amass many original fictional sketches and dialect tales. O. B. Mayer, a friend since childhood, was to publish his first backwoods tales there, beginning a career of some importance in the genre. "Nat Slocum" of Spartanburg District, a contributor to Porter's famous anthologies and the *Spirit*, provided original humorous sketches. So did "Pea Ridger" and "Phil Gilder," both contributors to the *Spirit*. One of the most skillful writers, "C.H.B.," a typesetter born in East Tennessee, did a series of comic mountain yarns set at quiltings, weddings, and corn-shuckings. This rustic talent wandered the South setting type, and

Summer reports his setting up his stories directly without writing first, jumping about illustrating by his actions the scenes he was setting. Summer reported that the "spiciest of the Western papers" were reprinting his stories from the *Carolinian*. Original pieces by "Some Punkins, Esq.," "Capting Luke Snuzeby," and Summer's own pseudonym "Vesper Brackett" were numerous. There were also unsigned original pieces such as "Smith, the Razor Strop Man," a good character sketch in the vein of Harden E. Taliaferro's famous "Ham Rachel."

The *Carolinian*'s pages also reprinted backwoods greats like Major Jones, Simon Suggs, John Robb, Sol Smith, and T. B. Thorpe. These were added to the original stories and a "Pickings and Pilings" column of humorous anecdotes. This was the humor which upcountry planters knew and enjoyed. The planters returned their own humorous sketches from Spartanburg, Newberry, Lexington, and Greenville, thus suggesting the paper's primary sphere of circulation in north and central regions of the state.

According to O. B. Mayer, Summer was a "rustic humorist who could hold his own with the roughest joker." He reluctantly gave over his position as editor, which he evidently enjoyed and despite knowing the ever increasing value of the journalist as powerful shaper of the course of affairs. He held an exalted and highly professional view of journalism, but the scrupulousness with which he adhered to his principles exhausted him at the height of his paper's popularity. With the issue of 29 December 1848, he gave up his editorship "to seek the quiet of rural retirement," and at the age of thirty-one he removed to his plantation "Ravenscroft" in present-day Newberry County, South Carolina.

Information Sources

BIBLIOGRAPHY:

Kibler, James E., ed. *Fireside Tales: Stories of the Old Dutch Fork*. Columbia, S.C.: Dutch Fork Press, 1984. Contains humorous stories by A. G. Summer and other authors originally published in the *South Carolinian*, 1846–1848.

————. "O. B. Mayer." *Dictionary of Literary Biography*. Detroit: Gale Record Research, 1979, 3: 213–217.

Mayer, O. B. *The Dutch Fork*. Columbia, S.C.: Dutch Fork Press, 1982.

————. *John Punterick: A Novel of Life in the Old Dutch Fork*. Spartanburg, S.C.: Reprint Co., 1981.

Meats, Stephen. "South Carolina Writers in the *Spirit of the Times*." In *Gyascutus: Studies in Antebellum Southern Humorists and Sporting Writers*. Atlantic Highlands, N.J.: Humanities Press, 1979, pp. 185–207.

INDEX SOURCES: None.

REPRINT EDITIONS: None.

LOCATION SOURCES: ScU and DLC have the known copies.

Publication History

MAGAZINE TITLE AND TITLE CHANGES: *South Carolinian*, 6 February 1845–29 December 1848.

VOLUME AND ISSUE DATA: Weekly, but semi-weekly during South Carolina State

Legislature sessions. With the 25 January 1848 issue (Vol. 10:4), permanently a semi-weekly.

PUBLISHERS AND PLACE OF PUBLICATION: 6 February 1845 (Vol. 7:23)–3 March 1847 (Vol. 9:39): A. G. Summer and B. R. Carroll, Columbia. 10 March–5 May 1847 (Vol. 9:40–48): B. R. Carroll, Columbia. 12 May 1847 (Vol. 9:49)–29 September 1848 (Vol. 10:74): A. G. Summer, Columbia. 3 October 1848 (Vol. 10:75)–29 December 1848 (Vol. 10:99): A. G. Summer and A. T. Cavis; Number 2 Main Street, Centre Range, Columbia.

EDITORS: A. G. Summer and B. R. Carroll, 6 February 1845 (Vol. 7:23)–3 March 1847 (Vol. 9:39); B. R. Carroll, 10 March–5 May 1847 (Vol. 9:40–48); A. G. Summer, 12 May 1847 (Vol. 9:49)–29 December 1848 (Vol. 10:99).

CIRCULATION: Unknown. The paper of record of the State of South Carolina. Extensive reprinting of selected items through "Exchange" was characteristic of its circulation.

James E. Kibler, Jr.

SOUTHERN PUNCH

Founded in Richmond, Virginia, on 15 August 1863, by John W. Overall, formerly of the New Orleans *Delta*, *Southern Punch* became the most popular humorous magazine of the Confederacy. Modeled after (London) *Punch*, *Southern Punch* was established at the most inauspicious time for the launchng a new literary venture. Cut off by the Civil War from the North and from Europe and from the supply of books and periodicals, which had heretofore been readily accessible, the South necessarily had to declare its literary independence, attempting in the process to uplift the morale and to awaken the sensibilities of a predominantly Southern readership for Southern literature. Overall, *Punch*'s first and, for most of its run, only editor and chief contributor, used the magazine as an organ for entertainment, for disseminating Confederate propaganda, and for castigating some of the more controversial social, political, and economic concerns affecting the war-ravaged Confederacy.

In his Salutatory, written for the maiden issue. Overall explained *Punch*'s sectional scope and editorial philosophy:

Our *Punch* is a genuine Confederate. . . . In a word, the young Punch is a Southron. He can be serious . . . when indulging his passion for polite literature; satirical, as the humbugs of his age will discover; and woe to him at whom he shakes his big-bellied fun, for his ridicule is more powerful than a thousand logicians.[1]

Adopting for *Punch*'s epigraph a well-known observation of Jonathan Swift—"to expose vice and make people laugh with innocence does more public service than all the ministers of State from Adam to Walpole"—Overall put this purpose into practice frequently, attacking Richmond extortioners, speculators, draft evaders, Confederate congressman, and Union military and political leaders, especially Abraham Lincoln. Anecdotes, military jokes, puns, dialect humor, sketches of Southern and European life and of famous personages, poems, invective, exposés, occasional travel sketches, communications from fictitious correspondents, and cartoons focusing on sociopolitical issues comprised *Punch*'s principal fare.

Like many periodicals of the Civil War era, *Southern Punch* was relatively short-lived, lasting only about a year and a half. Still, this was a considerably longer run than *The Bugle-Horn of Liberty*,* the South's other exclusively humorous magazine, which terminated publication after only three numbers. John Overall was the main impetus behind the magazine, serving simultaneously as co-publisher, promoter, and primary contributor, as well as editor-in-chief. Overall's Confederate loyalties determined *Punch*'s biasedly Southern flavor and defensive tone. Despite the difficulties posed by the war, Overall published the magazine weekly, except for several sporadic disruptions in the Spring, Summer, and Fall of 1864 and again in the Winter of 1865, when the editor and his staff had been summoned for militia duty or had to suspend publication temporarily because of a paper shortage. In August 1864, Overall announced his intention to expand *Punch* from eight to sixteen pages, thus making it the largest weekly in the Confederacy, but these plans never materialized.

The format of *Southern Punch*, except for the few issues of the third volume, remained fairly consistent. It was made up of eight four-column quarto pages measuring 10″ × 13½″. The cover, designed by John A. Elder, a young Richmond artist, and engraved by William C. Campbell, pictured a counterpart of London's *Punch*: a jolly elf-like man in a merry cap with a pipe and writing tablet in his hand seated in the midst of a basket of quills, ink, and books and surrounded by persons and scenes purporting to represent wartime Richmond. The yearly subscription rate was initially ten dollars, then twenty dollars, and finally, just before the magazine's demise in the Winter of 1865, thirty dollars. Near the end of the magazine's run, the price for an individual issue increased to one dollar, thus doubling the previous rate. The bulk annual rate was slightly less. Beginning with the third number of the third volume, the format of *Punch* was changed, with elimination of the separate cover page, reduction from eight four-column pages to four five-column pages, and use of a nearly illegible minuscule type. These changes—what might be better termed survival measures—can probably be attributed to the paper shortage, scarcity of printers, and increasing printing costs—all consequences of the South's losing effort in the war.

Labeled by its editor, John Overall, as "a hearty, laughing disciple of Momus" and "the legitimate son of that world-renowned London *Punch*,"[2] *Southern Punch* consisted mainly of prose by Overall himself, with some reprinted from other magazines and newspapers, although the first fifty issues also featured comically satiric illustrations as well. Typically, *Punch*'s first few pages contained fictitious communications, portraits, articles, anecdotes, and biographical sketches celebrating Southern military and political leaders such as General Robert E. Lee, Jefferson Davis, and General Stonewall Jackson and Southern writers, including William Gilmore Simms, Poe, Philip Pendleton Cooke, Paul Hamilton Hayne, John Esten Cooke, A. B. Meek, and Augusta Jane Evans. Some space would usually be devoted to sketches sharply criticizing Lincoln (portrayed as a Satanic figure), General Grant (his initials expanded to "Universal Slaughter"), General Butler, Seward, Henry Ward Beecher, and other Northern leaders and abolitionists. A recurring topic was Yankee puritanism and materialism which had infiltrated many areas of the South. Nor did the foibles of the Confederacy escape *Punch*'s scathing pen. Richmond's extortioners and speculators, who charged exorbitant prices for basic necessities, were frequently satirized. *Punch* also ridiculed Confederate congressmen, who prided themselves on their lofty and eloquent oratory and in so doing often delayed action on important legislative matters; the civilian militia, notorious for their unpatriotic stance toward the Southern cause and for their attempted evasion of military conscription; and Confederate Army leaders like General Bragg, the *enfant terrible* of the Army of Tennessee, infamous for his cowardice and ineptitude.

Sometimes *Punch* printed poems of Southern writers of the past or of contemporaries such as A. B. Meek and Thomas Davis. Sketches and letters of well-known humorists—Augustus Baldwin Longstreet, Artemus Ward, Seba Smith, Mortimer Neal Thomson ("Doesticks"), Sol Smith, Frances M. Whitcher, and Bill Arp—also appeared, borrowed from other sources. One of the magazine's most popular regular features was a column called "Punchiana." Overall, who had a penchant for puns, included brief jokes, sometimes of a topical flavor and heavily dependent on wordplay for their humorous effect. For instance, Yankees are the greatest musicians because they are "the most superb lyres (liars) in the universe," and the inept Confederate General Bragg most resembles a drum "because he is made to be beaten." In addition, comic illustrations treating current sociopolitical issues relating to the war or its consequences, some taking up a quarter or a half a page with captions or dialogue, appeared regularly. The magazine's back page consisted of several columns reviewing classical and Shakespearean plays currently on the boards at the New Richmond Theater, along with a half page or so of local advertising notices.

Some of *Southern Punch*'s best humor was found in its illustrations, most of which were the work of John A. Elder;[3] William B. Campbell, one of the co-publishers until he absconded in early 1864, did the magazine's engravings. Often blatantly satirical, *Punch*'s cartoons supported a Confederate viewpoint. A scene featuring a disconsolate Black woman, with the accompanying legend "Female Contraband," shows her among abolitionist sympathizers sweeping the streets of New York City while a contrasting scene pictures a contented slave woman in her comfortable home in the South. President Lincoln appears as the Prince of Darkness abducting the Yankee Goddess of Liberty and in another caricature is shown being lifted up on the ends of Confederate bayonets, an indication of how he would be removed from Washington by Lee's troops. Another illustration shows Confederate draft dodgers hiding from the reserve guard under a lady's hoop skirt. These and other cartoons graphically complemented some of the prevalent issues treated in *Punch*'s prose satires.

"The history of comic journalism in America," Brander Matthews once observed, "is merely a list of tombstones," and the comic periodicals of the Civil War era, including *Southern Punch*, were no exception.[4] The inferior quality of the few numbers of the third volume plainly demonstrated that in the closing days of the war *Punch* was faltering. *Punch*'s failure may be attributed to several factors: the scarcity of paper and other printing supplies, the difficulty of maintaining contact with its reading audience, the impending threat of a Union invasion of Richmond, rampant inflation coupled with the depreciation of Confederate currency, and the enforcement of a more inclusive, more stringent conscription law. Overcome by the financial exigencies of the war and deprived of its editor and chief sustaining force, John Overall, *Southern Punch* was quietly laid to rest in the Winter of 1865, thus becoming another tombstone.

Notes

1. "Salutatory," *Southern Punch* (15 August 1863): 2.
2. Ibid.
3. Frank L. Mott, *A History of American Magazines, 1850–1865* (Cambridge, Mass.: Harvard University Press, 1957), 2:113.
4. Brander Matthews, "The Comic Periodical Literature of the United States," *The American Bibliopolist* 7 (August 1875): 199.

Information Sources

BIBLIOGRAPHY:
King, Joseph Leonard, Jr. *Dr. George William Bagby: A Study of Virginia Literature 1850–1880*. New York: Columbia University Press, 1927, pp. 99–104, 116.
Linneman, William R. "*Southern Punch*: A Draught of Confederate Wit." *Southern Folklore Quarterly* 26 (June 1962): 131–36.
Mott, Frank L. "Magazines at the South." In *A History of American Magazines, 1850–1865*. Cambridge, Mass.: Harvard University Press, 1957, 2: 112–13, 155.
INDEX SOURCES: None.
REPRINT EDITIONS: None.
LOCATION SOURCES: CSmH, CtHW, DLC, ICN, MBat, MWA, NcD, NjP, OClWHi, ViU.

Publication History

MAGAZINE TITLE AND TITLE CHANGES: *Southern Punch*, 15 August 1863—early 1865. Since the final three numbers of Volume 3 are not extant, the date of the last number is unknown.
VOLUME AND ISSUE DATA: Weekly. Volume 1:1, 15 August 1863–Volume 1:25, 6 February 1864. Irregular for parts of Volumes 2 and 3, 13 February 1864 to early 1865.
PUBLISHER AND PLACE OF PUBLICATION: Overall, Campbell, Hughes and Co., Richmond, Virginia; after Campbell absconded in early 1864, published by Over-

all, Hughes and Co.; Volume 3 published by Overall and Co., beginning 8 November 1864, except for the last few numbers, of which the publisher is unknown.

EDITOR: John W. Overall; the editor of the last five issues, only two of which are extant, has not been identified.

CIRCULATION: Unknown.

Edward J. Piacentino

SPIRIT OF THE TIMES

The debut of *Spirit of the Times* on 10 October 1831 was an inauspicious one by any aesthetic or entrepreneurial standard. The smudged, unillustrated four-page tabloid was introduced as a sporting journal "on the model of *Bell's Life in London*," containing racing results, articles on hunting and angling, and bits of theatrical gossip. William Trotter Porter hoped to benefit from the absence of international copyright laws by filling his pages with pirated material from English journals. Certainly, there was little to suggest that the magazine would give significant impetus to a distinctive brand of humorous fictional writing from the American Southwest, causing its editor to become known as the father of the "Big Bear School of Humor." But the *Spirit* repeatedly expanded during its thirty-year history under editor Porter, finding a genuinely national readership and a circulation that may have reached 40,000. Porter became the literary patron of the most prominent Southwestern humorists of the mid-nineteenth century, including C.F.M. Noland, Thomas Bangs Thorpe, Johnson Jones Hooper, and George Washington Harris, who brought to the *Spirit* the vernacular dialects, yarnspinning techniques, and frontier characters and incidents of one of the most authentic versions of native American humor.

Porter was born to a wealthy family in 1809 in Newbury, Vermont. His biographer and brother-in-law, Francis Brinley, tells of Porter's early introduction to the spirited life of a gentleman, both in the cultivated conversation of the parlor and the sporting pursuits of the field. By the time he was twenty, he had learned printing and editing on various rural newspapers, including the *Farmer's Herald* of St. Johnsbury, Vermont. In 1830 he arrived in New York and became the foreman of John T. West's print shop. There he provided Horace Greeley with his first New York job, and thus began a life-long friendship. Greeley moved on with Porter in his next year to the shop of another young printer, James Howe, where the *Spirit of the Times* was born.

As Horace Greeley sarcastically assessed the *Spirit*: "It was a moderate sized sheet of indifferent paper, with an atrocious wood-cut for the head—about as uncomely a specimen of the 'fine arts' as our 'native talent' has produced." The journal struggled through the first five years with five titles, seven publishers, and at least seven editors, identifiable and unknown; only a handful of issues survive from the period. Porter sold out as early as 1832, but served as editor under two owners, while working for the *New-Yorker* and the *Constellation*. On

3 January 1835, there emerges from the confusion of this early history *The New York Spirit of the Times: A Gazette of the Literary, Fasionable and Sporting World*, with William T. Porter as editor and proprietor. Porter was to sell the journal once again in 1842 to avoid bankruptcy, but he remained editor of the *Spirit* without interruption from 1835 to 1856. The *Spirit of the Times* is significant for the editorial policy which Porter established in 1835 and fully implemented in the expanded eight-page triple-columned format of the New Series begun the following year.

From its earliest issues, the editorial mission of the *Spirit of the Times* was the cultivation of the *ideal gentleman*. The journal featured articles on turf racing and the pursuits of the active sportsman, but in 1835 Porter proclaimed a broader program: "Our course will be among the refinements, the luxuries and the enjoyments of society" (Vol. 5: 1/3/35). Moreover, the editor asserted that the *Spirit* was "designed to promote the views and interests of but an infinitesimal division of those classes of society composing the great mass . . . .we are addressing ourselves to gentlemen of standing, wealth and intelligence—the very corinthian columns of the community" (Vol. 7: 2/18/37). The assertions and manifestations of the *Spirit*'s fancied role as a journal of economic privilege were perhaps its most enduring characteristics. For the whole of its early history, the *Spirit* always managed to be more expensive than its competitors. In 1836, when the New Series began, the price jumped from three to five dollars per year, and in the midst of the depression year of 1839, in a move that apparently defied entrepreneurial logic, Porter raised the subscription price again to ten dollars (twice the usual cost of journals such as the *Spirit*). The cost of advertising rose as well, and in an editorial Porter guaranteed that the products and services offered in the *Spirit* would be of the highest quality.

The majority of articles in the *Spirit* imitated the manner and cultivation of English gentleman's magazines of the period, such as *Bell's Life in London*, *Punch*, and *Blackwood's*. Early issues featured "improving essays," the frequent publication of Charles Dickens's *Sketches by Boz* and William Thackeray's *Yellowplush Papers*, and tales and excerpts from the works of Frederick Marryat, Charles Lever, and Charles Surtees. Porter's choice of "Belle-Lettres of America," extracts of James Fenimore Cooper, Washington Irving, and William Gilmore Simms's *The Yemassee*, was similarly calculated to cultivate the gentlemanly tastes of the *Spirit*'s readership.

But despite these efforts to achieve a certain cultural elevation for men of leisure, the *Spirit of the Times* was devoted primarily to the active sportsman, who might combine the pursuits of the breeder, the hunter, the angler, and the farmer. Because Porter insisted that all "Gentlemen of wealth, leisure and spirit" must regard "the Turf not only as a National Sport, but as the manliest and most elegant of amusements" (Vol. 9: 3/4/39), the *Spirit* provided form charts, pedigrees, histories, listings and portraits of winning horses, as well as the most complete results from race courses across the country. In this latter endeavor, Porter enlisted the support of his readers, amateur correspondents who helped to develop the most significant category of original contributions to the *Spirit*—the "sporting epistle."

Even the *Spirit*'s determination to "abjure politics," "exhibitions of rancorous hatred," and "the railing spirit of party"—"No Smoking (Nor Politics) Allowed Here!" (Vol. 13: 11/11/43)—was an appeal to gentlemanly decorum. Despite Porter's professions of political neutrality, he himself was a Whig, and his distaste for the uproar of political factions seems to have been aimed directly at the raucous voice of Jacksonian Democracy. The *Spirit* never did banish politics from its pages, but it was more successful than most of its competitors. Porter recognized throughout the 1840s and 1850s that the retention of his national audience, and in particular his large Southern readership, depended on an avoidance of sectional tensions and an evasion of the major political issues of the day.

Given this editorial policy and the fancied social mission of the *Spirit of the Times*, Porter never intended his journal to be a forum for original American fiction, nor did he wish to articulate the claims of a new school of humorous writing. Humorous sketches of Southwestern characters, dialects, and incidents, which began to be featured in the late 1830s, may have been used to replace diminishing racing news during the depression years, as Norris W. Yates suggests. Yet, at no time during the depression years did the *Spirit* contain a significant proportion of humorous writing. The *Spirit*'s signifiance as a comic periodical is cumulative, based on the major writers to whom it offered first publication, and on the conventions of humorous writing and yarnspinning which its contributors introduced and refined over a thirty-year period.

The most notable change in the *Spirit of the Times* during the depression years was the proliferation of "sporting epistles," formal narratives by Porter's readers, which reflected their gentlemanly interests and beliefs. The correspondents emerged as the writers of frontier humor. Charles Fenton Mercer Noland of Arkansas, the first, the most prolific, and perhaps the most influential of these contributors is representative. A study of Noland's background and achievement as a humorist suggests that the depiction of frontier life was undemocratic in its intent. Faithful to the *Spirit*'s original aristocratic intentions, it expressed a distaste for the ignorance and bestiality of frontier people and frontier ways.

Born in Loudon County, Virginia, in 1810, Noland moved to Arkansas in 1826 to take up various occupations as a journalist. In 1836 he was admitted to the bar and began a successful career as a crusading Whig politician in a state legislature dominated by the Democrats. Although not himself a member of a hereditary planter aristocracy, he was a plantation owner and horse-breeder who freely associated with the elite of Southern society. His first contribution to the *Spirit of the Times*, a sporting epistle from a correspondent calling himself "N. of Arkansas," was entitled "A Glance at the Southern Racing Stables etc.," and it simply informed readers of the state of the breeder's art in Alabama. Through his more than 250 contributions to the *Spirit*, Noland concealed his identity behind the pseudonyms "N. of Arkansas," Colonel Pete Whetstone, and Jim Cole. Unlike his better known colleagues among contributors to the *Spirit*, he jealously preserved his status as a gentleman-amateur by refusing to publish his collected sketches in book form.

Noland's irresistible urge to digress on the more rustic and uncouth incidents of frontier life gradually changed the style of his sporting epistles. Sporting news became punctuated by bits of gossip about wilderness hunts, the presentation of comic sketches of frontier types, replete with vernacular dialect, and the spinning of celebrated yarns such as the one about the greenhorn who mistakenly fears that he has been bitten by a rattler, when he has in fact only been squatting on his own spurs. In "N.'s" sketches of frontier revels and pranks, the gentleman narrator establishes the pose of satiric observer commenting in a cultivated way on the boorish behavior of his social inferiors. This satiric distance and the framing of the tale by a cultivated narrator became the most distinctive narrative features of the Southwestern genre. Noland's creation of his second and most celebrated literary persona, Colonel Pete Whetstone, enabled him to depict the antics of backwoods characters from the perspective of an involved narrator. Pete is a breezy and irreverent prose stylist who punctuates the vivid, realistic details of frontier life with wild exaggeration, spicy metaphor, and the occasional oath. No subject is sacred to the digressive Pete. The topics which he addresses in his forty-five "letters" to the *Spirit* represent the gamut of frontier experience run by other writers of Southwestern humor: suspenseful hunts, quarter races, political debates, Fourth of July celebrations, quilting bees, Sunday meetings, weddings and funerals. There are also pranks played by the locals on the unsuspecting Eastern dandy; these are juxtaposed to the antics of the backwoodsman who comes to the big city (Little Rock) for the first time and is dumbfounded by the theater, the sight of his first piano, or the custom of eating raw oysters. But even the most solemn and decorous event in Pete Whetstone's world can degenerate instantly into a drunken brawl.

A number of the most popular humorists who contributed to the *Spirit*, including William P. Hawes, Francis Durivage (The Old'Un), and George P. Burnham (The Young'Un), were from New England and New York, and the journal's pages abound in tales of sharp Yankees. But the most significant of Porter's contributors were, like Noland, Southern gentlemen, plantation owners, breeders and sportsmen, often lawyers and other professionals, generally political foes of Jacksonian democracy, writing as anonymous amateurs. The conventions, characters, and incidents of their humorous writing reflect the influence of Noland's pioneering sketches.

Thomas Bangs Thorpe's first sketch, "Tom Owen, the Bee-Hunter," appeared in the *Spirit* in 1839 and was followed by dozens of sketches under the pseudonym, "The Bee Hunter." "The Big Bear of Arkansas" appeared on 27 March 1841, and it remains the quintessential Southwestern sketch for its development of vernacular dialect, manipulation of the framing device and setting aboard a Mississippi steamboat, and the fantastic tall-tale elements of Jim Doggett's pursuit of the "creation bear." Other humorists became renowned for their sketches developing a single backwoods persona, including the Major Jones letters of William Tappan Thompson (which appeared first in several Georgia newspapers before they received national circulation in the *Spirit*). Another direct offspring of the humorous writing of the *Spirit* is Johnson Jones Hooper's comic rogue, Simon Suggs. Sugg's motto, "It is good to be shifty in a new country," stands as an emblem of one kind of frontier spirit and much of its humor. Hooper depicts Simon's various swindles and tricks not merely to show the humor inherent in frontier opportunism, but also to offer a satiric criticism of the baser elements of human nature which Suggs represents in his drunkenness, selfishness, and treachery. Simon is a parasite on society, who pledges to stick "like a tick onder a cow's belly [*sic*];" he escapes the reader's moral censure only because the people he cheats are, on the whole, no better than he is.

This darker side of humanity which Southwestern humor exposes is epitomized by its most celebrated literary achievement, George Washington Harris's *Sut Lovingood: Yarns Spun By a "Nat'ral Born Durn'd Fool"* (1867). Harris, like C.F.M. Noland, made his first contributions to the *Spirit* in the early 1840s as a reporter of sporting pastimes in his native Tennessee. Writing under the pseudonyms "Mr. Free" and "Sugartail," Harris branched out in sketches such as "A Knob Dance—a Tennessee Frolic" to include vernacular dialects and the depiction of backwoods incidents which would characterize his more mature comic sketches. His final contribution to the *Spirit* in 1854 was his first Sut Lovingood sketch, "Sut Lovingood's Daddy Acting Horse," in which Sut's father flings off his clothing to pull the plough after his old nag drops dead. Being himself a "nat'ral born durn'd fool" (the curse he passes on to his son), he gets carried away by the metamorphosis. When hornets begin to attack his bald head, he breaks free of Sut who is driving and drags the plough over a bluff into the swimming hole below. There is broad slapstick humor in Daddy's wild attempts to escape the hornets, and in the torrent of curses he directs at hornets and humans from the pond. But there is human degradation in Daddy's perfect willingness to play the beast of burden, sadism in Sut's joy at bridling his father and selecting the switch to beat him with, and a grim pessimism about the hereditary disease of foolishness which will afflict Sut throughout his life.

The anonymity of the humorous sketches in the *Spirit* prevents a full roster of the journal's contributors. But the sketches of Thomas Kirkman (Mr. Snooks), Alexander G. McNutt (The Turkey Runner), Henry Clay Lewis (Madison Tensas), and John S. Robb (Solitaire) belong in any representative selection of native American humor. Editor Porter also developed a special relationship with two of his correspondents, George Wilkins Kendall and Joseph M. Field. Both men offered regular humorous sketches of their own to the *Spirit* as the editors of other newspapers, Kendall from the *New Orleans Picayune*** and Field from the *St. Louis Reveille*.* Both the *Picayune* and the *Reveille* distinguished themselves as the leading regional publishers of frontier humor, and Kendall and Field provided a steady current of materials for the *Spirit* to reprint. The *Spirit*, in turn, provided a national readership for sketches by several authors who had previously received only local attention.

In thirty years, the *Spirit of the Times* had few female contributors, and these remain unidentified. Porter fancied himself the editor of a gentleman's magazine, and both its matter and its manner are defiantly masculine. The *Spirit* may have served as a medium for Porter's correspondents slyly to debunk myths about the chaste, genteel, and mannered young women whom they met in their parlor society, and courted to become their wives. Women are depicted as the objects of bawdy stories told in taverns and around campfires. (There are repeated versions of "the one about the farmer's daughter.") Their quilting bees are disrupted; their attempts to urge men to temperance are mocked. Women, like livestock, are good chattel, fit to produce strong offspring.

In 1845, Porter gathered together twenty-one humorous sketches from the pages of the *Spirit* and published them under the title, *The Big Bear of Arkansas: Illustrative of Characters and Incidents in the Southwest*. Only in the Preface to this collection did Porter for the first time advance the claims of a new school of humorous writing: "A new vein of literature, as original as it is inexhaustible in its source, has been opened in this country, within a very few years, with the most marked success." As the pioneers pushed the frontier westward to the Pacific, "they have left behind them, on all hands, scores of original characters to be encountered nowhere else under the sun." The first edition of 4,000 sold out almost immediately, and the collection was reprinted four times in the next ten years. The companion collection of thirty-three sketches that followed in 1846, *A Quarter Race in Kentucky*, met with similar success. The second anthology took as its scope "The Universal Yankee Nation," but even the eight sketches that are set in the Northeast, in their use of dialect and the tallness of the incidents described, reflect the influence of the "Big Bear School of Humor." In addition, no fewer than eight of the authors represented in Porter's volumes published collections of their own by 1850, and Thorpe and Hooper at least received Porter's assistance in finding publishers. When Hooper dedicated *Some Adventures of Captain Simon Suggs* "To William T. Porter, Esq. Editor of the New York Spirit of the Times" he was signalling the transformation of a gentleman's sporting journal into a seedbed for a major school of American humor.

The demise of the *Spirit of the Times* was, perhaps, more chaotic than its early years. Porter remained the editor of the *Spirit* until 1856, even though he had surrendered ownership fourteen years earlier to John Richards, a wholesale printer. In 1856, Porter resigned from the *Spirit* to begin, along with George Wilkes, a new journal entitled *Porter's Spirit of the Times*. It was almost identical in format to the original *Spirit* and featured many of the same frontier humorists. Porter died in 1858, and his portion of the journal fell into the hands of Abraham C. Dayton. By 1859, Wilkes had broken with *Porter's Spirit*, only to begin yet a third journal entitled *Wilkes' Spirit*. By 22 June 1861, when the "old" *Spirit* ceased publication after thirty years, there were three journals with roughly the same name and a loosely connected chain of editorial influence. With three journals, correspondents did not always know which journal they were contributing to; subscribers could not be certain which journal they were actually receiving; and even today there is occasional confusion among critics and bibliographers about which journal is actually under consideration.

The *Spirit* ran continuously for thirty years, surviving dozens of competitors artistically and financially, and something of its "spirit" lived on in a journal of the same name until 1902. In the late 1850s, the *Spirit*'s finances seemed adequate, and in 1855 several issues were adorned with lavish mezzotint engravings (illustrations having never been a major appeal of the journal). Porter's resignation from the editorship may have been a factor, but the end of the *Spirit* does coincide with the onset of the Civil War in 1861. Despite the journal's professions of political neutrality, the alliance of Northern and Southern gentlemen in sporting pursuits was too tenuous to weather the sectional conflict. The suspension of the mails rather than political ideology may finally have been the most devastating blow. Barely two months after the firing on Fort Sumter, a new owner, Edward E. Jones, put the journal to rest.

Among journals of the nineteenth century, the *Spirit of the Times* was perhaps the most successful in fostering distinctive forms of humor from all parts of the United States, and in presenting regional dialects, characters, and incidents to a large national audience. Although the *Spirit* remained primarily a sporting journal throughout its history, it found both the original varieties of American humor and the receptive national audience which evaded those brief-lived periodicals devoted to humorous writing alone. Much research remains to be done on the *Spirit*. Countless tall tales and humorous sketches remain embedded in the sporting epistles where even the most diligent contemporary reader will require the spirit of the hunt to track them down.

Information Sources

BIBLIOGRAPHY:
Brinley, Francis. *The Life of William T. Porter*. New York: D. Appleton, 1860.
Collins, Carvel. "The *Spirit of the Times*." *Papers of The Bibliographical Society of America* 40 (Second Quarter, 1946): 164–68.
Fienberg, Lorne. "Colonel Noland of the *Spirit*: The Voices of a Gentleman in Southwest Humor." *American Literature*, 53:2 (May 1981): 232–45.
Meine, Franklin J. *Tall Tales of the Southwest 1830–1860*. New York: Alfred A. Knopf, 1930, pp. xxiv–xxix.
Yates, Norris. "The *Spirit of the Times*: Its Early History and Some of Its Contributors," *Papers of the Bibliographical Society of America* 48 (Second Quarter 1954): 117–48.
———. *William T. Porter and the "Spirit of the Times."* Baton Rouge: Louisiana State University Press, 1957.

INDEX SOURCES: None for Volumes 1–5. Volumes 6–31: title index at end of each volume.
REPRINT EDITIONS: University Microfilms reprints all known surviving issues. Index precedes some volumes.

LOCATION SOURCES: Volume 1–5: Fourteen issues are located in MWA. Additional issues are held by NN and CtY. Volumes 6–31: Largest holdings include N, Volumes 5–21, 23; NN, Volumes 13–24; University of Pittsburgh, Volumes 7–21; OU, Volumes 23–31.

Publication History

MAGAZINE TITLE AND TITLE CHANGES: *Spirit of the Times*, 10 October 1831–22 June 1861; 10 December 1831: *Spirit of the Times and Life in New York*: 1 December 1832: *The Traveller and Spirit of the Times*; 2 February 1833: *The Traveller, Family Journal and Spirit of the Times*; 3 January 1835: *The New-York Spirit of the Times: A Gazette of the Literary, Fashionable and Sporting World*. With the commencement of Volume 6:1, a New Series bears the abbreviated title, *Spirit of the Times*, which the journal was to carry until it ceased publication in 1861.

VOLUME AND ISSUE DATA: Volumes 1–31, published weekly; volumes 1–5: issue numbers are erratic due to ownership changes. Volumes 6–30: Numbers 1–52, 20 February 1836 (New Series); volume 31: Numbers 1–20 (22 June 1861).

PUBLISHER AND PLACE OF PUBLICATION: New York; volumes 1–5: Various mastheads from surviving issues include: William T. Porter and James Howe; William T. Porter and Co.; Freeman Hunt and John Jay Adams; William T. Porter and Thomas Renne; James D. Armstrong; Charles J. B. Fisher; Fisher and Inman. Volume 5 (3 January 1835)–12: William T. Porter. Volumes 12–29: John Richards. Volumes 29–31: Jones, Thorpe and Hays.

EDITORS: The sparseness of issues extant makes it difficult to determine editorial control during the early years. William T. Porter was the founding editor and had editorial control for several years between 1831 and 1835 when he did not own or publish the journal. Others who exerted editorial influence in the early years were Freeman Hunt and James Armstrong. Volumes 5–26: William T. Porter, sole editor; Volumes 26–31: Edward E. Jones.

CIRCULATION: Not precisely known. In 1856, Porter boasted to his brother-in-law Francis Brinley of a circulation of over 40,000, possibly a piece of frontier hyperbole. Porter made valid claims to a national and international circulation which encompassed every state and territory in the nation, and several countries and U.S. military installations abroad.

Lorne Fienberg

___ T ___

THE TABLET

The Tablet, a Boston weekly that ran for thirteen issues in mid–1795, was the first literary endeavor by Joseph Dennie, whom Timothy Dwight called "the Addison of the United States" and "the Father of American Belles Lettres." Each four-page issue, written primarily by Dennie and filled out with occasional selected verse, followed a format comprising a lead essay from Dennie's celebrated series, *The Farrago*, a short piece of biography or criticism, and miscellaneous back matter in prose and verse organized under such headings as "Levities," "Anecdotes," and "From the Shop of Mess. Colon and Spondee," in which Dennie printed the results of his collaborative efforts with Royall Tyler.

The Tablet is important primarily because of the thirteen *Farrago* essays that made up half of the completed series. These, along with the subsequent series, *The Lay Preacher*, constituted Dennie's major output and established his reputation as the foremost practitioner of the familiar essay in America before Washington Irving. *The Tablet* selections focused on eccentricities of character and manners. They lacked the stylistic finesse and gentleness of humor of the more famous *Lay Preacher* series, but they did reveal a liveliness and acidity of wit, particularly in their attacks on Harvard and in the essay for Number 10 in which Dennie ventured into Swiftian irony by arguing in favor of the murder of all bastards to ensure the complete eradication of genius.

Among Dennie's characters were Meander (Nos. 2 and 3), a transparent self-portrait of a youthful Dennie trying his best to study law; "My Aunt Peg" (No. 7), clearly modeled on Tristram Shandy's Aunt Dinah; and Charles Cameleon (No. 8), a satirical stereotype of the Renaissance man and bon vivant.

Taken together, the thirteen *Farrago* essays in *The Tablet* are an important document in Dennie's literary apprenticeship, revealing the strong influences of Jonathan Swift, Joseph Addison, Benjamin Franklin, and Lawrence Sterne.

Information Sources

BIBLIOGRAPHY:

Ellis, Harold Milton, *Joseph Dennie and His Circle: A Study in American Literature From 1792 to 1812*. Austin, Tex., 1915; rpt. New York: Johnson Reprint Corp., 1972

Granger, Bruce. *American Essay Serials from Franklin to Irving*. Knoxville: University of Tennessee Press, 1978.

Mott, Frank L. *A History of American Magazines, 1741–1850*. New York: D. Appleton and Co., 1930.

INDEX SOURCES: None.

REPRINT EDITIONS: University Microfilms.

LOCATION SOURCES: DLC, MWA, NN, CtY, OU, and approximately thirty others.

Publication History

MAGAZINE TITLE AND TITLE CHANGES: *The Tablet*, 19 May 1795 through 11 August 1795.

VOLUME AND ISSUE DATA: Weekly. Volume 1:1, 19 May 1795–Volume 1:13, 11 August 1795.

PUBLISHER AND PLACE OF PUBLICATION: William Spotswood, Boston.

EDITOR: Joseph Dennie.

CIRCULATION: Unknown.

Gary Engle

TALES FROM TOWN TOPICS

Tales from Town Topics was a lively quarterly of the early 1890s which featured light literary burlesques. Humorous sketches, witticisms, droll poems, and eventually a regular joke section identify it as a sophisticated comic journal with leanings toward society witticisms, "The Tourist," "The Rattler," "The Bachelor," and "The Dreamer" are typical author lines for the thirty or forty short stories in each 250-page, 5″ × 8″ issue. Representative is "The Tigress or the Lady" leading off Volume 3, lightly burlesquing Frank R. Stockton's acclaimed short story; the hero saves a lady by stabbing her trained tiger in the tail with his penknife, only to be rewarded by her biting a chunk out of his wrist when he later rejects her love. Signed novellas came to be a regular feature after the first few issues, but these tended away from the dominant comic mode of the shorter burlesque prose pieces. By the mid–1890s a joke section was a regular feature.

Tales from Town Topics was derived from William D. Mann's scandal sheet *Town Topics* in 1891. Two issue numbers were bound in each semi-annual volume, divided March/June and September/December. Although advertisements for back volumes confusingly state 1887 and 1888 as having two volumes per year and thereafter one volume per year, these references seem to be to *Town Topics*. As a humor magazine, *Tales from Town Topics* terminated in June 1905, becoming a fiction magazine, *Tales: A Magazine of the World's Best Fiction*, and, in December 1906, *Transatlantic Tales*; humor, except for some mild translated lines, disappeared. *Tales* was sold at fifty cents a copy and two dollars for a year, and had a number of pages of advertising in each issue. The original *Town Topics* has been praised for the quality of its writing, and some of that praise should rub off on the burlesque successor *Tales from Town Topics* as a comic magazine worthy of fuller study.

Information Sources

BIBLIOGRAPHY:
Mott, Frank L. "Town Topics." In *A History of American Magazines, 1885–1905*. Cambridge, Mass.: Harvard University Press, 1938, 4:751–55.
INDEX SOURCES: Tables of Contents at front of each issue.
REPRINT EDITIONS: None.
LOCATION SOURCES: CtY, DLC; scattered issues elsewhere.

Publication History

MAGAZINE TITLE AND TITLE CHANGES: *Tales from Town Topics*, September 1891 to March 1905; thereafter, no longer humor, published as *Tales, A Magazine of the World's Best Fiction* and *Transatlantic Tales*, through March 1908.
VOLUME AND ISSUE DATA: 1–44 (September 1891-June 1902) numbers each issue; 23–27 (September 1902-December 1904) numbers each volume of two issues per volume; Volume 28, March 1905. Successors published through Volume 38:1 (March 1908).
PUBLISHER AND PLACE OF PUBLICATION: William D. Mann, Town Topics Publishing Co., New York.
EDITORS: Unknown.
CIRCULATION: Unknown.

David E. E. Sloane

TEXAS SIFTINGS

Within a year of its initial appearance in 1881, *Texas Siftings* was well on its way to attaining the widest circulation of any Southwestern journal up to that time. Its sketches were from the beginning unmistakably regional in their taciturn style, satire of Texas and Western traditions, and use of typical Texas subjects such as the weather, regional animals, and the "Texan." At the same time, however, they were very much in the broader tradition of the literary comedians with their wise fool personae, general irreverence, amusing linguistic devices, and reliance on anticlimax. The combination of shrewd management and popular humorous copy—featuring homely metaphors and anecdotes, witty proverbs, gross overstatement, and excessive punning—catapulted J. Armoy Knox and Alexander E. Sweet's periodical into regional, national, and ultimately international prominence before its demise in 1897.

Sweet and Knox purchased the moribund *Weekly Review* from "Commercial College" Jones with the ambitious idea of making it "the weekly paper of the

State.'' The first issue of *Texas Siftings* on 9 May 1881 warned that the new weekly would not contain ''politics, vituperation, original poetry, a patent inside, catalogues of crime, coarse words nor expressions, nor anything that our wives and children should not read.'' Instead it would offer eight pages and forty-eight columns of news, humor, opinions, editorials, correspondence, historical notes, short paragraphs, sense and nonsense, ''New York Correspondence, Washington Correspondence, and many other features interesting to the general reader''— the last three pledges betraying even their ambition to achieve a national audience.

Alexander Edwin Sweet, a native of St. John, New Brunswick, but reared in San Antonio, turned to humor and journalism after being educated in New York and Germany, serving as an officer in the Confederate cavalry during the Civil War and practicing law for several years after the war. In 1869 he began writing ''San Antonio Siftings'' for the San Antonio *Express*, moving from there to win national fame writing ''Galveston Siftings'' for the Galveston *News*. He moved to Austin in 1881 to found *Texas Siftings* in partnership with John Armoy Knox, a young Irishman who had sold sewing machines before settling into a career in journalism. Although he unquestionably wrote a number of pieces for the journal, co-authored a Texas travel book with his partner, and served jointly as proprietor, editor, and sifter with Sweet, Knox's main function in the partnership seems to have been to look after its business affairs—a task he performed with great success. The first issue of the folio-size paper announced a circulation of 5,000, a number that had grown to 20,000 when the second volume began publication one year later. This immediate success was due almost as much to the efforts of the nine traveling agents hired to solicit advertisements and subscriptions from throughout the state as it was to the editors' ability to capture the reading public's fancy with their humorous fare.

In spite of its warning to the contrary, *Texas Siftings* soon developed into an important political organ: a series of editorials in 1882 exposed pervasive bribery in the leasing of Texas prisoners and prompted legislation that abolished the leasing system, and a number of its fiscal and land proposals were adopted by incoming Governor John Ireland in 1883. The mainstay of its success, however, was its humor, much of the best of which was cast in the form of short sketches such as ''The Drummer,'' ''The Razor Back Hog,'' ''Gunning for Quail,'' ''Sunday Reflections,'' and ''A Chapparel Cock.'' Typically, these sketches combine down-home metaphors with aphoristic wit: the roadrunner, for instance, ''makes better time standing still than is made by most railroad trains in Texas.'' Indeed, trains were among the favorite targets of their wry sarcasm: ''Accidents are every day becoming more frequent on the Central railroad. Yesterday the No. 1 passenger from Dennison ran into the Houston depot—on time.''

Perhaps the single most popular early feature was the 1882–1883 serial publication of what was to become their very successful book *On a Mexican Mustang, through Texas, from the Gulf to the Rio Grande*, a group of anecdotes, character sketches, humorous commentary on current events, and miscellaneous witticisms narrated in the first person by an unnamed New Englander. He and his companion—"the doctor"—satirize the state's history, traditions, cities and towns, and people: the herd of mustangs from which they buy their mounts was "as ignorant of . . . curry comb as the average Texas Justice of the Peace is of . . . the law"; "the majority of the people in the country lived by stealing cattle, and the balance died or went to the penitentiary by the same means"; the small town of East Bernard was "a store, a stable, and a large veranda with two small rooms attached to it." As the years wore on, Reverend Whangdoodle Baxter, Johnny Chaffie, and Colonel Snort of the Bill Snort Letters, a regular feature that was heavily political and satirical, achieved great fame and were widely quoted.

By mid–1883 Sweet and Knox had surpassed their goal of becoming the state weekly and had solidly established *Texas Siftings* as a national journal. Accordingly, they moved their main offices to New York, though they maintained a "branch" office in Austin as well. Although their subject matter broadened somewhat with the move, they continued to write and publish the same style of "Humorous and Descriptive Sketches (illustrated)" in the witty, satirical essay form that distinguished them from the typical news and comic "joke" journals of the day. They also broadened their stable of contributors, befitting the now national scope of *Texas Siftings*, to include Opie Read, Joaquin Miller, H. C. Lukens, Mrs. Fanny Darden, Bill Arp, and Bill Nye; staff artist W. H. Caskie had done almost all the early illustrations, but in New York he shared responsibility for the artwork with Frank Bellew, F. Ramsden, D. McCarthy, Thomas Worth (a Currier and Ives artist), and others. Although most of the *Siftings* staff worked anonymously, other known members included Frank P. Holland who later founded *Texas Farm and Ranch* and *Holland's* magazine, and William O'Leary, later city editor for the Dallas *Morning News*. In an attempt to capitalize on their swelling prosperity, Sweet and Knox opened a third office and began to issue a London edition in March 1884. It did not meet with the immediate success of the New York edition and was dropped in October of the following year.

In 1886 Volume 6 of *Siftings* began publication in a smaller quarto size and turned toward a typical magazine format; with Volume 7, semi-annual volumes replaced the annual ones of the first six years, and the Austin office was closed. Racial and ethnic humor, a staple of *Siftings* since its inception, also began to increase, particularly in its cartoons and illustrations. In June 1887, A. Miner Griswold ("Fat Contributor") joined Sweet as co-editor and wrote extensively for the journal until his death in 1891. In 1883 Knox had ceased to serve as editor and had formally become general manager, a position he maintained until he sold out in 1892. *Siftings* continued to flourish after Griswold's appointment and a "Western" business office was opened in Chicago in May 1888, and a second, more satisfactory, attempt at publishing a London edition began a month later. Indeed, England received the *Siftings* humor so well that *On a Mexican Mustang* continued to be reprinted there as late as 1905. Sweet served again as the journal's sole editor from 1891 to 1895, when he sold his share in *Siftings* after circulation had begun to decline. Although its new owner, Robert E. Morgan of New York, continued to publish *Texas Siftings* for two more years, with Sweet and Knox and most of the early staff gone, it was never able to recapture either its former quality or its former popularity. After sixteen years and twenty-six volumes, *Texas Siftings* finally closed its only remaining office in New York, two-thirds of a continent away from its roots in central Texas.

Information Sources

BIBLIOGRAPHY:

Miles, Elton. *Southwest Humorists*. Austin, Tex.: Steck-Vaughn Co., 1969.

Mott, Frank L. *A History of American Magazines, 1865–1885*. Cambridge, Mass.: Harvard University Press, 1938, 3:269–70.

Pickering, David. *Texas Siftings and Texas Journalism*. Austin: Department of Journalism Development Program, University of Texas at Austin, n.d.

Smither, Harriet. "Knox, John Armoy." In *The Handbook of Texas*. Ed. Walter Prescott Webb. Austin: Texas State Historical Association, 1952, 1:971–72.

Speck, Ernest B. "Sweet, Alexander Edwin." In *The Handbook of Texas*, 2:696.

———. *"Texas Siftings."* In *The Handbook of Texas*, 2:760.

INDEX SOURCES: None.

REPRINT EDITIONS: *Sketches from Texas Siftings*. Illustrated by W. H. Caskie. New York: Texas Siftings Publishing Co., 1882. *On a Mexican Mustang, through Texas, from the Gulf to the Rio Grande*. Hartford, Conn.: S. S. Scranton, 1883. *Three Dozen Good Stories from Texas Siftings*. With nearly one hundred illustrations by Thomas Worth and other artists. Chicago and New York: J. S. Ogilvie, 1887.

LOCATION SOURCES: There is no known complete file of *Texas Siftings*, but the two largest holdings are at TxU and N. Smaller partial files may also be found at DLC, MiU, NN, the Historical and Philosophical Society of Ohio in Cincinnati, and the North Texas State University in Denton.

Publication History

MAGAZINE TITLE AND TITLE CHANGES: *Texas Siftings*, 9 May 1881–1897.

VOLUME AND ISSUE DATA: Weekly, annual volumes, Volume 1:1, 9 May 1881–Volume 6:52, 30 June 1882. Semi-annual volumes, Volume 7:1, 7 May 1887–Volume 26, 1897.

PUBLISHER AND PLACE OF PUBLICATION: Alexander E. Sweet and John Armoy Knox, Austin, Texas, Volume 1:1, 9 May 1881–Volume 3:24, 20 October 1883. Texas Siftings Publishing Co., Austin, Volume 3:25, 27 October 1883–Volume 7:1, May 1887; New York, Volume 3:38, 26 January 1884–Volume 26, 1897, London, Volume 3:45, 15 March 1884–Volume 5:22, 3 October 1885, and Volume 9:7, 16 June 1888–Volume 26, 1897.

EDITORS: Sweet and Knox, 1881–1883; Sweet, 1883–1887 (with Knox as General Manager); Sweet and A. Miner Griswold, 1887–1891 (with Knox as Manager); Sweet, 1891–1895; Robert E. Morgan, 1895–1897.

CIRCULATION: More than 100,000 at its peak.

W. Craig Turner

THE THISTLE

The Thistle, ''an original work, containing a great many good things, by Roderick Rover, Esq.,'' was one of the brief spate of comic journals published in New England in response to the popular success of *Salmagundi*. Only three issues in octavo were produced between 4 August and 7 September 1807. Although Rover was never identified, there is internal evidence to suggest that he may have been Fisher Ames, a school teacher in Charlestown, or, more likely, one of Ames's former students. Much of the content of *The Thistle* made use of thinly veiled satiric allusions to educators and churchmen in the Boston area.

The humor of *The Thistle* was highly scholastic with material that included Latin puns, classical allusions, overt parodies of the literary tastes of the day (Robert Southey, William Cowper, Rousseau, Edward Moore), a broadly comic sketch in burlesque French dialect, and a three-page Latin eulogium for a ten-inch dog. The major accomplishment was a rambling, Shandian family history stretching over all three issues in which the editor and, presumably, sole author developed a meandering narrative of three generations of eccentric Rovers, the focal character being the editor's Uncle Isaac.

Information Sources

INDEX SOURCES: None.
REPRINT EDITIONS: University Microfilms.
LOCATION SOURCES: CtY, MBat, MWA, and one other holding.

Publication History

MAGAZINE TITLE AND TITLE CHANGES: *The Thistle*, 4 August 1807–1 September 1807.
VOLUME AND ISSUE DATA: Irregular, Number 1, 4 August 1807; Number 2, 15 August 1807; Number 3, 1 September 1807.
PUBLISHER AND PLACE OF PUBLICATION: Etheridge and Bliss, Boston.
EDITOR: Roderick Rover, Esq.
CIRCULATION: Unknown.

Gary Engle

THE TICKLER

The Tickler, by Toby Scratch'em, was George Helmbold, Jr.'s comic-satiric venture (begun in 1807), possibly the first truly comic newspaper in America and an important contribution to the growth of American humor. Its political and social satire scourged the venal and put forth ''pure American'' principles as an independently political, literary, and amusing paper. The corrosive of ridicule was reserved for those who could not be touched by the plain language of reason. Helmbold turned a keen satiric eye on politicians generally, and Henry Clay, William Duane, and the "embargaroons" in particular, but he is most important for his generalized humor, which pioneered the use of vulgar dialect and colloquial language in caricaturing local corruption.

Helmbold was one of several children of a well-to-do lower Marion township miller and paper-maker who had immigrated to America in 1771, and passed through indenture and the Revolutionary War to commercial success. George took his portion of the family inheritance to make paper and start a satiric newspaper. He went to war in 1812, leaving the paper in charge of his brother Henry K., returned in 1815 to start the Minerva Tavern, and reentered the satiric newspaper field with the *Independent Balance** in 1817, which illness and death parted from him in late 1821. Son of a self-made man, Helmbold manifested the attitudes later seen in post-Civil War humorists, reproaching greedy office-hunters and spoilsmen, attacking an ignorant "just-ass of the peace," and offering satiric toasts to city politicians and crooked contractors. Dialect letters and a variety of correspondents added to the fireworks. Lengthy series by the "Selector" and "The Extractor" provided essay continuity later in the *Tickler*'s run.

The Tickler sold for twelve and a half cents per issue, or four dollars per year. Its four-column pages were 11" × 18", with one page of comic letters and correspondence, and a fourth page of longer articles or verse. It was originally printed every Wednesday, but later by Henry on Tuesdays. The comic and satiric literature provided weighty reading matter, as it was closely connected to local, regional, and national politics—as well as being of the general sort that finds all politics corrupt. The post–1800 period was an era of increasing political depravity, according to the editor, and he picked a wide variety of targets. William Duane of the New York *Aurora* received special attention, and John Binns was tickled as the king of ignorance for his work as scape-gallows editor of the *Democratic Press*. Jailbirds, prostitutes, and politicians who pledged to Pennsylvanians, "Yis, I'll stick to them like wax," grafted through his pages, accompanied by scorn for such items as the comic dictionary definition of a proclamation: "A piece of paper used by great men to scare little rogues. The sheriff's proclamation (election notice) operates differently—he calls upon the people to convert little rogues into great men."

The paper was so closely tied to George as editor that during his illnesses some weekly issues were delayed, even though he maintained his numbering and subscription rates by extending the periods covered. Having begun on 16 September 1807, his first year ended with Number 52 on 8 February 1809. Henry K. Helmbold took over the paper on 20 July 1812, with Number 221, after a three-month lapse from Number 220 which had been issued on April 29. Following in his brother's editorial footsteps, he reasserted ridicule and correction as the driving motives of the paper. His brother, having recovered from an illness, shortly went to war against the British. In the last issue, 7 November 1813, Henry proposed a new twice-weekly *Tickler* which would appear in three months' time and sell at $6.50 per year, if interest warranted, but it seems never to have appeared. On his return from the war, George began the *Independent Balance*, hoping to pay off his remaining debts from the *Tickler*.

Information Sources

BIBLIOGRAPHY:
Becker, Gloria. "The Mill Creek Valley: Architecture, Industry, and Social Change in a Welsh Tract Community, 1682–1830." Ph.D. diss., University of Pennsylvania, in progress.
Mott, Frank L. *A History of American Magzines, 1741–1850*. Cambridge, Mass.: Harvard University Press, 1938, 1:170–71.
Scharf, J. Thomas, and Thompson Westcott. *History of Philadelphia, 1609–1884*. 3 vols. Philadelphia: L. H. Everts, 1884, 1:989.
INDEX SOURCES: None.
REPRINT EDITIONS: University Microfilms; Readex Microprint.
LOCATION SOURCES: PHi holds an extensive, though broken, run from Volumes 1 through 6, as does MWA. NN and DLC hold less complete runs, and scattered holdings exist in fifteen other libraries.

Publication History

MAGAZINE TITLE AND TITLE CHANGES: *The Tickler*.
VOLUME AND ISSUE DATA: Weekly but irregular; Volume 1:1, 16 September 1807– Volume 4:220, 29 April 1812; 221, 29 July 1812–?, 17 November 1813.
PUBLISHER AND PLACE OF PUBLICATION: 1807–1812: George K. Helmbold, Jr.; after 20 July 1812: Henry K. Helmbold, Philadelphia.
EDITORS: George K. Helmbold, Jr.; after 20 July 1812, William K. Helmbold.
CIRCULATION: Unknown.

David E. E. Sloane

TID-BITS and TIME

Tid-Bits, "an illustrated weekly for these times," started on 23 August 1884 as a cheap-paper reprinter of humor from all sources." It had a 10″ × 12″, sixteen-page format, and cost two cents a copy. But on 1 May 1886, it went into better paper, raised its price to five cents, and by 23 June 1888 in Volume 8, at ten cents a copy, became *Time*, with slightly more emphasis on the political and a more pointed quality of humor. *Time* lasted until Frank Munsey merged it with *Munsey's Magazine* on 22 February 1890. By then, partly boosted by Thomas Nast's double centerfold illustrations, it had achieved some merit as a humorous magazine. Throughout its life, it published columns of brief jokes, with some more impressive full-page cartoons later in its run.

The original *Tid-Bits* was published by the J. W. Lovell Company, New York, with a supplemental story paper and such devices as a weekly prize story. In 8½″ × 10″ size and three-column format on cheap paper, the early version offered such stories as "History of a Billiard Cue" and "Romance of a Spool of Cotton.'' Comic, poetic, and foreign tid-bits appeared as columns of humorous matter. The slick-paper expanded version which appeared on 1 May 1886 at five cents a copy was credited to Time Publishing Company and measured 9½" × 11½" Without sharply defined targets, its covers became more political by 23 June 1888, when the name was changed to *Time*. *Time* offered a page of political notes, some condensed dramas, jokes, and cartoons, and a page of ads in its sixteen pages. Uncle Bat's ''Horse Sense from the Quarters'' commented: ''Nebber hit de ole cow. She'll gib yo sumpen to eat arter yer naybur's chiken-roost am dun fur,'' and ''I likes fur ter see a young nigger wear a big bright wach-chain an a tremenjus dyermun pin. It makes up, in er great mesyer, fer his lack ob brains.'' City humor, social swells, class-race jokes against the Irish and Negroes, and some sappily maudlin humor filled its pages in this period, enlivened somewhat by color printing in addition to the coated paper.

By 1889, W. H. Bradshaw was listed as president of the Time Publishing Company, and John D. Adams appeared as the editor. Courtship and upper class jokes became more common. Double-page cartoons became prominent in the layout, and a subscription deal teamed *Time* with *Cosmopolitan*. G. R. Brill, A. Coles, and Thomas Nast provided illustrations at this time, and visual humor became more predominant than it had been previously. In the 19 June 1889 number, at the start of its second year in the new format, *Time* told its readers to expect two cartoons a week from Nast, and that with his help *Time*'s Republicanism would be stronger than ever, but *Time* would continue dealing with social, race, and literary foibles as well as politics. Nast's double-page center cartoons are arresting, and even the editorial paragraphs became somewhat sharper in content, although much of the humor was still aimed at general social life in America, with a variety of ethnic jokes. On 22 February 1890, *Time* announced that Frank A. Munsey and Company had purchased it and would merge it with *Munsey's Weekly*, ''the brightest and cleanest of all the clever journals.''

Information Sources

INDEX SOURCES: None.
REPRINT EDITIONS: None.
LOCATION SOURCES: DLC, NN have lengthy runs; four other libraries list small holdings.

Publication History

MAGAZINE TITLE AND TITLE CHANGES: *Tid-Bits*, 1884–1888; *Time*, 1888–1890.
VOLUME AND ISSUE DATA: Weekly, *Time* Volume 1:1, 23 August 1884–Volume 8: ?, 16 June 1888; *Time* Volume 8: ?, 23 June 1888–Volume 10:289, 22 February 1890.
PUBLISHER AND PLACE OF PUBLICATION: J. W. Lovell Co., New York; from 1886 as Time Publishing Co.
EDITOR: John D. Adams, circa 1889.

CIRCULATION: Unknown.

David E. E. Sloane

TRUTH

Truth had a varied career before it became a humor magazine. It was started as a society journal in 1881, suspended in 1884, and begun again in 1886. It called itself "A Journal of Society, the Clubs, Sports, Drama, and the Fine Arts." As a magazine of this type it had a circulation of 24,000. Then in 1891 another reorganization took place, and *Truth* took on the appearance of an illustrated comic. In little over a year its circulation grew to 64,000.

Frank L. Mott attributes *Truth*'s success to its new editor, Blakely Hall, who had been associated with several magazines that exploited "spicey" content. Like *Life*,* *Truth* was concerned largely with high society, and the problems of love and marriage, romance and money, temptation and gaiety. Like *Puck*,* its cartoons were in color. The front-page colored drawing was usually of fashionable women: statuesque, full-bosomed, and fine featured. They wore low-cut gowns exposing shoulders and a deep cleavage. The two-page middle illustration dealt with the themes of love.

Truth showed a spicier world than *Life*'s, a world of night clubs, chorus girls, champagne, and painted women. It was so racy on one occasion that the American News Company refused to distribute it. The back cover of each issue was usually a paneled colored cartoon, comparing manners on different social levels or telling a comic story. There were also black and white cartoons scattered throughout the magazine dealing with racial humor, bowery scenes, or fashionable life. The main artists were Charles Johnson, Archie Gunn, W. Granville Smith, and Thure de Thulstrup.

Like the drawings, *Truth*'s short stories were set in a world of opulence and high society. So well did *Truth* reflect this world that "Cholly Knickerbocker" praised it in his column, "Echoes from Dudedom," appearing in *The Recorder*: "That *Truth* Newspaper is great people, as we chappies say when we get gay and sportive. Upon my word, I see it every-where, in the clubs, the cafes, and the hotels. . . . *Truth* is par excellence the chappie's picture paper. . . . Its pictures are even better than its text, and altogether, it is a sort of French ball between the colored covers of a newspaper."[1]

James L. Ford, the literary editor, emphasized that *Truth* was realistic and not decadent. Ford criticized the quality magazines for their sentimentality and attracted new authors to *Truth* like Stephen Crane, Stephen Leacock, Albert Bigelow Paine, Bliss Carman, and Gellett Burgess. Tom Hall, a steady contributor, would become editor of *Truth* from 1895 to 1898.

Truth saw itself as the national humor magazine because it believed in beauty and fun and had no axes to grind. It said that *Judge*,* because of its Republicanism, did not find favor in the South, and Democratic *Puck* did not go over big in the West. *Life* appealed to the Eastern states and the college-educated. But *Truth* could be found everywhere, its middle lithographs framed for pictures in thousands of homes.[2]

But *Truth*'s success proved its ruin, for the American Lithograph Company, which did the printing, saw that the magazine was making money and bought out Hall's interest. Ford said that this was disastrous, for while the lithographers knew their trade, they did not know anything about running a humor magazine.[3]

Truth continued with the same format, the same society interest, and the same pretty girls, but the old sharpness and buoyant spirit were gone. In 1899 *Truth* became a monthly, lost its humorous disposition, concerned itself with women's fashions, ran articles by Theodore Dreiser on art, raised its price, and became even more elaborate in illustration, using large folded chromolithographs; it even published a serial by Henry James. The magazine folded in 1905.

Notes

1. *Truth* 12 (18 February 1893): 2.
2. *Truth* 13 (20 January 1894): 2.
3. James L. Ford, *Forty Odd Years in the Literary Shop* (New York: E. P. Dutton, 1921), p. 300.

Information Sources

BIBLIOGRAPHY:
Ford, James L. *Forty Odd Years in the Literary Shop*. New York: E. P. Dutton, 1921.
———. *The Literary Shop and Other Essays*. New York: Chelsea Co., 1899.
Mott, Frank L. *A History of American Magazines, 1885–1905*. Cambridge, Mass.: Harvard University Press, 1957, 4:84–85.
INDEX SOURCES: None.
REPRINT EDITIONS: None.
LOCATION SOURCES: Eleven libraries list short runs, including CSmH, IC, IU, MB, and MiU.

Publication History

MAGAZINE TITLE AND TITLE CHANGES: *Truth*, 1881–1905.
VOLUME AND ISSUE DATA: Weekly, no bound volumes. Volume 1 begins in 1881. With reorganization, Number 1 begins again in 1886, going to Number 608 in 1898. In 1899 the magazine became a monthly and started over with Number 1.
PUBLISHER AND PLACE OF PUBLICATION: Truth Co., New York.
EDITORS: Davison Dalziel, 1886–?; Blakely Hall, 1892–1894; Tom Hall, 1895–1898; E. H. Sylvester, 1898–1901; R. Bennett, 1901–1902; Fannie Humphreys Gaffney, 1902–1903; Charles Edward Burns, 1903; George William Hanna, 1904–1905.
CIRCULATION: 1890—24,000; 1894—64,000; 1897—45,000.

William R. Linneman

TWINKLES

Twinkles, originally subtitled "A serio-comic supplement to the *New York Tribune*," represented the *Tribune*'s first attempt at a Sunday newspaper magazine supplement. A mixture of cartoons, political commentary, social gossip, sketches, stories, and brief theatrical reviews, *Twinkles* was soon available separately until its transformation a year and a half later into a regular Sunday newspaper supplement.

Twinkles first appeared on Sunday, 25 October 1896. Printed on glazed stock, its sixteen pages, measuring 9″ × 12¼″, set the format for most of the issues that would follow. On the cover was a full-page color political cartoon, with a short editorial explanation on the second page. Page three held society news and photographs, followed by two pages of jokes and cartoons and two pages of world news and photographs. The center two pages were devoted to a color cartoon, political in nature. Another page of jokes preceded a page of theatrical gossip and photographs. A short story followed, with pages fourteen and fifteen filled with more jokes and advertisements. The final page, also in color, contained either a comic strip or two cartoons. This format changed little during *Twinkles'* run.

The supplement was published every Sunday. Each page held either two or three columns, with some cartoons and advertisements covering an entire page. Individual issues purchased separately cost five cents; an annual subscription was two dollars. No advertising rates were listed, although advertisements for a wide range of products appeared in each issue.

The conservative Republicanism of the *New York Tribune* was reflected in *Twinkles'* content. Cartoons burlesqued William Jennings Bryan, the 1896 Democratic presidential candidate; the "Tammany Tiger," which held New York City politics in its claws; and Democrat Grover Cleveland, the outgoing President, portrayed satirically in many guises. Also featured was a series of historical political cartoons.

Many of the stories and jokes were reprinted from other sources. Stereotypes abounded, both in dialect jokes and cartoons; puns were plentiful; and favorite topics included romance, society, and current fads and fashions, especially bicycling. Serious news items ranged from the treatment of the Armenians at the hands of the Turks to eulogies for William Morris and Ulysses S. Grant. The comings and goings of society matrons and debutantes were reported weekly, as were the latest triumphs of popular Broadway actors and actresses.

The last issue of *Twinkles* was dated "for the week ending May 29, 1897." There was no indication that this would be the final issue; indeed, a notice stated that the winners of a *Twinkles* "tournament" requesting witty sayings of children would be announced in the next issue. *Twinkles* was succeeded, however, by a *Tribune Illustrated Supplement* which contained more feature articles and fewer jokes. Eventually, this evolved into a Sunday magazine as we know it today.

Twinkles was a bright, cheerful, odd mixture of fact and fun, politics and society, wit and drivel. Like its parent *Tribune*, it was aimed at a prosperous and socially active audience, and presented in its pages a kaleidoscopic view of society during the last years of the nineteenth century.

Information Sources

BIBLIOGRAPHY:
Baehr, Harry W., Jr. *The New York Tribune Since the Civil War*. New York: Octagon Books, 1972 (1936), pp. 235–36.

Mott, Frank L. *A History of American Magazines, 1885–1905*. Cambridge, Mass: Harvard University Press, 1957, 4:70, 385–86.
INDEX SOURCES: None.
REPRINT EDITIONS: None.
LOCATION SOURCES: Complete runs can be found at ICN, Kansas State Historical Society, NjR, OO, and CtY; NN has a partial run.

Publication History

MAGAZINE TITLE AND TITLE CHANGES: *Twinkles; Serio-comic Supplement to the New York Tribune*, 25 October 1896–22 November 1896; *Twinkles; A Serio-comic Weekly Published by the New York Tribune*, 29 November 1896–9 May 1897.

VOLUME AND ISSUE DATA: Weekly for Volume 1:1, 25 October 1896–Volume 2:5, 29 May 1897. (Volume 1 comprised twenty-six issues.)

PUBLISHER AND PLACE OF PUBLICATION: Tribune Association, 154 Nassau Street, New York.

EDITOR: Unknown.

CIRCULATION: 84,000 copies of Sunday *Tribune*.

Eric W. Johnson

U

UNCLE REMUS' MAGAZINE

Uncle Remus' Magazine, the last effort of Joel Chandler Harris's literary career, indelibly bore his unique stamp in the scope, tone, and focus of the periodical's articles and fiction—even in the selection of advertising. The magazine was conceived and conducted with the same idealistic personal goals that had marked the entire body of Harris's very popular and influential writings. In it he sought to appeal to the better nature and the more humane sensibilities of his readers, and more specifically he strove to advance his life-long desire to explain the South to the rest of the nation. He hoped the magazine would help erase the lingering sectional antagonisms which, in 1906, continued to be the regrettable legacy of the Civil War. Harris's motto for the new periodical attempted to convey this synthesis: "Typical of the South—National in Scope."

Why, at the age of fifty-seven and in dubious health, the publicity-shy Harris was willing to leave retirement and take on the burdens and exposure of an editor-in-chief remains a matter of speculation. Possibly, he felt he had exhausted his sources of fictional material featuring the Old South, and that to carry out his mission as literary interpreter of the region, he must shift his efforts to a new, more vital contemporary form. The more likely explanation, however, is that Harris succombed to the unceasing appeals of the syndicate of promoters, Atlanta businessmen led by Harris's son Julian, who had been badgering the writer to serve as editor of the new monthly they planned. Toward its initiation, they had raised a working capital of $200,000, and contracted to succeed an existing family weekly, *Sunny South*, which had been published for many years in Atlanta.[1]

That Harris felt coerced to some degree is seen in a communication to James Whitcomb Riley of October 1906, in which Harris indicated his acquiescence to the promoters even as he voiced his irritation at them: " . . . they have bedeviled me until I have consented to become the editor . . . but not until I made the whole push sign a contract that I was to have absolute control of the contents."[2]. Once committed to the project, however, Harris devoted himself wholeheartedly to its success. His personal appeals quickly gained contributions from such notables as Riley, Thomas Nelson Page, F. Hopkinson Smith, and Ruth McEnery Stuart. He immediately engaged Don Marquis as associate editor.

The first issue of the magazine made it clear that *Uncle Remus' Magazine* was aptly named, for Harris, whom the country at large thought of as being one with his beloved literary character, wrote two-thirds of the articles. Marquis also authored a piece, and Richard E. Edmonds of Baltimore wrote another.

In his first editorial Harris laid out the magazine's tolerant philosophy, noting that the publication might well have taken the title *The Optimist*, and that its editor would strive to select articles and fiction that would promote harmony in areas where beliefs might conflict. Human brotherhood and unity among all people were seen as key goals. While attempting to clarify misconceptions regarding the South, Harris stressed, *Uncle Remus' Magazine* would be firmly, patriotically American, seeking to transcend sectionalism, partisan political views, and prejudice.

Defining his editorial policy, Harris said it would be conservative, and yet this conservatism would represent active commitment to strongly held beliefs, not repose. This stance left Harris in an awkward position. He was editor of a "New South" magazine, committed to conveying progressive Southern views on contemporary issues from time to time. At the same time, like the character who gave the magazine its name, Harris possessed a deep love for the harmonious old times. As such, could he address his readers with force and conviction on issues where a high degree of opinion was unavoidable? To do this, Harris needed a spokesman through whom he could air his views on contemporary affairs when necessary, a voice distinct, in his readers' imaginations, from Harris's identification with the Uncle Remus of Old South plantation folklore fame.

Harris had the solution to his problem ready to hand in his character Billy Sanders, a straightforward, independent, honest middle-Georgian, given to strong expression of his views and to use of the broad, vigorous verbal strokes of the Southwest humor tradition of A. B. Longstreet, J. J. Hooper, and W. T. Thompson. He was a great despiser of false show and pretense, and found the noisy facades of politicians easy to penetrate. Billy found the staff a bit too relaxed and unhurried, and wondered if the magazine, with its conservative focus, would really be able to succeed in the era of muckraking:

> You've got to git you some well-hooks an' a drag-net, an' a couple of sticks of
> dynamite, an' see what you can fetch up from the nasty deep, as the poet remarks.
> . . . you've got to let it be known to more than your families an' friends that you're
> ready for to jump up an' bite a piece out'n a pine wall.[3]

Yet Billy's fiery advice on dramatic investigative reporting was not largely heeded, even though he was to serve Harris on many occasions, at a lower pitch, to keep vigorous the strength of the magazine's opinions on current topics such as mob rule, violence, dishonesty in politics, and prejudice. Though following Billy's counsel on muckraking might indeed have sparked circulation, Harris stuck religiously by the restraining dictates of his morally sensitive nature. This may be seen with special clarity in the rather mystical meditative essay from the first issue of the magazine, "On Knowing Your Neighbors," an essay that shows how little Harris's philosophical mind was troubled by "the mania of owning things." The superiority of the reward found in the love of others and joys in nature are stressed. He urges his readers to consider practicing the oriental mental discipline of releasing their minds from the bondage of acquisition, counseling learning to unlearn all that is crassly material, advising them to clear their minds, and to "thus acquire something of the simple mysteries of the spirit and its infinite emanations."[4]

In the June number also appeared the first installment of Harris's new novel, *The Bishop, The Boogerman, and the Right-of-Way*. Reflecting a thematic debt to the *Silas Marner* tradition, the fiction traces the transformation of old Jonas Whipple, an avaricious, unsociable old bachelor, from his ugly introversion into an outgoing and likable person. The change is effected by the collaboration of Whipple's niece, Adelaide, and the ingenuity, plain talk, and good humor of Billy Sanders. The novel, like Harris's other writings, was more than entertainment, for it carried overtones of a changing South. Old Whipple symbolized an older generation of Southerners bound to resist change at all costs. Young John Somers, also a Southerner, who hopes to create a railroad right-of-way through Whipple's land, was not born in the area, had never lived there, and had hence never formed a sentimental attachment to it. His detachment, Harris commented, was not a misfortune, for, "being modern and practical, he was wholly free from the entanglements and misconceptions of prejudice that had outlived the issues that gave rise to them, and he went about his business with a mind at once clear, clean, and cheerful, bearing the signal of home in his forehead."[5] Harris believed that the South's best hope for the future lay in the hands of forward-looking young men like John Somers. While, like Uncle Remus, Harris frequently took a look backward toward an outlived time, he never suggested that the South should stand still and sentimentalize over days gone by.

Although the first number included an Uncle Remus folklore tale, "How Brer Rabbit Saved Brer B'ar's Life," for Old South flavoring, Harris minimized the folklore-based material, stressing his focus on the present and future, not the past of the South.

The magazine's book review section, written by Harris himself after he grew frustrated in his search for an acceptable reviewer, was conducted under the pseudonym of Anne Macfarland, supposedly a crotchety spinster who, according to Harris, was so touchy about her prose that only he could edit it. Harris/Macfarland stressed his strongly moralistic view of the role of good fiction, and the need for restricting oversophistication while maximizing earthy positivism in life and art. Although he admired the craft of Edith Wharton's *House of Mirth*, he sorrowed that such artistic skill had been expended on so degraded a set of characters. "Neither social agents nor biologists can deal adequately with the degenerates who figure in this tale."[6]

This issue established the pattern for *Uncle Remus' Magazine* under Harris, his own articles predominating. The material appeared as his own personal essays, as the Uncle Remus tales and poems, as book reviews by Anne Macfarland, and as commentary on a current social issue or political point by Billy Sanders.[7] While the rest of the staff, and particularly Marquis, regularly contributed significant articles, Harris remained his own best contributor. The periodical fulfilled richly, if briefly, the promise of its title, and of its creator's complex design for it.

In May 1908, *Uncle Remus' Magazine* absorbed *The Home Magazine* of Indianapolis, and *Uncle Remus' The Home Magazine* had a monthly circulation of 200,000.[8] Its founder was but little able to enjoy the success, however. Harris died on 3 July 1908 in Atlanta, of acute nephritis, complicated by cirrhosis of the liver, in some measure the outcome of the strains that the magazine put on him.

Notes

1. The *Sunny South*, a family weekly of miscellaneous contents, was published in Atlanta during 1875–1907. J. H. Seals was the publisher in the eighties. Among contributors were Sylvanus Cobb and Will Allen Dromgoole. Dromgoole edited for a period, and Henry Clay Fairman was editor in the nineties.

2. Julia Collier Harris, *The Life and Letters of Joel Chandler Harris* (New York: Houghton Mifflin Co., 1918), p. 528.

3. Joel Chandler Harris, "Mr. Billy Sanders, of Shady Dale, Makes Some Suggestions," *Uncle Remus' Magazine* 1 (June 1907): 7.

4. Ibid., 9.

5. Joel Chandler Harris, *The Bishop, the Boogerman, and the Right-of-Way* (New York: Doubleday, Page, and Co., 1909), p. 973.

6. Joel Chandler Harris, review of Robert Chambers, *A Fighting Chance*, *Uncle Remus' Magazine* 1 (June 1907): 40–41.

7. Published from June 1907 until May 1908, the magazine was in a 10½″ × 14½″ format, 48 to 54 pages in length, with extensive illustrations, including color tints.

8. It was published by Bobbs-Merrill, in Indianapolis, under Harris's son Julian after Harris's death. Lacking the elder Harris's touch, it was undistinguished.

Information Sources

BIBLIOGRAPHY:

Bickley, R. Bruce, Jr. *Joel Chandler Harris*. Boston: Twayne Publishers, 1978.

Cousins, Paul M. *Joel Chandler Harris: A Biography*. Baton Rouge: Louisiana State University Press, 1968.

Harris, Julia F. C. *The Life and Letters of Joel Chandler Harris*. New York: Houghton Mifflin Co., 1918.

Mott, Frank L. "Southern Magazines." In *A History of American Magazines, 1850–1865*. Cambridge, Mass.: Harvard University Press, 1957, 1: 46.

INDEX SOURCES: Index bound in the back of each volume.

REPRINT EDITIONS: None.

LOCATION SOURCES: *Uncle Remus' Magazine*: University of Alabama, University of Arkansas, University of Florida, Wake Forest, and GA. *Uncle Remus' The Home Magazine*: DLC, NN, OU, OO.

Publication History

MAGAZINE TITLE AND TITLE CHANGES: *Uncle Remus' Magazine* succeeded *Sunny South* in June 1907 and was published until May 1908. It then merged with *The Home Magazine* to become *Uncle Remus' The Home Magazine*, which published until June 1909.

VOLUME AND ISSUE DATA: *Uncle Remus' Magazine*: Monthly, annual volumes. Volume 1:1, June 1907–Volume 1:11, May 1908. *Uncle Remus' The Home Magazine*: Volume numbering irregular. Volume 23:3, immediately follows Volume 1:11. Following merger which produced *Uncle Remus' The Home Magazine*, both magazines numbered together, with pre-merger issues renumbered. Volume 1 begins 24 October 1907. Volume 2 is 1908, and the series ends in 1909 with Volume 3, number 6.

PUBLISHER AND PLACE OF PUBLICATION *Uncle Remus' Magazine*: Roby Robinson, for Sunny South Publishing Co., Atlanta; later, Julian Harris, Business Manager. *Uncle Remus' The Home Magazine*: Julian Harris, Bobbs-Merrill, Indianapolis.

EDITORS: *Uncle Remus' Magazine*: Joel Chandler Harris, Associate Editor, Don Marquis. *Uncle Remus' The Home Magazine*: Julian Harris.

CIRCULATION: *Uncle Remus' Magazine*: Unknown. *Uncle Remus' The Home Magazine*: Approximately 200,000.

St. George Tucker Arnold, Jr.

V

VANITY FAIR (1859–1863)

Vanity Fair was the answer to the demand for an American *Punch* and was widely acknowledged as the foremost American comic magazine of its era. With Charles G. Leland and Artemus Ward as editors, *Vanity* claimed the funniest men in America for its leadership and the self-proclaimed "Bohemians" of New York as its sustaining contributors. The pun, comic vernacular letters, and sociopolitical commentary and protest dominated *Vanity*'s prose and comic verse, and governmental, economic, and social issues were emblazoned in the graphics, dominated by Henry Louis Stephens's page-sized political cartoons. But *Vanity*'s centrist politics and its lukewarm resistance to emancipation, along with overt antagonism toward the Negro, irritated and finally alienated its abolition audience as the ongoing war polarized the Union. Personal problems in its management and managing philosophy, and its difficulty in finding an audience killed it, an extra casualty of the Civil War.

Frank J. Thompson, a Baltimore merchant, has been identified by F. L. Mott as most important to the birth of *Vanity Fair* by providing the financial backing to Henry Louis Stephens to start it in 1859. Stephens, a noted cartoonist of his day, was a close personal friend of Thompson, and *Vanity* provided him a wide scope to combine his artistic skills with social and political commentary. Joined by his brothers, William Allan Stephens who became managing editor, and Louis Henry Stephens who became publisher, agent "for the Proprietors," Stephens became art editor of *Vanity*. The Stephens brothers were pro-Union Democrats, and *Vanity* was an unenthusiastic commentator on Republican politics. Instead, they intended the magazine to take a more elevated course, attacking social and political folly evenhandedly wherever found. When Thompson withdrew toward the end of 1862, William Camac of Philadephia took his place as backer of the venture. The redoubling price of paper seems to have disrupted the weekly by the start of 1863, when it became a monthly, turned back into a weekly briefly in May and early June and died on 4 July, as Grant accepted Vicksburg's surrender and Lee prepared to retreat from Gettysburg.

In format, the paper was made up of twelve two-column quarto pages measuring 12″ × 16″. The subscription price for the weekly was originally three dollars a year, then $2.50 a year, less for bulk subscribers. Bound volumes were offered at various rates; an individual issue was at first five cents, but in late 1862 paper costs were given as the reason for raising the price to seven cents and later dropping it to six cents in a final effort to compensate for the rapid fluctuations in costs, and probably readership, at the turning point in the war. *Vanity*'s scope was intended to be national, but a fair amount of material reflects the New York City cultural scene and Northeastern occurrences; jibes at the South are common.

Vanity Fair combined text and pictures in a variety of ways that reflected its London model, *Punch*. Originally, the front page featured a Vanity Fair scene presided over by a devilish Punch-like jester, but in 1861 it changed to feature a half-page caricature of authors, newspaper editors, and political figures, Artemus Ward and P. T. Barnum, Parson Brownlow, Oliver Wendell Holmes, N. P. Willis, George Morris, and others, and a host of state and national politicians, primarily those with an anti-secession philosophy. A second page of advertisements was followed by several pages of short and long comic items in prose and verse, often including a letter from McArone on the war, "Hardee Made Easy"—a burlesque war handbook, or letters by Artemus Ward, Ethan Spike, or other comic correspondents; burlesque novels and plays were offered at one time or another, usually as a series over several issues. Before the firing on Sumter, local and state politics, contaminated foods, and slum and factory conditions were attacked, and lower and middle-class urban life, along with national, state, and city politics, dominated the magazine. Later, aspects of the war became the primary focus of the humor, moderated by occasional travel pieces and New York City theatrical events. Major items were illustrated, and cartoons with brief legends or dialogue appeared randomly. Comic commentary on political and social events appeared here and there in items of three or four paragraphs occupying a half column or so. One-line puns provided space fillers.

Engravings, which Franklin Meine has identified as the work of the engraving company of Bobbett and Hooper, "famous workers in their line," dominated the format visually. Among *Vanity*'s illustrators were Henry L. Stephens, Frank Bellew, John McClennan, J. H. Howard, Elihu Vedder, Edward F. Mullen, and Wilson Fisk. Stephens's half-page caricatures maintained the Democrat perspective, but the most dramatic of all were the full-page political cartoons by Stephens which ended each issue. These last cartoons were strongly pro-Union, visually inventive, and sometimes bordered on the surreal. An ugly machine labeled King Cotton—worshipped by a row of British merchants— chews on the bodies of Black men; President James Buchanan appears as a melting iceberg, one of a series which Stephens created and reprinted as a bound volume; Jeff Davis is seen as a shooting star trailing a tail of swords through the heavens. The Stephens cartoons are significant pre-Nast political-comic art.

Vanity Fair amassed an impressive list of contributors during its brief life, thanks in part to its location in New York City and the origination of its material in the Bohemians gathered in Pfaff's Cellar, a beer cellar at 647 Broadway, close to publishers and minstrel theaters. The Bohemians of New York modeled themselves on the denizens of the Parisian Latin Quarter, displaying the witty cynicism and vagrant life-style of the urban literati. Henry Clapp, acerbic founder of the *Saturday Press* (publisher of Twain's "Jumping Frog" story a few years later), was at the center of a group which included Fitz-James O'Brien (killed in the Civil War in 1862), Thomas Bailey Aldrich (author of the famed "Ballad of Baby Bell"), William Winter (drama critic of the *New York Tribune*), Fitz-Hugh Ludlow (notorious as the "Hasheesh Eater"), George Arnold (*Vanity's* "McArone"), Frank Wood and Charles Dawson Shanly (both editors of *Vanity Fair* during its brief life), Ada Clare (Queen of Bohemia), Walt Whitman, and others. Edward Mullen and Sol Eytinge, Jr., the illustrators, joined them, as did Artemus Ward—Charles F. Browne—on his arrival in New York. They provided *Vanity* with its mildly superior tone and its abundance of wordplay and verbal wit. Ward's literary and dramatic burlesques and comic letters expressed the vulgarized pragmatism of the Bohemian reporter toward religious sects, overwrought patriotism, and the rebellion.

The Bohemians in New York in the 1860s held some pretensions to social and political revisionism, and their viewpoint was consistent with *Vanity's* sense of itself as a national comic weekly. Attacks on mill owners who let buildings collapse, on slums, and on barkeepers-turned-politicians flowed from the pens of "The Undersigned" and "The Man Who Writes the Sonnets." With little hesitation, "V. F." in 1860 predicted that abolition was a disease that would soon kill off the nondescript candidate Abraham Lincoln. As blood flowed at Sumter, *Vanity* rose uncompromisingly to the Union, vilifying disunion and its causes: the South's greed for King Cotton, Buchanan's inaction, and Sambo the slave—whose freedom through abolition was not deemed worth the disruption of the Union. Even filler items showed the Bohemian stamp: North Carolina volunteers to the Confederate Army were sneered at as "Men of Mark" because 59 of them could only sign an X on their company roster. Notable successes included E. C. Stedman's "The Prince's Ball," published in October 1860— doggerel verse caricaturing Prince Albert Edward's visit to America. Artemus Ward caricatured the Shakers, defended Abe Lincoln from office-seekers, and caricatured free lovers, Confederates, and French romances. The longest series of comic letters was composed of the burlesque war correspondence of "McArone," George Arnold, making light of the indecisive events of the war front. Matthew Whittier, brother of the New England abolitionist poet, wrote countrified dialect letters under the penname of Ethan Spike, and John G. Saxe, America's most widely recognized poet of *Vers de Société*, William Dean Howells, and others contributed a scattering of pieces along similar lines.

The subject matter varied over the four-year life of the magazine but was roughly consistent with the interests of the intended audience of railway and urban readers. At first, social issues were prominently caricatured among lighter items concerning New York middle-class life. By the Spring of 1861, material was more hawkish, including R. H. Stoddard's political poem "King Cotton"; Artemus Ward letters appear regularly in June and July, indicating his editorial presence. By late 1861, war matters dominate, and one cartoon shows industry puncturing Jefferson Davis's soft-soap pipe dreams with her spindle. In April 1862, Artemus Ward writes to Secretary of War Edwin Stanton to keep his undergarments on, and Buchanan is described as good for a job as a wet-nurse in Hell. The politics of the *New York Tribune*, Buchanan as dough-face President, Henry Ward Beecher as a showman-politician-preacher, the danger of the Negro to the Union, and the doings of the Confederacy were regular subjects of burlesque comment.

In several ways the war worked against *Vanity*'s survival by causing editorial tensions as well as financial and philosophical problems. *Vanity*'s shaky status, financial and otherwise, may be inferred by the rapid turnover of editors. William Allan Stephens is generally listed as the editor-in-chief. Frank Wood was managing editor from 1859 to 1860; Charles G. Leland was editor from about February 1860 through May 1861; Artemus Ward joined the *Vanity* staff on 2 January 1861 as assistant editor and took over control on 16 May, publishing several of his own Old Showman letters and dramatic burlesques in the next few months. Ward's lecture career was launched in December 1861, and Ward, in turn, left *Vanity* in April 1862, replaced by Charles Dawson Shanly. Leland, in his *Memoirs*, gave as the reason for Wood's leaving that he had difficulties with Stephens, and such difficulties may have persisted with the other editors. Leland himself wanted the paper to come out strongly for emancipation as a war measure, and moved to *The Knickerbocker** and later *The Continental Monthly*** to state that position more strongly than he was able to do at *Vanity*. Ward said that the paper got to be a "conundrum" so he gave it up. Money was also a problem. Stedman's "The Prince's Ball" was supposed to have "saved" the paper from economic collapse in 1860; Ward cautioned Howells that he would never see payment for a sketch; and other evidences of marginal solvency appear.

Vanity Fair was so popular in the exchanges that the publishers lost distribution and advertising, the exchange system permitting wide circulation without the financial return that syndication would have offered. The lofty *Atlantic Monthly* spoke favorably of *Vanity* in its review columns and even purchased advertising space; consequently, there was evidenced at least a passing affinity with the Boston literati to boast of. The "Preface" to *Vanity*'s Volume 6 reflects the antagonism which abolitionist Republicans felt toward *Vanity Fair*'s anti-Negro leanings, commenting on hundreds of letters of vilification which it had received from them. Hostility from a major portion of the North's polarized readership, particularly for a nonaligned paper, must have been financially unpromising. Fluctuations in paper costs also seem a reasonable cause of problems in sustaining the paper, and other magazines such as *The Knickerbocker* suffered for the same reason. By 1863 political complexities of the war-Democrat position and the interplay between Editor Stephens and his managing editors seem most likely to have cost *Vanity* a regular and expanding readership, and the fluctuating economics of wartime production brought its end.

Information Sources

BIBLIOGRAPHY:

Hamilton, Sinclair. "Henry Louis Stephens." *Early American Book Illustrators and Wood Engravers, 1670–1870*. Princeton, N.J.: Princeton University Press, 1968, 1: xlii, 208–10.

Leland, Charles G. *Memoirs*. London: Heinemann, 1893, 2: 18–23.

Meine, Franklin J. "American Comic Periodicals: No. 2—Vanity Fair." *Collector's Journal* 4 (January-February-March 1934): 461–63.

Mott, Frank L. "Vanity Fair." In *A History of American Magazines; 1850–1865*. Cambridge, Mass.: Harvard University Press, 1957, 2: 520–29ff.

Murrell, William. *A History of American Graphic Humor*. New York: Whitney Museum, 1933, 1:209–12.

Nardin, James T. "Civil War Humor: The War in *Vanity Fair*." *Civil War History* 2 (September 1956): 67–85.

Seitz, Don C. *Artemus Ward*. New York: Harper and Bros., 1919, pp. 68–127.

INDEX SOURCES: Title index bound at the end of each volume.

REPRINT EDITIONS: University Microfilms.

LOCATION SOURCES: CU, CtY, MH, NN, NcD, NjP, OClWHi, PP, RPB, and fifty other libraries list holdings.

Publication History

MAGAZINE TITLE AND TITLE CHANGES: *Vanity Fair*.

VOLUME AND ISSUE DATA: Weekly, semi-annual volumes, Volume. 1:1, 31 December 1859–Volume 6:157. Irregular for Volume 7, 1863, January, Number 158; February, Number 159; 2 May–4 July, Number 160–170.

PUBLISHER AND PLACE OF PUBLICATION: Louis Henry Stephens "for the Proprietors" (Frank J. Thompson; William Camac), New York.

EDITORS: William Allan Stephens. Managing Editors: Frank Wood 1859–1860; Charles Godfrey Leland, 1860–1861; Charles Farrar Browne, 1861–1862; Charles Dawson Shanly, 1862–1863.

CIRCULATION: Unknown.

David E. E. Sloane

VANITY FAIR (1913–1936)

The *Vanity Fair* of the teens and twenties was the brain child of Frank Crowninshield—a New York socialite crony of Condé Nast who took over *Vanity Fair* in its fourth issue and transformed it into the spirit of the sophisticated twenties for the New York social-literary world. Crowninshield had editing credentials from better quality literary magazines, including *Bookman* and

Century, and with *Munsey's*; hence his experience was reasonably broad for the wide-based, culturally humorous style he gave to *Vanity Fair*. Interested in and committed to the New York socialite life, he drew his subjects, humor, and sensibility from the milieu. As a monthly, Condé Nast's *Vanity Fair* featured the best writers in New York and America, and the cleverest and most sophisticated commentators.

Vanity Fair was born out of an entertainment-oriented journal begun in 1892 and bought up and renamed by Condé Nast *Dress and Vanity Fair* for its first four issues beginning September 1913. Crowninshield's personality—worldly, urbane, polished, and snobbishly demure—was the formative influence, and it expressed fully his own hope for a "revival of Good Taste"—a willingness, as Robert Benchley put it, for anyone to say anything he wants to in the pages of *Vanity Fair* as long as he dressed it up in evening clothes. In his initial editorial statement on 14 March, Crowinshield wrote that his purpose was to believe in the progress and promise of American life and to chronicle it cheerfully and entertainingly. Most critics agree that the Depression—and the defenestration of many of its sophisticated stockbroker readers—accounted for the climate that killed it. It continued until its merger with *Vogue* following the February 1936 Number.

Vanity Fair was 9¾″ × 12¾″ and boldly designed, featuring advertising spreads and articles and fiction by the best writers of the day, humorous, sports, and belletristic—Alexander Woollcott, Robert Benchley, Paul Gallico, Grantland Rice, Gertrude Stein, and e. e. cummings, among a vast array of others. Dorothy Parker and Robert Benchley, along with Claire Booth Brokow—later Luce— were either notable writers or editorial staff under Crowninshield's urbanely eclectic editorship. Corey Ford's literary parodies and early work by the as-yet-unknown Noel Coward were also important acquisitions. "We Nominate for Oblivion" was a popular feature that mocked Hall of Fame recognitions. Other items, like an article praising the young Hitler as a gentle politician despite the people beaten at his rallies, were repugnantly memorable in a different way. Theodore Peterson reports that ad revenues were never large and that sales were in the 80,000 to 90,000 range, making it for its period a relatively limited circulation journal. Condé Nast's interest in it as publisher was that his publishing house gained "quality and prestige" from it, and such was the case.

A typical issue such as that for August 1922 (Vol. 18:6), at thirty-five cents, offered a gorgeous brown cover by Warren Davis of four graces dancing in bright smiles and gauzy veils—and little else—around a night fire. The first and last twenty pages were totally committed to advertising in spacious layouts. Regular sections were "In and About the Theatre," including Heywood Broun on Ring Lardner and Will Rogers in combination with the Ziegfeld Follies, and several photo displays, including one on showgirls, "The Favorite Follies of Mankind." "The World of Art" included items on Marsden Hartley and Max Eastman's "Washington Without a Wig," which is at least cheeky, if not actually tongue in cheek, on a lately discovered picture of the father of his country.

Aldous Huxley and John Bishop contributed to "The World of Ideas"; Thomas Beer wrote on Hart Crane and Henry James; Hugh Walpole discussed literature and drama; and Hendrik Van Loon in "Pigs in Clover" explained the dissatisfaction of World War I vets with American culture in the twenties. "Literary Hors d'Oeuvres" offered eight pieces covering contemporary social history: government control of temptation, liberty loans, and Edward E. Paramore, Jr., on "A School for Widows"—presenting courses on "Modern and Victorian Clinging Vines" and "Metaphysics of the Late Husband." "Satirical Sketches" featured the cartoonist Sto on "Why Do People Go to the Races?", Charles Martin on "Dangerous Affairs"(advising caution when a lover enjoys teasing by sitting on a windowsill and threatening to jump), Reginald Marsh's cartoons of New York yeggs at play on the beach—"The Coney Island Pharisees"—Fish's and Bonnotte's sophisticated deco line drawings on married couples and seaside life, and George Luks' charcoal sketches with captions making fun of baseball drama. "The World Outdoors," which focused on motor touring, and a miscellany on finance, dress, and culture rounded out the 104 pages. All in all, breadth, sophisticated lightness, and an amused "modern"-seeming attitude typified *Vanity Fair*. If anything, it was less whimsical than *The New Yorker*,* but without the overpowering heaviness of *Americana** or the *Art Young Quarterly** in tone or format. Twice the price of competing magazines, it offered twice the bulk as well.

As Theodore Peterson recounts, Condé Nast added Jay Franklin and Henry Pringle to the editorial staff in 1932 to give the magazine more cultural weight. But it never was intended to be truly profitable and was poorly suited to the passing of the Roaring Twenties New York socialite era. *Ballyhoo,** for all of its vulgarized and broadened appeal and million-plus circulation, encountered similar problems beginning in the middle thirties. Therefore, *Vanity Fair* could scarcely be faulted for being alone in its situation. Its collection of epitaphs place many memorable lines on permanent record, including W. C. Fields's "I would rather be living in Philadelphia," "Here lies Michael Arlen as Usual," and Dorothy Parker's "Excuse My Dust." *Vanity Fair* itself passed away with a modest whimper in 1936.

Information Sources

BIBLIOGRAPHY:
Amory, Cleveland, and Frederic Bradlee. *Vanity Fair*. New York: Viking Press, 1960, anthology.
Benchley, Robert. "Mr. Vanity Fair." *Bookman* 50 (January 1920): 429–33.
Hellman, Geoffrey T. "Profiles—Last of the Species, Parts I and II." *The New Yorker* 18 (19 September and 26 September 1942): 22–29, 26–33, respectively.
———. "That Was New York: Crowninshield." *The New Yorker* 23 (14 February 1948): 72ff.
Lawrenson, Helen. "First of the Beautiful People." *Esquire* 79 (March 1973): 98–106, 162–66.

Peterson, Theodore. *Magazines In The Twentieth Century*. 2d. ed. Urbana: University
    of Illinois, 1964, pp. 269–71.
"Smart Magazine Joins the More Popular *Vogue*." *Newsweek* 7 (4 January 1936): 31.
INDEX SOURCES: Individual Issues have table of contents.
REPRINT EDITIONS: University Microfilms.
LOCATION SOURCES: DLC; roughly seventy-five libraries list lengthy holdings.

Publication History

MAGAZINE TITLE AND TITLE CHANGES: *Dress and Vanity Fair*, (September-
    December 1913); *Vanity Fair* (January 1914-February 1936).
VOLUME AND ISSUE DATA: Monthly, Volume 1:1–Volume 45:6 (September 1913-
    February 1936). Irregular numbering.
PUBLISHER AND PLACE OF PUBLICATION: Condé Nast as "Vanity Fair Publishing
    Co.," New York.
EDITOR: Frank Crowninshield.
CIRCULATION: 1920—99,000; 1936—90,000.

David E. E. Sloane

---------- **W** ----------

THE WASP

When "Robert Rusticoat, Esquire," better known to his contemporaries as Harry Croswell, published the first number of his Federalist paper in July of 1802, he little imagined how short-lived the enterprise would be or how far-reaching its ultimate impact. Born in the small city of Hudson, New York, *The Wasp* was Croswell's answer to *The Bee*, a Democratic-Republican paper recently brought to Hudson from New London, Connecticut, by Charles Holt. Ostensibly devoted to political satire—to "the chastisement of a set of fellows . . . intrenched in filth" (*The Wasp*, 7 July 1802)—Croswell's paper frequently crossed the bounds of satire by dealing in open, vituperative attack. Though by no means unusual among political muckraking presses of the Jefferson era, *The Wasp* was nevertheless singled out by New York Attorney General Ambrose Spencer when the Jefferson administration sought to restrain Federalist town criers through charges of libel. *The Wasp*'s brief heyday (only twelve numbers in six months) ended just as its persecutors has hoped—almost. They had not reckoned on a brilliant defense by Alexander Hamilton who, though unable to win an acquittal for Croswell, nevertheless set in motion changes in state law regarding freedom of the press. American journalism still enjoys the fruits of Hamilton's efforts on Croswell's behalf.

In the paper's first number "Rusticoat" set forth his purpose:

My inducement for establishing this paper, may be stated in a few words:—A clan of unprincipled adventurers, totally destitute of talents, have for some years conducted the democratic presses of our country. They have reviled and calumniated our greatest and best men—they have slandered our wisest rulers—they have denounced our most worthy citizens. They have fattened on falsehood—they have drunk the blood of innocence—they have excelled in villainy, and have rioted on

its spoils. . . . Respectable federal papers [such as the Hudson *Balance and Columbian Repository*, perhaps, of which Croswell was junior editor] must not be engaged
in a "war of words" with such wretches. I have, therefore, thought proper to set
up "The Wasp" for the purpose of meeting my democratic neighbors on an equal
footing (7 July 1802).

Meet them Croswell certainly did, beginning with a series of "toasts," such as
this one to William Duane, editor of the Philadelphia *Aurora*:

> Some in the modern doctrines spy
> A new commandment—Thou shalt lie.
> And if there is, as who can tell,
> There's no one, sure, he keeps so well.
> (7 July 1802)

Croswell continued to fill the pages of his fledgling paper with similar samples
of "comic" verse and with articles responding to material appearing in Holt's
Bee. Excepting passages reprinted from other political papers, Croswell himself
seems to have been *Wasp*'s sole contributor, signing his pieces with a variety
of pseudonyms—Obidiah Oldnick, Bumbasticus Bimbernickle, Anti-Jaco'(bin),
Simon Sleekjacket, and the like, although frequently suggesting that "a friend"
sent him particular items. Most of *Wasp*'s assaults are aimed at personalities,
not events, unless certain "events" pertain to the political activities of various
Democratic-Republicans—alleged illicit campaign practices, for instance, on the
part of President Jefferson.

   Although Alexander Hamilton's New York *Evening Post* first printed the story
about Jefferson that brought Croswell an indictment for libel, Hamilton himself
was too much in the public eye for Jeffersonians to risk including his paper in
their selective enforcement of the Sedition Act of 1789. A small-town paper,
Wasp might be silenced without attracting the attention of prominent Federalists.

   Croswell had previously printed worse; the passage that actually effected his
arrest follows:

> Holt says, the burden of the Federal song is, that Mr. Jefferson paid Callendar
> [James Thomson, editor of the Richmond *Recorder*] for writing against the late
> administration. This is wholly false. The charge is explicitly this:—Jefferson paid
> Callendar for calling Washington a traitor, a robber, and a perjurer—For calling
> Adams, a hoary headed incendiary; and for most grossly slandering the private
> character of men, who, he well knew were virtuous. These charges, not a dem-
> ocratic editor has yet dared, or ever will dare to meet in an open manly discussion.[1]

Because "proof of the truth of the story was irrelevant and unnecessary" under
New York law, Spencer was able to prosecute Croswell merely for having
printed, but not without drawing heavy fire from defense counsel who disputed
the law on which the Attorney General rested his case.[2] When a new trial was

granted Croswell, Hamilton became his counsel; the case that Jeffersonians had hoped would draw little attention began to gather an extensive audience.

By this time, the heavy bond that Spencer had demanded Croswell post ($2,000) had effectively quashed the Federalist paper. In *Wasp*'s last number, 26 January 1803, "Robert Rusty-Turncoat" made his exit with one last series of bitter stings, beginning with a pointed comment:

> . . . why did the democrats call the federal sedition-law the "gag-law"? It only punished them for lying, while it left them at free liberty to publish the truth.— "Aye, there's the rub!" Nothing can so completely gag a democrat as to restrain him from lying. If you forbid his lying, you forbid his speaking. . . . The federalists were very willing to have the truth told, because they knew they had nothing to fear from it. Not so the democrats. They shudder at the voice of truth; for they are well aware that they might as well give up their power at once as to permit the circulation of correct information. Miserable, despicable, pitiful must the cause be, which shrinks from free investigation!—Such is democracy—and such will democracy ever remain (pp. 1–2).

Fortunately, history has not entirely fulfilled Croswell's predictions, but the idea behind the earlier portions of the statement caused Hamilton to stress that the press should be free to engage in investigative journalism, however distasteful the consequences. In February 1804 when Croswell's trial went before the Supreme Court in Albany, public sentiment in Croswell's favor had by then brought about a bill pending in the legislature to change the New York law on which Croswell had been prosecuted.

Hamilton had planned to summon Callendar as a witness to the truth of the statement in question, but to the shock of many, Callendar was found dead shortly before the date of the trial. Whether murder or accidental drowning had been the cause, no one was ever fully able to determine, and the coroner officially recorded Callendar's death as an accident. Croswell's counsel went ahead as best as possible without the star witness. Despite a forensic appeal which historians consider one of Hamilton's best, Croswell again lost.

The case to which *Wasp* had given birth proved in the long run a victory for American journalism: Hamilton's argument that, as the voice of the people, the press must retain the freedom to call public officials to account for their actions— lest a party in power become tyrannical—eventually effected the passage of the bill designed "to correct the outworn dictum [carried over from an archaic British law] that the truth could not be introduced as a defense to a charge of libel."[3] The change meant that Croswell might have a new trial, which would necessarily involve investigation of Jefferson's association with Callendar. Jeffersonians pursued Croswell no further. As other state legislatures followed New York's suit, Hamilton's appeal regarding freedom of the press and cases of libel translated into the law of the land.

Notes

1. *The Wasp*, 9 September 1802. For Croswell's full explanation of how the offending passage came to be printed, see the Hudson *Balance and Columbian Repository*, 16 August 1803.

2. Robert A. Hendrickson, *The Rise and Fall of Alexander Hamilton* (New York: Van Nostrand Rheinhold Co., 1981), p. 578.

3. Ibid., p. 583.

Information Sources

BIBLIOGRAPHY:

Brigham, Clarence S. *History and Bibliography of American Newspapers: 1690–1820*. Worcester, Mass.: American Antiquarian Society, 1962 (1947).

Chielens, Edward E. *The Literary Journal in America to 1900*. Detroit: Gale Research Co., 1975.

Emery, Edwin. *The Press and America: An Interpretative History of Journalism*. 2d ed. Englewood Cliffs, N.J.: Prentice-Hall, 1962.

Hendrickson, Robert A. *The Rise and Fall of Alexander Hamilton*. New York: Van Nostrand Rheinhold Co., 1981.

Hoornstra, Jean, and Trudy Heath, eds. *American Periodicals, 1741–1900; An Index to the Microfilm Collections*. Ann Arbor, Mich.: University Microfilms International, 1979. [Suggests that *The Wasp* "supported the Republican viewpoint" (p. 219) to oppose the "Democratic" *Bee*; this information is misleading, since separate Republican and Democratic parties as we know them today did not exist prior to Andrew Jackson's rise to political power in the middle 1820s. Both terms therefore suit *The Bee* but not *The Wasp*, a Federalist publication.]

Kribbs, Jayne K., ed. *American Literary Periodicals, 1741–1850: An Annotated Bibliography*. Boston: G. K. Hall, 1977.

Lewis, Benjamin Morgan. "A History and Bibliography of American Magazines, 1800–1810." Ph.D. diss., University of Michigan, 1956.

Mott, Frank Luther. *American Journalism, A History: 1690–1960*. 3d ed. New York: Macmillan Co., 1962.

INDEX SOURCES: None.

REPRINT EDITIONS: University Microfilms.

LOCATION SOURCES: Ten institutions hold all or portions of *The Wasp*. MWA and the Connecticut Historical Society each have all twelve numbers; partial holdings include PHi, ICU, NjR, Dartmouth College, NN, MH, the Massachusetts Historical Society, and the Long Island Historical Society.

Publication History

MAGAZINES TITLE AND TITLE CHANGES: *The Wasp* 7 July 1802–26 January 1803.

VOLUME AND ISSUE DATE: Irregular for Volume 1: 1–12.

PUBLISHER AND PLACE OF PUBLICATION: "Robert Rusticoat, Esq.," pseudonym for Harry Croswell, at the office of the Hudson *Balance*; Hudson, New York.

EDITOR: Harry Croswell.

CIRCULATION: Unknown; the first number proposes that *The Wasp* "will be issued occasionally, as may best suit the editor, at the moderate price of three cents a number. It will be printed with legible type, on good paper [quarto-sized sheets], and will make its appearance, as soon after Holt's *Bee* is announced, as possible, whether 350 subscribers are obtained or not'' (7 July 1802).

Allison A. Bulsterbaum

THE WHITE MULE

The White Mule, the first college humor magazine at the University of Arkansas in Fayetteville, was founded and edited by a student who later became a famous comic radio personality—Chester H. (Chet) Lauck (1902–1980), the "Lum" of the popular "Lum and Abner" show that ran from 1931 to 1955. It ran for three issues in March, May, and June 1924. Lauck's purpose for the publication was announced in the first issue:

> HIC! HIC! HOWDY!
> A college humorous publication—well, say a college publication that strives toward the humorous. If you are a gray bearded misanthrope viewing that portion of college life that includes petting, drinking, cuts and flunks as the curse of contemporary education, then you should read no further. In fact, you should throw the sheet in the nearest garbage can and tear your hair and ask: "Ye gods! What are the boys and girls coming to?" However, if college life does strike a responsive chord of irrepressible fun, and you don't think the boy-ed is eternally damned merely because he has powder all over his coat lapels, and hair nets hung on the buttons of his sleeves, then this magazine registers as a success. (p.7)

The "white mule" logo on the cover of each issue underscored the popularity of drinking on the college campus. Each number, however, had its own particular theme. March is the "Infant Number," the cover bearing the drawing of a toddler dancing a fancy step; May is the "Hang-Over Number," with the cover sporting the illustration of a convict in ball and chain at hard labor "Working off a Hangover," as the caption reads; and the last issue is the "Outlaw Number," with the figure of a masked bandit astride a get-away horse appropriately adorning the cover. Two of the three cover illustrations were drawn by Lauck himself, and he also created some of the cartoons scattered throughout the issues.

In content, the three issues contain a mix of jokes, comic anecdotes, essays, brief stories, mock plays, miscellaneous vignettes, and comic drawings and cartoons. Most of the material is original with the editorial staff or student contributors. The editor complains about the paucity of student contributors, but some pieces were taken from other publications, a practice that gave Lauck one good reason for dubbing the third issue the "Outlaw Number" ("After stealing jokes, poems, cartoons, etc., from every magazine we could get our hands on, we couldn't call it anything else").[1]

Since the magazine was pitched toward a college audience, the predominant subjects and tone are suited to the tastes and interests of students. Most common are jokes, stories, or other comic pieces that deal with such subjects as drinking, dating and petting, Greek life on campus, and the lighter side of college life. The May number contains a list of comic "Definitions from the Co-ed's Social Dictionary," another clever page entitled "A Line-a-day for the Arkansas Co-ed" (pat sayings and humorous explanations of them), and a spoof about an intellectually deficient student with great athletic skills. A brief mock drama on fraternity drinking, "Greek Tragedy," features two "Brothers" and a chorus. Other jokes and brief essays cover the usual topics of interest to college students: exams and grades, early classes and sleeping late, the settling of debts as summer vacation approaches, and the baleful effect of lingering winter weather. The racy nature of some of the jokes and one-line fillers is perhaps surprising for a campus publication of 1924 (and is likely a major reason that the magazine was discontinued after the first year). One highly titillating vignette in the "Outlaw Number" was disapproved by the censorship committee at the university, but Lauck published it anyway.

In the third and last issue, Chet Lauck takes leave of his readers and comments on the enthusiastic reception to the first two numbers. He wants this last one for the year to be the best "in order that the 'White Mule' may gain an impetus this year that will still be felt when the initial publication appears next fall." That next year never came for the magazine, but despite its short run, *The White Mule* had captured readers' attention at the University of Arkansas and had aptly displayed the humorous writing and cartoon skills of its soon-to-be-famous editor.

Printed in 8½″ × 11″ format and consisting of about twenty-eight pages of text and local advertising, the magazine sold for twenty-five cents a copy.

Note

1. (Chet Lauck), "OUTLAWS!" *White Mule* 1:3 (June 1924), p. 2.

Information Sources

INDEX SOURCES: None.
REPRINT EDITIONS: None.
LOCATION SOURCES: The three issues of the *The White Mule* are in the collection of the main library on the campus of the University of Arkansas in Fayetteville.

Publication History

MAGAZINE TITLE AND TITLE CHANGES: *The White Mule*, March, May, June 1924.
VOLUME AND ISSUE DATE: Volume 1:1–3, March, May, June 1924.
PUBLISHER AND PLACE OF PUBLICATION: Student body of the University of Arkansas, Fayetteville, Arkansas.
EDITORS: Chet Lauck; Managing Editor, Vincent Ripley; Art Editor, Doy Hancock.
CIRCULATION: Unknown.

David B. Kesterson

WORLD'S FAIR PUCK

World's Fair Puck, which ran from 1 May 1893 to 30 October 1893, was a Chicago offshoot of its New York parent, providing comic copy and colorful illustrations for the Chicago World's Fair-goer. Politics was supposedly excluded from its heavily illustrated colorful pages "devoted to the social, and picturesque and the humorous side of the great Exposition.'' Colored and black and white illustrations by Frederick Opper, Joseph Keppler—one of the editor-owners— F. M. Howarth, W. A. Rogers, and others gave the magazine its tone, holding up to ridicule all that is foolish and weak in our social and political life, but awkwardly forced into formats relating only to the Fair. The magazine was visually exciting by its extensive use of bright colors and adventurous placement of materials on the page. Its greatest asset was its visual comic material, including full-page colored cover cartoons, double-page centerfolds, and back cover cartoon sequences with the effect of comic strips.

Priced at twenty-five cents, or $2.50 for the proposed run of twenty-six weeks, the 11″ × 8″, twelve-page numbers boasted their lavish color illustrations, consistent with *Puck*'s* stature as America's most advanced illustrated humor magazine. Short jokes and cartoons predominated; uninteresting forced puns concerned the life of the Fair and Fair-goers. A shop clerk's date wants to go to the looking glass stand to see the optical delusions, and a wheel boasts to its friend the balloon that he's ''up and around'' as usual. Other humor is of similar calibre.

Information Sources

BIBLIOGRAPHY:

Mott, Frank L. "Puck." *A History of American Magazines, 1865–1885*. Cambridge, Mass.: Harvard University Press, 1957, 3: 520–32, and passim; and the following Volume 4: p. 100.

INDEX SOURCES: None.

REPRINT EDITIONS: None.

LOCATION SOURCES: CtY, IC, NjR, ICN, IEN 1–18, MiU, and Chicago Historical Society.

Publication History

MAGAZINE TITLE AND TITLE CHANGES: *World's Fair Puck*.

VOLUME AND ISSUE DATA: Weekly, Volume 1:1 (1 May 1893), Volume 1:2 (15 May 1893)–Volume 1:26 (30 October 1893).

PUBLISHER AND PLACE OF PUBLICATION: Keppler and Schwarzmann, World's Fair Grounds (Jackson Park), Chicago.

EDITOR: H. C. Bunner(?).

CIRCULATION: Unknown.

David E. E. Sloane

Y

THE YANKEE

John Neal was a controversial figure in his native Maine when he became the editor of *The Yankee* in 1828. A regular contributor to *Blackwood's Magazine* during a previous four years' stay in England, he had antagonized public opinion in his home country with caricatures of the American character. *The Yankee* constituted the eclectic response of this rash, erratic, but creative Down Easter to hostile popular sentiment. It was ostensibly devoted to the dissemination of Utilitarianism and carried as its masthead motto: "Utility—The Greatest Happiness of the Greatest Number." Benthamism shared space with Neal's slapdash efforts to encourage native writers. Seeking to vindicate himself, Neal thus intended to make his paper a forum for new talents. His interest in authentic Yankee characterization was conducive to vivid portrayals of New England life in a colloquial style which irreverently departed from the belletristic tradition of Washington Irving and James Fenimore Cooper.

First published on 1 January 1828 in Portland, Maine, by James Adams, Jr. and edited by John Neal for five hundred dollars a year, *The Yankee* "burst like a northern meteor on our people," in its editor's own words, and was continued for two years. After merging with Sarah J. Hale's *Monthly, The Bachelor's Journal,* and *The Boston Literary Gazette,* it became *The Yankee and Boston Literary Gazette* on 20 August 1828 and was published in Boston by William S. Wait, then Lilly and Wait, with John Neal and James W. Miller as co-editors.

There were contributors from all parts of the country including Grenville Mellen, Nathaniel P. Willis, and Daniel Webster. Neal also supported the fledgling endeavors of Edgar Allan Poe, Nathaniel Hawthorne, and John Greenleaf Whittier. *The Yankee* offered original and selected poetry, sketches, tales, anecdotes, and essays that illustrated the peculiarities of its first editor. A born humorist, Neal often combined affection with irony in his evocation of the

New England scene. His steady involvement with regional realism was particularly noticeable in two series of articles entitled "Live Yankees" and "Sketches from Life." In a humorous mood, Neal described the major traits of Down Easters: their indirection, materialism, fortitude, enterprising spirit, shrewdness, and mode of quarreling. An anecdote about a woodsman trapped in a tree served as a model for his "David Whicher," a tall tale later expanded into a short story. An anonymous contribution, "Johnny Beadle's Courtship," was first credited to James Brooks, but Captain McClintock also vehemently claimed the authorship; republished under different titles by several magazines, this typical Yankee story was emulated by Neal himself in another issue.

The Yankee readers were constantly submitted to a colloquial barrage of controversy. Neal harshly defended a theory of literature largely derived from Schlegel's doctrine of effects. He mocked the incongruous fusion of pretentious imagery and artificial diction in "Cooperish" fiction long before Mark Twain lampooned Cooper's "literary offences." In an issue of November 1828, Neal developed his conception of "jokology," noting that human nature was always flying from one excess to another and adding that the good storyteller was neither an idiot nor an actor; the humorist was a nobody, except he was natural.

The wide appeal of *The Yankee* could not save it from collapse. James Brooks, editor of the *New York Express* ascribed its failure to its being "a thousand miles too far Down East." This judgement foreshadowed James Russell Lowell's lines in *A Fable for Critics*:

> Thus swaggers John Neal who has wasted in Maine
> The sinews and cords of his pugilist brain.

Information Sources

BIBLIOGRAPHY:
Brooks, James. "Letters from the East—John Neal." *New York Mirror* 11 (1833–1834): 69–70.
Griffin, John. *History of the Press of Maine.* Brunswick, Me.: From the Press of John Griffin, 1872, pp. 55–56.
Kribbs, Jayne K. *An Annotated Bibliography of American Literary Periodicals, 1741–1850.* Boston: G. K. Hall, 1977.
Lease, Benjamin. *That Wild Fellow: John Neal and the American Literary Revolution.* Chicago: University of Chicago Press, 1972, pp. 129–36.
Neal, John. *Wandering Recollections of a Somewhat Busy Life: An Autobiography.* Boston: Roberts Brothers, 1869, pp. 336–45.
Sears, Donald A. *John Neal.* Boston: G. K. Hall-Twayne Publishers, 1978.
INDEX SOURCES: Title Index at the end of Volume 1.
REPRINT EDITIONS: University Microfilms.
LOCATION SOURCES: DLC, American Philosophical Society, and Portland Public Library.

Publication History

MAGAZINE TITLE AND TITLE CHANGES: *The Yankee*, *The Yankee and Boston Literary Gazette*.
VOLUME AND ISSUE DATA: Weekly, Volume 1:1, January 1828–Volume 2:26, 20 June 1829. Monthly, New Series 1, July-December 1829.
PUBLISHER AND PLACE OF PUBLICATION: James Adams, Jr., Portland; William S. Wait, Lilly and Wait, Boston.
EDITORS: John Neal, James W. Miller.
CIRCULATION: Unknown.

Daniel Royot

THE YANKEE BLADE

At the high tide of native New England humor, *The Yankee Blade* was considered the best repository of Down East lore. Self-styled as a home journal and fireside companion devoted to literature, education, morals, fun, and news, it devoted ample space to comic yarns and anecdotes. *The Yankee Blade* did not merely express those values identified with a rural experience. Given the realities of a nation rapidly becoming industrial and urban, it also reflected changing social attitudes in the mid-nineteenth century. As editor, William Mathews responded to the steady interest of the public in the comedy of locale while refining the Yankee stereotype. Firmly attached to the Union, he deliberately adopted a nonpartisan stand in a period of rampant sectionalism, when the press was prone to harsh political satire. Good-natured humor eventually proved detrimental to *The Yankee Blade*, which disappeared a few years before the Civil War.

A Harvard graduate, Mathews practiced law in Waterville, Maine, before launching a literary and family weekly known as *The Watervillonian* in May 1841. Within two years the paper was removed to Gardiner, Maine, and at the close of the first volume, its name was changed to *The Yankee Blade*. In 1847, Mathews moved the enterprise to Boston where he opened an office on Washington Street. In the early years of the paper, he admitted his brother Edward to a partnership, then other partners such as Moses Stevens joined efforts with him until 1856, when the enterprise was sold to *The Boston Mercantile Journal* and merged with *The Portfolio*, a periodical published by the owners of the *Journal*.

The Yankee Blade was a quarto of four to eight pages. Supported by mail-order advertisements which covered a full page, it increased its number of columns from six to seven in 1847. The subscription price was two dollars a year, and a single copy sold at four cents. Special terms were offered to clubs in order to save on postage. With agents in Portland, New York, Baltimore, and Philadelphia, Mathews numbered his subscribers by the thousands in 1848.

The Yankee Blade featured selections from American and foreign periodicals, miscellaneous news, a gossip column entitled ''Whittlings,'' innumerable jokes and anecdotes reprinted from *The Boston Courier*, *The Knickerbocker**, the *Spirit* *of the Times*,* and many other dailies or weeklies. Mostly anonymous, the original Yankee stories published by Mathews dealt with the peculiarities of New England dialect, the greenhorn's hardships in an urban culture, Yankee courtships, and peddling tricks. Folk material was generally stylized and added literary flavor. Such yarns as "The Ill-looking Horse," "The Yankee in a Cotton Factory," and "The Public Toothbrush" often served as models for the delineation of new Yankee types and were pirated by periodicals all over the country. Mathews frequently complained about such a habit of free appropriation, but himself reprinted some of William Tappan Thompson's Major Jones's Letters without credit. *The Yankee Blade* also gathered tall tales from various regions. A Gold Rush story described steel pens put into the ground overnight and found to be gold ones in the morning.

In Mathews's samplings of native humor, Yankees were confronted with Southerners or Midwesterners, and various stories illustrated the theme of the traveling Down Easter. Such was the case with "Yankee Doodle, Esquire, in Arkansas" or "Hez' Spalding's items and ideas of folks and fashions."

The wide dissemination of yarns either first published or reprinted by *The Yankee Blade* resulted in a growing standardization of the storytelling design among almanacs, jestbooks, journals, and magazines. Somewhat tired of puns, malaproprisms and parodies, Mathews turned to popular essays and adventure stories by 1851. Some of the new material retained the essence of Yankee humor but was primarily intended to convey a dramatic interest. At this time contributions often bore the names of such authors as Thomas Shaw, Nathaniel P. Willis, Joseph Green, Caleb Leathers, and M. C. Field. In 1851, "The Connors, or the New Year's Resolve, A Tale of New England Factory Life," by Aria Ashland, suggested that readers now sought more than mother wit in the pages of *The Yankee Blade*.

Mathews considered writing for the press to be an art by itself. Averse to rhetorical devices, he favored using short items to catch the attention of the reader, but he also thought each of the longer stories should be complete in a single issue. For him, quality lay in condensation. Spicy introductions and pithy paragraphs were the quintessence of true journalism. To newspaper-writers who advocated fast writing, he answered that the sword-blade needed forging, and long and weary polishing, and grinding had to follow before the blade had a sharp cutting edge. He ruled over *The Yankee Blade* until its very last year, when he shared editorial responsibilities with Joseph W. Paine. The fate of the paper was sealed after its sale in 1856. Mathews moved to Chicago where he first edited a financial weekly and then became a professor of English.

In 1862, *Harry Hazel's Yankee Blade*, a Saturday story paper, revived the name. In the early 1880s, Harry Hazel's name was dropped; the new weekly was published until 1894, but had nothing in common with the original *Blade* of Mathews's bonanza years.

Information Sources

BIBLIOGRAPHY:

Blair, Walter, and Hamlin Hill. *America's Humor: From Poor Richard to Doonesbury*. New York: Oxford University Press, 1978, pp. 181, 222, 225, 275.

Dorson, Richard. *Jonathan Draws the Long Bow*. Cambridge, Mass.: Harvard University Press, 1946, passim.

Griffin, John. *History of the Press of Maine*. Brunswick, Me.: From the Press of John Griffin, 1872, pp. 101, 105–106.

Kribbs, Jayne, K. *An Annotated Bibliography of American Literary Periodicals, 1741– 1850*. Boston: G. K. Hall, 1977, pp. 169–70.

Mathews, William. *Hours with Men and Books*. Chicago: S. C. Griggs, 1895, pp. 256– 61.

Mott, Frank L. "The Yankee Blade." In *A History of American Magazines, 1850–1865*. Cambridge, Mass.: Harvard University Press, 1957, 2:36, 4:18, 67.

INDEX SOURCES: Title index bound at the end of each volume.

REPRINT EDITIONS: None.

LOCATION SOURCES: MWA.

Publication History

MAGAZINE TITLE AND TITLE CHANGES: *The Yankee Blade*, 30 July 1842–26 January 1856.

VOLUME AND ISSUE DATA: Weekly, annual volumes. Volumes 1:1, 30 July 1842– Volume 4:24, 26 January 1856. Suspended between 25 March and 5 April 1847.

PUBLISHER AND PLACE OF PUBLICATION: 1842–1843: William and Edward Mathews, Waterville, Maine. 1843–1846: William Mathews and Moses Stevens, Gardiner, Maine. 1847: William Mathews, Gould and Co. 1848–1850: Mathews, Stevens and Co. 1851: Mathews and Stevens. 1852–1856: Mathews, Boston.

EDITORS: William Mathews, 1842–1856; Joseph W. Paine, Co-editor, 1855–1856.

CIRCULATION: Nationwide, several thousand.

Daniel Royot

YANKEE DOODLE

When *Yankee Doodle* plunged into the waters of New York weekly journalism on 10 October 1846, it seemed better adapted for survival than its numerous competitors. Its editor, Cornelius Mathews, was an accomplished satirist, and, as the co-founder of *Arcturus, A Journal of Books and Opinion* (1840–1842), he had obtained contributions by Hawthorne, Longfellow, and Lowell. Frank L. Mott numbers Horace Greeley and N. P. Willis among the writers for *Yankee Doodle*, although none of the articles in the journal are actually attributed to them. Published at an annual subscription of three dollars in the same building as Greeley's *Tribune*, *Yankee Doodle* was more lavishly illustrated than other New York weeklies (with engravings and political cartoons by Charles Martin, the Baker Brothers, and others), and from the first issue it was able to fill three of its twelve pages with quality advertising. Moreover, as its title suggests, *Yankee Doodle* had a mission: "to embody and reproduce in permanent form, that free spirit, that exuberant life, that creative energy, and refining enthusiasm which so eminently characterize us and distinguish the New World from the Old" (Vol. 2:40). And yet, after only 52 weekly issues, Mathews's journal had perished, at least in part because of its inability to discover a truly national subject matter and native American humor.

The journal's program as announced in the first issue as "the propagation of true genuine Yankee Doodleism" was broadly satirical: "We will laugh Politics out of its briberies and bullyings, Religion out of its bigotry and intolerance, Literature out of its leading-strings, Art out of its twaddling clothes, Trade out of its trickery, Society out of its false pretences [*sic*], and History out of its lies" (Vol. 1:1, 10 October 1846, p. 3). Yankee Doodle, assisted by his wife, Mrs. Columbia Yankeedoodle, found no lack of targets. The journal staunchly opposed the Mexican War and its prime movers, President James K. Polk and General Zachary Taylor. It was a vigorous foe of what it deemed the hypocrisy of the abolitionist movement. Closer to home, it mocked the execrable performances of three singers, Camillo Sivori, Heinrich Herz, and De Meyer, then popular on the New York stage. More timidly, it offered jibes at the New York journalistic establishment.

But *Yankee Doodle* was never able to create a format or an idiom suitable to its satiric intent or its assertions of a national mission. The journal's twelve double-columned pages (measuring approximately 9″ × 11 ¾″) featured a number of rather long articles, unrelieved by the shorter squibs, puns, or riddles that served as "fill" in other comic periodicals of the day. When *Yankee Doodle* went to a sixteen-page format after twelve issues, the ponderous nature of the contents seemed even more apparent. Each issue provided visual relief in the form of one or two full-page editorial cartoons, with the Mexican adventure the most frequent target. *Yankee Doodle* often published inferior drawings in the mistaken belief that any illustrations sold copies. This was particularly the case in one early issue which devoted two and a half pages to crude sketches of umbrellas being blown inside out on Broadway.

Yankee Doodle promised several regular columns and features, but none ever established itself firmly enough to become a weekly staple. "Notes for a Biography of a Distinguée," "City Characters," and even "The Philosophy of Omnibus Riding" appear for several issues and then disappear without warning. For several weeks, the cover of the journal puffed a comic series entitled "Handy Andy's Postbag," in which a Cockney servant mistakenly sends an English Lord's epistolary observations on New York to the *Yankee Doodle* offices instead of London. Handy Andy's comic bumblings and vernacular dialect also vanished after several installments. By issue 40, with the beginning of the sobering series entitled "Inequalities of Equality: A Daguerreotype of Social Democracy," there was firm evidence that *Yankee Doodle*'s editors and contributors were experiencing difficulty adhering to their original comic intent.

As *Yankee Doodle* aspired to informed social and political commentary for a cosmopolitan audience, it failed to exploit a genuinely American idiom. Like other American journals which professed originality and a national program, *Yankee Doodle* could not evade the influence and frequent imitation of the London *Punch*. Nearly every article is couched in elaborate Latinate diction, with a convoluted and artificial syntax. The editor's assertion that we will laugh "till our foaming beakers twinkle with cachinnatory sympathy" seems calculated to perplex rather than to amuse. Only rarely do series of "letters" experiment with the dialects of vernacular speakers, and they are seldom authentic American voices. More frequently, *Yankee Doodle*'s readers were treated to the Cockney barbarisms of a Handy Andy or the "Letters of Chang Foo," another set of observations of New York by an exotic foreigner. Such features betray the self-conscious Americans' fear that the culture of the United States would be found wanting by more cultivated outsiders.

Only several letters from a Corporal in the "Mecksikkin" War seemed to suggest the locale, the subjects, and the vernacular speech which would make a true American of *Yankee Doodle*. Perhaps the culture of New York, evolving as it was in conscious imitation or defiance of European models, provided too little scope for a unique brand of American comic writing. The humor of the backwoods South and the frontier West brought success to William T. Porter's *Spirit of the Times*,* with its original American subject matter and authentic American voices. Editor Cornelius Mathews could offer New York readers a stylish and well-written tabloid, but the limited social view and rather indistinctive format could not sustain circulation or reach out to a national audience.

Information Sources

BIBLIOGRAPHY:
Mott, Frank L. *A History of American Magazines, 1741–1850*. New York: Appleton and Co., 1930, 1:425.
Stein, Allen F. *Cornelius Mathews*. New York: Twayne Publishers, 1974, pp. 129–31.
INDEX SOURCES: Title index bound at the beginning of each volume.
REPRINT EDITIONS: University Microfilms.
LOCATION SOURCES: Complete holdings of *Yankee Doodle* are available at nine libraries, including NN, DLC, and ICN. Nine libraries list partial holdings.

Publication History

MAGAZINE TITLE AND TITLE CHANGES: *Yankee Doodle*, 10 October 1846–2 October 1847(?).
VOLUME AND ISSUE DATA: Volumes 1–2: 1–52.
PUBLISHER AND PLACE OF PUBLICATION: William H. Graham, New York.
EDITOR: Cornelius Mathews, with the assistance of Richard Grant and George G. Foster.

CIRCULATION: Unknown. After only two issues, the editor boasted a circulation of 10,000; even a later assertion of "several thousands" may be exaggerated but is possibly representative.

Lorne Fienberg

YANKEE NOTIONS

Twentieth-century scholarship has not been kind to *Yankee Notions*. It figures hardly at all in the accounts of American humor or in the studies of the many humorists it printed, including early work by Mark Twain. Frank Luther Mott mentions it briefly in *A History of American Magazines, 1850–1865*, dismissing it by saying that *Yankee Notions* was "Cheaply printed and its wit was usually cheap too" (2:182). Cheaply printed it may have been for the first few issues and for the last several years, and there was always plenty of cheap wit, what with three different attempts in twelve years for an illustrated pun on "Harriet Beecher's Toe." *Yankee Notions* did not become the "Funny Magazine of the Age; or, the Compendium of the Wit of all Nations" that it first intended to be, but beginning with the first issue in January 1852 and for at least fifteen of its twenty-four years, it was a representative anthology of the best as well as the worst of the native wit, humor, and satire of nineteenth-century America in word and in picture.

T. W. Strong began publication of *Yankee Notions* in New York in January 1952, as an extension of his publishing of comic valentines, penny ballads, and other inexpensive, highly illustrated publications, such as *New York in a Nutshell* and *The Hudson River Illustrated*. In 1853 he began *Young America*, a "comic of a somewhat higher grade" than *Yankee Notions*, Mott judges, but it did not survive a lawsuit. (It was revived briefly in 1856 as *Yankee Doodle: or, Young America*.) *Yankee Notions*, however, prospered, with a circulation of 33,000 copies a month and 25,000 subscribers announced at the end of the second year, figures far more reliable than the 1 million yearly readers claimed in 1857. In 1866, Strong sold *Yankee Notions* to R. M. DeWitt, whereupon the publication "deteriorated in paper, printing, and 'art'," as Mott says (2:182n). DeWitt claimed 10,000 readers in 1870, two years after A. S. Tuttle's American News Company took over distribution in 1868. With the December 1875 issue, *Yankee Notions* ceased publication and merged with two other comic periodicals—*Nick Nax** and *Merryman's Monthly***—to become *The Three Comics*, which lasted for at least three more years.

The format of thirty-two, two-column, 8″ × 11″ quarto pages changed little in twenty-four years, nor did the price. It stayed at twelve and a half cents until after the Civil War, when the price rose to fifteen cents a copy and then went down to ten cents in 1873, when a page or two of advertisements began to appear regularly. Early issues offered a year's subscription for $1.25 ($1.50 in 1865), but *Yankee Notions* was probably bought by the issue, certainly in the later years, aimed chiefly, as it seems to have been, at a New York City audience.

Every issue featured an original full-page cover illustration, a colored one was used in 1853, and in 1856, Strong offered twenty dollars for original cover illustrations. *Yankee Notions* had few special departments. "The Child's Corner" did not last the first year, and in 1856 Strong tried a "Musical and Dramatic" column, but it proved perfunctory and short-lived. "The Editor's Chip Basket," began the same year, survived to the end. At first, it offered commentary on politics, fashions, and fads, but it soon became and remained a page filled almost exclusively with comic conundrums, puns, and brief gags sometimes with a political or social barb to them. Above all, from the first issue in January 1852 to the last in December 1875, every page of every issue of *Yankee Notions* was filled with printed humor of all kinds, virtually all of it borrowed, and with humorous illustrations, virtually all of them original.

Illustrations were important to Strong, himself an engraver who was proud of the quality and the quantity of illustrations in *Yankee Notions*. He did not copy cuts from *Punch*, and even the initial, illustrated letters were original, he declared. The first volume contained over 1,000 illustrations, for which he paid $20,000 out of a total expenditure of $60,000, Strong announced, and over the years he employed most of the major illustrators of the time: Augustus Hoppin, T. B. Gunn, S. P. Avery, Frank Bellew, J. H. Howard, John McLenan, Thomas Worth, Jacob Dallas, and Carl A. Carlton among them. Strong himself occasionally contributed a signed illustration and probably did many of the unsigned ones.

The quality and quantity of the illustrations diminished over the years, but they were always important to the character of *Yankee Notions* as a comic periodical and were used in a variety of ways, less often to illustrate printed stories or jokes than as humor in their own right, with cartoons, caricatures, and visual puns being particularly popular. A captioned cartoon narrative often appeared through several pages and was sometimes serialized over several issues. Illustrations also provided the outlet for most of the political and social satire and commentary in *Yankee Notions*. Political satire appeared regularly during Strong's fifteen-year tenure and represented a watered-down version of his "Young America" Democratic party politics. During the early months of Lincoln's first term, *Yankee Notions* poked fun at the new President, but with the outbreak of the Civil War it came out strongly for Lincoln and the Union. A two-page cartoon in January 1863 shows Jefferson Davis making a deal with the devil, a Black man in chains at their feet. However, while *Yankee Notions* always took the high road in its denunciation of Southern slavery, it typically caricatured, usually grotesquely, Northern, urban Blacks and their aspirations for social and political equality.

As for the printed humor in *Yankee Notions*, it is typically anonymous, brief, and borrowed, and while virtually all of it is forgettable, as might be expected, it is an accurate representation of American popular humor of the time. All of the major "schools" that modern scholarship has assigned to native American humor are well represented—New England, backwoods, and the literary comedians—as well as others not so well documented, such as American Irish, Negro, and Dutch, Midwestern (called "Hoosier" in *Yankee Notions*), and Western.

All of the major humorists and their characterizations appear as well, with the exception of James Russell Lowell. Jack Downing, Sam Slick, and popular stories from the 1830s and 1840s are represented, but *Yankee Notions* is more remarkable perhaps for early recognizing and reprinting the work of a later generation of humorists. Strong reprinted several pieces by Mark Twain before the "Jumping Frog" story made Twain well known in the East, calling him "the witty correspondent of the San Francisco Golden Era" in a prefatory note to "Ladies' Toilets" in the March 1864 issue. The early work of Artemus Ward, Josh Billings, Sut Lovingood, and Matthew Whittier also found readers in *Yankee Notions*. The Civil War humorists were well represented with the pro-Union Petroleum V. Nasby, George Arnold, Artemus Ward, Doesticks, and Orpheus C. Kerr, but the Southern spokesman Bill Arp made a late appearance as well. After the war—after R. W. DeWitt took editorial control—few prominent writers appear, with the exception of Josh Billings, B. P. Shillaber as Mrs. Partington, and Mark Twain. There are fewer signed illustrations as well, and longer, nonhumorous fiction is featured more often.

To catalog those humorists and schools that twentieth-century readers have identified as meaningful to the study of American humor is probably to miss much of the character and function of nineteenth-century American humor to nineteenth-century American readers. In word and in picture much of the humor of *Yankee Notions* is urban and reflects the political, social, and cultural strains of a nation becoming increasingly democratized and urbanized. *Yankee Notions* portrayed persistently, but with consistently good humor, the comic pretensions of the urban middle class—its fashions, tastes, and romantic follies. It also portrayed, but with less good humor, the seamy side of urban low life—its poverty, vice, and violence generally—but with little sympathy for what caused such conditions or those forces that might change them. With uncharacteristic editorial forthrightness, *Yankee Notions* railed in October 1853 against the "Anti-Slaveryites, Temperanceites, Bloomerites, Women's Rightsites, and Devilites in general" who have "come to the rescue of the world."

In the abstract, *Yankee Notions* celebrated the social and political promises of the free and enlightened, "Universal Yankee Nation" that it ostensibly represented, but it had little use for the fulfillment of those promises in fact. Given the reality of Southern slavery, the American Negro represented an equivocal embodiment of that fulfillment, and thus the Irish immigrant, unequivocally urban, bore the brunt of *Yankee Notions* misgivings. A full-page cartoon titled "Paddy's Ladder to Wealth in a Free Country" features a leering, simian-like Irish hod carrier climbing up the scaffold. Recent Irish immigrants are regularly caricaturized over the years as new voters willing to trade their franchise for a drink, early and often. All of these kinds of urban humor, of course, had long been popular in English political and social satire, but in nineteenth-century America, a nation in search of an identity different from that of the mother country, they take on different meanings.

When *Yankee Notions* ceased publication at the end of 1875, it had been in print for nearly a quarter of the nation's first one hundred years, longer than any other humor magazine of the time. However ephemeral, even objectionable, as much of its humor may be today, it survived as long as it did because, above all else, it entertained its nineteenth-century readers. For readers today, the nearly 10,000 pages of *Yankee Notions* provide a good place to begin to understand not only what entertained those readers but also why it did so.

Information Sources

BIBLIOGRAPHY:

Mott, Frank L. *A History of American Magazines; 1850–1865*. Cambridge, Mass.: Harvard University Press, 1957, 2:182–83.

Murrell, William. *A History of American Graphic Humor*. New York: Whitney Museum, 1933, 1:182, and passim.

Sloane, David E. E., "Introduction." *The Literary Humor of the Urban Northwest, 1830–1890*. Baton Rouge: Louisiana State University Press, 1983, pp. 1–48.

INDEX SOURCES: None.

REPRINT EDITIONS: None.

LOCATION SOURCES: Several libraries have most of the first fifteen volumes, including DLC, MB, MH, MiD, MnU, NN, and NNC. The most complete collection is in OCLWHi. ULS is not accurate for many of the holdings of later volumes.

Publication History

MAGAZINE TITLE AND TITLE CHANGES: *Yankee Notions*, January 1852–December 1875.

VOLUME AND ISSUE DATA: Monthly, annual volumes, Volume 1:1, January 1852–Volume 24:12, December 1875.

PUBLISHER AND PLACE OF PUBLICATION: 1852–1866: T. W. Strong, New York. 1866–1875: R. W. DeWitt, New York.

EDITOR: Not known, probably the publishers.

CIRCULATION: In the early years, circulation was probably 20,000 to 30,000 a month and perhaps more in the mid- to late 1850s. After the Civil War, when *Yankee Notions* was sold primarily on newsstands, the publisher usually claimed 10,000 readers for each issue.

Cameron C. Nickels

Z

ZIFFS

Ziffs, was typical of the racy and breezy regional humor magazines of the 1920s, following the trail of *Sagebrush Philosophy*,* *The American Mercury*,* and *Captain Billy's Whiz Bang*.* November 1924 (Vol. 1:7) is the earliest seen. Following a revision in size and format, May 1925 was Volume 3:2 (probably a typographical error for Vol. 2:2), with an issue known at least as late as March 1926. Available monthly for twenty-five cents, *Ziffs* was published by the A. C. Auld Publishing Company of Maywood, Illinois; the editor was ''Badzib,'' the actual owner of the Auld Company, William B. Ziff, a proponent of liberal stands on temperance laws and postal regulations against obscenity, and an acerbic editorialist in favor of his positions. Through early 1925, *Ziffs* was in a ''red-headed'' cover in digest size, roughly 5½″ × 8″; it was changed to an 8½″ × 11½″ full-sized magazine as ''*Ziffs*—Badzib's Book of Art and Wit'' about March 1925.

The red-headed digest specialized in ''Bull Exterminating'' and stiletto pushing—its way of attacking political fakery in the press and on the national scene. Badzib's editorial in Volume 1:7 states that a ''Man'' is as good as a king, placing his ideology in the language and democratic mode of the comic tradition of Artemus Ward and Mark Twain in the previous century. Elsewhere, humor is in the twenties style: A lady complains to an urchin that she hasn't heard swearing like his since the day she was born, and the urchin replies, ''Why lady, did they cuss much when you wuz born?'' ''Hot Shots off the Press'' reprinted unintended comedy from the nation's papers. The large-format *Ziffs* rejected the cruder elements of regional styling in favor of colorful covers featuring pretty girls and the leading visual humorists of the 1920s. John Held, Jr., drew flappers and jellybeans; pin-up photos abounded; doggerel verse brought the old standards up to modern times: ''When the music's getting rotten, / And your Sheik is out of Gin, / Then go home and kid the milk man / As he meets you, coming in!'' Longer humor and dialect fiction punctuated pages of paragraph-length jokes and illustrations by Alberto Vargas, John Held, Jr., Nuytens, Russell Patterson, and Harold Delay. In the May 1925 number, four pages were devoted to the work of Heinrich Kley, the German surrealist cartoonist who enjoyed a renewal of interest in the 1960s. ''Hot Shots off the Press'' was supplemented by reprinted humor in ''Gas from Other Ranges.'' A long defense of *Broadway Brevities*,** in company with the artists just mentioned, suggests that *Ziffs* had matured into a highly conscious and thoughtful comic journal, worthy of further attention by scholars of humor in this period. W. B. Ziff Company was listed only as the advertising representative.

The *Dictionary of American Biography, Supplement*, identifies William B. Ziff (1898–1953) as the owner and editor of *Ziffs*. Ziff began as a commercial artist and cartoonist for the *Chicago Daily News*; after air service in the First World War, he began a Chicago advertising agency and eventually took over the E. C. Auld Company. Ziff edited his magazine for two years and then changed the name to *America's Humor*.** Ziff himself later becme widely recognized for his advocacy of air power and General Billy Mitchell and his thoughtful studies of international relations, particularly in relation to Palestine. Ziff-Davis, his New York publishing company, was successful with *Amazing Stories* and other popular magazines. Ziff's wide-ranging interests may help account for the high quality of his early comic magazine venture.

Information Sources

BIBLIOGRAPHY:
McCann, William. ''Ziff, William Bernard.'' *Dictionary of American Biography*, Supplement 5, pp. 760–61.
''Ziff, William B.'' *Current Biography*, 1946, pp. 676–78.
INDEX SOURCES: None.
REPRINT EDITIONS: None.
LOCATION SOURCES: None.

Publication History

MAGAZINE TITLE AND TITLE CHANGES: *Ziffs*.
VOLUME AND ISSUE DATA: Volume 1:1 (May 1923?)–Volume 3:3 (March 1926), and later.
PUBLISHER AND PLACE OF PUBLICATION: A. C. Auld Publishing Co. (sometimes appearing as E. C. Auld), Maywood, Illinois.
EDITOR: W. B. Ziff.
CIRCULATION: Unknown.

David E. E. Sloane

Part II
<u>BRIEF LISTINGS</u>

____ A ____

ABC (AMERICA'S BEST CARTOONS)

ABC was a brightly colored annual, 5¼" × 7¼" in size, with editorial and artwork by Harry "A" Chesler, Jr., father of a number of such World War II digests. It was first published in 1943. Private Bill, Riggin Bill, and A. Sapp's Fables were among the strip features that also appeared in magazines under their own names; "Private Chesler" and a collection of prose humor as "My Daze" by Vera Smart filled out the 64 pages, designed to be sold on newsstands and post exchanges. William H. Wise Company, New York, was the publisher, and it was published quarterly at ten cents a copy. Number 2 is 1944 and Number 3 is 1945, suggesting annual publication; it was never copyrighted.

A-LAUGH-A-MINNIT

This digest cartoon-gags magazine, 5¼" × 7¼" in size, was published by Minoan Publishing Corporation of New York; Number 15 was December 1955, with mostly girlie theme cartoons, a few printed in color. It may have also been copyrighted as *Laugh a Minute*. Numbers 12, 13, and 14 were copyrighted for August, September, and November 1955, respectively.

ALLEY UP

alley up—published without capital letters in the form of Don Marquis's archy and mehitabel—was a "weekly by the grace of God" by Jasmine Stone Von Dresser of Palm Beach, Florida. Volume 1:1 is dated 5 February 1926, and sold for twenty cents a copy. It was merely a four-page advertising sheet for the Everglades Arcade, with a circulation of 1,600, but four numbers—through 26

February—have been retained by DLC. Its phrases and style suggest free-form unedited reflections, and it was made up of breezy, conversational local alley news and city gossip. Its chief point is its lack of capitalization.

AMERICAN HUMORIST

American Humorist was a monthly publication by J. I. Rodale of Emmaus, Pennsylvania, who was later widely known for *Organic Gardening* magazine. In two-column format with 60 to 70, 5″ × 8″ pages per issue, *American Humorist* offered humorous anecdotes collected by topic, pages of jokes and gags, and some brief comic articles; a few page-size cartoons completed the mix of material, along with a movie-gags-of-the-month competition. Anecdotes were offered in a format suggesting similar *Reader's Digest*** departments, and some Thurber material and other light fiction was offered. Although its second-class mailing permit is dated 21 April 1933, and its first issue was probably in July, no issues have been seen prior to Volume 7:37 for August 1936—the last issue before it dropped its humorous format to become the nonhumorous *New Biography*. It sold for fifteen cents a copy, or one dollar for a year's subscription. One issue is available at NN; holdings of *New Biography* do not usually include the earlier publication, and the *Union List of Serials* is unreliable for locations.

AMERICAN HUMORIST/NEW YORK SUNDAY JOURNAL

William Randolph Hearst created the *American Humorist* in 1896 to compete with Joseph Pulitzer's successful Sunday supplements. Foreshadowing the comics of the twentieth-century newspaper, Hearst's papers claimed a circulation of 600,000 by 1898. See also *Sunday Comic Weekly/The Sunday World*.

THE AMERICAN MAGAZINE AND MONTHLY CHRONICLE FOR THE BRITISH COLONIES

Edited by the Reverend William Smith of the college of Philadelphia from October 1757 through October 1758, *The American Magazine* was a serious publication but among its contributors was satiric poet Francis Hopkinson. Its series of essays by "Timothy Timbertoes," titled "The Prattler," is a satire on the life of the town, women, and Quakers—early evidence of comic fiction in American serial publications. For more information, see Bruce Granger, *American Essay Serials from Franklin to Irving* (Knoxville: University of Tennessee Press, 1978), pp. 52–56, and Mott's *History of American Magazines* 1:80–82.

AMERICAN MASONIC REGISTER

L. G. Hoffman, a devoted Freemason with literary interests, founded his *American Masonic Register and Literary Companion* in Albany, New York, in 1839 to combat anti-Masonic feeling. Volume 1:1 was published 31 August 1839. It featured "Popular Tales," Masonic news, "Poetry" columns of reprinted verse, and "Miscellany" and "Intelligence" where most humorous pieces appeared, primarily borrowed from *The Knickerbocker** and *Bentley's Miscellany* of London. Various stories treated Jonathan the Yankee, Pat the Irishman, Black slaves, and wild Westerners. Bits on foreign countries were also published, but the humor tended to be short, unattributed, or signed by the likes of "Triptolomous Tindall, z. z.," "Timothy Titterwell, Esq.'', or "Philotheorus." Theodore S. Fay's "The Witness Box" was probably a reprint rather than an original. The lack of contributions from fellow Masons was a hardship, and the paper went from weekly to monthly, and terminated with August-September 1847, superseded by the *Masonic Review*. University Microfilms has reprinted it, and roughly thirty libraries list holdings.

Alan L. Kalish

AMERICA'S HUMOR

America's Humor was a jolly compendium of humorous short stories, cartoon gags, and jokes. Its graphics were varied and strong, leaning heavily on the entire range of the comic tradition of the 1900–1930 period from Zim to Russell Patterson. Both its humor and its visual appearance were boldly Roaring Twenties, although its viewpoint tended toward the conventional rather than the skeptical. Featured writers included E. P. Butler, Homer Croy, Opie Read, Everett Shinn, Parke Cummings, Will Rogers, and others. "The Circus of Life" was the subtitle found on many of its garishly crayoned romantic covers, dominated by twenties beauties. Selling at twenty-five and later thirty-five cents, 8½" × 11¾" in size, it varied from quarterly to monthly to bimonthly, with George Mitchell as editor for Walter Springer's Magazine Builders in New York for Volume 8, preceded by Harry Stephen Keeler for E. C. Auld of Chicago in Volume 7. Volume 7:1 appeared in April 1927, and Volume 8:7 for July 1928 was the last copyrighted. W. B. Ziff Company of Chicago was the advertising agent. William B. Ziff, later prominent as an international political analyst and president of Ziff-Davis Publishing Company of *Amazing Stories* pulp magazine fame, changed *Ziff's** into *America's Humor* and edited it for its first two years; see *Dictionary of American Biography*, Supplement 5, and *Current Biography*, 1946.

APPLE PIE

Apple Pie threw itself at conventional American social experience from March 1975 (Vol. 1:1) as a bimonthly, costing $1.25 per issue, or $7.50 per year, under the editorship of Dennis H. Lopez, published by Adrien B. Lopez and Histrionic Publications, New York. Trendy 1970s attitudes and counter-culture comix were combined in burlesques of old magazine formats, "Existential Follies" columns, and advertising takeoffs. National political targets also received soft satiric hits, including the Central Intelligence Agency. The format was slick magazine, measuring 8½" × 11", with articles like "My Most Unforgettable Character: I Remember Charlie Manson" by Patricia Krinkwinkle, and "Viet Kid Collecting: Tinseltown's Latest Craze"; comic sequences in black and white and color comix style attacked violence, big business, and related topics. A successor to *Harpoon*, another Lopez publication, it may have lasted as late as 1978, claiming a circulation of 100,000. Volume 2:1 for January 1976 is the last seen, however.

THE ARGUS

The Argus was established in Seattle, Washington, in 1894 as a breezy vernacular regional paper. It had a 12" × 18", three-column format, appeared weekly, and featured civic consciousness and a sarcastic but positive tone. Chadwick and Ambrose were the original publishers; H. A. Chadwick was alone by 1915. DLC holds Volume 5:1 (12 February 1898) through Volume 69:52 (28 December 1962); the last seen were edited by Russell Sackett and published by Thomas Meadowcraft at fifteen cents per copy.

ARKANSAW THOMAS CAT

Jefferson Davis Orear edited the *Arkansaw Thomas Cat* from Hot Springs, Arkansas, beginning in 1890 and lasting through 1948. In breezy and outrageous prose, he attacked the phony and the easy and praised the good old virtues of hard work. His motto was "God help the rich, the poor can beg" and the issues in the 1920s boasted that the *Thomas Cat* was "a journal of affirmation," not built for fanatics, reformers, mummies, or mammy club convention women. The "journalistic highball run by a heathen for people now on earth" sold for ten cents, in a 5½" × 8½" format. It claimed to be printed "just before midnight," allowing for legal Sunday appearance. The University of Arkansas has thirty-four numbers, and a few additional copies are held at the Arkansas Historical Commission. The Meine Collection at the University of Illinois has Volume 8:7 (7 March 1908) and Volume 40:1 (2 November 1929), but carries the next day's date on the cover.

In Fred W. Allsopp's *History of the Arkansas Press* (Little Rock: Parke-Harper Publishing Company, 1922), Orear is reported to have given up an early career in law and taken "to lying and drift[ing] into journalism," on the *Appleton City Picayune* (Mo.). Afterward, he purchased the *Browington Banner* (Mo.) and, as Allsopp vicariously writes, "lifted it into sudden and lasting fame" (p. 612). Orear then "immortalized" the *Democratic Standard* of Appleton with humor which he states was never equalled by any but himself (Allsopp, p. 612). In 1885, Orear started the *Thomas Cat* at Butler, Missouri, but sold it after nine months. The paper soon ceased publication. After a short time on the *Fulton Daily World* (Mo.), Orear secured a position on Kansas City's *Traveler*. In 1890, Orear "launched and jumped astride the *Arkansas Thomas Cat*, at Hot Springs, and rode it into glory," or so he states in Allsopp (p. 612.).

Orear described each issue of the Hot Springs publication as "a Necromatic Narrator of the Nigescent, Noxious, Nozzling Nuissance of a Nation swollen with ignorance and pride. It reads the Roasting Riot Racket and spreads sulphuric language occasionally, but for all that, it is a publication that can be taken into any family" (Allsopp, p. 168). At times, the *Arkansaw Thomas Cat* would rectify wrongs in the community. In 1917, the paper was sued for $40,000 by a man whose certain misdeeds had been exposed. Allsopp reports that eighteen attorneys served in the paper's defense, but the jury awarded the plaintiff, fining Orear a charge of one dollar. The Court Clerk is said to have donated the court costs (Allsopp, pp. 168–69).

Michael Pettengell

ARMY AND NAVY FUN PARADE

From 1942 through 1946, Alfred Harvey Publications, St. Louis, Missouri, brought out this digest size, 64-page cartoon and belly laugh, two-liner magazine, featuring "Camp Cuties" and similar departments, with Leon Harvey as editor in New York. Along with *Army and Navy Grins*,** *Hello Buddies*,** and *Army and Navy Jokes*,** it was intended to sell at PXs at $1.20, publishing every six weeks. Material was typical of the 1940s male humor viewpoint toward girls, dating, and marriage. Volume 4:7 (30 January 1946) is the last copyrighted.

ARMY AND NAVY GRINS

Volume 1:1 (February 1944) of *Army and Navy Grins* was digest size at 5½" × 7½", published every six weeks by Alfred Harvey Publications, St. Louis, Missouri, at fifteen cents per issue or $1.20 per year, and edited by Leon Harvey in New York. Harvey used the gals and gags format in uniform and wartime settings, leaning heavily on full-page cartoons with a slight mixture of two-liners. The last copyrighted issue was Volume 1:8 (Winter 1945), although it appeared at least through August 1946, with irregular publication dated by month or season, but apparently not in the six-weekly mode of *Army and Navy Fun Parade*.**

ARMY AND NAVY HOT SHOTS

Ampco Books published this 5¼″ × 7½″, fifteen-cent, 68-page gag cartoons book. It is typical of 1940s wartime humor digests featuring gobs 'n gals cartoons, one to a page, including contributions from Bill Wenzel and others listed on the first page. No publication date is given.

ARMY AND NAVY JOKES

Volume 1:1 (February 1944) through Volume 1:8 (Fall 1945) covers the copyrighted span of *Army and Navy Jokes* by Handy Publications: two numbers were issued as a monthly, and then the magazine was published quarterly. It may have survived to August 1946.

ARMY FUN

Digest-sized at 5¼″ × 7¼″, and varying from 64 to 96 pages of cartoons with a few paragraphs interspersed, *Army Fun* lasted from Volume 1:1 (November-December 1951) through Volume 12:8 (February 1975) and possibly beyond. The army gals and gags cartoons format under editor Samuel Bierman for Feature Publications corresponded to other Feature Publications, namely, *Broadway Laughs*,** *Army Laughs*,** and *Laff Time*.** By the mid–1970s, it increased from twenty-five cents to forty cents and to a sexier cartoon format under Crestwood Publications of Buffalo, New York.

ARMY LAUGHS (ARMY LAFFS and NEW ARMY LAUGHS)

Ninety-six pages of digest-size humor in uniform and in civilian life covered various topics, mostly in page-sized cartoon jokes with some brief prose pieces. Volume 1:1 for February 1941, as well as the following monthly three numbers, were copyrighted as *Army Laffs*. It continued as *Army Laughs*, including an annual edition, through Volume 5:12 (March 1946) copyrighted, and through new Volume 5:11, its twenty-second year, February-March 1961, as a bimonthly. The last issue seen, November 1965, Volume 16:9, claims to be its twenty-seventh year, so numbering seems somewhat arbitrary. Corporal Ken Browne edited and did covers and some inside pieces for Crestwood Publications of Buffalo, New York, through at least 1947 when it was fifty cents an issue and on through *New Army Laughs*. The size of the new digest was increased to 8½″ × 11″, and more of its revamped 64 pages were filled with advertising. It became bimonthly around 1949. Later, Samuel Bierman edited *Army Laughs* in the old format for Headline Publications of Holyoke, Massachusetts, and later New York, when it sold for a quarter as a Crestwood Publication possibly as late as September 1969.

AW, NERTS!

Aw, Nerts!, monthly from February 1932 at fifteen cents, was another of *Ballyhoo*'s* followers, with a similar 8½" × 11½" size and a format dominated by full-page burlesque advertisements and catchy 1930s cartoons. Fiction burlesques were akin to ''The Murder in the Marble Orchard'' by Sir Arthur Conan Nertz in the April 1932 (Vol. 1:3) number. George H. Guy was the publisher and editor; Jim Niles seems to have been responsible for much of the prose humor.

B

BALONEY

The Country Press, Louisville, Kentucky, produced *Baloney* in an 8½″ × 11″ quarterly format at fifteen cents. It aped *Ballyhoo*'s* splashy cartoons and society humor but without the burlesque advertisements that gave *Ballyhoo* its intellectual weight. Bedroom and outhouse cartoons, mostly full page, dominated its thirty-six-page, Summer edition, 1932.

BEDSIDE BOOK OF STAG HUMOR (ADAM STAG HUMOR)

This annual book of adult stag humor from *Adam Magazine*, a "men's" magazine, was edited by Richard Ashby. Number 4, dated January 1969 (8″ × 10½″), contains one hundred pages of jokes, humor stories, and cartoons, and uses 2002 A.D. and space humor as the theme for material on sex play and sexual activity.

BELLY LAFFS (1944)

Belly Laffs was issued by the Chardee Publishing Corporation, New York. Number 1 (1944), at ten cents, offered twenty pages of trite epigrams, and reprinted jokes in a three-column format and a scattering of cartoons with a center spread of all cartoons. Although the cover offered service-oriented cartoons and a claim as "America's Foremost Morale Builder," humor was general. "Advice to modern musicians—Look Bach" and "Sally complains that the new Sargeant who boasted he could read women like a book, uses the Braille system" are typical.

BELLY LAFFS (1955)

Belly Laffs was produced by the Minoan Publishing Corporation of New York. At twenty-five cents per issue, this 5¼" × 7½" magazine was all cartoons (with a number cheaply color printed) on sexy gold-digger themes, as when a young woman behind the perfume counter tells a propositioner, "I couldn't possibly come and look at your etchings on a night like this—unless, of course, I had a nice warm mink to go in." The issue seen is Number 5 for December 1955. Number 3 (for September 1955) and the November 1955 issue were copyrighted.

THE BIBELOT

In *The Bibelot*, Thomas Bird Mosher did not intend to produce a humorous magazine; however, wit was a natural byproduct of the miscellany of "exotics of literature" for which he hoped to create an audience. Although much of its material is serious to the point of gloom, the first issue featured François Villon ballads, and later Mosher offered twelfth-century Latin student songs, J. A. Symonds on medieval Norman songs, and Edward Burne-Jones on William Thackeray's humor, but little else to encourage the idea of humor generally. Duodecimo, at five cents an issue and fifty (later seventy-five) cents a year, twenty-four to forty-eight pages, it generally offered twelve choice pieces of literature per issue. Without advertising, and benignly ignoring copyrights and author payments, this little magazine survived for two decades, from Volume 1:1 (January 1895) through Volume 20 (December 1915) and an Index "Testimonial Edition" published in 1924. Circulation was about 1,650 by subscription, and 127 libraries list holdings of this magazine, which is considered one of the three or four best of the little magazines. University Microfilms has reprinted it.

E. Kate Stewart

BIG RIG SEX ON SEX

A coarser version of *Sex to Sexty*,** *Big Rig Sex on Sex*, first published in 1972, also claimed to be a book rather than a magazine. It featured physical sexual humor, emphasizing cartoons oriented toward the sexual act and bodies in sexual contact. Volume 2, at one dollar, 66 pages, in a 9" × 11" format with black and white cartoons purposefully scattered randomly in varying sizes, was published by CAT Enterprises, Fort Worth, Texas, in 1973, edited by Rick Gregson. No other issues have been seen.

BLACKOUT

Blackout was a 64-page bimonthly wartime humor digest, measuring 5⅜″ × 7½″, selling for fifteen cents, published by the Comic Corporation of America, New York. Blackout cartoons were oriented to kissing-girlie jokes of one sort or another, with a few pages of general jokes and five back pages devoted to rules for blackout and air-raid procedures. March 1942 (Vol. 1:1) is the only issue seen or copyrighted.

BLAH

"Now only 15 cents" raved the cover of Volume 1:12 for July 1933; *Blah* was cutie sleaze humor that hardly justified the twenty-five cent price of forerunner issues. Raymond Bargy was managing editor for Modern Life Publishing Company, St. Paul, Minnesota. The magazine was mostly cartoons and gags on mildly risqué dating themes; in format and on heavy cheap paper measuring 5½″ × 8″, it was reminiscent of *Hot Dog*** from Cleveland. Volume 1:1 was published in April 1932, and copyright listings are sporadic.

BOB'S DIGEST OF FUN AND FOOLOSOFY

Bob's Digest was crackerbarrel humor on dating, sex, and life of the 1940s. It claimed that it was "not" a periodical until after the war. It was published by Delta Publications of New York, with Bob Richman as editor. The one hundred page magazine measured 5¼″ × 7¾″ and cost twenty-five cents.

THE BONEVILLE TRUMPET

The Boneville Trumpet of Bridgeport, Connecticut, was edited by "Alderman M" and appeared from at least 5 September 1868 through 28 August 1869, according to a list supplied by Walter Blair and Franklin Meine to Mott.

THE BOOBY TRAP

December 1944 through October 1946 and Volume 1:1–5, 7–10 have been separately reported. The issue seen is Volume 1:6 for May/June 1945. Measuring 5½″ × 7½″, at fifteen cents a copy, and comprising brightly colored girlie joke covers, *The Booby Trap* was published bimonthly by the Goodman Publishing Company of Washington, Iowa, with editorial offices at Malibu Lake, California. Most of the cartoons were crudely executed and presented one to a page, with a page or two of gags thrown in. Typical is a lady lion tamer in torn clothing who complains to her film director about the lion, "He may not have teeth but he's certainly gumming h— out of me." On the cover a cutie holds a sign that reads, "10 cents a dance, 25 cents a wrestle." See also *The Nugget*.**

BOSTON LITERARY GAZETTE

The *Gazette* was a "Royal" sheet, 13" × 18½", in four pages of four columns, printed by John H. Eastburn for Jas. Wm. Miller, the editor; S. G. Goodrich was the general agent. It appeared in weekly numbers from 16 February 1828 through 9 August 1828 (Vol. 1:26). Favoring Washington Irving and John Neal to idolatry, and writing about them extensively, it was an enthusiast for Americanism and the American system. By March, it found itself needing to attack copiers and critics, without giving any clear explanation of why. Regular features included "A Rambler's Reminiscence" of a Western trip to Lake Erie and beyond, "Gossipiania," and "M'Going's Maxims": "If you have a puny enemy, buy him; if a potent one, crush him"; "Political colussuses in other countries are wonders, in ours weasels"; and "Love never stands upon ceremony but vanity can never dispense with it," among less pungent lines. "The Broken Down Gentleman" in the third number introduced "Jack Marrowfat" and "Toby Tipplewell" in an attempt to provide a racier form of humor than the epigrams and literary material allowed; "Tales of the Quizz Family" is also of minor interest. MWA has the only run.

BOSTON LITERARY MAGAZINE

This general monthly appeared from May 1832 (Vol. 1:1) through April 1833 (Vol. 1:12) with articles of a general nature, although some might be considered to show light humor and an elevated comic consciousness. Clapp and Hull printed it for "An Association of Literary Gentlemen," later W. G. Havaford and H. Bourne. Copies are at CU, DLC, CtY, MB, NN, and Colorado College, with partial runs at OC, MWA, NjR, MH, Massachusetts Historical Society-Boston, and Illinois State Library-Springfield. University Microfilms has reprinted the full run.

BREEZY

Breezy, cartoon jamboree, mixed a few cheesecake and sleazecake photos with an array of jokes and gag lines on sex and urban life, bimonthly at twenty-five cents. Number 5, which appeared in October 1954, featured whispering plumbers, gals in garters seducing groceryboys, and similar material; Jefferson Machamer, Bill Wenzel, and Reamer Keller appear frequently. By 1956, Humorama, Inc., was boosting it as a "gal-o-rama," possibly hoping for a men's magazine audience. February and August 1971 numbers have been seen, at thirty-five cents in a 5½" × 7" format, with very sexy photos, under the general banner of "Whizbanger's Entertainment."

BREVITIES

Tabloid-size at 10″ × 14″ on newsprint, *Brevities* claimed to be "America's First Tabloid Weekly," at fifteen cents a copy. The New-Broad Publishing Company, in New York's Flatiron Building, with Myron Hinsch, editor, took credit for Broadway *Brevities*'s hot humor, sexy bits, and varied cartoons; women were sexy or blowsily overblown, Negroes liver-lipped, and "pansys" slick and insincere: *Brevities* appealed to a wide range of social prejudices. Gossip columns and snappy public events commentary filled up various columns; "Fanny Hill" appeared in slangwich, and gangland hootch and Hot-cha-cha set the tone. Volume 1:1 as *New Broadway Brevities* was copyrighted in August 1930. Volume 8 appeared in the Fall of 1932. Volume 8:1 was 17 October 1932; Volume 9:2 was 2 January 1933, indicating quarterly volumes. Collections of three or four issues were also sold as *Albums of Brevities Gems* at fifty cents.

Whether sister publications or competitors, *Broadway Tattler* and *New York Tattler* appeared during the same period in similar format. *Tattler* (Vol. 1:1, March, 1934, monthly at fifteen cents) featured articles on "Welfairy Island" and Rudy Vallee's divorce: "To Hell with the Mules—I'll Take the Body," being a headline extracted from one salacious conversation from a lover to his nearly nude, but sandal-clad mistress. *Broadway Tattler* (Vol. 1:3, January 1933), "the lowdown on everything," was similar, copyrighted Volume 1:1 (November 1932) through Volume 2:1 (May 1933).

A *Brevities* monthly magazine appeared from 1938 through 1945 roughly, but the relation to the weekly tabloid is not known, and it was never copyrighted.

THE BRICKBAT

The only number of *Brickbat* known is for 1 February 1872, edited by "Bricktop" and published by Frank Leslie. Bricktop's humor was of the middle-class urban-suburban variety. The author behind the pseudonym was George G. Small, author of a number of comic pamphlets in the 1870s and 1880s published by Collins and Small and later Frank Tousey.

BROADWAY BREEZE

Volume 1:1 (15 October 1926), twice-a-month at fifteen cents (8½″ × 12″), the *Broadway Breeze* blew thirty pages of Broadway jokes, gossip, cartoons, and chorus line humor toward readers "to elevate the high-brow to a lower plain" and make Broadway a brighter and better place to those who never go there, at least through Volume 1:3. George Lait burlesqued true stories from life, Jack Farr did the most notable cartoons, and "Split-week Syd" provided the Broadway philosophy. Publication data were not given, and it was not copyrighted.

BROADWAY LAUGHS

In the blowsy 1950s style of light innuendo and suburban supermarket shopping jokes, *Broadway Laughs* (5″ × 7″, twenty-five cents), was a relatively innocent cartoon gag book. Published bimonthly by Feature Publications, Holyoke, Massachusetts, and later New York, with Samuel Bierman as editor, it was a sister to *Army Fun*,** *Army Laughs*,** and *Laff Time*,** with which it was probably published in tandem, sharing material. Volume 7:3 (December 1963) boasted its thirteenth year, possibly connecting it to *Broadway Romances*, begun in January 1950 by Comic Magazines. Crestwood Publications was the copyrighted publisher up to Volume 11:9 in September-October 1955; Samuel Bierman was editor. Feature Publications copyrighted Volume 12:2 (July-August 1956) through Volume 15:6 (April 1963).

BROADWAY NIGHTLIFE

Volume 1:1 (October 1933), monthly at twenty-five cents (9¾″ × 6¾″), *Broadway Nightlife*, published by the Bill Publishing Company in New York offered a "new, breezy, snappy" humor. It featured 74 pages offering eight or ten spicy stories, with presumably amusing twists, and photographs and cartoons of semi-nude or nude women. Volume 1:2 is the last seen; it is uncopyrighted.

BROADWAY NIGHTS

Volume 1:1 (July 1928), *Broadway Nights*, twenty-five cents (9¾″ × 6¾″), published by King Publishing Company, of Wilmington, Delaware, punctuated 56 pages of saucy stories with pictures of barely draped starlets and cartoons of half-dressed flappers. Women, like hothouse flowers, are often well-potted; Suzy swears she's never been kissed—enough to make any woman swear—are typical brief bits. Volume 1:3 is the last seen; the Tavern Publishing Company copyrighted Volume 10:1 in February 1933.

BROTHER JONATHAN

Brother Jonathan of the 1840s was issued by Wilson and Company of New York. Volumes 1–5 covered 1842–1843 at five dollars per volume, with extra numbers and supplements in oversize newspaper sheets for dates like the Fourth of July and Christmas. One such special "Mammoth" 22″ × 44″ sheet has been seen for 4 July 1845, and one is reported for 4 July 1848 featuring the Battle of Chapultepec, which took place in September 1847. The regular issue was weekly beginning 1 January 1842, advertising Belles Lettres, fine arts, standard literature, and general intelligence, primarily functioning as a "story" paper and reprinter of pirated European fiction. Also see Mott, 1:359–61. Approximately forty libraries list partial holdings.

BRUNO'S WEEKLY

This literary Bohemian teens product of Greenwich Village published Volumes 1–3 in 1915–1916, superseded by *Bruno's* with Volume 1:1 on 8 January 1917, *Bruno's Bohemian* for March and April 1918, *Bruno's Review of Life, Love, and Letters* in 1919, and *Bruno's Review of Two Worlds*, Volume 1:1 (November 1920) through November 1922 (Vol. 4:3). CtY, NN, and PP, and the New York Historical Society are among the holders of scattered issues of this rather little "Little Magazine" of very light verse, brief prose whimsies, and somewhat heavier Greenwich Village musings. Bruno collected a literary coterie for the *Weekly* which at one time included Madeleine and Charles Edison, daughter and son of the inventor, writing under pseudonyms to escape their famous father's notice. Charles Edison was the original publisher of the 4¾″ × 8″ weekly, which sold for five cents and contained sixteen pages plus stiff covers, with one or two cartoons among the prose.

THE BUBBLE

The Bubble, Volume 1:1 (20 October 1849) bubbled for one number as the American *Charivari* in New York. It intended to attack local dullness and national politics with sharply pointed wit, long doggerel verses, and cartoons. Henry Clay and General Zachary Taylor and his cabinet were burlesqued in the first issue. It was published in eight pages, measuring approximately 8½″ × 11″ and sold at six cents an issue. The known issue is at the New York Historical Society.

BUDDIES

Army and Navy gags and gals jokes appeared under the motto "Keep 'em Smiling" (Vol. 1:1, March 1942, fifteen cents, 5½″ × 7½″ monthly, the only copyrighted issue). Alfred Harvey, New York, was the publisher of this 84-page digest of cartoons punctuated by a few gags, all relating to service topics and soldier-sailor romancing. *Buddies* was a brother publication to Harvey's *Army and Navy Fun Parade*.**

BUNK

Bunk, as "The *bunk* of a Nation," was produced by W. M. Clayton, Clayton Magazines, New York. *Bunk* picked a theme most months—"Wrong Number," "What Every Young Man Should Know," or "Travel"—but cartoons were generalized around dolls and guys, with some Hoover and Roosevelt cartoons by Trent thrown in. Brief burlesque dramas and novels were featured, and *Bunk* also carried light movie and book reviews at a level that found Bela Lugosi bad in one horror movie but the six zombies "swell." F. Olin Tremaine edited many issues, and Clayton did others. April 1932 was Volume 1:1, cost fifteen cents, and measured 8½″ × 11½″, 54 pages; the last copy seen is Volume 3:2 (January 1933), although a February issue is advertised and *Bunk* was copyrighted through Volume 4:2 (May 1933), numbered four monthly issues to each volume number. Seeming a little more staid than *Ballyhoo** and more solid than *Bushwa,*** *Bunk* shared their orientation toward the mildly sexy cartoon humor of the Depression era big city.

BURTEN'S FOLLIES

Burten's Follies, Volume 3:8 (October 1925), twenty-five cents, 8″ × 10¼″, was the product of New York's Bohemian Publishing Company, and so it attempted to maintain the Parisian Bohemian tone of Greenwich Village. Joey Burten's motto was "The people be tickled," and his humor was mildly suggestive, with a scattering of scantily clad cartoon ladies, some pictures, and numerous prose fiction pieces, altogether milder than some of the "Broadway" humor magazines focusing almost solely on the sexsational. Burten later reunited with Celestine Vichy and others of the original racy *Follies*** in a continuation in the 1930s after an undetermined break in the publication history.

 Burten's publishing history is bizarre. *Follies* can be traced to *Cap'n Joey's Jazza-ka-jazza*, Volume 1:1 (February 1922), "a monthly magazine dedicated to the eliminating of blue laws. Strong for personal rights of men and women." The magazine measured 5″ × 8″, thirty-one pages, sold for two dollars per year, and was copyrighted by Joseph Bernstein. It was later copyrighted by J. Burten, or Jo., or Joe, depending on Burten's mood. With Volume 1:6 (September 1922) it became *Cap'n Joey's Follies*, then *Follies* for Volume 2:12 (October 1924), and then *Burten's Follies* in November 1924 (Volume 3:3) and December. "After a period of years," it returned as a quarterly *Burten's Follies*, with Volume 10:1 for Winter 1933 being the copy seen. The Burdon Publishing Company, made up of Burten and Harry Donenfeld, was also copyrighting *B-U-N-K* (not seen) and *Kookoo*** and publishing uncopyrighted *Hollywood Squawkies*** and *Radio Razzberries*** in the 1932–1934 period.

BUSHWA

Bushwa from March-April 1932 (Vol. 1:1) through at least May-June 1932 (Vol. 1:2) was an unabashed copy of *Ballyhoo,** measuring 8½″ × 11″, with parti-colored cover, fifteen cents an issue ($1.80 a year bimonthly), and with the same burlesque 1930s advertisements and splashy cartoon format. Stanley M. Estrow was editor with the assistance of Colvin M. Edwards; Bushwa Publishing Corporation, New York, John F. Edwards, President, with Colvin Edwards and Estrow as officers, was the publisher. The comic exposé format allowed for a John Held-style cartoon showing a woman with hairy armpits over the legend

"Has she ceased to care?" among a variety of features like "Jipley's Believe it or not." A few prose pieces and a varied lot of cartoons on sexual promiscuity and dating also appeared.

BUST OUT LAFFIN'

Minoan Publishing Company of New York published *Bust Out Laffin'* Number 6 in 1954. It was digest size with both black and white and color cartoons, all on promiscuous themes: one cutie responds, "Cut out the sweet talk, Mr. Pringle, is this a proposal or a proposition?" Another cutie in underwear says to her formal-dress date, "I simply didn't have a thing to wear"—and similar familiar favorites fill other pages, one cartoon per page on cheap paper. Numbers 10 and 11 were copyrighted for July and August 1955.

CALIFORNIA MAVERICK

The *Maverick* originated in small-town Stockton—in about 1883 and became the *California Maverick* in 1885, upon moving to San Francisco. According to an item in *Tid-Bits** for 20 March 1886, it became to the West what the *Arkansaw Traveler** was to the Southwest. *Tid-Bits* praised it for its sketches of frontier characters and its hatred of sham. William H. Marshall was editor; Mott lists its dates as 1883–1886.

CAMPUS COMICS QUARTERLY

Campus Comics produced *Campus Comics Quarterly* in the early thirties— Volume 1:3 (July, August, September 1931)—from the Collegiate World Publishing Company, Chicago, at thirty-five cents for each 8½" × 11¼", 80- plus pages issue. It offered all reprints of campus humor from the college magazines, with four or five by-line pieces thrown in. No other issues have been seen.

CAMPUS JOKES AND CARTOONS

Ribald fun from the pages of college magazines was offered by *Campus Jokes and Cartoons*, Volume 2:3 (June 1967), a late avatar of the college humor anthology magazine. Zenith Books, Inc., of New York published it at thirty- five cents, bimonthly, in an 8" × 10¾" format with pages of single cartoons and sets of cartoons and gags interspersed. One Hawaiian-looking collegiate wolf in front of a steaming volcano propositions a doubtful cutie, "Better believe it, kid. Tomorrow they're tossing all virgins into the bottomless well of the gods."

Martin Goodman was publisher with David Goodman as editor. Volume 1:2 for February 1966 was the first copyrighted, through Volume 2:6 for December 1967.

CARL PRETZEL'S MAGAZINE POOK

Carl Pretzel's Magazine Pook was the outgrowth of a popular Chicago German dialect magazine by Charles H. Harris (1841–1892). It began in 1872 as exclusively humorous, using dialect format, but its name changed to *Carl Pretzel's Weekly* and later *Carl Pretzel's Illustrated Weekly* with both plain English and German-American dialect pieces. It finally became the *National Weekly*, almost exclusively serious social and political commentary, lasting to 1893. Selections from it are reprinted in *Chicago's Public Wits*, edited by Kenny Williams and Bernard Duffey (Baton Rouge: LSU Press, 1983), the source of this information.

CARNIVAL COMBINED WITH SHOW

Show was a girlie magazine and *Carnival* was a circus and girlie magazine. Together they were a girlie magazine that presented burlesque cuties in various lingerie and panties photo articles, all with a light theme such as income taxes or learning to play the accordion. It was copyrighted as *Show*, by Show Magazine, Inc., of Dunellen, New Jersey, and New York (monthly, twenty-five cents, 8½" × 11½", 68 pages, with Tony Field as editor). Volume 2:10 was May 1942. The original magazines by themselves are closer to their title topics.

THE CARNIVAL OF AUTHORS

The Carnival of Authors was produced weekly for the Philadelphia Centennial, with Volume 1:2 dated 23 February 1876. It was dedicated to the Union and women's work, filling five three-column pages with comic historical and political writing with a vaguely literary flavor; the last three pages were filled with advertisements. A few cartoons appeared on the front page, and one page was given to theatrical listings. PHi has the only known copy.

CARTOON CAPERS

Sized 8" × 11", bimonthly at thirty-five cents, with Robert Mende, editor, *Cartoon Capers* at 68 pages closely followed *Cartoon Laughs*,** with fewer cartoons per page and slightly more emphasis on female breasts. A whale, following a submarine for years and passing out cigars every time it shot off a torpedo, is typical of the jokes; a bear reading a magazine in front of a stuffed hunter's head reflects the cartoons, derivative from earlier cartoonists like VIP.

Volume 1:1 appeared in January 1966; Volume 4:6 in December 1969 is the last seen. Magazine Management held copyrights from Volume 4:1 through Volume 10:6 for November 1975. See also *Cartoon Laughs*.

CARTOON COMEDY PARADE (CARTOON PARADE)

This was a Humorama bimonthly, thirty-five cents, one-hundred pages, 5½″ × 7″) featuring breezy eyefuls of cheesecake and sexually suggestive cartoons like one by Bill Ward in which a lecher says to his busty date in a restaurant, "You'd better go ahead and order—what I want isn't on the menu." *Cartoon Comedy Parade* is listed as the full cover title. Volume 1:17 for May 1963 has been seen. A Canadian publication with the same title appeared around May 1945. *Comedy Parade*, as it was also titled, seems to have used some of the same cartoons as *Comedy Riot*,** also by Humorama, with captions changed.

CARTOON FUN AND COMEDY

Number 5 of this girls and gags photo and cartoon digest was advertised in *Stare*** Magazine for October 1966, so it apparently belongs in the sleazecake family of humor. It was uncopyrighted.

CARTOON HUMOR

Measuring 8½″ × 11–11½″, originally one-hundred pages in 1939 but shrinking later to 84 in the early 1940s, *Cartoon Humor* was a more thoughtful presentation of the work of the best cartoonists of its period. Published quarterly at twenty-five cents in New York by Collegian Press, Robert A. Pines, editor, during the earliest years, and later by Better Publications and Standard Magazines, it intended to offer enough work of each of a dozen or so cartoonists—six to eight selections—to offer a course in cartooning, as well as a cure for the blues. Jefferson Machamer, Reamer Keller, Ross, Trent, Chon Day, Sydney Hoff, and Michael Berry were among the top-ranked humorous cartoonists represented in the full-page cartoons covering themes oriented toward dating, sex, and contemporary life. Even during the war, political and social humor was notable by its absence. Volume 1:1 was copyrighted for January 1939, quarterly with sporadic entries through 1946; Collegian Press, publisher at this time, was also publisher of *College Humor*.** It lasted through Volume 17:52 (1955) and possibly later.

CARTOON LAUGHS

Cartoon Laughs was one among several cartoon magazines published by Magazine Management, New York, including *Laugh Parade*,** *Cartoons and Gags*,** *Cartoon Capers*,** *World's Best Cartoons*, and *Best Cartoons from the Editors of Male and Stag*, two men's magazines. Robert Mende was editor of the 8″ × 11″, 68-page bimonthly, which sold at thirty-five and later forty cents; he seems to be responsible for the sexual orientation in terms of material to which his name is attached, although citations occur for Lord Byron, W. C. Fields, John Nance Garner, and others for brief epigrams of various kinds. The format allowed for two to six cartoons per page either randomly arranged or grouped in subject sequences with brief jokes throughout. The visual emphasis was strongly on sexy, whorehouse, and cutie humor; one large-busted coed says, "Gosh, mom, we may have had sex, but we weren't intimate." The attitude of the humor was of this consistency. Volume 1:1 January 1962 (with Volume 2:2 for December 1962 first copyrighted) through Volume 14:5 have been seen; October 1975 was the last copyrighted. Atlas Magazines published this periodical quarterly in the early sixties, and the numbering is thus irregular.

CARTOON PARADE

This "Whizgbang Entertainment"—eyeful of fun—digest, bimonthly, thirty-five cents, was published by Timely Features, Inc., of New York, and measured 5″ × 7¼″. It featured sensuous cuties with unrelated captions among "super humor cartoons" on sexual themes. Volume 10:7 was the April 1968 issue. It may follow *Cartoon Comedy Parade*.**

CARTOON ROUNDUP

At twenty-five cents a copy, *Cartoon Roundup* collected the best of the 1940s cartoonists, in an 8½″ × 11″ format, from *Collier's*, *Look*, *Life*,* the *New York Herald Tribune*, *This Week*, *Reader's Scope*, and *The Newspaper PM*. In addition, it featured one or two older cartoonists, John Held, Jr., and Percy Crosby, in the 1946 issue seen. The humor of middle-class American life and *Collier's* dominates. Round-up Publications and Florence T. Weiss published it in New York. Volume 1:1 for September 1946 is the only one copyrighted.

CARTOON WORLD

Cartoon World of Lincoln, Nebraska, edited by George Hartman, is a professional publication for cartoonists. Issue Number 471 was November 1981. Its thirteen pages of cheap offset information and advice to novices are stapled with a single staple.

CARTOONEWS (OK)

Cartoonews, Volume 1:1 (August 1936) through Volume 1:8 (December 1936), was a biweekly 8½″ × 11″, upgraded from typewriter print to linotype in Number 8 and superseded by *OK*, the official organ of the Cartoonist's Guild of America. Published in New York at ten cents a copy and containing eight pages per issue, it offered trade chat and cartoons as edited by Haile Hendrix. It claimed no politics, although it blacklisted *Gay Book Magazine*,* *Ten Story Magazine*, *Movie Humor*,** *Waldorf-Astoria Promenade*, *Real Screen Fun*,** and *Voyager* for undercutting the Guild minimum of fifteen dollars for "gag"drawings.

CAR'TOONS

Peterson Publishing Company, Los Angeles, California, publisher of *Hot Rod* and other car-related magazines, originated this bimonthly, 70-page, 8″ × 11″, car-oriented cartoon-story magazine. Number 1 was issued in August-September 1961, and the magazine continued in print as of December 1986, presently at $1.50 per issue. Don Evans is editorial director, Lee Kelley, publisher, and Dennis Ellefson, editor. Trend Publications copyrighted Summer and Fall quarterly numbers in 1961, possibly figuring in the numbering of issues. The counter-culture comix format is aimed at a youthful teens-twenties audience, and a few advertisements and decals of hotrods for tee-shirts are prominent among the cartoon strips with car themes. "CAR" is normally spelled in large letters on the cover, clearly identifying its interest.

CARTOONS & COLLEGIAN FUN

Cartoons & Collegian Fun sought to combine H. H. Windsor's *Cartoons Magazine** with the college spirit of the 1920s. Freeman H. Hubbard was editor for Cartoons and Movies, Inc.—an offspring of Hubbard Publications, New York (twenty-five cents, 76 pages, 7″ × 9¾″). Volume 29:5 appeared on 31 May 1926, claiming "Est. 1911." Articles by Zim (Eugene Zimmerman) on the Gillam brothers of *Puck*,* on cartooning and caricature, and on college cartoons typified the matter, punctuated by collegiate-oriented stories and verse and show-business oriented photos, including a nude Ziegfield girl. Guild Publishing Company of Philadelphia, also publishers of *Laughter*,** copyrighted 30:2 for September 1926.

CARTOONS AND MOVIES MAGAZINE

Cartoons and Movies Magazine, like *Cartoons & Collegian Fun*,** was an attempt to capitalize on *Cartoons Magazine*.* Measuring 6″ × 9″ and 68 pages, issued monthly at twenty-five cents per copy, the magazine was published by Hubbard Publishing Company, New York. Volume 2:4 was January 1925; Volume 2:11 and Volume 2:12 for October and December 1925 were copyrighted. One article was "Saving the Flapper by Punishment," written in response to the previous month's question, "Should a Flapper Be Spanked?" It also featured articles on cartooning by Zim (Eugene Zimmerman) and printed a number of jokes and gags from college humor magazines, along with one or two pin-up nudes and risqué jokes, which were mildly titillating. No editor is listed, which may account for the content of this magazine seeming to belong to its twin and vice versa.

CHAMPAGNE

Champagne, a garish journal that lasted for only the second half of 1871, represents a clear example of comic periodical publishing in transition. The journal (11″ × 15″, four column, in folio at ten cents per folio issue, fifteen pages) claimed that it was the illustrated journal of Society, Sparkle, and Sentiment. The Champagne Publishing Company of New York took credit for the monthly, Volumes 1–2 (Nos. 1–7) appeared from June to December 1871. Actually, Frank Leslie originated it with an eye toward his popular audience.

Pre-Gibson Girl bathing beauties and flashy women dotted its heavily illustrated pages, showing their indifference to the poor of the earth. Doggerel burlesques of women's rights caricatured the cigar-puffing women who wished to interfere with man's right to drink. Society belles and beaus were the targets of other lengthy prose satires. *Champagne* advised that if one married for property one should first find out what the property was, and it offered "Love in the Oil Districts: A Story of Mingled Affection and Nitroglycerin." "Flora MacFlimsey" was resurrected from Thomas Butler's popular poem "Nothing to Wear" from the late 1850s. Its treatment of New York's Seventh Regiment, more noted for social than for military prowess, allies it with Swift's proposal for babies in Ireland in "A Modest Proposal." *Champagne* was alert to the social mores of the New York world, and it managed to catch literary, social, and fashion items in a moderately exuberant profusion. DLC holds a copy.

CHAMPAGNE CLUB

Washington, D.C., in the 1830s was finding its social depth, and the *Champagne Club* intended to provide the plumbline. It was edited by "Ebenezer Lovemuch" and Captain Marcus Mucklewrath, aided and abetted by a secret society of bored gentlemen. Society was considered one polished horde, made up of the bores and the bored. The discussions and debates of the club were to be the content. The editors reflected admiration of a pretty ankle showing under a high hemline and reported the nature of city frolics. The effects of the President's message were described as limited to a duel and jailing at Hoboken. The *Champagne Club* was to be a "chronicle and critic of military and fashionable events and things, and criminal record of literary and other misdoings." Volume 1:1 was 6 December 1834 published by Mr. F. Taylor's Library, which possibly suggests F. Taylor as the editor. DLC holds a broken run through 21 February 1835.

CHEERS (CHEERS!)

Cheers, a quarterly digest of the 1940s, published Number 2 in February 1943 (twenty-five cents, 5½" × 7½", 132 pages, by Rockley Publications of Philadelphia) and featured wartime humor and gals and gags jokes and cartoons. The last issue copyrighted by Rockley was 13 for Winter 1946. Pages of ten to twelve gags faced single cartoons about equally. The last copy seen, Number 48 (Summer 1947), by Band Leader Publishing Company from the same office in Philadelphia, was all cartoons, with a few longer prose pieces thrown in. The humor is directed at postwar domestic life with no particular viewpoint evident. Following the Spring 1948 issue, *Cheers* became *Zing*, Numbers 52–60, from the Summer of 1948 through November 1949, copyrighted. Numbering discrepancies may be explained by more than one publication using this name. *Cheers* was copyrighted by a third corporate entity, Fifty Crosswords, Inc., Number 46 and 47 for Winter and Spring in 1948. Yet another was started in 1954; see copyright list.

CHICKS AND CHUCKLES

One of the 4" × 6" pocket-sized magazines of the late 1950s and early 1960s, *Chicks and Chuckles* offered one hundred pages of cartoon gags with some cheesecake photos thrown in. August 1957 was Volume 3:4. The magazine was issued bimonthly at fifteen cents by Sports Report, Inc., of Atlanta, Georgia, and was edited by Arthur C. Kohler. After Ben Bennett became editor in 1959, the price went up to twenty-five cents and the magazine featured a center color pin-up and slightly sexier humor. In 1960 it returned to a general humor format only to revert to the sexy format once again in 1961. Publication Management of Atlanta was listed as publisher from 1960 on. Photo caption humor was added to the cartoon gags; cover photos were even swapped with other publications such as *Bold*, from the same firm. The last issue seen is April 1961 (Vol. 6:2).

CLIPS

Clips (Zest of the Best; Wit of the World, weekly, illustrated, partly colored, Volumes 1, 2, and 3:1–7) was published from 21 November 1895 to 2 January 1897 in New York. The Clips Publishing Company was a nickel weekly reprinter which Mott describes as well printed and clever, with a gradually increasing amount of original material. H. B. Eddy was one of its editors. *Clips* consisted of sixteen pages and sold for two dollars yearly. The combined side and top measurement is given as 28½cm. by DLC. The DLC copy is missing on the shelf.

CLOWN

J. I. Rodale, publisher of *American Humorist*** and later of *Organic Gardening*, established *Clown*, "A Little Bit of Fun for Everyone" at five cents per monthly issue. It was issued by the Clown Publishing Company, in Emmaus, Pennsylvania; Volume 1:5 (April 1933) is the issue seen—8½″ × 11″, twenty pages of cheap paper with a primitive Chon Day cover. It offered answers to "Kwestions," reprinted college jokes, and presented "Laughs in the News" and some varied political humor, including a Roosevelt cartoon. Among longer pieces, "Dick Darewood" was a burlesque of high school heroes, and a low-German Baron Munchauson takeoff was offered. One bit of doggerel ran on a typically restrained sexual theme, foreshadowing Rodale's true interest: "Bare are the shivering limbs of shameless trees— / What wonder is it that the corn is shocked?"

THE CLUB-ROOM

With the same pretense of emanating from a literary club maintained by a number of humorous periodicals of the 1820–1830 period, *The Club-Room* in 1820 claimed to be founded by the "Pythagoreans," five literary men including W. H. Prescott, Edw. Everett, F. Dexter, and Dr. J. Ware. Ware wrote the introductory essay and was probably the editor. Timothy Swan of Boston was the publisher, and was replaced by Cummings and Hilliard with Number 4. The contributors claimed their motive was to make a profit, improve morals, and provide waste paper to a needy public. Of the four numbers printed, February, March, and July sold for thirty-seven and a half-cents and April for forty-five cents. It featured gentle Addisonian rambles, literary pieces, and light travel material, causing the editors to comment that they never could decide whether they were publishing a paper or a magazine. Ware's introduction promised to light his cigars with the best letters, for he could do better: "The worst we shall publish." University Microfilms has reprinted *The Club-Room*, and copies are available at DLC (with authors identified in pencil), CtY, MB, MBat, NN, PHi, and roughly fifteen other libraries.

COCKEYED

In 1955–1956 *Cockeyed* burlesqued the pulp exposé magazines of the late 1940s and early 1950s, borrowing their format and style. At twenty-five cents, first quarterly and then bimonthly, it offered "Jerry Lewis Returned to Central Park Zoo," "Liberace's Wig Maker Tells All!!", "Five Ways to Torture Your Mate," the best pear—a well-endowed young woman holding a fruit, chest high, and takeoffs on the $64,000 question, "Dragnet," Marlon Brando, and the school shortage—"fill 'em up with burlycue dolls and used up stuff!"—among other obvious targets of public and show life of the fifties. Volume 1 (1955), through Volume 1:5 (June 1956) are known; Burton Wohl was editor for Whitestone Publications, New York.

CO-EDS/FUN ON THE CAMPUS

Co-Eds was a tabloid (10½" × 13", thirty-two pages, featuring pretty girls from campus with mildly humorous captions or in photo sequences, and a mix of cartoons. It was published quarterly by Collegian Press at ten cents per copy. Volume 1:1 appeared in December 1940; the magazine was copyrighted through Volume 2:3 for Winter 1942.

COLLEGE COMICS

College Comics of the Du Pont Publishing Company of Chicago billed itself as "America's only humorous monthly" in Volume 1:3 for December 1924, the month in which it was combined with another Du Pont publication, *Co-Ed*, after one issue of *Comics* and two of *Co-Ed*. It sold for thirty-five cents, and measured 8½" × 10¾". James V. Spadea, publisher and later editor, took over from E. Du Pont. *College Comics* considered itself the happiest, snappiest journal in print, often featuring over one hundred pages of cartoons and jokes from the college humor magazines of the nation. It appeared to be thriving at Volume 4:6 (June 1926), the last seen, although paper and printing process had been cheapened from the earlier editions. The borrowed humor reflected the Jazz Age without emphasizing its sexy side, as did some other college-oriented humor magazines. The last copyrighted issue was Volume 5:3 for September 1926. Copyright listings show Volume 1:1 for November 1924 and Volume 1:4 for December of the same year.

COLLEGE FUN

A college humor magazine of the 1950s, *College Fun* (Vol. 1:2 for December 1950, published by College Fun, Inc. of New York, twenty-five cents, bimonthly, 8½" × 11") was somewhat more literary than its predecessors, with burlesque items on Gertrude Stein and Frank Harris, and serious ones on the likes of alumnus Booth Tarkington. Book Covers of the Month were burlesqued, and a speech by George Washington was given a D+; college pieces by Franklin Roosevelt and George Santayana were recaptured. Otherwise, format, cartoon styling, and general humor reflect the 1950s era in their conventionality and their avoidance of the sleazy and sensual.

COLLEGE HUMOR

College Humor (8½" × 11¼", 140 pages) was the greatest of the college humor reprinters of the late 1930s era, featuring beautiful girls done in pastels on its covers, short fiction, and jokes, gags, and cartoons.

August 1926 (Vol. 9:1) at thirty-five cents featured Donald Ogden Stewart, a continuing favorite, Mildred Cram, and others in fiction; drawings by John Held, Jr., and pages of college jokes gave the magazine its tone. By July 1930 it was in its ninth year, publishing Number 79.

College Humor was loaded with ads, fiction, and jokes in three-column format on good paper. In its ninth year it was briefly titled *College Humor and Sense*,** including a change in its numbering. Collegiate World Publishing Company of Chicago, J. M. Lansinger, president, was publisher with H. N. Swanson as editor. In 1931 the price per issue rose to twenty-five cents, and the editors were replaced. Dell copyrighted Volume 1:1 (November 1934) through February of the following year, when Collegian Press took over. Collegian Press of New York cited Robert A. Pines as editor and Ned L. Pines as publisher. The price was again reduced to fifteen cents, with cuties by Jefferson Machamer, articles by Gurney Williams, and cartoons by Syd Hoff and others, in a format closer to the middle-class popular magazines of the *Saturday Evening Post*** and *Collier's* variety. February 1936 was New Series Volume 1:5. By Volume 1:1 (January 1940) *College Humor* was reduced to a thin bimonthly, with a few more photos and cartoons relative to the varied prose. The last seen in this series is dated September 1940.

College Humor next appeared as a tabloid (10½" × 13", ten cents), with its gorgeousness reduced to wartime monotones. Replacing puppet-model covers of the late thirties and the earlier co-ed beauties were journalistic-seeming photos of pretty coeds. Volume 13:4 was issued in October 1941 in quarterly publication. This format continued at least through 1943, with gimmick photos and photo-articles, some cartoons by Lawrence Larier, Ted Key, Jefferson Machamer, and others, and varied matter including interest in the new craze—swing dancing. Volume 15:2 for Spring 1943 as a bimonthly is the last copyrighted. Other minor changes in publishing history also appear in the copyright notes.

COLLEGE HUMOR AND SENSE

College Humor and Sense (8¼" × 11¼", fifteen cents, 66 to 72 pages per issue) claimed to be in its twelfth year in its June 1933 issue (No. 113). Collegiate Reporter Company, owned by Stanley V. Gibson, was the publisher in Chicago. The magazine's Russell Patterson covers gave it a bright air, with a fashion column also by Patterson. It was mostly light fiction and prose, with a rotogravure section and a section of college wit. *College Humor* showed a much subdued *Esquire*** influence, with Robert W. Mickam as editor from New York and with monthly publication in the early thirties.

COLLEGE LAUGHS

Candar Publishing Company of Holyoke, Massachusetts, produced this 1950s bimonthly digest (twenty-five cents, 5½" × 7"). Volume 1:20 was for October 1960.

COLLEGE LIFE

College Life was published by Collegian Press, New York, at twenty-five cents per issue in a hundred-page, 8½" × 11¼" format from the late 1920s on. It was one of the weightier roaring college humor publications of the 1920s–1930s era. N. L. Pines was its editor, and it featured racy fiction and sexual innuendo cartoons, and girlies in lingerie. Its stories pushed the Jazz Age image. The earliest issue seen, Volume 3:1 (February 1926), offered eighteen pages of badly printed jokes and illustrated gags. The he-she joke was prominent: Billie—Are you fond of petting parties; Millie—Well, there are only a few parties I care to pet! Lengthier fiction and prose pieces became dominant in the larger magazine of the late twenties. It went from monthly to bimonthly in 1932 and to quarterly by 1936; Volume 5:3 was November 1928, and Volume 18:1 was January 1936, offering a William Faulkner story among the other college-centered light fiction. After Volume 18:1, it was restarted as Volume 19:1 for September 1940, the only later copyright listing; Collegian Press copyrighted issues from July 1928 through 1936.

COLLEGE YEARS

College Years, originating in New Haven, Connecticut, in the late 1930s, was an *Esquire***-styled magazine featuring the roaring collegiate years, college fashions, and mildly humorous views of life. Published first quarterly and then eight times during the college year, the magazine measured 9" × 12" and cost twenty-five cents. It was edited by Walter Camp III. Volume 2:1 for November 1939 marked its shift to the college-year monthly schedule. Cartoons were sprinkled among the fashion items and light college material. Copyrights cover Volume 1:1 for November 1938 through Volume 2:1.

COLLEGIATE WIT AND FRATERNITY FUN

Collegiate Wit, a Hubbard Publication from New York, Volume 1:5 for October 1925, was one of the lushly covered college humor reprinters, with Ziegfeld girls and rotogravure sections. Selling at twenty-five cents and measuring 8¼" × 11", it combined shorter college jokes and cartoons with full-page cartoons and some longer humorous prose. Compulsory chapel and how to eat a soft-shell crab were among matters of import given comic treatment in the issue seen. Volume 1:7 for December 1925 was copyrighted.

COLLIER'S COLLECTS ITS WITS

This magazine format collection of *Collier's* cartoons was on the order of *Cartoon Round-Up*.** It was edited by Gurney Williams and published by Avon Comics, selling for twenty-five cents in 1945. Other Avon laughbooks of the same sort included *Cuties*—cartoons by E. Simms Campbell—Harry Hershfield's *Book of Jokes* ("Now I'll Tell One"), and *Laugh Parade*.** Although in magazine format, this would not properly be classed as a periodical publication, but it does represent a subgenre of single-issue publications within the magazine world.

COMEDY (1938)

Comedy, Volume 1:1 (Winter 1938), measured 6″ × 9½″ and it sold at ten cents per issue. The quarterly, edited by Victor Bloom and published by the Dell Publishing Company, New York, contained one-hundred pages with about twenty pages of advertisements. It offered departments of "Radio Revels," "Nertzy Rhymes," "Film Frolics," and a vast array of uninspired jokes and gags relating to dating and middle-class problems. One figure on a movie screen says to two lovers in her audience, "Why don't you go home, this is where you came in." Two other American and one Canadian publication are named *Comedy* (see the following entry).

COMEDY (1942)

Digest-sized World War II *Comedy*, the second user of the name after Victor Bloom's 1938 publication, was a gals and gags cartoon book, 5½ × 7¾″ in size with both cartoons and gags on dating themes. It sold for fifteen cents. Volume 1:1 (January 1942) was a bimonthly, but it was published irregularly in Chicago by Comedy Publications through July 1943. It featured gags, cartoons, and sassy material, according to its cover. Another *Comedy*, from Duchess Printing in Toronto, Canada, sold at twenty-five cents and highlighted similar material; Volume 1:1 was May 1945. A later *Comedy*, half an inch shorter and with somewhat cheesier-sleazier content, including photos, was published by Stadium Publishing Company (Timely Features, Inc.) of New York. A quarterly (Vol. 2:6 was published in Spring 1951), it mixed domestic comedy with its sexual innuendo jokes. Humorama, another name for Timely Features, published *Comedy* at least through 1966, bimonthly, in sleazecake format, with entirely sexual innuendo cartoons and gags. The title page boasted "established 1941," that being the first "copyright" date cited in the older *Comedy*. Issues have been seen from 1954 through 1957 (Vol. 6:34) at twenty-five cents in a jazzy format with a girlie photo mixed on the cover with several cartoons. The earlier covers featured a single gal gag in bright pastel colors.

COMEDY RIOT

Also sometimes called simply *Comedy*, *Comedy Riot* by Humorama, New York, published Volume 6:35, in March 1957 as a bimonthly, claiming "established 1941." One cartoon, which looks like a recaptioned borrowing from another publication, has a sleazy middle-aged diner listening to his gigantic-busted cutie: "Well, I don't know, Mr. Bigby—your penthouse is a dream but I always get a nightmare after I leave!" It contained one hundred pages and sold for a dollar, digest-sized.

THE COMET

Boston's *Comet* of 1811 was edited by "Walter Wildfire," appearing weekly at twelve-and-a-half cents in twelve-page numbers, streaking through the skies only from 19 October 1811 (Vol. 1:1) to 11 January 1812 (Vol. 1:13). J. T. Buckingham of Boston was the publisher and solicited manuscripts for *Comet*, probably without success. It complained of the age of puffing, from the duchess to the Hottentot Venus, and it mentions the "Humbug" of the "quizzer" who thinks the editor a d—d fool because the editor does not think him a d—d liar, quoted from Browne's sketches. *Comet* has a somewhat theatrical orientation, as well as offering news, serious poetry, and foreign reprints with varied, often noncomic, content. DLC holds the copy seen; University Microfilms has reprinted it.

COMIC CUTIES

This 5¼″ × 7¼″ digest was published quarterly by Health Knowledge, Inc., of New York at thirty-five cents. Number 14 was Winter 1969, suggesting that Volume 1:1 should be approximately Fall 1966. Busty pin-up photos, clothed and unclothed, were interspersed with sex, honeymoon, and body cartoons in full-page format, with a few gag lines under photos and on one or two pages. Scattered advertisements for other spicy and busty books also appeared.

COMMODORE ROLLINGPIN'S ILLUSTRATED HUMOROUS ALMANAC

Not properly an almanac, although established as *Commodore Rollingpin's River Almanac* in 1871, *Commodore Rollingpin's* was one of the offsprings of the crackerbarrel philosophers. John Henton Carter, founder, publisher, and proprietor, was a St. Louis novelist and doggerel versifier. In April 1895, in its twenty-fourth year, the magazine entered into monthly publication, with outsized issues for the Spring, Summer, Fall, and Christmas numbers. It provided twenty pages in colorful folio size with Gibson Girl-style covers. The last issue was published in January 1899 (Vol. 28:1); it measured 10″ × 12½″ and sold for ten cents.

The magazine always featured brief jokes and plenty of cartoons, and Carter boasted that Joseph Keppler of *Puck** had contributed to his first issue in 1871. As a quarterly it had cost twenty-five cents, or one dollar per year, with Carter writing most of the material, including humorous local-color fiction and poetry. A poem on Susan B. Anthony in 1896 featured a belle wearing a handlebar moustache. The poem "Tobe Gray" was typical of the sentimental humanity of this school, "We loved him 'cause he war so human." Local-color material in the 1890s was typified by "All Round Sketches," Si Wiggins on love, poultry, and other topics, "Capt. Quimby's Mississippi Yearns," and similar material. Advertising revenue and biographies of St. Louis business poeple helped boost Carter's income. A color center spread provided a large double-size cartoon during this period. DLC holds later issues from the 1890s.

COMPANION AND WEEKLY MISCELLANY

Edward Easy, Esquire [pseud], edited this paper with the subtitle, "A Safe Companion And An Easy Friend—Pope" through 52 issues (two volumes) from 3 November 1804 to 25 October 1806. The weekly is arranged in eight-page, two-column installments and is devoted mainly to criticism and satirical attacks on manners, morals, and vices, excluding political and religious controversies. It contains some literary news, short comic sketches and anecdotes, poetry, and several ridiculous essays. The publication was supposed to be continued as *The Observer* by "Beatrice Ironside."

The first issue begins with a preface to the public, followed by the history of Edward Easy—including information on his grandfather, Ephraim Easy, and other characters. In the same issue a bizarre poem entitled "The Cambridge Scholar; or, The Ghost of a Scrag of Mutton" tells the story of an exorcism by a scholar of a ghost by changing him into a piece of boiled mutton after enticing him with mashed turnips and subsequently devouring the obnoxious fellow. A later issue, besides letters from one Nathan Scruple, offers a sketch entitled "Seduction," where, among much swooning and fainting, a daughter is wronged, a father revenged, a son-in-law disgraced, and a young lady seduced and left to die, all in less than one full page. It has been reprinted by University Microfilms.

Michael Pettengell

THE CONTINENTAL MONTHLY

"Devoted to Literature and National Policy" is displayed in the full title of *The Continental Monthly*. The publication, founded shortly after the start of the Civil War, was political, strongly backing Lincoln and the Republican party. The monthly ran for six volumes, and was published from January 1862 to December

1864: in Boston and New York by J. R. Gilmore (1862) and in New York by J. F. Trow (1862–1864). It provided a considerable amount of wit and humor, fiction, and also German writing. It was originally dominated by Charles Godfrey Leland (editor until April 1863), formerly of *Vanity Fair** and *The Knickerbocker.** Other writers included James Gilmore (the publisher), Henry Carey Lea, George H. Boker, N. L. Frothingham, Richard B. Kimball, and Martha Walker Cook (subsequent editor to Leland).

Among the interesting literary articles are titles such as "Jonathan Edwards' Family," "James Russell Lowell," and "Recollections of Washington Irving (By One of His Friends)" told in a light manner. Short stories and semi-historical pieces are accompanied by short poems of propaganda attacking slavery and Southern ideals. Leland's unsigned "Bone Ornament" describes a Southern belle with earrings of human bones, a brooch made from a Yankee's spine, and the young lady's fan handle from a finger of a "Lincoln man." Her lovers have pillaged graves to please her since she has been deprived of her slaves. Nearby sit pretty flowers in a human skull vase. It has been reprinted by University Microfilms.

Michael Pettengell

COO-COO

Coo-Coo, Volume 1:1 (1932) was a monthly issued by the Bob Edwards Publishing Company of Minneapolis, at ten cents a copy, with the "Let's all go nertz!" philosophy which was prominent among the followers of *Ballyhoo.** Humor focused on marital infidelity: "Rich boobs laboring under the impression that they are marrying pretty women, only to learn at Reno that they had just had them rented, at a dang high rental." Measuring 8½" × 11½" in a thirty-two-page format and edited by E. A. Sumner, *Coo-Coo* was dominated by half-page cartoons, with a few gags and varying sizes of cartoons. The copyright was listed in March. See also *Calgary Eye Opener*,* another Bob Edwards publication.

COOKOO NUTS

Cookoo Nuts (Vol. 1:1, March-April 1941) was an 8" × 11", thirty-six page collection of ordinary sayings illustrated in a humorous manner, such as "Split L ip." Hugo Gernsbeck was publisher and editor in New York. Five to twenty familiar phrases could be illustrated on a page, and prizes were given for the best submissions. The fifteen-cent bimonthly apparently had one issue, not counting an earlier *Cookoo-Nut Book* in the same format at twenty-five cents by Gernsbeck and the Experimenter Publishing Company in 1928. It had reprinted the original run of "Cuckoo Nuts" from a department in *French Humor*** and its successor *Tid-Bits.***

THE COUNTRY COURIER

Barent Gardenier was editor and publisher of this reprinter of comic material. Volume 1:1 was 3 June 1816, and the journal was issued twice a week at five dollars. Sarcastic wit was shown in appealing to Flibbertygibbet as a political and social motivator, but most material was not original; one September issue carried a dialogue between *Aurora* and the *Democratic Press*. The editor died in March 1817 and with him went his journal, the last issue being 24 March 1817. MWA, NN, and NjR have copies; it is available through University Microfilms.

CRACKED

Cracked is one of the longest lasting alternative *Mad Magazines*,* issued bimonthly and later eight times a year by Major Magazines of New York. The editor and publisher is Robert C. Sprout. The magazine began with Number 1, in February-March 1958 and reached Number 190 in October 1982, with Marion Sproul replacing Sprout as editor. Michael Delle-Femine became editor with Number 219 for May 1986, and the magazine is now published eight times a year. The format has remained the same: burlesques of television series, books, and feature items like "Great Moments in History" in extended comic strip format—8″ × 11″ and presently $1.25 per issue. The violence of *Rocky*, *Rambo*, and other such movies and television shows provides satirical matter for current issues. It has also spun off various annual editions like *Giant Cracked*, *Biggest Greatest Cracked*, *Cracked Collector's Edition*, *Extra Special Cracked*, *King-Sized Cracked*, and *Super Cracked*. The earliest copyright listed is 1960, and some special editions like *Cracked Shut-Ups*, 1972–1973 have reprinted hundreds of "Shut-up Jokes": "Mommy, why does Daddy run down the road like that?"— "Shut up and reload." It is listed by Overstreet in his comic guides. The most recent edition is a *Cracked Digest* in digest size, quarterly, with Number Two for January 1987.

CRAZY

Crazy is yet another of the *Mad** copiers. It originated in October 1973 (Vol. 1:1), bimonthly and later as a monthly, from the Marvel Comic Group, New York, as a "Stan Lee" presentation. It sold at forty cents an issue and measured 8″ × 11″. Paul Laiken, Marv Wolfman, and Larry Hama have been successive editors. "The magazine that dares to be dumb" burlesques magazines and various feature items from television shows and other sources. The first issue cover showed a dynamiter blowing up *Mad*,* *Sick*,** *Cracked*,** and *National Lampoon*,* although its satire is milder. Volume 1:87 was the June 1982 issue, and it continues in print. Overstreet lists it and offers more information.

CRAZY, MAN, CRAZY

This magazine was another of the *Mad**-derived adult-oriented comics, with burlesques of sexy paperback covers, war movies, and beauty magazines, among other conventional targets. Measuring 8½″ × 11″ in a 68-page format, it sold for twenty-five cents and was closer to magazine format than to comics. Volume 2:1 was December 1955 and Volume 2:2 was June 1956, although it claimed to be bimonthly. Humor Magazines, Inc., of Charlton Press, Derby, Connecticut, was the publisher, and it was classed with their comic group rather than with their cartoon group.

THE CRITIC

The Critic was an intellectual attempt at humor conducted by "Geoffrey Juvenal, Esquire" from 29 January to 10 May 1820 in Philadelphia. Each of the twenty numbered issues contains one or two essays which rely on Latin phrases and occasional letters or poems to stimulate interest.

The ramblings of Juvenal are upbraided in one letter by Abigail Briar. It is unclear whether or not Briar is a fictional character, but at any rate, her objections are well founded. This attack forces the sole writer of the paper to draw up a treaty between "Geoffrey Juvenal, Critic General, of the one part and His Miscellaneous Magesty, commonly known by the name of The World, of the other part." One redeeming essay in *The Critic*, however, involves the adventures of a bored Satan who comes to earth for a little excitement.

The Critic attacked the stamp of imbecility and the pygmy race of literati invading every action of its "once classic metropolis." Geoffrey Juvenal, Esq., was the nominal editor of the eight-page journal attacking pretenders to literary quality. J. K. Paulding is the "cabbage bard," and later the "Homer of the Backwoods." Ladies' letters also come in for criticism, but before the critic himself was fairly started, he claims the nightwatch put an end to his activities. DLC and NN hold copies, and it has been reproduced by University Microfilms.

Michael Pettengell

THE CURIOSITY SHOP

The Curiosity Shop was a four-page—actually a folded single sheet—give-away which appears to have been primarily an organ for advertising the Boston Museum, a commercial institution along the lines of Barnum's establishment in New York but with muted showmanship in comparison. General interest matter predominated, although some humor appeared. The publication measures 11½″ × 17¼″, in a four-column format, and only two numbers are known, Volume 1:2 for March 1856 and Volume 1:4 for September 1856, suggesting quarterly publication. The back page was oriented toward actors, actresses, and current Museum theater productions. MWA holds the only copies.

THE CYNICK

"We'll snarl, and bite, and play the dog—For dogs are honest," is the caption of Volume 1:1 on 21 September 1811 of *The Cynick*. Led by "Growler Gruff, esquire" and his "confederacy of lettered dogs" in Philadelphia, the paper attacks other theatrical magazines, the local government, politics, and the theater itself. "Gruff's" and his associates' snarls were short-lived, however, since the paper's last issue appeared on 12 December 1811.

An early issue of *The Cynick* contains a humorous letter criticizing and banning Mr. Gruff from the theater, which the reader finds addressed from the "Manager's Dog." The vanity of the masses is attacked on another issue in a two-part poem entitled "The Groans of the Town." The paper's response to the presumably negative reaction to its views is summed up as follows: "We wanted to make our readers grin, we say grin because we do not believe they can laugh." *The Cynick* saw the theater in Philadelphia as a stage where "no good actor dares appear / Because foul envy riots there, / Seats now fill'd with dirty doxies, / Wooden plays and golden boxes." University Microfilms has reprinted it.

Michael Pettengell

D

DASH

Dash was typical of the oversize tabloid humor magazines of the World War II period at 10½″ × 13½″ and featuring a pretty, partly-clad young lady on the cover. Volume 1:1 appeared in June 1941; it was published monthly by Elite Publications of New York at ten cents. Thirty-two pages were filled with full- and half-page jokes, a "Laugh with Dash" collection of gags and articles featuring young ladies wrestling over skirts, having skirts torn off by ostriches at the zoo, falling down with raised skirts, and skirting similarly eye-catching revelations of the girls behind the men at the front, representing "The Best of Humor in Pictures." The first three issues were seen; Volume 1:8 for January 1942 is the last copyrighted.

DIOGENES, HYS LANTERN

Diogenes, Hys Lantern—alternately known as *The Lantern* and thus confused with an English counterpart—lit up Volume 1:1 as a weekly on 10 January 1852, at six pence per issue, lasting through a seventy-eighth number in June 1853. Edited by Diogenes, Jr., from the Lantern Office in New York, it proposed to "take the shine" out of humbug, folly, pride, and vain-glory, and provide the Atlantic community with rays of humor from Yankeedoodledum. Theodore Jones, publisher, and Jackson and Company, subscription agents, are mentioned in text and may have some connection with the journal. For its July 4th *Pictorial Lantern* special issue, it advertised costs of $2,000 for material and a publication of 50,000, although it only identified its own circulation at about 8,000. A copy of the 4 July issue does not appear with the regular volumes, if it appeared.

Diogenes stayed relatively close to the *Punch* format, with blocks of humorous items rather than columns. British material was reprinted with humor oriented toward foreign issues, including Kossuth—brooded over by a cartoon George Washington worried about foreign entanglements. Full-page cartoons were frequent, including a 14 February piece attacking the forces of disunion. Claiming the largest variety of pictorial humor in the United States, *Diogenes* regularly attacked the "viciousness of virtue" but also burlesqued Thomas Hood's "Song of the Shirt." As "Mose" in one piece yells at a bearded foreigner: "Jest shet off de gas, will ye! If you want to raise a muss, why don't ye do as we do—run wid yer own Ma-chine, and do yer own fightin'—sa-ay!" Various columns chided dollar-admiration on Broadway, Lucretia Mott, and the Bloomer movement. Other pieces used folk-songs to burlesque political candidates. Regular series included "The Adventures of Mr. Papplewick," the *Lantern's* own political columns, and the full-page comic political illustrations. Locations are DLC (Rare Book Room), MWA, NN, ICN, and ten other libraries; CtY lists a copy not found; Mott, 2:179, 182–83, 188 offers information on it.

DOLLS & GAGS

Published bimonthly by Crestwood Publishing Company of Canton, Ohio, and New York with Samuel Bierman, editor, *Dolls & Gags* offered 98 pages of full-page (5″ × 7″) cartoons mixed with a few pages of gags. Humor was not only girlie but also domestic, husband and wife, and householder jokes; the per issue cost was twenty-five cents. Volume 2:2 was December-January 1953–1954; copies have been reported as late as 1962, though without verification.

DROLL STORIES

The monthly *Droll Stories* may not qualify as American Balzac; however, from 1923 to 1927, it offered titillating stories of gold-diggers who ended in conventionally moral poses, appealing to a generation seeking "frolicsome reading." A pulp of the C. H. Young Company's "Newsstand Group" of similar publications including *Breezy Stories*, it and its peers claimed a combined circulation of 1.5 million. Peggy Gaddis's racy novellette "Fly by Nightie" in the November 1924 issue is typical. The magazine was about 120 pages an issue, 7″ × 10″ in size, twenty cents monthly, and printed on cheap paper with suggestive covers, with twelve pages of slick paper ads bound in. It followed a racier line than *Wayside Tales* had followed in Chicago a year or two earlier.

By 1927, E. R. Crowe was handling the advertising for the magazine, boasting "Thrills—gay girls and dazzling lights! Sportive youths and Bohemian nights!" "One Arm" is a representative brief bit of doggerel: "I met her in a one-arm lunch / (The proper name to call it) / She used one arm to get her food, / And one to get my wallet." O'Henry-style surprise endings were *Droll Stories'* stock in trade, including an "other" woman assaulting a wife only to find out that the wife wants to ditch her obnoxious husband, or a "frolicsome" story where a poor girl is almost seduced by her boss, but ends up landing a good job for the-young-hero-who-saves-her, with only a moderate amount of blackmail; titillation is provided by an undressing-for-the-bath scene. *Droll Stories* is best classed as 1920s fictional/sexually oriented humor of the naively salacious sort. A full run is located at DLC. The first copyrighted is Volume 2:1 for September 1923; the last copyrighted is Volume 9:4 for June 1927.

DUKE'S MIXTURE MAGAZINE

This tobacco advertising sheet was published in New York and carried sixteen pages of humorous anecdotes, colored cartoons in a center page, and various bits of information and brief jokes, along with material on tobacco-related products. It cost five cents an issue and measured 8″ × 11″. Its 1909 "Midwinter Holiday Number" was Volume 2:6.

E

ESQUIRE

Esquire belongs in the category of general magazines but deserves citation for its impressive array of cartoons, including the Vargas and Petty girls—notorious successors to Gibson's more archly caricatured ladies. Articles like Helen Norden's "Latins Are Lousy Lovers" are rightly pointed out by Henry Pringle, in "Sex, Esq.", *Scribner's* 103 (March 1938): 33–39, as spicing up the magazine's image, but even the Watch and Ward Society of Boston later found its humor merely "slapstick" in the face of legal obscenity charges. Cartoons and comic covers made humorous what began as a slick, oversized men's fashion magazine, but became a major publisher of serious fiction and commentary. It is accorded partial credit for undermining the hold of *Life*,* *Puck*,* and *Judge** in the 1930s by Theodore Peterson in *Magazines in the Twentieth Century*. At fifty cents per copy, the 10″ × 13″ magazine was expensive compared to the other magazines of the 1930s, but sales expanded rapidly from 100,000 to 750,000 by mixing visual spice with its more intellectualized matter. The editor was Arnold Gingrich in New York, and the publisher was Alfred Smart in Chicago. It is still published today, following its first appearance as a quarterly in October 1933 and its rapid rise in circulation following its shift to monthly status. The present *Esquire* (Volume 106:5 for November 1986 being the last seen) has little of the earlier humorous style.

EVERGREEN REVIEW

The bimonthly *Evergreen Review* of New York featured a number of comic elements in Number 40, April 1966 (8½″ × 11″, one dollar per issue), although at other times its status as an avant garde literary periodical has not qualified it as humorous. The April 1966 number featured Allen Ginsburg's poetry, Jack

Kerouac, Henry Miller on George Grosz, with Grosz illustrations, and the "Phoebe Zeitgeist" comic strip among other cartoons scattered variously. Barney Rosset was editor. It ran from April 1957 through summer 1973 (Vol. 17:97), with its claimed circulation rising from 25,000 to 170,000. Volume 1:1 was Grove Press's copyright for 1 April 1957; the last copyright by Evergreen Review, Inc., was Volume 17:97 for Summer 1973.

EXPERIENCE ANNUAL/EXPERIENCE MONTHLY/ FLAPPER'S EXPERIENCE

The Experience Publishing Company of Chicago produced the *Annual* (5¼" × 8¼"), at fifty cents a copy as an offshoot of its monthly *Experience* and *Flapper's Experience*. In *The Experience Annual*, 130 pages were filled with pictures for correspondence, jokes and gags, starlets, and letters on themes like "My Most Embarrassing Moments." Number 2 was 1925. The Experience Publishing Company became Experimenter, publisher of *French Humor*** and *Your Body* among other magazines. *Experience*, copyrighted September 1923 (Volume 1:1), was published irregularly between monthly and bimonthly through Volume 3:4 (March 1925), with *Flapper's Experience* copyrights continuing from Volume 3:6 for May 1925 through Volume 4:6 for June 1926. *The Flapper*** is a separate unrelated publication along similar lines.

EXTRAVAGANZA

Published semi-monthly by the Extravaganza Publishing Company of Chicago, *Extravaganza* described itself as the successor to *The Magazine of Fun.*** It featured short and long prose burlesque Roaring Twenties romances. It was thirty-two pages, printed on cheap paper for ten cents an issue, with a sprinkling of gag cartoons and doggerel, and 7¼" × 10½" in size. The issue seen is Volume 1:3 for 1 November 1923. Volume 1:1 (for 1 October 1923) through Volume 1:3 were copyrighted.

THE EYE

The Eye was edited by Obadiah Optic in Philadelphia, weekly, from 7 January 1808 (Vol. 1:1) to 22 December 1808 (Vol. 2:25) at three dollars per year. Published by John W. Scott, it featured original papers under headings including "The American Idler," "Mushroom," "The Spectacles," "The Tortoise," and "The Expatiator," in various letters and essays. It advanced morality with essays sanctioned by Joseph Addison, the *Edinburgh Mirror*, and *The Looker-On*. Its most interesting pieces of social satire appeared in "The Mushroom Papers" by "Fungus," which burlesqued modish Philadelphia customs. An index appears at the front of each section. DLC holds the original, reprinted by University Microfilms.

EYEFUL

An eyeful and an earful were provided by cuties in silk underwear and burlesque costumes, punctuated by full-page cartoons of burlesque show humor. Volume 1:1 was published in March 1943 by Eyeful Magazines of New York; Tony Leeds was editor; the 8½″ × 11½″ format sold at twenty-five cents and was primarily a girlie magazine. First copyrighted was Volume 1:4 for Summer 1944 by Personality Publications; then Eyeful Publications published it quarterly through Volume 3:5 for February 1947 and on through Volume 11:5 for April 1955 (publishing as Eyeful Magazines). *Eyeful of Fun* may have been an alternate title for the smaller 1950s version.

FAT CONTRIBUTOR'S SATURDAY NIGHT

A well-known colleague of Artemus Ward's, the "Fat Contributor," A. Minor Griswold, founded his own weekly newspaper in Cincinnati from 1872 to 1875, according to Mott's dates. Volume 1:23 was 21 December 1872; the 26″ × 20″, eight-column, four-page publication in standard newspaper format for the era, cost five cents an issue. It was a literary and humorous journal for family reading, with poems by Will Carleton, clips from the exchanges, various comic doggerel written for itself, city notes, and local advertisements. "Light Laughter" and "Lines Upon Lines" columns were regular features playing with exaggeration, irony, and one-liner humor of various sorts, and the prose expanded elsewhere in the paper up to long stories. One issue is at RPB.

FIGARO! OR CORBYN'S CHRONICLE OF AMUSEMENTS

Wardle Corbyn brightened the Manhattan literary scene with his "Chronicle of Amusements" weekly beginning on 31 August 1850, although he withdrew by Number 19 just after the turn of the new year and was long gone by the demise of the paper with Volume 2:23 on 10 May 1851. Art, music, and drama were the focus of *Figaro!*, particularly including the Jenny Lind madness which romped through its pages. Intelligent humor, however, was a notable product of Corbyn's pen, from puns suggesting that New York's Negro regiment should be named the Black Guards to thoughtful articles on George P. Morris and Herman Melville. Volume 2's masthead featured the barber Figaro himself surrounded by heads on poles, a grisly rendering by T. W. Strong, who later went on to publish *Yankee Notions*.* "The Topic of the Week" column led off the magazine and set the tone for it, usually commenting on one or another human foible. Personal sketches, burlesque dramas—"The Providential

Thunderbolt'' being one outstanding example that includes hits at slavery along with its vulgarization of the sentimental, humorous ''Instructions to the Police,'' ''Green Room Gossip'' on theatrical topics, or articles like ''On Humbugs'' in the 15 March 1851 number—filled up each issue, with four pages of advertisements rounding out its sixteen pages. The urbane irony and slapstick burlesque of much of this writing stands among the best of the era, perhaps because of the paper's orientation toward literary and theatrical life and the New York theater, which included a wide range of farce, Barnum's ''moral'' dramas, and legitimate plays.

Originally, *Figaro*! was an impressive quarto, better printed on good paper than most comic weeklies, 8½″ × 11″ in two-column format at six and a quarter cents, edited by ''wit and wisdom''—Corbyn and Professor Hows, its drama critic. S. French was the publisher, later replaced by Bunnell and Price. Corbyn announced his withdrawal with the last issue of Volume 1 on 4 January 1851, and his name disappeared from the masthead. No publisher was listed until Bunnell and Price appeared on 21 March. On 12 April, there was a significant decline in the quality of illustrations and the journal's overall appearance, and a shift to cheaper paper. The last issue seen is Volume 2:23, for 10 May. The two bound volumes are at the NN Annex; MH and DLC list partial holdings.

FIGARO (Chicago)

The Chicago *Figaro*, published from 1888 through 1893, showed relatively little humor under the editorship of J. C. B. Andrews or J. C. Vynne. A few one-liners and society chit-chat dominated, with lengthier fiction by Opie Read, Caroline Kirkland, J. Percival Pollard, and lesser lights. W. J. F. Dailey was publisher and proprietor from March 1892. Volume 2:40 was 4 December 1890. Incomplete runs are at DLC, ICN, NN, and one other library.

THE FLAPPER

The Flapper (Vol. 1:1, May 1922) was the voice of the liberated women of its era, treating itself as a club magazine and urging a ''Flapper Flock in every town.'' Monthly, 5⅞″ × 9¾″, at twenty cents, in white covers with black photos and masthead, it offered 52 pages of flapper theme humor, gags, cartoons, and miscellaneous pieces. It published plenty of newsy, humorous material and a multitude of columns on various flapper concerns. Thomas Levish was managing editor in Chicago for the Flapper Publishing Company, owned by S. A. Cousley. Four issues have been seen for 1922. The last copyrighted was Volume 2:6 for June 1923.

FLICKS

Parliament Magazines of North Hollywood, California, produced *Flicks* in the 1960s as a "crazy caption kook book." A slick-paper quarterly, 8″ × 10½″, at $1.50, February-March-April 1966 is the only issue seen, the first of two numbers copyrighted. Humorous captions are attached to movie stills, usually with undressed women or a crude double entendre in the caption.

FLIP

Flip was a large size—10¼″ × 13″—magazine of the 1940s offering "cartoons with a kick." It contained thirty-four pages, cost fifteen cents monthly, and was issued by G. I. Publishing Company of New York. It was mostly four cartoons to a page in the styles of prominent cartoonists; one or two prose features were also included. The humor was general, with a little of the "hard-boiled" Broadway style in the prose pieces. June 1946 (Vol. 1:1) through August 1946 (Vol. 1:3) were copyrighted.

FLOPHOUSE NEWS

Flophouse News, a tabloid newspaper from K. R. K. Publishing Company in New York during the World War Two era, measured 12″ × 16¼″ and sold for ten cents. Volume 1:2 for April 1944, edited by Bert Dooley, offers twenty-four pages of Bowery brevities, flophouse chatter, jokes and gag cartoons of "sense, nonsense, and fun for a liberal clientele." Beside the lines urging readers to buy war bonds, jokes on marriage, flappers, bowery business life, and soldiers filled its columns. A brief article on Gypsy Rose Lee on page 23 justified a double headline advertising "Strip-Tease"; otherwise jokes are a representative sampling of humor from gagbooks of the 1890 period to its own era.

FLUMGUDGEON GAZETTE AND BUMBLE BEE BUDGET

Charles E. Pickett handwrote twelve copies of each issue of the *Flumgudgeon Gazette and Bumble Bee Budget* in Oregon City in the Oregon Territory from about June 1845 through August 1845 to criticize the corrupt doings of the Legislative Committee. The only known copy—for 20 August 1845, 12½″ × 7½″, thirteen pages written and one blank—is at the Oregon Historical Society in Portland. In his "Newspaper of the Salmagundi Order and Devoted to Scratching the Follies of the Times," Pickett noted that the legislators acted more like turkey coop robbers. According to Warren J. Brier, "The *Flumgudgeon Gazette and Bumble Bee Budget*," *Journalism Quarterly* 36 (Summer 1959): 317–20, copies of the paper sent to President James K. Polk caused one corrupt

Indian agent to be dismissed. Brier is the source of the information used here and a larger body of interesting details about the "first English-language newspaper to appear in the Far West."

FOLLIES

Follies was a renewal of *Burten's Follies*** of the 1920s by "Cap'n" Joey Burten and Celestine Vichy and was so numbered with the Winter 1933 issue as Volume 10:1 at twenty-five cents a copy. *Follies*, in digest size at 6" × 9", was all girlie gags, girlie line drawings, and a few photographs. The most notable works were color prints in blue and red featuring comic wisdom concerning flappers showing a deco-Parisian influence. A spread of jokes and brief prose pieces dealt skeptically with sexual themes. It is not known how long it lasted. See also *Burten's Follies*.

THE FOOLISH BOOK

The Foolish Book was listed in 1903–1904 as "Sis Hopkin's Sister," and featured Ida Melville in that role on its covers. Volume 1:1 for June 1903 and Volume 2:12 for May 1904 represent the run at DLC. Rose Melville supposedly became editor in August 1904, but it is not clear if the magazine was still publishing at this date. Offering similar humor, it was taken into the combination of *Judge's Library*** and *Sis Hopkin's Own Book*,** which eventually became *Film Fun*.*

FOR LAUGHING OUT LOUD (LAUGHING OUT LOUD)

For Laughing Out Loud was a quarterly general humor magazine of the late 1950s and early 1960s published by Dell Publishing Company at twenty-five to thirty-five cents per copy over its lifespan. The first copyrighted is Number 3 for February-April 1957; a copy seen for January-March 1958, in 7½" × 10½" format, lists Bill Yates as editor. John Norment moved up to the editorship in the early 1960s. A sprinkling of light prose by Gurney Williams, Parke Cummings, and others and cartoons by popular cartoonists filled its pages. Number 22 was January-March 1962, the last seen; Number 23 was the last copyrighted, although it may have continued.

FRANK LESLIE'S BUDGET OF HUMOROUS AND
SPARKLING STORIES

This journal was published from May 1878 through April 1896 as a monthly by Frank Leslie in New York City. One copy is at Yale; MWA has discarded it; DLC has a broken run; and a few other issues are scattered. It is primarily a story paper.

FRANK LESLIE'S BUDGET OF WIT, HUMOR, ANECDOTE, AND ADVENTURE

This monthly (Vol. 1:1, May 1878), priced at fifteen cents per copy or $1.50 yearly, attempted to be varied in content and attractive to travelers. As claimed, it was a melange of adventure fiction and miscellaneous items. DLC has copies.

FREELANCER

The *Freelancer* Magazine was a Drukel Publication, issued bimonthly from Waterbury, Connecticut, and devoted to the interests of freelance cartoonists, artists, and humor writers. Volume 1:1 appeared in March-April 1966 at fifty cents, measuring 8½" × 11" and twenty-six pages. It featured an article on Gurney Williams, advice to gag writers and cartoonists, and advertisements for other trade-related magazines such as *The Super Market Magazine*—listing sales sources for the Cartoonists' Guild of America—and *The Gag Recap*—distilling over 900 gags monthly for the trade.

FRENCH CARTOONS AND CUTIES

Mild sexually oriented cartoons characterized *French Cartoons and Cuties*, a digest-size monthly of the late 1950s and early 1960s which confined itself to the simpler variety of line-drawn cartoons. Volume 1:21 appeared in December 1960. Candar Publishing Company of Holyoke, Massachusetts, and New York offered it at twenty-five cents an issue.

FRENCH FROLICS

French Frolics (Vol. 1:1, January 1925), edited by Harry A. Glynn, worked hard to obtain a sleazy sexual comedy appropriate to its subtitle *La Vie Parisienne*, "An American Magazine in the Parisian Style." Published monthly by the French Frolics Publishing Company of Newark, New Jersey, it sought French material of all types, "translated before submitting." One flapper in garters tells a wealthy gent, "Love You? No I hate your wife." Other cartoons, drawn in deco style and colored with reds and blues, featured undressed flappers in sexy situations. Oversize at 9" × 12", it filled twenty-eight pages with gags, jokes, and cartoons sporting the Parisian view of sex as interpreted by Newark. It cost thirty-five cents per issue and five dollars annually.

FRENCH FUN

French Fun was a gags and gals magazine of the late 1960s featuring nude photos and sexually oriented cartoons. It was digest-size, 5¼" × 7¼", cost thirty-five cents, and was published quarterly by Health Knowledge, Inc., of New York City. The issue seen is Number 7 for Winter 1969.

FRENCH HUMOR

"All illustrations by French Artists" proclaimed the covers of *French Humor*, a ten-cent cheap-paper weekly of reprints from half a dozen leading French humor magazines. Experimenter Publishing Company of New York copyrighted it as a weekly from Volume 1:1 for 16 July 1927 through Volume 1:45 for 23 June 1928. Its twenty-four page, 8″ × 11½″ format was filled with stories and jokes suggesting amoral comic philosophies: "My weak spot is faithfulness," says one French flapper, "Every time I love a man it is always forever!" The Experimenter Publishing Company also published *Radio News, Amazing Stories, Your Body, Know Thyself,* and other journals, including four devoted to television in 1928. Volume 1:10, the earliest issue seen, was for 27 September 1927. *French Humor* became *Tid-Bits** with the 23 June 1928 issue at twenty-five cents a copy. *Tid-Bits* reached Volume 2:6 on 29 September 1928, the last issue seen or copyrighted, under the editorship of Valentine Erskine. *Tid-Bits* offered a wider number of humorous topics, puzzles, and a story or two to round out a thirty-six page journal in a finished-paper cover replacing the cheap-seeming newsprint cover of the old *French Humor*.

FRENCH SCANDALS

French Scandals was a monthly issued by H. M. Publications of New York (Vol. 3:4, February 1937) in a 6¾″ × 9¾″ format at twenty-five cents per issue. It featured sexy stories with clever endings, nude photos, and some infidelity jokes.

FUN

Fun was the eight-page humor section of the *New York World* newspaper published during 1910–1920. The issue seen is dated 19 September 1915. Printed in orange and blue on a single folded sheet of newsprint, it measures 9″ × 11″. Its pages are filled with illustrated gags and jokes of a general nature: holes in a suit are "moth proof," or my tailor's suit against me is being aired in court, for example. Puzzles, rebuses, and hidden proverbs rounded out the family-oriented humorous material.

FUN & FROLIC

Fun & Frolic was copyrighted by Guaranteed Rural Mailings and, later, Play Magazine of Minneapolis, Minnesota, with Number 1 for Spring 1944. It was published irregularly and achieved Number 6—its seventh issue—in June 1946. It was made up of cartoons typical of its era; it is not the same magazine as *Fun Frolic.***

THE FUN BOOK

At thirty-six pages, measuring 6½″ × 9½″, and selling monthly for a dime, *The Fun Book*, by Dennis, Harvey and Remington, Inc., "progressive publishers" of Chicago, was a throwback in its humorous attitudes and subject matter to the turn of the century small-town outlook. It reached Volume 2:8 by June 1922, with Albert Dennis as editor and art director. Gently humorous prose dominated the scattering of cartoons by E. W. Kemble and others resembling those popular before 1900. Humor was epigrammatic—"greasing the palm usually cures the itching thereof"—or genteel, masquerading as low-brow. Volume 1:1 was copyrighted for September 1920 by Progressive Publications of Wheeling, West Virginia, with the last copyright as Volume 2:10 for August 1922.

FUN FROLIC

Fun Frolic offered two issues in the Gals and Gobs format and was copyrighted for Volume 1:1, Winter 1944, and Volume 1:2, Spring 1944. It cost twenty-five cents, measured 8½″ × 11″ and 86 pages, and presented mostly full-page cartoons, some four-to-a page cartoons, and some pages of light prose. Pin-up girls deluxe by George Janes and a cutie cover by James Trembath set the mood, pieced out with a variety of general and service jokes, predominantly on sex and flirtation. The humor covered varied topics, and a spectrum of contemporary cartoonists appeared. Phil Painter Publications of Dunellen, New Jersey, and New York was the publisher.

FUN HOUSE COMEDY

Fun House Comedy was typical of the 1960s sleazecake formula of Humorama Magazines—sometimes as Timely Features, Inc.—of New York in *Laugh Digest*,** *Zip!*,** *Stare*,** *Joker*,** *Eyeful of Fun*, *Jest*,** *Humorama*, *Popular Jokes*,** *Comedy*,** *Laugh Riot*, *Gaze*,** *Romp*,** *Fun House*, *Laugh Circus*, and *Instant Laughs*. Bimonthly, at thirty-five cents, 5½″ × 7½″, it offered one hundred pages of cartoons by Bill Wenzel, Jefferson Machamer, and others; jokes and gags; and half-nude girlies with suitable captions: "A man with no sense of values is one who throws away a pin-up calendar just because he ran out of dates." Issues from 1964 have been seen, carrying no volume numbers. Many of the jokes deal with sex in business, gold-digging, and sexual propositioning on dates. It may have lasted to 1970.

FUN OUTDOORS PICTORIAL

Not a girl scouting magazine, *Fun Outdoors* was an outdoors and sports-girlie humor magazine with a bit of adventure prose, some cheesecake and mildly humorous captions, and lots of cartoons and shorter humorous fiction. Volume 1:1 was the Autumn 1937 issue; it cost thirty-five cents and was edited by Wm. H. Kofoed from

Philadelphia. As a pictorial, *Fun Outdoors* took full advantage of its opportunity to offer bathing suit girl pictures, but in 8½″ × 11½″ format, it took a higher line of comic prose than the gals and gags digests of the 1950s and 1960s.

FUN PARADE

Fun Parade was a World War II digest-size monthly of service-oriented and general jokes, gags, and short material. Volume 1:1 was issued in December 1941 by the Alfred Harvey Publishing Company of New York at fifteen cents. It featured 68 pages of chestnuts like "She said it was love at first sight, but then took a second look." A cartoon shows bombs and rolling pins falling with the caption: "It looks like they've mobilized their women." Nevertheless, it was still publishing city-life, domestic, and flirtation jokes in Fall 1947, Number 35, with Leon Harvey as editor. Hence, its mix of jokes and cartoons must have maintained an appeal to readers looking for varied jokes of a retellable sort. *Fun Parade* also escaped the trap of being solely sexually oriented. In fact, a back page surveys its readers for the type of humor they would like in future issues, even though it was slipping from bimonthly to quarterly publication as it conducted the survey.

FUN QUARTERLY

DLC lists incomplete holdings, Volume 1 from September 1903 by the Arkell Company, New York, but it does not appear on their shelves.

FUN RIOT

Military Mirth, Navy Nifties, and Marine Merriment were offered by *Fun Riot* in the 1940s, with cartoons, gags, gals galor [sic], as depicted in the James Trembath and Frank Beaven covers. Mostly cartoons, with a slight mix of prose humor by William Lieberson and others and pin-ups by George Janes, *Fun Riot* adhered to the wartime humor-sex-flirtation formula of the 1940s pulp humor magazines, but with a significant number of Rosie-the-riveter theme cartoons by servicemen-cartoonists. Volume 1:1, bimonthly, October 1943, was the first number for Baffling Mysteries, Inc., of Mount Morris, Illinois, and New York. It lasted at least through an eleventh number, July 1946, the last copyrighted, with jokes on city and dating themes. Although intended as a bimonthly, it seems to have appeared quarterly and then triannually.

FUN WITH CY SCUDDER

Fun with Cy Scudder was a racier, folksier version of *Life** spun off from *Sis Hopkin's Own Book*** for a two-volume fling from August 1903 through December 1904 (Vol. 2:17). Measuring 7″ × 11½″ and published in both New York and London, the monthly was offered by Arkell Company at ten cents a month or a dollar a year as part of the stable of journals Arkell ran against *Life—Fun Quarterly,*** *Foolish Book,*** and *Just Fun That's All.***

Like *Life* and some others of this period, *Fun With Cy Scudder* introduces sexual themes into its humor, including marital infidelity: Mrs. Suburbs hysterically berates her husband for kissing the maid, and he defends himself by declaring that he was convincing her to stay in their employ—to which the Mrs. responds, "Tell me quick, John, dear, did she promise?" Among its thirty pages were tall tales, jokes, busty Gibson Girl types, Blacks, and children in profuse illustrations, and four pages of ads. In Volume 2, photos show up on inside pages for the first time. In August 1904, Rose Melville, fresh from her success in the stage role of Sis, began offering "Sis Hopkin's Own Column" and was announced as the editor of *The Foolish Book*.

THE FUNNIEST OF AWL AND THE PHUNNIEST SORT OF PHUN

Under the rubric "Laff and Grow Phat," the monthly *Phunniest* claimed a sellout of its first ten-cent issue in 1865. Sixteen pages of cartoons, burlesque Down East dialect novels, one- and two-line jokes, and a double-page centerfold cartoon characterized its 12″ × 16¼″ four-column pages. Shoddy manufacturing and cruelty to children were attacked, and expediency, miscegenation, and Irish immigrants came in for barbed criticism. Urban slang fitted easily into its columns of jokes and burlesques, and it urged social leadership on colleagues like the *Tribune*. Politics also came in for comment. One two-page cartoon shows Lincoln as a monkey riding the hobby horse of expediency while John C. Fremont frees the slaves, supported by *vox populi* and constitutional law. Josh Billings was reprinted and Frank Bellew's illustrations were prominent, along with Bellew's series "How to be Amusing." Local items around New York, as well as items from as far away as Philadelphia, accompanied railroad anecdotes; page 15 was advertisements, and the back cover was made up of cartoons. By 1866, the price had increased to fifteen cents, or $1.50 per year. The magazine disappeared in 1867.

Harvard and the American Antiquarian Society have the few known issues: Volume 1:1 (1865) through Volume 3:24 (1867). A. T. Bellew was publisher of the monthly, although Mott lists W. Jennings Demorest as publisher. Frank Bellew was editor, making this paper a potential touchstone for the socially oriented comic consciousness which Bellew represented during his career.

FUNNY FACTS AND FICTION

Funny Facts and Fiction was an off-size, 8¼″ × 4¾″, yellow-covered quarterly of 52 pages which sold for a quarter. W. A. Keller and the Keller Publishing Company, who also published *Today's Humor,*** produced it from St. Paul, Minnesota, with Volume 1:3 as the Autumn (July) 1931 number. The crude illustrations give *Funny Facts* an old-time look, which is reinforced by its humor boosting the commonplace virtues of home and family and its preference for nineteenth-century humor of the likes of Josh Billings and John G. Saxe. It had many nonprofessional Midwestern contributors of clean family humor in dialect verse and plain prose. Volume 2:1, January-March 1932, was copyrighted. From April 1932 to Spring 1933 it continued as *Today's Humor/Today's Best Stories*. NN holds copies.

FUNNYBONE (1916)

Funnybone was a 9″ × 6″, two-column, thirty-two page magazine published by the Funnybone Publishing Company of New York as "a quarterly magazine for comic entertainers." Twenty-five cents an issue, and later thirty-five cents, or $1.00 a year, it was copyrighted for April-June 1916 (Vol. 1:1) through July-September 1917 (Vol. 2:6), corresponding to the issues seen. James Madison was editor and owner, and collected the crackerjack minstrel routines, snappy sidewalk patter, sketches, parodies, and gags which provided both the amateur and professional with sure-fire "stuff." The "Wedding Bells" monologue noted that the wife speaks five languages, "but thank Heaven, only one at a time." A Hebrew in "The Highest Bidder" hears that someone lost a wallet with $100 and will pay $50 to get it back; the Hebrew bids $55, and the act continues from there. Whole minstrel acts—with Interlocutor and Bones, in classic minstrel show format—and sections of song parodies filled out the patter routines from the vaudeville stage of the 1915–1920 period.

THE FUNNYBONE QUARTERLY

Published quarterly by the Anthony Publishing Company of Chicago and New York, Volume 1:1 of *The Funnybone Quarterly* appeared in April 1942. S. J. Perelman and F. P. A. were among the notable contributors, and the cartoons were consistently witty and well executed. An ad at the back of the magazine offered a monthly *Funnybone*, also with Perelman, Franklin P. Adams, Ted Shane, Frank Sullivan, and dozens of others. The 8½″ x 11″, twenty-five-cent *Funnybone* was Norman Anthony's bid to blaze a new 1940s trail after his hit with *Ballyhoo** a decade before, but there is no evidence that he succeeded. Like all of Anthony's work, however, it has a racy, updated classiness which, in this case, suggests a genuine entry into the 1940s. Volume 1:3, November 1941, is probably the only copyright listing for the monthly. A *Funnybone* comic published around 1944 is not related.

G

GAG STRIPS

Gag Strips, like *Gags*,** was a World War II bimonthly issued by Triangle Publications of Philadelphia with Charles Rubino editing in Chicago. Volume 1:1 appeared in August 1942 at fifteen cents in tabloid size. Whereas *Gags* offered single cartoons, *Gag Strips* was devoted to sequential story cartoons of varying subject matter from muggers to newspaper photographers and detectives. Twenty-four cartoonists were represented in Number 1. The length of the run is unknown.

GAGS

Gags, "The New Book of Jokes and Cartoons," was a garish comic-book format cartoon journal featuring "Grin and Bear It" sequences by George M. Lichty. The 7″ × 9¾″, ten-cent quarterly (Vol. 1:1, Summer 1937) was a product of the United Features Syndicate, New York. The orientation reflects lower-middle-class viewpoints toward the rich and the poor, with comic cartoon material and three-liners on family and marital themes sharing equal space. The name was taken over by Triangle Publications for a tabloid-size journal in 1941.

GAGS (HERE! IS AMERICA'S HUMOR, HERE)

Gags of the 1940s and 1950s was produced by Triangle Publications of Philadelphia at ten cents on a bimonthly basis. In the beginning it was one of the oversize World War II cartoon magazines, thirty-six pages, measuring 10½″ × 13″, with bold poster-style color cartoon covers. Later, it edged up to forty-four pages. Triangle Publications copyrighted Volume 1:2 (May 1941) through Volume 10:7 (July 1951) and *Here* from Volume 10:8 (August 1951) through

Volume 11:3 (March 1952). Charles Rubino in Chicago was the editor for Volume 1:5 (November 1941), the first seen following the first publication date of March 1941. The whole issue was a running gag with cartoons built around a hole drilled through the upper right corner of the magazine. *Gags* offered a splashy cartoon format with some racy dating gags, a magic trick or two, and a puzzle, and favorite prose gags from the contributing cartoonists. Volume 2:8 lists Del Poore as editor, and the format was somewhat squared up and boxed, although still posterlike. Publication became monthly, but it returned to bimonthly in 1944. The armed services figured more heavily in the cartoons. By July 1944 (Vol. 3:7), editing functions with Poore had been transferred to Philadelphia; the price was fifteen cents, as it had been in 1942. War humor and general themes continued. By 1947, *Gags* was still in the same format but at twenty-five cents an issue.

By the 1950s, *Gags* underwent a transformation, having been reduced to comic-book size, $7\frac{1}{4}'' \times 10\frac{1}{2}''$. Advertising, which had held the inside covers and back pages of the tabloid *Gags*, vanished. Cartoons were now solidly middle class in orientation and were similar to those found in *Colliers* and the *Saturday Evening Post*,** among other purveyors of middle-class reading matter. The comic-book size *Gags* contained 64 pages, each page presenting one, two, or six cartoons, although the format was not rigid. It lasted at least to 1951, when service jokes for a new war began to appear. Del Poore was editor through 1951.

GAL SNAPS

Gal Snaps was an early form of the digest-size girlie cartoon magazine, issued in a $5\frac{1}{2}'' \times 7\frac{1}{2}''$ format at twenty-five cents by Palace Promotions of New York. It appears to be from the late 1940s, with a wide splay of business, cutie, and general humor of no particular merit. See also *Jolly Dolls*.**

THE GALAXY

The Galaxy, An Illustrated Magazine of Entertaining Reading (May 1866-January 1878), known as *The Galaxy* from 1872 on, was a fairly somber publication important chiefly for publishing Mark Twain's "Memoranda" column in 1871, when readership rose from about 6,000 to 23,000, thereby suggesting Twain's drawing power even at this early stage in his career. Twain had published brief articles in the magazine in 1868, and in 1870 he contracted with *The Galaxy*'s proprietors, W. C. and F. P. Church, for ten pages of copy for each issue for $2,000 to $2,400 yearly, roughly $20 a page versus J. W. DeForest's three to eight dollars per page for his novel *Overland* running at the same time. May 1870 offered the first "Memoranda," and Twain retreated in April of 1871, after missing March, due to family illnesses. A humor department was continued as "The *Galaxy* Club-Room" by Don Piatt and later Kate Sanborn. C. A. Bristed also attempted some humor before his death in 1874. University Microfilms has reprinted *Galaxy*. Twain's *Contributions to the Galaxy, 1868–1871, by Mark Twain*, edited by Bruce McElderry, Jr., was published by Scholar's Facsimiles and Reprints of Gainesville, Florida, in 1961.

Michael D. Butler

THE GALAXY OF COMICALITIES

The Galaxy of Comicalities is one of America's early introductions to folk and frontier comedy as a staple. It was issued in forty weekly numbers from 2 October 1833 through 5 July, 1834—the first eleven issues on Wednesdays and thereafter on Saturdays—at $1.25 per year. In physical format, it was an eight-page, two-column octavo measuring 15 × 24 centimeters, profusely illustrated. At the end of its run in 1834, it made a single bound volume of 320 pages. Printed in Philadelphia by Lesher and Shelly, the *Galaxy* is silent about its editors, publishers, or writers. Some pseudonyms of the Yankee caricature variety are affixed to some articles, but no names are associated with the periodical.

The subtitle of the *Galaxy of Comicalities* was "*Short Stories Well Told (Containing) Extracts of History, Tales, Wit, Fun, Anecdotes, Conundrums, & c. & c. (Embellished) With Upwards Of Two Hundred Cuts.*" The paper was ambitious to excel in popular humor both visually with its illustrations and intellectually with its content. Early numbers are filled with typical Yankee, or Jonathan, stories as well as representative Irish or Dutchman jokes. As the issues advance, *Galaxy* printed more songs and poems, including *My Long Tailed Blue* and *The Star Spangled Banner*. By the latest issues, its columns were frequently filled with high-flown romances: *The History Of Rinaldo Rinaldini—Captain Of Bandits and Elizabeth* (or) *The Exiles of Siberia* are typical. In addition to the rich Yankee humor in the earlier numbers, there are several Davy Crockett stories of the exaggerated almanac variety.

Galaxy's interest in comic slang is one of its notable points. Number 39, dated 28 June 1834, contains this brief item: "Names—A writer in the Illinois Pioneer says that the following nicknames have been adopted to distinguish the citizens of the following states:—In Kentucky, they're called Corn-Crackers, Ohio—Buckeyes, Indiana—Hoosiers, Illinois—Suckers, Missouri—Pukes, Michigan—Wolverines, The Yankees are called Eels." One representative bit of humor in Number 13, dated 28 December 1833, listed the terminology of frontiersmen and Yankees:

Cracker Dictionary

Bodiaciosly	Coperously.
Cattywampusly	Obliquely: bias.
Chawed up	Having ear, nose and lip bit off.
Contraption	Contrivance appendant.

Bombesticle	Between a contrivance and a trapping.
Corn Steeler	Thumb and four digits.
TatterGrabber	[as above.]
Fifified	Subject to fits.
Flugens	Fire and faggots.
Forked	How came you so. [A pun on a Shakespeare line.]
Fotch	Did fetch.
Flustrated	Flustered and prostrated; greatly agitated.
Jimber Jawed	Having the tongue always moving.
Lambasting	A severe licking.
Moccasin	Green Whiskey.
Obsquatulate	To mosey, to abscond.
To Mossey	To clear out.
Persnickety	Squeamishly fastidious.
Pisin	Violent in politicks; on the wrong side, i.e. against us.
Mogamatorial Writ	A process that takes a man as well where he is not as where he is.
Ramsquattled	Rowed up salt river.
Ring-Tailed Roarer	A most violent fellow.
Rip Roarous	Ripping and tearing, very outrageous.
Rumbunctious	[as above.]
Scrouger	Ringtailed Roarer.
Scrimptious	Minutest atom; the little end of nothing sharpened.
To Swagger	To strut with free negro dignity.
Sockdolager	In fighting, a lick that tells.
Slantendicular	Slanted from perpendicular.
Spontinaciously	Of one's own accord.
Sarsafarari	Legal proceedings of any kind.
Smartic	One who thinks himself right sharp.
Swimpey	Forked.
Sniptious	Farcically nice.
To Chunk	To brickbat with chunks, not with stones.
Tetotally Twisted	Confoundedly contorted.

Never reprinted, *The Galaxy of Comicalities* is held by the Franklin Meine Collection at IU; partial runs are at MNU, DLC, and PHi.

John Grant Alexander

GALS AND GAGS

Gals and Gags takes its name from a genre of digest-sized cartoon and sleazecake magazines dominant in the 1950s and 1960s. Health Knowledge, Inc., published Number 9 of this quarterly in Fall 1969 in New York at thirty-five cents in a 5½" × 7½" format. It offers jokes, cartoons, and busty pin-up photographs, with all the humor oriented toward physical sexuality.

GAY BOOK MAGAZINE

Gay Book Magazine attempted to cross the formulas of *Film Fun,* 1000 Jokes,*** and *Breezy Stories*. William Kofoed, later editor of *Fun Outdoors Pictorial,*** was editor of the quarterly, which sold at ten cents in an 8½" × 11½", 68-page format. Volume 1:3 (Spring 1934) sported a flapper cutie cover, "My Night-club Nights" by Jimmy Durante, a Manly Wade Wellman story, and a host of dressed and undressed cuties in a variety of light articles, still photo shots in lingerie, and movie out-takes. When a mother asks her daughter if "he tells you any questionable stories," she answers, "No, mother, he makes them so plain I never have to ask him a thing." A steno explains to her boss that she is looking in the mirror because his wife told her to watch herself while he was around. Gay Book of Philadelphia was the publisher, and the last copyrighted was Volume 5:3 (August 1938), after it became monthly in 1937.

GAYETY (1942)

The World War II version of *Gayety* was a tabloid, 10" × 13½", thirty pages. The November 1941 issue, like some of the other tabloids, is printed in only two colors—in this case, brown with a few splashes of red, giving a somber appearance. Cartoons appear in a format using a pasted-on look. The content is poolroom and bar cartoons dominated by cartoon gags around luscious cuties in nighties, with lines like, "Your sargeant stopped to tell me he trusts you so—he's going to let you stand guard again tonight." Volume 1:3 appeared in February 1942. Comedy Publications also copyrighted a *Gayety*, Volume 1:1 and Volume 1:2 for April and October 1943; it is not clear if these are the same or related publications.

GAYETY (1947–1950)

Gayety, "the spice of life," offered a "Big 132 pages" of grand new cartoons and "oh! so lovely girls!," once it worked into its finished format, at about Volume 1:9 (November 1950). It offered cheesecake, believe-it-or-not style cartoon pages, comic sequences, and a large number of girlie cartoons on sexual themes. One sequence is in Basil Wolverton's style and content. A sprinkling of one-liners and brief paragraphs completes the contents. It was published quarterly by Skyline Publications of New York, although Timely Features, Inc., claimed the copyright. It was digest-size and advertised *Joker*** and *Snap* in full-page ads. Volume 1:3 was copyrighted in September 1947, and Volume 1:9 was the last copyrighted.

GAZE

Humorama, Inc.'s *Gaze* is the ultimate example of the sleazecake formula in American humor magazines. Don Q. Shane was the editor of this sister publication to *Popular Jokes*,** *Popular Cartoons*,** *Romp*,** *Stare*,** *Zip!*,** *Fun House*,** *Laugh*, *Joker*,** and *Cartoon Parade*** in the late 1950s and 1960s. Volume 12:89 of the bimonthly, the last seen, appeared in October 1970 at thirty-five cents, measured 5¼" × 7¼", and contained 102 pages filled with large bare-breasted girlies, mostly with a funny epigram or sex-oriented caption having no relation to the photo. Cartoons on sexual topics, concentrating on half-clad girlies, honeymoon themes, and the like, were scattered among the pictures. A few jokes were also mixed in.

GEE WHIZ!

Gee Whiz!—a magazine for amazing gazing—was one of Humorama, Inc.'s bimonthly sleazecake cartoon and picture digests. Volume 1:11 was issued in July 1957; the magazine cost one dollar and had one hundred pages. A typical screamer has a cutie berating her lover: "It's no use saying it's your wife's hair—I happen to know she's a redhead!"

GIGGLES

Giggles is turn-of-the-century commercial humor. The Pratt Food Company of Philadelphia sent out Volume 1:9 in April 1909 with a posted price of five cents. It was four 9" × 12" pages of humor and ads. The outside pages were brightly colored comic strips of Kafoozalem and Deacon Wheyback adventures; the inside pages were filled with country-style humor about school boys, milkmen, and maids, mixed with ads for Pratt animal feeds.

GOOD HUMOR

Good Humor, (Vol. 1:1, Fall 1947) is still being published as a bimonthly by Charlton Press, Derby, Connecticut, with emphasis now on sexually oriented adult cartoons. Sales peaked at 75,000 copies at one time but have diminished to about 17,000. *Good Humor* has undergone several transformations. Volume 1:1 by Picture Detective Publishing Company, published at Charlton, gave way to Volume 1:1 (Summer 1948), 68 pages by Capitol Stories Inc. through Summer 1955 (Vol. 1:17), with covers by Stanley Rayon. It began as a girlie humor magazine. The older version was probably edited by Burton N. Levey, at which time it had a pin-up photo section. Later, with Chad Kelly as editor, it became a quarterly, selling for twenty-five cents and measuring 8½" × 11¾", with pages of jokes, gags, and cartoons mixed. Volume 3:1 (February 1957), however, abandoned the subtitle "Goofy Gags and Gorgeous Gals" in favor of "Satire for Sophisticates," featuring long prose stories following the men's magazine model, punctuated by nude girlie photos. Robert Weston was editor; the men's magazine format lasted for about three or four issues, still quarterly, 8" × 10", thirty-five cents. By June 1958, it even offered a centerfold. It did not return to the all-cartoon format until after it died as a men's magazine.

Number 1 of the new *Good Humor* appeared in Spring 1962, its first two issues oriented toward show biz jokes and pictures, including "Good Humor from Hollywood" and similar features. By 1963–1964 all traces of the men's magazine format were gone. Bill Kish was editor for Volume 4:11 (Spring 1966), with more one-liners organized in various departments. "Wild" Bill—Bill Anderson—was editor through the October 1967 number (Vol. 4:18), with more than 200 girls, grins, and giggles. From 1970 through 1979 it continued in much the same format with gradual increases in price; 6½" × 10" eventually became 8" × 11", $1.50, all adult sexy cartoons and gags.

As of 1986, *Good Humor*'s adult sexy humor format continues, featuring jokes and cartoons scattered randomly on the page and dealing largely with the physical aspects of sex acts and sexual relationships: in 1980s' style, the new "discovered cheating wife" says to her outraged husband as she lies in bed with her lover, "Don't be angry, dear—I was fantasizing about you the whole time." It continued bimonthly, as it has been since the late 1960s, through Volume 21:130 (February 1987) after which its publication is to be suspended. JoAnn Sardo is the present editor of both *Good Humor* and its sister bimonthly, *Cartoon Carnival*.* ($1.75, 7¾" × 10¾"), which is boldly sexy in its covers and its jokes and gags. For more information, see *Cartoon Carnival*.

GOOD THINGS OF "LIFE"

Good Things of "Life" was a hardcovered publication which reprinted cartoons from the parent *Life*** from 1884 to 1893. J. Å. Mitchell took out the first copyright. The firm of White, Stokes, and Allen copyrighted through the third volume. The "Fourth Series," copyrighted by Frederick A. Stokes, New York, 1887, offered 64 pages of cartoons in a 10" × 8" volume, oblong quarto. The cartoons burlesque the pretensions of the American aristocracy, although a fair sprinkling of sentimentalism is thrown in. It was an annual with cartoons by Rudolf Bunner, E. W. Kemble, and Palmer Cox among others. The 1887 volume was priced at two dollars.

THE GRIDIRON

The Gridiron is thought to be the oldest representative of a Dayton, Ohio, magazine, beginning with Volume 1:1 on 29 August 1822 and ending with Volume 1:26 on 8 May 1823. The weekly, published by John Anderson, is a good example of partisan journalism of the day. Focusing strongly on local affairs, it was known for its abusive political satire, captioned by the couplet, "Burn, roast meat burn, / Boil o'er ye pots, ye spits forget to turn." It was advertised in 1939 in Wesson's *Midland Rare Book Catalog* as "one of the rarest and most colorful of early Ohio periodicals," and it is also credited with the first political cartoon to appear in the Western country. The charge was one dollar annually, payable half yearly in advance.

Besides political satire, *The Gridiron* contains literature, poetry, and humor (including puns, anecdotes, and riddles). There are comments on the judicial system by "Fat Fiddlemaker," and parodies using biblical language in a column, "Chronicles," portraying Dayton's citizenry as Old and New Testament figures. "A Play" by "Tim Troublesome" involves the fall of a politician who is informed by his confidante, "Turkeybuzzard," that he lost the election through dishonesty. The play ends with one vote being bought for one hundred "segars," and the words, "If one hundred segars procure one vote—How many hogsheads of leaf tobacco will elect a congressman?" It has been reprinted by University Microfilms.

Michael Pettengell

GRIN

Grin—The American Funny Book is listed in Overstreet's comics guide as a magazine, although, with its 8½" × 11" size and in bright comic-style covers at forty cents it looks like a comic book. Bimonthly, Number 1 was issued in November 1972 by APAG House Publications and offered 54 pages of satiric comic strip sequences on "Penu's," the ghetto version of "Peanuts," "Kissinger," "Blandie in the Capitol" with Richard Nixon as Dagwood, and "The Godmother," among other contemporary political-social, pop culture, and movie-television targets for satire. Gerald Rothberg took credit for the magazine; it reached at least a third number in April 1973, aiming sharp adult criticism at Nixon as a prostitute and at the carefully laundered life-styles of movie and television shows like *The Godfather* and "All in the Family."

GRIN AND BEAR IT

Dell Publishing Company of New York offered *Grin and Bear It* in a large feature comic, reprinting George H. Lichty cartoons featured in the *Chicago Times*; Number 28 was published in 1941. In periodical format, it is not fully a periodical in the sense of most magazines in this volume but is one issue of a varied series; see Overstreet.

GRIN—HUMOR IN PICTURES

The pictorial tabloid *Grin* was an early 1940s magazine featuring some cartoons and jokes but mostly clothed or bathing suit girlie pictures and sequences with a supposedly amusing story covering the captions and providing a general motif, such as "cute contortionist cuts capers." Volume 1:1 was issued in August 1940, at ten cents, 10½" × 13", thirty-two pages, by Elite Publications, of Dunellen, New Jersey, and New York. One of the sequences was an obvious borrowing of a Robert Benchley routine, and none of the sequences was challengingly innovative. *Grin* was identified by its posed photographs of showgirls for the covers. Most of the humor had a girlie orientation. The last seen or copyrighted is Volume 2:7 for February 1942; Volume 1 provided a Number 13 without seeming to have altered the sequence.

H

HA

Ha was the early 1960s version of "the new American humor magazine," featuring general jokes and cartoons and light prose humor of a noncommittal generality. It adhered to the *Saturday Evening Post*** sort of material, relatively bland middle-class-oriented comedy. No serious political satire or commentary was included. A few burlesque ads appeared in a weak reminiscence of *Ballyhoo*.* George H. Levy was publisher in New York, John Bailey was editor and Mel Brookstein editor-in-chief. The magazine cost thirty-five cents from its beginning in 1963.

HALT!

Halt! "The Pause That's Fun," was a digest-sized monthly issued by Crestwood Publishing of New York at fifteen cents a copy in a 5½″ × 7½″ format. The editor, "Wilkinson," in September 1946 (Vol. 5:10) published general cartoons, a few jokes, and a crossword, all directed at servicemen, but not service humor as such. He even offered originals of the cartoon artwork free to servicemen who wrote in. Volume 1 (December 1941) was copyrighted by Crestwood Publications; the last copyrighted is Volume 5:7 for June 1946.

HALT FRIENDS!

A small, 4¼″ × 5½″, thirty-two page magazine priced "Pay What You Please," *Halt Friends!* was a publication by ex-servicemen which cartooned the fifth rider of the apocalypse as "unemployment" and showed the jobless veteran in the guise of Art Young's "Poor Fish" in other cartoons. Articles like "Americanism—What Does it Mean?" described patriotism, but seemed also to protest bitterly the lot of servicemen; in one cartoon an amputee is reduced to watering a small tree to grow his own wooden leg. The issues seen are from 1928, and it shares with *Hello Buddy*** the subtitles "Comics of War/ Facts of Service" and its format.

HARPOON

Harpoon billed itself in 1974 as the "new" American humor magazine. One of several Adrian B. Lopez publications, edited by Dennis Lopez, *Harpoon* tried to capture the slick format and to mix comix-style cartoon pieces, burlesque advertisements, and takeoffs on the American political scene. The first issue— September 1974, bimonthly at one dollar in standard 8″ × 11″ magazine format— was dedicated to W. W. Scott, who was then producing the gals and gags magazines *Zowie*** and *Jackpot*** and was former contributor to *Ballyhoo** and *Movie Humor.*** It lasted at least through a third number by Histrionic Publications with the same burlesque and slick pseudo-counter-culture ad and fiction parodies.

HELLO BUDDIES

This wartime digest, 5″ × 7½″ in size and fifteen cents in price, featured gals and gags. Leon Harvey was the editor for Alfred Harvey Publications, with issues published bimonthly through March 1945 and then every six weeks. Volume 2:3 was for September 1943, with issues known from March 1942 through April 1946. Volume 4:7 for 30 January 1946 is the last copyrighted. *Army and Navy Fun Parade*** was a sister publication. Sixty-six pages of service-oriented jokes about camp life and dating dominated *Hello Buddies* as full-page cartoons, with a few pages of gags thrown in.

HELLO BUDDY

Measuring 4¼″ × 5½″, *Hello Buddy* was a fifteen-cent cartoon and joke magazine published by the Veteran's Service Magazine Company of New York in 1928 to provide work for disabled and unemployed vets of World War I. Its thirty-six pages featured both the sad and the less tragic side of war. Full- and part-page cartoons and war and returning vet jokes give the magazine a somber mood, and economic injustice is indicted in several items. A copy is in the Harris Collection at Brown University. *Halt Friends!*** subtitled "Carrying On," and priced at "Pay What You Please," was similar and may have been interchangeable with *Hello Buddy*.

HELP!

Help!, a follower of *Mad Magazine*,* is significant largely for Harvey Kurtzman's role as editor. It was published monthly beginning in August 1960 at thirty-five cents a copy. Emphasis was on whacky dubbed-quip photograph articles, which it favored over *Mad*'s comic cartoon sequences. Literary, theatrical, cultural, and political burlesque was the chief fare. It was published in New York by the Help! Publishing Company in an 8″ × 11″ format. Number 26 (September 1965) is the last seen or copyrighted.

HERE! IS AMERICA'S HUMOR

Del Poore edited *Here!* from Philadelphia as a monthly for Triangle Publications. Volume 11:2 appeared in February 1952; the magazine was 8″ × 11″ in size and cost twenty-five cents per issue. *Here!* was a cheap-paper 60-page collection of cartoon humor and funny stories based on middle-class life. A few lengthy comic articles were interspersed to piece out the cartoon fare and to provide a format approximating a general magazine. It was derived from *Gags*.** According to copyright information, Volume 10:1 was for November 1951; the last copyrighted was Volume 11:3 for March 1952. For more information, see *Gags*.

HILARIOUS 'LAFF RIOT'

Published by Ziegelheim in New York with a 1946 copyright date claimed *Hilarious Laff Riot* (5¼″ × 8¼″) offered 68 pages of single-page cartoons and some gag pages. It cost fifteen cents per issue. Inside the front cover, the cartoon shows a spinster admonishing a speechless traffic cop, "I most certainly do know what a raised hand means . . . I've been a teacher for 20 years!" Hobo, marital, convict, and office cartoons filled out the magazine.

HIT!

Hit! was one of the early Adrian Lopez publications, under the heading of Volitant Publications, New York. A thirty-two-page tabloid of World War II vintage, it started as the serviceman's gazette packed with pin-ups punctuated by some cartoon pages and a joke page or two, with general material at fifteen cents, 10¼″ × 13″ in size. It was first copyrighted for February 1945 (Volume 2:9). A man wounded in the African campaign is asked if he's married and responds, "No, this is the worst thing that's ever happened to me." It made the transition to peacetime by changing its subheading to "a pictorial peek at life" while maintaining the sexy pin-up and trendy article format and dropping the humor.

October 1950 was Volume 7:7. In addition, an *Annual Hit* followed the monthly at least from 1943 through 1952. Volume 8:3 for September-October 1951 is the last copyrighted issue.

HIT! JUNIOR

Hit! Junior was a twenty-five cent digest-size bimonthly published by Picture Magazines, with Volume 1:4 being January-February 1954. It featured cartoons on the 1950s' life-style, the service, and dating, with gags thrown in randomly.

THE (LANCASTER) HIVE

Beneath the running title, *The Hive*, which includes an illustration of swarming bees, a caption reads,

> "Be Thou The First, Our Efforts To Befriend—
> His Praise Is Lost, Who Stays Till All Commend."

As this example suggests, the four-page miscellany by Charles McDowell and William Grear published essays on morality, along with biographical sketches and humorous anecdotes. *The Hive* was published from Lancaster, Pennsylvania, from 22 June 1803 to 12 June 1805 on a biweekly basis. The paper invited philosophers, moralists, satirists, candid inquirers, humorists, and poets to submit material, and its annual cost was two dollars—payable in half-yearly advances— or two dollars annually in advance for issues by mail.

Articles such as attacks against swearing and slander, and guides for correct manners dominate the paper; examples of humor are found mostly in short anecdotes and fillers. One such anecdote involves a Duke who mistakenly places his watch "in between the lining of his breeches and his shirt." Later, he thinks it has been stolen and promptly searches everyone on the premises. After realizing his mistake, he asks one young man why he refused to be searched, being assured of his innocence. The man replies that, "not knowing where to dine this day, I put a cold fowl in my pocket, and would sooner fight any man in England than it should be discovered there." *The Hive* has been reprinted by University Microfilms.

Michael Pettengell

HOBO NEWS

Hobo News ($11\frac{1}{4}'' \times 14''$) was a twenty-four-page tabloid newspaper of the World War II era which offered "a little fun to match the sorrow," and proclaimed, "War stamps stuck in your book are better than Jap bayonets stuck in your back." Patrick Mulkern, in New York, was the owner. The weekly cost ten cents (21 May 1945 was Volume 5:21) and featured a mix of show biz interviews, city columns, cartoons, and longer light comedy prose pieces in the 1940s style. *Hobo News* appears in copyright listings irregularly in the 1950s and is apparently the same publication that continued from Volume 2:86 (November 1953) through Volume 2:99 (December 1954).

HOKUM

Hokum was copyrighted by Graphic Arts Corporation, Volume 1:2 for February 1932, although the actual issue claimed to be produced by Modern Humor Company of Minneapolis. Captain Billy Fawcett, however, had a hand in its publication. It offered jokes and some doggerel poetry. The only issue known, Volume 1:2, sold for fifteen cents.

HOLLYWOOD SQUAWKIES

Hollywood Squawkies (7½″ × 10″, fifteen cents, thirty-four pages) was closely allied with *Burten's Follies*,** *Radio Razzberies*,** *Nudies, Passion Stories*, and *New York Life*—the content of the last three being overtly sexual. Produced by Joe Burten, it offered "the inside of movieland," staged by Celestine Vichy, who offered a cheeky view of Hollywood with stories like "Chiselin' Cherub" and nude photos in the "Turkey Number," Volume 1:3 (November 1933). By 1934, the F. G. Wilson Company published it in Brooklyn, with plenty of gossip, a few cartoons, a Walter "Snitchell" column, and photo montages of Hollywood's Miss (Marlene) "Dootrick." The length of the run is uncertain beyond early 1934. See also *Burten's Follies*.

THE HOMBRE

The Hombre was one of the wild effusions of the San Francisco literary landscape in 1851. William Rabe listed himself as the "responsible editor" and threatened to publish the paper if he couldn't sell his press in three days. Only one issue is known of the weekly at twenty-five cents in 10″ × 12½″, two-column format, located at Harvard.

Rabe was a lawyer and dry-goods salesman, among other odd-ball activities, and epitomized acerbic, rough-house San Francisco and California political humor. The cover featured a hanging Chinaman, three-card monte, and a bear holding the acts of the California legislature: brimstone, brass, and soft solder were identified as major constituents of California life. Rabe's comments on juries and legislators were written in educated vernacular language, neither elevated nor cute, but fresh and direct.

HOOEY

Hooey was the most successful copier of the *Ballyhoo** style beginning in December 1931 and lasting at least into the early war years. The regular issue cost fifteen cents, and the *Annual*—the second dated 1932—was twenty-five cents, measuring 8½" × 11¼" and featuring large cartoons of the Prohibition thirties. By World War II, gals and gags cartoons and war cartoons became more prominent. *The Annual* for 1940 was particularly rich in the sexy cartoons of the 1940s style, but the eleventh, for 1941, leaped to greatness with a cover showing Hitler with both feet flying in a double goosestep for his troops—when the reader lifted a tear flap, a goose was goosing him in the rear end. Originally, it was the product of Popular Magazines, Louisville, Kentucky, and later Long Prairie and Minneapolis, Minnesota, and still later Country Press, Greenwich, Connecticut. The humor was a little sexier as time passed but never approached the adult humor of other magazines. The cartoon styles remained varied, and "Newsreels" and burlesque advertisements maintained the *Ballyhoo* effect closely. Volume 1:1 was copyrighted for January 1932 in November 1931, suggesting that it is the December 1931 issue. The last copyright was Volume 5:8 for August 1936 by Popular Magazines, then publisher of *Captain Billy's Whiz Bang** and *Smokehouse Monthly.***

HORNYTOONS

This quarterly (Vol. 1:1, 1980), published by Nuance, Inc., of Van Nuys, California, offers pornographic cartoon sequences, keeping company with other "raunchy, lustful laughs" from the same publisher, including *Nasty Funnies* and the like sexual-content cartoon publications. Jervis Hill is the perpetrator, burlesquing traditional comic strips like "Dagwood" for the most part.

HORSESHIT

Horseshit, subtitled "The Offensive Review," edited by Bob Dunker of Scum Publishing Company, Hermosa Beach, California, produced its first issue in 1965 at two dollars, and reprinted it up to at least a sixth edition, 8½" x 11", in clean-looking, white, heavy-stock covers. Sex, censorship, politics, and disgust were the main themes of the editor and his brother, who promised more numbers but couldn't predict when. Its attitudes typify the counter-culture humor of the period. An American eagle excretes missiles; on the cover, a ribboned soldier-hunter holds up a baby like a dead rabbit; the prose material focuses on sex themes and prostitutes.

HOT-CHA

Hot-Cha by F. S. C. Publications, New York, appears to be a late Roaring Twenties offering at fifteen cents, 6″ × 9″, featuring lots of flapper girls, Black jokes, and Noel Meadow's gag columns: "We understand that out in Hoboken the women have their cans ready when the garbageman calls." It lasted for at least three numbers, with some photo cuts that seem to be throwbacks to the teens. The only apparent date is 1933. Longer stories and flashy cartoons dominate.

HOT DOG

One of the jollier and sexier of the skeptical regional humorous commentators, Jack Dinsmore was editor of *Hot Dog* throughout its run in the 1920s. "The Regular Fellows Monthly" was a twenty-five-cent digest-size publication, 6″ × 9″ and thirty-four pages, in breezy slang. The Merit Publishing Company of Cleveland, later the Erie Publishing Company, was the publisher, first in rough brown covers and later in slick paper. Volume 1:1 was copyrighted for August 1922, with a later by-line, "a journal of humor and satire." Humor included limericks, short gags and one-liners, and some longer jokes of the comic tough guy type: "Ignatz's girl tells him she'd return his engagement ring—but she can't find the ticket"; "Hot Hanna Says: There is one nice thing about posing in the nude; there's no danger of your bloomers showing." Volume 3:12 was September 1924 and Volume B:10 was October 1928; by November 1933, Dinsmore was in Volume G:4 in New York City as Nationwide Publications in 5½″ × 7″ format, and had cheapened both his paper and his image with more nudie photos and cartoons and somewhat increased political content. The cover price was fifteen cents with a ten-cent over-sticker on the cover. Consolidated Press and Printing Company copyrighted Volume E:12 for December 1931; the volume lettering system began after a thirteen-month hiatus from October 1926 (Vol. 6:1) to November 1927 (Vol. A:1).

HOT ROD CARTOONS

Hot Rod Cartoons was copyrighted by Peterson Publishing Company of Los Angeles bimonthly from November 1964 (No. 1) through September 1974 (No. 60) and with a change in numbering format through January 1975 (Vol. 28:1). The March 1970 (No. 33) issue features brief cartoon articles and sequences on hot rod subjects, punctuated by humorously recaptioned old movie stills. In the early 1970s, the magazine (8″ × 11″, approximately 54 pages) was edited by Pappy Lemmons; its cartoon art clearly reflected the influence of *Mad.**

HOT SHOTS FROM THE FUNNY BOYS

Edited by Hugh Mustlaff (George Wade Snoddy) for Laird and Lee Publishing of Chicago, *Hot Shots* was Number 6 in the Happy Go Lucky Library and reprinted cartoon jokes from *Puck*,* *Judge*,* and *Life** and more vulgar sources in 1901. It probably should not be classed with the periodicals, but it does anthologize their humor.

HOT SOLDIER

A monthly from the J. L. Perkins Company of Chicago as an advertising humor newspaper, this journal is listed by DLC (holding two to four) as two volumes, illustrated, 20 cm, but is missing on the shelf and has not been seen. Its dates are given as Number 1 from 1901 through April 1904. Mott particularly notes the "Sandy Pike" stories of a city boy in Chicago, apparently a 1900s Midwestern version of the Yankee greenhorn in Boston and New York of the 1800–1850 period.

HULLABALOO

A fifteen-cent bimonthly offspring of *Ballyhoo*,* *Hullabaloo* was edited by Lester Grady—"edited evenings by the editors of *Ballyhoo*"—from December 1931, copyrighted as Volume 1:1, the only bimonthly issue, through issues appearing in April, May, June, and July 1932, copyrighted in each previous month, in the standard thirty-two-page, 8½" × 12" format. It was Dell's own spinoff to absorb some of *Ballyhoo*'s public and dampen the competition. Comic letters and entertainment-oriented humor dominate. Garish and energetic, it was heavily visual with full-page photos and comic captions: Gandhi and Jimmie Walker over "clothes make the man," and a profile of Greta Garbo's dream man with Jimmy Durante's nose. A Bran Flakes ad said, "Keep regular and bring back posterity," and French cartoons added some lingerie for spice. Some amount of marriage and sex humor and speakeasy material set the thirties' tone.

HUMBUG'S AMERICAN MUSEUM

Humbug's American Museum of 1851–1852, a 7" × 12" half-monthly containing four plates, was produced by the lithographic office of Nagel and Weingartner as "lithographic caricature." Barnum's humbuggery was the motif rather than the target; one plate showed the nation's capital as Barnum's "Happy Family" populated by congressmen-animals; another burlesques Mrs. Oakes-Smith's lectures on emancipation; and a map of the United States emphasizes California, Gotham, and Gomorrah. Theater life in New York and political life in Washington were both humbug shows. A special target as more prose appeared in later issues was *The Lantern** (*Diogenes, Hys Lantern*), an "ignis fatuus" with which *Humbug's American Museum* declined comparison. The quality of the engravings, signed AW, sets this apart from other journals except Johnston's annual folio titled *Scraps*** which had been a prominent satiric cartoon publication of the 1830s. Number 1, at one shilling, appeared in June 1851, and a second series was begun with Number 7 on 1 March 1852 and ended with Number 8 on 15 March; publication was irregular with only eight issues known, of which the most complete run is at Harvard.

HUMOR

Humor was a bimonthly at twenty-five cents offering a range of anecdotes, feature essays, fiction, and cartoons in an 8" × 11" magazine format. Volume 1:1 was April 1945, copyrighted by Alexander Segal, reissued as Volume 1:1 by Humag, Inc., for June 1946. Ilka Chase, Jimmy Durante, Stephen Leacock, Jefferson Machamer, and H. Allen Smith were contributors, with Alan Seigel listed as editor. *Humor* covered a range of contemporary topics with greater or less degrees of whimsy, humor, or lightness—or seriousness in a few of the essays. Volume 1:2 was dated August-September 1946, and Volume 1:3 for October-November 1946 was the last copyrighted.

HUMOR DIGEST

Humor Digest (7" × 9½", fifteen cents) offered one hundred pages of cartoons and comedy quarterly. Volume 1:1, the only issue identified, was copyrighted by Better Publications for Spring 1939 with a cutie cover and college humor throwbacks to the twenties. Longer prose humor was produced by Gurney Williams, Paul Gallico, Allan Eppes, and Dorothy Dow, and concentrated on the contemporary scene: sports, dating, and related materials.

HUSTLER HUMOR

Raunchy sexual humor (although raunchy political and social humor also appears) is the forte of *Hustler Humor*, a comic spinoff of Larry Flynt's *Hustler* sex magazine. Volume 1:1 was copyrighted in February 1978 by Hustler Magazines of Columbus, Ohio, as a monthly, but with only irregular numbers copyrighted. By Volume 3:5, published in September 1980, it became bimonthly. By 7:4, published in July 1984, it appears to be a bi-monthly, 8" × 11", of roughly 64 pages, priced at $2.95, a dollar above its price in 1980. Dwaine Tinsley is the present editor from Los Angeles; the magazine presently sells for $2.95, publishing eight times a year. Volume 9:8 is for January 1987.

I

THE IDLE MAN

The Idle Man of 1821 was a stiff and mostly unhumorous irregular periodical attributed to Richard Henry Dana, senior. It was published by Wiley and Halsted in New York in 5″ × 8¼″ size, with the number of pages varying radically according to the length of melodramatic fiction published in the six issues in 1821 and 1822 (through Volume 2:1, as numbered, but without dates). A genteel collection of Shandyian stories, essays, and poems was intended. It is a dubious inclusion in the humor category; DLC, MWA, CU, MBat, and several others list holdings.

INTERNATIONAL INSANITY

Phi Publishing Company, Phil Hirsch, publisher, and Bill Skurski, editor, listed Harvey Kurtzman as their inspiration under their masthead. This bimonthly, 8″ × 10¾″ in size, was copyrighted for July 1976 (Vol. 1:1). Superwoman gives way to "Singlewoman meets Mr. Wright," a parody of women's lib and an older comic heroine. "The Hughes Collection" features designer bras with propellers and rocket-booster G-strings. "Horny Hippie Housewives" is a burlesque of pornographic films, and "Excerpts from the Final Daze," in color, covers the fall of Richard Nixon. It continued through at least May 1977, although the last copyrighted is Volume 1:5 for March 1977. Data on this periodical are generally confusing as a Volume 1:2 has been seen for July 1976, although Volume 1:2 is copyrighted for September.

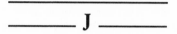

J

JACKPOT (1952)

Jackpot (Volume 2:1, December 1953) by Youthful Publications of St. Louis, Missouri, at twenty-five cents, 5″ × 7¼″, offered cartoons and gags, but maintained the format of the service humor cartoon and joke books of the 1940s, including a section on service jokes. A cheap-paper monthly joke magazine, it mixed cartoons and gags on a wide variety of 1950s themes, but without any social or political humor. *Zowie!*** (1953) was its sister publication.

JACKPOT (1958)

Jackpot, "The Cad's Home Companion," was an outright burlesque of men's magazines like *Rogue* and *Cavalier*. Olympic Publishing, Inc., of Somerville, New Jersey, published the January 1958 issue at fifty cents, in an 8¼″ × 11″, 52-page format. It presented a burlesque *Peyton Place* and articles on "Will Sports Cars Make Girls Obsolete," featuring exaggerated cheesecake, and a comparison of *Playboy* and *"Plowboy"* magazines. J. M. Stewart Gordon was editor.

JACKPOT (1966)

Jackpot, "The Best in Cartoons and Jokes," a bimonthly, was issued by Picture Magazines of New York at thirty-five cents per copy in 5½″ × 7¼″ format (Volume 3:6 for October 1968 and Volume 7:6 for October 1972). It was an interchangeable sister publication to *Zowie!*** which was also published in the 1966–1973 period. Gag cartoons were of the girlie and general variety.

JEEPS

"Army and Navy Fun" (No. 1, February 1942), published in digest-size by the Comic Corporation of America in New York, contained 66 pages at fifteen cents per copy. It was typical of the milder gals and gags service-oriented humor of its era, with short jokes and cartoons randomly arranged.

JEST (1932)

The *Jest* of the 1930s was a magazine of social satire beginning in April 1932 as a monthly in the same format as *Ballyhoo*,* fifteen cents, but with some variations in size from 7½″ × 10½″ to an inch larger on top and side. One burlesque lingerie ad in Volume 2:2 (March 1933) offered "Quickoff Stepins— The Handy Garment for the Ready Girl." The Rembrandt Art School touted "Study the Human Torso and Get Big Ideas!" Robert Young was editor for G. S. S. Publishing Company in New York. Unlike many of the other humor magazines copying *Ballyhoo*, *Jest* commented on national political figures both in prose and cartoon items and showed an awareness of social issues which justified its claim to deal in social satire. Some prose humor and cartoons reflecting the harsher style of *Americana** or reprinted from European sources give *Jest* a more serious humor than its counterparts.

JEST (1941)

Jest—The Zest of Life was a 1940s tabloid bimonthly from New York and has no relation to the 1930s *Jest*. Bathing beauties and chorines shared space with sports and joke photo sequences showing some humor and much leg. Volume 1:1 appeared in July 1941, at ten cents; the periodical ran at least through Volume 2:9 (January 1943), when it was last seen or copyrighted. It measured 10″ × 13″ and had thirty-two pages. When cartoons appeared among the dominant funny photo features, they dealt with sexual, crime, or big-city nightlife themes.

JEST (1950)

The third user of the *Jest* name was a digest bimonthly of Humorama, belonging to its stable of cheesecake-sleazecake publications. Since it claimed lineage to 1940, it probably represents the purchase of the previous *Jest*. One tag line beside a chorine in pasties and G-string says that in the ten years she's been on the legitimate stage, she hasn't fallen off the runway once. The periodical, 5½″ × 7¼″ in size, cost twenty-five cents per copy. It was dominated by one cutie joke per page, with some gags thrown in along with pin-ups. With significant irregularities in publication dates, *Jest: The Spice of Life* was copyrighted by Timely Features, Volume 1:10 (November 1950) to Volume 2:2 (November

1951), and as *Jest Magazine* through Volume 4:7 (May 1953) and Volume 4:3 (July 1953) as misnumbered; Volume 6:19 was March 1956. It was advertised as late as June 1966.

JESTER (1845)

Boston's 1845 *Jester* is known only by the Volume 1:1 (14 June 1845) number at MB. H. L. Williams published it at six and a quarter cents per weekly issue in 9" × 11¼" format. It promised no quarter to hypocrisy and led off with a manifesto and a burlesque of Saratoga parvenues. "The Turkey" burlesqued "Poe-try." Various other illustrated witticisms appeared with an eye toward literary humbugs; a full-page political cartoon showing America squaring off for a prize fight with John Bull was also featured. Cited in Mott 1:425, 807.

JESTER (1890)

Philadelphia's 1890 *Jester* advertised itself as a better buy than *Puck*,* *Life*,* *Judge*,* and *Texas Siftings** when it went from sixteen to twenty-four pages for five cents, in an 8½" × 11" format. A weekly, it boasted a front-page cartoon, some clipped humor from other sources, ads, and two or three longer pieces, along with paragraphs, poetry, and occasional short stories. One of the best cartoons suggests for a Chicago World's Fair fountain the image of a big-footed goddess holding sausages, mounted side-saddle on a pig spewing water. Verse was doggerel: "Only a little dandy, / Only a city dude, / Cigarettes and candy / Answer him for food." A potpourri of illustrations reflected the socialite world of the 1890s, in keeping with the prose humor. DLC has a run beginning with Volume 1:18 (1 March 1890) to Volume 1:26 (26 April 1890). Mott gives the dates 1889 through 1891, singling out the illustrations of "Matt" Morgan, Edwin H. Blashfield, and Charles H. Johnson.

JOKER

Joker originated as a digest-size cartoon and gag magazine on general American life themes, publishing three times a year. Volume 1:1 was October 1944 by Comedy Publications of Chicago, although edited from New York; Volume 2:1 was Summer 1946, at twenty-five cents, copyrighted by Skyline Publications, New York, through Volume 2:12 for October 1947 and Volume 1:13 for March 1948. As time passed the cuties grew lusher in the Bill Wenzel, Jefferson Machamer, Pico style. By Volume 6:48 (February 1956), Humorama had modernized the title into the cheesecake formula of its other publications, boasting that it originated in 1938. It was a 1950s cheap-paper, digest-size gags and gals magazine; cartoons, gags, and gagvertisements filled up its pages with more or less sex-oriented material. Timely Features copyrighted Volume 1:14 (September 1948) through Volume 4:29 (June 1953). Humorama continued to publish *Joker*, with Ernest N. Devver listed as editor through the 1960s, the last seen being Volume 18:12 for May 1969. It called itself the "only magazine with JEsT propulsion" but was really propelled by photo pin-ups of half-dressed cuties. It may have lasted into the early 1970s.

JOLLY DOLLS

Jolly Dolls was a twenty-five cent, mostly girlie cartoon and gags magazine published by Palace Promotions in New York. It did not bother to give itself a masthead or publication information, but it is in the 1940s digest style and shape with gags and pin-ups. It may be related to *Gal Snaps*,** a similar publication, and may be a "one-shot" publication.

JOY STORIES

Joy Stories (Vol. 1:4, March 1930) by Irwin Publishing Company, twenty-five cents, featured titillating sex stories with a twist, with one or two departments of clever lines and brief jokes thrown in. It reflects the sexy cleverness of the flapper era, but may not be eligible for inclusion as a humor magazine. Irwin also published, but copyrighted, *Paree Stories* and *Peppy Humor* in the Spring of 1930.

JUDGE (1963)

The 1960s *Judge* (Vol. 1:1, October 1963) considered itself a successor to the old *Judge**; it had an 8¼″ × 11¼″ thirty-four-page format and sold at twenty-five cents a copy. It set itself up as an intellectualized magazine of satire and humor. Mabel Search was editorial director, and Victor Lasky, Ted Shane, Homer McCoy, and Arthur Lippman contributed to the first issue. The humor seems general and mild, however, with no particular focus beyond an overview of contemporary middle-class American life.

JUDGE'S LIBRARY

Judge's Library was the successor to *Judge's Serials*** and predecessor of the *Magazine of Fun*** and *Film Fun*.* It ran from January 1880 to August 1912, Numbers 11–280, monthly. Copies seen for 1902 show country and crackerbarrel cartoons and jokes. November 1902 was number 164, featuring Tambo and Bones and a minstrel on the cover. The 8″ × 11¼″ monthly sold for ten cents or one dollar a year. Its humor was of cheap hotels and lower-middle-class concerns. Whisky was advertised inside the front cover, and an opium seller offered free samples in one of the smaller ads at the back. Jews had big noses; Irishmen had pugs and carried hods; and Negroes sported liver lips in uglier cartoons. See *Film Fun* for more information. DLC and NN list holdings.

JUDGE'S QUARTERLY

Judge's Quarterly ran from July 1890 through 1913 and cost twenty-five cents an issue; circulation was 60,000 in 1899, according to Mott, 3: 554. Number 1 is at N.

JUDGE'S SERIALS

Judge's Serials kicked off with Number 1 of the quarterly story magazine for August 1887. It measured 7½″ × 10½″, cost ten cents an issue or thirty-five cents a year, and totaled 52 pages, including the covers and with many pages split for advertisements. Punctuated with a few comic illustrations, it offered longer prose burlesques and comic stories from *Judge*,* its parent magazine issued by the Judge Publishing Company, New York. The quarterly became the monthly *Judge's Library* after Number 10 for January 1890, which in turn eventually led to the *Magazine of Fun*** and *Film Fun*.* The entire first issue was composed of a burlesque of Victor Hugo's *L'Homme qui Rit*, a long-standing target of burlesque writers, including Artemus Ward and Mark Twain, titled "The Man Who Talks; or The Drummer on the Rail." Comedy was made out of the adventures of emissaries of trade named Lang, Cusby, and Brown who "have more cheek than a monkey with the mumps." They meet local society in the Midwest, businessmen, and even Psyche Hogpen, "a leader in the great cause of Women's Rights," among other popular targets of the conservative humorists of the late 1880s. CtY has the first number.

JUST FUN THAT'S ALL

Just Fun (Vol. 1:1, June 1903 through at least Vol. 3:16, September 1904), was one of W. J. Arkell's many comic publishing ventures around the turn of the century aimed at the suburban and village audience. Subscription was one dollar a year, and the format was 8″ × 11″ random two-column cartoons and joke materials with various larger illustrations. It was part of the group, including *The Foolish Book*,** *Just Fun*, and *Fun with Cy Scudder*,** which tried to rival *Judge*,* *Just Fun* featured Grant E. Hamilton, an illustrator from *Judge*, Eugene Zimmerman—"Zim"—and W. J. Merritt, with Hamilton as publisher for Arkell in New York. Each month, a different grinning cover face offered boy and girl readers prizes for subscriptions, with a first printing claimed at 50,000. The humorous side of life had some bite, as when a sarcastic maid tells her mistress that if she breaks a $2,000 vase, the price can be deducted from her wages. Despite the claim not to reprint humor, some of the jokes had a familiar air, as "In two she broke her heart / and Jim and Bob each got a part," or "Oh, my goodness, if your rat powder didn't kill your rats, it must be the party that ordered the baking powder who got your order instead." Hayseed jokes and romantic jokes abound, and *Just Fun* assumed that any girl at a piano wanted to be kissed and all women overdrew bank accounts. The last cover, of Teddy Roosevelt grinning over the phrase, ''Dee-Light-Ed,'' was the most stunningly garish of all *Just Fun*'s illustrations.

K

KALEIDOSCOPE (1818)

The Boston Kaleidoscope and Literary Rambler was N. H. Wright's successor to *The Idiot** on 2 January 1819. It offered romantic tales, humorous matter, and even religious verse. Hews and Goss were the publishers, and the four-page, three-column sheet sold for two dollars annually. The *Kaleidoscope* appeared as Volume 1:1 on 5 December 1818 and joined with *The Idiot* with the 9 January 1819 issue; it terminated with Volume 1:50 on 13 November 1819. *Kaleidoscope* offered mock-definitions like "caucus" as coming from the Latin "corkus": we are stoppered. Original comic stories and literary dialect humor appeared, and some attention was paid to poverty and wealth and greed and generosity. Some regional jokes also appeared, such as the 1878 Vermont inn-keeper who marvelled that a traveler from Boston had come 150 miles, "Dear me, how can you live so far off." Later in its life, Goss alone was the publisher, and he announced *The Ladie's Port Folio* for January 1820 with humor included in its literary department as a successor to the *Kaleidoscope*. Readex Microprint has reprinted it with the *Boston Mirror*.

KALIEDOSCOPE (1869)

The one *Kaliedoscope* issue dated July 1869, headed "intermittent," promised a journal of "many reflecting surfaces," and a full harvest of "Shoddy," the 1860s term for a cheapened life style. Wealthy Fifth Avenue butterflies were to be ridiculed for abandoning the good old hard work ethic, and the content is socially conservative. "Verdict $100,000" assaulted women's rights and breach of contract law suits, using octets in a comic verse travesty of "Sucker" marriages. Travel letters, fillers, and scattered illustrations completed the offerings. It listed the "Brothers Triplex—Roderic, Roger, and Robert" as editors of the 6″ × 10″ magazine, offering gooseberries as the only subscription premium. It is interesting chiefly because it originated in the publishing firm of G. W. Carleton, prominent humor publisher of the period. Copies are located at CtY, MB, NN, and NHi.

KEEP 'EM LAUGHING

Keep 'em Laughing from Comic Corporation of America, Number 3 (January 1943), digest-size at 5½″ × 7¼″, fifteen cents a copy, carried the same general sort of cartoons and gags as *Jeeps*,** from the same publisher. Copyright information indicates Number 1 as July-August 1942 and Number 8 as March 1944; other sources suggest a Number 10 for Spring 1945. Comic Corporation also published *Khaki Wacky*.**

THE KEYHOLE

From Youthful Magazines of St. Louis, like *Jackpot*,** *The Keyhole* was a bimonthly, digest-size, that sold at twenty-five cents. Volume 1:9 was issued in January-February 1954. Mostly mild sex-life and general cartoons were featured, with some gags thrown in.

KHAKI HUMOR

Khaki Humor, Number 1 (November 1941), a bimonthly from the Comic Corporation of America, New York, cost fifteen cents per issue and was in a 8½″ × 11½″, 52-page format. It was a digest of the "cream" of humor from the various formal and informal papers, mimeos, and slicks of the mushrooming army. Jokes were service-based, and prose predominated over cartoons. At least a Number 2 was published; both were copyrighted, with the second for January 1942.

KHAKI WACKY

This "Army and Navy Fun" magazine published Number 1 of *Khaki Wacky* in December 1941, by Comic Corporation of America; the digest-size, 5¼″ × 7½″, fifteen-cent monthly had 68 pages. It was oriented toward slightly sexier cartoons and gags than *Khaki Humor*,** from which it reprinted a few cartoons of the girls and gags sort. From February through August 1942, the last copyrighted, it ran as a monthly; it was from the same publisher as *Keep 'em Laughing*.**

KIT 'O WIT

Kit 'O Wit appears to be an annual collection of jokes and cartoon gags published by National Research Bureau of Chicago at twenty-five cents in a 5½" × 8½" format. The 1942 edition has been seen. Humor is conventional 1940s general humor.

THE KNAPSACK

The 1865 *Knapsack*, intended to support the Philadelphia Soldiers' and Sailors' Home through a little comedy, was a souvenir from the Philadelphia Fair of 1865, with eleven daily eight-page numbers published from 24 October through 4 November 1865 at ten cents per copy. Riter Fitzgerald was the editor, and the fare consisted of burlesque melodrama, travel pieces, and various material, along with two pages of paid advertisements. Although its light amusement was meant to carry beyond the Fair, it does not seem to have traveled well. Library holdings include CSmH, DLC, MB, MWA, N, NB, NN, OClWHi, PP, PHi, and MnU.

KOOKOO

Kookoo was another of the 1930s followers of *Ballyhoo*,* (thirty-six pages, fifteen cents, 8" × 10¾") with the same garish presentation. The cover of Volume 1:2 (April 1932) shows one eunuch saying to another, "Aw Gwan! Tell us about your operation!" in the center of an elaborate bullseye design, an obvious variant for *Ballyhoo*'s bright patchwork. Darnation Milk, Canada Rye, and Veneral Electric were among the travesties of advertisements, tilted toward the sexy. One page shows Gandhi brooding over an invitation to a strip poker party. At the bottom of pages, running thumbnail biographies chronicled the fate of high rollers in the Depression. Burdon Publishing Company, New York, published this under the "supervision" of Joe Burten and the "advice" of Harry Donenfeld; the editor was actually listed as "Herman Pfss." Its manifesto was "From the cradle to the grave life is just a lot of kookoo." The only copyrights were for Volume 1:1 and Volume 1:2, both taken out in February 1932. See also *Burten's Follies*.**

L

LAFF and LAFF ANNUAL

Laff was Adrian Lopez's folio-size humorous picture magazine issued by Volitant Publishing Company, a sexy humor pictorial. At 10½″ × 13½″, *Laff*'s thirty-four-page monthly numbers showed girls' legs in every photo: "City Girls Visit a Farm" in bathing suits, "Society Lifts Its Skirts," and "Strip Tease Girl" are three typical features from Volume 1:11 (December 1940), at ten cents. Each combined a mildly humorous caption with a titillating photo. Among the light showgirl articles were pages of jokes and cartoons oriented toward sexual themes. By 1945, Tony Field was editor and Adrian Lopez was listed as "publisher on leave with the armed services," but the legs 'n laffs format remained the same. Unlike the other forties tabloids, *Laff* survived the war and the late forties. Volume 12:10 (January 1952) was priced at a quarter and adhered to the same format, except that more skin and fewer "laffs" characterized the fifties' material. Volumes 13 and 14 for 1952 and 1953 dropped the size down to 8″ × 10½″ and emphasized the girlie content even more; the ending date for the magazine is uncertain. *Laff Annual* appeared at least from 1941 through 1951, with more emphasis on girlie photos and less on cartoons, although some of the photo stories were intended to be "light" humor.

LAFF JUNIOR

The Volitant Publishing Company's pocket-size edition of *Laff*—the *Junior*—was a 5¼″ × 7¼″, twenty-five-cent bimonthly digest (Vol. 1:3, January-February 1954). A typical chorine cartoon is captioned, "Imagine Flopsie marrying that rich Spaniard! She never could stand spicy food!" Other cartoons depended on similar cultural stereotypes.

LAFF TIME

Crestwood Publishing Company's *Laff Time* was a cartoon and nudie magazine, a digest-sized bimonthly at thirty cents, edited by Paul Epstein. *Army Fun,*** *Army Laughs,*** and *Broadway Laughs*** were similar publications. Volume 11:5 (July 1972) at thirty-five cents features sex-oriented jokes and provocative pin-ups; this was its twentieth year.

THE LAMB

Wall Street found its humor magazine in *The Lamb*, which lasted from Volume 1:1 (13 May 1916) through at least Number 26 (28 April 1917), fortnightly, at ten cents an issue or $2.50 per year. The first three numbers were 8″ × 9″ and the following were 8½″ × 10½″, roughly twenty-one pages per issue. A. Newton Plummer was the editor and publisher. He offered to give a free copy to anyone who couldn't afford a dime, and to publish their name in his next issue as well. His general idea was to circulate the humor of "The Street" in magazine form. Norman Anthony was art editor, as a walk-in hire, and illustrations were well drawn; Wall Street advertisers were prominent. Humor was centered around money matters with a Wall Street orientation, and one of Plummer's own ads called *The Lamb* "The Wall Street Punch." Thomas Masson, Arthur Guiterman, and Homer Croy contributed, and various bright witty bits of prose were featured, along with an "All Joking Aside" column on corporate news and other informative matter. The "Lamb Chops" column covered social and travel news related to brokers. Anthony later gave as the reason for its demise that the broker-editor had lost the money made from a previous killing in the market. DLC has a bound volume. Volume 2:10 for 15 September 1917 is the last copyrighted.

THE LANCET

In a preface dated "Newark, May 3, 1803" in the June 1803 issue of *The Lancet*, Dr. Sangrado, jun. [pseud.], explains that the paper he edits will battle "political fever" and "disease" in New Jersey. Having a run of only one issue (No. 1) of four pages, the paper consists of satirical material attacking the Newark government and politicians.

An inventive sketch entitled "Anecdotes of a Great Man" portrays the character of "Josey" in childhood, adolescence, and manhood, at which time, with years of bungling behind him, he becomes one of the "demagogues of New Jersey." As a youngster, Josey gets tricked into filling his house with oysters, much to the dismay of his visitors. When courting a young lady, he lays his hand on her soft, "snowy bossom." She smiles and says that she will put it on a "softer place." The outcome illustrates *The Lancet*'s views toward the mentality of Newark politicians: "Fir'd with nameless, blissful expectation, he immediately delivered his yielding hand to her implicit direction—when, O cruel!—she laid it on his own head!" It has been reprinted by University Microfilms.

Michael Pettengell

LAUGH DIGEST

Laugh Digest was a thirty-five cent bimonthly publication from Humorama, Inc., New York, 5½" × 7½" in size. Number 74 was the June 1966 issue, featuring racy humor and "bunnyfunnies," as edited by "Huckleberry Flynn, Editor." Cuties and sexually oriented humor filled up its 102 pages, including bare-breasted sleazecake photos and scantily-clad women in cartoons punctuated by some gags and a few longer gag items. The only one signed is a two-page essay by Joseph S. Russotto on falling asleep in lectures. Typical cartoons are by Wenzel and Ward, and feature gals undressing for various reasons, or pajama-clad lovers being caught in closets by angry husbands. Issues from October 1968 through April 1969 have also been reported.

LAUGH FACTORY

Laugh Factory offered Volume 2:3 (April 1985) in 8½" × 11" format. It is a yuppie burlesque of show business and financial advice slick magazines on the order of *People* and *Money*, with articles such as "Tax Advice from the Celebrities," "Trivia Pursoot," and "Celebrity Tombstones." The 84-page periodical sells for $1.95 per issue; it is edited by Jamie Masada and published bimonthly by *Laugh Factory*, Inc., Los Angeles.

LAUGH PARADE

Over 200 cartoons and fun gags, oriented mostly toward wedding night and desert island sexual humor, were featured in each thirty-five-cent, 8" × 11" bimonthly issue of *Laugh Parade*, from Magazine Management Company, edited by Robert Mende. Volume 1:1 (July 1961) was copyrighted by Non-Pariel Publishing Company, bimonthly; Volume 15:5 (October 1975) was the last copyrighted. Volume 10:2 (March 1970) featured "sexy slip-ups," "fast show biz," and "on the make—wild bachelors on the loose," but the jokes were conventional stereotypes from earlier eras, and some cartoon gags can be found in alternate publications from the same company.

LAUGHING ALL THE WAY

Laughing All the Way was a typical digest-sized girlie humor magazine featuring cartoons of sexy cuties. For thirty-five cents it offered "A Tickling Variety of Comedy Cartoons and other fun-filled pages of racy humor," including a bathing-suit cutie with a tag hanging off her suit reading "Special One Piece $3.50"; she says to her friend "I'm so pleased with my new bathing suit—it's certainly attracting attention," as various guys look and leer rather innocently. An "Information" giant-breasted cutie says to her store manager, "So far it's been easy . . . all men ask the same question." Timely Features published it bimonthly in the 1960s.

LAUGHTER

Laughter, "a magazine of good humor," offered its 1920s readers a thousand chuckles in story and picture, derived from longer prose stories by Ellis Parker Butler, James House, Jr., and other writers of amusing stories with general themes. A variety of gags, cartoons, and jokes appeared as filler between the stories. The Guild Publishing Company, of Philadelphia, originated *Laughter* at twenty-five cents in a 7" × 10", one-hundred-page size; Volume 1:1 appeared in October 1925, and Volume 4:3 for June 1927 is the last seen; Volume 5:3 for December-January 1928 is the last copyrighted and the only bimonthly issue. Subjects ranged from burlesques of Shakespeare to dialect gold miner's stories. DLC has four issues of this pulp humor magazine in its pulp magazine collection; size may vary.

LAUGHTER IS OUR ALLY

Progressive Publishing Company, New York, brought out this one-time publication in magazine format to present prose and cartoon humor, mostly from Europe in 1942, attacking the Axis partners and supporting the allies—"The jokes are on our enemies." The cartoon on the last page showed a sinking face of Hirohito and an American bomber titled "shadow over the land of the rising sun." It was edited by Emery Kelen, cost fifteen cents, and used an 8" × 11", 52-page format.

LET'S LAUGH

More than 1,000 jokes, boasts the cover of *Let's Laugh* by Ace Magazines, New York, A. A. Wyn, president. The jokes are in three columns covering, with the addition of some cartoons, the 52-page, 8½" × 11½" magazine in column after column of puns and wordplay. Each page had a theme, such as the "Nudist Nonsense" page: "When your girl insists on joining a nudist cult, the only thing you can do is to bare with her." Volume 1:15, Summer issue, quarterly, at fifteen cents carries no year date, but it appears to belong to the late thirties (1938?).

LIBERTY LAUGHS

Number 1 (December 1942), by Dell Publishing Company, New York, was a 54-page, 8½″ × 11½″, ten-cent collection of wartime gags and cartoons compiled by a group of Chicago sorority women to aid the Army Emergency Relief. Its premise was that humor could help the war effort with a smile.

LIP PARADE

One issue of this cheap-paper wartime digest, 5½″ × 7½″, at twenty-five cents has been seen, published by Green Publishing Company of New York. Most of the cartoons were reprinted from King Features Syndicate, 1944. One fishing cutie returns to her partner with a farmboy, "Hey, Margie! Look what I caught about three blocks upstream!" in a typically derivative cartoon, mostly printed one to a page with occasional bits of prose gags.

LITERARY MAGAZINE

Editor Isaac McLellan, Jr., of Boston proposed to issue a periodical entitled the *Literary Magazine* on the first day of each month beginning 1 January 1835. To be sold for three dollars per year, this forty-eight page publication was to consist "entirely of original articles from the pens of individuals of high literary reputation." In the prospectus to the first number of Volume 1, the editor promises to offer "articles of every description" including satires, essays, poetry, sketches, tales, legends, translations, and editorials, not to mention engravings and pieces of music. Unfortunately, the first number of the *Literary Magazine*, as published by E. R. Broaders, was also the last. This single issue is available from University Microfilms prepared from the copy held by MWA; MBat also holds a copy.

Barbara McMillin

LITTLE JOKER

The *Little Joker* was a Civil War children's magazine published in New York and edited by "Cousin Lizzie" under the watchful eye of "Uncle" Robert Merry of *Merryman's Monthly*. A three-column, 9″ × 12″ monthly whose price drifted upward from fifteen to twenty to twenty-five cents a year due to paper costs, *Little Joker* offered a page or two of comic anecdotes mixed with general material to fill out each four-page issue. Although claiming to be apolitical, it offered one cartoon at least that identified a vote for McClellan with cheap liquor. Among the rebuses and brief moral stories by Uncle Robert Merry, J. D. C., and "Clara Augusta," other items showed antagonism toward Northern Copperheads. Circulation was approximately 1,500 according to a printer's ad. Two volumes were printed beginning in January 1863; MWA has a run of Volume 2. It is an uncertain inclusion as a humor magazine.

LONE STAR

Lone Star, $1.95 an issue, is currently being published bimonthly under the editorship-ownership of Lauren Barnett Scharf of San Antonio, Texas. Volume 1:6 was November/December 1983. It measured 5½" × 8½" in thirty-four pages. Volume 2:1 for Spring 1984 gives its price as $3.50 for a thirty-two-page issue. Its humor is a light counter-culture commentary on the national scene in typewriter/photo offset form.

THE LORGNETTE

The Lorgnette of 1850 was a weekly publication from an anonymous source who viewed the world through opera glasses and was pictured on each cover as a dapper, sideburned gentleman standing on the globe observing continents labeled fashion and politics. The portrait, in fact, was a good rendering of the author Donald G. Mitchell, better known for *Reveries of a Bachelor* by "Ik. Marvel," appearing in the same year. *The Lorgnette* sometimes escapes mention in Mitchell's biographies because he only acknowledged his authorship with the publication of the fourth edition. It also escapes note as a periodical because it has been considered fiction, and is so listed in Lyle Wright's *American Fiction 1774–1850* (San Marino, Calif.: Huntington Library, 1969, p. 247).

Light first glinted through *The Lorgnette* on 20 January 1850, when it promised weekly numbers at a shilling, published by Henry Kernot of New York City. The prospectus described a journal of twenty to thirty pages in yellow covers, "working for the entertainment of all spinsters who wanted husbands, all belles who admire their own charms . . . all critics confident of their own taste, and all sensible men who are content to be honest." "Timon," the author, corresponded to his friend Fritz about the different social stages and fashionable gradations of the town, with each number representing a gossipy letter. He claimed to puff no books and no tarts, but innocently suggested that he would be glad to have the tarts delivered to the office. A number of society and literary figures in the upper crust of New York were mentioned, although any satire is more by implication than by direct attack. Tophanes, a character intended to be an intruder into the higher caste, reports with a naive enthusiasm that carries some of the humor. Notices of the critics, which were freely reprinted from Number 9 on, varied between interest in the concealed author and a sense that the well-bred satire was vapid.

The first series was completed with Number 12 on 24 April, when Mitchell told critics who found the satire purposeless that he intended to fire a yellow salvo among the poets and poetasters of the city. The second series resumed as a biweekly with the 10 May number, lasting until 9 October, accounting for the total run for the year of twenty-four issues. Stringer and Townsend of New York published the second series, which is most commonly found as a bound volume. The first series was originally bound as a series of pamphlets. *The Lorgnette* as a book achieved at least a fourth edition by 1851. Copies are held at MWA, DLC, CtY, MH, and several other libraries. It is available on microfilm in the Research Publications series, although it is not listed as a periodical. Volume 1:1–24 is normally dated 20 January 1850 through 9 October 1850; the last twelve biweekly issues, however, are described by the author as the new or second series.

LU LU

Lu Lu (6¾″ × 10″, twenty-five cents, 72 pages) was a late 1930s girlie humor magazine "For Men Only" featuring racy cartoons dealing with dating, sex, and related themes. Published quarterly by Sun Publications, Chicago, it was "directed" by A. J. Gontier, Jr., and seems to have published around the period December 1937 through December 1939, extending both earlier and later. It became a monthly after five issues and was published by the same people who produced *10 Story Book* and *Girl Parade*. R. C. Dell did many of the more notable illustrations. A Canadian publication took the name in 1945.

MACK'S POCKET CARTOONS AND JOKES MAGAZINE

The monthly *Mack's* was a digest of 1930s gags and crudely drawn and lettered cartoons in a 5″ × 7½″ format. It was sold for fifteen cents by the Pocket Magazine Company of New York. Volume 1:5 was February 1931. Typical jokes include, ''Nobody in this chicken coop but us chickens, Boss,'' and a cartoon jelly-bean suitor who tells his girl that she is a shadow of her former self: ''You used to undress with the shades up.'' There were a number of advertising pages and a round table for reader exchanges; jokes were solicited and a general distribution was the target. The only copyrighted issue was Volume 1:1 for December 1930 by Gilbert Patten Corporation.

MADHOUSE

Madhouse, published in standard 8″ × 11″ format at twenty-five cents, was a 1945 attempt at a slap-happy cartoon and gag magazine directed at adults but featuring general cartoons and humor. One unnumbered issue from 1945 by the Milrose Publishing Company, New York, has been seen; Jesse Merlan was editor. The jokes were dismal: one cartoon has a publisher looking at a fish typing ''Sea Stories'' and commenting, ''We like an author who knows his material.'' Qwhacky Questions and Reasonless Replies and Daffy Dottie's Daffy-Ni-Tions were departments: ''How can I stop my boyfriend from buying me presents?—Marry him. That'll stop it.''

THE MAGAZINE OF FUN (1912)

Judge's Library** and *Sis Hopkin's Own Book*** combined to make Leslie-Judge's monthly *Magazine of Fun*, with Homer Croy as editor, ten cents per issue, 8½″ × 11″. E. P. Butler and Carolyn Wells were featured writers. Humorous stories and cartoons seem to have been directed at a youthful audience; it offered the humor of society, social life, middle-class city, and rural American life "with jests, verses, and a wealth of timely illustrations." *Judge's Library* had been the top listing of this journal until the August 1912 issue, but *Magazine of Fun* retained top billing through Number 315 (June 1915), following which time *Film Fun** emerged. DLC holds copies.

THE MAGAZINE OF FUN (1921)

The Magazine of Fun (Vol. 1:5, December 1921) was a Chicago-based digest of 68 pages which boosted regular fellows, depicted Hell as a place where booze was served to the regular guys while the reformers agonized, and argued that water was a dangerous agent capable of corroding metal and much more damaging than booze to the tender stomach lining. Girls love hugs and, it is hinted, even more, as the sexual humor remains coy. At twenty-five cents for a monthly issue, 5¼″ × 7½″, 66 pages, it is one of the better of the regional humor digests, composed solely of prose pieces, doggerel poetry and limericks, and two-line jokes and gags in a relaxed Roaring Twenties spirit. Its last pages carried its editor's endorsement of *College Humor*,** 1920–1921, the hardcover edition relating to the magazine from Collegiate World Publishing Company. Volume 3:2 for October 1922 was the only issue copyrighted, and Volume 3:5 for April 1923 is the last seen, by Magazine of Fun Publications, Chicago.

THE MANUSCRIPT

Dedicated to "the liberal American, disposed to patronize the efforts of native literature," *The Manuscript* originated in New York in 1827. Publication ceased in 1828, two volumes of six numbers each having been issued. Oddly enough, the first volume bore the label "Second Edition." The first number contained an essay in which the editors proposed "to provide, in short, a series of essays to amuse an idle hour, and promote the best interests of literature and morality." Besides such humor stories, *The Manuscript* contained biographies, literary criticism, historical accounts, and even love stories. Both volumes, published by G. and C. Carvill and Elam Bliss, are available on University Microfilm prepared from the copies held by DLC. Copies are also available at ICN, NjR, MBat and ten other libraries.

The first issue of Volume 1 offered an amusing anecdote about a sagacious dog able to locate any item lost or misplaced by its master. Wise Romeo proves himself by retrieving a marked silver dollar fallen into the hands of a wily pedlar.

The wisdom of the animal contrasts sharply with the foolishness of man exemplified in "The Money Dreamer" (Vol. 1, pp. 85–96). In this story the central character is an old German whose manner of storytelling inspires more laughter than the matter of his tales. Convinced by a vagrant that treasure lies buried in his pasture, old Boniface digs for riches while the conniving wanderer steals his horse. Another piece that satirizes the foolishness of humankind has the form of a travel sketch and is entitled "Trenton Falls" (Vol. 1, pp. 75–84). As is characteristic of Twain, the author of this piece satirizes tourists who expect to find greater beauty in Europe than in America. The theme of people's folly continues in Volume 2, with the first issue offering a fabliaux similar to those of Chaucer. "The Reward of Avarice" is the tale of a greedy *senex amans* whose money is stolen by his jealous wife. Apparently, to keep their promise to amuse, the editors and writers of *The Manuscript* chose the one topic most likely to generate laughter—human shortcomings.

Barbara McMillin

MERRY-GO-ROUND

Not to be confused with the British children's magazine of the same period, the New York *Merry-Go-Round*, published by Cartoon Reviews, Inc., was an 8½″ × 11″, fifteen-cent monthly which closely followed the themes of *Ballyhoo*,* *Bunk*,** *Hooey*,** and the other magazines of its genre. It was primarily cartoons, with occasional college-humor prose pieces inserted, including credits. Volume 1:1 was dated June 1932. The first inside back cover featured a monument to Hitler fenced off with signs reading "Juden Ferbotten" and showing excited Huns watching the third empire ground into sausage meat through a cannon mouth. Most of the dominant cartoons—exaggerated in a sort of distorted close-up which makes them distinctive from other magazines of the genre—were oriented toward society, infidelity, and allied light sexual and general themes. Harry Gronich copyrighted Volume 1:1, 2 only and published *Modern Psychologist* as well.

MERRYMAN'S MONTHLY

Mr. Merryman's Monthly, as it was sometimes called, was one of the longer running and more densely packed humor magazines of the Civil War and post-Civil War period. The first issue seen is Volume 2:1, dated January 1864, thirty-two pages, ten cents, 7″ × 10½″ in two-column format. As published by J. C. Haney and Company, *Merryman's Monthly* described itself as a family magazine of amusement and recreation. Advertisements in *Frank Leslie's Budget of Fun** in October 1863 described a magazine that featured 60 or more comical and satiric pictures illustrating the social foibles of the day, accompanying thirty-two pages of amusing literature: "It is the perfect melange of Wit and Humor," a pleasant companion for railroad, steamboat, or summer stroll. Its *Punch*-like front page, and distribution by the American News Company, assured its recognition as a comic paper and its easy accessibility. Lasting for thirteen years, it finally merged with *Nick Nax** and *Yankee Notions** from 1876 through 1879 to make the *Comic World*.

Merryman's Monthly featured a fair amount of regional humor in the form of anecdotes and longer humorous stories. Its two-column pages were broken up visually by cartoons and by various illustrative cuts in the columns. Some bolder double-page cartoons took up Civil War issues during that period, but without the stridency of more committed journals. Humor was often oriented toward literary topics, such as burlesques on Blackbeard or "The Ballad of Lord Bateman." One full-page cartoon was devoted to the war between Fogeyism and Bohemia—the dashing world of the *Tribune* reporters, Artemus Ward, and Walt Whitman, but a two-page sentimental cartoon on St. Valentine's Day in an army camp suggests the popular direction of much of the content. Some of Frank Bellew's cartoons were reminiscent of *Vanity Fair*,* but with less social and political stress. A typical cartoon indicating the generalized political humor is one of Brother Jonathan debating whether or not to woo the old maid Britannia while "C. S." says, "Please Misses trust me a penny till I sell my niggers & my cotton." "Travelling on the Mississippi River" is a longer moralized story in which a governor routes three gamblers who are cheating a New York greenhorn and drops the three on a sandbar, admonishing the greenhorn to give his money to an orphan asylum. Featuring cheaters cheated for good purposes rather than ill, the piece is of the more refined type of frontier literary humor.

By 1866, the paper was comfortable in its format as the only humorous paper in the country "intended expressly for family reading." Rebuses and prize puzzles were regular features, and the exposure of the "Sphinx Mystery" caused the June issue to be reprinted. The price was raised to fifteen cents a copy. Bellew provided a comic history of America, and the run of frontier and local stories continued, frequently including rough-house elements. Artemus Ward's letters from London were reprinted, a baseball number was offered in November 1866, and some snappy letters and responses completed the fun. As a reprinter of regional stories and humor along with *Yankee Notions*, *Merryman's Monthly* deserves more serious study in relation to the post-Civil War era, even though much of its humor in the 1860s seems a throwback to before the war. INE holds Volumes 6–10, and N has part of 1873; MWA–2; NN 2–3–4; Vassar 6–7.

THE MICROSCOPE (Albany)

Not to be confused with *The Microscope* of New Haven (1820) or *The Microscope and General Advertiser* of Louisville (1824–1825), the periodical called simply *The Microscope* originated in Albany, New York. Introduced in 1821 as the *Microscope and Independent Examiner*, this miscellany ran through seven volumes, the last being issued on 29 December 1827. After 1823 the title was shortened. A weekly publication issued every Saturday, *The Microscope* offered its readers satirical essays, anecdotes, poetry, snatches of Albany gossip, letters to the editor, legends, marriage announcements, book reviews, advice columns, and even illustrated advertisements. A subscriber could enjoy twelve numbers of *The Microscope* for fifty cents, an entire volume for two dollars, or a year's worth for three dollars. Portions of Volumes 2 through 5 are available through University Microfilms. Copies of *The Microscope* are held by NHi and MWA.

Although not intended as humor, the bits of "gossip" dotting the pages of this magazine provide the modern reader with as much enjoyment as the actual comic pieces. Among the best of the comic pieces is the account of a drunken pidgeon hunter whose breath catches fire, found in the 11 October 1823 number. The explosion blows the foolish hunter's head off, killing a snapping turtle on impact. In the issue dated 13 March 1824, one will find a witty set of rules for good housekeepers and gentle folk to follow, while the September 18 issue offers a sample of poet "Jeremiah See-All's" satiric verse. Contrasted with the New Haven and Louisville *Microscopes*, the Albany version most deserves the label "comic periodical."

Barbara McMillin

MICROSCOPE (New Haven)

Edited by "a fraternity of gentlemen" from Volume 1:1 (21 March 1820) through Volume 2:50 (8 September 1820), the four-page *Microscope* was published in New Haven by A. H. Maltby and Company, twice weekly. Its final closing statement described its diversity of taste—actually the product of its four chief contributors, including the editor Cornelius Tuthill—and its "innocent and rational amusement" rather than lampoon and sectarian bitterness. Lighter essays appeared along with general material. Indexed at the end on pages 198–200, it was octavo, eight pages, four cents an issue, and was supposed to have paid for itself, but no more. Most important is its "Memoirs of Gabriel Gap," appearing in Numbers 9, 13, 19, and 47, an inconclusive biography of a backwoodsman which anticipates the tone of James Russell Lowell's Birdofredum Sawin by twenty-five years. One or two other folk-humor items appeared. CtY holds a copy; it is available through University Microfilms.

Each issue begins with a lengthy untitled essay introduced by a quotation from the classics. The most humorous section, besides an extended sketch of "The Adventures of Gabriel Gap" complete with drawings, is the editors' response to reader mail. They caution many would-be poets; for example: "Flora's description of the rose, is so much inferior to that flower, that it would require the skill of a botanist to discover the resemblence."

Michael Pettengell

MICROSCOPE AND GENERAL ADVISOR

On 17 April 1824 *The Microscope* was established in Louisville, Kentucky, by "Tim Tickler, Jr., Esq.," and this four-page weekly resolved "to shoot folly as it flies." The first issue was published by T. H. Roberts with preceding numbers published by Johnston and Roberts. Because of its activities, the paper was raided and burned to the ground, after which it reappeared in New Albany, Indiana, on 22 September 1824 under the name *Microscope and General Advisor*. The paper ceased publication on 10 September 1825.

Before the fire, *The Microscope*'s caption read, "To lash the rascals naked through the world," and it attempted to do so with articles concerning unfaithful wives and ads for "500 first rate speech-writers to transcribe certain Great Hickory speeches." Articles by Phelim O'Fuggy and Timothy Twist headed the assault against the public. With the change of name and location, the paper was tamed down considerably. The cost in Indiana was two dollars annually, payable quarterly in advance. Those not paid in advance would be charged twelve and a half cents each issue. Although the *Microscope and General Advisor* contains letters from such characters as Dr. Puke, Sarah Pleased, and Big Whisker'd John, the whimsical writing does not match the fire of the earlier publication. It has been reprinted by University Microfilms.

Michael Pettengell

A MILLION LAUGHS MAGAZINE

Volume 1:1 (May 1966) by Laughs Publications, New York, edited by John Norment, was a thirty-five-cent, 8½″ × 11″ magazine of 52 pages featuring Gahan Wilson and John Dempsey cartoons and a variety of general humor including quips from "Bob Hope's Greatest Gag-Bag," "Campus Clips," and miscellaneous humor materials such as "Classic Tales for Frisky Males," which was a parody of *Playboy*. The last copyrighted issue (Volume 1:2) was dated 1 September 1966.

MIRTH

According to one cover spot, *Mirth* had amused America since 1950; by March 1956, it had reached Number 42 as a 5½″ × 7½″ bimonthly digest at twenty-five cents. The magazine was published in Silver Spring, Maryland, but sometimes claimed New York editorial offices and H. K. Publications as publisher. Bill Wenzel's covers of lush 1950s cuties typified the innocent soft sexuality of the cartoon material, with a few scattered gags. Originality was not sought, and the cartoon material reflects the *Saturday Evening Post*,** *Collier's* style with only slightly more adult overtones.

MOMUS

A pre-Civil War comic paper lasting three months, *Momus* was a daily from Volume 1:1 through Volume 1:23 (28 April through 24 May 1860) and a weekly through 21 July, at six cents an issue, originally publishing six days a week and then only on Saturday. To *Momus* illustrators, Lincoln was the Western luminary and Douglas was a Nero fiddling while Rome burned, despite *Momus*'s claim that it adhered to no party but would gladly sell out to any. Cartoons were similar to those in *Vanity Fair*,* with Frank Bellew and William North establishing a fairly bold pro-Republican position. "Gotham Dirt" and the "Dollar-ocracy" provided a full range of targets beyond the political scene. The graphics of the Charleston Convention populated by wire-pullers and drunken plug-uglies and Bellew's two-page cartoon of the ship of the Democrat party splitting on a rock of a Negro face are the most memorable images. City localities and old Know-Nothings on prize fighters and theatrical events filled out the two-column pages.

Mott lists an Englishman named Addie as editor, and cites a series of articles on city comic types as a particular strength of *Momus*. "Miss Charity Dodge's" letters from the city are also noteworthy along with the "Sketches by our Japanese artist, Sli-Po-Kum" on New York City street life. Originally, *Momus* claimed a circulation of several thousand for the daily and twice that for the weekly, but gave 72,939 as a number for sales of the first weekly; it claimed sales of 175,076 for the third weekly number but projected that weekly sales of 220,000 would be needed to meet expenses. Although its life was short, it stands as one of the more interesting of the Civil War era sources of imaginative comic political graphics. The DLC copy is housed in the Rare Book Room.

MONOCLE

Monocle, a magazine of the early 1960s, offered itself as "politics, polemics and satire for the sub-influential" at one dollar per 5½" × 11" oddly sized issue of 82 pages. Number 1 was copyrighted in September 1961, apparently as a quarterly. Volume 5:4 was Spring 1964, quarterly, with Victor Navasky as editor. Marvin Kitman, Richard Lingeman, and Eleanor Deinstag were the most active editors in shaping the magazine. It might be said to have updated *Americana** to a slightly more optimistic 1960s posture. Its previous form was titled *The Outsider's Newsletter*.* Since a "Preview Issue" was copyrighted as Volume 5:1 in May 1962 and the last copyrighted issue was Volume 6:5 in March 1967 (noted as 1966), following Volume 6:4 copyrighted in December 1965, numbering may require further verification.

THE MORALIST

After its first appearance on 27 May 1814, *The Moralist* of New York appeared infrequently. Printed "once a week or oftener, or less frequently, just according to the whim, or convenience of our association," each issue of this publication offered a single essay composed by one or more of its seven editors. These essays typically consisted of personal reactions to theatrical productions, fashionable amusements, or intriguing conversations. Publishers Garrit C. Tunison and Thomas Snowden produced the eleventh and final number of this single volume publication on 7 November 1814. This volume is available on University Microfilm. A copy can be found at DLC and one other library.

Barbara McMillin

MOVIE FUN

Movie Fun was one of the pictorial tabloids of the World War II period, featuring photos of starlets with light captions and a page or two of jokes, cartoons, and show biz gossip. Volume 1:1 was September 1940; the periodical was 10½″ × 13½″ in size, cost ten cents, and was published monthly by Crestwood Publishing Company, New York.

MOVIE HUMOR

Movie Humor, subtitled Hollywood Girls and Gags, was published in the 1930s under the editorship of M. R. Reese. Its 8½″ × 11½″ Quintana covers gave it a gaudy, girlie appearance true to its contents. Silk stockings and showgirl photos had humor captions like "Many a girl who calls a spade a spade calls a rake a darling." Various one-liners, quotes from the stars, and stories using movie titles provided comic filler. Volume 1:3 was July 1934, and it ran through at least Volume 4:3 (October 1937), and probably thereafter. It sold at twenty cents an issue, by Ultem Publications, New York, and its issues bore a strong resemblance to *Film Fun*.*

MOVIE MERRY-GO-ROUND

The bimonthly *Movie Merry-Go-Round* (Vol. 1:3, November 1936) is typical of the starlets-in-lingerie format of the Hollywood girlie photo magazines of the twenties and thirties. Captions were humorous puns and gags: "A sheer silk stocking over a knee," says Eleanor Powell, "makes it a high class joint." It is in standard magazine format with gaudy covers; Periodical House, presided over by A. A. Wyn, was the publisher, with Frederick Gardener as editor. The price per issue was fifteen cents, and the size was 8½″ × 11½." Volume 1:2 (September 1936) through Volume 5:5 (April 1939) were copyrighted.

MR.

Mr., a men's digest-size, 5½″ × 8″, twenty-five cents, 130 pages, featured men's stories and about fifty pages of cartoons along girlie themes, some old standbys from other magazines. It was published by the Exposed Publishing Company, in New York, bimonthly, Number 1 appearing in 1937; Volume 1:4 was July 1938. Number 2 was copyrighted in February 1938, as *Mister* Volume 1:3 in May, and *Mr.* Volume 1:4 for December 1938. At least one full-page advertisement for *Ballyhoo** indicates a connection between the two.

N

THE NATIONAL CRUMB

This magazine from Mayfair Publications, New York (bimonthly, fifty cents, 8″ × 10¾″) followed *Mad** in format. Volume 1:1 was August 1975. It offered burlesques of movies and a series of good news-bad news jokes on poorly printed offset pages. Joe Simon was editor.

NATURAL GAS

This spinoff of reprinted material from *Judge*,* 10″ × 14″ at twenty-five cents, is dated 1888. A copy is housed at DLC. *Natural Gas* was probably part of the regular run of secondary printings in quarterly and annual form from the regular *Judge*.

NEW BROADWAY BREVITIES.   See BREVITIES.

NEW JOKES

New Jokes (Vol. 1:4, Fall Edition, 1939–1940) was a 6½″ × 9½″ digest of gags and short jokes with a number of indifferently executed cartoons. Examples of new jokes include an artist backing up to see his painting and falling over a cliff, in cartoon format, and "One way to brighten the corner where you and the girl friend are, is to turn out the lights." It was published quarterly by Dell Publishing Company, New York, at ten cents per issue and edited by Victor Bloom. It was uncopyrighted.

NEW ORLEANS PICAYUNE

One of the best sources for comic clips in the 1830s was Vermonter George W. Kendall's *New Orleans Picayune*. The periodical began with Volume 1:1 for 25 January 1837 and continued (long after Kendall's departure and death) to 1877, in conjunction with Francis Lumsden. The Picayune is a coin worth one-sixteenth of a dollar—a sixpence in New York—and at four issues for twenty-five cents, the *Picayune* has been called the first cheap paper in the South. Immediate circulation was 1,800 and eventually higher, although fires and other setbacks dogged it. Kendall wrote amusing local comments, and his "The Devil's Walk in New Orleans" offered jokes in doggerel verse on vice and civil corruption. As a result, Kendall also was challenged to duels. The popularity of his paragraphs in the exchanges of other newspapers was widely recognized. After Kendall left for jingoistic expeditions to Mexico in the 1840s, the paper became less lively. For more information on this periodical, see Fayette Copeland, *Kendall of the Picayune* (Norman: University of Oklahoma Press, 1943).

THE NEW VARIETIES

The New Varieties was a sensationalist tabloid newspaper of the 1871–1875 period. It featured illustrated articles on catastrophes, murders, and stories of vice and sin, along with material on a variety of titillating social matters. However, it also published lurid cartoons, local-color stories, and jokes. So much of its "news" reporting borders on burlesque that the modern critic may want to identify it as totally humorous. Such is not the case, however, and it merits consideration primarily for its cartoon illustrations and its consciously published humorous stories and paragraphs.

A sixteen-page, four-column, $11'' \times 16''$ folio newspaper, *The New Varieties* appeared as a weekly on 9 January 1871; the last issue recorded is Volume 6:147 (25 October 1873), still at ten cents. Mott gives 1875 as the terminal date. The Independent News Agency in New York served as general agents, and John Stetson distributed it in Boston. The orientation was toward the urban life of these two metropolitan Northeastern areas and their satellite watering places. Included in the coverage were exaggerated cartoons of Satan producing a chorus girlie leg-line on a stage in Boston—"The Black Crook" melodrama being the play—and prostitutes waving at passersby out of Greene Street windows in New York City, among other graphic and titillating depictions of licentiousness drawn so boldly as to border on travesty. In its opening salvo, titled "The Paper of the Period," *The New Varieties* promised to combine striking sensation with the vigor of "life," vaunting female beauty in its purest form and illuminating the whole with flashes of wit and genial humor and sarcasm. Graphic depictions of women in cartoons suggest the pre-Gibson era, as his style of line and detail is clearly anticipated.

Among the sensational items are a broad play of Western stories, local-color poems, and news humor items. However, the tone of the dominating graphics and the news stories is so provocatively and consistently sexual that *The New Varieties* may be seen as representing the first thrust toward the coming age in which sexual humor would replace political humor as a dominant cultural mode. The last issue seen, Volume 2:49 (9 December 1871), features a bold cartoon cover attacking the Tweed Ring, but the contents adhere to the sex-legs-busts visuals and vile seducer/adultery stories characteristic of the journal. A column or two of humor material was also admitted to the mix regularly. Along with *Chic** of the 1880s, *The New Varieties* represents an important point in popular culture where humor and sensuality become part of the mainstream of post-Civil War American culture, a trend that would be elevated and refined by Gibson's girl in *Life** in the following thirty years. The copies seen are at MH.

NEW YORK NIGHTS

New York Nights was a sleazy sexsational story magazine with comic twists and a few comic verses (6¾" × 9¾", 66 pages, twenty-five cents) with a genuine slick-paper section of nude photos. Volume 1:1 (Summer 1933) was copyrighted by the Bow-man Publishing Corporation; Volume 4:3 was February 1937. It probably should be excluded from the humor category except for its story lines.

NEWSWRECK/WRECK. See WRECK/NEWSWRECK.

NIFTY

World War II-era *Nifty* was a tabloid featuring gags and cartoons on the girlie theme. Service humor was also prominent in the wartime issues seen. Typical of cartoons is one gob saying to another, "On ship we got sea legs—on shore we got to see legs!" Issues were thirty-six pages long with cartoons irregularly splashed across 10½" × 13½" pages. It was edited by Charles Rubino in Chicago and published by Par Publishing Company of Mt. Morris, Illinois. At fifteen cents in 1942, *Nifty* seems to have been a quarterly, with Volume 1:6 as August and Volume 1:8 as February (1944?), both bearing copyright notices for 1943, reflecting the year in which they were printed. Twenty-four numbers are known from 1942 through 1947 with somewhat erratic publication dates; Volume 1:2 for November 1942 was the first copyrighted issue, and Volume 2:14 for April 1947 was the last copyrighted. See also *Nifty Gags* in the Copyright Listings of Humor Magazines.

NIFTY GALS AND GAGS

Nifty Gals and Gags was a 5" × 7¼", twenty-five cent digest from the 1950s offering one-page cartoons and three or four pages of jokes and brief comic paragraphs with a sexual orientation that was mildly crude. A May 1951 and a May 1952 issue of this bimonthly listed Dearfield Publishing Company of New

York City as the perpetrator. "Nicky Goes to a Convention" is typical of its humor. Nifty Nick is sent to the IWW Convention—International Working Wolves—to represent Broadway; meeting a coy redhead struggling to become a singer, Nick promises to introduce her to a Broadway producer if she promises to stop struggling.

THE NUGGET

The Nugget for September, October 1945 (Vol. 1:7), 7¼″ × 5¼″, fifteen cents, 68 pages, by Goodman Publishing Company of Washington, Iowa, and Malibu Lake, California, was typical of the wartime cartoon digests coming home from the war, along with its sister publications like *The Booby Trap*.** Most of the cartoons are gal n' guy jokes.

O

OGILVIE'S FUN BOOK

J. S. Ogilvie of New York City was a popular publisher of low-cost self-help books, fiction, and comic and joke books. *Ogilvie's Fun Book* was presented in the format of a cheapened *Life*,* with much the same look to its cartoons and a similar sense to its jokes. The 8" × 11¼", ten-cent magazine offered approximately thirty pages of wit, humor, and fun of popular cartoonists and writers in the 1905 period. Other than being numbered (a broken run from Numbers 3 through 15 seen), the issues carry no identification by date or publisher. Number 10, "The Rogers Bros. in Funville," bore a 1904 copyright notice and was oriented toward country and small-town jokes featuring the Rogers brothers.

OLD ABE

Old Abe (The War Eagle) is representative of the early commercial use of humor in conjunction with advertising pages to form periodical humor publications. It was originated by George Kelly's dry-goods store in Philadelphia in 1879. Distributed free, the three-column, four-page monthly lasted at least from September through the following March, claiming a distribution of 100,000. Jokes and general items were mixed with general interest materials, household hints, and funny pieces by comic writers including James T. Fields. Advertising for Kelly and Company was prominent and was waved more dramatically than the bloody shirt of the Civil War. Volume 1:1 and 1:6, for September 1879 and March 1880, respectively, are located at PHi.

OLD DOC GAGS

Grace and Charles Ubert published *Old Doc Gags* in New York City, by the Reprint Publishing Company, from July 1920 through June 1922. It was priced at ten cents, monthly, in a 6″ × 8½″, two-column format. Its twenty-four pages were dedicated to the old country doctor who would rather tell you funny stories than dose you with drugs. Offering reprints and soliciting contributions, its best feature was "Homespun Phoolosopay" by Zim, the prominent illustrator, although "Old Doc Says" offered a column of crackerbox humor on politics. A June 1922 editorial referred to winning a war with a large distributor in 1920 and tried to sell $10,000 in stock to expand, but *Old Doc* folded without ever achieving a new format or gaining enough advertisers to cover more than a single back page. It may have died because its typical gags were outdated for the twenties—Customer: I want some underclothes; How long?—How long? I don't want to rent 'em, I want to buy 'em. DLC holds a volume donated by the editors.

150 NEW CARTOONS/175 NEW CARTOONS

Charlton Press of Derby, Connecticut, published *150 New Cartoons*, and for a brief period a successor *175 New Cartoons*, from 1963 through 1979 as a bimonthly digest, in company with several other cartoon publications oriented around adult sexual material. Typical is a full-page color cartoon in which a doctor hits a young lady's knee in an examination and her bare breast hits him in the eye in reflex. The magazine measured 6¾″ × 10″, cost thirty-five cents in July 1967, and was bimonthly from Number 18 (September 1967). Volume 1:1 was published in February 1962 originally as a quarterly; it became *175 New Cartoons* with the August 1977 (No. 77) issue and ended with Number 83 in February 1979. Sales in the early 1960s ranged from 40,000 to 50,000, peaking in September 1967 at 65,500. By the early 1970s, sales dropped into the 40,000 range and gradually drifted lower; the series was discontinued while sales were still around 25,000. The makeup of Charlton's magazine was done by a single editor selecting cartoons through mail submissions, which may account for the tendency of sales to decline as the selection of material became conventionalized.

1000 JOKES MAGAZINE

Dell Publishing Company, in New York City, originated *1000 Jokes Magazine* (8½″ × 11½″, 54 pages) in 1936 as a semi-annual, then quarterly, beginning at ten cents and rising gradually to thirty-five cents by the late 1960s. It crammed twenty to thirty jokes on a page, punctuated by a scattering of cartoons. Sources were primarily radio humor in the earlier period, including Burns and Allen, Alice Frost, Hammerstein Music Hall, and unnamed gag writers. By Number 24, Summer 1942, edited by Charles Saxon, cartoons were larger, and three or four lengthier prose pieces appeared. In 1944, with Ted Shane as editor, the format was closer to a popular magazine than a gag book, with features by Gracie Allen and Ed (Archie) Gardner, stories, satire, and gag features. In the 1950s, Bill Yates took over the editorship and cartoons dominated the prose gags; subject matter was general and middle class in orientation and tone. In the 1960s, C. Mitchell Freeman became editor, maintaining the same format with the addition of some comic-caption stills from the movies. Circulation was stated as 101,600 as listed in Number 129 (March-May 1969), the last issue seen. Dell, which copyrighted this magazine irregularly, was no longer copyrighting it at that time.

1000 NEW JOKES

1000 New Jokes was a Dell Publishing Company offering in the same format as *1000 Jokes*.** The quarterly cost ten cents and was in an 8½″ × 11¾″, three-column format with lines of gags and an infrequent cartoon. Issues from 1937–1938 have been seen. Summer 1936 and two 1937 issues were copyrighted, with the last being September-November 1937.

1001 LAUGHS

1001 Laughs, edited by J. J. Robinson for the Experimenter Publishing Company, New York, 1927, at fifty cents for Volume 1, is a collection of 1,000 jokes and more than 350 illustrations "from the best humorous periodicals of the world." The 10″ × 11¾″ publication was crammed with jokes. It is not clear whether it was a periodical or an anthology, but its republication of humor from college sources and American and international sources makes it a broad index to the humor of its era.

ORION

The *Orion* (March 1842-August 1844) was a "Monthly Magazine of Literature and Art" which was established and published in Penfield, Georgia, and moved to Charleston, South Carolina, shortly before its failure. According to its editor and founder, William Carey Richards, the son of a Baptist minister, the *Orion* was a general-interest magazine for "the advancement and refinement of intellectual taste and habit in the South."

Probably fewer than twenty humorous items were printed in the two-year run (twenty-four numbers) of the magazine. The humorists of the Old Southwest, including Georgians A. B. Longstreet and William Tappan Thompson, did not submit sketches to the *Orion*, at a time when they were frequent contributors to the New York *Spirit of the Times** and numerous regional newspapers. Among the most notable humorous pieces published in the *Orion* were five "Smithville sketches" by the editor William C. Richards, which derive their humor from the naiveté of a rural community introduced to such "modern" things as electricity and laughing-gas. Richards also occasionally wove humorous anecdotes into the "Editor's Department" of the magazine.

Mark A. Keller

P

PACK O' FUN

The 1950s provided a blast of digest-sized, girlie humor magazines, and *Pack o' Fun* was one of the early forerunners of the type. The magazine—Volume 1:1 (August 1942), 5½" × 7½", one hundred pages, twenty-five cents—was originally a bimonthly but was then published quarterly through August 1949 and thereafter bimonthly in tandem with *Nifty*.** The original *Pack* had large swatches of prose and doggerel and was service-oriented; "Call me a cab," said one drunk to an admiral, who protested he was in the navy—"Okay, call me a boat." *Pack o' Fun* in the 1950s was typified by its Bill Wenzel covers: one has an intently collegiate "Packy Fun" removing spots from a cutie's dress by cutting them out with a scissors. During the late forties, it was edited by Red Kirby for Magna Publications of New York; other editors are unknown. Its one hundred pages were filled mostly by cartoon gags punctuated by a few pages of ads or jokes. The November 1948 number (Vol. 5:2) offered a "calendar" in the style of Vargas and Petty by Donnelly, and the general run of girlie and sexual jokes fit this pattern. By that time whole-page cartoons, almost all on seduction and dating themes, dominated the magazine and prose had disappeared.

PANIC

Panic was a satire magazine different from an earlier *Panic* published by EC Comics as a companion to *Mad*,* although the later *Panic* also appears to be one of many clones of *Mad* Magazine. It was published in New York City by the Panic Publishing Company, in an 8" × 11" format, for thirty cents an issue, and edited by Robert W. Farrell. Burlesqued subjects included teachers, advertisements, movie and television plots, and a general run of cultural denominators. April 1966 was Volume 2:12, bimonthly, and appears to be the last issue, reprinting an earlier issue according to a note in Overstreet. The earlier *Panic* first appeared in 1958, and five numbers are reported, although later numbering suggests more issues.

PARIS FOLLIES

Paris Follies (6½" × 10", twenty-five cents) is yet another of the cheap-paper "peppy snappy stories" genre, with pages of jokes and photo nudes among sexy stories with humorous and titillating components. Volume 1:3 is December 1933, 76 pages. "Rod, Reel, and Sex Appeal" is glossed as "The second adventure of those Hot Hitch-hikers, Laurette and Sue, finds them one bedroom scene closer to Hollywood." Jokes approximated, "That front row chorus girl is a good tennis player—Oh, yes, she gives fine service."

PARIS LIFE

Paris Life claimed to be the "American Edition" of *La Vie Parisienne*; Volume 1:16, quarterly, Fall 1954, was published by Paris Life, Inc., of New York at the Charlton Press in Derby, Connecticut. The 9¾" × 12½", twenty-five cents periodical is a throwback gals pictorial to the World War II era, featuring chorines in pasties and light captions. It may be more a girlie magazine than a humor magazine.

PARIS NIGHTS

Paris Nights is typical of the liberated sexual humor that Americans thought made Paris and New York roar in the Roaring Twenties. Volume 7:1 was August 1928; Volume 11:4 was November 1932. The twenty-five cent, 7½" × 10½", fifty-page magazine offered "The Merry Whirl of the World in Story and Picture." Shade Publishing Company of Philadelphia published it monthly, offering humorous fiction on sexy courtship themes, one-liners on sexy and general topics, and a variety of cartoons interspersed. Some slick sections offered nudes and more cartoons. One-liners were of the sort where a mistress tells the maid that she saw the maid kiss the milkman and will take in the milk in future; response, "It wouldn't be no use, mum. He's promised never to kiss anybody but me." One double-page center cartoon translated from Ch. Herourd shows the ancient and modern fires of love—a Trojan dragging off a Sabine on one side and a flapper shooting her lover with a handgun on the other side. A relation to *Gayety*** and *Zippy*** is suggested by advertisements. Paris Nights Publishing Company copyrighted Volume 1:1 for April 1925.

PARIS THRILLS

Paris Thrills was a titillating sexy humor magazine which didn't even bother to list publisher or other information. The 6" × 9", twenty-five-cent magazine refers to the Depression in several jokes. Cartoons were leering, and pin-up photos were of nude French girls of a decade or two previous. Humor was of the he-she variety: "Will you be my companionate wife?"; "Yes—if you let me have enough companions."

PARODY

Parody identifies itself as a *Mad** knockoff with its subtitle "Entertainment for Clods." Volume 1:1 was April 1977, 8" × 10¾", fifty cents, bimonthly, and was issued by Armour Publishing Company in New York. "A City Dweller's Night Before Christmas" was a noteworthy parody of Clement Clarke Moore's poem in an urban-dweller's nightmare of drug-crazed burglary, although in a stilted middle-class tone. The second issue parodied Ripley's Believe It or Not— a tried and true parody subject, King Dung, L'il Abnerd, and Woody Allen. Twelve cartoon sequences were offered covering that many subjects, punctated by a few burlesque advertisements. Number 2 is dated June 1977.

PARODY PENTHOUSE

This 8" × 11", 90-page magazine is issued by TSM Publishing Corporation of New York and sells for $3.95. It is one of a series of annual publications parodying a popular magazine—*Playboy* in 1983, *Cosmopolitan* in 1984. Masturbation is substituted for bisexuality to obtain most of the humorous effects.

THE PARTERRE

Promising to guide "the inexperienced in the paths of literature," *The Parterre* was a weekly periodical published from 15 June 1816 through 28 June 1817. "Conducted by a trio," this magazine offered a variety of forms, including poetry, epigrams, short anecdotes, biographical sketches, and sentimental prose passages. Published by Probasco and Justice, of Philadelphia, the two volumes are indexed and a list of subscribers is provided. Both volumes are available on University Microfilm. Copies of *The Parterre* may be found at DLC, PU, CtY, TxU, NcD, and four other libraries.

Combining amusement and instruction, this magazine contained humorous reviews of current and past fashions in both male and female attire. Entitled "The Chamber of Fashion," this series was complemented by another which provided a comic analysis of human behavior. In "The Escritoire" "Simon Scribble, Esq." advised his readers on such subjects as the loss of self-possession (19 April 1817) or the hazards of yielding to "an extreme and romantic sensibility'' (3 May 1817). Though limited in number, *The Parterre* offers modern scholars much insight into the fads and foibles of early nineteenth-century America.

Barbara McMillin

PASTIME

W. W. Scott edited *Pastime* to provide five hours of entertainment, with Volume 1:1 appearing in November 1932, copyrighted by Howard-Scott Publishing Company and carrying a notice that *Pastime* was not an imitator of *Ballyhoo.** Its thirty-six pages, in 8½″ × 11½″ format, at fifteen cents, featured a wide variety of general cartoons interleaved with various pages of puzzles. Howard-Scott Publishing Company, New York, produced the monthly, advertising "clean humor" from the likes of Robert Benchley, Gluyas Williams, and Donald Ogden Stewart. It appears to have lasted through at least April 1933.

PAUL PRY

New York's *Paul Pry* offered "New Series Number One" on 31 August 1839; Number 3 was later identified as whole Number 41 of the weekly "theatrical, sporting, quizzical, critical, and satirical journal." It was four pages, 12″ × 19″, in three-column format published Saturdays at three cents by Wardle Corbyn, later of *Figaro*** (New York), and A. W. Noney. Corbyn and Noney offered "Green Room" (theatrical) gossip, political comment, jokes, anecdotes, burlesques of the puffery dominating theatrical criticism of the day, and comic character sketches such as "The Supernumerary, The Amateur Actor." Mrs. Anne Royal edited a *Paul Pry* in Washington, D.C., from November 1831 to 1836, as a gossip sheet. According to Mott (1:356), it was superseded by *The Huntress*, but this earlier paper does not seem to be related to the New York bearer of the *Paul Pry* name. Volume 2:11 for 15 February 1840 was prepared by Noney alone and offered "Peter Funk," a sketch by "Boz of Gotham" as one attraction. The New York *Paul Pry* is at DLC.

PEEK/PEEK ANNUAL/PEEK QUARTERLY

Peek was a tabloid monthly of the World War II era in the gals and gags format, emphasizing light photo-articles around cuties in bathing suits among the cartoon pages. The 10½″ × 13½″ periodical sold at ten cents as a monthly and at fifteen cents as an annual. *Peek* was a product of the Bilbara Publishing Company, of Mount Morris, Illinois, and New York City. Adrian Lopez was listed as editor of earlier issues. Volume 1:8, the first seen, was June 1939—almost entirely photo sensationalism—and Volume 3:12 appeared in February 1941; Volume 5:2 for April 1943 was the last copyrighted. "A Humorous Look at Life" served as subtitle, although "A Humorous Look at Legs" would be more accurate.

Peek Quarterly has been seen for Autumn 1942; it is almost entirely cheesecake with one or two pages of jokes at most, but its cartoon covers and large cartoons on dating and marriage themes give it the air of a cartoon magazine more than a photo book. Copyrights were taken for Volume 1:3 (Winter 1942) and for Volume 1:4 (Autumn 1943). At least three *Peek Annuals* appeared in the early forties along the same content lines.

PEPPER

Pepper of the 1940s is not the same as *Red Pepper*,** the offshoot of the *Calgary Eye-Opener.** The 1940s *Pepper* in fact may be two little *Peppers* rather than one. One *Pepper* appeared in February 1943 (Winter) and was copyrighted by H. K. Publications as a quarterly, but it published Number 15 in May 1946 as Comic Corporation of America; it has not been seen. The other *Pepper* is a digest-sized 5¼" × 7½" cartoon magazine of indistinguishable merit, featuring cartoons on general themes with something of a girlie slant, a number of one-liners, a pin-up or two, and a couple of longer prose humor pieces. It was a product of Band Leader Publications, New York, and sold at twenty-five cents. Number 11 of this monthly was issued in July 1949.

THE PICAYUNE. See the NEW ORLEANS PICAYUNE.

THE PICK. See THE NEW YORK PICK.

PICTORIAL CHUCKLES

In 8¾" × 12", 72-page format, *Pictorial Chuckles* tried to capture the range of service on the home front in dating cartoons. Sally Carter was editor of Volume 1:1 (1945, no month) of the monthly. It featured splashes of dating cartoons with crude coloring, mixed in with gags mostly generated by George Posner. Depictor Corporation of New York published it in Wilkes-Barre, Pennsylvania, at twenty-five cents a copy. The cover cutie says to her pal, "It's the violinist with the army band—he wants me to send him a g-string," but inside humor was even milder.

PICTORIAL MOVIE FUN

A World War II gals and gags tabloid, *Pictorial Movie Fun* was one of many Crestwood Publications products. The monthly was 10½" × 13½" in size and sold for ten cents. Volume 2:4 was published in June 1942, and Volume 2:7 in September 1942. Roughly six pages of cartoons complemented the cheesecake photo articles oriented toward humorous themes and filling each thirty-two-page issue.

PICTORIAL REVIEW

The New York *Journal American* provided *Pictorial Review* as a tabloid section copyrighted by the King Features Syndicate in the 1940s. Writers included Paul Gallico, Westbrook Pegler, George Dixon, and a host of others providing light stories for the front pages. Bruce Patterson conducted a double-page cartoon-joke centerfold, and movie and Broadway material filled up most of the back pages. Copyrighted from 17 June 1951 as *Sunday Pictorial Review*, *Pictorial Review* copyrights extended from 6 January 1946 to 21 April 1963.

PICTORIAL WAG

What little is known about the *Pictorial Wag* is described in Frank L. Mott's *A History of American Magazines* (1:425, 805). According to Mott, the *Pictorial Wag* was a comic newspaper published in New York, probably from 1842 to 1843. It was founded by Thomas Nichols, a physician, and Robert H. Elton, a wood-engraver, both of whom were joined in the enterprise by the artist John H. Manning. Extant issues of the *Wag* have not been found, but one can surmise from the title of the paper that its contribution to humor came from its illustrations. The paper apparently failed in its second year of publication, and its proprietors turned to the more profitable field of publishing comic valentines.

Mark A. Keller

PIN-UP FUN

Published quarterly by Health Knowledge, Inc., of New York, *Pin-Up Fun* (No. 1, Winter 1968) provided sleazecake pin-ups and sexy cartoons in digest format, $5\frac{1}{4}'' \times 6\frac{1}{2}''$, and sold for thirty-five cents. Although Health Knowledge copyrighted a number of titles, *Pin-Up Fun* was not among them.

PIZZAZZ

Pizzazz was a production of the Marvel Comics Group, New York, in a magazine format, published by Stan Lee in the 1970s. Originally edited by Bobby Miller, it was edited by Jeff Lewis as of Number 13. The price was $7.50 per year. It was directed at younger teens and offered articles like "Adults Through the Ages"—an illustrated cartoon piece—and "Sci Fi: Test Driving the Great Spaceships." Issue Number 13 was published in October 1978, and the last copyrighted was November 15 (December 1978). Bulk rates were offered to schools and institutions.

THE PLANTATION

The Plantation was a short-lived product of the Old South which upheld the standards of Southern gentility in literature and life with a slant toward American humor. It claimed to be addressed to all classes, but it also defended slavery unreservedly. One review acridly attacks *The Life of P. T. Barnum* and George Burnham's *The History of the Hen Fever* as abominations by swindlers, and the sales of Doesticks and Sam Slick are bemoaned in comparison to Dryden and Longfellow. Elsewhere "The Old Farm-House of My Uncle Simon" by Abraham Goosequill demonstrates that Southern humor could be rather washed out at times. The quarterly journal was edited by J. A. Turner, later an influence on Joel Chandler Harris, at Eatonton, Georgia, from March 1860 (Vol. 1:1) through September 1860 (Vol. 2:1), at five dollars per year. DLC has the copy seen.

PLAYGIRL'S BEST CARTOONS

Playgirl, the feminist answer to *Playboy*, spun off the quarterly publication *Playgirl's Best Cartoons* about 1979. Volume 3:4, copyrighted in 1982 in an 8" × 11" format sold for $2.95, and features a slick magazine cover but plain uncoated stock pages. It offers cartoons from a feminist viewpoint, many with an overtly sexual orientation. For instance, one piglet says to another: "I think its an obscene phonecall—there's a lot of huffing and puffing"; in another, a woman complains to the marriage counselor, "I'll tell you what turns him on!— nineteenth-century poetry." Ritter/Geller Communications, Inc., of Santa Monica, California, is the publisher. The issue seen offers two or three cartoons per page for 82 pages, including covers. Of the eighteen "Playgirl's Cartoonists" given brief biographies on pages two and three, none are female; R. W. Claire is editor.

A POCKETFUL OF PEPPER

A Pocketful of Pepper, a 5¼" × 7½" quarterly issued by H-K Publications of Springfield, Massachusetts, was a World War II cartoon book with pages of one-line gags thrown in. October 1945 was Number 13. Some of the humor was dating humor put in uniform, but most of the cartoon gags were conventional. Number 1 was copyrighted for Winter 1942; Comic Corporation of America copyrighted Number 6 (February 1944), and H-K copyrighted Numbers 7–8–9 for May-July-October 1944. H. K. (varying H-K slightly) published *Mirth*** in the 1950s. See also *Pepper*.**

THE POLITICAL MANIA

The Political Mania (1833), a pamphlet in two parts, at PHi, is not a periodical per se although it is similar in form to periodicals of the period.

POPULAR CARTOONS

Published quarterly by Visual Varieties, Rockville Center, New York, *Popular* Cartoons featured bare-breasted cheesecake and lush cutie cartoons by Jefferson Machamer, Bill Wenzel, Bill Ward, and others on adolescent-adult sexual themes. Volume 8:24 was issued in July 1973 at forty cents in an 8″ × 11″ format. The editor is listed as "Ernest N. Devver."

POPULAR JOKES

Popular Jokes, "The Big Laugh Magazine," was standard magazine size at 8″ × 11″ and cost twenty-five cents. Ernest N. Devver was the editorial pseudonym here as it was with *Popular Cartoons*,** and jokes and cartoons were so freely mixed that similar jokes appear on different pages of the same issue, although a number of items by Basil Wolverton—one of the leading illustrators of the counter-culture comix—appear. Jokes and gags have a general breadth, with a slight "girlie" slant. Volume 2:9 is dated May 1963. The editorial contents, according to a note in the magazine, were previously published by Humorama Magazines, which establishes the connection to Visual Varieties of Rockville Center, New York, the current publisher. It was advertised at least through June 1966.

POPULAR PARODY SONG HITS

Thirty-two pages of parodies contributed by its World War II readership filled the pulp pages of *Popular Parody*, published monthly by Song Parodies, Inc., of New York at ten cents an issue and a dollar a year. Volume 1:1 was published in July 1942 in an 8½″ × 11″ format. Hy Rosen provided most of the crude cartoon illustrations, and various hands provided inept parodies of popular and traditional favorites.

PORCUPINE'S GAZETTE

William Cobbett created *Porcupine's Gazette* as a Philadelphia daily on 4 March 1797, originally titled "Porcupine's Gazette and United States Daily Advertizer." It lasted as a daily in Philadelphia until 28 August 1799 (Vol. 4:770). With two of its four pages filled with advertisements, the journal's claim of a circulation of 2,000 may have been justified. Cobbett, fleeing the yellow fever epidemic, continued in a Philadelphia suburb identified by Bingham as Bustleton for six weekly issues from 6 September through 11 October (Nos. 771–776) and two duodecimo pamphlets on 19 October (No. 777) and 26 October (No. 778), each of twenty-four pages. His final shot was fired from New York on 13 January 1800 (No. 799). A tri-weekly called "The Country Porcupine" was published from 5 March 1798 through 28 August 1799 (Vol. 3:232) as a reprinting of material from the *Gazette*. See Brigham for more information; DLC and about twenty other libraries list varied holdings of both journals.

Porcupine's Gazette is possibly the best example of sarcastic invective in American literature. Staunchly Tory but in other ways modern, Cobbett was vituperative in attacking the Philadelphia government, democracy, and particularly Dr. Benjamin Rush. Cobbett claimed that Rush's commitment to bleeding as a treatment for yellow fever had killed thousands. Losing a libel suit to Rush, Cobbett was forced to flee the city and finally the country. Mott in *American Journalism* (p. 130n) offers the following quotation on Benjamin Franklin as evidence of the brilliant Cobbett's tendency to excess, from the *Gazette* for 31 July 1797, he vilifies the Philadelphian saint as "Crafty and lecherous old hypocrite of a father, whose very statue seems to gloat on the wenches as they walk the State House yard." Such language was typical of the strength of Cobbett's imagination, which finally alienated him from both foes and friends.

PUCK: THE PACIFIC PICTORIAL

San Francisco's *Puck* burst into life for seventeen issues on 7 January 1865 at the office of Loomis and Swift. Originally a weekly designed to promote local engravings rivalling *Punch*, *Puck* was lively and literate, contrasting favorably with its best New York counterparts.

Chaffing the "old granny Alta" (the *Alta California*, which sponsored Mark Twain's first travel letters in 1866–1867), *Puck* offered six pages of comic matter sandwiched between two pages of ads at the front and back. The San Francisco Merchantile Library was just an "intellectual boarding house" to *Puck*, and Jeff Davis skedaddling in a woman's dress was ridiculed; a full-page cartoon showed an unchained Black slave raising his hands to heaven beside the goddess of freedom, and "Negro Suffer-age" has Sambo and Uncle Sam in dialogue: Uncle Sam, "Wait, *Just a Little*, Sambo, and I won't be particular to a shade like I have been." / Sambo, "All right, Massa Uncle Sam, jes as you say—only wanted to know ef I WAS a man now." Commercial and social San Francisco provided much of the basis for local humor, which abounded.

Fourteen numbers were indexed at the end of Volume 1, beginning with the first four-page issue, in $9'' \times 11\frac{3}{4}''$ format at twelve and a half cents a copy; it consisted of eight pages by Number 3 and was a monthly by Number 4 at fifteen cents a copy. Thus, December 1865 was Volume 1:14, and it ceased with Volume 2:3 in March 1866. Its strongest point was its impressive engravings on good paper by Loomis and by L. Nagel, among others. At the end of Volume 1, *Puck* announced its success and intention to return to weekly status, but it never carried out that plan. Franklin Meine has written on it briefly in *The Collector's Journal* Volume 4:2 (January-March 1933): 437–38. Copies are held at CU-BANC, CSmH, MBat, and NN.

PUNCHINELLO

Veterans of Henry Louis Stephens's *Vanity Fair** founded *Punchinello* with what they felt was adequate financial backing, reported by Frederic Hudson in *Journalism in the United States, from 1690 to 1872* as $50,000. However, its one volume covers only weekly numbers from 2 April 1870 to 24 December 1870. Stephens was to provide the art, and Charles Dawson Shanley and William A. Stephens were the editors. Jay Gould, Jim Fisk, and the Tammany bosses were supposed to be the backers. "Dick Tinto," "Matador," and others offered comic pieces; satirical hits at New York life, political doings in Washington, and similar material were the standard fare. Orpheus C. Kerr's "The Mystery of E. Drood," purporting to finish Charles Dickens's unfinished novel, was the dominant feature of its short life. Mott (4:440–42) offers more information on this periodical. Forty libraries list holdings.

— Q —

THE QUILL

The Quill was a thirty-eight-page Greenwich Village magazine of the late teens and twenties which claimed to be the only international amateur magazine in America. June 1924, *The Quill*'s anniversary seventh-year number, was Volume 14:6 of the twenty-cent, 6″ × 7″ offering of art, letters, songs, Blah!!! sentiment, "& serious stuff, like humor." Bohemian, it offered "no compromise with sanity or popular dumbness." Robert Edwards was editor and publisher in 1924, having inherited the sheet from its founder Art Moss and Moss's successor Millia Davenport. Seven pages of ads and a Greenwich Village guide accompanied brief humor items, some poems and illustrations, and varied light material. March 1924 through Volume 17:4 (October 1925), with some irregularities in the last three months, were copyrighted.

QUIPS

Quips was a 1950s digest of general and light dating and sex humor by Humorama of New York as "Quips!—For Pleasure Only." The bimonthly was all cartoons, 5¾″ × 7¼″, one hundred pages, and cost twenty-five cents. Volume 1:4 was issued in June 1955. One cartoon gag has a luscious cutie standing by an office door as two employees comment, "The boss is going to present his new incentive program this morning." A masher pleads with his resisting girlfriend in another, "Have a heart, honey, I've already been rejected by the army, navy, and air force."

THE RADIO HUMORIST

Volume 1:9 (June 1936) of James Madison's *The Radio Humorist* was typical of this thirty-page monthly, typed humor sheet. It offered Routines for Two Males, for Male and Female, and Miscellaneous—stories, parodies of old-time songs, and minstrel and variety gags. *Radio Humorist* was intended for radio and commercial users and sold at one dollar a copy. Three issues from 1936 at least are held by the San Francisco Public Library. It was preceded by an annual *Madison's Budget*, a compilation of vaudeville material that ran to nineteen numbers.

THE RAMBLER (1884)

The Chicago *Rambler* from 1884 through 1887 was not originally designed as a humor magazine, but by early 1885 it had made a dramatic change into one of the Midwest's most formidable comic spokesmen, openly boasting that it was the only Western paper sold on the Manhattan Elevated Railroad. Reginald deKoven, Harry Smith, and later Elliot Flower were the editors behind the change from commonplace Chicago social narrator to national humor magazine, and they blended longer social humor with comic bits and some well-drawn cartoons on local city life.

The original *Rambler*, "a journal of men, manners, and things," sold at five cents when the first sixteen-page issue appeared on 29 March 1884 in a 10″ × 13″ format with only a scattering of humor under editor Ion Lewis. Reginald deKoven and Harry Smith revolutionized the format with Volume 3:41 on 3 January 1885, decreasing the size to 8½″ × 11″, adding articles such as B. B. Vallentine's "Fitznoodle in the West," and poking fun at middle-class city and suburban life and upper crust new rich Chicago. This new *Rambler* was "devoted to its own interests" and provided more generalized comic items, verse of humorous sentiment, notes on Chicago theaters, and other varied fare with a scattering of sophisticated graphics. Later, the last three or four pages of its sixteen were advertisements. Editor deKoven may have left as early as June 1885 when the masthead stopped listing editors; editors' names returned with only Smith and Flower in September. The final issue was Volume 11:145 (1 January 1887). Typical lightly ironic humor has the meat-king Armour advising a reporter to go to bed at nine and get up at five, while the reporter covers a fire at nine and eats his dinner at five in the morning. A "Boston" version of an old poem is, "of all the sad words of tongue or pen, the saddest are these: it might have bean." The bad puns in the "Follies of the Day" section especially stand out. The humorous format stayed the same, but *Rambler's* humor loses interest due to its upper class and literati focus. MB (1–8) and MH (8–11 broken) together have an almost complete run from Volumes 1 through 11, and two other libraries list Volume 1.

THE RAMBLER (1916)

John Kendrick Bangs created his humorous *Rambler* in 1916 as an elevated Boston soapbox. The magazine was 6″ × 9½″ in size, totaled first sixteen and, later, twenty pages, and sold at ten cents per monthly issue, or one dollar a year. It was devoted to literature and the arts, but most notably to politics. Luther Burbank's spineless cactus was not as amazing, wrote Bangs, as the spineless U.S. President, and the journal's "steel rivetted Republican" stance was barely covered in Bangsian gentility. In 1917, Bangs scourged "old Midas Moneybags" who pays in pelf while others sacrifice their brawn in the fight against the Kaiser, the "Supreme Manifestation of Malign and Brutish Force." Bangs was both editor and vice-president of the Rambler Company. The last issue seen is Volume 1:10 (July 1917), at MH. The journal is an interesting example of genteel humor gone to war. Only Volume 1:1 for October 1916 was copyrighted.

RAW

Raw, an oversized slick graphix magazine of the 1980s, is a Greenwich Village publication with a cosmopolitan flavor. Dedicated by its publisher co-editors, François Mouly and Art Spiegelman, to expanding the possibilities of the comic strip—or recapturing the original possibilities of the form as seen in the early 1900s, *Raw* treats each issue as a "one shot" publication moving in various directions in the avant-garde art/new-wave comix world. Number 1 appeared in 1980 at $3.50 with a tribute to Alfred Jarry, one of the fathers of the punk movement. *Raw*, Number 6, is subtitled "The Graphix magazine that overestimates the taste of the American public"; it is dated 1984, is 10½″ × 14″ in size, and appears semi-annually at $5.00, although the original intent was to offer a quarterly. Continental and primitive cartoon artists provide graphics stories dominated by dark lines and chaotic page formats. Number 8 in 1986 features Spiegelman's "Maus," color pages by Sue Cole and Bruno Richard, "Jimbo" by Gary Panter on the post-nuclear explosion world, and a section of "Raw Gagz." *Raw* is now an annual at $9.00.

Each issue since Number 2 includes a magazine-within-a-magazine titled "Maus" which tells the compelling story of Jewish survival during the holocaust; characters are transformed into mice, cats, and pigs. On cheaper paper, the small comic-format story book is an independent tuck-in which achieved its own status as a book by Pantheon Press in 1986. The *New York Times Book Review* for 26 May 1985 identified "Maus" as an important literary event in itself. The *Village Voice* for 4 June 1985 has also accorded *Raw* serious extended treatment as an important innovator in stimulating an expansion in the American comix form. Circulation is given as 12,000; it sells out regularly, and consistent with the intent of its creators to assert through style the importance of the magazine as graphics event rather than being merely a disposable comic book, it has been seriously reviewed by a number of other periodicals.

RAZZBERRIES and RADIO RAZZBERRIES

Joe G. Burten, of *Squawkies*** and *Burten's Follies*,** was also responsible for *Razzberries* and its counterpart, *Radio Razzberries*. *Razzberries* was co-edited by Wayne Sabbath, issued monthly at fifteen cents, and 7½″ × 10″ and thirty-four pages in size on cheap paper except for a slick nudie center section. It featured genuine nudes, including a nude cover girl superimposed on the National Recovery Administration eagle in the "Buy American" number.

November 1933 has been seen, and the journal completed at least two volumes, but numbering is uncertain. Number 2 in 1932 and November and December issues in 1933 were copyrighted. One proposed Hollywood theme song was titled, "I was engaged to a girl with a wooden leg, but I broke it off." Cartoon sequences have elephants blowing ladies' dresses off; prose stories deal with infidelity and innuendo, all treated as humor, or burlesques like "Peradventures of Flintlock Shomes."

Radio Razzberries was bimonthly, begun in January-February 1934 without volume numbers, and published by Independent Magazine Company, Brooklyn, at fifteen cents, in the same size and general format as *Razzberries*. In "Fun from the Airways," Gracie Allen tells George that the height of nerve is sitting down to a strip poker game in your nightie. In "Coming out of Ether," it claims, "After the radio gets hot we'll gargle that old sweet song of matrimony entitled: The First Hundred Beaus are the Hardest." Other prose burlesques, cartoons, and joke items are oriented toward the show biz and glamor side of radio and sex, although it may be hard for present-day readers to imagine radio as "sexy" in the way that Burten treated it. A caricature of "Reefer Madness" was titled

"Camp Followers of the Program Prowlers," exposing shady radio dives using the lure of young hostesses and easy money to lure nice girls into crime. See also *Kookoo*.**

READER'S DIGEST

Reader's Digest, published in Pleasantville, New York, since 1922, is not a humorous magazine. However, its several humor departments have been impressive reprinters of humor since its founding. Humor departments have included "Humor in Uniform," "Laughter is the Best Medicine," "Life in These United States," "Personal Glimpses," and "Quips." Other humorous one-liners frequently appear as fillers; among hardcover reprints are *Reader's Digest Treasury of Wit and Humor* (1958) and *Funfare* (1948) and softcover pamphlets such as *Best Stories from Life in These United States* (1967). Among typical stories is one that has a group sargeant yell at troops huddled together in the face of a thunderstorm, "Stand apart, men, and give the good Lord his chance to pick and choose." Another story describes a man christened R. B. Jones, with initials only, as happens in the Southern United States, who is required to fill out his army forms R(only) B(only) Jones. As a result in future documents he is addressed as Ronly Bonly Jones. Middle-class American ideology is as well represented in *Reader's Digest* humor as in the *Saturday Evening Post*'s** longer short fiction.

REAL SCREEN FUN

"Girls-Gags-Cartoons-Stories," "with Radio and Stage Fun," was the boast of this thirties Hollywood-oriented film humor magazine. Photo cuties and comic captions were mixed in with a substantial amount of paragraph humor in sections on "Radio Fun," "Screen Fun," "Movie Tattler," and similar sections featuring both jokes and undressed cuties. The 66-page, twenty-cent, 8½″ × 11½″ magazine was published monthly by Tilsam Publications of New York, although Louisville, Kentucky, and F. M. Lippincott are the names associated with the postal notice. Volume 1:1 was issued in August 1934 and Volume 4:4, the last copyrighted, in February 1938. "Keen Kracks" offered, "She's got the devil in her tonight." "Yeah, and it cost me ten dollars a quart."

RED PEPPER

Red Pepper claimed a printing of 100,000 for its fifth monthly number in November 1924. Harry A. Glynn was editor for the Red Pepper Publishing Company of Newark, New Jersey. At twenty-five cents a copy in 5½″ × 7½″ format, it brought forty-four pages of relatively sedate flapper-era humor to its readers, lightly sprinkled with photo pages of barely covered showgirls. Volume 1:1 (July 1924) through Volume 1:6 (December 1924) were copyrighted.

REEL HUMOR

"Gorgeous Girls! Gay Gags!—Jazz a song at twilight" was the offer of *Reel Humor*, a late 1930s magazine featuring Broadway charmers in burlesque costumes or stockings and lingerie. Volume 1:1 of the fifteen-cent bimonthly was issued in August 1937, and the last copyrighted was Volume 2:4 (July 1939). The editor was Frederick Gardener, and the publisher was A. A. Wyn in New York through Periodical House in Mount Morris, Illinois. Starlet photos were captioned "humorously": "I don't want you to wear my new silk stockings to the party." "Oh, don't worry. They'll be in good hands." or "Sometimes a girl is just like a third rail—dangerous when exposed." Two or three of the fifty pages of photo-gags were given over to show biz comic paragraphs by "The Keyhole Reporter."

THE ROLLER MONTHLY

The Roller Monthly, also calling itself the Khaki Kovered Book, was a magazine of "Breezy Stuff" at a dime per issue, or one dollar for a year, in a 5¼" × 7¾" format. It originated in Canton, Ohio, and praised the traditional virtues while burlesquing the rest. It featured plenty of poetry and homilies, as "Be wise at forty, a fool with speed is a food indeed," fitted to its slower era. The only number seen is for November-December 1918, which claimed its thirty-fourth year since 1885. T.B.C. Voges and A. Claus Shear were editors of it as a monthly for the Roller Printing and Paper Company.

ROMP

Romp was a 1960s "gags for stags" production of Humorama, Inc., the parent company for *Jest*,** *Gaze*,** *Comedy*,** *Gee-Whiz!*,** *Eye*,** *Snappy*,** *Joker*,** *Stare*,** *Laugh It Off!*, and *Breezy***—all sexually oriented humor digests. It was bimonthly at thirty-five cents and offered 102 pages (5½" × 7¼") of lush cutie cartoons on dating and lovemaking topics by Bill Ward, Bill Wenzel, Reamer Keller, and others, with a few pages of prose humor. Later, it added photos of cuties. The May 1961 issue and Number 36 for July 1966 have been seen.

THE ROUNDTABLE

The Roundtable has only been seen in its first issue dated 23 August 1819; it was put out by George Bickerstaffe and others of Hartford, Connecticut. It was intended to amuse and improve the public with satiric cuts and thrusts at vices, not persons, and the warning was given that jokes would be cracked. Productions were intended as Swiftian satire from a variety of pens. Travelers' observations on Hartford noted money-getting as its chief vice. The copy seen is at CtY.

ST. LOUIS LIFE

Measuring 9″ × 12″, *St. Louis Life* followed the format of the national *Life** published in New York. It combined regional, society-oriented material with *Life*-style illustrations and advertised the New York *Life*. The monthly sold at five cents a copy, and beginning in 1889, Mrs. S. V. Moore was the publisher. The first seen is Volume 1:10 for 15 February 1890. Later, W. D. Alexander was manager and publisher, followed by Ballard Turner as editor in 1892. The last issue seen is Volume 4:20 for 23 April 1892, all at DLC. Mott (4:65) chronicles further changes when Grace L. Davidson bought the magazine in 1896 and changed its name to *Criterion*.

SATIRE (1911)

Although the name *Satire* was taken by more than one magazine, Walter Pulitzer's weekly was the most notable, running from 20 September 1911 (Vol. 1:1) through 14 September 1912 (Vol. 5:4), copyrighted. *Satire*'s illustrated humor was supposed to shock snobs and snub shams. Its limited-color bold covers gave it a more modern appearance than the magazines of the 1900–1910 period, and its two- and three-column pages mixed college and post-collegiate humor. One cover opened Woodrow Wilson's head and showed a White House inside, and a later comment suggested that the insertion of a few corset ads would brisk up the *Congressional Record* wonderfully. Elsewhere, however, the tenor was deeper, with the last grisly cover a man drowning in quicksand while grasping at a wall marked with a dollar sign—harsh fare for a humor magazine that had featured a typical bathing beauty issue in August. Theatrical reviews, book reviews, a scattering of advertisements, and longer articles added to the mix, with a few memorable cartoons, such as trusts snakily swallowing people behind a Roosevelt bulldog growling for public appearance's sake.

SATIRE (1927)

The 1927 *Satire*—"The Funniest Book in the World," according to the subtitle of its editor Jack Dinsmore—a monthly from the Merit Publishing Company, of Cleveland, Ohio, was an 8″ × 11½″, thirty-four-page magazine featuring breezy, slangy humor burlesquing a variety of topics. "The Scarlet Sweater" has an old maid knitting a cover for her hot water bottle and thus almost getting locked into the Puritan alphabet soup by the kluck of a governor. A variety of full-page cartoons by Verschuuren, Herb., and one or two others gave a visual appearance consistent with the flapper era and its humor. Volume 1:1 (October 1926) through Volume 2:3 (January 1928) were copyrighted. Dinsmore and Merit also published *Secrets* and *Hot Dog*.**

SATURDAY EVENING POST

The *Saturday Evening Post* was a general rather than a humor magazine, dating from 1821, although it claims origination with Benjamin Franklin; it perished in the 1960s. It is significant to students of humor because of the editorship of George Horace Lorimer, which began in 1899, two years after Cyrus H. K. Curtis bought the magazine. Lorimer was a business-oriented humorist whose light letters of a self-made merchant drew attention under various titles including *Old Gorgon Graham* and *Letters of a Self-Made Merchant to His Son* around the turn of the century. He also recruited other writers and by the teens was publishing Ring Lardner, H. L. Wilson, P. G. Wodehouse, Irvin Cobb, and Montague Glass. In the thirties, "Tugboat Annie" was a popular favorite, and the cartoons from the forties and fifties were frequently reprinted as books; Ted Kay's "Hazel" ultimately achieved her own television show. Mott cites its whole-hearted devotion to material prosperity as its driving force, and its humor may be interpreted in that light as the humor of the complacent middle-class American. For further information, see Mott and John Tebbel's *George Horace Lorimer and the Saturday Evening Post* (Garden City, N.Y.: Doubleday, 1948).

SCRAPS

Scraps was an annual publication of cartoons by D. C. Johnston and ran from 1828 to 1834 and 1836, 1839, and 1848. It may not properly be a periodical, but Johnston's reputation as the American Cruickshank and the satirical power of the illustrations of social and city settings give *Scraps* interest in relation to comic periodical humor. The annuals were issued as an unbound portfolio, and the illustrated characters were given their own speeches in various situations.

See David Tatham, "D. C. Johnston's Pictorialization of Vernacular Humor in Jacksonian America," in *American Speech: 1600 to the Present*, the Dublin Seminar for New England Folklife 1983 Annual Proceedings, Volume 8 (Boston: Boston University, 1985), pp. 107–19.

SCREW

Overtly sexual, *Screw*, edited and published by Al Goldstein in New York, reached weekly Number 867 on 14 October 1985, and continues in publication at $1.50 per issue, 11″ × 13″ in newsprint paper, by Milky Way Productions of New York City. A 56-page tabloid devoted to sex and subtitled "The Sex Review," it exaggerates the typical tabloid exposé style of the 1960–1980 period. *Screw* advocates sexual intercourse but usually develops material through irony, satire, and self-satire; covers are frequently cartoons, and language is oriented toward slangy humor. One photo gag showed New York Mayor Ed Koch's notorious grinning face atop a male undergoing fellatio. "Smut from the Past" in the same issue featured nude pictures of long-dead models. Most readers will consider this journal pornographic, but its comic element is integral and worth study. Circulation for 1969 was listed as 100,000. Number 84 for 12 October 1970 is the first copyright listing.

SCREWBALL

Beginning in 1941, *Screwball* was published by Crestwood Publishing Company of Buffalo, New York, with editorial offices in New York City. The last seen, Volume 7:2 (January 1948), at twenty cents monthly, is in a digest format at 5½″ × 7¼″, offering mostly full- and half-page cartoons with a few one-liners and one or two crossword puzzles. Typical of the generally oriented humor is "Diamond mystery solved—heiress charged with snuggling," a reprint of a *New York Gazette* headline, although some of the humor is even less pointed.

SEA BREEZES

San Diego, California, offered *Sea Breezes* by a publishing company of the same name as a flapper-era joke magazine drawing from Western and Pacific fleet humor sources. Edited and owned by Carl Stanley Fish, it measured 7¾″ × 10¾″ and was sold monthly at twenty-five cents. Volume 3:5 appears to be the April 1927, "Pirate" number, showing a pretty Vampirate wielding a sword over her soldier and sailor galley slaves. Three-liners and joke paragraphs on contemporary social life predominate, with one or two melodramatic short stories per issue.

SERVICE SNICKERS

"Gags and Gals Galore," boasted this bimonthly by Magnum-Royal Publications, New York—publishers of *Dapper*, *Swank*, and *Sexplosion*. At fifty cents per copy, *Service Snickers* offered one hundred pages of bathing suit girlie photos and cartoons and jokes—"Beautiful Gals! Rib-tickling Laffs! Cartoon Giggles—A Jackpot of Breezy Humor." Service and sexually oriented jokes were more general than explicit. Volume 1:3 was published in January 1969, copyrighted, and Volume 1:10 appeared in April 1970. The magazine was digest size, 5½" × 7".

SEX TO SEXTY

Issues of *Sex to Sexty* claim it is a book, not a magazine. At first, beginning in about 1965, it was published quarterly (although a Vol. 1:1 for 1964 has been listed by one comic dealer). Number 9 is the last issue for 1967 at $1.25, 68 pages in 8½" × 11" two-column pages. It intersperses adult sexual cartoons and comic paragraphs—three of four cartoons and a variety of jokes to each page. Richard Rodman and Ken Idaho are listed as editors, published by the SRI Publishing Company, Fort Worth, Texas. By Volume 24 in 1973, six issues a year were offered with Rodman as editor, and by Volume 43, *Sex to Sexty* was a monthly; Number 170, 1983, sold at $2.95 an issue. It continues in the same format, although the sexual humor is somewhat more explicit and more oriented toward sexual organs than earlier issues of this adult sexual humor magazine. *Super Sex to Sexty*, 10" × 14", fifty pages, was also offered. Numbers 2 (March 1969) and 26 (1972) have been seen; they are bimonthly, claiming 300 cartoons and as many jokes on adult sexual themes.

SHAKESPEARE'S BONES

Adrian Hitt edited *Shakespeare's Bones* from New York in 1884 at ten cents a copy, in a 4¾" × 6⅞" format. Volume 1:2 for April 1884 is paged 63–98. This monthly was pro-Irish and opposed petticoat government, drink, and capital punishment. Woodcuts by Hitt punctuated doggerel verse on widespread contemporary social topics.

SHANTYTOWN NEWS

Appearing in 1944 (Vol. 1:1), *Shantytown News* was a 12" × 14", twenty-four page magazine that appeared in newspaper format and sold for fifteen cents. Published by K.R.K. publications, the publisher of *Flophouse News*,** it filled its tabloid pages with "100 Peppy Cartoons—Snappy Stories," and bits including

"Under the Bed," a rhyme in which a spinster catches a burglar under her bed and says that now that she's finally caught a man, he's going to be married or dead.

SH-H!

Sh-h!, "Secrets—Mysteries: No Blabberteurs" was a 64-page "Laffs with Army Navy Defense" humor digest sold bimonthly at ten cents a copy in a 5½″ × 7¼″ format. It was published along with its sister World War Two publications, *Eek!*, *G.R.R!*, and *Boo!*, all of which were issued bimonthly by Consolodated Magazines of New York, run by J. A. Ruby, with George Kapitan as editor. The editorial in Volume 1:2 for June 1942 warned against blabbing but said we'll laugh our boys to victory and the Japnastys to Hari-kiri. Girlie and uniform service jokes were the chief fare; one marine says to his well-endowed date, "I could demonstrate a frontal attack easier than I could describe it." At least three numbers were published; Volume 1:1 for April and Volume 1:2 for June were copyrighted.

SICK

Sick is a later follower of *Mad*,* issued first quarterly from Volume 1:1 (August 1960) and then eight times a year, at twenty-five cents in 8″ × 11″ comic magazine format with running comic stories, burlesques of ads, movie posters, and similar cultural artifacts to those which provided the content for *Mad*. Its run is at least through Number 137 by Feature Publications, Headline Publications, Crestwood, Hewfred, Pyramid, and finally Charlton—from Number 109 to Number 134 as the last—and some "Specials" interspersed with regular issues in the last six months of its life. *Annuals* appeared in 1969 through 1971.

Charlton's records show a peak of 110,000 copies sold for the August 1976 issue and sales plunging into the twenties and teens in 1979 and 1980. Joe Simon was editor through the Headline era, followed by Frank Roberge. Jack Sparling, sometimes spelled by George Wildman, was editor from the June 1977 issue, after which it moved more completely into television show burlesques. Television, movies, and contemporary life offered subjects for satire. The last *Sick Special*, with sales of only 13,187 copies, offered one of its best visuals, Rembrandt's Dutch Masters eyeing girlies' stockings. Issues are readily available through comic-book outlets.

SILK STOCKING STORIES

The fifteen-cent, 8″ × 11½″, thirty-six-page *Silk Stocking Stories* was a glamorously covered story publication by Ultem Publications, New York, featuring romance. Lingerie girlie shots and stories were leavened by "Sheer Nonsense"—"A girl can be as green as grass and still ripe for love"; "Garters hold a girl's stockings and a man's interest"—and boxed jokes among the stories; Volume 1:3 is dated January 1937. (This is on the borderline between titillation and humor.) *Handies Silk Stocking Review—New Jokes and Gags* has been noted as Number 2 for December 1936, and it may be related to *Silk Stocking Stories*.

SIS HOPKIN'S OWN BOOK AND MAGAZINE OF FUN

Sis Hopkins, as depicted by E. Flohri on her covers, was a folksy popular culture figure at the turn of the century who represented the crackerbarrel philosophy. However, she was clearly pointed toward a nostalgic and somewhat self-aggrandising middle-class audience by the Judge Publishing Company from Volume 1:1 (September 1899) through July 1911—as a bimonthly through May 1901, and then as a monthly. It was 8½″ × 11¼″, cost ten cents, and was printed on slick paper with high-quality illustrations. By 1903, *Sis Hopkin's* was claiming 1 million readers. *Sis Hopkin's Own Book* merged with the *Magazine of Fun*** in December 1906 (Vol. 7:77) and with *Judge's Library*** (No. 270) in September 1911. The three magazines were roughly identical throughout their runs, published by Judge, Leslie-Judge, and finally Leslie-Judd publications. *Magazine of Fun* became the top listing in August 1912, through Number 315 (June 1915). This lineage leads to *Film Fun*.*

Local farming and country figure types were the focus of cartoons and brief jokes in the early days. A pig-tailed Sis dominated most covers, and humor often employed dialect and dealt with early nineteenth-century neighborhood and country topics. Tramps, Negroes, dating and courting, and upper crust society provided butts, all mixed together as separate joke and cartoon and doggerel items from one up to six or eight items per page. A "below-cost sale" is called "another lie nailed" as it is tacked to a merchant's wall in one cartoon; another brief bit has a beau and his girl disparage marriage but decide they are exceptions since they are in such perfect sympathy. Inside cover ads touted pictures of Stanlaws "smartest" girls and Flagg beauties printed by the Judge Company.

Later in the run, starting in 1905, longer stories appeared with by-lines and an index. By 1909, longer signed items in a two-column format dominated; jokes became filler items or were grouped on joke pages. Norman H. Crowell's "Bill's Derby Winner" is a shaggy horse story in which Bill's nag finally wins by sticking out its eight-inch tongue at the finish line. A. B. Lewis contributed "Diary of a Summer Boarder" on summer vacationing experiences. Penrhyn Stanlaws's jaded post-Gibson Girl cartoons offer beauties mourning the fall of the year, only to be told by their stockbroker beaus that the fall of copper is even worse. Political and international jokes do not appear, and the mode of humor is a suburban precursor of Jazz Era cynicism: "Man is like a nail. When he's crooked, you may be sure he's been driven to it by a woman." Eugene Zimmerman, James Montgomery Flagg, J. K. Bangs, Art Young, and Otto Lang were prominent contributors.

SLAPSTICK

Volume 1:1 (February 1932) through at least Number 4 (May) was edited by Hugh Layne for the Red Band Publishing Company, Harold Hersey, President; M. J. Keiley was art editor. At fifteen cents a month, the magazine sported zebra-stripped covers and full-page jokes on 1930s Broadway and city-life themes, including convicts, police, bridge-players, and businessmen, but relatively little of courtship or sexual pursuit. In a forty-two page, 8½" × 11¾" size, it was almost wholly given over to full-page cartoons. *Slapstick* can be placed in the genre of magazines spawned by the success of *Ballyhoo.**

SMILES

Smiles, Number 1 (May 1942), issued by the Comic Corporation of America, New York, was a digest-sized quarterly featuring 132 pages of cartoons and jokes. After the war, it continued at twenty-five cents an issue, featuring more girlie and dating humor, with covers by Bill Wenzel and other drawers of lush cuties. Another *Smiles* may have started up in the Fall of 1953, beginning a new numbering system but still quarterly, switching to a larger format for a time. Number 71 was published in October 1975, as a bimonthly, and was the last seen. After the war Edward Murphy was editor for Band Leader Publications, Silver Spring, Maryland. *Smiles* also experimented in a modest way with short stories; all the later issues seen are in the 5¼" × 7½" format featuring single-page cartoons.

SMOKEHOUSE MONTHLY

"The Nit Wit Brother to Whiz Bang" was the Official Organ of the American Bar Flies, edited as a spinoff of *Captain Billy's Whiz Bang** by W. H. Billy Fawcett himself in Minneapolis. Originally, Fawcett published a book of poetry as *Smokehouse Poetry* for one dollar, dated 1 May 1920, including such doggerel as "The Ballad of Steam Beer" and about a hundred more poems. The magazine took up where the poetry book left off. It was dedicated to glorious guzzlers, woozy warblers, and other good people who still believe in the joy of living. From the beginning in February 1928, in *Whiz Bang* format but with a woodcut-styled cover and an emphasis on Hobo Ballads and sexy doggerel and cartoons of gold-diggers, *Smokehouse* sold for twenty-five cents. In the October 1928 number, Captain Billy claimed a circulation of 250,000. By 1930, it had colorful covers in the John Held, Jr., style but changed over to the size of *Ballyhoo*-Slapstick**-Hooey*** (the last being a sister publication). It charged fifteen cents by Volume 10:60 (December 1932) and listed "Popular Magazines" as the publisher. In both formats, *Smokehouse* adhered strictly to its formula of sexy, jazzy, somewhat breezy humor, doggerel, and cartoons. The last issue copyrighted is Volume 14:112 for April 1937.

SNAPPY

The original full-size *Snappy* was a sexy story magazine of the 1930s, its illustrated fun and fiction intended to be boldly seductive. However, the title returned on a digest-sized "Men's Gag Mag" which published Volume 5:31 in May 1959, as a bimonthly from Humorama, Inc., of New York for mankind and kind women. Any familiarity between any person or joker is a wonderful coincidence, its disclaimer offered. Panties, bare breasts, and stocking tops were featured in the photo pin-ups and the cartoons. Gags and stories were also included in the same sexy mode.

SNAPS

Snaps was a magazine of relatively long humorous prose stories with little or no comic illustration. Number 7 was published on 22 November 1899 and Number 70 on 6 February 1901. It sold for four or five cents weekly and $2.50 per year, and was published by Frank Tousey, New York. Mott thought that it might have succeeded Tousey's Comic Library. NN lists Number 23 as a holding.

SNICKER SNACKS

"A Monthly Pestilence of New-fangled Humor," *Snicker Snacks* was a 4¾″ × 6½″, fifty-page monthly, published in Oak Park, Illinois, by the Snicker Snackers, at twenty-five cents. Leigh Metcalfe was the editor. Humorous jokes and jokey prose dominated, with a few cartoons, a limerick contest for readers to fill in the last line, and pages designed to be torn out and placed in your auto window, such as "Danger! 10,000 Bolts!" Volume 2:6, the last seen, is dated October 1926; it seems to have lasted beyond 1926.

SO THIS IS PARIS MAGAZINE

Bathing-suited flappers and twenties-style cartoons and jokes filled the 68 pages of *So This is Paris* in the mid–1920s. "Gus the Editor" advised that "girls who kiss and run away, are safe to pet 'most any day," and "A soft drink turneth away company, and a pint to the wise is sufficient." The 6½″ × 9″ monthly cost twenty-five cents and was published by the Paris Publishing Company of Minneapolis. Since manuscripts were to go to Robbinsdale, Minnesota, this magazine can be identified with the Fawcett publications, although its bathing beauty photos and half-tints and its run of humor have a more sophisticated air than *Whiz Bang*** or *Smokehouse*.** It also featured a few burlesque short-short stories and a July Bathing Beauty number. "America's review of Art and Folly," Volume 1:1 appeared in March 1925; *Paris Magazine* by Fawcett, with name changes in the copyright listings to *So This Is Paris and Hollywood* lasted from October 1925 to December 1926. At about this time it may have been abandoned in favor of, or submerged in, an international movie review of Fawcett's *Paris and Hollywood* (1927), later *Paris and Hollywood Screen Secrets* (1927–1928), and variations on *Screen Secrets* thereafter.

SOMETHING

Something, edited by "Nemo Nobody, Esq.," a pen-name of James Fennell, was a satirical periodical issued in Boston during the six-month period beginning on 18 November 1809 and ending on 12 May 1810. Offering a moralistic viewpoint, this publication covered topics involving manners, moral and religious issues, and marriage. It typically included essays, reviews, poems, and a section that solicited readers' questions on diverse subjects. Numbers 1 through 7 (18 November 1809–30 December 1809) and Numbers 8 through 26 (6 January 1810–12 May 1810) are available on University Microfilm prepared from the DLC copy. This periodical may also be examined at CSt, ICU, MH, NN, MBat, and ten other libraries.

Barbara McMillin

SPECTACLES

Only eleven numbers of the comic periodical *Spectacles* were published, the first issued on 6 June 1807 and the last on 18 July 1807. Edited by Joseph Harmer, this Baltimore-based weekly sold for two dollars per annum. Its four pages were filled with poems, letters, riddles, romances, marriage announcements, editorial comments, and fashion reviews. Only Numbers 5, 6, and 11 of this single-volume publication are available on University Microfilm. These numbers are in the possession of MWA.

The first issue of *Spectacles* contained a letter to "Mr. Spectacles" from one Theophilus Rusty on the subject of the ill treatment of bachelors. Similar exaggerated grievances and tirades on trivial topics accounted for much of the humor found in this small comic magazine. Representing the best of these articles is a playful notice in the June 13 number for the arrest of one "Barber-ian" who had "disordered the heads" of many well-meaning citizens. Had *Spectacles* endured, it might have contributed much to our knowledge of early nineteenth-century urban humor.

Barbara McMillin

THE SPICE BOX

The Spice Box (Vol. 1:1, August 1926, 5" × 7¼", fifteen cents monthly), was edited and published by Edward H. Austin at Rockland, Massachusetts. Its twenty-eight pages were filled with short quips and jokes with a vaguely Yankee air and generally forced quality.

SPICY FUN

Spicy Fun, subtitled "Gags and Gals Galore," published in a 5¼" × 7" format at thirty-five cents quarterly by Health Knowledge of New York, was another of the 1960s adult sexy humor magazines with "Busty pin-ups!" and cartoons on adult themes. Number 7 is dated Winter 1969.

SPICY STORIES

In 1932, *Spicy Stories* by King Publishing offered humorous sexy stories with twists and some pages of dating jokes. By 1933, Merwil Publishing Company had eliminated the humor and heated up the spice. From New York in an 8" × 11" format at twenty-five cents monthly, King's January 1932 number is given as Volume 7:2, but Merwil's August 1933 number is given as Volume 3:8; Volumes 3:9 (September 1933) through 4:1 (January 1934) were copyrighted.

THE SPY

Under the full title *The Spy in Philadelphia and the Spirit of the Age*, William Hill and Company started this weekly with Volume 1:1 on 6 July 1833, in a four-column 11" × 16" newspaper format. The ailing Hill was replaced by W. C. Armstrong and Company (who later gave Joseph C. Neal his start in Philadelphia) on 7 September, claiming at that time 1,700 subscribers and listing a hundred agents. Blackwood and Company appears to have published the last issue, Volume 1:26, on 28 December 1833. It censured the vices of the time and argued for purity in politics, "holding the court of Momus" through columns of humorous paragraphs and fillers among a wide spectrum of literary material. It sold for two dollars annually.

In the last number a skeptical American traveler, who denigrates a dirty phial, is told that it contains the darkness Moses spread over Egypt—one of the earliest models for the American vandal and innocent abroad. Elsewhere some comic poetry was offered. A number of pieces including American dialects appeared: travelers' comic anecdotes, a Kentucky tall tale in the 7 September issue, and some city stories such as the "Philadelphia Militia System" in the 10 August number. One of the best stories in the August issue is "Saratoga Springs," in which a resourceful Miss Simper outwits the sharper who married her in a burlesque of humor stories about marrying for money. *The Spy* holds a modest place in the distinguished run of humor periodicals in Philadelphia.

SQUADS RIOT

A World War II magazine in 8½″ × 11″ format, 68 pages, at twenty-five cents quarterly, *Squads Riot* from the Country Press, Greenwich, Connecticut, was a "military mirthquake" with jokes, cartoons, and some "he-man" stories. Humor was along the sexy service line of the early 1940s. Some issues do not carry publication data, but issues from 1941 through at least May 1943 have been identified. James Thurber appeared among the writers, and covers featured James Trembath's cartoons, along with Ben Roth, Mel Casson, and Robert Pilgrim cartoons inside. Number 5 is dated 16 September 1942, and Number 6, 1 January 1943 with Rod Reed as editor and Carlton Brown as associate editor. One of the more imaginative covers uses a comic cut-out to show a naked body, which turns out to be a goat on the inner page. Volume 2:7 for 3 March 1943 is the only copyright.

STAG

Stag billed itself as the man's home companion, featuring prose by F.P.A., Robert Benchley, Jack Benny, plenty of girlie cartoons, a center double-page girlie cartoon by Peter Driben in the format later developed by *Esquire*** and *Playboy*, and jokes and adventure stories. A 10″ × 14″ tabloid, it was flashy and smart rather than crude, selling at twenty-five cents monthly, published by Martin Goodman from Dunellen, New Jersey, with Joe Lesly as editor and Mel Barry as art director. Volume 1:3 is dated February 1942, and Volume 1:4 for May 1942 was copyrighted.

STAND

Seven numbers of this periodical were published, the first being issued on 21 December 1819 and the last on 14 August 1820. Strangely enough, the number issued on the former date reads "Second Edition." Published by a Hartford, Connecticut, society known as the "invincibles," a group of young men opposed to chivalry and the superiority of the "fair sex," *Stand* contained poetry and satirical essays that criticized the follies of both men and women. All numbers except six are available on University Microfilm prepared from the copy housed at MBat. One other source is known. Preliminary pages, tables of contents, and indexes are lacking, and only the final issue boasts a title page.

Barbara McMillin

STARE

Stare was digest-sized, 5½" × 7¼", and cost thirty-five cents. It is typical of the gals and gags format of Humorama, publisher of the Volume 5:26 (October 1957) number and Timely Features, Inc., which published the Volume 12:90 (February 1970) number. Nude girls predominated over the cartoons and over the articles with titles like "Smatter of Tact!," "Giggles and Wiggles!," and "Bo-ing Went the Strings of My Bra!" Issues ran one hundred pages. A typical cartoon has a luscious cutie in a bathrobe welcoming her plumber with "I don't know what the trouble is; one minute I'm running hot and then suddenly I'm running cold!" The numbering suggests a switch from quarterly to bimonthly in about October 1958, but this is not yet confirmed.

STOP! MAGAZINE

Stop! is a slick counter-culture burlesque of 1980s American culture. Number 8 was published in 1983 at $1.95 for forty-eight pages; J. D. King is listed as editor-in-chief. Most of the contents of the issue seen are given to a parody of sex and scandal magazines and a take-off of "All My Children" titled "All My Dead Children." Although Stop Publications of New York is listed as publisher, Independent Publications of Chicago advertised burlesque calendars—with dates for events like the first auto accident—along with counter-culture magazines including *Fabulous Furry Freak Brothers*, and books by Art Spiegelman, R. Crumb and other illustrators involved in the modern comix graphics movement. John Holmstrom's anti-artistic cartoon style dominates both the style and content of the issue seen.

STRICTLY STAG

Monarch Publishing Company of New York offered this 5¼" × 7" quarterly beginning in 1947. This one-hundred-page pulp digest presented humorous stories, cartoons, and gags, with a few pin-ups thrown in at the end among the ads for sexy joke books. Adult humor here showed post-collegiate sophistication with Robert Benchley, Ted Key, and Thomas Hardy—"The Ruined Maid" in Volume 1:2—among others, and some reprints from *Life*,* *Judge*,* and elsewhere. Volume 1:2 was copyrighted in October 1947.

THE SUNDAY COMIC WEEKLY/THE SUNDAY WORLD

The Sunday Comic Weekly, the *New York Sunday World*'s comic supplement, began in about 1894. Garish, heavily illustrated, and popularly oriented, it boldly provided its humor from all sources, borrowing cartoons from continental sources, *Puck*,* and providing its own full-page renderings of the masquerades in Hogan's Alley, featuring Richard Outcault's pug-nosed, slummy "Yellow Kid," as the other side of the cartoon pages showing Wall Street bankers trying to steal away the national treasury. Four of its eight pages, including the yellow-colored Yellow Kid himself, were in color.

The Comic Weekly had a circulation of 600,000, which it proclaimed "The Greatest Circulation on Earth," in circus-style letters on the front of its eight-page sections, as early as 1896. Joseph Pulitzer copyrighted it as the "Press Publishing Co." in New York. In content, it married the sensational to wage-earner attitudes. One cartoon claimed not to be able to tell the difference between a woolly haired "Harvard Yalepen" and a fuzzy haired anarchist, and most humor on economic issues was similarly oriented toward the lower-middle-class viewpoint. The Children's Corner was conducted by "Uncle Tommyrot," and farmboys from Ridgefield, New Jersey, were the stuff of which New York "mashers" were made in new dandy dress.

When William Randolph Hearst took over the *New York Journal* to contest the New York and national newspaper market with Joseph Pulitzer and the *World*, he hired away the entire staff of the *Sunday World*, in order to start his own Sunday humor section, *The American Humorist*. (For Frank Luther Mott's informative account in *American Journalism* see Selective Bibliography.) Richard Outcault, the originator of the Yellow Kid, went with Hearst, but George Luks began to draw the same figure for the *World*, offering New York two Yellow Kids as the phenomenon of 1896. By 1898, Mott notes that Hearst's circulation for *The American Humorist* had also 176sed 600,000.

SUNNY SOUTH

DLC and GA hold various early issues. See UNCLE REMUS'S MAGAZINE.

SUPER SEX TO SEXTY. See SEX TO SEXTY.

SWINGLE

Swingle, published quarterly by Magnum-Royal Publications, New York, at 75 cents an issue with a $7\frac{1}{2}'' \times 11''$ magazine format, offered adult sexual humor and half-nude pin-ups: a boy on a beach looks at a cutie's body and exclaims, "Wow! Have you ever got the mumps!" Other jokes were of comparable quality.

November 1969 was Volume 16:1. Number 202 was copyrighted in April 1970. The same name was copyrighted as a bimonthly with Volume 2:3 (May 1971) using a more modern interpretation and orientation of swinging than the earlier one.

THIS WEEK

This Week, subtitled "An Editor's Table," was edited by A.J.H. Duganne, who had been a writer of humorous and sentimental stories for *The Knickerbocker*.* It ran from 3 October 1868 (Vol. 1:1) through 7 November 1868 (Vol. 1:6); it was twelve pages long, 11″ × 20″, cost ten cents, and was published in New York. Despite Duganne's authorship of "The Fastest Funeral on Record" and "The Quod Papers," *This Week* was more closely allied to his sentimental romances. It intended to attack the age of cant, but there is little discernible humor. The copy seen is at DLC.

THISTLETON'S ILLUSTRATED JOLLY GIANT

San Francisco of the 1870s offered local and regional readers sarcastic humor in the form of gross and disgusting portraits of local figures, acerbic attention to "Bible Pounders" in starched frocks, and round-house attacks on the Irish savages and their priests arrayed against American freedom and unity. Publisher and proprietor Colonel George Thistleton stridently attacked papist invaders, and Tom Flynn's letters to the "Iditor" boasted, "Wance put God in the Constitution, an' the rest follows as natural an' aisy as atin' potatoes. The people will niver detict the trick": the Pope will take over as easily as changing a dissolving lantern slide.

The 4 July 1874 number (Vol. 3:1) described how the *Giant* grew to its present size—a twelve page, 9″ × 11½″, three-column weekly—from a "modest little handbill." Thistleton claimed that his subscriptions were increasing by 500 weekly. He described the journal as a newspaper rather than a magazine, and so it maintained a newspaper appearance. The cover sported a bristly Popeye head—the critical giant himself—and a half-page cartoon. Local political issues were taken up with acrid humor, and most vice was attached to Catholics and the Roman Catholic Church. One notable two-page cartoon shows Liberty weeping as a boatload of Papal infallibility lands on U.S. shores with the aid of General Sherman.

The periodical was issued bimonthly from February 1873 (Vol. 1:1) through August 1873; semi-monthly from September 1873 through 1 January 1874; and weekly from 17 January 1874 through 8 March 1880 (Vol. 12:9). The per issue price was ten cents. DLC has a lengthy broken run. CSt lists Volume 5, and NN lists Volume 8.

TICKLE-ME-TOO

A knockoff of *Ballyhoo*,* *Tickle-Me-Too* (Vol. 1:1, December 1931), in the same format, offered a whirl of American subjects at fifteen cents a ride. Whereas *Ballyhoo* was all burlesque, the self-help and breast-development ads in this magazine were for real. The December 1931 cover featured a woman shaving her armpit—other humor was much at the same level. Merry-go-round, Inc., in New York, published it, with Harold Hersey as president and barker. Some Depression humor was included in the cartoons and captioned photos: it contained forty-four pages in an 8½" × 11½" format. No other issues have been seen.

TICKLES

Modern Sports Publishing Company of New York published this 6½" × 9½", 66-page collection of jokes in magazine format in 1931. It does not seem to have been a periodical.

TID-BITS

*French Humor*** became *Tid-Bits* in 1928; for more information, see *French Humor*.

TITTER

Titter provided 60 pages of pulp-paper slapstick photo humor sequences and mild pin-ups in bathing suits and lingerie, along with funny essays like "Are You a Character?" and one or two varied articles. The 8½" × 11½" bimonthly sold at twenty-five cents a copy and was edited by Roy Harmon. Volume 7:2 was dated October 1950. In its earlier days it was one of the oversized Second World War magazines offering gals, giggles, and gags.

TNT

TNT (Vol. 1:1, March 1941), published by Cinema Comics in New York, was one of the tabloid-size humor magazines of the World War II era, measuring 10½" × 13" and thirty-two pages. It sold for ten cents per issue and listed only Eric Godal as art editor. It offered a variety of cartoons in a variety of styles, covering contemporary issues and international politics as well as the American political scene generally. Cultural and political personalities were burlesqued in *TNT*'s dedication to harassing sacred cows: "the snobs, the agents of oppression, the disseminators of political poisons" and other fun-banishers of the world. Burlesques of exposé-magazine writing also figured prominently in the spread of prose humor.

TODAY'S HUMOR

Today's Humor, combined with its sister Chicago publication *Snicker Snacks*,** was a digest, 4½" × 6½" in size, selling for twenty-five cents monthly. Leigh Metcalfe was the editor for Snicker Snackers, Inc., of Oak Park, Illinois. Humorous essays with some line-drawing cartoons provided its "monthly pestilence of new-fangled comedy" of a gentler gay twenties sort. *Today's Humor*, Volume 3:1, was dated November 1926, at which time it advertised "combined with *Snicker Snacks*" on its cover; *Snicker Snacks*, Volume 2:3, appeared in July 1926. For another appearance of this title, see Copyright List.

TOKYO PUCK

One of the most fantastic offshoots of American comic periodical publishing is the *Tokyo Puck*, published by The Yuraku Sha—a Tokyo Publisher—in Tokyo, Japan. It boldly followed the format of *Puck*,* but it was a Japanese propaganda magazine. The Atsumido Watanabe Press in Japan was the printer, with Kitazawa Racten, editor; the price was thirteen sen a copy, with issues on the first and twentieth of the month. A supplement, *Zieroku Puck*, was available on the tenth of the month. The publication measured 10½" × 14". As brightly colored as its inspiration, *Tokyo Puck* offered a double centerfold cartoon on political themes, and a variety of single cartoons and action strips. All of them were in Japanese, but many had English subtitles, and virtually all were on the theme of American corruption and abuse aimed at the Japanese, either through Pacific expansion or continental violence toward Japanese immigrants.

In politics, *Tokyo Puck* was anti-Yankee and identified Japan and Germany as peace bringers. One historical joke goes, "A lie, declared the American, never passed George Washington's lips. / The Englishman retorted with a sneer: I suppose he talked thru his nose, like the rest of you Yankees." The centerfold shows Dr. Puck at the Peace Conference at the Hague on "The Limitation of the Powers' Armaments" presenting the idea that each country send an individual rather than an army to end disputes: the cartoon shows two mounted Samurai ready to do battle. On the front page of one issue, a worried William Howard Taft feels the pulse of Miss Rising Sun before hurrying home from the Philippines. Crude caricatures of C. D. Gibson cartoons have a lady preparing to shoot a Japanese because she caught a cold from him; another lady has her seat changed in a theater so as not to be next to a Japanese gentleman. A cartoon of Teddy Roosevelt slapping a dog asks, "Ought we to forever trust our neighbors and pocket insults?"; another suggests sending a warship to blow up "Frisco." Many others deal with anti-Japanese violence in the San Francisco affair. Internal text suggests the issue seen is 1908–1909; Volume 3:17 is the only one identified by volume and issue number.

TOUCHSTONE

Sherwin Cody, a Chicago English teacher and proprietor of the Old Greek Press, published five monthly numbers of this 6″ × 9″ little magazine from January through May 1906, sixteen pages each, at five cents a number. He offered the "little joker of the magazines" as America's best high-class humor periodical, with lampoons, parodies, and satires on nonpolitical subjects by Bert Lester Taylor. Sexual mores and courtship practices were burlesqued along with literature and the classics, such as "Jack Liverpool's" "evaporated" novel *The Game* as a burlesque of Jack London. It is a slight, marginally clever, regional offering.

TOWN CRIER

The *Town Crier* was a *New Yorker** copy bent on "relieving the tedium of Philadelphia." The 14 March 1930 number at fifteen cents, 9″ × 12″, was Volume 1:6 of this weekly. Justin Herman was the editor, and the humor followed predictable lines and format, except that Philadelphia life replaced New York as the orbit of interest.

TRASH

Trash, "All the Junk Unfit to Print," was a *Mad**-styled humor magazine, bimonthly, with Volume 1:2 appearing in June 1978 and selling for 60 cents, by Trash Publishing Company, New York. Slightly smoother illustrations and a less pointed sense of satire characterized its 52-page issues.

TV GIRLS AND GAGS

From July 1954, *TV Girls and Gags* offered television-oriented dating jokes at fifteen cents an issue in a digest-size, one-joke per page format (4″ × 6″). R. E. Damon of Atlanta seems to have started it, with Bruce Elliot editing at least in 1956. By 1957, Sports Report, Inc., had taken over publication from Pocket

Magazines, and pin-ups and a few jokes appeared with the full-page cartoons. Humor continued to be innocuously sex-oriented in this format into the 1960s, published by Magazine Management Corporation at the same address throughout the period, although the number of pin-ups and stag film ads gradually increased. The last issue seen is Volume 7:1 (January 1961), selling at twenty-five cents.

$$\underline{\qquad} \; U \; \underline{\qquad}$$

UNCLE SAM (1879)

Uncle Sam; The American Journal of Wit and Humor was a weekly lasting for eleven numbers from 12 April 1879 through 21 June 1879; it was issued by the Uncle Sam Publishing Company of New York in a 9″ × 12″, two-column format for ten cents. Twelve pages of content and two pages of ads made up the typical issue, with two or three full-page cartoons. On 10 May it claimed a million readers, and on 17 May it announced that it would become a monthly for the Summer with Number 12 on 15 July, but instead it disappeared. The DLC Rare Book Room has a copy.

Uncle Sam's content was oriented toward the amusing side of national life, with substantial borrowings from foreign exchanges. Congress, modern philanthropy, and landladies came in for equal licks. One full-page cartoon shows Justice preventing a policeman from beating a crowd—a Manhattan topic that remains current. "Uncle Remus's Political Theories," more interested in a smokehouse than a fight, were reprinted from the *Atlanta Constitution*. The 17 May cover cartoon responded to the Vicksburg Convention by showing a "hard leak to stop" from a splitting barrel (Immigration)—"500,000 Chinamen to fill the place of the ungrateful nigger!"—a slap at the demand for cheap labor and black subservience. "Sheer nonsense," a back page of one-liners from the exchanges, finished each issue.

UNCLE SAM (1894)

Chicago's *Uncle Sam* was a subscription-only monthly which published Volume 1:1–12 from June 1894 through May 1895, announcing at that time a semi-monthly publication that has not been seen and might not have appeared. This *Uncle Sam* was for Americans, by Americans, and adhered violently to the proposition that American institutions must be protected from foreign immigrants and the Pope. The same publishing group, including James W. Scott, James Butler, and Dwight Baldwin as editor, was responsible for *Coin's Financial School*. *Uncle Sam* was brightly illustrated in color, and the first cover set the tone by showing Uncle Sam holding a gun on Chinamen and thugs who want to destroy the schoolhouse, which is viewed as a preserver of the American way of life.

The American Protective Association provided the strong anti-Catholic impulse for *Uncle Sam*, claiming that it would be to Americans what *Judge** was to the Republicans and what *Puck** was to the Democrats. In 10" × 13", sixteen-page format it aped the appearance of its two models. Each issue offered two colored cartoons and a two-page color center spread by C. DeCrimm on "Issues of the Day." One cartoon showed the Pope stuffing a ballot box, leading Irishmen on a neck-chain; another showed the Tammany tiger skin draped over a gaunt Chicago wolf—noting the Chicago "machine" was in the progress of construction. A few pithy paragraphs on the American self-protection movement and some socialite cartoons and jokes appeared, along with strong editorials attacking the intertwining of church and state. The copy seen is at DLC.

UP TO DATE

Up to Date, subtitled "Everybody's Magazine," was another Chicago rival to *Life** and *Judge** in the 1890s. It was twenty-four pages, 8½" × 11", in two-column format. It published every other Saturday, beginning in 1895: the first issue held by the Library of Congress is Volume 3:1 for 7 February 1896. John Mahon is listed as managing editor of the early numbers; the Will H. Dilg Publishing Company published it, with Alvah Milton Kerr as editor in 1896; Kerr's name disappeared when the Barrett Publishing Company took it over in 1896 and cheapened both the paper and the style. It sold for five cents, or one dollar per year.

Up to Date reprinted many jokes and quips, with credit to other sources, and offered family humor with a modest degree of political comment and less sex orientation than the flirtatious *Vim,** Wit and Wisdom,*** and some of the other colored comics of the era. Of the German-American trade war, it mused that the government's policies on pork were a striking example of pigheadedness. When Mrs. Lillypad says, "As a wife—I want to be loved," Miss Tartline responds, "By whom, for instance?" Ellis Parker Butler offered columns; cartoons covered Atlantic cruises and local bars with equal interest. Editorials attacked Charles Yerkes, Wolf Wyler the Cuban beast, and the Department Store Trusts. Humor toyed with society, infidelity, and the Jingo Quickstep as practiced in the Caribbean. One of the publication's most impressive double center-page political cartoons shows William Jennings Bryan rushing to save American producers from the knife of monopoly wielded by William McKinley and Mark Hanna.

In April 1897, in cheaper format, *Up to Date* added photographs of pretty actresses from the stage and a "Woman's Corner" column by a big-lipped Negro "Miss I. McComin Honey." Illustrations included Mikesell's tramps, C. L. Emmons's Gibson Girl lookalikes, and Jos. P. Birren's colorful pretty girls for front covers; Otto Lang drew the back cover. Domestic comedy and dramas and satires of middle-class life were more notable; the Cuban War—which became the subject of a number of dramatic covers—and local Chicago ward politics were treated in columns and cartoons. Some stiff humorous reportage was even offered from Alaska in 1898 in a "Fresh from the Klondike" series. The last number seen is Volume 7:12 for 18 June 1898.

V

THE VERDICT

The Verdict, Volumes 1–4 (19 December 1898 through 12 November 1900), was published by the Verdict Publishing Company, O.H.P. Belmont, President. The editor was A. H. Lewis, sometimes known as "Dan Quin," who published his "Wolfville Stories" as part of *The Verdict*'s fiction offerings. It was twenty-four pages and was priced at ten cents weekly. *Verdict* offered some harsh satire, but was more political, social, and fiction-oriented than humorous or comic. DLC has a complete run, and MH, NN and three other libraries list holdings; MWA holdings were discarded.

THE VERMONT GRAPHIC

The Vermont Graphic was an illustrated weekly that provided a local takeoff on *Life** for a single year of 53 issues from 13 April 1895 through 11 April 1896. David A. Rowe was editor in Burlington, Vermont. Twenty-page issues sold for five cents a copy, with a double plate between pages 8 and 13 and a large number of local advertisements. It planned to "amuse and entertain by comic cuts and witty words, short paragraphs and copious illustrations related to Vermont." As time went on, one-liners became more prominent. Its "scintillating foolings" were thought to silence foreigners and to make sensible Vermonters even more grave as it covered local and state issues—including the funny men and comic cultists of the Vermont desert—but maintained some awareness of New York and Europe. Its normal circulation was around 750, reaching 3,000 in some weeks; it died "anemic but solvent" when it sold out to the News Publishing Company. Centercuts were provided by C. D. Gibson and Howard Cort, among others, and it offered a range of 1890s cartoons. DLC has a complete run.

THE VILLAGE FIREFLY

The Village Firefly has some importance as a transitional humor publication of the 1830 period, looking forward to the pre-Civil War era as much as backward to the Federalist period. It was published weekly in Taunton, Massachusetts, by Thomas Prince at fifty cents yearly; Volume 1:1 was dated 28 March 1831, and the last seen is Volume 1:52 for 15 April 1832. Always on cheap paper, it was terribly printed toward the end of its year. It flatly proclaimed that it intended to amuse rather than instruct, under the legend "Laugh and be fat," which provided the banner for many English and American humorous works.

Firefly jumbled short and long prose items, humor and verse together. The first page often reprinted comic dialect pieces, such as "Grand Review" from the Boston *Galaxy*, a burlesque military drill description. Detailed descriptions of locals were also notable, with jokes on jolly tars and "darkies" as well. Dialect letters, jestbook jokes, and anecdotes finished the mix. When a Louisiana gent offers to duel anyone with their own weapons, a tar comes forward with a pump-break. In the 31 October number, Yankee dialect appeared in "Enoch's Bargain"; "Jonathan's Trip on the Railroad" commented in Down East dialect, "I've seen oceans o' strange things in my time, Joe, I tell you; but let me be trod to a pancake in deacon Lames' hogen, if I ever saw nothing like a railroad.— Didn't we streak it?" The plain-language, un-Addisonian, light humor was typical: of disguise parties *Firefly* wrote, "Go sober, for once in your life, and I shall undertake that not one of your friends will know you." When it ended its run, *Firefly* claimed that its subscriptions were paying, but other reasons forced an end to it. The copy seen is at DLC; MWA also lists a holding.

VIM

The 1898 *Vim* was as full of vigor as its title suggested, claiming to be "better, brighter, and more aggressive" than all the other colored weekly humor journals of its era. Not only did it accuse *Judge** of copying its cartoons, but it also took on the vampire department stores and monopolistic street railways of New York and Tammany, bossism, and Crokerism in the City. For its vigorous political positions, it claimed to have been banned for sale on stands of the Manhattan Railroad, and this was probably the case. Although it attacked yellow journalism, it splashed more actual yellow coloring through its garish cartoons by Leon Barritt than any other of the colored weeklies. It enthusiastically chronicled and cartooned the great naval victories of the Spanish-American War, which it energetically supported as an "independent" weekly.

Twenty pages, with fourteen in black and white and six in color, *Vim* was tailored to jingo tastes and politics. Some socialite and social topics were mixed with comic poems and brief jokes, but it boasted that it was a fighter for the right and wouldn't stand meekly by with no position. Its political cartoons fulfilled that claim: 100,000 was stated as the sales figure for the first issue on 22 June

1898, at five cents—half the price of the competing weeklies—measuring 8½″ × 11″. The Vim Publishing Company of New York was run by H. Wimmel, who had been *Puck*'s* secretary and manager for twenty-two years; Roy L. McCardell, also from *Puck*, served as editor. On 10 August it claimed sales of 70,000. It tried to boost its appeal with artistic nudes gazing at water lillies and with similar subjects. The last seen is 24 August 1898 at DLC. Five other libraries list broken runs.

W

WACKO

Wacko, a quarterly comic-format journal oriented toward teens, was a *Mad**-type comic book. Volume 1:3 was dated October 1981 by the Ideal Publishing Company; John Krach and Paul Laikin were editors. It offered satire on Ronald Reagan, magazine covers, Shakespearean language, and similar targets in its 86-page, 8″ × 11″ format. It sold for $1.75.

WAR LAFFS

War Laffs was a tabloid-size World War II journal featuring "hundreds of army jokes," humor photo sequences, cartoons, and plenty of pin-ups. It was published as a quarterly in 1943 by Blue Swords, Inc., and then bimonthly by Volitant Publishing Company, New York, for twenty-five cents, in 10¼″ × 13½″ size, 70 pages. Subtitled "Fun for Fighting Men," *War Laffs* revised standard jokes into service format: The first soldier asks if that's a new girl and the second soldier says, "No! Just the old one repainted." Cartoon and pin-up captions were similar. Issues have been seen for 1943 and 1944.

(San Francisco) WASP

The San Francisco *Wasp* stung with Ambrose Bierce's venom in the 1880s and stands from its first issue on 5 August 1876 as one of the earliest and most important printers of bold satiric political cartoons. The Korbel Brothers of San Francisco, first printers and later vintners, founded the magazine as a satiric corrective of California politics, and George Mackrett, its first editor, gathered a stinging mix of cartoons, political commentary, and literature. The Korbels sold the journal in 1881 and Ambrose Bierce became editor. E. C. Macfarlane

& Co. were listed on the masthead as publishers and proprietors; The Wasp Publishing Company, owned by John P. Jackson, took over the publication in 1885 and Bierce soon departed, and with him much of the sardonic humor of the paper. By the late 1890s, humor had largely disappeared and the bold color lithographs which had given the front, back, and two center pages striking political force on the West Coast faded to black and white; they disappeared altogether by the turn of the century. The *Wasp* itself lasted to 25 April 1941, but it had long since ceased to be of interest to students of American humor. The *Wasp* was a weekly at ten cents, or five dollars for the year, during Bierce's editorship. Mott estimates circulation at 14,000–18,000 in its heyday. Copies seen from the middle 1880s are at DLC, and a number of libraries have holdings although it is not cited in the Union List consulted. Bruce L. Johnson has published an excellent essay on the *Wasp* in Edward Chielens, *American Literary Magazines* (Westport, Conn.: Greenwood Press, 1986), pp. 433–37.

At 10″ × 14″, the *Wasp* made a dramatic presence in the 1880s with its boldly colored front and back page cartoons. The two center pages of the 14-page journal were also taken up by a single large political cartoon. G. Frederick Keller was the primary cartoonist during the 1870s and until his death in 1883, and his boldness rivals Thomas Nast's; his targets, however, are somewhat more generalized and thus not quite as forceful politically or emotionally as Nast's attacks on secession, Tammany, and Tweed. In three-column format, the prose of the *Wasp* was molded by Ambrose "Bitter" Bierce from 1881 through early 1886; editorials, comment on local and national matters, and poetry reflect his irony. *The Devil's Dictionary* first appeared as bits and pieces to fill out columns, and even clips from other papers are shaped by Bierce's chilling wit. Volume 9:327 (4 November 1882) burlesqued "Maud Miller," after Whittier's poem: Maud Levy escapes marriage to a "High Tycoon" by returning to her fiancée the dry-goods clerk—the realistic poem has the young Mrs. Blumenthal shuddering when she thinks what might have been if she had married a rich but repulsive old man. Several pages of Volume 16:495 (23 January 1886) have been reprinted in Franklin Walker's *The Wickedest Man in San Francisco* (San Francisco: Colt Press, 1941). Bierce attacks Mark Twain as softening into "Mark the money-worm" and Frank Pixley of the *Argonaut* is pilloried as a manipulator of anti-Chinese sentiment—among other things—exploiting "the incendiary goose which dropped so many eggs into Mr. Pixley's till." The *Wasp* was never as strong after Bierce's departure.

THE WEEKLY VISITANT

Salem, Massachusetts's *The Weekly Visitant* published 52 weekly numbers from 1 January 1806 through 27 December 1806 at two dollars a year. Eight pages long, printed and published by Haven Pool, it offered elevated discourse to improve humankind in a pleasant semi-formal style. Pool's regular page of light articles offered humorous material in plain language, often reprinting English and American sources as well as original items, including Joseph Dennie's Lay Preacher from *The Port Folio*.* In "Flimflams" (31 May 1806), the author's uncle is described as an experimentalist who puts pants on frogs and hatches eggs by putting them between the housemaid's breasts. RPB, MWA, and MBat hold volumes, and it is reprinted in University Microfilms.

WEIRDO

Weirdo is one of the counter-culture comix from California during the early 1980s. R. Crumb is the dominant cartoonist, with various stories caricaturing straight culture fiction. There is a fairly heavy sexual content. The publisher is Last Gasp Eco-Funnies, Berkeley, California; Number 4 is dated Winter, 1981–1982, indicating quarterly publication. The periodical measured 8¼″ × 10¾″, cost $2.25 per issue, and had an initial printing of 10,000. The first issue was published in March 1981. For more information, see Kennedy, *Official Underground and Newave Comix Price Guide*.

WESTBROOK'S FUN BOOK

Westbrook's Fun Book (thirty-two pages, 8″ × 10½″, ten cents) was a monthly magazine of humor published by the Arthur Westbrook Company of Cleveland, Ohio, in the 1910s. It devoted each issue to a loose theme—summertime, ginger snaps, the fire department. An old maid suffragette carries a sign in one cartoon that proclaims the human being to be nature's sole mistake. Other gags deal with wife-husband jokes about money, dating, village humor, or suburban jokes. One cutie flapper in a full-page cartoon says she wants to meet her step-papa in public at the train station after her show so he won't want to kiss her. Tootsie the *Fun Book*'s steno started a column of advice, such as don't eat peanuts at the opera. Illustrations were relatively crude, but much along the lines established by *Life*.* In the summer, photos of starlets began appearing. Volume 1:1 (November 1908) through Volume 1:10 (August 1909) have been seen at DLC.

   Westbrook's Big Budget of Fun and *Westbrook's Stage Favorites* also appeared during this period; they seem to have been intended as periodicals similar in format to *Fun Book*, with *Stage Favorites* featuring photos of actresses. Volume 1:4 (February 1909) of *Fun Book*, subtitled "Frivolities," was copyrighted.

THE WESTERN EXAMINER

"Edited by an association," the St. Louis-based bimonthly journal *The Western Examiner* was first published on 19 November 1833. This "specimen" number included a prospectus in which the editors proposed "to advocate liberal principles West of theAllegheny." When the first regular number was issued on 1 January 1834, readers noticed a slight change in plans; the editors were now promising to investigate "the credibility and general tendencies of the Christian

Religion.'' Most of the articles reflect non-Christian values and often satirize Christianity. In addition to satirical essays, *The Western Examiner* offered anecdotes, biographies, poetry, travel sketches, and historical articles. Published by John Bobb on the first and fifteenth of every month, this journal sold for $1.50 per annum in advance. The last of forty-six numbers was issued on 10 December 1835, completing two volumes. Both volumes, including the specimen number, are available on University Microfilm prepared from copies held by DLC, IU, and NN. Copies are also available at four other libraries.

Barbara McMillin

WHAM!

Wham! was a monthly, digest-size, sexy gags magazine of the 1950s which offered three hours of fun and cartoons in color on cheap paper. Most of the cartoons, which occupy a full-page measuring 5¼" × 7½", show curvaceous cuties throwing or catching sexual passes. In earlier issues "Tessie" gave her views of life and held off wrestlers and referees, or egged them on, in various fight cartoons. The editors provided pages of humor, and a few pages of gags also appeared. Typical cartoons include two guys passing a door where cats run out and a girl is standing, and one says, "It's damned obvious what kind of house this is!" Issues have been seen from 1954 through 1957. It belongs to the *Pack o' Fun*,** *Nifty*,** and *Zip*** family. Kirby Publishing Company of New York was publisher.

WHAT'S COOKIN'!

Comic Corporation of America, New York, published *What's Cookin'!* from July-August 1942 through Fall 1945 in the gals and gags in uniform style, with a sprinkling of army life jokes. It offered full-page cartoons, brief jokes, some comic sequences, and a few informative brief humor articles. The 5½" × 7¾", 68-page periodical was originally published bimonthly but possibly quarterly later at a cost of fifteen cents. The last copyrighted was Number 8 for March 1944.

WHIZ BANG

Captain Billy, although he had tried his magazine in a larger format in 1932, was not the dominant influence on the 1940s *Whiz Bang*, which took up his style and merged it with the brightness of *Ballyhoo** to make a girls and gags service-oriented magazine, 70 pages long and 8½" × 11¼" in size. Country Press of Greenwich, Connecticut, was the publisher with Rod Reed as editor. Reamer Keller, Henry Boltinoff, and Laurence Larier cartoons gave the magazine an *Esquire*** feel, filled out with pin-up sequences and five or six humorous prose articles. Some of the cartoons dealt with war themes, but most were of the sexy socialite variety. For example, one busty cutie says to another, "So I said to myself, today I'm going out and get a job with my references or bust—and I got one." Volume 1:5, for November 1942, sold at twenty-five cents.

WILD!

Wild! or *This Magazine is Wild!* (8¼" × 10⅓", thirty-five cents, fifty pages) was a Dell Publishing Company establishment version of a counter-culture comix. It looked like a college student's *Mad,** with less content. The "Wild Book Review" reviewed the telephone directory and matchbooks. "Would you believe it?" had jokes like "Wilbur Tush of East Happenstance, Kansas, grew a turnip one inch long," accompanied by a cartoon. D. J. Arneson was the editor; Number 1 was published in 1967.

WILD CHERRIES

Wild Cherries was a titillating sexy humor magazine of the 1930s. The monthly (twenty-five cents, 7" × 10") offered 68 pages of prose pieces like Asap's Fables, Harlem Nites by M. Hardway Brown, "She Knew What She Wanted," and five or six other pieces per issue. Short gags and cartoons asked, "Remember when pansies used to come in bunches instead of groups?" and "What can I do to keep my husband from running after other women?—"Cut his—er—legs off!" A number of cartoons punctuated its pages. Volume 1:2 for September 1933 has been seen. Worth B. Carnahan copyrighted Volume 1:1 for Summer 1933.

WILD OATS

Wild Oats, in folio size at 11" × 15", was a venture by the publishing firm of Winchell and Small: an illustrated weekly journal of fun, satire, burlesque, and hits at persons and events of the day in the 1870s. It began as a monthly in February 1870 at fifteen cents an issue, became biweekly on 29 February 1872 and weekly on 15 October 1874, apparently terminating in 1876. In four-column, sixteen-page format, it concentrated on prose offerings by Bricktop (pseudonym of George G. Small), who was its editor, B. Dadd, and Si Slokum, among other phunny phellows writing localist humor items. Country humor was well represented, mixed with infrequent illustrations and cartoons. Watts O'clock offered amusing burlesque novels. In 1871, the Erie Railroad and Tammany were attacked in cartoons, and the April 1871 cover presented a notable graphic of New York City as a pig being carved up by gloating devils. DLC has the first two years.

WISE CRACKS (1929)

Wise Cracks (5" × 8", fifty pages) bowed in with the May 1929 number by the RASHEA Publishing Company of New York. It sold for twenty-five cents. The contents were a loosely strung collection of wisecracks, with some pleasant illustrations and one or two cartoons. "A wise cracker knows its own oyster," boasted the back cover; other jokes were along the same lines as the lady who says, "No, we don't want no books," to a salesman who replies, "How about a grammar?" This is the only issue seen.

WISE CRACKS (1955)

In the 1950s *Wise Cracks*, by Minoan Publishing Company, New York, offered a mix of colored and black and white gag cartoons by Jack O'Brien, Bill Wenzel, and others, oriented toward sexy situations and curvaceous cuties. One vacationer says to another, "I'd marry a girl like that in a minute, but my wife would never give her consent." Number 2, at twenty-five cents, carries a 1955 date; it was digest-size (5¼" × 7¼"). Number 3 (July 1955) and Number 7 (December 1955) were copyrighted.

WIT

Wit was another of the World War II tabloids—10" × 13", thirty-two pages— devoted to "Loads of Pictures/Loads of Laughs." Volume 1:1 was issued December 1941 by Elite Publications of New York, monthly at ten cents. It was devoted mostly to photo-journalism on cheesecake themes like "Beauty—by the Pageful" and "Wrestling Girls Show New Holds," sometimes in lingerie, sometimes in bathing suits. Cartoons dominate, with an occasional page of two-liners, all on similar themes. Volume 1:4 (January 1942) was copyrighted.

WIT AND WISDOM (1881)

Wit and Wisdom in the 1880s drew from a vast number of national papers for city-life humor items. Fit for the home circle, it intended to contain the choice of humorous articles, sketches, stories, poems, and paragraphs of the funny men of all the papers in the country—"the fun that is going, fresh in every issue." As a reprinter, *Wit and Wisdom* offered pages like "Shear Wisdom" and "Wittiscissors," while championing the cause of credits in reprint, praising those who did and shaming those who did not give credit, including the San Francisco *Wasp*,** which began crediting snips in 1881 under *Wit and Wisdom*'s sting. Alex Sweet, Opie Read, G. W. Peck, and a host of less prominent comedians found a place in its pages and were frequently described in pictures and brief squibs themselves. On 6 October 1881, Mark Twain was so featured as the "best known living humorist." Nor was the magazine without critical discernment, praising the second number of *Judge*,* a magazine destined for a long run, on 3 November 1881. Because it was newspaper oriented, most humor was in the two-three paragraph or newspaper column format.

Wit and Wisdom used a sixteen-page, 8″ × 11″, three-column format. It sold weekly at five cents and was distributed by the American News Company. A. C. Wurtele and Harry J. Shellman were the original editors and publishers in New York, later joined by John F. Oltrogge. Volume 2:1 (No. 27) is 21 July 1881 and Volume 2:22 (No. 48) is 15 December 1881 in the single volume held by DLC. Probably no better index to the newspaper humor of the era of the Phunny Phellows could be found than a complete run of this journal. CtY, MH, NB, and NN list runs.

WIT AND WISDOM (1943)

Wit and Wisdom of the 1940s claimed that its entire content was derived from Norman Lockridge's book *World's Wit and Wisdom* (1936), based on world humor of great thinkers. However, a mixture of popular 1940s sexual jokes and cartoons seems indicated by such full-page cartoons as one of the panty-clad coeds of Gimma Bitta Pi visited by a zoot-suiter who asks if a high-powered buyer of second-hand clothes had been that way. It was one-liner in format, and hundreds of one-liners and epigrams followed each other: ''Nothing is a greater impediment to being on good terms with others than being ill at ease with yourself,'' or ''Ignorance is like a delicate fruit: touch it, and the bloom is gone.'' (This is recognizable as Oscar Wilde's, although Wilde is not one of the handful of exemplary ''masters'' listed on the title page as typical sources for the ''wisdom'' portion of the magazine.) The ''wit'' was usually 1940s jokes and gags, mixed with cartoons.

Wit and Wisdom (in 5½″ × 7½″ format) offered a hundred or more pages of one-liners and cartoons to its readers, with a mixture of ads for other publications. It sold for twenty-five cents. Volume 2:1 for May 1944 and Volume 2:2 for December 1944 were copyrighted; Volume 4:5 was copyrighted in 1947 and was probably the June number. Palace Sales Company was the publisher in New York, and Norman Lockridge was the original editor, replaced by Monroe Mendelsohn.

WIT O' THE WORLD

Edited by Norman Anthony, *Wit O' the World* republished jokes and cartoons from all over the world, but with particular emphasis on *Judge*,* *Gayety*,* *Punch*, and the college humor magazines. Anthony borrowed some of his own prose items from *Judge*, and the John Held, Jr. covers gave it a Roaring Twenties air. Later issues featured some longer humor fiction and photos of starlets. New Fiction Publishing Company, New York, published *Wit o' the World* monthly at twenty-five cents; it was 6¾″ × 10″ in size, with 126 pages of jokes and cartoons and an additional advertising supplement because of its syndication as part of the "Newsstand Group" of advertisers. Volume 1:1 appeared in August 1925, and Volume 3:2 for August 1926 was the last copyrighted. DLC has the first five numbers; NN also lists holdings.

WRECK/NEWSWRECK

Wreck started as *Newswreck* in May 1977 but abandoned the title under threat of a lawsuit from *Newsweek*. It was published as *Wreck* in July 1977 but retained its parody aspect. The one dollar monthly, published by Newswreck, Inc., of Chicago, consisted of 64 pages and measured 8¼" × 11". Its parodies were crude and oriented toward adolescents, for example, "Up yours Pained-Webber" and "Why Howard Hughes Never Gave a Crap." Photo articles toyed with the Mafia, drug dealing, mugging, and ugly fashions, among other contemporary topics. An August issue is reported.

THE YALE LITERARY MAGAZINE

"Conducted by the students of Yale College," *The Yale Literary Magazine*, according to Hoornstra and Heath, ranks among the most successful of all college magazines. First issued on 1 February 1836, this periodical was published monthly during the school year; it is now published irregularly. Considered to be the earliest of the long-lived college monthlies, the young *Yale Literary Magazine* contained biographical pieces, essays, travel sketches, and many satirical and humorous works. As Hoornstra and Heath report, following the suppression of the February 1864 number, the editorial board subdivided, each group publishing a magazine for February, March, and April of that year. Herrick and Noyes were the original publishers. Volumes 1 through 16 (February 1836-July 1851) are available on University Microfilm prepared from copies held by CtY and DLC. Copies are also available at MH, RPB, MBat, and dozens of other libraries.

The humor of the earlier numbers was confined primarily to a series entitled "Confessions of a Sensitive Man" in which the writer pokes fun at the speech, social life, and customs of Droneville, Massachusetts. Milder satire is evident in another series labeled "Conversations with a Man of Taste and Imagination." The second installment of this series (March 1836) provides a biting appraisal of dueling in the Old South, namely, Natchez, Mississippi. That the magazine is produced by students explains the variety of humorous school teacher characterizations which frequently appear. Among the most notable are "Miss Tabitha Tunk" (October 1836) and "Our School Mistress" (April 1850). Foreshadowing the clever wit of Twain's Hawaiian recollections in *Roughing It* is a travel sketch entitled "A Trip to the Tropics" in the April 1843 number. Among the best anecdotes is a tale found in the August 1841 publication. Here a cynical bystander dressed in black dupes a crazy Alabama preacher into believing that he has come face to face with Beelzebub. Offering pieces both local and regional in flavor, *The Yale Literary Magazine* serves as a repository of early American humor.

Barbara McMillin

YANKEE HUMOR

Yankee Humor (Vol. 1:1, November 1927) was not very Yankee, particularly in comparison with earlier comic journals that had carried the epithet "Yankee," but it offered plenty of uncomplicated jokes that could easily be retold by its readership. Motor cop: "Didn't you see me wave my hand?" Flapper: "Yes, but I'm not that kind of girl." Another typical joke is the answer to the question of what causes most auto accidents: "The nut that holds the steering wheel." There were also some longer bits and a variety of cartoons. Bathing beauties occupied the center pages.

Yankee Humor was thirty-six pages long, measured 8" × 11", cost fifteen cents an issue in 1927, and was published by Consolidated Features of New York. Dic Loscalzo was the editor. Its second issue claimed that in response to demand it was going to raise its print number. Volume 2:1 (May 1928) is the last copyrighted.

THE YELLOW KID/YELLOW BOOK MAGAZINE

The Yellow Kid was a gay product of the Gay Nineties, published fortnightly by Howard Ainslee and Company in New York. It obviously borrowed the name of Richard Outcault's "The Yellow Kid" of 1895, who appeared in 1896 as America's reputed first comic strip character and became the notable subject of an ownership war by William Randolph Hearst and Joseph Pulitzer. As a result, the figure was omnipresent in New York City for years and gave the field of "yellow journalism" its name. Under Joe Kerr's editorship, the "Five Cent" magazine *Yellow Kid* (forty-eight pages, 7" × 10¼") offered four or five short stories per issue, accompanied by sketches, jokes, poems, and pictures by the leading cartoonists of the day. Volume 1:1 was published on 20 March 1897, and it became *The Yellow Book* following the issue of Volume 1:9 for 17 July 1897.

The first six issues of *The Yellow Kid* proudly noted that the shapeless and deformed refugee from Hogan's Alley was the type described in Max Nordau's *Degeneracy*. In content, however, *The Yellow Kid* intended to appeal to the middle class. It boasted of stories by M. Quad, Will Gridley, and Ellis Parker Butler and illustrations by Penrhyn Stanlaws, Fisher, and other humorous social illustrators of the day. Humor represented the 1890s period. "Snap Shots By The Kid" gave slangy critiques of "da jays whut rigs out dere woikers in unniforms, and other subjects around Noo York, Amurrica." Photos showed pretty ladies, including a nude Psyche; cartoons dealt with the upper crust. One classy Vassarine replies languidly to the question "Do you love me?" in a full-page Gibson-style cartoon: "Would it be any harder than Greek?"

The Yellow Book "Bicycle Number" was promised for 31 July 1897, marking an "improved and more general character for the magazine." It was to include jokes, skits and four "absolutely up-to-date" bicycle stories.

The Yellow Book was published monthly through January 1898 with more stories by E. P. Butler and others. In February 1898 it became *Ainslee's Magazine*, taking up a new volume and issue numbering. As a "general" magazine *Ainslee's* included writers such as John Kendrick Bangs and Dorothy Parker, but was not "humorous" in overall direction.

YOO HOO!

Yoo Hoo! was another "Army and Navy Fun" digest-sized publication from World War II. Volume 1:1 appeared in November 1941, bimonthly, although it appears to have varied its publication to monthly and quarterly at times. The last copyrighted by H-K Publications was Number 40–41 for April 1946. Comic Corporation of America was the earlier publisher in New York at fifteen cents an issue and 5½″ × 7″ in size. It featured service and dating cartoons, a few jokes, and a crossword. Parachuting WACs on the cover are described as "Fannies from Heaven"; another joke has a recruit boasting that he lived the life of Riley on home leave; he is warned, "Wait until Riley hears about it."

YOUNG SAM

Young Sam, a short-lived humor paper of the 1850s, supported infant liberty on a foundation of the Monroe Doctrine and the Declaration of Independence and attacked Black Republicanism. It took an elevated tone against the "awful political doings in Shecargo" and used slangy misspellings to play with political issues. *Sam* noted that an up-country editor who paid $50 for a new head for his paper was advised that the money would have been better spent on a new head for its editor. *Sam* offered satire, political attacks, and skepticism about political and cultural payoffs; one cartoon shows a good book review being purchased for five dollars. Letters came from Cone-cut Corners, Connecticut, and burlesques included "The Last of the Kickaways." It was anti-Pierce as well, and caricatured the British Lion flapping its wings and crowing on a fence.

MWA has Volume 1:4 dated 29 December 1855, but *Young Sam* is cited in UL and Mott as having twelve issues in 1852. Abbott and Company in New York were the publishers at five cents weekly. Mott (2:182) lists Thomas Powell, later of *Diogenes, Hys Lantern*,** as editor and Henry Watson and George Arnold as contributors, along with illustrator Charles Rosenberg.

Z

ZIP!

Zip! was a digest-sized 1950s cartoons and sexy gags magazine in the family of *Pack o' Fun,*** *Nifty,*** and *Wham.*** Sex was the theme. Issues were bimonthly, 5¼″ × 7¼″ in size, cost twenty-five cents, and had about one hundred pages of cartoons. Some page-long prose pieces featured "Zippy" as the subject of a string of gags. August 1955 through January 1957 have been seen; there are no volume or issue numbers. "Red n' Dave" signed off on the advertisements. Another *Zip* was published by Humorama (Timely Features, Inc.) monthly, and an issue for May 1965 has been seen, adding sleazecake pictures to the cartoon matter. Whether or not these are related publications is not clear.

ZIPPY

Zippy was a large-format World War II tabloid featuring showgirl and gold-digger humor; "America's gayest gagmen" offered one hundred cartoons, with some pages, *Zippy* boasted, in color. The cartoons featured the bodily attributes of women, and the gag lines revolved around love for profit. Volume 1:1 (May 1941) cost ten cents and was 10½″ × 13″ in size; the length of the run is unknown. Manvis Distributors published it bimonthly from Dunellen, New Jersey.

ZOWIE! (1953)

Zowie! is the first bearer of this name in the 1950–1960 period, identical in format with a later publication by the same name. It was a monthly, selling for twenty-five cents, subtitled "Spicy Cartoons and Gags" in digest size at 5¼″ × 7¼″. General humor dominated, with some dating and social orientation; cartoons, liberally sprinkled with prose gags, occupied its pages. An efficiency expert says his prayers once a year on New Year's Day; the rest of the year he just jumps out of bed and says, "Ditto." Youthful Magazines of St. Louis, Missouri, published the issue seen (Volume 2:4 for March 1954), but it seems to have been edited in New York, possibly by W. W. Scott. See second *Zowie!* entry.

ZOWIE! (1966)

The second bearer of the *Zowie!* name was a sister publication of *Jackpot*** and was subtitled "Snappy Cartoons and Jokes." Both magazines are almost identical to their 1950s predecessors and may be considered continuations of those titles by a different publisher and with a similar format and slightly sexier humor. *Zowie!* was thirty-five cents an issue, in the same digest size and appearance as before, but with more prose among the cartoons. Picture Magazines of New York was the publisher, bimonthly in tandem with *Jackpot*. Volume 2:1 appeared in January 1967 and Volume 3:6 has been seen for November 1968. Humor was somewhat oriented to sexy themes, but the later *Zowie!* was less sexy than its contemporaries in the later 1960s. A deaf and dumb man wiggling his fingers wildly under his coat is explained as telling dirty stories. An article on W. W. Scott in *Harpoon*** (Volume 1:1 for September 1974) identifies him as editor of *Zowie!*, following his work with *Harvard Lampoon** in 1924, *Life** in 1926, *Ballyhoo** in the 1930s, *Pastime*** in the 1940s, *Movie Humor*** in the early 1930s, *Laff*** in the 1940s, and a variety of comic books; neither the *Jackpot*s nor *Zowie!* shows any particular influence or relationship to any of these.

Part III
ADDITIONAL MAGAZINES

Copyright Listings of
Humor Magazines

This list includes titles from the copyright listings of the United States Copyright Office, *Catalogue of Copyright Entries: Periodicals* (Washington, D.C.: U.S. Government Printing Office, 1906–1979, and continuing), based on submissions of periodicals by publishers as required to obtain copyrights. The periodicals listed here have not been seen, and it is possible that some listings are not appropriately classified as humor magazines. Copyright listings from 1906 to 1979 have been searched; the list was compiled by Bonnie Fausz Sloane.

Aardvark. Copyrighted by Williard R. Espy and Marvin R. Bendiner, September-October 1933 (1:2) only.

Anecdotes, Fun and Jokes. Copyrighted by William S. Brewer of New York; Volume 2 is December 1920.

Arkansas Hillbilly. Copyrighted by P. A. Tofft of Mount Ida, Arkansas; semi-monthly, "a clear cut highly educational comic paper"; eight pages, 9″ × 12″, one dollar per year; 1:1 copyrighted 14 April 1920.

Axe Grinder. Copyrighted by Raye Bidwell; monthly from 1:1 in January 1933 through 1:5 May; 6–8, listed as June-July, is the last found.

Ax-Grinder. Copyrighted by the Ax-Grinder Publishing Company, Inc., 19 May 1933 (1:1).

Backstage Follies. Copyrighted by Humor Digest, Inc., October 1957 (1:5) and December 1957 (1:6).

Bananas. Copyrighted by Scholastic Magazine, Inc., September 1975 (1:1); bimonthly through January 1976 (No. 3). Issues are reported through 1978 (No. 23).

Bayburn Breveties. Copyrighted by Lawrence P. Bliss, September 1934 (1:9) only.

The Bazoom. Copyrighted by Russell Thompson of Chicago; issues were sporadic and unnumbered from March 1928 through September 1931.

Bean Spiller. Copyrighted by the Kentucky Lithographing Company, Inc. Monthly issues were listed as vine and beans instead of volume and issue; 1:6 listed for 18 June 1921.

The Bell-Cow. Copyrighted by the Bell-cow Company of Cleveland, Ohio; monthly with issue 1:2 in March 1914, through 1:4 in May 1914.

Belly Button. Copyrighted by Calgo Publishers, Inc.; 1:1 for June-July 1970 is the first bimonthly issue, with 3:1 for April-May 1972 the last copyrighted.

Best Cartoons from the Editors of Stag and Male (later Male and Stag were reversed). Copyrighted by Magazine Management Company; the first issue copyrighted is No. 3 in September 1970. Issues were quarterly and became bimonthly with 4:6 in November 1973, with sporadic copyright listings through 6:3, April 1975.

Blast. First listed as copyrighted by Blast, Inc., for September-October 1933 (1:1), then by Fred R. Miller for November-December 1933 (1:2).

Blue Mule. Copyrighted by the Blue Mule Publishing, San Francisco; eight issues are copyrighted from 2:1 in February 1907 through 2:10 in November 1907.

Boloney from Hollywood. Copyrighted by H. Charles Anderson, March 1932 (1:1) only.

Boo. Copyrighted by Consolidated Magazines, Inc., April 1924 (1:1) and June 1942 (1:2).

Booze. Copyrighted by Cooperative Publishing Company, Pittsburgh; 1:2 for August 1915 only.

Briefed. Copyrighted by Brief Publishing Company, issues listed as monthly for 12:7 in July through 12:12 in December 1955.

Broad Lynes. Copyrighted by Leon A. Silverman of Detroit, 1:1 for Fall 1929 only.

Broadway Follies. Copyrighted by White Way Publications, 1:1 for July 1933 only.

Broadway Parody Songs. Copyrighted by Song Parodies, Inc., 1:1 for July 1942 only.

Bubbles. Copyright data state that it is "published occasionally for the promotion of merriment, common sense, good health, and public decency." Five cents is listed as the price for the eight-page, 9″ × 12″ issue of 10 June 1910 (1:1).

Buddies Review. Copyright data for the introductory number of the monthly states that it is "dedicated to our buddies who fought so valiantly in the Great War." Data also list the price of two dollars for a thirty-two page illustrated 10½″ × 8″ magazine; issue 1:1 is 3 April 1922.

Buffoon (Humor Magazine). Copyrighted by Apollo-Graphics; issue No. 2 is May 1965.

Bughouse Bugle. By the Columbia Nuts and Bolts Company of Bridgeport, Connecticut; copyrighted issues are February 1922 (2:10) through May 1923 (4:1).

Bumbledom Journal. Copyrighted by Bulfin Printers for 22 June 1932 (1:1).

Bunk. Copyrighted by Leon Kaufman; the only listed issue is March 1942 (1:1).

B-U-N-K. Copyrighted by Burdon Publications; the only issue is listed for 1 February 1932 (1:1). See *Burten's Follies*.**

The Buzzer. Copyrighted by Swift and Company of Chicago; monthly issues are copyrighted from January 1921 (8:5) through March 1923 (10:7).

The Buzzer. Copyrighted by Louise Aimee Patterson, 16 October 1922 (1:2).

The Cactus Needle. First copyrighted by John Tombs in Banning, California, for August (2:8) and September (2:9) 1921, then listed by E. Ganson of Tucson for November (3:11) and December (3:12) 1922.

Campus Humor. Copyrighted by the Official Magazine Corporation, December 1966 (1:1) only.

Campus Jaybird. Copyrighted by Jaybird Enterprises, October-December 1968 (1:1) only.

Campus Parade. Copyrighted by Campus Parade, Inc.; seven issues are listed from November 1947 (1:1) monthly through May 1948 (1:7 listed as *Graduation*).

Cap'n Joey's Follies. Also copyrighted by Joe Burten, New York, February 1923 (2:1) only. See *Burten's Follies*.**

Cap'n Joey's Jazza-Ka-Jazza. First copyrighted by Joseph Bernstein from New York in February 1922 (1:1) and then by Joe Burten, New York, for March (1:2), this monthly magazine was "dedicated to the elimination of Blue Laws" and "strong for the personal rights of men and women." Copyright data list price as two dollars yearly for thirty-one pages, size 8″ × 5″. Two more issues were monthly and issue 1:5 is for June-July. Last listed is 22 September 1922 (1:6). See *Burten's Follies*.**

Caricature. Copyrighted by Haile Hendrix; issues are listed from June 1947 (1:6) monthly through December 1948 (2:12).

Cartoon Comedy. Copyrighted by Zenith Publication Corporation, Summer 1947 (1:1) only.

Cartoon Cuties. Copyrighted by Minoan Publishing Company; three issues are listed: July (No. 1), September (No. 2), and November 1955 (No. 3).

Cartoon Review. Copyrighted by Roland B. Westerlund, October 1968 (1:1) through December 1968 (1:3).

Cartoon-A-Vision. The only copyright is for Karl-Joy, Inc., for May 1965 (1:2).

The Cartoonist. Copyrighted issue by the National Cartoonists' Society, Spring 1958 (No. 57 only).

Cartoonist Profiles. Copyrighted by Cartoonist Profiles, Inc., three issues from Winter 1969 (1:1) through February 1970 (1:5); issue No. 64 was published in 1984 and continued from Fairfield, Connecticut. Reprinted by University Microfilms.

Cartoonist's and Gagwriter's Supermarket. Copyrighted by the Cartoonist's Guild of America, Inc., 30 March 1955 (1:1).

The Cartoonists' Comic. Copyrighted by Kenneth J. Lizorty, March 1954 (1:1) only.

Cartoons and Gags. Originally copyrighted by Newsstand Publications, Inc., bimonthly from February 1958 (1:1); later taken by Perfect Films and Chemical Company by December 1968 (11:6) and then copyrighted by Magazine Management Company from February 1969 (12:1) through September 1975 (22:7).

Cartoons for Men Only. Also copyrighted by Newsstand Publications, Inc., sporadically from February 1958 (1:2) through August 1959 (2:4) and continued as *Cartoons and Gags* with issue 2:6 for December 1959.

Cartoons Marooned. Copyrighted by Zenith Books, October 1968 (1:1).

Cartoonus Sexualis. Copyrighted by American Art Enterprises, May-July 1972 (1:1) through February-March 1973 (1:5).

Cheers. Sporadically copyrighted, first by Cheers Publishing Company, January (1:4) and June (1:9) 1954, and then copyrighted by Henry P. Lankenau from August (2:11) through December 1955 (3:3).

Choppertoons. Copyrighted by Magazine Management, Inc., Fall 1971 (No. 2) only.

Chuckles. Copyrighted by Esrom Corporation for May and June 1939, both listed as 1:1.

Clever Truths. Copyrighted by Clever Truths Publishing Company, Inc., Chicago for August 1925 (1:3); became *Best Stories of All Time* in September 1925 (1:4) through 1926.

Co-ed Campus Comedy. Copyrighted by Collegiate World Publishing Company of Chicago, November (1:3) and December 1924 (1:4).

College Stories. Copyrighted by James Vincent Spadea, New York, from July (1:1) to Fall 1926 (1:2).

Comic Cuts. Copyrighted by H. L. Baker Company, Inc., 19 May (1:1) and 26 May (1:2) of 1934.

Comic Tabloid. Copyrighted by United Features Syndicate, 7 July 1934 (1:38).

The Comics. Copyrighted by Steve Slesinger, Inc., beginning March 1937 (1:1) through September 1937 (1:5).

Comics Magazine. Copyrighted by Comics Magazine, with monthly issues from May (1:1) through September 1936 (1:5).

Corning's Quarterly Razoo. Begun as *The Razoo* in 1905, Leavitt Corning of St. Paul copyrighted from November 1906 (2:3) through the name change. The last issue was listed as Winter 1934 (29:4, although Fall 1934 was numbered 30:2).

Crazy. Copyright information shows issues from December 1953 (1:1) monthly through May (1:6), with July 1954 (No. 7) as the last by Classic Syndicate, Inc.

Cylcetoons. Quarterly by Peterson Publishing; the first issue listed is February 1968 (No. 1) through February 1974.

Cynic. Copyrighted by Cynic, Cincinnati, September (2:1) monthly through December (2:4) 1926.

The Dart. Copyrighted by Sidney Cox of Hanover, New Hampshire, 15 March 1929 (1:1) through May 1930 (2:2). Probably a collegiate humor publication.

The Devil. Copyright data state that it is "a monthly magazine to stimulate the best there is in man." Price quoted as one dollar per year for the 12" × 9" illustrated, sixteen-page issue for October 1916 (1:1).

Diogenes. Copyrighted by Arthur Blair and Frank Jones, December 1940-January 1941 (1:2) and Autumn 1941 (1:3) only.

Doughboy's Fun and Facts. Copyrighted by Albert W. Brice of New York, January 1921 (No. 3), only.

The Dumbook. Copyrighted by The Dumbook, Mill Valley, California, monthly from April (1:1) through August 1925 (1:5).

Eek! Copyrighted by Consolidated Magazines, May 1942 (1:1) only.

Excitement. Copyrighted by Street and Smith Publications, Inc., New York, January (21:5) monthly through April 1931 (22:2) only.

Facts, Fun, and Satire. Copyrighted by St. Luke's Bible School, from 13 July (No. 75) to 7 December 1950 (No. 80).

Fads and Fancies. Copyrighted by Kenbridge Press, Philadelphia; copyright data state that it is "devoted to various interests of human life." The fourteen-page illustrated, 9″ × 6″ magazine cost five cents; the only listing was for 25 March 1916.

Farmer Dick's Pitchfork. Copyrighted by Emma Jaqua of Indianapolis, April (1:1) and May (1:2) 1928.

Featheredge Quills. Copyrighted by Etheredge Guano Company, Spring 1940 (1:1).

The Fig Leaf. Copyrighted by Sam A. Cousley of Lancaster, Wisconsin; copyright data state that it was "a monthly magazine of American modernism"; the price was two dollars yearly for thirty-two pages, 7″ × 5″ issues beginning December 1922 (1:1) through June 1923 (3:6).

Flit Buzz. Copyrighted by Stanco Distributing Company, beginning 15 January 1927 (1:1), published every ten to fourteen days to December 1928 (1:34), continuing through 4 May 1929 (2:8), with a last unnumbered issue 11 May 1928.

The Follies. Copyrighted by Boulevards Publishing Company, Inc., New York; copyright data state that it was formerly *The Parisienne Monthly Magazine.* Issues are listed from July 1921 (1:1) through April 1922 (2:4).

Follyology. Copyrighted by Clark Publishing Company, Minneapolis, November (1:7) and December 1924 (1:8). See *Jim Jam Jems.**

The Fool. Copyrighted by John Serrigan, New York; copyright data state that 1:1 for June 1921 is a four-page 9″ × 6″ pamphlet for five cents.

Fool Killer. Copyrighted by George Damrel Beason of Washington, D.C.; copyright data state that it is a forty-page 6″ × 5″ "magazine of general interest in the home." The price is $1.50 yearly; three issues are listed: October 1918 (1:1), February (1:2), and April 1919 (1:3).

For Men and Men Only. Copyrighted by Popular Magazines, Inc., from 1:2 copyrighted 16 February 1937 to No. 5 in August 1937; then apparently as *For Men Only*, still by Popular Magazines, monthly from September (1:6) to December 1937. The title continues, copyrighted by Fawcett in March 1938 (1:12) monthly to May 1938 (2:2); then apparently by Country Press of Connecticut, as *For Men* in June 1938 (2:3), then monthly from August 1938 (2:4) to December (2:8), and then bimonthly through August 1938 (2:12).

Frantic. Copyrighted by Pierce Publishing Company, October 1958 (1:1) only. Issue 2:2 has been reported; similar to *Mad.**

French Follies. Copyrighted by Tavern Publishing Company, 4 February 1933 (10:1) only.

French Follies. Copyrighted by American Art Agency; quarterly issues are occasionally copyrighted from February-April 1963 (1:1) through August-October 1969 (6:3).

French Frills. First copyrighted by Jaybird Enterprises from December 1960 (1:2) monthly, then quarterly, last listed, October-December 1970 (9:4); two issues are by American Art Agency in 1969 (8:1,2).

Fun and Frolic. Copyrighted by Fun and Frolic, Stoughton, Massachusetts; copyright data list a price of five cents a copy or fifty cents a year for the five-page 12″ × 9″ issues. June 1910 (1:1) is the only listing.

Fun and Funds. Copyrighted by C. R. Van Nice of Morrill, Kansas, September 1929 (1:1) only.

Fun Finder. Copyrighted by Fun Publishers, 3 June 1933 (1:1).

Fun for All. Copyrighted by Popular Publications, Inc., May 1939 (No. 3) only.

Fun for One. Copyrighted by Popular Publications, Inc., April (1:1) and May 1938 (1:2).

Fun 'n Facts from the Wall Street Journal. Copyrighted by Dow Jones and Company, January 1959 (4:1) through name change to *Fun 'n Facts* in 1960, until July 1961 (6:7).

The Funnies. First copyrighted by Film Humor, Inc., 16 January and 28 January 1929 (1:1,2), then by Dell Publishing Company. It was bimonthly for two more issues, then monthly through early 1930, becoming weekly for a brief period, with the last listed 28 October 1930 (No. 36). A sixteen-page tabloid, it featured Foxy Grandpa.

The Funnies. First copyrighted by Steve Slesinger, Inc., for April 1939 (1:30), monthly through October 1939 (1:36), and then copyrighted again by Dell for December 1941 (1:62) through June-July 1942 (1:65). The strange numbering makes unclear exactly what happened. Dell may have added the numbers of its previous magazine of the same title.

Funny Bone. Copyrighted by Anthony Publishing Company, Inc., from November 1941 (1:3) through May 1942 (1:6).

Funny Book. Copyrighted by Parents Institute, December 1942 (1:1) only.

Funny Funnies. Copyrighted by Nedor Publishing Company, April 1943 (1:1) only.

Funny Pages. Copyrighted by Centaur Publications, Inc., from March 1938 (2:6), usually monthly through a numbering change in 1940 with the last, No. 42, in October 1940.

Funny Picture Stories. Copyrighted by Centaur Publications, Inc., March 1938 (1:6), monthly to May (2:8), then bimonthly through May 1939 (3:3).

Funny Stories. Copyrighted by Erie Publishing Company of Cleveland, which also published *Hot Dog*,** December 1928 (1:1) through June 1931 (D:6).

Funnyman. Copyrighted by Magazine Enterprises, Inc.; issues are irregular from December 1947 (1:1) through August 1948 (1:6).

Funtest. First copyrighted by William Russell Pine in March 1934 (1:1), then by Funtest Publishing Company for November 1934 (1:2) and February 1935 (1:3).

Gag, Plot, and Title. Copyrighted for January 1928 (1:1) only.

Gals. First copyrighted by Robert Harrison in Summer 1946 (1:1); two issues are by Par Publishing Company for September and Fall 1946 (both listed as 1:2); then again by Harrison for Spring (1:3) and Fall (1:4) 1947.

Gals A-Go-Go. Copyrighted by American Art Agency, 13 April 1965 (1:1).

Gay Ninety's Magazine. Copyrighted by Vogel Magazines, September 1936 (1:1).

Gay Parisienne. Copyrighted by Merwil Publishing Company, 5:1 is dated January 1934.

George Fuller Golden Journal. Copyright data state that this journal was "a little book of motley moods; wisdom for the foolish and folly for the wise." 1:1 was described as 6½" × 4", thirty-two pages, froms Saranac Lake, New York, in February 1907.

Gesundheit. Copyrighted by Schuster Company of Cleveland; monthly issues are listed as cask and glass instead of volume and issue (sometimes numbered irregularly) from February 1916 (4:1) through May 1917 (6:5).

G'Eye News. Copyrighted by Robert Wilson Tribble and James Earle Tribble; 1:4 was 15 March 1946.

Ginger Goes Places and Sees Things. The only copyright listing is for September 1931

(1:1) by Eleanor Richey Johnson and Ruby Holland Rosenberg, Kansas City, Missouri; adult nudie, uncopyrighted issues are reported through May 1936 as *Ginger*.

The Grid. "A quarterly published to disseminate some sense and a little nonsense among users of storage batteries." This twenty-two page, 9" × 6" illustrated magazine by the Edison Storage Battery Company, West Orange, New Jersey, had copyrighted issues from October 1919 (1:1) through July 1920 (1:4).

The Grizzly. Copyrighted by the Baer Brothers and Prodie, Chicago, 1:1 for March 1928.

GRR. Copyrighted by Consolidated Magazines, Inc., 1:1 for May 1942.

Gulf Comic Weekly. Copyrighted by Gulf Refining Company for 28 April 1933 (No. 1) through 19 May (No. 4). Name changed to *Gulf Funny Weekly* with issue No. 5 for 26 May 1933; other sources state it was a four-page tabloid size through No. 300 on 2 February 1939; became comic book size with No. 301 on 10 February 1939, and continued through 23 May 1941 (No. 422); freely circulated at Gulf stations.

Ha Ha. First copyrighted by Dell Publishing Company, December 1941 (No. 1), then by Ha Ha Publishing Company for June (No. 2), August (No. 3), and September 1942 (No. 4); an uncopyrighted No. 5 is also reported.

Happiness. Copyrighted by John Merkens, October 1933 (1:1).

Happiness. Copyrighted by Arthur Bruce of Bennington, Vermont, September 1939 (1:1).

Happiness-for All the World. Copyrighted by George Blumenstock, Spring 1933 (1:1).

Happiness Magazine. Copyrighted by Ray Woodworth Hutton of Minneapolis, Fall (2:3) and Winter (2:4).

Harpoon. Copyrighted by Katharine Lord, June 1934 (1:1), with three issues yearly (June, July, August) until 5:1 for June-July 1938, 5:2 August 1938, and 6:1 Spring 1939 last.

Harpoon. Copyrighted by Walter Weems, 1:1 for March and 1:3 for May 1942.

Harpoon. Copyrighted by Harpoon Press, solely owned by Jo Ann Townsend and Steven C. Levi of Anchorage, 1:1 in 1979 and 2:2 in Fall 1980. Copyright data state that they publish three issues yearly; possibly a literary magazine.

Have You Told Your Wife? Copyrighted by H. S. Koster and Company, one issue for January 1948.

Heads Up! Copyrighted by Rudolph Wurlitzer Company, March (1:1), May (1:2), and December 1938 (1:4).

Hellzapoppin. Copyrighted by Anthony Associates, one issue in August 1939 (1:1).

Hi Fellers. Copyrighted by Truefax Publishing, Inc., one issue for February 1945 (1:1).

Hi-Jinx. Copyrighted bimonthly by B. and I. Publishing Company, Inc., July-August 1947 (No. 1) through July-August 1948 (No. 7).

High Spots. Copyrighted by Hagan Corporation, irregular issues, monthly and bimonthly from July 1935 (2:4) through 1 July 1937 (4:4). For a period in late 1935 the volume number is listed as 7.

Hold It! Copyrighted by Robert B. Knight, monthly from July 1946 (1:1) through December 1947 (2:9).

Homeresque. Copyrighted by Laurelle Miller, for 1 February 1945 (1:1).

Horse Feathers. Copyrighted by Horse Feathers Magazine, November 1944 (2:1) and April-June 1945 (2:4).

Horsing Around. Copyrighted by James Lynch, 7 May 1946 (1:1).

Hot After Cold Business. Copyrighted by Trilling and Montague, February 1932 (2:1).

Hot Dog. Copyrighted by Magazine Enterprises, Inc., bimonthly for June-July (1:1) through October-November 1954 (1:3), with another issue copyrighted in July 1955 (1:4).

Hot Lynes (For Flaming Youth). Copyrighted by Leon A. Silverman, December 1929 (1:1); also a second issue with by-line "for flaming youse" in January-February 1930 (2:2).

Hot Sheet! Skip List. Copyrighted by Walter B. Barr and C. S. DeWeese, 7 September 1933 (No. 105).

Hot Spark. Copyrighted by R. C. Banker and Company of Detroit, unnumbered monthly issues from January through March; June; then monthly for September to December 1924.

Howdee. Copyrighted by Eugene V. Thornton ('Gene) biweekly from 30 November 1932 (1:1) through 28 February 1934 (2:7).

Humor. Copyrighted by Humor Publishing Company, New York, June 1930 (1:1).

Humor-Esq. Copyrighted by Humor-esq Publishing Company, March 1946 (2:1).

Humorist of the Week. Copyrighted by Humorist of the Week Publishing and Printing Association, beginning 20 November 1932 (1:1) through 4 December 1932 (1:3).

Humorous Verse on Current Events and Other Topics. Copyright data state that it is a thirty-page, 6½″ × 4¾″ "monthly get-up, take-off and opinion" by David V. Bush of Lake Preston, South Dakota. Price was $1.50 yearly for August 1916 (1:1) irregularly through November 1916 (1:4), with the last word in the title changing to *Things* in the last three issues.

Imp. Copyrighted by Frances C. and Elizabeth Mortimer, January through May 1925 (1:1–5).

Imp. Copyrighted by the Botz Printing and Stationary Company, Jefferson City, Missouri, January, February, March 1930 issues.

Insanity Fair. Copyrighted by Insanity Fair Publishing Company, Lincoln, Nebraska, February 1930 (1:4).

The Jester. Copyrighted by the Masquers Club, with Key E. Kuter and John Reinemund, co-editors, October-November 1959 (1:10) and January-February 1960 (2:2).

Jokes by Cracky. Copyrighted by Western Publishing Co., New York, Joseph Connaughten, publisher, July 1971 (1:6) and February 1972 (1:7).

Kistler Kootie. Copyrighted by the Walter Kistler Stationary Company, Denver, Colorado, March 1920 (1:4) through August 1920 (1:7).

K. Lamity's Harpoon. Copyrighted by John S. Bonner; later as J. S. Bonner and A. B. Coffee, of Houston, Texas, June 1920 (18:4) through February 1926 (26:5), with frequent uncopyrighted issues in between.

The Knocker. Copyrighted by the Knocker Publishing Company, New York, April 1917 (13:3).

Kollege Kwips. Copyrighted by the George Muse Clothing Company, October 1933 (1:1) and Christmas 1933 (1:2).

Laffalog. Copyrighted by C. A. Lutz Company, York, Pennsylvania, first four issues of Volume 1 for January through April 1925.

Lamp of Diogenes. Copyrighted by Nicolas Bessaraboff, March 1933 (1:1).

Latest Gags. Copyrighted by Robert Makinson, monthly January-June 1976.

Laugh and Learn. Copyrighted by Reinhold A. Aman, February 1971 (1:1); may not be humor.

Laugh-in. Copyrighted by George Schlatter, editor, and Friendly Publications and Romart, Inc., October 1968 (1:1) through October 1969 (1:12). Apparently the same as *Laugh-in Magazine*, reportedly based on the Rowan and Martin television show of the same name, published monthly by Laufer Publishing Company, fifty cents, reported during the same time period.

Laugh-Maker, The Professional Comics Gag File. Copyrighted by Johnny Cavallo, August 1971 (1:1).

Laugh We Must, by Zing Cornell. Copyrighted by Leon D. Cornell, 5 October 1963 only.

Laughing Horse. Copyrighted by Roy E. Chanslor, Berkeley, California, January, February, and March 1923 (1:5,6,7); may not be humor.

Laughing It Up. Copyrighted by Star Publications, January 1955 (No. 1).

The Laughing Man. Copyrighted by The Laughing Man Institute for Traditional and Esoteric Studies, February 1976 (1:1) and March 1976 (1:2).

Lightnin'. Copyrighted by Elmer Lynn Williams, February 1936 (6:12) and March 1936 (7:1).

Limerick Magazine. Copyrighted by William G. Bearhope, New York, January 1922 (1:1). "A Monthly Magazine of humor, wit, poetry, and minute stories and a prize limerick contest," sixteen pages, 10½" × 7", twenty-five cents.

Literary Huckster. Copyrighted by Huckster Publications, January 1945 (3:1).

Little Wit. Copyrighted by Edmund Kelly Jones, January-February 1939 (1:1).

Live Wire. Copyrighted by Live Wire, Local 64, National Federation of Postal Clerks, April 1945 (30:1); may not be humor.

Loose Lips Sink Ships. Copyrighted by Madonna Datzman, Mark Ross, and Marguritte Taliafaro, Winter 1975–1976 (1:1).

Marine Comedy. Copyrighted by Mohawk Publication Corporation, Winter 1944 (1:1).

Mascalines. Copyrighted by Earl Barron Publications, Inc., July-August 1957 (1:4) to November-December 1957 (1:6), bimonthly.

Medical Pickwick. Copyrighted by Medical Pickwick Press, New York; January 1915 (1:1) through February 1927 (13:2); "A monthly literary magazine for and by physicians"; forty-eight pages, 11" × 9", two dollars. May be general rather than humor.

Medical Quip. Copyrighted by Quip Publication Company, Inc., New York, January 1922 (1:1) and January 1923 (3:1); "A Monthly publication devoted to humor, wit and satire pertaining to the medical, dental, and pharmaceutical professions"; thirty-two pages, illustrated, 9" × 6", three dollars annually.

Monsters to Laugh With. Copyrighted by the Non-Pareil Publication Corporation, August and December 1964 (Nos. 2 and 3).

Moonshine. Copyrighted by Moonshine Publication Company, Minneapolis, Minnesota, May 1922 (1:5).

National Bootlegger. Copyrighted by A. J. Shortell and H. G. Comfort, Paso Robles, California, September 1924 (1:1) only.

Nifty Gags. Copyrighted by Edwin E. Zoty, October 1942 (1:1) only.

Nuttylife. Copyrighted by Fox Features Syndicate, Summer 1946 (No. 2).

Odd Things. Copyrighted by Edward G. Pettee, Cleveland, Ohio, December 1929 (1:2).

The Orben Comedy Letter. Copyrighted by Robert Orben, 22 April 1971 (1:1) biweekly through 20 September 1972 (2:12).

Orben's Comedy Fillers. Copyrighted by Robert Orben, Wilmington, Delaware, January 1972, (1:3) continuing through 30 September 1980 (9:11) as Number 107.

Orben's Current Comedy. Copyrighted and edited by Robert Orben, Wilmington, Delaware, first appearing as a monthly in July 1961 (3:9), also as a biweekly through 4 November 1981 (25:6, No. 457), the limit of this search; not all issues copyrighted.

Original Cartoons. First copyrighted January 1969 (1:1), bimonthly; last copyrighted November 1969 (1:6) by Hampshire Distributors, Ltd.

Oyez. Copyrighted by Portia Publishing Company, Inc., New York, November 1916 (1:1) and December 1916 (1:2); "A monthly magazine evading the worn ruts and pitfalls of fads and isms, seeking instead the high levels of originality, with, humor, and good cheer"; thirty-two pages, 12″ × 9″, one dollar annually.

The Pagan. Copyrighted by Joseph Kling, New York, June-July to October-November 1921 (6:2–3 through 6:6–7), bimonthly. "A magazine for Eudaemonists," it was begun in 1916; INE holds copies.

Parade. First copyrighted by Parade, Inc., 28 March 1928 (1:1), weekly; last copyrighted by W. Holden White, Cleveland, Ohio, 31 December 1931 (2:5).

Paree Stories. Copyrighted by the Merwil Publishing Company, October, November, December 1933 issues (Vol. 4); possibly titillating stories rather than humor; see *Pep* below.

Pep. Copyrighted by the Merwil Publishing Company, January 1934 (4:1); also holders of copyrights for *Gay Parisienne* and similar titles of sexsational titillation and humor.

Peppy Humor. Copyrighted by Irwin Publishing Company, New York, 19 March 1930 (1:1).

Playboy. Copyrighted by Egmont H. Arms, New York, 1 June 1921 (1:7).

Printers Hell Box of Southern California. Copyrighted by Hell Box Publishing Company, Los Angeles, May 1923 (1:1).

The Quamahoochian. Quarterly official organ of the Ancient Order of Quamahoochies, Brooklyn, New York, December 1921 (1:1); twenty-two pages, illus., 11½″ × 9″, twenty-five cents.

Red Devil-Ry. Copyrighted by Smith and Hemenway Company, Inc., New York, March 1923 (1:1).

Red Hot. Copyrighted by Red Hot Publication Company, Inc., Baltimore, April 1925 (1:1).

Rooseveltian—Look Out. Copyrighted by Samuel Rudd Cook, Rockport, Indiana, January-February 1909 (2:1); may be nonhumorous political magazine.

Ruff-Nek-News. Copyrighted by James L. Foss of Bell, California, 28 September 1929 (1:8).

Salute. One of the two titles copyrighted by two publishers may be humor: Vet Publishers through 1948, April 1946 (1:1); Weintraub Bros. and Company, January 1946 (2:1), through 1950 and after.

The Satyr. Copyrighted Louisville, Kentucky, December 1927 (7:3) through December 1930 (8:3); copyrighted by B. F. Jay as *Satyr*, March 1932 (1:1).

Saucy Stories. Copyrighted by Intercontinental Publishing Corporation, monthly, January 1920 (7:6) and February 1920 (8:1). Begun in 1916 by H. L. Mencken and G. J. Nathan in response to competition for *The Smart Set** from *Snappy Stories*.

The Scandalizer. Copyrighted by Boris O'Sullivan, New York, January 1907 (1:2).

Semi-Occasionally. Copyrighted by Occasional Publisher, Cincinnati, April 1908 (1:1); bimonthly publication "containing miscelaneous [*sic*] matter, fiction, travel, & c."; ten cents a copy, fifty cents yearly, sixty-four pages, 5" × 7½".

Sextra Laughs. Copyrighted by Knight Publishing Co., Numbers 1–7 beginning with an April 1968 submission and continuing irregularly to October 1970.

SFZ. Copyrighted by Marcel Honore, July 1936 (2:2); may not be humor.

Shed Row News. Copyrighted by A. Gurwitz, Louisville, Kentucky, 27 April 1928 (1:5).

Sh-h-h-h. Listed as a "new publication" in the back of the January-June 1956 copyright listings but does not appear in the front listings.

Sierra Breeze. Copyrighted by John Tombs, editor of the *Cactus Needle*, Banning, California, August 1921 (1:2) and September 1921 (1:3).

Slices. Copyrighted by Behr-Manning Corporation, Troy, New York, February-March 1930.

Smile-a-While Magazine. Copyrighted by Alphonse N. Wagner, Newport, Kentucky, 1 March 1919 (1:1); "A monthly of smile provoking character"; thirty-two pages, illustrated, 6½" × 5", $1.25 annually.

Smile Club Messenger. Copyrighted by C. S. Stright, Brooklyn, New York, April 1910 (1:2).

Smiles. Copyrighted by Nathan L. Teeple, Brooklyn, New York, December 1919 (1:2); January to December 1925 (8:3 through 9:2) also copyrighted.

Smiles. Copyrighted by Faussett and Parmenter, 27 May 1932 (1:1), 30 June 1932 (1:2), and 3 August 1932 (1:3); copyrighted by Smiles Feature Service, September through December 1932.

Smiles and Giggles. Copyrighted, Newark, New Jersey, May (1:1) and June (1:2) 1925.

Smiling Thru. Copyrighted by Walter Edwin Ulrich, January 1936 (1:1).

Smoke. Copyrighted by Charles C. Stoddard, New York, December 1906 and January 1907; "A magazine of humor and good fellowship"; 6" × 4¾", forty-five pages. NN holds 1, 2, and 3 (February/March 1907).

Smoke. Copyrighted by Susanna Valentine Gammel, Summer 1934 (3:3), an Autumn number, and Winter 1935 (4:1).

Smoke. Copyrighted by Wally Frank Limited, July 1953 (1:1) through February 1954 (1:3).

Smoke/Smoke from the Corn-Cob Pipe Club of Virginia. Copyrighted by Larus Bros. Company, Inc., August (1:3) and September 1934 (1:4) as *Smoke*; the later title copyrighted by Larus from October (1:5) through August 1935 (2:8).

Snap. Copyrighted October 1958 (1:1) through March-May 1970 (9:3) as quarterly, monthly, and bimonthly; the varying copyrights were taken by a succession of publishers, each of which specialized in sexually-oriented rather than humorous material.

The Sniper. Copyrighted Lexington, Virginia, 24 January 1925 (1:3) through December 1927 (4:3).

Spectator. Copyrighted by Freud-Boudon Publishing Company, Chicago, "for the entertainment and instruction of its readers," November 1908 (1:1); 13½″ × 10½″, fourteen pages, fifty cents yearly.

Spitzpippin. Copyrighted by C. T. Colt, Roseburg, Oregon, August 1910 (1:7).

Squeeks. Copyrighted by Lev Gleason, October 1953 (1:1) and June 1954 (1:5).

Stuffed Club for Everybody. Copyrighted by J. H. Tilden, Denver, Colorado; 1906 (7:8); four or five issues appeared yearly through 1907; continued from 1908 as *Stuffed Club*; bimonthly in 1914; continuing through April 1915 (15:12) monthly.

Tale Spins. Copyrighted by Clifford A. Wright, Houston, Texas, semi-monthly, 5 July 1919 (2:5); also as *U.S. Talespins*, copyrighted by C. Anderson Wright, Chicago, 1 June 1920 (3:6–11).

Tatler. Copyrighted by Waterson, Berlin, and Snyder Company, Brooklyn, New York, June 1919 (1:4), with 3:10 listed in 1921.

Tatler and American Sketch. Copyrighted by Carlton Publishing Company, July 1930 (6:7).

Tattler. Copyrighted by Sidney W. Williston, Chicago, September 1919 (1:9) and October 1919 (1:10).

Telephony. Copyrighted by Telephony Publishing Company, Chicago, December 1906 (12:6)—ten times a year, then weekly from 1 May 1909 (17:18) through 31 July 1909 (18:5).

Tenafly Humbug Magazine. Copyrighted by Edward S. Evans, February 1932 (1:1) and March 1932 (1:2).

Thacker's Joke Sheet. Copyrighted by Thacker's Root Beer Stands, Dallas, Texas, 7 July 1928 (1:1).

Today's Humor. Copyrighted by William A. Keller, April 1932 (2:2), October-December 1932 (2:4), January-March 1933 (3:1). See entry for *Today's Humor*,** circa 1926, for previous use of this title.

Toots. Copyrighted by C. M. Lovsted, Seattle, Washington, June 1921 (1:8).

Treat'em Square. Copyrighted by Treat'em Square Publications Company, November 1921 (1:3) through January 1924 (3:2); no listings in 1923.

Tucker's Magazine of Scandal. Copyrighted by Fred L. Walker, Walnut, Illinois, June 1923 (1:1).

TV Carnival. Copyrighted by Hillman Periodicals, April 1954 (1:4).

Uncle Jerry Says. Copyrighted by Jerome P. Fleishman, Baltimore, August 1922 (3:11) and September 1922 (3:12).

Unk Ebenezer's Tiny Magazine. Copyrighted by A. F. Meserve, June 1935 (4:3) and April 1937 (6:1); four issues yearly.

Varieties. Copyrighted by Varieties and Lynne Young or Gene Schneider for Varieties, September 1944 (14:1) to May 1947 (16:9).

Verse and Worse. Copyrighted by Cyril A. Smack, Sea Bright, New Jersey, January through March 1924 (1:3–1:5).

Whimsies. Copyrighted by George Wahr, Ann Arbor, Michigan, irregularly, May 1921 (1:3) through December 1923 (4:1).

White Mule. Copyrighted by Eldon Langeven, Omaha, Nebraska, September 1921 (1:1); "Omaha's own magazine of frivolity and nonsense," sixteen pages, 7½″ × 5½″, $1.50 yearly.

Whose Is It. Copyrighted by A. N. Swallow, Baltimore, Maryland, 1 March 1909.

Wieboldt's Wampum Club. Copyrighted by the Wampum Club of America, October 1934; may not be humor.

Wink. Copyrighted by Wink, Inc., December 1954 (10:3) and February 1955 (10:4); it featured "a whirl of girls" and cutie covers by Peter Driben.

Wise House. Copyrighted by the Whys-hows Company, March 1932 (1:6) through January 1936 (5:1), bimonthly.

Wit and Humor. Copyrighted by Wit and Humor Publishing Company, New York, June 1921 (2:6) through July 1921 (3:1) and through October 1921 (3:4), copyrighted by Maurice Battista, New York.

The Witamii. Copyrighted by Robert Hoot, Canton, Ohio, January 1925 (1:1) to March 1926 (2:3), monthly, copyrighted irregularly.

World Humor Flashes. Copyrighted by Thorn Publishing Company, Inc., January 1933 (1:1); fifteen cents; featuring "international fun in pictures."

Wot Sat. Copyrighted by John Wanamaker, New York, September 1915 (2:2) in September 1923.

Yankee Hustler. Copyrighted by John J. Vincent Wilcox, Newport, Rhode Island, November 1921 (5:7) and December 1921 (5:8).

Your Naborhood. "Who's who—and what?" Copyrighted by Michael D. Pellitier for 15 February 1931 issue; may not be humor.

Zest. Copyrighted by Zest Publication Corporation, Inc., New York, November 1926 (1:2).

Zest. Copyrighted by Natamsa, semi-monthly from 16 November 1923 (1:1) through 22 June 1928 (5:21).

Zest. 1940s *Zest* copyrighted by Zest Publication Company, Inc. from November 1940 (3:6) to October 1942 (5:3) with some omissions.

Zing. Copyrighted by L. M. Umsted and Co., New York, 4 October 1920 (1:1) through 27 June 1921 (3:13), weekly with thirteen issues to a volume.

Zip 'n Tang. Copyrighted by Zip 'n Tang, Cedar Rapids, Iowa, October 1929 (1:2) to November 1930 (2:2).

Zowie. Copyrighted by Wm. D. McJunkin Advertising Agency, Chicago, January 1915 (1:3) and May 1915 (1:4).

Bonnie F. Sloane

Unverified Data: Magazines Identified and Described, but Not Examined

The following periodicals have been described with enough information to indicate that they are not ghosts, but they have not been examined in preparing this volume. Listings from the Newberry Library holdings are derived from Jerold J. Savory, "An Uncommon Comic Collection: Humorous Victorian Periodicals in the Newberry Library," *Victorian Periodicals Review* 17 (Fall 1984): 94–102. A number of listings identified as "before 1900" are contained in a list supplied to F. L. Mott by Walter Blair and Franklin Meine and are used with the permission of the Joint Collection University of Missouri Western Historical Manuscript Collection-Columbia and State Historical Society of Missouri Manuscripts.

The Album and Ladies Weekly Gazette. Philadelphia, 1820.

American Comic Annual. 1831. Illustrated by D. C. Johnston and edited by Henry Finn. Held by Newberry Library. Possibly an alternate name for *Scraps*.**

The Bachelor Book. Light humor for bachelors published by two women, Marion Egbert and Page Sampson, in Chicago; ICN holds March-August 1900.

The Bang. Weekly from 27 April 1907 to 29 March 1909, edited by Alexander Harvey, *The Bang* is reported as 2″ × 5″ and is filled with chatty gossip, comic poems, parodies, and miscellaneous material, including Theodore Dreiser material. ICN holds the copies noted.

The Barber. January 1924 issue reported.

The Bare Facts. Winter 1951 and Fall-Winter 1952 reported.

The Bauble: Contemporary. "A literary burlesque" by "anti-faddists," pocket-sized, from July 1895 to February 1897, for younger writers; ICN holds one issue.

The Beacon. "Erected and supported by Lucidantus and his Thirteen Friends," *The Beacon* was published by W. Brown in Philadelphia for two numbers, 27 November and 11 December 1811, to expose the "machinery" of Philadelphia Society. Cited in Albert Smyth, *Philadelphia Magazines and Their Contributors, 1741–1850*.

Best Cartoons from Escapade. Number 5 for 1964 reported; this would be an annual review of the men's magazine cartoons.

Bijou Funnies. First issue is September 1972. It is one of the leading adult-oriented counter-culture comix, and the only one listed here, although *Fabulous Furry Freak Brothers*, *Wonder Warthog* and *Zap* are equally representative of the genre.

The Bilioustine: A Periodical of Knock. Nos. 1–2 for 1901, published by William S. Lord, Evanston, Illinois, are held at ICN.

Blast. Number 2, May 1971, illustrated humor magazine.

Blitz Bang. World War II era with September 1945 and a Volume 5, Number 3 being separately reported.

The Blue Devil, A Journal of Disapprobation. February 1906 through September 1908, monthly, from Louisville, Kentucky, edited by P. T. Ridsdale at ten cents per copy, satirized religion and superstition in favor of reason; pocket-sized. ICN holds copies.

Bombshell. "Devoted to the diffusion of knowledge and the confusion of butternuts" was published at New Harmony, Indiana, in 1864. The Illinois State Historical Library, Springfield, holds the known copy.

Breeze. Chicago, 1883, weekly.

Broadway Hollywood Blackouts. Bi-monthly, March-April 1954 (No. 1) through July-August 1954 (No. 3); Stanhall, ten cents, cartoon gags in comic-book format.

Broadway Magazine. New York, 1892–1894, merged with Benjamin Hampton's *Hampton Magazine*; see *Union List of Serials*.

Bubble. Mott cites a New York 1853 *Bubble* with two issues; this may be the 1849 *Bubble*.**

Budget. New York, 1852–1853; noted by Mott as possibly continuing as *City Budget*, 1853–1854.

Buffoon. Number 2, 1976, illustrated humor magazine.

Bul. "A Monthly Journal Devoted to Hoo-Hoo" published in St. Louis and Nashville, Tennessee; 1–31, 1896–1921, according to Mott's unpublished notes.

Burlesque Jokes and Stories. 1930s, digest-sized publication reported; silhouette cartoons.

Burlington Hawkeye. The newspaper home in Iowa of Robert J. Burdette came to national prominence in 1879–1880 largely owing to Burdette's short humorous pieces.

Campus Howl. Number 2, February 1960, illustrated humor magazine.

Captain Wag. February 1941 through February 1942 (Nos. 1–7) reported.

Cartoon. 1 May 1872 is reported as Number 1 of this New York publication; MWA may have holdings.

Cartoon. October 1941 to April 1951, monthly, reported. August 1973 through April 1975 is also reported, but this may be a separate publication.

The Cartoon. Later name of the New York *Saturday Cartoon*, as of 18 August 1888 when *The Cartoon* was published as a quarto, according to Mott.

Castigator. Referred to by the *City Firefly*** on 23 November 1822 as published by Mr. (Lorenzo?) Hall. See *City Firefly* entry.

Chaff. Before 1900.

Chameleon. Sherwin Williams Paint Company publication from Cleveland, Ohio; Number 1 was 1898. DLC, NN, and OC list holdings through Number 31, monthly.

Charivari. New Orleans before 1900.

Cheerful Liar. New York, September 1915-May 1916 (1:1–16); held by MH and NN.

Cheerful Pessimist. New York, October 1908-April 1914 (1:1–6:1). Held by DLC.

Chic. New York, March 1908-December 1909 (1:1–2:2). DLC and IU list holdings.

Chip Basket. John Silver published *Chip Basket* as a cheap monthly in New York City from 1869 to 1871 for fifty cents yearly.

City Budget. See *Budget*.

Clicks. Cartoon annual; Philadelphia, 1940; fifty cents.

Cocktails. Four or five numbers published by Stetson in Boston from July to November 1871.

The Comic Bouquet. Philadelphia, 1859, offered "Fun, Fancy, and Philosophy" at ten cents per issue with 1:10 reported for October 1859, with a three-color cover cartoon. Mott cites a verse from it, and the Newberry Library lists a holding. J. L. MaGee was the proprietor.

The Comic Library. Described by Mott as a cheap comic weekly published by Tousey in New York from 1894 to 1898. *The Five Cent Comic Library* was also published in New York from 1889 to 1892, but it is not known if they are related.

The Comic Mirror. Philadelphia, before 1900.

The Comic News. New York monthly, 1869–1872.

The Comic Times. Before 1900.

Comic Ventilator. Boston, monthly, cited in Mott from E. Steiger, *The Periodical Literature of the United States* (New York, 1873).

Comic Weekly. Richmond, Virginia; cited in Ernst(?) Steiger and Lester J. Cappon, *Virginia Newspapers 1821–1935* (1936); no known copy.

Comic World. New York, April 1855 (1:2) monthly, reported as held by MWA.

Comic World. January 1876 through December 1879, identified on the cover as a combination of *Yankee Notions*,* *The Merrymans*,* *Comic World*, and *Nick Nax*.* OClWHi and one other library list holdings.

Constellation. New York, 1829–1834; edited by Asa Green, William T. Porter, and others, as an early comic newspaper.

Corrector. New York, 1815–1817; ICN, DLC, NN, and several other libraries hold copies.

Corrector. Philadelphia, weekly; volume 1:7 (16 September 1814) cited by C. Brigham. James Fuller and L. P. Frank were the publishers; "Cadwallader Crabtree" (Lorenzo Hall) was editor. MWA has one issue.

Curiosity Cabinet. New York, Volumes 1–4 (September 1870 through 1877); Numbers 1–12 (through August 1871) as *Kuriosity Kabinet*. CtHW, OClWHi, and one other library list holdings.

Curiosity Shop. San Francisco, published for a few weeks as an illustrated quarto in 1854.

Current Anecdotes. See *Expositor and Current Anecdotes*.

The Daily Blab. 1981.

Daffy Comics. Winter 1944 issue reported.

Der Gag Bag. Norman Anthony's comic attack on Hitler as "Mein Chump." Number 1 was published in 1939, probably the only issue; the price was fifteen cents or fifteen days in a concentration camp.

Diogenes. Utah, before 1900.

Dizzy Detective Magazine. 1930s satire, undated.

Dizzy Parade. 1944 issue reported.

Drag Cartoons. Number 1 (June-July 1963) through at least March 1973 as bimonthly and monthly. Related titles include *The Best of Drag Cartoons* with four numbers issued from 1968 through 1970 and *Wildest Drag Cartoons*, undated in the 1960s, with issue number one featuring "Wonder Warthog."

Echo. Boston, circa 1808–1812, Augustan satire.

The Echo. Numbers 1–12 (1 May 1895–15 April 1896) provided a Chicago-based review of international comic journals; ICN holds copies.

Ed Big Daddy Roth. Number 1, 1964, illustrated humor.

Everybody's Own. Buffalo, New York, 1853.

Expositor and Current Anecdotes. Volumes 1–7:6 (October 1899-March 1906) as *Current Anecdotes*; Number 1 of the combined magazine was October 1899; length of run unreported. It was published in New York and Cleveland according to Mott's unpublished notes.

Eye Opener. Number 1, 1957; Charlton Press, with Bill Ward cartoons.

Fantasia. Numbers 13 and 14 in 1959 through reprints in 1962 are reported for this risqué adult comic art magazine.

Figaro in Albany. Number 1, 1 April 1837, edited by Paul Pepperpod, Esq., in Albany, New York; MWA holds this issue. DLC also has several listings under *Figaro* which do not appear to be humorous.

Film Humor. Spring 1949 (1:4) featured Marilyn Monroe on the cover.

First Class Male. Number 1, December 1943.

Flashes. Circa 1928.

Foo. Number 4, May 1952; *Mad** style.

Fooey. 1:1 (1964) reported, through Number 4.

French Frolics. Number 3 (December 1933) reported.

Frenzy. Numbers 1 (1958) through 5 reported; similar to *Mad.**

Frolics. "Or, *Paris Frolics*"; June 1931 issue reported.

From Here to Insanity. October 1955 issue reported.

Fun. New York, 1901, produced by C. L. Riker to present British-style humor in America.

Fun Follies. 1944 and 1945 issues reported.

Fun House. March and May 1971 issues reported.

Fun Yearbook. 1946 issue reported.

Funnyboy. Number 1 (Spring 1966) of this sexy humor magazine of cartoons and gags was advertised in Humorama's *Laugh Digest*** for June 1966. It sold for twenty-five cents.

Funny Funny World. 6 December 1982 (12:25) and continuing, Los Angeles, thirty-five dollars per year, edited by Martin A. Ragaway. Jokes and gags on contemporary life, survey style.

Funny Side. 1901–1917.

The Gag Recap. October 1954 (1:2); in 1956 referred to as a trade journal with 900 gags every month in *The Freelancer*;** Earle Temple, ed., mimeographed.

Gas. Brooklyn weekly of the early 1880s edited by Allan Forman and illustrated by Hillary Bell; it lasted for one or two years according to Mott's unpublished notes.

Gay Broadway. Winter 1934 through Spring 1938 reported, twenty-five cents per issue, breezy stories and pin-ups.

Gay French. 1930s.

Gayety. Number 7 was May 1933, as reported; breezy stories, pin-ups, jokes, fun; twenty-five cents per issue.

Genius of Comedy. New York, 1830–1831.

Get Lost. February-March 1954 and June-July 1954 (No. 3); *Mad*-inspired satire by Mikeross Publications.

Gilhooley's Etchings. Pittsburgh, 1883, weekly.

Girlie Fun. Fall 1970 reported.

The Gleaner. Boston, 1845–1849, resembling the *Spectator*. ICN lists holdings.

Gobs and Gals. 1:1 reported; apparently World War II era.

Good Things of Life. Before 1900.

Goose. 1 (1976) and 2 reported; illustrated humor.

The Goose-Quill. Chicago monthly edited by John Cowley-Brown at ten cents per issue from 1901 through 1904, held by ICN and nine other libraries.

Hallo. By Carl Hauser of *Puck** (1903–1904); the same title has also been reported as a Denver publication, 1893–1895.

Handies Silk Stocking Review. Number 2 was December 1936, offering movie stars, new jokes, and gags; fifteen cents.

Happy Variety. November 1952 reported.

Harlequin, or the Grotesque Magazine. Monthly, "now publishing" was advertised in New York's *Paul Pry*** in December and January 1839–1840. It offered thirty-two pages of human eccentricity, satirical selections from other sources, and absurdities, in Royal Octavo pages, with ten to fifteen illustrations per issue. Number 1 was offered September first at twelve and a half cents per issue by publisher and proprietor Robert H. Elton.

Haywire. 1:1 (1932), following *Ballyhoo.**

Hee Haw. Number 1, May 1970, bimonthly, through July 1971.

The Hint. New York, 1854, was edited and illustrated by William North for eight issues, possibly six as a daily, according to Mott (2:183).

Hiye. 1945.

Hollywood Nights. October 1931; sexsationalism possibly, rather than humor.

Hot Shots. 1946.

Hub Budget. Boston, 1872–1877.

Humor. 7 December 1951 issue reported should be different from *Humor*** described in the brief descriptions.

Humorama. Girlie humor of the 1950–1960 era.

Humor Exchange Newsletter. New York, 1962–; George Q. Lewis, editor for Humor Exchange Network, circulation by membership: 200.

The Humorist. Boston, circa 1855.

Humorist. New York, 1874; J. H. Rochacker, editor with strong Democratic politics.

Humorist. New York, 1:1–1:7 (February-August 1909), in Yiddish; NN lists holdings.

The Humorous Scrap Book. Number 1, January-March 1931 reported; slick humor magazine.

Innocent Weekly Owl. New York, 1860.

Instant Laughs. Girlie humor of the 1950–1960 era.

Iris Magazine. Indianapolis, 1892, in small format featuring witty writing; held by ICN.

Is My Face Red! 1945, stories of embarrassing moments.

Jester. Boston, 1891–1892, ten cents; the title was also carried by a Canadian publication in Montreal, 1878–1879.

Joke Parade. 1946 through 1950 reported.

Jolly Hoosier. Indianapolis, 1867, four pages, monthly.

Jolly Joker. New York; 1:3, 5, 7, 10 for May, July, September, December 1866; Volume 1: 4–10 for June-December 1867 as a small folio monthly featuring political humor with full-page and double-page cartoons. Mott cites this title as a New York monthly, later semi-monthly, from 1862 to 1877 (2: 185n); 6:8 was October 1868 at ten cents; actual dates are September 1862 through May 1878. It was published by the Frank Leslie Company in New York.

Judge and Jury. Before 1900.

Just for Fun. Fifty-six pages, *Puck** size, in colors, available from *Puck* for twenty-five cents, according to a *Cosmopolitan* advertisement in November 1895.

Laffboy. Parody of *Playboy*; 1:2 (April 1965) reported.

Lantern (New Orleans). *Lantern* provided varied prose and cartoons of social and political satire; it lasted from 1886 through 1889.

Lantern (Cincinnati). The Cincinnati *Lantern* from 1907 to 1908 was a furniture company's monthly featuring one-liners and aphorisms (ICN).

Laugh. 1960s girlie humor.

Laugh Circus. Girlie humor of the 1950–1960 era.

Laugh It Off! Advertised in *Romp.***

Laugh Out. Spring 1969 issue reported.

Laugh Riot. August 1961-December 1965 issues reported; issues advertised at least through June 1966.

Laughter-Magazine of Adult Humor. July 1976 issue reported.

Let's Have a Good Laugh. Circa 1945.

Lies. New York, 1889; produced by Alfred Trumble, New York journalist.

Life's Monthly Calendar. Ten cents or one dollar a year by mail, advertised in February 1892 *Life**.

Light. Ohio, Chicago (1889–1901); holdings at DLC and University of Arizona.

Light. San Francisco; Volumes 1–2 (1896–1897).

The Lion's Mouth. Cincinnati, December 1900-March 1901; "official journal of the society of those who do not need Diogenes"; brief comic essays; held by ICN.

Little Corporal. Chicago; 4:6-Volume 17 (June 1867-December 1873) in quarto and octavo.

Little Devil. A "journalistic highball" for everybody but "mental mendicants and moral runts" (1905–1908), merged into the *By Stander*.

The Lounger. By George Goodfellow, Esq., from Hudson, New York; 1:1–26 (16 September 1815–15 June 1816) by W. L. Stone. MWA holds the complete file.

The Low Down. "A magazine for hypocrites"; ICN has Number 1 (May 1925) and a special June number.

Luncheon. July 1815-January 1816; Lewis P. Franks, editor; discontinued to escape a libel suit. See Albert H. Smyth, *Philadelphia Magazines and their Contributors, 1741–1850*.

March of Fun. Circa 1945.

Mascot. New Orleans; Mott gives both 1882–1895 and 1881–1900, and the *Union List* gives 1882–1894. *Mascot* was an illustrated weekly with political and social satire in varied prose and cartoons. Holdings of scattered issues are at NN and NcD.

Maybe You're Screwy Too. 1950 issue reported.

Merry and Wise. Mott lists this title as 1867, New York, but issues seen at MB are for *Merry and Wise* preceding *Old Merry's Annual*, published in 1867–1869 by Hodder and Staughton in London. This may be an American reprint of the British periodical.

Merry Masker. New York, 1876.

Merry Moments. Before 1900.

Mirth of a Nation. Harry "A" Chesler and William Wise and Company produced *Mirth of a Nation* beginning in 1941 as a color comic digest at ten cents; Numbers 1–5 have been reported.

Native Virginian. Gordonsville, Virginia, 15 November 1867 to 1 March 1870.

Neal's Saturday Gazette. More properly considered a general fiction magazine, *Neal's Saturday Gazette* is significant because of Joseph C. Neal's founding and editing of it from 1844 until his death in 1847. It included his own "Charcoal Sketches" and encouraged "Solitaire" and "Widow Bedott." PHi holds copies.

New Cartoons, Jokes & Gags. July 1956 issue reported.

New Comedy. March 1962-November 1963 issues reported.

New Hampshire Republican. Concord, New Hampshire, 26 July through 8 November 1890 reported.

New Milk and Cheese. Boston, 16 April–2 May 1807; complete file held at MWA.

The New Satirist. Volume 1:1 was issued in late 1981; Randy McAusland, editor; bi-monthly at $10.00 per year from New Canaan, Connecticut; serious intellectual humor.

New World. June 1840-May 1845; five libraries list holdings, and it is reprinted by University Microfilms.

New York Gazette. 4 March 1846–10 June 1846 are 2:1–12, "devoted to fun, frolic, etc." MWA holds the issues cited.

New York Humorist. 1869 publication reported.

New York Time-Piece. Four-page folio with comic woodcuts, 1853.

Nugget. Quarterly, September 1944 through March 1946 (1:1–9).

Nuts. February 1958 (No. 1) reported.

Nuts & Jolts. Number 22 reported, probably World War II humorous digest.

Nutz! July 1945 reported as a very large paperback book.

O.K. New York, 1853.

Oy' Oy I'm Leffin. Circa 1930.

Pardon My Sex, Doctor! 1950 and 1954 issues reported.

Paris Frolics. One of many titles including the words "Paris," "French," or "Parisian" in the 1930s which lie somewhere between sexual titillation and humor, leaning to the former. Monthly at twenty-five cents, issues are reported from September 1931 through March 1932.

Paris Gayety. February 1934 through February 1935 issues reported, along the same lines as other "Paris" pulps.

Parisian Follies. Number 21, at fifty cents, is reported in the 1930s, and a 2:2 is reported in 1943.

Parissienne. A 1915 cheaply satirical paper begun by H. L. Mencken and G. J. Nathan.

Pen and Pencil. January-June 1853, features caricatures and comical editor's portfolio; ICN holds copies.

Photo Fun. Girlie humor of the 1950–1960 era.

Pickles. New York, August 1855–1956? reported.

Pictorial French Follies. May (No. 4), November 1930 issues reported, monthly.

Pip. Summer and Winter 1944 issues reported.

Pleasure. Number 1 (1946) reported, with cartoons by Flagg, Soglow, Gross, and others.

Poker Chips. 1:1, June 1896 to November 1896.

Polyanthos. Boston, December 1805-September 1814, in three series with some interruptions, monthly; a general magazine particularly devoted to the theater, but edited by Joseph T. Buckingham and with contributions by Royall Tyler. See Joseph T. Buckingham, *Personal Memoirs and Recollections of Editorial Life* (Boston, 1852). CtY, MB, MH, NN, and three other libraries list holdings; reprinted by University Microfilms.

Portland Figaro. Portland, Maine; 1–2, August 1890-November 1891 issues reported.

Private Bill. One of the Chesler digest humor books from 1943 and 1944 named after one of his stock comic figures; see *ABC*.**

Puck's Calender. Part of the *Puck** array of magazines.

Punch and Judy. 1:1 was August 1882, Boston.

Punster. The Mobile, Alabama, *Punster* is referred to in Hudson's book on comic journalism (1871) as "recent."

Pup. 1941 issue reported.

Quampeag Coyote. Calaveras County, California, May 1855.

Quote. "The Speaker's Digest that Grows into a Book" proclaimed its forty-third year in 83:12 (15 June 1983). From Atlanta, Georgia, twenty-three pages, 5" × 7½", it provides jokes and stories for speakers; similar to material found in the *Reader's Digest.***

Racin' Toons. April 1972 issue reported.

Racket. New York, circa 1890. A five-cent humorous pictorial weekly.

Reveille. The New York *Reveille* (1851–1854) was edited at one time by Cornelius Mathews. Mott reports that it was founded by Englishmen named Charles and Barton.

Riggin' Bill. Another Harry Chesler product of World War II in 1943 and 1944 was *Riggin' Bill*, a stock comic figure along with *Private Bill* from the *ABC*** comic digests; four numbers are reported.

Rutland (Vermont) Times. A weekly listed as comic by E. Steiger, *The Periodical Literature of the United States* (New York: Steiger, 1873).

The Salmagundi: The News of the Day. Philadelphia, 3 January 1836–1837?

Salute. April 1943 issue reported.

Sam, the Scaramouche. Cincinnati, 1885, weekly, sixteen pages, 9" × 11", eight dollars annually; listed in Ayer's *Directory of Periodicals* for 1885.

The Satirist. Boston, 16 January 1812; titled *The Boston Satirist* from 20 April 1812; discontinued on 9 May 1812. James L. Edwards, formerly the publisher of Merrill Butler's Boston *Scourge,** was the proprietor. MWA, MB, MHi, and DLC list holdings; University Microfilms has reprinted it.

The Satirist. New York, 11 January 1845–?

Screen Comedy. Number 2 was October 1931; movie glamor girls were featured in pin-up poses.

Screen Humor. Number 1, January 1934, twenty cents, featuring starlets in lingerie.

Sexplosion. Advertised in a Magnum-Royal Publication in 1969 as one of their offerings.

Shanghai. Ellicott's Mills, Maryland, 1855–1856.

Shook Up. Number 1 for 1958 reported; *Mad** inspired.

Slick. May 1945 issue reported.

Snafu. March 1956 reported, Marvel Comics response to *Mad.**

Snap. January 1934 issue reported; Numbers 1–5 also reported separately, probably for a cartoon digest like *Gayety.***

Sporty. Number 1 for 1958; sports magazine parody.

Strictly Private. Two numbers reported; probably World War II service humor.

Suppository, A Magazine of Contemplation. Santa Barbara, California, 1970 quarterly;

edited by Eustace Trevache. "A satirical expose of what some think is wrong with dogmatic thought"; forty pages, offset, three dollars annually.

Texas Sifter. Published briefly by Alex Sweet, 1:1–38 (29 December 1895–12 September 1896) after he left *Texas Siftings*.* North Texas State University holds five issues.

Thimk. Six numbers beginning in 1958; *Mad** inspired.

Thistle. New York, 1872; edited by F. S. Saltus and printed by S. M. Howard.

Tops in Humor. Numbers 1 and 2 reported for 1944; a second source reports Number 1 for 1941 from Chesler studios.

The Town. New York, 15 February–26 July 1845.

Trump. New York, (1) January and (2) March 1957, edited by Harvey Kurtzman and published by Hugh Hefner, after Kurtzman left *Mad*,* satirical material, fifty cents per issue.

Uncle Sam. Boston, 1842-?

Wag. Boston, 1868; Mott describes *Wag* as a cheap South Boston monthly.

Wang Doodle. Chicago, October 1858-January 1859, four numbers reported.

Whim. Philadelphia, 14 May through 16 July 1814; a dramatic paper edited by John Bioren.

Whim. The later *Whim* was a "little magazine" of comic froth and whimsy from 1901 to 1904; a number of libraries have holdings, including DLC.

Whip. St. Louis weekly, 1885–1886.

World Humor. November 1925 issue identified; thirty-five cents, supplying a "comedy digest" of the world; the issue cited contains four George Ade "Fables in Slang," among other material more reflective of the flapper era in Europe and America.

Yankee Comics. Issues reported circa 1943.

The Yankee Miscellany. Boston, January-November 1839; eleven numbers held by MWA.

Yell. Number 3 for February 1966 and June issue reported.

You Chirped. Possibly titled *You Chirped a Chinful*, December, 1943 (Number 2) reported.

Young America. T. W. Strong, proprietor of *Yankee Notions*,* began *Young America* in 1853, edited by Charles Gayler; sued for libel in 1854, it was discontinued, to be revived in 1856 briefly as *Yankee Doodle; or, Young America*.*

Young America on the Pacific. California, 1853–1854.

Zany. 1958, Numbers 1–4 reported.

Henry Clay Lukens in "American Literary Comedians" in *Harper's Magazine* 80 (April 1890): 791–92, gives a list of humor magazines which provides no dates and in several obvious cases gives a partially inaccurate name. Titles which seem to fit in Part III.B are *The Torch, Uncle Sam* (prior to the Chicago version), *Flying Leaves, Gas*, and *Snap* ("Mr. Vallentine's short-lived bantling"). Among newspapers Lukens lists the *Oil City Derrick*, edited by Robert W. Criswell, the *Virginia City Territorial Enterprise*, which included Dan DeQuille and Mark Twain, *Solid Muldoon, Denver Hello, Tombstone Epitaph, Jimpelcute, Chaff, Breeze* and *Sunday Morning*, among others which may have varying degrees of comic content. These items cited in Lukens do not appear in the date listings.

Part IV

GENRE ESSAYS

College Humor Magazines

Student humor and the academy have been related in a tradition that goes back to at least the twelfth and thirteenth centuries in Europe. Wandering "scholar-poets" produced "goliardic" verse that satirized the Church (which controlled the universities of the time) and the popes while glorifying wine, women, and song. Later at Oxford University the *terrae filius* (a son of the earth) satirized graduates and university officials alike as part of the four-day commencement ceremonies. The satiric speech eventually became so popular that the occasion was moved from the chapel to where the ceremonies were usually held in a theater. This secularizing step gave greater freedom to the *terrae filius*, and the speeches became so unrestrained that in the early eighteenth century the speech was abolished. The preoccupation of the goliardic poets with libations and the opposite sex, the humorous aggression of the *terrae filius*, and the banning of his satire, these anticipate to a large extent much that is typical of student humor magazines in the United States.

Although referred to as magazines, such student publications include mimeographed sheets stapled together as well as highly professional periodicals printed on coated stock. The sizes of such magazines have ranged from octavo to tabloid, and frequency has varied from fortnightly and monthly to highly irregular, even fugitive. The contents have generally included sketches, stories, jokes, cartoons, and other graphic humor, verse, and photographs. What kind of humor material dominated and what was excluded depended on the era the magazine was published in, the amount of money and printing facilities available, the availability of someone who could draw or cartoon, and finally the predilections of the editors and their staffs. Early versions tended to feature stories and sketches, later, jokes and cartoons dominated, and photographs made a still later appearance.

Such magazines have been published under a variety of arrangements. Some of the earliest magazines were published by classes, the sophomore class at Princeton putting out the *Nassau Rake* in the 1850s, the senior class at Allegheny College putting out *Whiskers* ("watch us grow") in 1911, and the freshmen at

Duke University issuing the *Blue Imp* and the *Duke 'n Duchess* in the 1930s. Various clubs and fraternities have published the humor magazines of their schools. The Ambrose Bierce Society issued *The Vulture* (1965–1967) at Swarthmore College, while the Scribbler's Club published *The Giggler* (1913–1914) at Louisiana State University. Local chapters of Sigma Delta Chi, the journalism fraternity, were in charge of publishing Grinnell College's *Malteaser* (1920–1936), Minnesota's *Ski-U-Mah* (1921–1949), and Maine's *Maniac* (1921–1929). The *Royal Gaboon* (1921–1932; 1949–1967) at Hamilton College was produced by the local chapter of Pi Delta Epsilon. The Hammer and Coffin Society published the Oregon State *Orange Owl* (1920–1928). Informal self-appointed groups of students have also succeeded in publishing humor magazines. *Tar Baby* (1911–1912; 1919–1921) and *Boll Weevil* (1922–1924) at the University of North Carolina and *The Coyote* (1908–1911) at the University of Texas were such magazines. But being published by informal and unofficial groups does not necessarily mean being short-lived. Tulane's *Urchin* was published from 1936 until 1961. In fact, the most successful college humor magazine, the *Harvard Lampoon,** exists independently of the University, incorporated, in a building donated by William Randolph Hearst. But for the most part college humor magazines, like most other student publications, have existed with the blessing of the campus student government, sometimes supported with allocations from that organization, using the school's name. In addition, such magazines usually operated from premises on the campus, a dorm room, an office, or a building. Such connections were the source of the conflicts that often arose between editors of the magazines and school administrators when differences of opinion arose over the contents of the magazines. The matter of what rights, freedom, and responsibilities each party has and how the parties will decide on their application has been the source of much friction and the cause for many a magazine closing down. Such conflicts may be said to be endemic to college humor magazines.

Full-fledged magazines dedicated solely to humor and published regularly did not begin until the 1870s, but there were forty years of germination during which a great variety of publications on college and university campuses contained humor. Frank Luther Mott mentions in passing *Thistle* (1834) and *Chameleon* (1835), both published at Princeton, as "pioneer college comics" (1:427). The *Chameleon* was a pioneer in that it took a lighthearted approach in its contents, promising to publish "all violent deaths, romantic marriages as well as authenticated ghost stories, . . . the most important foreign intelligence, such as the sacking of cities, the discovery of new continents, the death of kings and queens, the birth of princes and princesses, the eruption of volcanoes, and the reformation of drunkards." Its first issue (2 March 1835) contained a dialect joke, a parody, and a short squib against early rising by Theophilus Sleeper, among other items, some serious, some humorous. In short the *Chameleon* was a literary magazine with a heavy emphasis on humor.

Much different was a series of periodicals published from 1852 to 1869 at Princeton and from 1857 to 1892 at Allegheny College. Published annually at

Princeton by members of different classes and anonymously at Allegheny, varying in length from four pages to more than a hundred, and bearing such names as *Paul Pry, Whangdoodle, The Thunderbolt, The Vindicator*, and *The Scorpion*, the magazines lampooned faculty and students alike. The attacks included references to physical and personal attributes so exaggerated that one suspects exaggeration as part of the humor. One professor at Princeton is described as a "dandy" who acted as if he had been "employed to teach the Sophs the science of dress, and the art of wooing to the fair sex." A professor at Allegheny is called an "odious villain" in a "malformed carcass." Such scurrility caused one president of Allegheny College to attempt to prosecute the perpetrators, offering a $500 reward and hiring a detective to catch them. One suspected editor was brought to trial but was judged not guilty. *The Surveyor* at Rensselaer Polytechnic Institute in its second issue (23 December 1865) advanced as its slogan: "With or without offence [sic] to friends or foes / We shall sketch Students [sic] life exactly as it goes." Within months *The Rod and Leveller*, a rival magazine, accused it of publishing "filthy billingsgate."

Humor in literary magazines remained a viable alternative to the lampoon sheet. At Washington and Lee in 1873 a literary magazine, the *Southern Collegian*, with a well-developed sense of humor, hoaxed the student body and a considerable number of newspaper editors around the country as well with a deadpan "eyewitness" account of the burning of the Natural Bridge, a structure fourteen miles south of the W & L campus in Lexington, Virginia. *The Collegian*, which had started in 1868, continued to feature satire and parody down to the 1930s when it finally became a full-fledged college humor magazine in keeping with the trend of the period.

The first student literary magazines in which the emphasis was more on humor than on literature were at Columbia, Yale, and Harvard. At Columbia *Cap and Gown* (1868–73) the *Acta Columbiana* (1873–1885) fit this description. The Columbia yearbook of 1870 described *Cap and Gown* as "filled with wit and humor, poetry and prose, and as such it cannot fail to recommend it to all true lovers of college literature." It failed to flourish, however, but was followed immediately by *Acta Columbiana*, which metamorphosed into a full-fledged humor magazine when John Kendrick Bangs became editor in 1879. Writing under such pseudonyms as Shakespeare Jones, T. Carlyle Smith, and the Collegiate Vituperator, Bangs served his apprenticeship for a career as a popular comic writer, the first of a long line of humorists to emerge from the seedbeds of college comic magazines. Bangs graduated in 1883, and *Acta Columbiana* folded the following year. It would be nearly twenty years before Columbia University would have another humor magazine.

Meanwhile, students at Yale and Harvard had begun humor magazines, the *Yale Record* in 1872 and the *Harvard Lampoon** in 1876, that would become among the longest lived in the country. Both conceived of themselves as dedicated solely to purveying humor in a magazine format. The founders of the *Lampoon* talked of putting out a college *Punch* and subtitled their first issue, "Cambridge

Charivari.'' By the turn of the century, college humor magazines existed on campuses from coast to coast. New magazines started on the East Coast at City College of New York (*College Mercury*, 1880), Lehigh (*The Burr*, 1881), Princeton (*The Tiger*, 1882), Cornell (*The Widow*, 1894), and Bryn Mawr (*The Fortnightly Philistine*, 1895–1903). (Although *The Philistine* was never exclusively a humor magazine, it took a lighthearted approach to college affairs and published some excellent humor. It was also the first such publication at a women's college.) The first college humor magazine in the Middle West was Michigan's *The Wrinkle* (1893–1905), followed by Wisconsin's *Sphinx* (1899–1905). The oldest college humor magazine on the West Coast is *Chaparral* at Stanford, begun in 1899. Of these early magazines *The Lampoon*, *The Tiger*, and *Chaparral* have continued to the present, more or less without serious interruptions. The *Yale Record* also continues, but it did not publish from 1973 to 1976.

Slow but steady growth continued up to the outbreak of World War I and produced such long-running magazines as Columbia's *Jester* (1901-current?), California's *Pelican* (1903-current), Dartmouth's *Jack-O-Lantern* (1909-current but with interruptions), and the Naval Academy's *Log* (1913-current). The first full-fledged college humor magazine in the South was *The Coyote* (1908–1911) at the University of Texas, at first an unofficial student publication that soon received official recognition. Hard on the heels of *The Coyote* was Georgia Tech's *Yellow Jacket* which in 1909 evolved into a humor magazine from the literary *Georgia Tech* (1897). In 1911 the *Tar Baby* popped up at the University of North Carolina, and in 1913 a group of women students at Louisiana State under the name of the Scribblers' Club issued *The Giggler*, which was not only the first humor magazine at LSU but also the first exclusively humor magazine put out by women students. It lasted a little over a year. Although *The Giggler* denied being a ''militant maid,'' the editors pointed out some inequalities in a university only recently turned coeducational. Other humor magazines started in the pre-World War I period were Penn State's *Froth* (1910–1982?), Ohio State's *Sundial* (1911–1960s), and the University of Kansas' *The Sour Owl* (1914–1956).

By 1914 students at between twenty-five and thirty colleges and universities were regularly issuing humor magazines. But within ten years the number had nearly tripled as approximately seventy schools claimed humor magazines. Not only were students at the large public and private universities publishing humor magazines, but students at small liberal arts and women's colleges were turning out comic magazines as well. In the early 1920s Grinnell, Davidson, Hamilton, Denison, Bowdoin, Pomona, Colby, Middlebury, Wabash, and Whitman Colleges were in the act. Following the short-lived *Giggler* at LSU came the *Campus Cat* at Smith (1918–1930; 1948–1952), *The Vassar Vagabond* (1925–1927), and Randolph-Macon's *Old Maid* (1926–1953), for some time the only humor magazine at a women's college until Smith's *Campus Cat* returned in the late forties.

The outbreak of new comic magazines on college campuses began seriously in 1919 when at least seven new journals appeared. In 1920 at least ten more new magazines started up, and a year later a dozen more. During the rest of the 1920s twenty more began publication. Although the 1920s was the period of most rapid growth for college comic magazines, the Depression and World War II failed to appreciably reduce the introduction of new magazines (1930–1939, ten new magazines; 1940–1949, a dozen new magazines; 1950–1959, eleven more new magazines). But even when the burgeoning of new magazines was most dramatic, the mortality rate kept pace. Some magazines lasted only a few issues, for example, Bowdoin's *Blowout* (1917), Brigham Young's *Y's Guys* (1922), Arkansas' *White Mule** (1924), and Michigan State's *Green Onion* (1925). Fifty-five magazines closed down between 1930 and 1959, two dozen in the 1950s alone. The golden age of college humor magazines was a period of rapid expansion and equally rapid turnover.

The humor magazine on the college campus was far from dead in the sixties. Some that had died in the 1930s and 1940s came back in the 1950s and 1960s: *The Wesleyan Wasp* (1919–1930; 1967–1968), the University of Chicago's *Phoenix* (1920–1937; 1958–1967), Pennsylvania's *Punch Bowl* (1900–1940; 1965–current), Williams's *Purple Cow* (1907–1943; 1946–1950; 1952–1963), and Middlebury's *Blue Baboon* (1923–1929; 1963; 1965; 1967). Some campuses tried new names for new magazines, perhaps unaware that earlier comic magazines had existed on the same campuses: Washington State's *Fo-Faws* (1949–1951) and *Spark* (1956–1961) were successors to WSU's first humor magazine *Cougar's Paws* (1921–1929); New York University's *Plague* (1977; 1978) followed NYU's *Medley* (1913–1950); Kansas State's *Bitter Bird* (1946–1950) and *Squat* (1955–1958) replaced *The Sour Owl* (1914–1956). Some schools that had never had comic magazines were launching them: Texas at El Paso's *El Burro* (1943–1974); Occidental's *Fang* (1946–1968); Purdue's *Rivet* (1946–1967); San Jose State's *Lyke* (1946–1961); Florida State's *Smoke Signals* (1951–1970); Rochester's *Ugh* (1957–1966), Rutgers's *Rut* (1961–1974) and Swarthmore's *Vulture* (1965–1968).

But by the late 1970s and early 1980s, fewer than two dozen college humor magazines were in existence. To a large extent they survived where college humor magazines had begun or had first flourished, mainly in the Ivy League and on the West Coast. The *Harvard Lampoon*, the *Princeton Tiger*, and Columbia's *Jester* have continued without interruption since their inception, the *Lampoon* and *Tiger* issuing centennial anthologies. Dartmouth's *Jack-O-Lantern* suffered only a brief interruption during World Wars I and II. The *Yale Record* closed down for three years in the mid–1970s but began again in 1976. Pennsylvania's *Punch Bowl* began again in 1965 after having been closed since 1940. Elsewhere in the East, Amherst's *Sabrina* tried again for the third time (1950–1953; 1971; 1981-current), Navy's *Log* continued uninterrupted since 1913, while Massachusetts' *Yahoo* (1969-current) and Massachusetts Institute of Technology's *Tool and Die* (1983-current) were new vehicles for schools with traditions going back many decades. In the West, Stanford's *Chaparral* and

California's *Pelican*, the earliest humor magazines in that area, continued to flourish. The University of California at Los Angeles' *Satyr*, which began in the early 1960s, exists as an insert for the college newspaper. In 1979 students at Northwestern started *Rubber Teeth* and at Michigan State *Stale News*. At Emory University the tradition is being kept alive by *Spoke* (1976-current), the last humor magazine there disappearing in 1974. Two long-lived humor magazines, Penn State's *Froth* (1910-?) and Michigan's *Gargoyle* (1919-?), were reported in precarious state in 1983. Student humor magazines have survived but are at best marginal publications on most campuses.

What has been the legacy of college humor magazines for humor in the United States? Some may not think it funny, but the Metro Goldwyn Mayer lion trademark was inspired by the laughing lion decoration on the Columbia *Jester*. The growling lion of MGM was the work of Howard Dietz, an editor of the *Jester*, one of the leading lyricists of the American musical theater, and chief of publicity and advertising at MGM when he came up with the famous trademark. According to Dietz in his 1974 autobiography *Dancing in the Dark*, the laughing lion of the *Jester* comes from the symbol of Columbia University, which in turn comes from the lion on the crest of King's College, the name given to Columbia when it was founded. The legacy of the college humor magazines also reaches into *Bartlett's Quotations* and similar collections with Graham Lee Hemminger's doggerel, "Tobacco is a dirty weed. I like it. / It satisfies no normal need. I like it. / . . . It's the worst darn stuff I've ever seen: I like it," which appeared in the Penn State *Froth*, November 1915 (p. 9). Hemminger may or may not have had in mind Benjamin Waterhouse's quatrain by way of Oliver Wendell Holmes:

> Tobacco is a filthy weed,
> That from the devil does proceed;
> It drains your purse, it burns your clothes,
> And makes a chimney of your nose.

But the full legacy of college humor magazines is seen in the number of humorists, cartoonists, graphic artists, or writers whose work contains a significant comic orientation who served apprenticeships on such periodicals:

Acta Columbiana: John Kendrick Bangs

Arkansas *White Mule*: Chet Lauck ("Lum" of the radio comedy team, "Lum and Abner")

Arizona *Kitty Kat*: Virgil Partch

Brown Jug: S. J. Perelman

California *Pelican*: Rube Goldberg; Ted Key (creator of cartoon and TV character "Hazel.")

Colgate *Banter*: Andy Rooney

Columbia *Jester*: Charles Saxon; Ed Koren; David Cort; Bennett Cerf; Robert Paul Smith; Herman Wouk

Cornell *Widow*: St. Clair McKelway; George Jean Nathan; E. B. White

Dartmouth *Jack-O-Lantern*: Theodor J. Giesl ("Dr. Seuss''); Abner Dean; Budd Schullberg

Harvard Lampoon: Robert Benchley; Christopher Cerf; Henry Beard; James Montgomery Flagg; Doug Kenney; J. P. Marquand; George Plimpton; John Updike; George W. S. Trow; Gluyas Williams

Minnesota *Ski-U-Mah*: Max Shulman; Thomas Heggen

Missouri *Showme*: Mort Walker

Occidental *Fang*: Terry Gilliam

Penn State *Froth*: Ed Zern

Pomona *Sagehen*: Richard Armour; Wright Morris

Princeton *Tiger*: Whitney Darrow, Jr.; F. Scott Fitzgerald; Booth Tarkington; Ring Lardner, Jr.; Struthers Burt

Ohio State *Sundial*: Elliott Nugent; James Thurber; Earl Wilson

Oklahoma *Whirlwind*: Sam Cobean

UCLA *Satyr*: Tony Auth

USC *Wampus Cat*: Art Buchwald

Yale *Record*: Robert C. Osborne; Peter Arno; Garry Trudeau

In addition to serving as a greenhouse for the humorously disposed, alumni of college humor magazines have from the onset of such magazines enhanced American humor by founding and staffing commercial humor magazines. Alumni of the *Harvard Lampoon* are responsible for founding two of the important humor magazines of the twentieth century: *Life** (1883–1936) and *National Lampoon** (1969-current). *Life* was founded by Edward Sanford Martin and John Tyler Wheelright, both of whom were members of the founding staff of the *Harvard Lampoon*. Several generations later, Doug Kenney and Henry Beard put their experience on the *Harvard Lampoon* into founding the *National Lampoon*. *Life* in turn served as the inspiration and prototype for many college humor magazines, among them the Dartmouth *Jack-O-Lantern* and the Cornell *Widow*.

College humor magazines also served as stepping stones into the world of commercial humor magazines. Harold Swanson, staffer of the Grinnell *Malteaser*, eventually became editor of *College Humor*,** the monthly anthology that claimed to publish the best from all college humor magazines of the time. In the early 1940s people from the California *Pelican* flocked to *The New Yorker*,* according to an article on the *Pelican* by the *Daily Californian*. College humor magazines have also been conduits for a variety of writers and graphic artists whose later works are not basically humorous, among them Vance Packard (Penn State *Froth*), Kenneth Roberts, Whitney Baillet, and Hendrik Van Loon (Cornell *Widow*), Allen Ginsberg, Thomas Merton and Ad Reinhardt (Columbia *Jester*), Clay Felker (*Duke 'n Duchess*), Frederick Faust, pseud. Max Brand (California *Pelican*), John McPhee (Princeton *Tiger*), and many others.

A final legacy of college humor magazines is the magazine parody. The *Harvard Lampoon* claims to have parodied *Life* in 1901 but also claims that Robert Benchley, an editor of the *Lampoon* in 1910, "invented" the magazine parody. The first college humor magazine to devote a full issue to parody was the Princeton *Tiger* which parodied *Alice in Wonderland* in 1882. In any case, the magazine parody became and remains a humor form especially associated with college humor periodicals. Popular magazines no longer in existence (*Liberty, Literary Digest, American*) found favor with the editors of the *Lampoon*, the Penn *Punch Bowl*, and the Cornell *Widow*. Magazines with specialized content were also popular: *Popular Mechanics, Photoplay, Snappy Stories, The American Mercury*, and *Town and Country*, for example. The Smith *Cat* parodied not only popular magazines (*Kitterary Digest*) but also traditional campus publications, that is, the *Cat-ologue* and the *Calumnae Quarterly*. In the 1940s the Pomona *Sagehen* did *Time* (*Dime*, a Nickel's Worth of News for Fifty Cents) and *Esquire* (*Squire*, The Magazine for When). More recently, *Harvard Lampoon* has taken on *Cosmopolitan, Mademoiselle*, and *Sports Illustrated*.

College humor magazines have served an important function in American humor almost from their beginning. The list of comic writers, cartoonists, and graphic artists whose apprenticeships coincided with their years as students suggests that, for many, such magazines took the place of the print shop and the lecture platform as the training grounds for printed and visual humor. In addition, college humor magazines have inspired or supplied material and personnel for important commercial humor magazines from *Life* to the present. As vaudeville provided much talent for radio and television comedy in their early days, so college humor magazines supplied newspapers and magazines with literary and graphic humorists.

Bibliography

Information about college humor magazines consists almost entirely of nostalgic articles and anthologies. *A Century of College Humor* (New York: 1971; slightly updated, 1982, reissued as *College Humor*) by Dan Carlinsky is the most accessible source of examples of college humor, but its organization and analysis are suspect. Four anthologies from individual institutions are available: *The Harvard Lampoon Centennial Celebration 1876– 1973*, edited by Martin Kaplan, foreword by John Updike (Boston: 1973); *The Cornell Widow Hundredth Anniversary Anthology*, edited by Joey Green (Ithaca, N.Y.: 1981); *Roaring at One Hundred: The Princeton Tiger Magazine Centennial Album* (Princeton, N.J.: 1983); and *Laughter on the Hill: A Treasury of Allegheny College Humor*, edited by Nels Juleus (Meadville, Pa.: 1979). Each contains selections and historical commentary. Alumni magazines, student newspapers, and college histories are also sources of information; typical examples include Martin Barolsky, "Champions of Obnoxious Humor," *At Rensselaer* (November 1984): 5–8; *Columbia College Today: Special Issue* (Spring-Summer 1981) devoted part of an issue to the eightieth Anniversary of the *Jester*; Dick Corten, "The Long Flight of the California *Pelican*," *Daily Californian Weekly Magazine* (31 October 1968): 1, 7–8; Virginius Dabney, *Mr. Jefferson's University—A History* (Charlottesville, Va.: 1981), passim; Robert T. Hilton, "It was Frivol-ous and

Fun,'' *The Iowan* (Spring 1981): 34–41, 50–51; Debbie Shell, ''Forty Years of Showme,'' *Missouri Alumnus* (November/December 1981): 16–21; Hope Waingrow, ''Whatever Happened to College Humor?'' *Claremont Courier* (24 September 1970): 1–4; and Charles A. Wright, ''When Punch Bowl had some punch,'' *Pennsylvania Gazette* (November 1975): 21–25, among others. Also see *Max Shulman's Guided Tour of Campus Humor: The Best Stories, Articles, Poems, Jokes, and Nonsense from over Sixty-five College Humor Magazines* (Garden City, N.Y.: 1955).

George A. Test

Scholarly Humor
Magazines

The union of humor and scholarship in periodical form has occurred only in the last twenty-five years but at an increasingly rapid pace in the last ten. Although two periodicals devoted to Mark Twain began in the 1930s, they are special and isolated cases in the movement to give more attention to humor in the scholarly community. *Worm Runner's Digest: Journal of Biological Psychology* (1959–1981), *Satire Newsletter* (1963–1973), *Subterranean Sociology Newsletter* (1967–current), and *The Journal of Irreproducible Results* (1955–current) were among the earliest manifestations of the incursion of humor into scholarship. In the 1970s at least six periodicals dedicated to humor or related aspects appeared for the first time: *Journal of American Humor, American Humor Newsletter, Studies in Contemporary Satire* (all 1974–current); *Scholia Satyrica* (1975–1981); *Maledicta* (1977–current); and *Thalia: Studies in Literary Humor* (1978–current).

But the alliance of humor and scholarship has not been a simple one. It has taken a variety of forms, and, as with comic periodicals in general, its spawn has led a marginal existence at best or a short-lived one at worst (compared, that is, to most scholarly journals). Broadly speaking, such periodicals have taken two routes in combining scholarship and humor: one is the marriage of the two in more or less traditional scholarly journals or newsletters; the other the mock-marriage, that is, the parodying of the scholarly periodical with humorous articles and other spoofery. A third somewhat miscellaneous category includes periodicals similar in some ways to trade journals and others (often newsletters) directed to those who share a particular interest or taste in a kind of humor (for example, puns or limericks).

The most general of scholarly periodicals devoted to humor is *Thalia*, edited by Jacqueline Tavernier-Courbin at the University of Ottawa. Launched as a thrice yearly periodical in folio size, it has since become a biennial in a smaller format. Bilingual, it has issued special issues on "Humour Québec" (Vol. 8:1), "Humor and Religion: Friends or Foes?" (Vol. 6:1), and "Satire: Language and Style" (Vol. 5:1), among others. *Thalia* also publishes humor and book reviews from time to time. *Studies in American Humor* and *American Humor: An Interdisciplinary Newsletter* began as separate publications in 1974 but in 1983 merged while retaining the logos of each periodical. *Studies in American Humor*, founded by Jack Meathenia at Southwest Texas State University, and edited by him until his death in 1981, concentrated on literary humor and published news, queries, and book reviews. Published three times a year from 1974 to 1976, a news series under the editorship of John O. Rosenbalm was begun in 1982. Volume 2, Numbers 1 and 2, were special issues honoring Thomas Berger. *American Humor: An Interdisciplinary Newsletter*, founded and edited by Lawrence Mintz of the American Studies Program at the University of Maryland, was more eclectic than *Studies in American Humor*, publishing short articles on ethnic humor, stand-up comics, the roast, and *Playboy* as well as extensive annotated checklists, book reviews, and news of meetings of humor organizations. The *Newsletter* came out twice a year in folio size, the pages stapled in the upper left-hand corner.

Interest in satire has generated a number of periodicals, although the mortality rate has been high. The first was *Satire Newsletter*,* conceived as a newsletter but issued from the beginning in journal size. Then came *PUCRED* (or Publications of the University of California at Riverside English Department), issued from San Francisco by Richard Desson, a former graduate student at Riverside. It rarely exceeded forty-eight pages and was in fact a parody of *PMLA* (*Publications of the Modern Language Association*) and other literary learned journals. Between 1968 and 1974 eleven issues appeared as well as a *Directory cum* "PUCRED Text Society Reprint" (1972) and a *Style Manual* (1973). In 1975 *Scholia Satyrica* appeared from the University of South Florida under the editorship of Ralph Wyly. It announced that it had "absorbed" *PUCRED* but was expanding the scope of the original journal to include "genuine criticism, particularly . . . explorations devoted to 'the tradition of learned wit'." It continued to be mainly a vehicle for satire, academic and otherwise, and never attracted sufficient scholarly submissions. It was discontinued in 1981. The sole surviving journal devoted to satire is *Studies in Contemporary Satire*, edited by C. Darrell Sheraw at Clarion State College, Clarion, Pennsylvania. Published annually, it combines criticism; original satire, literary and graphic; and occasional book reviews.

The field of periodicals dealing with the humor of specific writers is nearly monopolized by Samuel Clemens. Five periodicals devoted to Mark Twain appear from time to time, but only one devotes itself exclusively to Twain scholarship. Devotees of H. L. Mencken share a newsletter, and for a short time the Washington Irving Society of the Sleepy Hollow Restorations put out *Postscripts* (1982–1984) for Irving buffs. *Menckeniana* (1962-current) is sponsored by the Mencken Society from the Enoch Pratt Free Library in Baltimore. Edited by Frederick Rasmussen, *Menckeniana* publishes articles, book reviews, bibliographic checklists, and miscellany about Mencken and the Society.

Mark Twain's life and writings support several periodicals, although only the

Mark Twain Journal is, strictly speaking, a scholarly journal. The others tend to be associated with places where Twain lived and are newsletters more concerned with biographical matters than with literature or humor. The Mark Twain Boyhood Associates (Hannibal, Missouri) publishes *Fence Painter* (1981-current), a quarterly newsletter edited by the curator of the Twain Home Foundation, Henry H. Sweets III. *Twainian* (1939-current), published by the Mark Twain Research Foundation (Perry, Missouri) concentrates on publishing newly discovered facts about Twain's life and writings. The Mark Twain Memorial which maintains the Twain home in Hartford, Connecticut, also publishes a quarterly newsletter. The Mark Twain Society of Elmira, New York, concentrates on Twain's connection with that community through the *Society Bulletin* (1978-current). The most prestigious is the *Mark Twain Journal* begun by Cyril Clemens, Twain's cousin, named as a quarterly of the now inactive Mark Twain Society. The four-times-a-year schedule proved too ambitious, and in 1954 it slowed to a one-a-year schedule. It has published short pieces by Anthony Burgess, Langston Hughes, W.E.B. Du Bois, Carl Sandburg, among others, as well as articles by leading Twain scholars. Cyril Clemens retired in 1982, and the journal has been moved to the College of Charleston, South Carolina, under the editorship of Thomas A. Tenney.

Although it is literary humor that tends to beget the most periodicals, interest in humor occurs in other academic areas as well. Whereas periodicals in other disciplines may not focus directly on humor, they nevertheless contribute to understanding its nature and scope. The American Anthropological Association, for example, sponsors the Association for the Anthropological Study of Play which publishes the *TAASP Newsletter* edited by Ann Marie Guilmette. Sociologists look at humor through the *Subterranean Sociology Newsletter*, edited by Marcello Truzzi of Eastern Michigan University. Started in 1967, it has appeared irregularly during the early 1980s. The humorous vagaries of language turn up in *Glimpse* and in *Word Ways: The Journal of Recreational Linguistics*. *Glimpse*, published by the International Society of General Semantics since 1977 and edited by Russel Joyner, is a four-page newsletter containing brief items on how signs, symbols, and other means of communication influence thought and behavior, frequently in humorous ways, however unintentional. *Word Ways*, founded in 1968 and edited by A. Ross Eckler of Morristown, New Jersey, is also a four-page newsletter. It publishes articles on manifestations of wordplay in names, headlines, and other linguistic phenomena. It devotes much attention to word games and puzzles. *Glimpse* and *Word Ways* are published four times a year. *Maledicta: The International Journal of Verbal Aggression* (1976-current) collects examples of and publishes articles on verbal aggression: insults, curses, nicknames, ethnic and sexual slurs, and all known forms of aggressive slang. Founded and edited by Reinhold Aman, *Maledicta* appeared irregularly in its early years but since 1981 has been an annual supplemented, irregularly, by *Benedicta* (1982-current), a newsletter of Aman's International Maledicta Society. *Maledicta* publishes articles on verbal aggression from all ages, times, and cultures as well as examples in cartoons or other visual forms and current "folk" forms (mock-letters, graffiti, etc.). Aman also works in checklists, bibliographies, book reviews, and commentary.

Theologians and nurses have turned their attention to humor and now publish newsletters to promote the study of humor in their callings. *Salvation and Laughter Together* (SALT), a newsletter founded in 1983 by Robert J. Larremore of Fort Worth, Texas, publishes biographies, bibliographies, and research aimed at developing a nonsectarian theology of humor. *Nurses for Laughter* also supports research into the therapeutic use of humor in health care. *PRN: Playfulness, Revelry, Nonsense* (1982-current), edited by Elaine Teutsch and Pat Rushford, compiles data for nurses and other health care professionals. Both newsletters are published quarterly.

Although the periodicals in the previous category are concerned mainly with collecting and studying humor, the periodicals in the next category concentrate on publishing humor. They are in effect parodies of scholarly or professional journals, mocking the methodology, the jargon, the pretentiousness of traditional learned journals. Such periodicals cover the academic spectrum from the sciences to the arts.

The most comprehensive and the oldest of the mock learned journals is *The Journal of Irreproducible Results*, begun in 1955 and edited from the beginning by Alexander Kohn of the Israel Institute for Biological Research. Its more than four dozen associate editors represent academic disciplines in the sciences, the social sciences, and the legal and medical professions. The thirty-two-page journal which appears five times a year reprints items from other journals as well as original humor and satire. Its humor is drawn from articles replete with mock footnotes, charts, diagrams, and mathematical formulas as well as from photos, cartoons, and anything else that undercuts academic pretensions. *The Best of the Journal of Irreproducible Results*, edited by George H. Scherr, was published in 1983. The *Worm Runner's Digest* (1959–1981), published simultaneously with the *Journal of Biological Psychology*, founded and edited by James V. McConnell, covered much of the same territory as *JIR*, although not so comprehensively. The humor of the *Worm Runner's Digest* appeared back to back with the serious articles of the *Journal of Biological Psychology*. Each had its own cover, but its half of the journal was upside down to the other. Begun as a mimeographed handout (facetiously labeled Volume 1, Number 1) to satisfy requests for information on research on planaria worms at the Planaria Research Group at the University of Michigan, the journal became the only journal with a seriously split personality. *The Worm Returns: The Best from the "Worm Runner's Digest"* appeared in 1965. A second gathering, *Science, Sex and Sacred Cows: Spoofs in Science from the Worm Runner's Digest*, appeared in 1971. Readers of these journals are likely to find such items as "The Effect of a Prefrontal Lobotomy on the Tsetse Fly" (*WRD*) and "Weekend Scientist: Let's Make a Thermonuclear Device!" (*JIR*). Some of the humor is esoteric and depends on the reader's having specialized knowledge and background; some of the humor is available to general readers.

In the social sciences, two journals spoof psychology. *The Journal of Therapeutic Humor* (1977–1981) satirized various aspects of the mental health field. Edited by Jack Solomon, *JOTH* included a "Hostility Corner" for readers to vent their "rage and indignation on controversial issues, professional injustices, and clerical errors." "Book Previews" reviewed books that hadn't been written, and articles mocked all aspects of psychology. Following in the footsteps of *JOTH* is *Journal of Polymorphous Perversity* (1984-current), edited by Glenn C. Ellenbogen. The twice-annual periodical has published articles on "The Etiology and Treatment of Childhood," "New Improved Delusions," and a case study of Nicholas Claus, a.k.a. Santa.

Traditional art and music are the targets of *Vile* and *The Peter Schickele Rag*. The latter, founded in 1979, chronicles the activities of Schickele and his creation P.D.Q. Bach. The eight-page newsletter also contains music, puzzles, and miscellaneous humor. *Vile* (1974–1983) is at once a parody of *Life*, *File*, and traditional art journals. Edited by Anna Banana in San Francisco, *Vile* is a product of the counter-culture movement as well as of dadaism and surrealism. It became the chronicler of the international mail-art movement as *File* magazine turned away from that movement. Profusely illustrated, it combined nonsense, obscenity, and social comment. *About Vile: Mail Art, News & Photos from the Eternal Network* (1983) is at once the last issue as well as a sampling of previous issues, together with a brief history.

Two other periodicals in the mock parody category are *Libsat* and *International Journal of Creature Communications*. *Libsat* is a newsletter for librarians edited by John Love from the Gananoque Public Library in Gananoque, Ontario, Canada. Started in 1982, it is published approximately twice a year. Its subjects include washroom libraries: a wave of the future with guard swans and book decoys. *The International Journal of Creature Communication* (1980-current), edited by Charles U. Larson, claims to be devoted to the scholarly study of sport-fishing while publishing parodies of scholarly research by using the jargon of specialized disciplines (e.g., "The Berlo Model and Fisher Guide/Trout Interaction Feedback Loops" and "Ichthymanuel Kant: Fishing and Philosophy").

Periodicals containing humor may be specialized in various ways. Some may specialize by devoting themselves to particular kinds of humor, while others may specialize by providing humor as a service. The latter are commercial enterprises but not for a mass market. They provide jokes or cartoons to professionals or to others who need humor, speechwriters, public speakers, disc jockeys, or persons who need a regular source of humor in their work. Since 1981 nine such services have opened for business. Whether any will attain the longevity of *Orben's Current Comedy* (1958-current), a newsletter published twenty-four times annually costing $72.00 or *Latest Jokes* (1974-current), $18.00 for six issues a year newsletter, remains to be seen. Cartoonists may draw on the services of *Gag Recap* (1954-current) and *Cartoon World* (1936-current). Both appear twelve times a year and cost $40.00. A specialized journal for professional and amateur clowns is *Calliope* (1968-current). Information about humor magazines and humor organizations is available in Glenn C. Ellenbogen, ed., *Directory of Humor Magazines and Humor Organizations in America (and Canada)* (1985).

Punsters and limerick buffs can chuckle over newsletters devoted to specialized forms of wordplay. The International Save the Pun Foundation (Toronto, Canada) issues *Pundit* (1978-current) twelve times a year, and Lee Gershuny edits *Play On, Words* from the City University of New York's Manhattan Community College. Limerick lovers may choose from *Limerick Sig*, a publication of a special interest group of Mensa, from Moffett, California, and *Letters from Limerick* from the Limerick League of Philadelphia. *Thoughts for All Seasons: The Magazine of Epigrams*, which appears irregularly from State University of New York College at Geneseo, devotes itself to that often humorous form.

Humor and articles about humor are also sprinkled throughout the world of learned and specialized periodicals. Articles on humor in its various manifestations occur in such journals as *American Speech, Names, Journal of Reading* as well as traditional literary journals. Special topical issues of periodicals include, for example, "Comedy in Children's Literature," *The Lion and the Unicorn* 1:1 (1977); "Humor and Satire in the English Classroom," *Arizona English Bulletin* 16:1 (1973); "Humor in the Classroom," *English Journal* 70:6 (1981); and "American Humor," *American Quarterly* 37:1 (1985). Humor itself is sometimes published in professional journals, for example, *The Physics Teacher* and *Physics Today* and journals for English teachers. Graduate students in linguistics at Indiana University published *Lingua Pranca* and *Son of Lingua Pranca*, fugitive issues containing learned parodies of articles on linguistics and anthropology.

Two professional organizations in academia cultivate the production of scholarship on humor. The Workshop Library on World Humor describes itself as a "non-profit organization established to explore the use of humor from the earliest societies to the present." For this purpose it publishes the *Humor Events and Possibilities* newsletter four times a year containing brief news items and reviews from around the world. It is edited by Barbara Cummings from Washington, D.C. Since 1980 World (formerly Western) Humor and Irony Membership (WHIM) has sponsored an annual interdisciplinary humor conference and published abstracts and extracts from all the papers presented. Don and Alleen Nilson of Arizona State University founded WHIM and co-edit the proceedings. The worldwide extent of the union of humor and scholarship may also be seen in the International Humor Conferences held for the first time in 1976 in Wales, subsequently in 1980 in Los Angeles, 1982 in Washington, D.C., 1984 in Tel Aviv, and 1985 in Cork, Ireland. Although no formal organization exists to sponsor these conferences, the worldwide network of academicians and humorists that has emerged to put on such affairs is another tangible instance of the emergence of the union of humor and scholarship.

George A. Test
Don Nilsen

Humor in American Almanacs: From the Colonial Period to the Civil War and After

Perhaps the best record of the development of America's popular taste in humor can be found in its almanacs. The almanac was virtually the first production from Stephen Daye's printing press—only "The Freeman's Oath" preceded the 1639 appearance of "an Almanack calculated for New England, by Mr. Pierce"—and for most of the century almanacs continued to be produced at Cambridge, usually by Harvard graduates calling themselves "philomaths." In many colonial households, these almanacs were, along with the Bible, the only available reading. Although the Cambridge almanacs were largely serious affairs, they also show the beginnings of American humor in their poetry, essentially Spenserian verse that appeared on the calendar pages.

By the late seventeenth and early eighteenth centuries, humorous prefaces, aphorisms, epigrams, and poems became a large part of the appeal of almanacs— particularly by the most successful families of almanac makers: Daniel and Titan Leeds, Nathaniel Ames and his son (also Nathaniel), and James and Benjamin Franklin. At the end of the eighteenth century, Robert B. Thomas began *The Farmer's Almanac*, which became extremely popular in the early years of the nineteenth century and is still running today. (Of almanacs still publishing, only *Webster's*, begun in Albany in 1787, predates it.) *The Farmer's Almanac* depended on humor for a large part of its appeal. As its major historian, George Lyman Kittredge, says, Thomas was no astrologer, "but he was a humorist."[1]

During the second quarter of the nineteenth century, beginning with *The American Comic Almanac* in 1831, whole almanacs were devoted to humor. The most important of the "comic almanacs" were the Crockett Almanacs, published under various names, imprints, and locations. The last of the *Crockett Almanacs* was published in 1856, and by the Civil War the comic almanac as a major organ for American humor had passed into history.

The Cambridge Almanacs

In format, the first colonial almanacs were, of course, similar to those in England, giving information about eclipses, the sun's rising and setting, the turning of the tides, the place of the moon in the zodiac, and similar calculations useful to sailors and farmers. The almanacs issued at Cambridge from 1639 to 1692 (by different authors under varying titles) were usually no more than eight leaves, or sixteen pages, and measured about 6" × 4". Twelve of these pages were calendars, one for each month; the remaining ones were usually devoted to some astronomical discussion.

About half of these almanacs carried verse, usually at the top of each calendar page, and, although these poems could be tedious displays of learning, they could also display metaphysical wit. Sometimes this wit remained at the level of the pun, one of the most recurring ones depending on the "ear" of corn. Thus, in 1647, Samuel Danforth predicts for August, "Many this month I do fore-see / Together by the eares will bee." The observation is also a comic, mock prediction, as is the verse for November: the winter "shall be milde, let such be told / If that it be not over cold. / Nor over cold shall they it see, / If very temperate it bee." The mock prognostication recurs throughout the century, indicating the skeptical attitude of many of these learned colonists to the astrological almanac.

It was not until John Richardson's almanac for 1670, however, that we see the kind of humorous hard sense later associated with Benjamin Franklin. Richardson's almanac includes a poem, "A Perpetual Calendar, fitted for the Meridian of Babylon, where the Pope is elevated 42 degrees," which Harold Jantz calls "one of the sharpest anti-Catholic satires of early New England."[2] "The Country-Man's Apocrypha," from the same almanac, is a humorous satire of both astrology and the rustic believer. The poem makes use of the corny pun ("Hunger will so prevail for many years, / Rather than famish, some will *Roast* their *Ears*"), as well as of the mock prediction, saying that men will resort to eating the offspring of their mother (earth). Country bumpkins will have to interpret not only the signs of heaven but also the signs of earth: when they visit their city cousins, they will find *"Trees walking* with their *Roots* toward the Sky / and if (as wonted) Winters Air be clear / Men not a few, with *Swines heads* will appear"—city men wearing either three-cornered hats or wigs of animal hair.

In 1676, John Foster, who had published the almanac at Cambridge the previous year, was authorized to set up the first printing press in Boston, where for the next five years he helped to expand the American almanac and widen its possibilities for humor. He doubled the number of calendar pages, added illustrations, and in 1678 introduced the "Man of Signs" popular in European almanacs. He accompanied the figure with a humorous poem, titled "The Dominion of the Moon in Man's Body."

Almanacs of John Tulley

The title of "the first humorous almanac-maker" is usually given to John Tulley. Tulley illustrates the lightness of his touch when he says about his craft (1688), "For all predictions do to this belong / That either they are right, or they are wrong." As Marion Stowell says, Tulley "was just bawdy enough to be refreshing and just shrewd enough to know what his audience wanted and needed: so he gave them smiles. Attitudes were changing, and Tulley's almanacs reflected these changes."[3] Tulley's verse for January of 1688 reveals the new tone of his almanacs: "The best defence against the Cold, / Which our Fore-Fathers good did hold, / Was early a full Pot of ale." Similarly, whereas the philomaths punned on ears, Tulley puns on lads and lasses making hay: "Now wanton Lads and Lasses do make Hay, / Which unto lewd temptation makes great way. / With tumbling on the cocks, which acted duly, / Doth cause much mischief in this month of July."

The Leeds Almanacs

As almanacs entered the eighteenth century, they were still largely useful for the astronomical information they provided, but as they expanded to meet the needs of a growing society they soon began giving useful local information, such as times for court and religious meetings, and helpful guides for the traveler: lists of roads and places of entertainment along these roads, distances between towns, and names of taverns. As competition among rival almanacs grew, compilers also recognized the need to amuse their readers by interspersing entertaining crumbs of wisdom and snatches of light verse and jests. Commonplace wisdom and moral advice were frequently presented in the dress of the witty aphorism. As Isaac Briggs announced in his 1798 preface, "I shall endeavour to the utmost of my power, that the moral pieces it may contain, both original and selected, shall appear in a pleasing dress; and that (although wit and humour shall be respected) low ribaldry and filthy jests shall be cautiously excluded." Americans were exhorted to practice industry, temperance, and piety in maxims that were the natural outgrowth of earlier exhortations on when the weather would be best for planting or the stars best for bleeding.

One of the first to use such aphorisms was Daniel Leeds, whose almanacs were begun on the Philadelphia press of William Bradford in 1687, continued thereafter on Bradford's New York press, and after 1714 compiled for the next fifty years by his sons, Titan and Felix. Leeds added variety to the almanac's offerings, included narratives and anecdotes, placed sayings on the calendar pages, and interspersed verse from first to last page. Sometimes the humor of the Leeds was aimed at themselves as prognosticators, as when in 1738 Titan predicts "A bad time for somebody" in December. And sometimes it could touch on the bawdy, as Titan foresees that in August (1714), "*Dick* on the Hay doth tumble *Nell*, / Whereby her Belly comes to swell." Among the favorite targets for satire and humor among the Leeds and their contemporaries were physicians and lawyers, as we see in the following two representative verses. The first is from Daniel's *American Almanack* for 1708; the second is from 1706 and repeated in 1707 and 1708:

> The learned *Physicians*, such as were of old,
> *Galen* and *Hippocrates* lie and mould,

Now *Paracelsus* claims the curing part
And most men practice the spagyrick art,
Yet *Herbs* when gathered in their proper seasons
More harmless physic makes, for diverse reasons.

Lo, here's a Trade surpasseth all the rest,
No Change annoys the Lawyers Interest:
His Tongue buys Land, builds Houses without toil:
The Pen's his Plough, the Parchment is his Soil.
His Storms disturb not, nor militia Bands.
The Tree roots best that in the weather stands.

When Leeds attacks the lawyer for using his pen as his plow, we see the poet wearing a mask different from that employed in "A Country-Man's Aprocrypha." Perhaps this change is best illustrated by a quatrain Leeds gives us for May 1693: "I dread to touch at State affairs, for fear / Lest the Apollo pull me by the Ear / I'm safe while moving in my proper Sphere. / In Plowing, Planting, there's no treason there." In fact, Leeds identifies himself on the title pages of his early almanacs as a "Student of Agriculture"—he was not a "Harvardine" showing his academic prowess with poetry based on classical and scientific learning. The mask Leeds wore (perfected by Benjamin Franklin as "Poor Richard") was not that of the learned man who patronizes the superstitions of the country bumpkin, but rather of the countryman himself—a man like most of his readers, who knows his proper sphere, in which he plants and plows and does not touch affairs of state which are beyond him. In truth, of course, he believes himself superior to the learned physicians and lawyers who do not know an honest day's work as they make their pens their plows. Leeds's humor is thus homely and earthy—as Stowell says, "It reflected, at its highest, the level of comic perception we associate with the British squirearchy rather than with the nobility."[4]

Nathaniel Ames, Father and Son

According to Max Savelle, the best place to study early American wit is in the country's almanacs, such as those of Ames and Franklin: "Colonial newspapers . . . are interesting. . . . The almanacs are much more fun."[5] Nathaniel Ames compiled the *Astronomical Diary and Almanack* for 1726 when he was just seventeen, and until 1764 his almanacs were the standard in New England. Although printed for Massachusetts, they were also sold in Maine and Vermont, where the printing press was not introduced until after 1778, and reprinted in New Hampshire and Rhode Island. Eventually, these almanacs reached a circulation of 60,000. The first to recognize their historical importance was Moses Coit Tyler, who, while stressing their humor, compared them favorably to those of Franklin:

[E]ight years before Benjamin Franklin had started his almanac, Nathaniel Ames was publishing one that had all of its best qualities—fact and frolic, the wisdom of the preacher without his solemnity, terse sayings, shrewdness, wit, homely wisdom, all sparkling in piquant phrase. . . . [H]e freely predicted future events, but always with a merry twinkle in his eye, and always ready to laugh the loudest at his own failure to predict them aright. He mixes, in delightful juxtaposition, absurd prognostications, curt jests and aphorisms of profound wisdom, the whole forming a miscellany even now extremely readable, and sure, at that time, to raise shouts of laughter around thousands of fireplaces where food for laughter was much needed.''[6]

Ames also made use of satirical verse, telling his readers to take his poetry "as some men take their wives, for better or worse" (1729). In a typical barb aimed at lawyers, priests, and doctors, one of Ames's poems answers the question, what would have happened if Adam had not fallen: "Nor *Lawyers, Priests* nor *Doctors* ne'er had been / If Man had stood against th'Assaults of Sin. / But oh, He fell! and so accurs'd we be / The World is now oblig'd to use all Three" (1738). By his own writing and by the selections he printed from contemporary English writers, like Alexander Pope, John Dryden, and Joseph Addison, Ames encouraged in colonial America a taste for urbanity and wit.

The Franklin Almanacs

Better known than the eighteenth-century almanacs of the Ames family are those by the Franklins. James Franklin's *Rhode-Island Almanack* (1728), by "Poor Robin," shows much of the same shrewdness and humor that are associated with his more famous brother. Although he is not a fully created character like Poor Richard, Robin also has a clearly identifiable and likable personality. *Poor Robin* was published regularly from 1728 to 1741, except for 1736, the year after James's death. From 1739 to 1741, the almanac was compiled by "Poor Robin, revived," most likely James's widow Ann, the official colony printer and one of six women in America printing almanacs before 1800. Their son, James Franklin, Jr., carried on the family tradition with *Poor Job* (1750–1758). Like those of his father and uncle, his almanacs were put together with care and humor.

Benjamin Franklin detailed the achievement of his famous almanac in his *Autobiography*: "In 1732 I first publish'd my Almanack, under the name of *Richard Saunders*; it was continu'd by me about twenty-five years, commonly call'd *Poor Richard's Almanack*. I endeavor'd to make it both entertaining and useful, and it accordingly came to be in such demand, that I reap'd considerable profit from it, vending annually near ten-thousand." If Franklin was not the first to employ witty aphorisms, humorous anecdotes, and amusing prefaces, he used these devices with greater success than any of his predecessors. A number of the witty sayings of "Poor Richard," which Franklin found in other sources but then shaped and sharpened to a fine point, were collected in a preface to the last almanac of the series in 1758.

The preface is in the form of a speech by "Father Abraham," often reprinted as "The Way to Wealth." In response to a series of questions about the nature of the times, wise old Father Abraham answers with moral sayings culled from the past twenty-five years of *Poor Richard*, sayings that emphasize the need for industry, frugality, and virtue. Less moral sayings, although not repeated by Father Abraham, were nonetheless also sprinkled throughout the almanacs over the second quarter of the century. The worldly humor of "There's more old Drunkards than old Doctors" and "Neither a Fortress nor a Maidenhead will hold out long once they begin to parley" were probably just as responsible for the success of Franklin's almanac as "God helps them that helps themselves."

No almanac-maker made better use of the preface to amuse his readers than did Franklin. In early almanacs, the preface followed a predictable formula, by which the almanac-maker would bear his readers' indulgence for his humble efforts and ask them to forgive his errors. By the time Franklin began *Poor Richard*, it had evolved into an opportunity for the compiler to address other concerns and reveal some of his personality and humor. Franklin had the advantage of knowing how to develop a humorous character, the shrewd, outspoken Richard Saunders, whose problems with his wife readers of the Almanac soon came to know. In the first issue, for example, Richard tells how he started the almanac because Brigit was tired of spinning while he did nothing but gaze at the stars.

The funniest moments in these prefaces, however, were at the expense of Titan Leeds, whose death Richard predicts when Sol and Mercury will be in conjunction. When the moment passed, Leeds called his rival "a fool and a Lyar," but in his 1734 almanac Richard insisted that Leeds indeed did die. After all, Titan himself would not have written such an uncivil preface; moreover, no living man could have written such bad verses as appeared in Leeds's 1734 almanac. Extending the hoax in his 1740 almanac, Richard presented a letter supposedly from Titan's ghost, predicting that another rival almanac-maker, John Jerman, would become a priest on 17 September. When like Leeds before him Jerman wrote to deny the prophecy, Richard stood his ground, citing as evidence lines in one of Jerman's own almanacs: "When any trouble did me befall / To my dear Mary then I would call."

Although Franklin's battles with Titan Leeds are best known, feuds between rival almanac-makers were not uncommon. Beginning with Samuel Clough's almanacs (1700–1708), which ridiculed Nathaniel Whittemore, there were also feuds between Daniel Leeds and Jacob Taylor; Taylor and both John Jerman and William Ball; Nathan Bowen and Whittemore; James Franklin and Nathaniel Ames; Ames and Bowen; and finally, at the end of the century, Isaiah Thomas and Robert B. Thomas. Although some of these feuds may be seen as simply nasty, most often they allowed the almanac-maker to make use of wit and satire to liven up his preface and gain readers for both himself and his rival.

Other Eighteenth-Century Almanacs

Of course, Leeds, Ames, and Franklin were not the only almanac-makers of the eighteenth century who included humor in their work. By the time of the skirmishes at Lexington and Concord, every city and many a town in British America had its own almanac. Almost all included verse, of which over half (excluding the seasonal poems on the calendar pages) was humorous or satirical. The mock-prognostication continued to be a device for humor, with predictions being either intentionally self-evident or obviously ludicrous (as when Rittenhouse's *Maryland, Virginia and Pennsylvania Almanack* for 1780 assures readers that "A Cow shall be heard to speak Latin.") Puns continued to be painfully present in these almanacs. For example, in the *American Country Almanac* for 1768, a lady is told by her doctor that her husband needs "an *Appetite*." The wife, "thinking he said an *Ape tied*, got an Ape, and tied it to his Bed."

Frequently, the men who issued these almanacs made the foibles of women their subject. A sextet in *The Kentucky Almanac* (1797) compares women to books, closing with the lines, "If they are books, I wish that my wife were / An Almanac, to change her ev'ry year." *Daboll's New England Almanack* (1775) treats the hypocrisy of widows: "Before my face, my handkerchief I spread, / To hide the floods of tears I did————not shed." Such inconstant women are quick to make cuckolds of their husbands. *Gentlemen's and Ladies' Diary and Almanac* of 1804 includes a poem about "fretful James" and his wife. When "fretful James" says he would just as soon send all cuckolds tumbling into the Thames, "La! cried his wife, a buxom lass, / How could you think of such a whim? / For, prithee, should it come to pass, / Have you, my dearee learn'd to swim?" At times the humor could be bawdy or scatalogical, as in the story told by the *Virginia Almanack* (1775) about a man who on a bet was closeted unknown in a woman's room at a resort. Thinking herself alone, the woman breaks wind "with the voice of a cannon," causing her visitor to exclaim: " 'Well said, madam, by Heaven it was a rouzer; I hope you are better, madam; I think I never heard such a banging f————t in my life.' " Occasionally, more serious satire was attempted. In 1768, *Hutchins Improved* castigated contemporary society in "A Description of the Land of Promise." The mythical land in this allegory is one of wealth and opportunity, in which people run "to and fro, regardless of everybody but themselves," while "wearing the face of care and importance."

By the end of the eighteenth century, some almanacs were competing for stories with the joke books that had begun to appear in the new republic. The first extensive joke book, *The American Jest Book* (1789), lifts the following example of the "bon mot" from Rivington's *New Almanack and Ephemeris* (1774): a countryman gets back at "two smart Fellows" who in riding past remark, " 'Well, Honest Fellow . . . 'tis your Business to sow, but we reap the Fruits of your labour.' " To this the countryman replies, " 'Tis very likely you may, truly; for I am sowing Hemp.' " In both jest books and almanacs of the time, a frequent target was the scholar, a comic figure because he is either a pedant or a fool, who is not as smart as he thinks he is or else is too ingenious for his own good. The following anecdote appears in Briggs's almanac for 1798:

A SCHOLAR, a bald man, and a barber, were traveling together, agreed each to watch four hours at night, in turn, for the sake of security; the barber's lot came first, who shaved the scholar's head when asleep, then waked him when his turn came. The scholar scratching his head, and feeling it bald, exclaimed, you "wretch of a barber, you have waked the bald man instead of me!"

The anti-intellectualism implicit in such humor became more apparent in the *Crockett Almanacs* of the next century.

It really mattered little who the compiler was or from where the almanac was issued—the objects of humor remained the same: astrologists, lawyers, physicians, priests, scholars, fools, cuckolds, women, and rival almanac-makers.

The Farmer's Almanac

The most popular almanac during the first part of the nineteenth century was *The Farmer's Almanac*. It was begun by Robert Bailey Thomas in 1792, and it has been running ever since, changing its name after fifty years to *The Old Farmer's Almanac* in order to distinguish it from its many imitators. It included a "Farmer's Calendar," illustrated by old-fashioned cuts, brief poems, the weather prognosis for the year, agricultural guides, fish and game laws, recipes, anecdotes, and astrological lore treated with some skepticism. What helped to distinguish the almanac was Thomas's homely sense of humor. He introduced in his almanac humorous sketches concerning a number of mythical characters, whimsically named but so near the mark that Thomas had to assure his readers no particular individuals were intended for his satire.

These characters included "Ben Bluster," "Captain Swash," "Goody Shipshod," and the village gossip, "Old Betty Blab." Betty is a "dabster" on the instrument of rumor, who "knows exactly how to time and to key her tune to give the proper effect; she can perform in diatonic, cromatic, or enharmonic with vast variety and astonishing modulation" (1817). Another comic character was Tim Twilight, an enterprising door-to-door seller of, among other things, almanacs. Tim even interrupts a wedding ceremony to sell almanacs: "And now, my good friends, will you suffer me to introduce the contents of a poor peddler's pack; and give me leave to say, Sir Simon, that the next thing, after a wife, is an *almanack*" (1825).

In its subject for satire, *The Farmer's Almanac* followed its eighteenth-century predecessors. For example, in 1813 Thomas identified five kinds of pestilence: "From quack lawyers, quack doctors, quack preachers, mad dogs and yellow fever, good Lord, deliver us!" In an extended analogy between lawyers and tailors, Thomas places his tongue in his cheek as he suggests why we would do better to have business with lawyers (1796):

Tis true, they both furnish you with suits; but which is the best workman, the tailor, who must have matter to work upon, or the lawyer, who can make a long suit out of nothing? Your tailor's suit is gone in half a year, but the lawyer's will last often to your posterity; suppose he hurries you out of breath upon a wrong scent, yet then he will give you time by a writ of error or demurrer, to recover yourself, and keep in fast friendship to you whilst you have the strength of one fee left. And though he runs some out of their estates, he often gives to others other people's estates, which is yet some compensation.

Different from the humor of the previous century, however, were occasional tall tales that showed the influence of the frontier. In 1809, for example, we hear of the feats of a "mighty hunter" named "Vermont Nimrod," who once killed with a single bullet a "stately buck" and a "huge sturgeon" that had leaped out of the river. The same ball entered a hollow in a tree, which began running honey, and when Nimrod reached to grab something with which to stop it he found he had taken hold of a rabbit. Nimrod then flung the rabbit with such force that it killed three cock partridges and a wood cock.

The American Comic Almanac and Its Imitators

The nineteenth century also saw the specialization of almanacs. There were almanacs to support movements and causes, such as masonry and temperance, and to oppose them. State boards of agriculture sponsored agricultural almanacs. Almost every religious denomination had its own almanac. By the 1840s there were the *Phrenological Almanac* (1840), *The Musical Almanac* (1842), and *The Angler's Almanac* (1848). Patent medicine almanacs began to proliferate, beginning with *Bristol's Free Almanac* in 1844. Understandably, then, the nineteenth century also saw the birth of almanacs which specialized in the comic. According to Constance Rourke,

> Few materials are more important for a view of American humor than those provided by the comic almanacs during the period from 1830, when they began to appear, to 1860, when they had grown less local and flavorsome. These fascinating small handbooks yield many brief stories and bits of character drawing not to be found elsewhere; more than any single source they prove the wide diffusion of a native comic lore.[7]

Inspired by George C. Cruikshank, whose *Comic Almanac* in England was a predecessor of *Punch*, America's comic almanacs amused a public ready to be entertained by works free from statistics, moralizing, and special interests. The first almanac devoted to humor was *The American Comic Almanac*, issued by Charles Ellms in Boston beginning in 1831. The series changed its name in 1839 to the *Old American Comic Almanac* and continued until 1846. Its jokes could be crude and uncouth, but they found a ready audience. The humorous stories were accompanied by illustrations that were frequently funnier than the text. At first, the almanac was mostly indigenous in its use of material, but as its supply needed to be replenished it began borrowing freely from other publications.

There were many imitators of Ellms's success; between 1830 and 1860 in Massachusetts alone more than thirty different comic almanacs were issued. These almanacs boasted such titles as *Comic Tokens, Broad Grins, American Comic Annual, The Rip Snorter, The Merry Elephant, The Devil's Comical*

Texas Oldmanick, Finn's Comic Almanac, Whim-Whams, and *Tragical and Piratical Almanac.* The longer running series included *Elton's Comic All-My-Neck* and *Fisher's Comic Almanac,* but their highwater mark was reached by the *Crockett Almanacs,* which originated in Tennessee around the figure of the legendary Davy Crockett.

The Crockett Almanacs

The common-sense aphorisms we associate with the Eastern almanacs can also be found as fillers in the *Crockett Almanacs*—for example, "Riches, like manure, do no good till they are spread." But the importance of these almanacs is that they captured and fostered like none other the spirit and the humor of the American frontier. Davy Crockett—hunter, militia officer, United States congressman—was a master of the tall tale, and he helped to create his own legend.

As a frontiersman who rose to the halls of power, Crockett was readily identified as a "ring-tailed roarer" whose spontaneous responses and home-spun wisdom were unspoiled by book-learning. Crockett himself fostered this image, saying "I ain't used to oily words; I am used to speak what I think, of men, and to men . . . I have made my way to the place I now fill, without wealth, and against education." Fantastic stories circulated about him, whether in the image of Nature's Nobleman or as crude barbarian, but in either guise Crockett became a favorite subject for frontier humor. Many of these stories had been told before about other figures, real or mythic, but they were now retold about Crockett, who in a song popular a hundred years later was still being extolled as "king of the wild frontier."

Davy Crockett's Almanac of Wild Sports of the West, and Life in the Backwoods was first issued in Tennessee in 1835, the year before Crockett died in the Battle of the Alamo. The almanacs continued with the dubious claim that they were being issued by Crockett's heirs; later they were said to have been compiled by Ben Hardin, or Harding, Crockett's mythical companion. From 1835 to 1856, *Crockett Almanacs* were published under various titles and in various places, from Nashville and Louisville to Baltimore, Philadelphia, Boston, Albany, and New York. While most of the *Crockett Almanacs* depicted the legendary exploits of the title character, they varied widely in the degree to which they were actually devoted to him, and some, like *Sprees and Scrapes in the West* and *Life and Manners in the Backwoods and Exploits and Adventures on the Prairies,* involved a number of other characters.

Nonetheless, the Crockett myth conveyed by these almanacs is the closest America comes to having a national epic, a crude and grotesque epic infused with the bawdy humor of the frontier. Crockett is America's comic hero, raised not on mother's milk but on whisky sucked out of a bladder, on the eggs of rattlesnakes and the meat from wild bears. The issue for 1837 reported a "Speech of Colonel Crockett in Congress," in which the frontier congressman boasts:

> I can outlook a panther and outstare a flash of lightning: tote a steamboat on my back and play at rough and tumble with a lion, and an occasional kick from a

Zebra. Goliah was a pretty hard colt but I could choke him. . . . I can walk like an ox; run like a fox, swim like an eel, yell like an Indian, fight like a devil, and spout like an earthquake, make love like a mad bull, and swallow a nigger whole without choking if you butter his head and pin his ears back.

The language of the *Crockett Almanacs* is characteristically vivid and metaphoric, filled with extravagant similes and invented words, as when Crockett says his throat is "exfluctoficated" with influenza and informs his readers that he was not "choked by the weeds of education, which do not grow *spontinaciously*." Sometimes the language and humor, as in the boast quoted above, can be seen as racist, as well as crude and violent: for example, "I kept my thumb in his eye, and was just going to give it a twist and bring the peeper out, like taking up a gooseberry in a spoon." This, however, was the aggressive humor of the American frontier, of which we have no better examples than can be found in the *Crockett Almanacs*. Their devices were the devices of this regional humor: hypberbolic boasts, extravagant threats, colorful language, and crude earthiness. As folklorist Richard Dorson says,

The gusty, lusty frontier humor sketch is alive and fresh today as it was in the newspapers and almanacs of a hundred years ago. It is the most distinctive and enduring strain of American humor, and though partaking of characteristics in common with the national blend—the American penchant for exaggeration and burlesque, the American delight in mocking the finer things and the higher places— it remains unique in the compost of its nature-spattered imagery, its sly delineation of the quirks and eccentricities of frontier folk, its vibrant realism and virility.[8]

By the time of the Civil War, both the frontier humor tale and the comic almanac were rapidly becoming part of America's past, but important vestiges remained. *Frank Leslie's Comic Almanac* appeared from 1866 through 1895. *The Comic Almanac* continued from the 1870s through the turn of the century, published by King and Baird of Philadelphia. In several years, a crude cut on the front page even maintained one year's date for two or three years in copy while altering the large-print date below the cut and text. Its humor was a country version of common turn-of-the-century themes, including the following comic verse from 1903:

The Ice is on the River,
The Snow is in the Air;
The Coal is in the Cellar,
And the Wood beneath the Stair.
The Bill is in my Pocket,
All folded up with care;
But the where-with-all to pay it
Isn't with it, I declare.

Even the "Introduction" of these later almanacs remained the same from year to year, with only the date changed. *Fisher's Comic Almanac*, published by Fisher and Brother in Philadelphia, existed from at least 1871 through 1883, and undoubtedly longer. Josh Billing's "Comic Allminax" proved so popular in the 1870s that they were published in a hardcover collection by Dillingham. Mark Twain's letters to his publishers reveal that he considered competing with Billings through a "Mark Twain's Annual—1871" to be published by the Galaxy magazine company. Appealing though the idea seemed to him in the fall of 1870, it did not come to fruition, and Billings held the field. Although the San Francisco literati might be thought above this form of humor, Gelett Burgess brought forth the *Lark Almanac* with simple limerick-style poems and block prints in 1899. Kin Hubbard used his character "Abe Martin" for a series of almanacs yearly from 1908 through 1925 which fit more clearly in the tradition, as they were attached to the Indiana crackerbarrel humorist personality. The legacy continues today in the form of burlesque *Old Farmer's Almanacs* printed from time to time either independently or as sections of other magazines.

Notes

1. George Lyman Kittredge, *The Old Farmer and His Almanack* (Boston: William Ware and Co., 1904), p. 50.

2. Harold Jantz, *The First Century of New England Verse* (New York: Russell and Russell, 1962), p. 49.

3. Marion Stowell, *Early American Almanacs* (New York: Burt Franklin, 1977), p. 60.

4. Marion Stowell, "Humor in Colonial Almanacs," *Studies in American Humor* 3:1 (April 1976): 34–47.

5. Max Savelle, *Seeds of Liberty* (New York: Alfred A. Knopf, 1948), p. 427.

6. Moses Coit Tyler, *A History of American Literature* (1878; rpt. New York: Cornell University Press, 1949), p. 366.

7. Constance Rourke, *American Humor* (New York: Harcourt Brace and Co., 1931), p. 305.

8. Richard Dorson, *David Crockett* (New York: Arno Press, 1977), pp. xxi, xxii.

Information Sources

BIBLIOGRAPHY:

Blair, Walter, and Hamlin Hill. *America's Humor: From Poor Richard to Doonesbury*. New York: Oxford University Press, 1978.

Brigham, Clarence S. "An Account of American Almanacs and Their Value for Historical Study." *Proceedings of the American Antiquarian Society* (October 1925): 195–226.

Dorson, Richard, ed. *Davy Crockett: American Comic Legend*. New York: Arno Press, 1977.

Jantz, Harold. *The First Century of New England Verse*. New York: Russell and Russell, 1943; rpt. 1962.

Kittredge, George Lyman. *The Old Farmer and His Almanack*. Cambridge, Mass.: Harvard University Press, 1924.

Marble, Annie. "Early New England Almanacs." *New England Magazine* 19 (January 1899): 548–57.

Murrell, William. *A History of Graphic American Humor*. New York: Whitney Museum, 1933.

Nichols, Charles L. "Notes on the Almanacs of Massachusetts." *Proceedings of the American Antiquarian Society*, New Series 22 (10 April 1912): 15–40.

Rourke, Constance. *American Humor: A Study of the National Character*. New York: Harcourt, Brace, 1931.

―――. *Davy Crockett*. New York, 1934.

Sagendorph, Robb. *America and Her Almanacs: Wit, Wisdom & Weather 1639–1970*. Boston: Little, Brown and Co., 1970.

Savelle, Max. *Seeds of Liberty: the Genesis of the American Mind*. Seattle: University of Washington Press, 1948.

Stowell, Marion Barber. "American Almanacs and Feuds." *Early American Literature* 4, No. 3 (Winter 1975): 276–85.

―――. *Early American Almanacs: The Colonial Weekday Bible*. New York: Burt Franklin, 1977.

―――. "Humor in Early American Almanacs." *Studies in American Humor* 3, No. 1 (April 1976): 34–47.

Tyler, Moses Colt. *A History of American Literature During the Colonial Time*. New York: G. P. Putnam's Sons, 1878.

INDEX SOURCES:

Drake, Milton. *Almanacs of the United States*. 2 vols. New York: Scarecrow Press, 1962.

Evans, Charles. *American Bibliography*. 14 vols. Vols. 1–13 ed. by Clifford K. Shipton, Vol. 14 ed. by Roger Pattrell Bristol. Varying publishers and publication dates, 1941–1959.

National Index of American Imprints Through 1800: The Short-Title Evans, 2 vols. Ed. by Clifford K. Shipton and James E. Mooney. Worcester, Mass.: American Antiquarian Society, Barre Publishers, 1969.

Stowell, Marion. *Early American Almanacs* (see Bibliography above), Appendix A ("Major Almanac Series in America Before 1800"), pp. 315–320.

REPRINT EDITIONS:

University Microfilms, for almanacs to 1800. A large, well-annotated selection from the Ames almanacs can be found in Samuel Briggs's *Essays, Humor, and Poems of Nathaniel Ames, Father and Son, of Dedham, Massachusetts, from their-Almanacs 1726–1725* (Cleveland, Ohio: Short and Forman, 1891). One of the more elaborate reproductions of the Franklin almanacs is *Poor Richard: The Almanacs for the Years 1733–1758*, with an introduction by Van Wyck Brooks (New York: Heritage Press, 1964). For generous samplings of *The Farmer's Almanac* see Kittredge, above; also *The Old Farmer's Almanac Sampler*, edited by Robb Sagendorph (New York: Ives Washburn, 1957). For selections from the *Crockett Almanacs*, see Dorson above.

LOCATION SOURCES:

Virtually every library has some collection of almanacs, but the largest collection by far is at the American Antiquarian Society, which owns over 4,000.

Publication History of Major Almanacs Mentioned

Ames, Nathaniel (the elder). *An Astronomical Diary* (1726–1764). Boston; also Portsmouth, N.H. Continued after his death by his son.

Ames, Nathaniel (the younger). *An Astronomical Diary* (1765–1775). Boston; Newport R.I.; Portsmouth, N.H.; New Haven, Hartford; and New London, Conn.

Cambridge Almanacs, 1639–1692. Although these almanacs are believed to have been published continuously, there are no extant copies before 1646 or from 1651 to 1655. The compilers of the almanacs usually changed each year, although occasionally a single author might issue two or three almanacs. Titles vary.

Crockett Almanacs (1835–1856). Nashville, New York, Boston, Philadelphia, and other cities. About fifty separate issues, with varying titles and by different publishers, under the name of Davy Crockett, or his "heirs," or by "Ben Hardin" or "Harding."

Ellms, Charles. *The American Comic Almanac* (1831–1846). Boston. From 1839 to 1846 titled *Old American Comic Almanac*. From 1837 by Thomas Groom for Ellms.

Elton, R. H. *Elton's Comic-All-my-nack* (1834–1850). New York.

Fisher, James. *Fisher's Comic Almanac* (1841–1847). New York, Philadelphia, Boston.

Foster, John. *An Almanack* (1675–1681). Cambridge (1675) and Boston (1676–1681).

Franklin, Benjamin. *Poor Richard's Almanac (1733–1758)*. Philadelphia. From 1748, published as *Poor Richard Improved*. Series continued from 1759 until 1766 by the firm of Franklin and Hall. Other publishers used the name thereafter.

Franklin, James, Sr. *The Rhode-Island Almanac*, by "Poor Robin" (1728–1735). Newport, R.I. Series continued from 1737 to 1741, by Joseph Stafford and Ann Franklin.

Franklin, James, Jr. *Poor Job*, by Job Shepherd, pseud. (1750–1755; 1758). Newport, R.I.

Hutchins, John Nathan. Title varies: *An Almanac* (1753–1754), *Hutchins* (1755–1759), *Hutchins Improved* (1760–1818). New York. Continued after Hutchin's death by various publishers, both as *Hutchins Improved* and *Hutchins Revived*.

Leeds, Daniel. *An Almanack* (1687–1700) and *The American Almanack* (1701–1714): Philadelphia and New York. Continued by Titan Leeds.

Leeds, Titan. *The American Almanac* (1715–1738). Philadelphia and New York. Printed by the Bradfords, who continued the series to 1746 after Titan Leeds's death.

Thomas, Robert B. *The Farmer's Almanac* (1793–   ): Boston. Title changed to *Old-Farmer's Almanac* in 1832. Thomas died in 1846, but the series has continued with his name as editor. Current publisher: Robb Trowbridge of Yankee, Inc., Dublin, N.H.

Tulley, John. *An Almanack* (1687–1702). Boston (except 1791, 1792: Cambridge).

Robert Secor

Chronological List of Humor Magazines

This list locates journals in a time line and in relation to one another. Not every journal listed here is solely a comic magazine, as several magazines are included because of the importance of a humorous component. In many cases, particularly in the 1920–1980 period, dates may be approximate. Dates in parentheses are tentative placements; vagaries of dating and numbering in some magazines make any "computed" date unreliable.

The symbol after each title indicates the list in which it appears: I—Magazine Profiles; II—Brief Listings; III.A—Copyright Listings; III.B—Unverified Data. Journals described in the essays on the subgenres of scholarly sources and collegiate humor are not included.

1757	*American Magazine and Monthly Chronicle*, II
1765	*The* (Philadelphia) *Bee*, I
1784	*New Haven Gazette*, I
1793	*Farmer's Weekly Museum*, I
1795	*The Tablet*, I
1796	*Political Censor (Porcupine's)*, I
1797	*Porcupine's Gazette*, II
1800	The *Rush-Light*, I
1801	*The Port Folio*, I
1802	*The Wasp*, I
1803	*The* (Lancaster) *Hive*, II
	The Lancet, II
1804	*Companion and Weekly Miscellany*, II
	The Corrector, I
1805	*Polyanthos*, III.B
1806	*The Weekly Visitant*, II
1807	*The Barber's Shop*, I
	The Fool, I

Moonshine, I

New Milk and Cheese, III.B

The Thistle, I

The (Philadelphia) *Tickler*, I.

Salmagundi, I

Spectacles, II

1808 *Abracadabra*, I

(1808) *Echo*, III.B

The Eye, II

1809 *Omnium Gatherum*, I

Something, II

1810 *The Scourge* (Baltimore), I

1811 *The Beacon*, III.B

The Comet, II

The Cynick, II

The Scourge (Boston), I

1812 *Satirist* (Boston), III.B

1814 *The Corrector* (Philadelphia), III.B

The Moralist, II

Whim, III.B

1815 *Corrector*, III.B

The Lounger, III.B

Luncheon, III.B

1816 *The Aeronaut*, I

The Country Courier, II

The Parterre, II

1817 *Independent Balance*, I

1818 *The Idiot*, I

Kaleidoscope, II

1819 *The Red Book*, I

The Roundtable, II

Stand, II

1820 *The Album and Ladies Weekly Gazette*, III.B

The Club-Room, II

The Critic, II

The Microscope (New Haven), II

1821 *The Idle Man*, II

	The Microscope (Albany), II
1822	*Castigator*, III.B
	City Fire-Fly, I
	The Gridiron, II
1824	*Microscope and General Advisor*, II
1826	*The ———*, I
1827	*The Ariel*, I
	The Manuscript, II
1828	*Boston Literary Gazette*, II
	The Yankee, I
1829	*Constellation*, III.B
1830	*Genius of Comedy*, III.B
	Scraps, II
1831	*Cincinnati Mirror*, I
	Spirit of the Times, I
	The Village Firefly, II
1832	*Boston Literary Magazine*, II
1833	*The Galaxy of Comicalities*, II
	The Knickerbocker, I
	The Political Mania, II
	The Spy, II
	The Western Examiner, II
1834	*Champagne Club*, II
1835	*Literary Magazine*, II
1836	*Every Body's Album*, I
	Baltimore Monument, I
	Salmagundi, III.B
	Yale Literary Magazine, II
1837	*Figaro in Albany*, III.B
	The Oasis, I
	New Orleans Picayune, II
1838	*South Carolinian*, I
1839	*American Masonic Register*, II
	Harlequin, III.B
	Paul Pry, II
	Yankee Miscellany, III.B
1842	*Brother Jonathan*, II

	Orion, II
	Pictorial Wag, II
	The Satirist (Albany), I
	Uncle Sam, III.B
	The Yankee Blade, I
1843	*The Rover*, I
1844	*Neal's Saturday Gazette*, III.B
	St. Louis Reveille, I
1845	*Flumgudgeon Gazette*, II
	Jester, II
	The Satirist, III.B
	New World, III.B
	The Town, III.B
1846	*Judy*, I
	New York Gazette, III.B
	Yankee Doodle, I
1847	*The New York Picayune*, I
1848	*The Elephant*, I
	The John-Donkey, I
1849	*Aurora Borealis*, I
	The Bubble, II
1850	*Figaro!, or, Corbyn's Chronicle of Amusements*, II
	The Lorgnette, II
1851	*The Carpet-Bag*, I
	The Hombre, II
	Humbug's American Museum, II
	Reveille (New York), III.B
1852	*Budget*, III.B
	Diogenes, Hys Lantern, II
	The New York Pick, I
	Yankee Notions, I
(1852)	*Young Sam*, II
(1853)	*Bubble*, III.B
1853	*Everybody's Own*, III.B
	New York Time-Piece, III.B
	O.K. (New York), III.B
	Pen and Pencil, III.B

	Young America, III.B
	Young America on the Pacific, III.B
1854	*Cozzens Wine Press*, I
	Curiosity Shop, III.B
	The Gleaner, III.B
	The Hint, III.B
1855	*Comic World*, III.B
	The Curiosity Shop, II
(1855)	*The Humorist*, III.B
	Pickles, III.B
	Quampeag Coyote, III.B
	Shanghai, III.B
1856	*Nick Nax (For All Creation)*, I
1858	*Frank Leslie's Budget of Fun*, I
	Wang Doodle, III.B
1859	*Comic Bouquet*, III.B
	Comic Monthly, I
	The Phunny Phellow, I
	Vanity Fair, I
1860	*Innocent Weekly Owl*, III.B
	Momus, II
	The Plantation, II
1862	*The Continental Monthly*, II
	Jolly Joker, III.B
1863	*The Bugle-Horn of Liberty*, I
	Little Joker, II
	Merryman's Monthly, II
	Southern Punch, I
1864	*Bombshell*, III.B
1865	*The Funniest of Awl*, II
	The Knapsack, II
	Mrs. Grundy, I
	Puck: The Pacific Pictorial, II
1866	*The Galaxy*, II
1867	*Jolly Hoosier*, III.B
	The Keepapitchinin, I
	Little Corporal, III.B
	Merry and Wise, III.B

	Native Virginian, III.B
1868	*The Boneville Trumpet*, II
	New York Humorist, III.B
	This Week, II
	Wag, III.B
1869	*The Comic News*, III.B
	Kaliedoscope, II
	Chip Basket, III.B
1870	*Curiosity Cabinet*, III.B
	Punchinello, II
	Wild Oats, II
1871	*Champagne*, II
	Cocktails, III.B
	Commodore Rollingpin's Illustrated, II
	New Varieties, II
1872	*The Brickbat*, II
	Carl Pretzel's Magazine Pook, II
	Cartoon, III.B
	Fat Contributor's Saturday Night, II
	Hub Budget, III.B
	Jubilee Days, I
	Thistle, III.B
	Thistleton's Illustrated Jolly Giant, II
(Before 1873)	*Comic Ventilator*, III.B
(Before 1873)	*Comic Weekly*, III.B
(Before 1873)	*Punster*, III.B
(Before 1873)	*Rutland Vermont Times*, III.B
1874	*Ye Giglampz*, I
	Humorist, III.B
1876	*The Carnival of Authors*, II
	Comic World, III.B
	Harvard Lampoon, I.
	Merry Masker, III.B
	The (San Francisco) *Wasp*, II

1877	*Puck*, I
	Judge's Serials, II
1878	*Frank Leslie's Budget of Humorous Stories*, II
	Frank Leslie's Budget of Wit, II
1879	*American Punch*, I
	Burlington Hawkeye, III.B
	Uncle Sam, The American Journal of Wit, II
1880	*Chic*, I
	Puck's Annual, I
	Puck on Wheels, I
1881	*The* (Laramie) *Boomerang*, I
	(The) *Judge*, I
	Texas Siftings, I
	Truth, I
	Wit and Wisdom, II
1882	*The Arkansaw Traveler*, I
(1882)	*Gas*, III.B
	The Mascot, III.B
	Punch and Judy, III.B
1883	*Breeze*, III.B
	California Maverick, II
	Gilhooley's Etchings, III.B
	Life, I
	Pickings from Puck, I
1884	*Good Things of "Life,"* II
	Jingo, I
	The Rambler (Chicago), II
	Shakespeare's Bones, II
	Tid-Bits (*Time*), I
1885	*The Roller Monthly*, II
	Sam, The Scaramouche, III.B
	Whip, III.B
1886	*Lantern* (New Orleans), III.B
1887	*Puck's Library*, I
1888	*The Cartoon*, III.B
	Figaro (Chicago), II
	Natural Gas, II

1889	*Lies*, III.B
	St. Louis Life, II
	Light, III.B
1890	*Arkansaw Thomas Cat*, II
	Jester (Philadelphia), II
	Judge's Library, II
	Judge's Quarterly, II
	New Hampshire Republican, III.B
	Racket, III.B
1891	*Jester* (Boston), III.B
	Portland Figaro, III.B
	Tales from Town Topics, I
1892	*Broadway Magazine*, III.B
	Iris Magazine, III.B
	Life's Monthly Calendar, III.B
	Nast's Weekly, I
1893	*World's Fair Puck*, I
1894	*The* (Seattle) *Argus*, II
	The Comic Library, III.B
	The Rolling Stone, I
	The Sunday Comic Weekly, II
	Uncle Sam (Chicago), II
1895	*The Bauble: Contemporary*, III.B
	The Bibelot, II
	Clips, II
	The Echo, III.B
(1895)	*Just for Fun*, III.B
	The Lark (*Epi-Lark*), I
	Philistine, I
	Texas Sifter, III.B
	Up to Date, II
	The Vermont Graphic, II
1896	*Bul*, III.B
	Light (San Francisco), III.B
	Poker Chips, III.B

	Puck's Quarterly, I
	Twinkles, I
1897	*Life's Comedy*, I
	The Yellow Kid/Yellow Book Magazine, II
1898	*The* (New York) *Bee*, I
	Chameleon, III.B
	The Verdict, II
	Vim, II
1899	*Expositor and Current Anecdotes*, III.B
	The Jolly Joker, I.
	Saturday Evening Post, II
	Sis Hopkin's Own Book and Magazine of Fun, II
	Snaps, II
(Before 1900)	*Chaff*, III.B
(Before 1900)	*Charivari*, III.B
(Before 1900)	*The Comic Mirror*, III.B
(Before 1900)	*The Comic Times*, III.B
(Before 1900)	*Diogenes* (Utah), III.B
(Before 1900)	*Good Things of Life*, III.B
(Before 1900)	*Judge and Jury*, III.B
(Before 1900)	*Merry Moments*, III.B
1900	*The Bachelor Book*, III.B
	The Kansas Knocker, I
	The Lion's Mouth, III.B
	The Smart Set, I
(1900)	*Stuffed Club for Everybody*, III.B
(1900)	*Telephony*, III.A

1901   *The Bilioustine*, III.B

Fun, III.B

Funny Side, III.B

The Goose-Quill, III.B

Hot Shots from the Funny Boys, II

Hot Soldier, II

Whim, III.B

1902   *Calgary Eye Opener*, I

1903   *The Foolish Book*, II

Fun with Cy Scudder, II

Fun Quarterly, II

Hallo, III.B

Just Fun That's All, II

1904   *The Knocker*, III.A

Sagebrush Philosophy, I

1905   *Little Devil*, III.B

1906   *The Blue Devil*, III.B

Corning's Quarterly Razoo, III.A

(1906)   *K. Lamity's Harpoon*, III.A

The Scandalizer, III.A

Smoke, III.A

Tokyo Puck, II

Touchstone, II

1907   *The Bang*, III.B

Blue Mule, III.A

George Fuller Golden Journal, III.A

Lantern (Cincinnati), III.B

Uncle Remus' Magazine, I

1908   *Cheerful Pessimist*, III.B

Chic, III.B

Duke's Mixture Magazine, II

Giggles, II

Semi-Occasionally, III.A

Spectator, III.A

Westbrook's Fun Book, II

1909   *Humorist* (Yiddish), III.B

Rooseveltian—Look Out, III.A

Whose Is It, III.A

1910	*Bubbles*, III.A
(1910)	*Fun*, II
	Fun and Frolic, III.A
	Smile Club Messenger, III.A
	Spitzpippin, III.A
1911	*Satire*, II
1912	*Cartoons Magazine*, I
	Jim Jam Jems, I
	The Magazine of Fun, II
1913	*Vanity Fair*, I
1914	*The Bell Cow*, III.A
	Wot Sat, III.A
	Zowie, III.A
1915	*Booze*, III.A
	Bruno's Weekly, II
	Cheerful Liar, III.B
	Film Fun, I
(1915)	*Live Wire*, III.A
	Medical Pickwick, III.A
	Parisienne, III.B
1916	*The Devil*, III.A
	Fads and Fancies, III.A
	Funnybone, II
	Gesundheit, III.A
	Humorous Verse on Current Events, III.A
	The Lamb, II
	Oyez, III.A
	The Pagan, III.A
	The Rambler, II
	Saucy Stories, III.A
1917	*Yankee Hustler*, III.A
1918	*Fool Killer*, III.A
(1918)	*Hello Buddy*, II
	The Quill, II
	Tale Spins, III.A

1919	*Captain Billy's Whiz Bang*, I
	Good Morning and *Art Young Quarterly*, I
	The Grid, III.A
	Kistler Kootie, III.A
	Smile-a-While Magazine, III.A
	Smiles, III.A
	Tatler, III.A
	Tattler, III.A
1920	*Anecdotes, Fun and Jokes*, III.A
	Arkansas Hillbilly, III.A
(1920)	*Excitement*, III.A
	The Fun Book, II
	Playboy, III.A
	Toots, III.A
1921	*Bean Spiller*, III.A
	The Buzzer, III.A
	The Cactus Needle, III.A
	College Humor and Sense, II
	Doughboy's Fun and Facts, III.A
	The Follies, III.A
	The Fool, III.A
	The Magazine of Fun, II
	The Quamahoochian, III.A
	The Satyr, III.A
	Sierra Breeze, III.A
	Treat'em Square, III.A
	Uncle Jerry Says, III.A
	White Mule, III.A
	Whimsies, III.A
	Wit and Humor, III.A
	Zing, III.A
1922	*Buddies Review*, III.A
	Bughouse Bugle, III.A
	Burten's Follies, II
	The Buzzer, III.A
	Cap'n Joey's Jazza-Ka-Jazza, III.A
	The Fig Leaf, III.A
	The Flapper, II

Hot Dog, II

Laughing Horse, III.A

Limerick Magazine, III.A

Medical Quip, III.A

Moonshine, III.A

Reader's Digest, II

1923   *Cap'n Joey's Follies*, III.A

Droll Stories, II

Experience Annual/Experience Monthly/Flapper's Experience, II

Extravaganza, II

Printers Hell Box of Southern California, III.A

Red Devil-Ry, III.A

Tucker's Magazine of Scandal, III.A

Verse and Worse, III.A

Zest, III.A

Ziffs, I

1924   *The American Mercury*, I

The Barber, III.B

Cartoons and Movies Magazine, II

Co-ed Campus Quarterly, III.A

College Comics, II

College Life, II

Follyology, III.A

Hot Spark, III.A

National Bootlegger, III.A

Red Pepper, II

Sea Breezes, II

The Sniper, III.A

Today's Humor, II

The White Mule, I

1925   *Clever Truths*, III.A

Collegiate Wit, II

The Dumbook, III.A

French Frolics, II

Imp, III.A

Laffalog, III.A

Laughter, II

The Low Down, III.B

The New Yorker, I

Paris Nights, II

Red Hot, III.A

Smiles and Giggles, III.A

So This Is Paris Magazine, II

Tatler and American Sketch, III.A

The Witamii, III.A

Wit o' the World, II

World Humor, III.B

1926   *alley up*, II

America's Humor, II

Broadway Breeze, II

Cartoons & Collegian Fun, II

College Stories, III.A

Cynic, III.A

Satire, II

Snicker Snacks, II

The Spice Box, II

Zest, III.A

1927   *Flit Buzz*, III.A

French Humor, II

Shed Row News, III.A

Yankee Humor, II

1928   *The Bazoom*, III.A

Broadway Nights, II

Farmer Dick's Pitchfork, III.A

(1928)   *French Follies*, III.A

Funny Stories, III.A

Gag, Plot, and Title, III.A

The Grizzly, III.A

Halt Friends!, II

Parade, III.A

Smokehouse Monthly, II

Thacker's Joke Sheet, III.A

Tid-Bits, II

1929	*Broad Lynes*, III.A
	The Dart, III.A
	Fun and Funds, III.A
	The Funnies, III.A
	Hot Lynes (For Flaming Youth), III.A
	Odd Things, III.A
	Ruff-Nek-News, III.A
	Wise Cracks, II
	Zip 'n Tang, III.A
1930	*Humor*, III.A
	Imp, III.A
	Insanity Fair, III.A
	Joy Stories, II
	Mack's Pocket Cartoons and Jokes Magazine, II
	New Broadway Brevities, II
(1930)	*Oy' Oy I'm Leffin*, III.B
	Paree Stories, III.A
	Peppy Humor, III.A
	Pictorial French Follies, III.B
	Slices, III.A
(1930)	*Smoke*, III.A
(1930)	*Spicy Stories*, II
	Town Crier, II
1931	*Ballyhoo*, I
	Campus Comics Quarterly, II
	Frolics/Paris Frolics, III.B
	Funny Facts and Fiction, II
	Ginger Goes Places and Sees Things, III.A
	Hollywood Nights, III.B
	Hooey, II
(1931)	*Hot Sheet! Skip List*, III.A
	Hullabaloo, II
	The Humorous Scrapbook, III.B
	Lightnin', III.A
	Paris Frolics, III.B
	Pep, III.A
	Screen Comedy, III.B
	Tickle-Me-Too, II

	Tickles, II
	Today's Humor, III.A
	Wise House, III.A
	Your Naborhood, III.A
1932	*Americana*, I
	Aw, Nerts!, II
	Baloney, II
	Baloney from Hollywood, III.A
	Blah, II
	Bumbledom Journal, III.A
	Bunk, II
	B-u-n-k, III.A
	Bushwa, II
	Clown, II
	Coo-Coo, II
	Gayety, III.B
	Haywire, III.B
	Hokum, II
	Hot After Cold Business, III.A
	Howdee, III.A
	Humorist of the Week, III.A
	Jest, II
	Kookoo, II
	Merry-Go-Round, II
	Pastime, II
	Razzberries, II
	Slapstick, II
	Smiles, III.A
	Tenafly Humbug Magazine, III.A
	Unk Ebenezer's Tiny Magazine, III.A
(1932)	*Varieties*, III.A
1933	*Aardvark*, III.A
	American Humorist, II
	Axe Grinder, III.A
	Ax-Grinder, III.A
	Blast, III.A
	Broadway Follies, III.A
	Broadway Nightlife, II

(1933) *Burlesque Jokes and Stories*, III.B
(1933) *Dizzy Detective Magazine*, III.B
Esquire, II
Follies, II
French Frolics, III.B
Fun Finder, III.A
Gay Book Magazine, II
(1933) *Gay French*, III.B
Gulf Comic Weekly, III.A
Happiness, III.A
Happiness—For All the World, III.A
Hollywood Squawkies, II
Hot-cha, II
Kollege Kwips, III.A
Lamp of Diogenes, III.A
New York Nights, II
Paris Follies, II
Wild Cherries, II
World Humor Flashes, III.A
1934 *Bayburn Brevities*, III.A
Broadway Tattler (see *Brevities*), II
College Humor, II
Comic Cuts, III.A
Comic Tabloid, III.A
Funtest, III.A
Gay Broadway, III.B
Gay Parisienne, III.A
Harpoon, III.A
(1934) *High Spots*, III.A
Movie Humor, II
Paris Gayety, III.B
(1934) *Paris Thrills*, II
Radio Razzberries, II
Real Screen Fun, II
Screen Humor, III.B
Smoke, III.A
Snap, III.B
Wieboldt's Wampum Club, III.A

1935	*French Scandals*, II
	The Radio Humorist, II
	SFZ, III.A
1936	*Cartoonews (OK)*, II
	Comics Magazine, III.A
	Gay Ninety's Magazine, III.A
	Handies Silk Stocking Review, III.B
(1936)	*Lu Lu*, II
	Movie Merry-Go-Round, II
	Silk Stocking Stories, II
	Smiling Thru, III.A
1937	*The Comics*, III.A
	For Men and Men Only, III.A
	Fun Outdoors Pictorial, II
	Gags, II
	Mr., II
	Reel Humor, II
1938	*Chuckles*, III.A
	College Years, II
	Comedy, II
	Fun for One, III.A
	Funny Pages, III.A
	Funny Picture Stories, III.A
	Head's Up!, III.A
(1938)	*Let's Laugh*, II
	Peek, II
	Zest, III.A
1939	*Cartoon Humor*, II
	Der Gag Bag, III.B
	Fun for All, III.A
	The Funnies, III.A
	Happiness, III.A
	Hellzapoppin, III.A
	Humor Digest, II
	Little Wit, III.A
	New Jokes, II

(1940)	*Bob's Digest of Fun*, II
1940	*Co-eds*, II
	Diogenes, III.A
	Featheredge Quills, III.A
	Grin, II
	Grin and Bear It, II
	Laff and *Laff Annual*, II
	Movie Fun, II
	Quote, III.B
1941	*Army Laughs (Army Laffs)*, II
	Captain Wag, III.B
	Cartoon, III.B
	Carnival Combined with Show, II
	Comedy Riot, II
	Cookoo Nuts, II
	Dash, II
	Funny Bone, III.A
	Fun Parade, II
	Gags (Here! Is America's Humor), II
	Gayety, II
	Ha Ha, III.A
	Halt!, II
	Jest—The Zest of Life, II
	Khaki Wacky, II
	Khaki Humor, II
	Mirth of a Nation, III.B
	Pictorial Movie Fun, II
	Pup, III.B
	Screwball, II
	Squad's Riot, II
	Stag, II
	TNT, II
	Wit, II
	Yoo Hoo!, II
	Zippy, II

1942	*Army and Navy Fun Parade*, II
	Blackout, II
	Boo, III.A
	Broadway Parody Songs, III.A
	Buddies, II
	Bunk, III.A
	Comedy, II
	Eek!, III.A
	Funny Book, III.A
	The Funnybone Quarterly, II
	Gag Strips, II
	Grr, III.A
	Harpoon, III.A
	Hello Buddies, II
	Jeeps, II
	Kit 'o Wit, II
(1942)	*Laughter Is Our Ally*, II
	Liberty Laughs, II
	Literary Huckster, III.A
(1942)	*Marine Comedy*, III.B
	Nifty, II
	Nifty Gags, III.A
	Pack 'o Fun, II
(1942)	*Parisian Follies*, III.B
	A Pocketful of Pepper, II
	Popular Parody Song Hits, II
	Sh-h!, II
	Smiles, II
	What's Cookin'!, II
	Whiz Bang, II
1943	*ABC*, II
	Cheers, II
	Eyeful, II
(1943)	*Facts, Fun, and Satire*, III.A
	First Class Male, III.B
	Funny Funnies, III.A
	Fun Riot, II

	Hit!, II
	Keep 'em Laughing, II
	Pepper, II
	Private Bill, III.B
(1943)	*Riggin' Bill*, III.B
	Salute, III.B
(1943)	*Strictly Private*, III.B
(1943)	*Titter*, II
(1943)	*War Laffs*, II
(1943)	*Wit and Wisdom*, II
	Yankee Comics, III.B
	You Chirped, III.B
1944	*Army and Navy Grins*, II
(1944)	*Army and Navy Hot Shots*, II
	Army and Navy Jokes, II
	Belly Laffs, II
(1944)	*The Booby Trap*, II
(1944)	*Cartoonist*, III.A
(1944)	*Daffy Comics*, III.B
	Dizzy Parade, III.B
	Flophouse News, II
	Fun Follies, III.B
	Fun Frolic, II
	Fun & Frolic, II
(1944)	*Gobs and Gals*, III.B
	Hobo News, II
	Horse Feathers, III.A
	Joker, II
	Laugh Book Magazine (Charley Jones'-), I
	Lip Parade, II
	Marine Comedy, III.A
	The Nugget, II
(1944)	*Nuts & Jolts*, III.B
	Pip, III.B
	Shantytown News, II
(1944)	*Tops in Humor*, III.B
	Wink, III.A

(1945)	*Blitz Bang*, III.B
1945	*Collier's Collects Its Wits*, II
	Hi Fellers, III.A
	Hiye, III.B
	Homeresque, III.A
	Humor, II
	Is My Face Red!, III.B
(1945)	*Let's Have a Good Laugh*, III.B
	Madhouse, II
	Nuts!, III.B
	Pictorial Chuckles, II
	Salute, III.A
	Slick, III.B
1946	*Cartoon Roundup*, II
	Flip, II
	Fun Yearbook, III.B
	Gals, III.A
(1946)	*Gal Snaps*, II
	G'eye News, III.A
(1946)	*Hilarious 'Laff Riot'*, II
	Hold It!, III.A
	Horsing Around, III.A
	Hot Shots, III.B
	Humor-Esq, III.A
	Joke Parade, III.B
	Jolly Dolls, II
	Nuttylife, III.A
	Pictorial Review, II
	Pleasure, III.B
1947	*Campus Parade*, III.A
	Caricature, III.A
	Cartoon Comedy, III.A
	Funnyman, III.A
	Gayety, II
	Good Humor, II

	Hi-Jinx, III.A
	Strictly Stag, II
1948	*Film Humor*, III.B
	Have You Told Your Wife?, III.A
	Pepper, II
1950	*Broadway Laughs*, II
	College Fun, II
	Comedy, II
	Jest, II
	Maybe You're Screwy Too, III.B
	Mirth, II
	Pardon My Sex, Doctor!, III.B
	Paris Life, II
1951	*Army Fun*, II
	Here! Is America's Humor, II
	Humor, III.B
(1951)	*Nifty Gals and Gags*, II
(1951)	*Stare*, II
(1951)	*The Bare Facts*, III.B
1952	*Dolls & Gags*, II
	Foo, III.B
	Happy Variety, III.B
	Mad, I
1953	*Belly Laffs*, II
	Cheers, III.A
	Crazy, III.A
	Hit! Junior, II
(1953)	*Humorama*, III.B
	Jackpot, II
	Laff Junior, II
	Smoke, III.A
	Squeeks, III.A
(1953)	*Swingle*, II
(1953)	*Zowie*, II

1954	*a-Laugh-a-Minnit*, II
	Breezy, II
	Broadway Hollywood Blackouts, III.B
	The Cartoonists' Comic, III.A
	The Gag Recap, III.B
	Gaze, II
	Get Lost, III.B
	Hot Dog, III.A
(1954)	*Instant Laughs*, III.B
	The Keyhole, II
	Laugh Digest, II
	Quips, II
	Snappy, II
	TV Carnival, III.A
	TV Girls and Gags, II
(1954)	*Wham!*, II
1955	*Belly Laffs*, II
	Briefed, III.A
(1955)	*Bust Out Laffin'*, II
	Cartoon Cuties, III.A
	Cartoonist's and Gagwriter's Supermarket, III.A
(1955)	*Chicks and Chuckles*, II
	Cockeyed, II
	Crazy, Man, Crazy, II
	From Here to Insanity, III.B
	Gee Whiz!, II
	Laughing It Up, III.A
	Wise Cracks, II
(1955)	*Zip!*, II
1956	*Mascalines*, III.A
	New Cartoons, Jokes & Gags, III.B
	Sh-h-h-h, III.A
	Snafu, III.B

1957	*Backstage Follies*, III.A
	College Laughs, II
	Evergreen Review, II
	Eye Opener, III.B
	Fantasia, III.B
	Humbug Magazine, I
	Trump, III.B
1958	*Cartoon Parade*, II
	Cartoons and Gags, III.A
	Cartoons for Men Only, III.A
	Cracked, II
	Frantic, III.A
	Frenzy, III.B
	Jackpot, II
	The Jester, III.A
	Nuts, III.B
	Orben's Current Comedy, III.A
	Panic, II
	The Realist, I
	Shook Up, III.B
	Snap, III.A
	Sporty, III.B
	Thimk, III.B
	Zany, III.B
1959	*Fantasia*, III.B
	French Cartoons and Cuties, II
	Fun 'n Facts from the Wall Street Journal, III.A
	Funtasia, III.B
(1959)	*The Best Cartoons from Escapade*, III.B
1960	*Campus Howl*, III.B
	French Frills, III.A
	Help, II
	Romp, II
	Sick, II
1961	*CAR' Toons*, II

(1961)	*Laff Time*, II
	Laugh Parade, II
	Laugh Riot, III.A
	Monocle, II
(1961)	*Popular Jokes*, II
1962	*Cartoon Carnival*, I
	Cartoon Comedy Parade, II
	Cartoon Laughs, II
	Humor Exchange Newsletter, III.B
	New Comedy, III.B
	The Outsider's Newsletter, I
1963	*Drag Cartoons*, III.B
	French Follies, III.A
	Ha, II
	Judge, II
	Laugh We Must, by Zing Cornell, III.A
	Satire Newsletter, I
1964	*Ed Big Daddy Roth*, III.B
	Fooey, III.B
(1964)	*Fun House Comedy*, II
	Hot Rod Cartoons, II
	Laughing All the Way, II
	Monsters to Laugh With, III.A
	Panic, II
(1964)	*Sex to Sexty*, II
1965	*Buffoon*, III.A
	Cartoon-a-Vision, III.A
	Gals a-Go-Go, III.A
	Grump, II
	Cartoon Fun and Comedy, II
	Horseshit, II
	Laffboy, III.B
(1966)	*A-Laugh-A-Million*, II

1966	*Campus Jokes and Cartoons*, II
	Campus Humor, III.A
	Cartoon Capers, II
	Comic Cuties, II
	Flicks, II
	Freelancer, II
	Funnyboy, III.B
	Jackpot, II
	A Million Laughs Magazine, II
	Yell, III.B
(1966)	*Zowie*, II
1967	*Gals and Gags*, II
(1967)	*Popular Cartoons*, II
	Wild!, II
1968	*Campus Jaybird*, III.A
	Cartoon Review, III.A
	Cartoons Marooned, III.A
	Cycletoons, III.A
	French Fun, II
	Laugh Circus, III.B
	Laugh-In, III.A
(1968)	*Photo Fun*, III.B
	Pin-Up Fun, II
	Screw, II
	Service Snickers, II
	Sextra Laughs, III.A
	Spicy Fun, II
1969	*Bedside Book of Stag Humor*, II
	Cartoon World, II
	Cartoonist Profiles, III.A
	Laugh Out, III.B
	Original Cartoons, III.A
	Sexplosion, III.B
	Super Sex to Sexty, II
1970	*Belly Button*, III.A
	Best Cartoons from the Editors of Stag and Male, III.A

(1970)	*Funny, Funny World*, (*Martin Ragaway's*), III.B
	Girlie Fun, III.B
	Hee Haw, III.B
(1970)	*Jokes by Cracky*, III.A
	National Lampoon, I
	Suppository, III.B
(1971)	*Blast*, III.B
1971	*Choppertoons*, III.A
	Laugh and Learn, III.A
	Laugh-Maker, III.A
	The Orben Comedy Letter, III.A
	Orben's Comedy Fillers, III.A
1972	*Big Rig Sex on Sex*, II
	Bijou Funnies, III.B
	Cartoonus Sexualis, III.A
	Grin, II
	Racin' Toons, III.B
1973	*Crazy*, II
1974	*Harpoon*, II
1975	*Apple Pie*, II
	Bananas, III.A
	Loose Lips Sink Ships, III.A
	The National Crumb, II
1976	*Buffoon*, III.B
	Goose, III.B
	International Insanity, II
	Laughter-Magazine of Adult Humor, III.B
	Latest Gags, III.A
	The Laughing Man, III.A
1977	*Parody*, II
	Pizzazz, II
	Wreck/Newswreck, II
1978	*Hustler Humor*, II
	Trash, II
1979	*Harpoon*, III.A
	Playgirl's Best Cartoons, II
1980	*Horneytoons*, II
	Raw, II

1981	*The Daily Blab*, III.B
	The New Satirist, III.B
	Wacko, II
	Weirdo, II
1982	*Lone Star*, II
	Stop! Magazine, II
1984	*Laugh Factory*, II
1985	*Parody Penthouse,* II

Selected Bibliography

American Comic Book Co. "Magazine List, Part 1 and 2." Studio City, Calif., 1984.

Ayer Directory of Publications. Philadelphia: N. W. Ayer and Sons, 1880 and ongoing.

Blair, Walter. "Burlesques in Nineteenth-century American Humor." *American Literature* 2 (November 1930): 236–47.

———. *Native American Humor*. San Francisco: Chandler Reprint, 1960.

———. "The Popularity of Nineteenth-Century American Humorists." *American Literature* 3 (May 1931): 175–194.

———, and Hamlin Hill. *America's Humor: From Poor Richard to Doonesbury*. New York: Oxford University Press, 1978.

Brigham, Clarence S. *History and Bibliography of American Newspapers, 1690–1820*. Hamden, Conn.: Archon Books, 1962, reprinted from the American Antiquarian Society.

Catalog of the Schmulowitz Collection of Wit and Humor. San Francisco: San Francisco Public Library, 1962.

Chielens, Edward E. *The Literary Journal in America to 1900*. Detroit: Gale Research Co., 1975.

———, ed. *American Literary Magazines: The Eighteenth and Nineteenth Centuries*. Westport, Conn.: Greenwood Press, 1986.

Dorsan, Richard M. *Jonathan Draws the Long Bow*. Cambridge, Mass.: Harvard University Press, 1946.

Fulton, Len, ed. *International Directory of Little Magazines and Small Presses*. Paradise, Calif.: Dustbooks, 1976, 12th ed., noncumulative indexing.

Gabor, Mark. *The Illustrated History of Girlie Magazines*. New York: Harmony Books, 1984.

Hagood, Patricia, ed. *Standard Periodical Directory*. New York: Oxbridge Communications, 1982, 8th ed., updated regularly.

Hoornstra, Jean, and Trudy Heath. *American Periodicals 1741–1900/An Index to the Microfilm Collections*. Ann Arbor, Mich.: University Microfilms International, 1979.

Hudson, Frederic. "The Comic Papers." In *Journalism in the United States from 1690 to 1872*. New York: Harper and Bros., 1873.

Inge, M. Thomas. "Collecting Comic Books." *American Book Collector* (March–April 1984): n.s.5:3–15.

Katz, Bill, ed. *Magazines for Libraries*. New York: R. R. Bowker, 1969, regularly updated.

Kennedy, Jay. *The Official Underground and Newave Comix Price Guide*. Cambridge, Mass.: Boatner-Norton Press, 1982.

Kery, Patricia F. *Great Magazine Covers of the World*. New York: Abbeville, 1981.

King, Alexander. "The Sad Case of the Humorous Magazines." *Vanity Fair* 41 (December 1933): 26–27, 68–71.

Koppe, Richard et al. *A Treasury of College Humor*. New York: William Penn, 1950.

Kribbs, Jane K. *An Annotated Bibliography of American Literary Periodicals, 1741–1850*. Boston: G. K. Hall, 1977.

Leutheusser, O. G. "The Comic Supplement." *The Illustrated Home Journal* 12 (November 1907): 427–29.

Lukens, Henry Clay. "American Literary Comedians." *Harper's New Monthly Magazine* 80 (April 1890): 783–97.

Marschall, Richard, and Carol J. Wilson. "Selected Humorous Magazines." In Stanley Trachtenberg, ed., *American Humorists, 1800–1950*. Detroit: Gale Research, 1983, 2:655–78.

Matthews, Brander. "The Comic Periodical Literature of the United States." *American Bibliopolist* (August 1875) 7:199–201.

Mott, Frank Luther. *American Journalism*. New York: Macmillan Co., 1941.

———. *A History of American Magazines*. 5 vols. Cambridge, Mass.: Harvard University Press, 1938–1965.

Murrell, William. *A History of American Graphic Humor*. New York: Whitney Museum, 1933.

Overstreet, Robert M. *The Comic Book Price Guide*. New York: Harmony Books, 1984, 14th ed., annual price guide.

Peterson, Theodore. *Magazines of the Twentieth Century*. Urbana: University of Illinois Press, 1964, 2d ed.

Richardson, Lyon. *A History of Early American Magazines, 1741–1789*. New York: Thomas Nelson & Sons, 1931.

Savory, Jerold J. "An Uncommon Comic Collection: Humorous Victorian Periodicals in the Newberry Library." *Victorian Periodicals Review* 17 (Fall 1984): 94–102.

Serials in Microform, 1984. Ann Arbor, Mich.: University Microfilms International, 1984, updated annually.

Sloane, David E. E. "American Humor Periodicals." In Larry Mintz, ed., *Humor in America: A Research Guide to Genres and Topics*. Westport, Conn.: Greenwood Press, forthcoming.

———. *The Literary Humor of the Urban Northeast, 1830–1890*. Baton Rouge: L.S.U. Press, 1983.

———. "Nineteenth-Century American Magazines and Illustration." In *Drexel's Great School of American Illustration: Violet Oakley and Her Contemporaries*. Philadelphia: Drexel University, 1984, pp. 8–9.

Smythe, Albert H. *Philadelphia Magazines and Their Contributors, 1741–1850*. Philadelphia: Robert M. Lindsay, 1892.

Tebbel, John. *The American Magazine: A Compact History*. New York: Hawthorn, 1969.

Titus, Edna B., ed. *Union List of Serials in Libraries of the United States and Canada*. New York: H. W. Wilson Co., 1965, 3d ed., regularly updated.

Ulrich's International Periodicals Directory. New York: R. R. Bowker Co., 1983, 22d ed., regularly updated.

Wood, James P. *Magazines in the United States*. New York: Ronald Press, 1949.

Various hardcover reprints of *Life*, *Collier's*, *Reader's Digest*, *Saturday Evening Post*, *Esquire*, *Playboy*, and *New Yorker* humor and cartoons, and now even counter-culture and other humor, as well as various period anthologies like *Clips from Jonathan's Jack-knife* as early as the 1870 period, may be located individually.

Individual state histories of journalism will offer local additions to the list of statewide humorous publications.

The *Dictionary of National Biography* and other general biographical collections are often helpful in researching individual writers and editors.

Index

Note: **bold** page numbers indicate main subject entries.

27, 159; on comics, 158; counter-culture, 470; fiction, 103; literary, xx, 177–78, 237–38, 280; of men's magazines, 407; of nineteenth century scientific organizations, 162–63; political, 75–76; of pulp expose magazines, 356–57; sophisticated, 25–27; of women's rights, 354; yuppie, 419
Burlesque show humor, 373
Burlington, Iowa, xxiii
Burlington, Vermont, 483
Burlington Hawkeye, 18, 518
Burne-Jones, Edward, 340
Burnet, Dana, 225
Burnham, George P., 274, 447
Burns, George, 438
Burr, Aaron, 59, 60
Burr, The, 534
Burten, Joe, 346, 378, 399, 415, 455, 505
Burten's Follies, **346**, 378
Burton, William E., 66
Bush, Charles Green, 144
Bush, David V., 510
Bushwa, **346–47**
Bushwa Publishing Corporation, 346
Business-oriented humor, 460
Bust Out Laffin', **347**
Butler, Ben, 13
Butler, Benjamin Franklin, General, 269
Butler, Ellis Parker, xiii, xxiv, 333, 420, 426, 480, 496, 497
Butler, James, 480
Butler, Merrill, xviii, 258–59
Buzzer, The (Louise Aimee Patterson), 504
Buzzer, The (Swift and Company), 504

C.A. Lutz Company, 511
C.H.B., 265
C.H. Young Company, 368
Cabell, James Branch, 260
Cackles, xxiv
Cactus Needle, The, 504
Cadwalader, Thomas, 217
Cady, Harrison, 148
Cain, James M., 7
Caldwell, Charles, 214, 218
Caldwell, Eleanor B., 205
Calgary Eye Opener, xxv, xxix, **39–40**, 41
Calgo Publishers, Inc., 504
Calhoun, John C., 193, 240
California, University of, 536, 542
California Gold Rush, 245
California Maverick, xxiii, xxv, **349**
Callendar, 309

Calliope, 546
Calvin, John, 204
Camac, William, 299
Cambridge, Massachusetts. *See Harvard Lampoon*
Cambridge Almanacs, 549–50
Camp, Walter, III, 358
Campbell, E. Simms, 360
Campbell, Thomas, 216, 256
Campbell, William, 268, 269
Campus Cat, 534
Campus Comics Quarterly, xxvii, **349**
Campus Howl, 518
Campus humor, 349–50
Campus Humor, 505
Campus humor: *See also* Collegiate humor
Campus Jaybird, 505
Campus Jokes and Cartoons, xxvii, **349–50**
Campus Parade, 505
Canadian magazines, 39–40, 360
Candar Publishing Company, 358, 379
Canton, Ohio, 368, 457
Cap and Gown, 533
Capitalism, satire on, 80–81
Capitol Stories, Inc., 390
Cap'n Joey's Follies, 346, 505
Cap'n Joey's Jazza-ka-jazza, 346, 505
Capone, Al, 15
Capote, Truman, 184
Capp, Al, 82
Capper, Arthur, 125
Captain Billy's Whiz Bang, xv, xxix, **40–44**, 465
Captain Wag, 518
Caravan Books, 51
Caricature, 505
Caricatures, 155, 301, 323, 402
Carleton, G.W., 414
Carleton, Will, 375
Carlisle, David, 69
Carl Pretzel's Magazine Pook, xxv, **350**
Carlson, Wallace, 53
Carlton, Carl A., 323
Carlton Publishing Company, 514
Carman, Bliss, 205, 289
Carnahan, Worth B., 491
Carnival, **350**
Carnival of Authors, The, xxiii, **350**
Carpenter, William H., 28
Carpet-Bag, The, xix, **44–51**: format of, 48–49; national reputation of, 46; philosophy of, 45–46

Contributors

JOHN GRANT ALEXANDER is Associate Professor of English at Parkland College.

ST. GEORGE TUCKER ARNOLD, JR., is Associate Professor of English at Florida International University, and author of articles on modern Southern fiction, Eudora Welty, and American humor.

ERIC AUSTIN is a doctoral candidate at the University of Iowa.

DEBRA BROWN is a doctoral candidate at the University of Mississippi.

ALLISON A. BULSTERBAUM is a doctoral candidate at the University of Mississippi.

JAMES LESTER BUSSKOHL is Associate Professor of English at Eastern Washington State University, author of poems and studies on Mark Twain, and a student of Thai literature and culture.

MICHAEL D. BUTLER is Assistant Professor of English at the University of Kansas.

DOUGLAS R. CAPRA is an independent scholar in Seward, Alaska, and author of numerous articles on nineteenth- and early twentieth-century American culture, including sleighing, Elbert Hubbard, and Rockwell Kent.

FRANZ DOUSKEY is Associate Professor at South Central Community College, New Haven, Connecticut. He has published over 400 stories, essays, and poems in magazines including *The Nation*, *Rolling Stone*, and *The New Yorker*; his most recent book of poetry is *Rowing Across the Dark*, University of Georgia Press.

GARY ENGLE is Associate Professor in English at Cleveland State University, editor of *The Grotesque Essence: Plays from the American Minstrel Stage*, and contributing editor of *Cleveland* Magazine and *Northern Ohio Live*; he has written over one hundred articles on American culture.

DAVID C. ESTES is Assistant Professor of English at Loyola University, New Orleans, and a specialist in Thomas Bangs Thorpe and American bibliography.

LORNE FIENBERG is an Assistant Professor of English at Millsaps College.

GARY ALAN FINE is Professor at the University of Minnesota and author of *Rumor and Gossip* (with Ralph Rosnow), *Shared Fantasy, With the Boys*, and various articles on the sociology of culture and art.

BENJAMIN FRANKLIN FISHER IV is Professor of English at the University of Mississippi and author of numerous articles on Poe, the Gothic, and English Victorian authors; he is also editor of *Mississippi Studies in English* and forthcoming books on Thackeray, Poe, and others.

STEVEN H. GALE is Professor of English and American Studies at Missouri Southern State College and editor of the forthcoming *Encyclopedia of American Humor*.

THOMAS GRANT is Associate Professor of English at the University of Hartford and author of *The Comedies of George Chapman* and various articles on American drama, humor, and western film.

DAVID W. HISCOE is Assistant Professor of English at Loyola University of Chicago.

JON CHRISTOPHER HUGHES is Professor of English at the University of Cincinnati and author of *The Tanyard Murder: On the Case with Lafcadio Hearn, Ye Giglampz, The Jolly Book*, and numerous articles and reviews in journals, magazines, and newspapers.

ERIC W. JOHNSON is chief research librarian at the University of Bridgeport Library.

ALAN L. KALISH is a doctoral candidate at Indiana University with an M.A. from Cleveland State University in 1986. His unpublished thesis is "Pynchon and Joyce: An Annotated Bibliography."

MARK A. KELLER is Associate Professor at Middle Georgia College and author of numerous articles on antebellum American humor in *American Literature, New England Quarterly*, and elsewhere.

DAVID B. KESTERSON is Associate Dean of Arts and Sciences and Professor of English at North Texas State University. His books include *Josh Billings, Bill Nye's Western Writings*, and *Bill Nye*, and various articles on American humor and Nathaniel Hawthorne.

JAMES E. KIBLER, JR., is Assistant Professor of English at the University of Georgia.

STUART A. KOLLAR is Director of Publications at Cleveland State University and author of articles in *The Gamut, Cleveland Magazine*, and the *Encyclopedia of American Humorists*.

WILLIAM E. LENZ is Assistant Professor of English, Chatham College, and author of *Fast Talk and Flush Times: The Confidence Man As a Literary Convention* and articles on Mark Twain, William Dean Howells, and various other American humorists of the nineteenth century.

WILLIAM R. LINNEMAN is Professor of English at Illinois State University.

KENT P. LJUNGQUIST is Associate Professor of English at Worcester Polytechnic Institute and author of *The Grand and the Fair: Poe's Landscape Aesthetics and Pictorial Techniques* and co-editor of James Fenimore Cooper's *The Deerslayer*, as well as author of numerous articles in *American Literature*, *Poe Studies*, and elsewhere.

RICHARD E. MARSCHALL is editor of *Nemo: The Classic Comics Library*, author and researcher of books and articles on American cartoons, comics, illustration, and humor, instructor at various colleges of art, and director of museums devoted to comic art.

BARBARA McMILLIN is a doctoral candidate at the University of Mississippi.

CAMERON C. NICKELS is Professor of English and co-chair of American Studies at James Madison University and has written extensively on early American literature and on American humor.

DON NILSEN is Professor of English Linguistics at Arizona State University and co-author with Alleen Pace Nilsen of *Language Play: An Introduction to Linguistics*. He is also chair of "World Humor and Irony Membership" (WHIM) and author-editor of numerous books, articles, and reviews in linguistics and humor.

ROBERT H. O'CONNOR is Assistant Professor at North Dakota State University and is the author of fiction, poetry, and articles on American poets and English dramatists.

MICHAEL PETTENGELL is a doctoral candidate at the University of Mississippi and a specialist in the humor, literature, and folklore of Arkansas.

EDWARD J. PIACENTINO is Professor of English and Director of the Honors Program at High Point College and author of numerous articles on nineteenth- and twentieth-century American literature and culture.

JEAN RAINWATER is Reader Services Librarian at the John Hay Library, Brown University.

DANIEL ROYOT is Professor at the Université Paul Valéry, Montpellier, France, and author of *L'Humour American*, *Dex Puritains Aux Yankees*, and various books and articles on American culture.

RICHARD ALAN SCHWARTZ is Associate Professor of English at Florida International University and author of articles on modern literature, science and literature, American humor, and of short fiction.

ROBERT SECOR is Professor of English and American Studies at the Pennsylvania State University; his books include *The Rhetoric of Shifting Perspectives: Conrad's Victory*, *Pennsylvania 1776*, editor; *John Ruskin and Alfred Hunt*, *The Return of the Good Soldier*, and *Joseph Conrad and American Writers*, and numerous articles.

L. MOODY SIMMS, JR., is Professor of History at Illinois State University and author of over one hundred articles on American cultural, intellectual, and social history, including articles on J. G. Baldwin and H. Allen Smith.

BONNIE F. SLOANE is a nurse specializing in obstetrics-gynecology, which explains why she took the job of extracting titles from the government copyright lists.

DAVID E. E. SLOANE is Professor of English at the University of New Haven and author of *Mark Twain as a Literary Comedian* and *The Literary Humor of the Urban Northeast: 1830–1890*, and numerous articles on American literature and linguistics in the teaching of writing.

GREGORY S. SOJKA is Assistant Vice-President for Academic Affairs and Associate Professor of American Studies and English at Wichita State University. He is the author of *From Icarus to Concorde: Air Flight and Travel in American Culture* and *Ernest Hemingway: The Angler as Artist*, and articles on American literature and popular culture.

E. KATE STEWART is Visiting Associate Professor of English at Worcester Polytechnic Institute and author of *Arthur Sherburne Hardy: Man of American Letters* and various articles on Edgar Allan Poe.

THOMAS HUNTER STEWART is a doctoral candidate at the University of Mississippi studying ministers in Southwestern humor. He has authored various articles on American literature and folklore.

GEORGE A. TEST is Professor of English at the State University of New York College, Oneonta; founder and editor of *Satire Newsletter* (1963–1973); and author of various articles on satire and humor.

W. CRAIG TURNER is Professor and Head of the English Department at Mississippi College; he is author of *The Poet Robert Browning and His Kinfolk* (1983) and co-editor of *Critical Essays in American Humor* (1984) with William B. Clark.

CLYDE G. WADE is Associate Professor of English at the University of Missouri, Rolla, and author of essays on British and American humor.

JACK D. WARREN, JR., is a doctoral candidate in History at Brown University and author of various articles on political and legal culture in early America.

RICHARD SAMUEL WEST is editor of *Target, The Political Cartoon Quarterly* and author of the forthcoming *Satire on Stone: The Political Cartoons of Joseph Keppler* and various articles on nineteenth- and twentieth-century American political cartoonists.